# American Aquarium Fishes

NUMBER TWENTY–EIGHT

W. L. Moody, Jr., Natural History Series

# American Aquarium Fishes

## Robert J. Goldstein

*with* Rodney W. Harper *and*
Richard Edwards

*Photographs by*
William F. Roston, Richard Bryant,
Fred C. Rohde, Garold Sneegas, *and*
Robert J. Goldstein

Texas A&M University Press
*College Station*

Library of Congress Cataloging-in-Publication Data

Goldstein, Robert J. (Robert Jay), 1937–
        American aquarium fishes / Robert J. Goldstein
    with Rodney W. Harper and Richard Edwards ;
    photographs by William F. Roston . . . [et al.].—1st
    ed.
            p. cm. — (Moody natural history series ; no. 28)
        Includes bibliographical references (p. ).
        ISBN 0-89096-880-2 (cloth : alk. paper)
        1. Aquarium fishes.    2. Freshwater fishes—North
    America.    I. Harper, Rodney W.    II. Edwards,
    Richard.    III. Title.    IV. W.L. Moody, Jr., natural
    history series ; no. 28.

SF457 .G648 2000
639.34—dc21
                                          99-043786

# Contents

# Illustrations

# Acknowledgments

Many persons have contributed to this book, from collecting with me over many decades to providing research papers or reviewing the manuscript. Foremost is the gratitude I owe my wonderful friend, the late H. Ross Brock, Jr., whose love of wielding a long-handled dip net throughout the swamps of Georgia and the Gulf Coast was infectious to every aquarist fortunate enough to have known him. Others with whom I have happily collected over the years include Rick Edwards, John and Dennis Everett, Steve Yonke, and Scott Van Cleave in the Missouri Ozarks, Dave Herrema in Florida, and Todd Wenzel and Gerald Pottern in North Carolina. Dan Logan provided live Oregon fishes. Sallie Boggs took me collecting in Pennsylvania, Kirk Winemiller near Texas A&M University, and Dick Stober in Alabama.

Vadim Birstein and Boyd Kynard provided information on the sturgeons. Bruce Turner and Jim Thomerson reviewed the killifishes. Larry Page reviewed parts of the section on darters, acknowledging my right to be flat wrong in my taxonomic organization of that family. Carole Johnston reviewed parts of the section on minnows, pointing out errors until she could no longer stand it. Bob Jenkins reviewed and graciously corrected much of the chapter on suckers. Jay Stauffer helped considerably with the chapter on sunfishes.

The spectacular photographs were taken by William F. Roston, Richard Bryant, Frec C. Rohde, Garold Sneegas, and myself. Following each caption are the initials of the photographer. Any exceptions are noted by giving the full name of the photographer. The plant illustrations were drawn by Richard Edwards, author of the plant chapter.

All the reviewers recommended that an ichthyologist of broad training and stature provide technical editing of the entire manuscript, but none was cruel enough to direct me toward a specific colleague. Fortunately, I have been around almost as long as binomial nomenclature, and immediately thought of ambushing Carter Gilbert of the Florida State Museum. Using all the guile at my disposal, I prevailed upon Carter to agree to technically edit the manuscript sight unseen, fully realizing that he might bolt were he to see the manuscript first. Not to be ruffled by so puny an effort compared to his usual fare, Carter quickly tore through the entire manuscript and sent me thirty-three single-spaced pages of helpful comments and recommendations.

I owe much to Dr. Gilbert and all the other reviewers. I have incorporated their recommendations as much as practicable, meaning that while they were stepping on the gas for detail, my editor, Noel Parsons at Texas A&M University Press, was stepping on the brake to limit the size of the book to something H. Ross Perot could afford.

All authors end their acknowledgments by taking responsibility for errors that may slip through. Readers in the ichthyological community will sagely agree that, in my case, that conclusion is so obvious as to make the remark superfluous.

American Aquarium Fishes

# I  Introduction

THE United States is home to over 700 species of freshwater fishes, some extending into Canada. One-third to one-half are sufficiently small and attractive to qualify as aquarium fishes. Canada and the coastal waters of the Atlantic, Gulf, and Pacific offer a hundred or more additional fishes readily collected and suitable for aquaria, such as the marine blennies and gobies.

Certain fishes are not suitable because they: (1) are mainly game fishes; (2) grow too large for aquaria; (3) escape too easily from aquaria (e.g., freshwater eels); (4) have exceptionally rigorous feeding or reproductive requirements; or (5) are simply uninteresting. These include the lampreys (family Petromyzontidae), mooneyes (Hiodontidae), smelts (Osmeridae), trout and salmon (Salmonidae), freshwater eels (Anguillidae), striped bass and their relatives (Percichthyidae), mullets (Mugilidae), herrings (Clupeidae), surfperches (Embiotocidae), snooks (Centropomidae), and mojarras (Gerreidae); all are excluded from this book. Other families including the marine soles (Soleidae), butterflyfishes (Chaetodontidae), angelfishes (Pomacanthidae), spadefishes (Ephippidae), and drums (Sciaenidae) are delightful aquarium fishes collected easily from shallow Atlantic and Pacific waters; they are also excluded due to extensive coverage in existing aquarium books.

Nonnative fishes are not included here. Many exotics have been released in domestic waters by game and fish agencies for sportfishing, bait dealers, state mosquito control agencies, fish farms (accidentally), and home aquarists (through ignorance). Not all released fishes, however, persist. For example, barbs and tetras have never become established in Florida, despite untold numbers dumped or escaped from ponds during floods. Some exotic fishes have become established; e.g., some cichlids have displaced local native fishes. Those effects may extend to extirpation (local extinction) to complete extinction of native species. The risk to American fishes should be clear from the impact of introduced Nile perch *(Lates niloticus)* to Lake Tanganyika in Africa for sportfishing and a new commercial fishery; the result was the inexorable species-by-species extinction of much of the endemic cichlid fauna, a process that could be completed during our lifetimes. Some Asian and European exotics have reached North America in ship ballast through transportation of oysters from one coast to another for aquaculture, or were brought here a hundred years ago by the federal government (e.g., brown trout, carp). The developing impacts of newly imported exotic invertebrates (e.g., zebra mussels, corbicula clams, spiny daphnia), however, may be more damaging than exotic fishes because of their ability to alter habitat and the food web.

This leaves hundreds of attractive U.S. and Canadian fishes about which aquarists know little regarding care, housing, feeding, and breeding. These fishes have been ignored for various reasons. The older literature is replete with remarks that native fishes require cold water, overwintering outdoors, living foods, and strong currents. Many were difficult to keep in the days of metal frame tanks, rotary electric motors, and hot incandescent lamps. Authors such as William T. Innes did discuss sticklebacks, sea horses, bluefin and golden-ear killies, and *Heterandria* and mollies as representative of our native fishes, but left the impression these were the only natives worth keeping. Innes and others merely scratched the surface of the beautiful fishes of North American rivers and streams.

Today, the knowledge, skills, and equipment to solve once insoluble problems and to breed fishes previously thought impossible to maintain alive are readily accessible. A network of hundreds of aquarists anxious to jump into a creek, lake, or pond, to swipe with a dip net or drag a seine and pack fishes home to the 10-gallon aquarium or the 100-aquarium fish room also exists, as members of local and national aquarium societies. Today's aquarist has power, trickle, and diatomaceous earth filters, myriad powerful air pumps, blowers, identification books on the fishes of every state or region, and a choice of live foods never before available. With the option of trading fishes through the postal services throughout the world, we now have an international community anxious to offer their native fishes and hungering for ours.

Several important books are essential for identifying North American fishes. Two that belong in every library are Page and Burr's (1991) Peterson Field Guide, *A Field Guide to Freshwater Fishes, North America North of Mexico,* and the Lee et al. (1980) *Atlas of North American Freshwater Fishes.* Almost every state or region has a dedicated fish book essential to knowing the local species and their distributions. If starting a career in ichthyology, try to locate the two volumes of Carlander's (1969, 1977) *Handbook of Freshwater Fishery Biology.* Taxonomists needing to examine type specimens from specific localities will appreciate the guidance in Gilbert's (1997) *Type Catalogue of Recent and Fossil North American Freshwater Fishes.* For an up-to-date treatment of aquarium equipment and theory of operation, including lighting, filtration, water quality, pumps, chillers, meters, fish diseases, medicaments, and growing live foods, see Goldstein's (1997) *Marine Reef Aquarium Handbook.*

I have slogged through the gluey, gray sediments of Atlantic, Gulf, and Pacific coastal marshes for killifishes, and slipped in swift, algal-glazed bedrock streams of the Ozark, Rocky, and Appalachian Mountains in search of darters, sculpins, and minnows. I have seined and trapped sculpins and gobies, cast-netted, block-netted, electrofished, bought beauties from bait dealers, and traded fishes through the mail. The fun is not just in collecting and keeping; philatelists do that. Real aquarists breed their fishes. Not only do native North American fishes offer opportunities to apply modern tropical fish breeding techniques used on egg scatterers, bottom nesters, and cave spawners, but they also offer new modes of spawning not previously seen among tropicals (e.g., eggs on vertical rock walls and in clumps beneath sand or rocks). Thus far, no North American native fish has been found to be a bubblenester, but their range of breeding behaviors is still remarkable. For the aquarist, challenges await.

In many states, while it is legal to catch small native fishes, it is illegal to keep them in a home aquarium. The wildlife agency people with whom I have spoken do not believe that native fishes should be harvested for commercial purposes but generally agree that if a few are caught for personal use and bred, the fate of the offspring is not their concern.

Review your provincial or state laws, get a fishing license, and determine the legal methods for taking bait. In most states, legal means include dip nets, small seines ( ≤ 4 × 10 ft.), and minnow traps. Seining is best with two people holding the net, one to kick the substratum toward the net, and one to hold the collection bucket. Your local aquarium society will have many people who will enjoy a collecting trip, even during December.

## Geologic Features

The more than 700 species of freshwater fishes of the United States and Canada are not distributed evenly. Some locations have great diversity while others have little, attributable to the amount of water, the number of waterways, and the history of those waterways. The present only partly tells the story of fish distribution, for the past is equally important.

The United States and Canada average 3,000 miles from the Atlantic to the Pacific. The United States extends 1,500 miles from Canada to Mexico in the west and to the Gulf of Mexico in the east. Canada is equal in area to the United States, extending from the Maritimes and Hudson Bay to the Yukon south of the Arctic Circle. Within these 8 million square miles occur mountain forests and swamp forests, mangrove swamps and grassy wetlands, coral reefs, lakes, wet savanna, and arid deserts. Much of the continent's fish fauna is concentrated in the southeastern and south central United States. Canada's depauperate fauna (< 200 spp./4 million sq. mi.) is compensated for its lack of numbers of families by the diversity within some families (e.g., the sculpins [Cottidae] and trout and salmon [Salmonidae]).

Weather separates the United States into climatic zones, and rivers and mountain chains divide the warmer and wetter states into regions. In the west, the Sierra Nevada mountain range runs northward from Baja California, Mexico, to the Pacific northwest where it is punctuated by enormous volcanoes. East of this range is the Great Basin, a vast desert containing the Great Salt Lake, source of much of the world's brine shrimp eggs and very little other fresh water. Dessication of the Great Basin resulted from the uplifting of the Sierra Nevada in the west and the Rocky Mountains to the east combined with scouring of the basin by Pleistocene glaciers. Many historical fishes have died out from natural climate changes during the past two hundred years, and more will soon become extinct because of groundwater depletion associated with agriculture and development.

Beyond the eastern edge of the desert are the 400-mile-wide Rocky Mountains, their deeply cut canyons formed by once great rivers from another time. The Rockies extend southward from western Canada into Mexico and continue into Central and South America under other names.

East of the Rockies, the great Mississippi River drains the entire central third of the United States and part of Canada, and pours into the Gulf of Mexico, its brown silt rolling a hundred miles seaward. From the west, the Mississippi's most important tributaries are the Missouri and Platte Rivers. From the east, its largest tributary is the Ohio River. Most of the rivers of the central United States drain into the Mississippi, while a few reach the Gulf of Mexico independently to the west or the east.

Two important areas in the central United States are the Ozark Plateau in Missouri and Arkansas (and the Ouachita Mountains immediately to the south) and the Cumberland Plateau in Kentucky and surrounding states. Ancient elevated plains, they have been severely eroded by myriad tributaries cutting through the rocks, and fish speciation has been rampant.

The eastern United States has another important mountain range, the Appalachians, arising in Quebec and extending to Georgia and Alabama. The western slopes of the Appalachians drain into the Tennessee and other tributaries of the Ohio River. The eastern slopes drain into two dozen separate rivers along the Atlantic seaboard.

From the middle Atlantic Coast, north to New Jersey, southward around the end of the Appalachians, and all the way around Florida, the hilly land below but close to the mountains is known as the Piedmont Plateau. Downslope of the Piedmont is a broad, flat, sandy reach known as the Coastal Plain, the remnant of an old sea bed when the ocean was much higher. The Coastal Plain extends around the Appalachians and continues northward up the Mississippi Valley almost to Canada. A small portion of the Coastal Plain in Virginia and the Carolinas, known as the Sandhills, has a unique fish and herpetological fauna.

# 2 Distribution of Fishes

*T*HE western United States today is largely dry and wanting in big rivers with widely separated tributaries. Much of the present desert southwest consists of old, dry basins that once supported many species of fishes; isolated springs and pools are all that remain, yet the remaining fishes in these widely disjunct locales demonstrate a shared evolutionary history.

The Northwest has a few old rivers (e.g., Columbia and Snake Rivers) damaged by dams, agricultural withdrawal for irrigation, and pollution from silt and farm chemicals. Inland, many of the tributaries suffer from impacts passed on to their final rivers. Many smaller isolated streams that drain small coastal watersheds are often deleteriously affected by transplantations that displace small native populations.

The western states have many endangered or threatened species, including many of the pupfishes (*Cyprinodon* spp.). Many species, once wide-ranging, are now restricted to tiny pools or streams. In some ancient western rivers (e.g., tributaries of the Colorado River), now dried by eons of climatic change and further drained for farming or altered for hydroelectric power, some relict fishes (e.g., squawfishes) remain in imminent danger of extinction.

Much of Canada and the northern United States has been dramatically carved by glaciers to leave behind a series of massive lakes extending in an arc from Great Bear Lake and Great Slave Lake in the Northwest Territories north of Alberta and British Columbia, eastward and south of Hudson Bay to the somewhat smaller Great Lakes of the Canada-U.S. border. The almost pristine northwestern Canadian lakes remain largely unaffected by the problems of the east, whereas the Great Lakes have suffered from alteration of flow, massive pollution from industrial and residential development, and invasion by sea lampreys and by exotic fishes in ships' ballast. Today, continued biological alteration to serve sportfishing and commercial fisheries constituencies has rendered the Great Lakes of little interest to aquarists.

The greatest variety and abundance of freshwater fishes occur where the greatest diversity and abundance of river drainages exist—the eastern United States. Here, climate and topography produce great rivers, myriad tributaries, and thousands of streams extending into the upper slopes of the eastern mountains. Where streams are old, present-day related species have differentiated from a common ancestor to become subspecies or new species. On the slopes of the eastern mountains, for example, many streams only yards apart have different species of common ancestry that have been separated for eons by a thousand feet of elevation prior to the rivers converging many miles below. Near the tops of the mountains along the Continental Divide, some streams drain to the east toward Atlantic rivers, while others just a hundred yards away drain westward toward the Mississippi basin and the Gulf of Mexico. Long separated, the fishes in the upper reaches of these streams are now different.

Continued erosion and stream capture mixes and reshuffles the distribution of species, confounding interpretations of relationships. That, however, is what ichthyologists enjoy unraveling, and reports such as Hocutt and Wiley's (1986) *The Zoogeography of North American Freshwater Fishes,* Holt's (1971) *The Distributional History of the Southern Appalachians,* and Mayden's (1992) *Systematics, Historical Ecology, and North American Freshwater Fishes* have interpreted geology, climate, the fossil record, and genetic changes in fishes over time to provide a modern and substantially complete and rational record.

*Climate*    In brief, the western part of the continent is dry, especially in the southwest; the eastern half of North America is wet, especially in the southeast. Wind and geography are responsible.

The prevailing westerlies from the Pacific Ocean drive most of the weather in the United States. Moist Pacific air or dry Canadian air sweeps southward and eastward to bring winds or rain to the northwestern coastal states. The Sierra Nevada mountains remove the moisture from these air masses and prevent it from reaching farther east, resulting in desert conditions as the dried winds sweep from the Sierras to the Rockies. The desert absorbs enormous amounts of solar heat and produces its own weather in the form of powerful, sustained hot winds that may blow into southern California, fanning fires during drought conditions.

Eastward across the desert and the Rockies into the wide basin of the Mississippi, the land once more flattens, softens, and becomes a yellow-and-green checkerboard of farmland divided by great meandering brown rivers. Continuing eastward, the land changes again as the lush green Appalachians loom skyward. Now, all is green, and the landscape is fractured by glinting slivers of silvery rivers.

As the prevailing air masses from the north and west approach the Atlantic, they crash into oceanic easterlies and turn abruptly northward along the coast. At their meeting point off Cape Hatteras, North Carolina, turbulent weather is common, for this is the birthplace of the great gales of the eastern seaboard.

High and low pressure systems are associated with these air masses, and both can generate strong winds. When cold air drops southeastward from Canada, it frequently meets hot, moist air pushing northward from the Gulf of Mexico or westward toward the North Atlantic. These conditions are strong weather makers, producing drenching rains, severe thunderstorms, hail, and occasional tornado outbreaks when the jet stream is directly overhead. But these are not the only major rainmakers.

When strong low pressure systems develop in west Africa and move across the Atlantic toward the United States, they can develop into hurricanes that sweep into the Gulf of Mexico or veer northward before making landfall anywhere from Florida to Canada, sometimes sustaining tornadic strength for great distances inland. Should they veer south of the United States, they can drop two *feet* of rain over large areas, as did Hurricane Mitch in 1998, resulting in an estimated 10,000 to 15,000 human fatalities in Nicaragua and Honduras from floods and mudslides.

*Water Quality*    The water chemistry of the United States and Canada varies by region and geology. Western and southwestern waters are sometimes saline to hypersaline, leaching salts from long-dead inland seas (and agricultural chemicals from farms). The salts are concentrated in small depressions fed by rain, with no outlets or places to redeposit the minerals except at the margins during drought.

At the opposite end of the continent, the swamp forests of the southeast often drain old sphagnum deposits from dead, fossilized forests. Here, the frequent rain flushes the tannins and other acids from the decayed vegetation while absorbing or holding onto minerals, and the water can be soft, acidic, and as darkly stained as the black waters of the Rio Negro of Brazil.

The Appalachians and Rockies generally are composed of sandstones and granites, with water usually cold, clear, neutral, and soft to moderately hard. On the deeply cut Cumberland and Ozark limestone plateaus, the water arising from springs is clear, cool, highly oxygenated, and usually slightly alkaline and moderately hard. Eventually it flows into large rivers with high sediment loads, and the fish fauna of the smallest and largest streams may differ dramatically.

# 3

# Collecting and Transporting Native Fishes

WHEN preparing to collect in any state, one should have a: (1) state fishing license (usually required); (2) collector's permit (if required); (3) field guide and the best available book on the fishes of a state or region; (4) a state DeLorme atlas of the rivers and roads; (5) county map from private sources or the State Department of Transportation; and (6) a plan. Carry a notebook to record when, where, and what was collected.

Plan on what to collect and where to get it. Confirm that collection will not violate the law on protected species or localities (e.g., designated trout waters). Collect at road crossings to avoid trespassing on private property. Record the road and river crossing in tenths of a mile (using the automobile odometer) in a specific direction from X to Y. Even if the name of the stream is not known, you can find it on a map later and determine the basin from this information. Stream identification can facilitate the identification of a fish that may be difficult to distinguish from other species except by its endemicity to a drainage.

A long-handled dip net is essential for working banks or deep water. Most dip nets on the market are rounded and have hammered sheet aluminum collars that kink and break. Nets used by zoological institutions are better built and include both rounded and straight-edge types. These latter (D-nets) are excellent for working the cavities of undercut banks, often the preferred habitat of certain darters and minnows. The best rounded and D-type dip nets are solid rings of steel or aluminum without collars, the pins buried in the pole.

Good seines are well floated and fitted with additional weights on the lower line. I use PVC pipes as poles, tying the seine's four corner strings to drilled holes in the PVC, and I carry monofilament fishing line for field repairs. You can purchase inexpensive cotton seines at sporting goods and discount stores; more expensive nylon seines last longer and do not need to be dried after use. If you order directly from a manufacturer, you can get seines in ⅛-inch mesh, excellent for juveniles and small or thin animals such as swampfish, salamanders, eels, and lampreys.

My standard gear is a straight 4 × 10 feet, ¼-inch mesh seine, the type that can be purchased in any sporting goods shop. Other people use bag seines for large nets (15–30 ft.) that cannot be pulled quickly due to the force of water on so large a surface area. The bag is a deep pocket in the middle of the seine (like the pocket in trousers) that keeps fishes from rebounding off the seine by trapping them in a deep recess. Many professional ichthyologists prefer a ³⁄₁₆-inch mesh bag seine for making large collections; a ¼-inch mesh seine can also be used to collect small specimens. Any kind of seine can be made to order by specialty companies.

How a seine is operated depends on the waters and the number of people

Collecting darters from an Ozark riffle, Missouri. RJG

working together. For collecting darters, madtoms, sculpins, and other riffle-inhabiting stream fishes, the standard technique is to have two persons facing upstream, holding the seine poles at an angle. The top of each pole points to the rear and somewhat down from the vertical, the foot of the pole pointing upstream while digging into the bottom. Each pole holder slips one foot behind the pole to keep it from slipping backward under the strain of a heavy load and water pressure. The weighted line should hug the bottom with no gaps, and the floated upper line should form a deep U at the surface or just below. The entire seine should form a deep purse; it is not necessary to use the full length of a seine to maximize the distance between the poles. A deeper purse is obtained by moving the pole holders closer to one another, which also reduces the water pressure on the crew holding the net. A third (or third and fourth) member of the team then walks downstream from one-half to two seine lengths toward the net, kicking over stones and disrupting the bottom vigorously with both feet in a zigzag path. This action disturbs all bottom in the area immediately upstream of the net, chasing the fishes downstream into the seine. The seine is then lifted, weighted line first, to form a purse, and the entire unit carried clear of the water to the bank, where the catch is sorted and unwanted animals quickly returned to the water undamaged. Trash is piled away from the working area or removed altogether, but branches, sticks, plants, and other natural materials should be returned to the water, as they provide both habitat and friction that slows the flow of the stream and retards erosion.

For working a quiet sandy area of a river, pond, or lake, walk the net toward shore in a sweeping curve (one person making an arc around a stationary partner) or in a sheet (both pole holders walking together toward shore). For areas with debris, have both pole holders walk toward a corner with a kicker in advance of the net. For collecting minnows and suckers in faster rivers, have both pole holders walk rapidly downstream with the current (trying to keep the bag open can be difficult) to overtake fleeing fishes. Another method useful in riffles or in dense vegetation is for both pole holders to start far apart, then kick while they move toward each other to form a closed circle.

Cast nets are excellent for coastal, estuarine, and lakeshore schooling fishes over clean sand bottoms. Cast nets can be made in any size; a 6-feet or smaller diameter net with ¼-inch mesh is most practical. Never throw a cast net into a location you are unwilling to wade, because it is often necessary to enter the water and release the net from an obstruction. The cast net's cord should always be attached to your wrist before throwing.

A lift net consisting of a meshed frame is little more than a modified dip net, but many sizes and shapes can be built for local vegetated pond and lake edges or for lowering into a habitat from a pier, dock, or boat. Carter Gilbert prefers a Goin dredge (Goin 1942) to capture small fishes in dense vegetation.

For most of the year, waders or hip boots are unnecessary. It is easier to simply stomp through muck, sand, gravel, and onto slippery rocks in sneakers or tennis shoes. For great comfort, visit a dive shop and purchase a pair of foam booties (used by scuba divers and snorkelers to fit inside open-heeled swim fins). A zippered pair large enough to fit over sneakers will exclude gravel.

In winter, chest waders will maintain warmth. Purchase high quality (and expensive) 3 to 5 mm neoprene waders and avoid lightweight, inexpensive nylon or rubberized waders that readily crack or tear and require bicycle patches until the damage

Throwing a cast net into a North Carolina borrow ditch. RJG

becomes extensive. Chest waders should be worn outside the clothing, supported by suspenders, and tightened around the waist with a belt to keep water from entering.

Where water quality is excellent (viz., cool, clear, moderately hard and alkaline), captive fishes should be placed into the ambient water in disposable styrofoam fish shipping boxes available from pet stores. Because styrofoam allows gas exchange and plastic bags do not, bare boxes will support fishes longer than boxes lined with bags. Aerators are usually not necessary, but when using nonstyrofoam containers or containers with little surface area, a D-cell battery powered aerator is helpful. Fishing tackle dealers sell larger aerators (bilge pumps) with alligator clips to power from a 6- or 8-volt boat battery; the clips can be replaced with a cigarette lighter attachment. A bait-saver system operating off a car battery that circulates water through a cooler is available at sporting goods stores.

Where water quality is poor (turbid, low pH, low dissolved oxygen concentration), I prefer to carry treated tap water into the field. I fill my coolers one-half or more with tap water treated to provide dechlorination, dechloramination, and ammonia removal, and to stimulate the production of protective coatings. For sensitive fishes from soft waters, I also carry sea water, brine, or solid salt; a small amount of salt added to the water will often prevent skin infections that do not manifest until two or three days following collection.

Fishes can be shipped to other aquarists through the mail or by next day and 2-day commercial carriers. Not all carriers accept live fish shipments. The U.S. Postal Service's guaranteed next day and 2-day delivery services are, in my experience, unreliable, and even worse is Canada's postal service. My best results have been through United Parcel Service.

When shipping fishes, water is less important than air. The fishes need only enough water to remain wet; having sufficient atmosphere to capture carbon dioxide produced during transit is critical. Fishes seldom die of oxygen depletion, but rather from carbon dioxide toxemia when there is insufficient atmospheric space into which the carbon dioxide can exit the water. Fishes should be placed in the largest bag available. The bag should contain one part water to ten or more parts atmosphere, either air or oxygen. Compressed oxygen is valuable for shipping and in some cases for field collections. Shipping costs are usually based on weight (large shipments substitute volume as an estimate of weight) and thus the cost of excess atmosphere is minimal in small packages.

A tranquilizer such as a mixture of quinaldine and acetone or 10 percent quinaldine in 95 percent ethanol dissolved in water is recommended. Quinaldine is commercially available and, when used at six drops to the gallon, reduces oxygen demand and stress on fishes for up to five days. Some fishes become torpid while others show no visible effects, but all benefit when the anesthetic dose is correct.

The bag containing fishes, treated water, and atmosphere is twisted closed and sealed with two rubber bands. It is then inverted into a second bag to eliminate all corners that might trap the fishes; the second bag is sealed with one or two rubber bands. The double bag is placed into a large box (styrofoam or otherwise insulated) and shipped by next day or second-day air.

# 4  Collecting Regulations and Protected Species

SPECIES may need protection from the public or from other species. The most frequent causes of population decline are habitat degradation and competition from introduced species. Habitat degradation may be insidious, as when siltation and sedimentation occur during land development, or overt, as when a dam converts a river into a lake. Many species cannot survive turbidity, lowered dissolved oxygen levels, or alterations in current velocity; these particular habitat characteristics may be necessary for specialized feeding or spawning. In general, stream fishes do not survive in lakes, and vice versa.

Dams have eliminated or threaten to eliminate many species, not solely by interfering with spawning migrations but by changing the nature of the habitat. Dams often remove spawning microhabitat requirements (e.g., riffles) and favor lake fishes, including potential predators.

Agricultural practices also threaten fishes. Farming introduces fecal waste and toxic ammonia from livestock that may induce noxious algal blooms that in turn deplete oxygen and introduce cyanotoxins. Pesticides kill daphnia and other microcrustaceans, and the aquatic stages of stream insects (e.g., midges, blackflies, mayflies, stoneflies) that comprise the most common foods of stream fishes. Herbicides eliminate diatoms and useful green algae, and fertilizers alter the nitrogen to phosphorus (N:P) ratio (and their loads) in streams, causing noxious blue-green algae (cyanobacteria) blooms. Mud and silt from runoff where vegetation has been removed from stream banks covers spawning and feeding microhabitats such as diatom-covered boulders and cobblestone coated with aquatic insect larvae.

Competition from introduced species, leading to extinctions or depletions of native fishes, has often and unfairly been blamed on aquarists, but government policies in support of anglers are more often responsible. In the western United States, the introduction of mosquitofish has been a frequent cause of extinctions and depletions. Mosquitofish *(Gambusia)* were widely introduced by state mosquito control agencies, and secondarily transferred by a public seeking to extend the benefits provided by government. Other widely introduced species include largemouth bass, bluegill and green sunfish, golden shiners, red shiners, fathead minnows, and other easily collected or propagated bait fishes. In the southeastern states, transplantations by state fish and game agencies and by sportfishing enthusiasts or farmers stocking ponds have introduced predators into lakes and streams, eliminating native species. Red shiners, members of a large genus *(Cyprinella),* are more prolific and better competitors than their cogeners, displacing other native *Cyprinella* species (and other minnows) having lower reproductive potential.

Underground waters, visible both in caves and at springs, are remarkably specialized habitats, often with unique species of invertebrates, amphibians, fishes, and plants (at outflows). Most springs are outflows of surficial aquifers with their rainfall recharge zones at a higher elevation and often some distance away. Alternatively, the recharge zone may be nearby, upslope atop a mountain, and the spring a surface leak somewhere downslope. If the aquifers flow through limestone, the water may be hard and even alkaline; if through sand or fractured granite, other water quality characteristics reflecting the physical conditions underground will be evident.

Aquifer waters are often low in dissolved oxygen, clear, and a uniform temperature year-round. Aquifers can grow and contract with annual recharge during the rainy season and drought, changing both their belowground elevation and head pressure at the spring. Some springs arise from deeper, confined aquifers that have broken through a confining layer and have considerable head pressure. Surficial aquifers are common everywhere. Deep aquifers, layered one above the other with intervening confining layers, are only common in coastal zones. They formed as changes in ocean levels associated with multiple ice ages that gave rise to a surface aquifer that was subsequently buried by deposits of sand and silt. Surface aquifers may contain cave fishes; confined aquifers never do.

While spring water quality, and even quantity of flow, may be constant at the source, the downstream flow (spring run) can be very different. At some point, the downstream flow is influenced by mixing with surface water, rainfall, flooding, porosity of the ground, evaporation, and a change in plant life adapted to seasons, substrata, and hydrologic regimes that favor their growth over that of spring species of vegetation.

These differences among springs, nearby spring runs, and the downstream regions (now predominantly surface water) prompted Hubbs (1995) to review the importance of springs in maintaining rare and endangered species. In case after case, Hubbs described spring endemics at the source and slightly downstream that disappeared farther downstream as they were replaced by widespread, tolerant species. In some cases, the spring species were more tolerant of lower oxygen levels or higher temperatures than the widespread species.

The greatest danger to these rare species, and to rare species everywhere, does not come from collectors but from developers who alter habitats. In the case of spring endemics, human use of aquifers beyond their capacity for recharge lowers the levels of the aquifers. Springs can contract and even dry up, eliminating species that exist nowhere else.

Today, concern by state and federal resource agencies is changing the ways aquifers are permitted to be used by municipalities, although industrial users are generally unregulated. Agencies now ask municipal water purveyors, who rely on groundwater for part of the year, to evaluate the feasibility of storing excess water in deep aquifers (from either surface supplies or treated wastewater) for reuse during periods of low surface water supply. This aquifer storage and reuse (ASAR) promises to reduce the need for new water supplies (and dams) by reserving and reusing water.

For many spring and spring run species, however, it is already too late. Collecting rarely eliminates a species. Of far more importance is loss of specialized habitat through nutrient and silt pollution, alteration of hydrology that increases erosion, removal of cooling and filtering streamside vegetation and canopy, sand mining, or excessive withdrawal of source waters. Protect the habitat and the species will take care of themselves.

It is important not only to protect habitats from alteration or degradation, but to prevent the introduction of species not native to that particular stream. Aquarists and many professional biologists cannot distinguish individuals of closely related populations of fishes; often even the ichthyological community does not know or has not yet studied the genetic characteristics of fishes from adjacent streams (i.e., whether the same or different species, subspecies, or another category). Thus, even a common fish such as a red shiner or a bluegill from one body of water should never be introduced into another; the introduced fish could displace and eliminate the native fish. In addition to competition, introduced species may be better predators and could potentially eliminate a food source, introduce an infectious disease, destroy spawning or feeding habitat, or through interbreeding destroy a unique genetic population.

Native fishes can often be removed safely from nature when populations are large. Excess stock collected or raised by aquarists should go to one of two end points: either to another aquarist or into the aquarium of a large predator. *You should never return fishes to any water body other than the precise location from which they or their parents were collected.*

Many fishes of the United States are protected under the federal Endangered Species Act of 1973 (ESA) and amendments. Protection categories include E (endangered), T (threatened), PE (proposed endangered), PT (proposed threatened), and C1. An endangered or proposed endangered species is one on the verge of extinction in a large portion or all of its range. A threatened or proposed threatened species is one likely to become endangered in the foreseeable future. C1 denotes that the species is unprotected at present, but is likely to be listed as protected in the near future.

Protection under the ESA is enforced with severe penalties for interfering with any E or T species, proposed threatened or endangered (PT, PE), or those likely to come under protection (C1). Sanctions are directed against taking, defined in part as harassing, harming, pursuing, trapping, capturing, collecting, or attempting to do any of the foregoing: trading, importing and exporting, and handling any federally listed species that moves naturally between countries. In some regions, as in the desert Southwest, many species endemic to a particular spring or lake are now afforded protection from collecting or habitat degradation (Minckley and Deacon 1968). Specific subspecies or populations of a species are protected in certain cases. Violation of the ESA is a federal offense with severe civil and criminal penalties.

Mexico has its own laws to protect species. Canada does not at present have a federal law comparable to the ESA, although it has frequently identified species at risk (McAllister et al. 1985). Some states in the United States and Mexico and provinces in Canada can have individual laws to protect species under threat from overharvest, habitat degradation, and competition from exotic species.

In the United States, state laws can be largely ineffective (e.g., protection against fish collection but not bulldozing the habitat, or penalties with negligible fines), or may be as rigorous as the ESA. Information for individual states on collection conditions follows; consult with state agencies to determine if protection extends to collection for propagation purposes. States also use the designation SR, referring to species that are significantly rare. In some states this designation affords legal protection; in others it does not. In most cases, many species of desirable fishes are available to aquarists; protected species tend to be few, limited in range, and too rare to be found by amateurs with simple collecting gear. Always carry licenses, permits, and copies of the regulations on collecting trips and avoid any area identified as a known habitat for a protected species.

The best freshwater fish books for Canada are Scott and Crossman's (1973) *Freshwater Fishes of Canada,* Leim and Scott's (1966) *Fishes of the Atlantic Coast of Canada,* Nelson and Paetz's (1992) *The Fishes of Alberta,* and McAllister et al.'s (1985) *Rare, Endangered, and Extinct Fishes in Canada.*

Two books are essential for collecting, trading, and identifying freshwater fishes of the United States: Page and Burr's (1991) *A Field Guide to Freshwater Fishes, North America North of Mexico* and Lee et al.'s (1980) *Atlas of North American Freshwater Fishes.* An excellent key and training in ichthyological terminology is provided by Eddy (1969) in *How to Know the Freshwater Fishes,* sometimes available from antiquarians.

Regional or state guides are recommended as are the books for surrounding states. Most books can be ordered through university of commercial bookstores or the American Fisheries Society. Out of print books may be located through antiquarians. Maps providing details of rivers and watersheds are published by the U.S. Geological Survey and available from surveyor supply stores. The DeLorme Company publishes *Atlas and Gazetteer* editions for many states, which are available at convenient stores and gas stations. Details of rivers are in Patrick's (1994–96) six volume *Rivers of the United States.*

States usually protect both federally and locally important species, with laws addressing collection, possession, and damage to habitat. For each state in which collections are to be made, contact the appropriate agency for information. Many states list State Extirpated as a protected category; extirpated means that the fish is locally extinct. Be aware that states do not change species names as often as they are changed in the scientific literature; names you do not now recognize may be represented in other genera. Contact the U.S. Fish and Wildlife Service for federally protected fishes.

# Species

| Common Name | Scientific Name | Federal Status |
|---|---|---|
| Catfish, Yaqui | *Pangasianodon gigas* | T |
| Cavefish, Alabama | *Speoplatyrhinus poulsoni* | E |
| Cavefish, Ozark | *Amblyopsis rosae* | T |
| Chub, bonytail | *Gila elegans* | E |
| Chub, Borax Lake | *Gila boraxobius* | E |
| Chub, Chihuahua | *Gila nigrescens* | T |
| Chub, humpback | *Gila cypha* | E |
| Chub, Hutton tui | *Gila bicolor* ssp. | T |
| Chub, Mohave tui | *Gila bicolor mohavensis* | E |
| Chub, Oregon | *Oregonichthys crameri* | E |
| Chub, Owens tui | *Gila bicolor snyderi* | E |
| Chub, Pahranagat roundtail | *Gila robustajordani (= bonytail)* | E |
| Chub, slender | *Erimystax (= Hybopsis) cahni* | T |
| Chub, Sonora | *Gila ditaenia* | T |
| Chub, spotfin | *Cyprinella (= Hybopsis) monacha (= turquoise shiner)* | T |
| Chub, Virgin River | *Gila robusta semidnuda* | E |
| Chub, Yaqui | *Gila purpurea* | E |
| Cui-ui | *Chasmistes cujus* | E |
| | | |
| Dace, Ash Meadows speckled | *Rhinichthys osculus nevadensis* | E |
| Dace, blackside | *Phoxinus cumberlandensis* | T |
| Dace, Clover Valley speckled | *Rhinichthys osculus oligoporus* | E |
| Dace, desert | *Eremichthys acros* | T |
| Dace, Foskett speckled | *Rhinichthys osculus* ssp. | T |
| Dace, Independence Valley speckled | *Rhinichthys osculus lethoporus* | E |
| Dace, Kendall Warm Springs | *Rhinichthys osculus thermalis* | E |
| Dace, Moapa | *Moapa coriacea* | E |
| Darter, amber | *Percina antesella* | E |
| Darter, bayou | *Etheostoma rubrum* | T |
| Darter, bluemask (= jewel) | *Etheostoma* n. sp. | E |
| Darter, boulder (= Elk River) | *Etheostoma wapiti* | E |
| Darter, duskytail | *Etheostoma (Catonotus) percnurum* | E |
| Darter, fountain | *Etheostoma fonticola* | E |
| Darter, goldline | *Percina aurolineata* | T |
| Darter, leopard | *Percina pantherina* | T |
| Darter, Maryland | *Etheostoma sellare* | E |
| Darter, Niangua | *Etheostoma nianguae* | T |
| Darter, Okaloosa | *Etheostoma okaloosae* | E |
| Darter, relict | *Etheostoma chienense* | E |
| Darter, slackwater | *Etheostoma boschungi* | T |
| Darter, snail | *Percina tanasi* | T |
| Darter, watercress | *Etheostoma nuchale* | E |
| | | |
| Gambusia, Big Bend | *Gambusia gaigei* | E |
| Gambusia, Clear Creek | *Gambusia heterochir* | E |
| Gambusia, Pecos | *Gambusia nobilis* | E |
| Gambusia, San Marcos | *Gambusia georgei* | E |
| Goby, tidewater | *Eucyclogobius newberryi* | E |

| Common Name | Scientific Name | Federal Status |
|---|---|---|
| Logperch, Conasauga | *Percina jenkinsi* | E |
| Logperch, Roanoke | *Percina rex* | E |
| | | |
| Madtom, Neosho | *Noturus placidus* | T |
| Madtom, pygmy | *Noturus stanauli* | E |
| Madtom, Smoky | *Noturus baileyi* | E |
| Madtom, yellowfin | *Noturus flavipinnis* | T |
| Minnow, loach | *Rhinichthys (= Tiaroga) cobitis* | T |
| Minnow, Rio Grande silvery | *Hybognathus amarus* | E |
| | | |
| Poolfish (= killifish), Pahrump | *Empetrichthys latos* | E |
| Pupfish, Ash Meadows Amargosa | *Cyprinodon nevadensis mionectes* | E |
| Pupfish, Comanche Springs | *Cyprinodon elegans* | E |
| Pupfish, desert | *Cyprinodon macularius* | E |
| Pupfish, Devils Hole | *Cyprinodon diabolis* | E |
| Pupfish, Leon Springs | *Cyprinodon bovinus* | E |
| Pupfish, Owens | *Cyprinodon radiosus* | E |
| Pupfish, Warm Springs | *Cyprinodon nevadensis pectoralis* | E |
| | | |
| Sculpin, pygmy | *Cottus pygmaeus* | T |
| Shiner, beautiful | *Cyprinella (= Notropis) formosa* | T |
| Shiner, blue | *Cyprinella (= Notropis) caerulea* | T |
| Shiner, Cahaba | *Notropis cahabae* | E |
| Shiner, Cape Fear | *Notropis mekistocholas* | E |
| Shiner, Palezone | *Notropis albizonatus* | E |
| Shiner, Pecos bluntnose | *Notropis simus pecosensis* | T |
| Silverside, Waccamaw | *Menidia extensa* | T |
| Smelt, delta | *Hypomesus transpacificus* | T |
| Spikedace | *Meda fulgida* | T |
| Spinedace, Big Spring | *Lepidomeda mollispinis pratensis* | T |
| Spinedace, Little Colorado | *Lepidomeda vittata* | T |
| Spinedace, White River | *Lepidomeda albivallis* | E |
| Springfish, Hiko White River | *Crenichthys baileyi grandis* | E |
| Springfish, Railroad Valley | *Crenichthys nevadae* | T |
| Springfish, White River | *Crenichthys baileyi baileyi* | E |
| Squawfish, Colorado | *Ptychocheilus lucius* | E |
| Stickleback, unarmored threespine | *Gasterosteus aculeatus williamsoni* | E |
| Sturgeon, Gulf | *Acipenser oxyrhynchus desotoi* | T |
| Sturgeon, pallid | *Scaphirhynchus albus* | E |
| Sturgeon, shortnose | *Acipenser brevirostrum* | E |
| Sucker, June | *Chasmistes liorus* | E |
| Sucker, Lost River | *Deltistes luxatus* | E |
| Sucker, Modoc | *Catostomus microps* | E |
| Sucker, razorback | *Xyrauchen texanus* | E |
| Sucker, shortnose | *Chasmistes brevirostris* | E |
| Sucker, Warner | *Catostomus warnerensis* | T |
| | | |
| Tango, Miyako (Tokyo bitterling) | *Tanakia tanago* | E |
| | | |
| Woundfin | *Plagopterus argentissimus* | E |

**Alabama.** Contact: Division of Fish and Game, Environmental Coordinator. Minnows and shad may be taken by cast net, minnow trap (≤ 1 × 2 ft.), dip net, and minnow seine (≤ 4 × 25 ft.) for use as bait. It is unlawful to drag nets except minnow seines in public waters. Commercial or nongame fishes are freshwater drum, buffalo, carp, all catfish (Ictaluridae), spoonbills, all suckers (Catostomidae), bowfin, and gars.

Recommended regional fish book: Boschung's (1992) *Catalogue of Freshwater and Marine Fishes of Alabama.*

**Alaska.** Contact: Department of Fish and Game for an application to collect nongame fishes. Scientific and educational permits are issued to eligible individuals and institutions at no cost to collect nongame fishes using nets, traps, etc., as specified on the permit. Any fish taken, held, or transported live, requires a Fish Transport Permit or FTP.

Recommended regional fish book: Morrow's (1980) *The Freshwater Fishes of Alaska.* A DeLorme atlas and gazetteer is available.

**Arizona.** Contact: Game and Fish Department. A fishing license is required to transport bait fishes, including fathead minnow, mosquitofish, red shiner, threadfin shad, and golden shiner. Accepted taking methods are: minnow trap (≤ 1 × 2 ft.); cast net (≤ 3 ft. radius); seine (≤ 4 × 10 ft.); and dip net.

Recommended regional fish books: Rinne and Minckley's (1991) *Native Fishes of Arid Lands,* Minckley's (1973) *Fishes of Arizona,* and Sigler and Sigler's (1987) *Fishes of the Great Basin: A Natural History.*

**Arkansas.** Contact: Game and Fish Commission. Only licensed fish farmers, minnow dealers, and certain others may sell or trade native fishes. Bait fishes include minnows, darters, shad, killifish, small carp, goldfish, and sunfish under 4 inches. The regulations are not clear on methods for collecting nongame (rough) fishes, including bait fishes. Wire traps and dip nets are prohibited except under license. For a permit to take "species of special concern," contact the Chief of the Endangered, Nongame, and Urban Wildlife Section.

Recommended regional fish book: Robison and Buchanan's (1988) *Fishes of Arkansas.* See also Buchanan (1973) for a key to the fishes.

**California.** Contact: Department of Fish and Game, License and Revenue Branch. Scientific collecting permits to qualified individuals are sometimes waived. Common bait fishes are longjaw mudsucker, golden shiner, red shiner, fathead minnow, mosquitofish, sunfish, molly, sargo, bairdiella, inland silverside, lamprey, staghorn sculpin, oriental gobies, Lahontan redside, tui chub, Tahoe sucker, Lahontan speckled dace, mountain sucker, and Paiute sculpin. Bait fishes may be taken by handheld dip net, or traps (≤ 3 ft. in greatest dimension with diagonal mesh size ≥ 2 in.).

Recommended regional fish books: Moyle's (1976) *Inland Fishes of California* and Miller and Lea's (1972) *Guide to the Coastal Marine Fishes of California.* Two DeLorme atlas and gazetteers cover the state.

**Colorado.** Contact: Division of Wildlife, Department of Natural Resources. Collecting by cast net, dip net, trap, or seine requires a fishing license. A seine may not block free passage without a special permit. Only minnows (except protected species) are considered bait fishes. No rules exist on net dimensions and the taking of small fishes for private aquarium use. Collecting is prohibited in certain locales.

Recommended regional fish book: Woodling's (1985) *Colorado's Little Fish*. A DeLorme atlas and gazetteer is available.

**Connecticut.** Contact: Department of Environmental Protection. A scientific collector's permit is not available without an institutional affiliation. The following species may be taken for personal use: common shiner, golden shiner, spottail shiner, blacknose dace, cutlips minnow, killifish, common sucker, silversides, chub sucker, fallfish, longnose dace, bluntnose minnow, fathead minnow, creek chub, and pearl dace. Accepted methods are the use of seines ($\leq 4 \times 15$ ft.), bait traps ($\leq 20$ in. long and 15 in. diam.), and umbrella nets ($\leq 4 \times 4$ ft.). In lakes and ponds, the above species may be taken at any time with traps and umbrella nets of the previous dimensions; during the open season, they also may be taken by hand, angling, and scoop net. Seines may be used only in lakes and ponds designated by DEP as open to commercial taking of bait.

Recommended regional fish book: Whitworth et al.'s (1968) *Freshwater Fishes of Connecticut*.

**Delaware.** Contact: Department of Natural Resources and Environmental Control, Division of Fish and Wildlife for current fishing guide. Tidal nongame fishes include: minnows and shiners (Cyprinidae), killifish (*Fundulus* spp.), anchovy (*Anchoa* spp.), sand lance (*Ammodytes* spp.), mullet (Mugilidae), and all food fishes less than 7 inches long and not otherwise protected. Bait fishes may be taken from tidal waters by trap, dip net, lift net, push net, cast net, seine, or bag net when hand operated without power. Minnow traps ($\leq 1 \times 1 \times 2$ ft.) are permitted in tidal waters. Use of nets in fresh waters is prohibited without a scientific collecting permit.

Recommended regional fish book: Rohde et al.'s (1994) *Freshwater Fishes of the Carolinas, Virginia, Maryland, and Delaware*. A DeLorme atlas and gazetteer is available for Maryland-Delaware.

**Florida.** Contact: Division of Fisheries, Game and Freshwater Fish Commission. Nongame freshwater fishes (defined as bait in Florida) include: bowfin, carp, catfish, eel, gar, shad, shiner, tilapia, killifish, and sucker, which may be taken by hook-and-line and other specified methods for human consumption. Nongame fishes except catfish may be taken by cast net, minnow dip net ($\leq 4$ ft. diam.), minnow seine ($\leq 4 \times 20$ ft.), or minnow trap ($\leq 1 \times 2$ ft. with a maximum 1 in. funnel). Cast nets and minnow lift nets are prohibited in the St. Johns River Water Management District lands adjacent to Lake Griffin in Lake County. Cast nets are legal in the south and central regions.

Recommended regional books: Carr and Goin's (1959) *Guide to the Reptiles, Amphibians, and Fresh-Water Fishes of Florida,* Tagatz's (1967) "Fishes of the St. Johns River, Florida," Gilbert's (1979) "Part 4. Fishes," and Rohde et al.'s (1994) *Freshwater Fishes of the Carolinas, Virginia, Maryland, and Delaware,* the latter containing valuable information on many fishes that extend into Florida. In fact, the area bounded by the Cape Fear River at Wilmington, North Carolina and the St. Johns River at Jacksonville, Florida is arguably a unique ecological zone. A DeLorme atlas and gazetteer is available for Florida.

**Georgia.** Contact: Department of Natural Resources, Fisheries Management. Minnow seine (< 20 ft. long, $\leq \frac{3}{8}$ in. mesh) is permitted, except in designated trout waters.

Recommended regional fish books: Dahlberg's (1975) *Guide to the Coastal*

*Fishes of Georgia and Nearby States* and Dahlberg and Scott's (1971) "The Freshwater Fishes of Georgia."

**Hawaii.** Contact: Department of Land and Natural Resources, Division of Aquatic Resources. Hawaii's laws are included in this book because transport to and removal of fishes from Hawaii are regulated, and Hawaii is a port of entry into the United States. Any person with facilities for keeping live fishes in reasonably good health may apply for an aquarium fish permit to use fine-mesh traps or nets (other than throw nets) for taking certain aquatic life. Noncommercial aquarium fish collectors are limited to five fishes or aquatic life specimens per person per day. Trading fishes through the mails may prove awkward, because the state has live import rules. For information, request Olin (1993), "Importing Live Organisms to Hawaii, Procedures and Permitting," from University of Hawaii Sea Grant. Accepted taking methods are lay, fence (similar to lay), scoop, draw, drag or seine net, or other nets with a minimum size of 2-inch stretched mesh. One may not intentionally take, break, or damage any stony coral or "live rock" to put into an aquarium.

Recommended regional freshwater fish book: None.

**Idaho.** Contact: Department of Fish and Game. Nongame fishes are carp, suckers, chubs, and squawfish. Accepted nongame fish-taking methods include no more than one minnow net or seine (≤ 4 × 4 ft.), and not more than five minnow traps (≤ 12 × 18 in.). All fishes netted must be killed immediately. For scientific collecting, a scientific collecting permit is required.

Recommended regional fish book: Simpson and Wallace's (1978) *Fishes of Idaho.* A DeLorme atlas and gazetteer is available.

**Illinois.** Contact: Department of Conservation. A fishing license is required for cast nets, shad scoops, and minnow seines to collect minnows for personal use as bait. Cast nets may not exceed 8 feet in diameter or ⅜-inch mesh. Minnow seines may not exceed 6 × 20 feet or ½-inch bar mesh.

Recommended regional fish books: P. W. Smith's (1979) *The Fishes of Illinois,* Pflieger's (1975) *The Fishes of Missouri,* and Burr and Warren's (1986) "A Distributional Atlas of Kentucky Fishes." A DeLorme atlas and gazetteer is available.

**Iowa.** Contact: Department of Natural Resources. Nongame collecting requires a fishing license. Minnows are chubs, shiners, suckers, dace, stonerollers, mudminnows, redhorse, bluntnose, and fathead minnows. Other nongame fishes are green sunfish, orangespotted sunfish, and gizzard shad. Nongame fishes may be taken by dip net (≤ 4 ft. diam.), cast net (≤ 10 ft. diam.), or minnow seine (≤ 20 ft. long with a mesh ≥ ¼ in. bar measure).

Recommended regional fish book: Harlan and Speaker's (1951) *Iowa Fish and Fishing.*

**Indiana.** Contact: Department of Natural Resources, Division of Fish and Wildlife. A scientific collector's permit is available. No person may possess any *Scardinius erythrophthalmus* (European rudd) or any member of the exotic catfish family Clariidae except by permit. Minnows include all members of the minnow family (Cyprinidae) and the young of all species not otherwise protected. It is legal to take minnows. Seines cannot be larger than 4 × 12 feet with ½-inch stretch mesh. Dip nets cannot exceed 3 square feet without sides or walls and a ½-inch stretch mesh. Minnow traps cannot exceed 2 feet in length or an opening diameter of 1 inch. Cast nets must be no larger than 10 feet in diameter and the stretch mesh not larger than ¾ inch.

Recommended regional fish books: P. W. Smith's (1979) *The Fishes of Illinois* and Trautman's (1981) *The Fishes of Ohio,* 2nd edition.

**Kansas.** Contact: Department of Wildlife and Parks, Fisheries and Wildlife Division for permit requirements and current protected species list. Fee is required for a scientific, education, or exhibition permit. Legal bait fishes include minnows (Cyprinidae), suckers (Catostomidae), killifish (Cyprinodontidae), shad (Clupeidae), and sunfish (Centrarchidae) except black basses *(Micropterus)* and crappie *(Pomoxis).* Bait fishes may not exceed 12 inches, and the possession limit is 500 per person. Bait fishes exclude fishes specifically named as threatened, endangered, or in need of conservation. Accepted methods are seine (≤ 4 × 15 ft. with ¼ in. mesh), minnow trap (¼ in. mesh and throat ≤ 1 in. diam.), and dip or cast net (mesh ≤ ⅜ in.). Seining is prohibited on state fishing lakes.

Recommended regional fish book: Tomelleri and Eberle's (1990) *Fishes of the Central United States.*

**Kentucky.** Contact: Department of Fish and Wildlife Resources. A fishing license is required to seine nongame fishes and possess up to 500 minnows. Accepted methods are dip net (≤ 3 ft. diam.), minnow trap (≤ 3 ft. long and 19 in. diam. with 1 in. throat openings), and seine (4 × 10 ft. with ¼ in. mesh; 6 × 30 ft. in the Ohio and Mississippi Rivers and Kentucky and Barkley Lakes). A permit is available for scientific collecting, educational wildlife collecting, or commercial nuisance wildlife control. A collecting permit cannot be used in lieu of a fishing license.

Recommended regional fish book: Burr and Warren's (1986) *A Distributional Atlas of Kentucky Fishes.*

**Louisiana.** Contact: Department of Wildlife and Fisheries. Minnows and nongame fishes may be taken by seine (≤ 30 ft. and ≤ ¼ in. mesh), cast net (< 8½ ft. diam.), dip net, and minnow trap. The taking of bowfin *(Amia calva)* with nets is prohibited during December, January, and February. The taking of paddlefish *(Polyodon spathula)* is prohibited.

Recommended regional fish book: Douglas' (1974) *Freshwater Fishes of Louisiana.*

**Maine.** Contact: Inland Fisheries and Wildlife. For collecting permits, contact Chief of Marine Patrol. No length or limit restrictions apply to nongame fishes. Regulations on collection vary according to gear type and disposition of the fishes (i.e., for sale or personal use).

Recommended regional fish book: Everhart's (1966) *Fishes of Maine.* A Delorme atlas and gazetteer is available.

**Maryland.** Contact: Department of Natural Resources, Freshwater Fisheries. Residents may take up to 35 bait fishes daily by seine (≤ 4 × 6 ft.) or dip net from April 16 through December 31, but not from designated trout streams or their tributaries.

Recommended regional fish book: Rohde et al.'s (1994) *Freshwater Fishes of the Carolinas, Virginia, Maryland, and Delaware.* There is also a key to the fishes (Davis 1974). A DeLorme atlas and gazetteer is available.

**Massachusetts.** Contact: Division of Fisheries and Wildlife. Shiners may be taken for personal use by seine (≤ 36 sq. ft.), hoop or circular net (≤ 6 ft. diam.), or with a fish trap with openings not exceeding 1 inch.

Recommended regional fish book: Mugford's (1969) *Illustrated Manual of Massachusetts Freshwater Fish.*

**Michigan.** Contact: Department of Natural Resources, Fisheries Division. Nongame fishes may be taken without limit. Dip nets (≤ 9 sq. ft., without walls, and lifted vertically) may be used for suckers, smelt, bowfin, gar, and carp on nontrout streams during May in Upper Peninsula and from April 1 through May 31 in Lower Peninsula. Minnows for personal use may be taken by seine, dip net, and trap from all waters except trout streams, where minnow traps may be used. Minnows may be taken by seine (≤ 4 × 12 ft.), hand net (≤ 8 sq. ft. without sides or walls), or minnow trap (≤ 24 in. long). Cast nets (≤ 8 ft. diam.) may be used for minnows in Great Lakes and connecting waters, but not within 100 feet of a dam.

Recommended regional fish books: The 1974 edition of Hubbs and Lagler's (1958) *Fishes of the Great Lakes Region,* Trautman's (1981) *The Fishes of Ohio,* and Scott and Crossman's (1973) "Freshwater Fishes of Canada." A DeLorme atlas and gazetteer is available.

**Minnesota.** Contact: Department of Natural Resources. Those licensed to fish may take minnows for personal use with handheld dip nets (≤ 24 in. diam.), traps (must have a waterproof tag bearing the name and address of the owner), or seines (≤ 25 ft. long or 148 meshes deep with ¼ in. bar measure or 197 meshes deep with ¹⁄₁₆ in. bar measure). Minnows may not be taken from trout waters except with a DNR permit. Live fishes may not be transported; however, special no-fee permits are issued to take, possess, and transport fishes as pets and for scientific, educational, and exhibition purposes.

Recommended regional fish book: Eddy and Underhill's (1974), *Northern Fishes.* A DeLorme atlas and gazetteer is available.

**Mississippi.** Contact: Department of Wildlife, Fisheries and Parks. A scientific permit is available to those qualified. Minnows may be taken for bait using seines (≤ 4 × 25 ft.) and minnow traps or jars (without wings or leads; ≤ 12 × 30 in. with a 1 in. diam. entrance).

Recommended regional fish book: Cook's (1959) *Freshwater Fishes of Mississippi.*

**Missouri.** Contact: Department of Conservation. A scientific collecting permit is available to qualified university or agency affiliated investigators. Up to 150 nongame fishes (≤ 12 in.) may be taken by minnow trap (throat opening ≤ 1½ in. diam.), dip net, cast net, or seine (≤ 4 × 20 ft. and ½ in. bar mesh). Fishes may not be taken by hand.

Recommended regional fish books: Pflieger's (1975) *The Fishes of Missouri* and Pflieger and Belusz's (1982) *An Introduction to Missouri Fishes.*

**Montana.** Contact: Department of Fish, Wildlife and Parks. A collector's permit for scientific studies is available. Native American reservations may have separate rules and permits. No limit is imposed on sculpin, carp, goldfish, sunfish, bullhead catfish, yellow perch, and rainbow smelt (nongame fish). A screen or a net (≤ 4 ft. long or wide) may be used to take sculpins. In Central and Eastern District, where live fishes are allowed for bait, nongame species (except carp, goldfish, sunfish, bullhead catfish, yellow perch, and rainbow smelt) may be taken by seine (≤ 4 × 12 ft.) or minnow trap (≤ 10 × 18 in.). Landing nets may not be used to take nongame fishes.

Recommended regional fish book: Brown's (1971) *Fishes of Montana.* A DeLorme atlas and gazetteer is available.

**Nebraska.** Contact: Game and Parks Commission. Nongame fishes may be taken year-round: buffalo, carp, gar, quillback, sucker, and gizzard shad. A possession limit of 100 minnows exists, and to take minnows from any lake, reservoir, or bayou, to leave minnows in a minnow trap for more than 24 hours, or to possess live diploid grass carp (*Ctenopharyngodon idella;* also known as white amur) is illegal. Dipping, seining, and trapping are prohibited in all closed areas of trout streams and streams with endangered species. Acceptable bait and minnow taking methods are seine (≤ 4 × 20 ft. and ¼ in. mesh), dip net (≤ 36 in. diam. and ¼ sq. in. mesh), and minnow and bait trap (≤ 16 × 24 in. and ¼ sq. in. mesh with a 1½ in. diam. throat).

Recommended regional fish book: Tomelleri and Eberle's (1990) *Fishes of the Central United States.*

**Nevada.** Department of Wildlife. The transport of live fishes is illegal, except under special permit or for use as bait in authorized waters. Approved live bait fishes are Lahontan redside shiner, speckled dace, Tahoe sucker, mountain sucker, mosquitofish, carp, tui chub, sacto blackfish, Paiute sculpin, golden shiner, fathead minnow, red shiner, threadfin shad, and goldfish.

Recommended regional fish book: LaRivers' (1962) *Fish and Fisheries of Nevada.*

**New Hampshire.** Contact: Fish and Game Department. No bag or possession limit is imposed on nongame fishes. A circular drop net (≤ 48 in. diam.), or a square net of equal area, may be used for minnows in nonbrook trout waters. Minnow traps in other trout waters may not exceed 18 inches in length and a throat opening of 1 inch in diameter.

Recommended regional fish book: Scarola's (1973) *Freshwater Fishes of New Hampshire.* A DeLorme atlas and gazetteer is available.

**New Jersey.** Contact: Department of Environmental Protection and Energy, Division of Fish, Game and Wildlife. Bait fishes include all species of *Alosa, Notemigonus, Fundulus, Lampetra, Noturus, Notropis, Pimephales, Rhinichthys,* and *Semotilus.* Other species may be taken with a scientific collecting permit. Bait fishes may be taken by seine (≤ 50 ft. in ponds and lakes larger than 100 acres and ≤ 30 ft. in other fresh waters) but not in trout waters. In trout waters, no bait fishes may be taken in spring, except as and where specified; in winter and summer, up to 35 bait fishes per person per day may be taken by trap (≤ 24 in. long with a funnel mouth ≤ 2 in. diam.).

Recommended regional fish book: Smith's (1986) *The Inland Fishes of New York State.*

**New Mexico.** Contact: Department of Game and Fish. A permit is available for scientific or educational purposes. Nongame fishes are sunfish, carp, carpsucker, buffalo, red shiner, and shad. Nongame fishes may be taken by seine (≤ 20 ft. long and ¼ in. mesh), cast net (≤ ¼ in. mesh), and minnow trap (≤ 24 in. long and 1 in. diam. entrance opening, with mesh between ¼ and 1 sq. in.).

Recommended regional fish book: Sublette et al.'s (1990) *The Fishes of New Mexico.*

**New York.** Contact: Department of Environmental Conservation, Division of Fish and Wildlife. Any licensed person may collect minnows, killifish, mudminnows, darters, sticklebacks, stonecats, smelt, alewives, cusk, and blueback herring for personal use. Dip nets may be used for smelt, suckers, alewives, and blueback herring only. Other allowable gear are seine (≤ 36 sq. ft.; 25 sq. ft. for alewives) and minnow trap (≤ 20 in. long and 1 in. entrance diam.).

Recommended regional fish book: Smith's (1986) *The Inland Fishes of New York State*. A DeLorme atlas and gazetteer is available.

**North Carolina.** Contact: Wildlife Resources Commission. Fishing device license required for taking and selling nongame freshwater fishes with nets, traps, gigs, or baskets. A scientific collector's license is available. Acceptable nongame taking methods are: dip net (≤ 6 ft. diam.), seine (≤ 12 ft. with a mesh of ¼ in.), cast net, and minnow trap (≤ 12 in. diam. and 1 in. diam. throat opening). Up to 200 nongame fishes may be taken year-round. Bait fishes may not be taken from Bear Creek and Rocky River in Chatham County, from Fork Creek in Randolph County, from Deep River below Coleridge Dam in Randolph County, and from Deep River in Moore, Chatham, and Lee Counties. In Lake Waccamaw, any length seine may be used to collect bait fishes, but some species are protected.

Recommended regional fish books: Rohde et al.'s (1994) *Freshwater Fishes of the Carolinas, Virginia, Maryland, and Delaware* and Menhinick's (1991) *The Freshwater Fishes of North Carolina*. Also see Menhinick (1975) and Menhinick et al. (1974). A DeLorme atlas and gazetteer is available.

**North Dakota.** Contact: Game and Fish Department. A scientific collector's permit is available. No possession limit is imposed on nongame fishes; a possession limit of 144 applies to bait-minnows. A license allows the use of one minnow trap (≤ 12 × 30 in. and 1¼ in. throat opening) and/or one dip net (≤ 2 ft. diam. and 3 ft. deep) for smelt or fathead minnows to be used as bait.

Recommended regional fish book: Scott and Crossman's (1973) *Freshwater Fishes of Canada*.

**Ohio.** Contact: Department of Natural Resources, Division of Wildlife. A scientific collecting permit is available. Possession of up to 100 nongame fishes is allowable. Legal taking methods are minnow seine (≤ 4 × 8 ft. inland; no limit on Lake Erie), dip net with mesh larger than ½ inch (≤ 4 ft. per side; 6 ft. in Lake Erie), and cast net (≤ 10 ft. diam. in the Inland Fishing District) with mesh between ¼ and 1 inch.

Recommended regional fish book: Trautman's (1981) *The Fishes of Ohio*. A DeLorme atlas and gazetteer is available.

**Oklahoma.** Contact: Department of Wildlife Conservation. Nongame fishes include carp, buffalo, flathead catfish, drum, river carpsucker, gar, and paddlefish. The daily limit for flathead catfish is ten (20 in. minimum) and two for paddlefish (no size limit), with no limits on other nongame fishes. Seines may not exceed 20 feet in length and ¼-inch mesh. Cast net mesh may be no greater than ⅜ square inch. Seines, cast nets, and dip nets are not allowed in department fishing areas, Lakes Taft and Lone Chimney, and in the Wichita Mountains Wildlife Refuge.

Recommended regional fish books: Tomelleri and Eberle's (1990) *Fishes of the Central United States* and Miller and Robison's (1973) *Fishes of Oklahoma*.

**Oregon.** Contact: Department of Fish and Wildlife. A scientific collecting permit is available. Unprotected suckers, squawfish, carp, chubs, sculpins, and other nongame fishes may be taken without limit by angling, hand, bow and arrow, gaff, and snag hook. A collecting permit and special gear permit are available, which are more useful for smaller fishes.

Recommended regional fish books: Wydoski and Whitney's (1979) *Inland*

*Fishes of Washington* and Bond's (1994) *Keys to Oregon Freshwater Fishes*. A DeLorme atlas and gazetteer is available.

**Pennsylvania.** Contact: Fish and Boat Commission for license information. For a permit to collect a limited number of protected species based on no demonstrable adverse impact on the population, contact the Herpetology and Endangered Species Coordinator, Bureau of Fisheries. Bait fishes may be taken by dip net, minnow seine (≤ 4 sq. ft. diam.), or minnow trap with an opening not more than 1 inch in diameter. The limit is 50 combined species, including all unprotected species of minnows, suckers, chubs, darters, killifish, and stonecats (madtoms).

Recommended regional fish book: E. L. Cooper's (1983) *Fishes of Pennsylvania and the Northeastern United States*. A DeLorme atlas and gazetteer is available.

**Rhode Island.** Contact: Department of Environmental Management, Division of Fish, Wildlife, and Estuarine Resources. A scientific collector's permit is available. Freshwater minnows may be taken by minnow trap, dip net, or seine (≤ 8 × 4 ft. and ¼ in. sq. mesh).

Recommended regional fish books: Whitworth et al.'s (1968) *Freshwater Fishes of Connecticut* and E. L. Cooper's (1983) *Fishes of Pennsylvania and the Northeastern United States*.

**South Carolina.** Contact: Wildlife and Marine Resources Department. A scientific collecting permit available. Accepted nongame fish taking methods include seine (≤ 4 × 20 ft. and ¼ in. mesh) and dip net (mesh ≤ 1½ in. and the bow ≤ 6 ft. in any direction).

Recommended regional fish book: Rohde et al.'s (1994) *Freshwater Fishes of the Carolinas, Virginia, Maryland, and Delaware*.

**South Dakota.** Contact: Wildlife Division. Licensed anglers may take up to 144 combined bait fishes, including Cyprinidae (except carp and goldfish), Catostomidae (except buffalo and carpsucker), and Gasterosteidae. All other nongame fishes are rough fishes or protected species. Minnow seines may not exceed 6 × 30 feet and ⅜-inch mesh; lift nets may not exceed 4 × 4 feet (same mesh); dip nets may be up to 30 inches in diameter (same mesh); minnow traps may not exceed 1 × 3 feet with a 1-inch entrance; and bait fishes may not be collected within 100 feet of designated spawning beds or other management areas.

Recommended regional fish books: Eddy and Underhill's (1974) *Northern Fishes* and Bailey and Allum's (1962) *Fishes of South Dakota*.

**Tennessee.** Contact: Wildlife Resources Agency, Ellington Agricultural Center for a permit to take wildlife requiring management for propagation in captivity. It is legal to take (but not sell) up to 20 of any one nongame fish, up to 50 in the aggregate of bait fishes (Cyprinidae), and unlimited numbers of stoneroller, fathead minnow, and golden shiner. A permit is required to possess buffalofish. All other nongame native fishes may be possessed, unless otherwise protected. Acceptable taking methods are seine (≤ 4 × 10 ft.), umbrella net (≤ 5 sq. ft.), commercial minnow traps (with openings ≤ 1 in. diam.), cast nets (≤ 6 ft. radius), and handheld bow nets (≤ 20 in. diam. with a handle ≤ 8 ft. long).

Recommended regional fish book: Etnier and Starnes' (1993) *The Fishes of Tennessee*. A DeLorme atlas and gazetteer is available.

**Texas.** Contact: Parks and Wildlife Department. With a special permit, an aquaculturist may sell broodfish to another aquaculturist. Upon receipt of a broodfish collection report, the Parks and Wildlife Department will request restitution for the value of the fishes collected. Nongame fishes may be taken by seine (≤ 60 ft. long and mesh ½ sq. in.), cast net (≤ 14 ft. diam.), minnow trap (≤ 24 in. long with a throat ≤ 1 × 3 in.), or dip net (no restrictions). Cast nets or 20-feet minnow seines may be used in coastal waters.

Recommended regional fish books: Chilton's (1998) *Freshwater Fishes of Texas* and Knapp's (1953) *Fishes Found in the Fresh Waters of Texas*.

**Utah.** Contact: Division of Wildlife Resources. Nongame fishes, including carp, suckers, chubs, and minnows, may be taken by seine (≤ 10 ft.) by licensed fishermen, but may not be kept alive, displayed, or held in an aquarium. A certificate of registration is required to take, propagate, or display nongame fishes or aquaculture products in an aquarium; no certificate is necessary for ornamental aquarium fishes. Only those species listed on a certificate of registration may be possessed or transported.

Recommended regional fish book: Sigler and Sigler's (1987) *Fishes of the Great Basin: A Natural History*. A DeLorme atlas and gazetteer is available.

**Vermont.** Contact: Fish and Wildlife Department. No size or possession limits exist for nongame fishes. A minnow seine (≤ 75 ft.) may be used to take nongame fishes from waters not listed as trout waters; however, seines are allowed in the Black, Clyde, Johns, and Barton Rivers. A minnow trap may be used for taking nongame fishes in water inhabited by trout, provided such trap does not exceed 18 inches in length and the entrance hole does not exceed 1 inch in diameter. More than 2 quarts of fishes may not be transported without a permit.

Recommended regional fish book: Smith's (1986) *The Inland Fishes of New York State*. A DeLorme atlas and gazetteer is available.

**Virginia.** Contact: Game and Inland Fisheries. A fishing license is required to collect nongame fishes for personal use. One may legally take up to 20 of any nongame fishes, 50 in the aggregate of bait fishes (Cyprinidae), and unlimited numbers of carp, bowfin, longnose gar, mullet, bullhead, sucker, gizzard shad, blueback herring, white perch, yellow perch, alewife, stoneroller, fathead minnow, golden shiner, and goldfish. A special permit is required to possess buffalo fishes. Acceptable taking methods are seine (≤ 4 × 10 ft.), umbrella net (≤ 5 sq. ft.), minnow trap (with opening ≤ 1 in. diam.), cast net (≤ 6 ft. radius), and handheld bow net (≤ 20 in. diam. with a handle ≤ 8 ft. long).

Recommended regional fish book: Jenkins and Burkhead's (1994) *Freshwater Fishes of Virginia*.

**Washington.** Contact: Department of Wildlife. A scientific collector's permit is available for research or display purposes in public zoos and aquariums, but not to the general public for collecting wildlife to use in home aquariums. It is illegal to keep nongame native fishes in a private aquarium.

Recommended regional fish book: Wydoski and Whitney's (1979) *Inland Fishes of Washington*. A DeLorme atlas and gazetteer is available.

**West Virginia.** Contact: Division of Natural Resources for a permit to collect nongame fishes for propagation. A fishing license or scientific collecting permit allows taking of up to 50 minnows for personal use as bait. Accepted methods are seine (≤ 4 × 6 ft.), minnow trap (with throat ≤ 1 in. diam.), cast net (≤ 6 ft. diam. with maximum ⅜ in. mesh), and dip net (≤ 36 sq. ft. and ¼ in. mesh) from February 1 to April 30.

Recommended regional fish books: Jenkins and Burkhead's (1994) *Freshwater Fishes of Virginia* and Stauffer et al.'s (1995) *The Fishes of West Virginia.*

**Wisconsin.** Contact: Department of Natural Resources. Possession limit is 600 minnows except for bait dealers and residents under 16. Shiners are the only minnows to be taken in Lake Superior and tributaries upstream to the first dam or falls, except upstream from Highway 13 on the Marengo River and upstream from Highway 2 on the Middle and Poplar Rivers. Nongame fishes may be taken by seine ($\leq$ 35 ft. long with a mesh $\leq$ ½ in. in inland waters; 50 ft. in Minnesota and Iowa boundary waters), dip net ($\leq$ 8 ft. diam. or sq.), or trap ($\leq$ 16 × 24 in. and throat $\leq$ 1½ in.).

Recommended regional fish book: Eddy and Underhill's (1974) *Northern Fishes.* A DeLorme atlas and gazetteer is available.

**Wyoming.** Contact: Game and Fish Department. A license for bait-minnow seining and trapping is available. Seines ($\leq$ 5 × 25 ft. and ¼ in. mesh) and traps ($\leq$ 1 × 3 ft. with throat $\leq$ 1 in.) may be used to take fishes. To collect native fishes for aquaria, request a letter of approval from the Chief of Fisheries. Approval will depend upon the purpose for collection, the species and number of individual fishes involved, the methods of collection and transport, and where the fishes are to be held.

Recommended regional fish book: Baxter and Stone's (1995) *Fishes of Wyoming.* A DeLorme atlas and gazetteer is available.

# 5 Plants in the Aquarium

*Richard Edwards*

LANTS and fishes interact. Plants provide oxygen in the presence of strong light, and absorb and reduce the concentrations of dissolved carbon dioxide, nitrates, ammonia, phosphates, and heavy metals. Some plants release chemicals that influence fish color, behavior, and disease resistance. Many fishes require plants directly as food, or indirectly as the hunting grounds in which they forage for small animals such as amphipods and insect larvae. Many fishes spawn among plants. Of practical importance is the calming effect of plants in providing refuge from bright light or predators in open water. Plants add beauty to the aquarium. Some plant types are associated with certain fishes, such as dense vegetation with the Poeciliidae (livebearers). A more subtle association exists between plants growing on rocks in swift currents and some plant-spawning darters (Percidae).

When collecting plants, note the water and substratum conditions to provide similar conditions at home. Try to collect plants with roots intact, with sufficient substratum (gravel, sand, muck, mud, rock) to fill a small flower pot, and protected by a plastic bag. Wild plants should be washed before placing them in an aquarium. Wrap the roots, if loaded with muck, in a segment of old nylon stocking, and then bury the base of the plant under the aquarium gravel, being careful not to bury the growing crown from which the leaves emerge. Alternatively, place the plant in a clay flower pot; a layer of sand or gravel covering the substratum will prevent mud from escaping to cloud the water.

The principal limitations to growing native plants are temperature and light. Many beautiful plants occur only in springs or cold-water creeks and cannot tolerate the high temperatures in fish rooms. Water willow, *Justicia americana,* is a hardy plant accepting any temperature but requiring intense light. The beautiful *Elodea nuttallii,* on the other hand, requires a spring habitat for success, and does not do well at room temperature.

The following species are just a sample of widespread North American plants suitable for aquaria. Trial and error may be the best teacher.

## Plant List

### Characeae
*Nitella* spp.
*Chara* spp.

These plants are green algae with no true leaves. They appear as sticklike segments, each segment (perhaps several inches long) an individual cell. Excellent oxygenators, they provide cover for fry, and tolerate a range of temperatures and light intensities.

*Nitella* species are soft and flexible; *Chara* are usually encrusted with lime. Having no roots, they can be floated, buried in the gravel, or attached to driftwood or rocks.

| | |
|---|---|
| **Ricciaceae**<br>*Riccia fluitans* | An aquatic liverwort similar to the terrestrial *Marchantia, Riccia* does well either floated on the surface or attached to floating driftwood, and rots if submersed. It tolerates warm temperatures but needs strong light. It is an outstanding spawning medium for many killifish, provides cover for fry and invertebrates, and most Poeciliidae will feed on it. |
| **Ranunculacea**<br>*Ranunculus flabellaris*<br>*R. longirostrus*<br>*R. trichophyllus*<br>*R. reptans*<br>*R. sceleratus* | These aquatic buttercups occur in shallow water with their flowers above the surface. Most are stream plants of flowing water. Requiring cool temperatures and intense light, they provide cover for small, bottom fishes and egg substratum for stream plant spawners such as *Etheostoma blennioides.* They do well rooted in plain gravel.<br><br>*Ranunculus sceleratus,* alone in this group, is found in quiet water. It has an open and upright growth habit and provides good cover for larger fishes. |
| **Cabombaceae**<br>*Brasenia schreberi* | This plant is similar to the water lily, but smaller, with individual plants only 16 inches in spread. The leaves are flat, round, and float on the surface. The roots reach to the bottom. The 1-inch flowers are red. In the aquarium, it survives on the surface, but a root mass soon forms to provide food, cover, and spawning substratum. It serves as an excellent cover plant to calm jumping fishes. |
| **Ceratophyllaceae**<br>*Ceratophyllum demersum*<br>*C. echinatum* | Better known as hornwort, *C. demersum* is compact and stiff, while *C. echinatum,* or giant hornwort, is more open, soft, and limp. Hornworts have no roots. They occur in quiet waters on the surface or along the bottom, grow fast, and tolerate all temperatures and low light. They can be floated or anchored, and provide cover, spawning substratum, oxygenation, and containment of jumpers. |
| **Brassicaceae**<br>*Armoracia lacustris*<br>*Rorippa nasturtium-aquaticum* | *Armoracia,* or lake cress, grows both submersed and emersed. The plant grows upright from the bottom, quickly filling a 55-gallon aquarium. The submersed leaves are deeply dissected, the emersed leaves entire with a finely toothed (serrate) margin. The flowers are typical of all the mustards. This beautiful plant can be maintained in the submersed form by trimming. It tolerates cool to moderately warm temperatures and requires soil for the roots.<br><br>*Rorippa,* or water cress, is an outstanding aquarium plant. It tolerates cool to moderate temperatures, but strong light is required and it should be rooted in soil for long-term growth. If floated, it develops quantities of drifting roots, providing cover for fry and invertebrates, adults, and an excellent spawning medium. |
| **Onagraceae**<br>*Jussiaea decurrens*<br>*J. diffusa (= J. repens)*<br>*Ludwigia palustris*<br>*L. lacustris*<br>*L. alternifolia* | *Jussiaea* and *Ludwigia* are identical in growth habit and appearance, differing in flowers and fruits. *Jussiaea* usually has yellow flowers 1 inch across, while *Ludwigia* usually small green flowers without obvious petals (*L. alternifolia* is an exception with yellow flowers). Both genera must be rooted for long-term growth, but the plants will last for months if floated. When floating, they produce thick, spongy white roots at the nodes. The leaves are 1 to 3 inches long and shiny above. These plants remove ammonia, nitrate, and phosphate, and tolerate all temperatures, but need plenty of light to flower. |

## Haloragaceae
*Myriophyllum* spp.
*Proserpinaca* spp.
*Hippuris vulgaris*

All three genera grow submersed until flower production. *Myriophyllum* species grow as single stalks covered by whorls of finely dissected, threadlike leaves. *Proserpinaca* species have a dissected leaf but a flattened blade, and are intermediate between *Myriophyllum* and *Hippuris vulgaris* in appearance. *Hippuris vulgaris* resembles a robust *Elodea*. All can be started by stem cuttings inserted into soil, tolerate cool to moderately warm temperatures, and need intense light. They provide excellent cover and spawning media, and are outstanding oxygenators. The native species are more vigorous than the tropicals cultivated for the commercial aquarium trade.

## Podostemaceae
*Podostemum ceratophyllum*

This is an important and widespread alga-like plant, usually found in fast-moving water attached to rocks. It resembles filamentous algae or a *Fontinalis* moss. Collect the rock to which it adheres to avoid damaging the holdfasts. It needs cool temperatures, current (a submersed powerhead is adequate), and strong light. In the wild, *Podostemum* is home to small crustaceans and aquatic insect larvae, and important foraging habitat. It is the preferred spawning medium for certain darters and an excellent oxygenator.

## Callitrichaceae
*Callitriche heterophylla*

This plant needs a soil substratum and produces a submersed, shrubby growth. Each stem eventually reaches the surface and forms a rosette of leaves. It tolerates cool to moderately warm temperatures but requires intense light. It provides fair cover for fry and adults and is a good oxygenator.

## Acanthaceae
*Justicia americana*

Growth is similar to a small willow tree, with a central stem and many narrow willowlike leaves. It blooms in early summer, the 1-inch flowers resembling lavender orchids. Growth is all emersed and the plant is of limited use, although the flowers are attractive. Gravel is a suitable substratum. It needs intense light.

## Najadaceae
*Najas* spp.
*Potamogeton* spp.

*Najas* species are very similar to one another, requiring comparison of fruits under magnification to identify the species. They have a shrubby growth with narrow filiform leaves and are totally aquatic, even during flowering. They require soil but tolerate all temperatures.

*Potamogeton* is a diverse genus. The leaf ranges from broadly ovate to filiform. Those with two different leaf forms usually occur in calm waters, grow up from depths of 6 feet, tolerate moderate light and warm temperatures, and require soil. The submersed forms usually have one leaf type, fruit below the surface, and filiform or ovate leaves, or even crinkled leaves; there is no typical form or pattern. This group has species adapted to currents and cool temperatures. Most tolerate a poorer substratum, but all need intense light.

*Potamogeton* species are excellent aquarium plants. With care, show specimens will grow to fill a 100-gallon aquarium. They readily root from stem cuttings in the spring, but easily bruise and rot. Try to start with an entire rooted plant. Many are adaptable and hardy given a good start.

## Pondetariaceae
*Heteranthera dubia*
*H. limosa*
*H. reniformis*

*Heteranthera dubia* is hardy and attractive with long elliptical leaves like a willow. It is usually found in some current, and can form beds several feet long. In early summer, small, star-shaped, yellow flowers appear at the ends of stems. In aquaria, it grows in gravel and sand, forming a sizable shrub that may need trimming. Its leaves

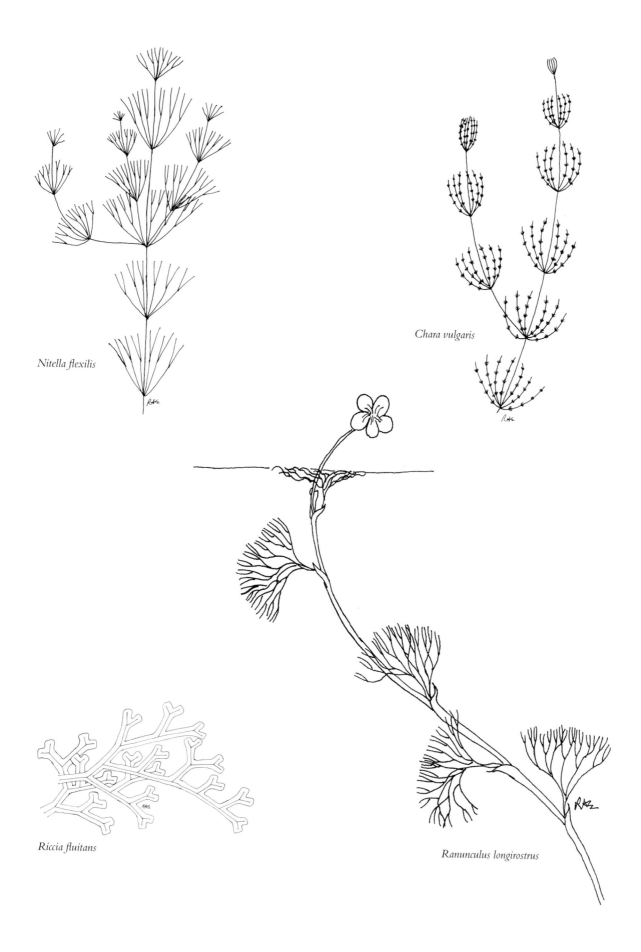

*Nitella flexilis*

*Chara vulgaris*

*Riccia fluitans*

*Ranunculus longirostrus*

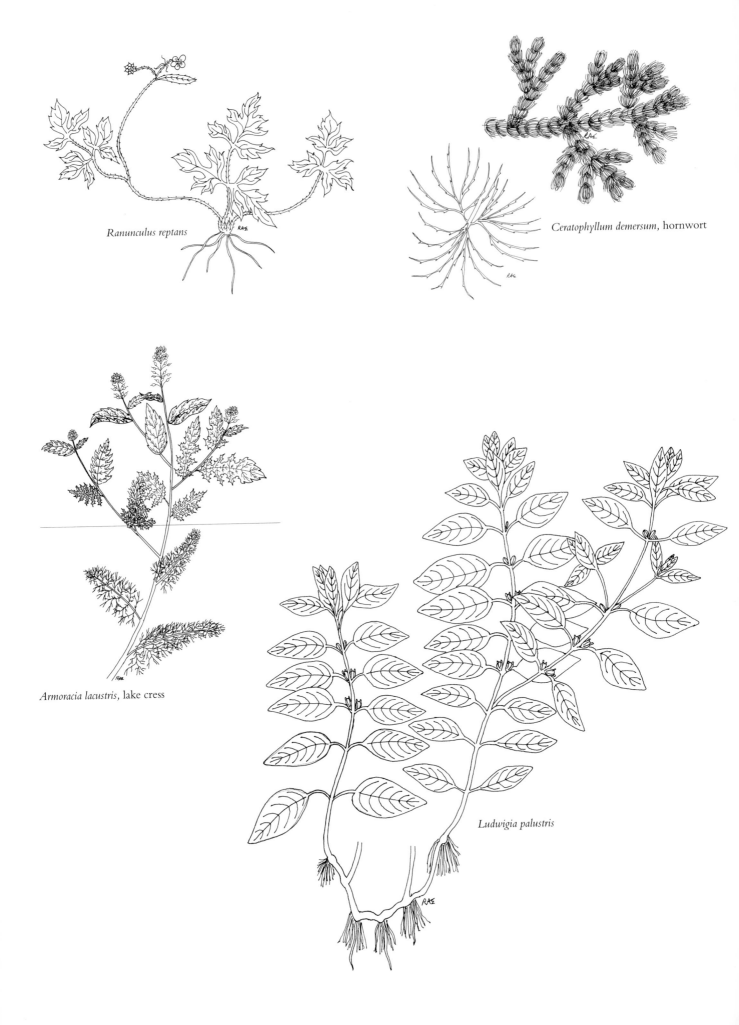

*Ranunculus reptans*

*Ceratophyllum demersum*, hornwort

*Armoracia lacustris*, lake cress

*Ludwigia palustris*

*Myriophyllum heterophyllum*

*Callitriche heterophylla,*
water starwort

*Justicia americana,* water willow

*Najas flexillis*

*Najas flexillis*, detail

*Potamogeton diversifolius*, waterthread pondweed

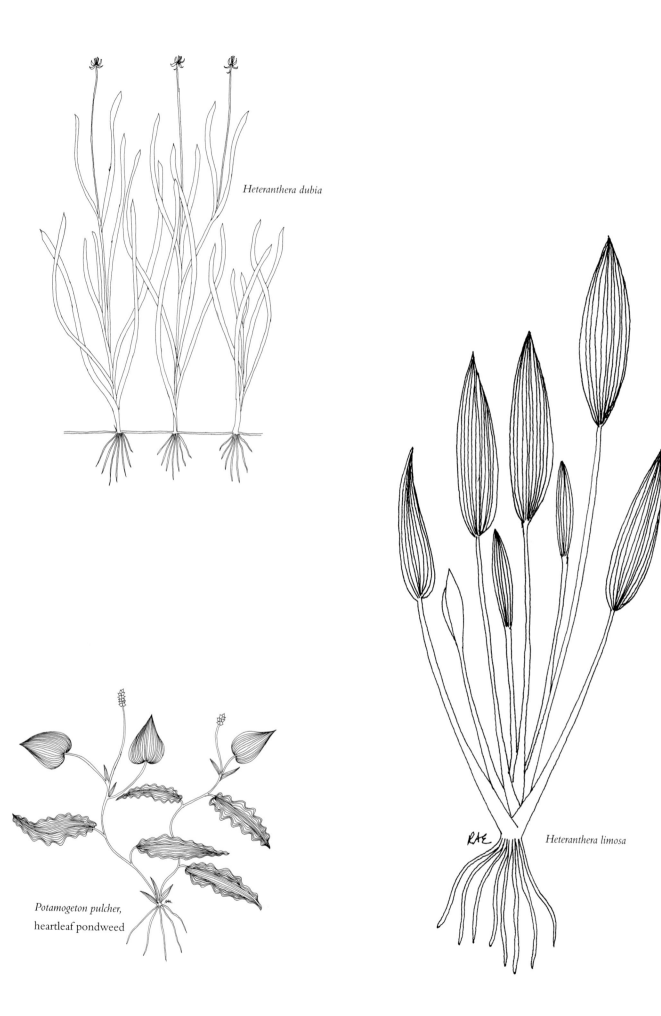

*Heteranthera dubia*

*Potamogeton pulcher,*
heartleaf pondweed

RAE

*Heteranthera limosa*

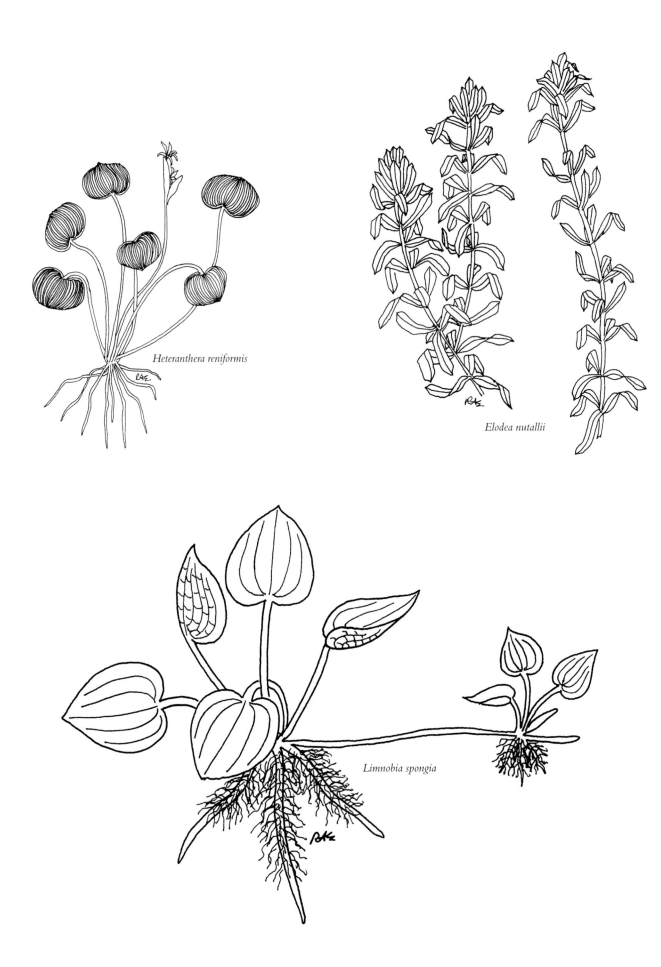

*Heteranthera reniformis*

*Elodea nutallii*

*Limnobia spongia*

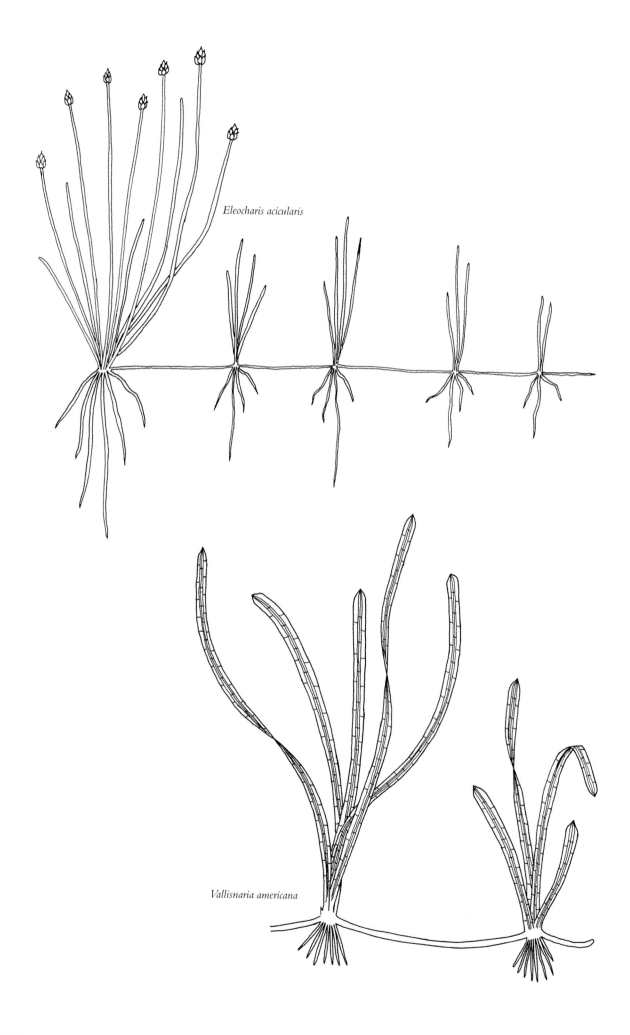

*Eleocharis acicularis*

*Vallisnaria americana*

*Juncus militaris*

*Marsilea quadrifolia*

must be kept clean or will rot. It needs plenty of light and clear water, tolerates cool to moderately warm temperatures, and provides good cover.

*H. reniformis* is a bog plant requiring soil, plenty of light, and warm to hot temperatures. It has heart-shaped leaves and small spikes of blue flowers. It lends itself to shallow aquariums suitable for breeding killifish or *Elassoma* spp. *H. limosa* is similar, its leaves more elliptical.

## Hydrocharitaceae
*Limnobia spongia*
*Elodea* spp.
*Vallisnaria* spp.

Although the physical appearances of these plants are different, their close relationship is revealed by the reproductive structures. *Limnobia spongia* looks like an African violet with white flowers 1 inch across. It usually floats on the surface with root masses reaching toward a muddy bottom. It requires warm temperatures and prefers acidic water, but can tolerate low light for weeks at a time.

*Elodea* spp. are native plants. *Elodea canadensis* is robust, tolerant of all temperatures and low light. It does well in gravel but flourishes in soil, a single strand sometimes reaching more than 2 feet long. *E. nuttallii* is a dwarf species reaching 6 to 8 inches in length. It requires cooler temperatures, and is hardy. *Egeria densa,* formerly known as *Elodea densa,* is the common species of the aquarium trade; some escaped populations exist. All species provide excellent cover for fry and adults, security, and oxygenation.

*Vallisnaria* spp. have ribbonlike leaves. Hardy, they tolerate cool to moderately warm temperatures, do well in gravel, but require intense light. They provide security for larger fishes and are excellent oxygenators.

## Cyperaceae
*Eleocharis acicularis*
*E. obtusa*
*E. palustris*

The Cyperaceae are wetland plants known as sedges or spike rushes. *Eleocharis* is the only genus with plants suitable for the aquarium. All have the same growth habit: (1) they form a clump with round stems standing upright; (2) there are no other vegetative parts; and (3) the fruits appear at the ends of the stems and are used to identify the species. *E. acicularis,* hair grass, attains a height of 6 inches but remains submersed. *E. obtusa* and *E. palustris* are taller at 2 feet. They can be planted into gravel in 10 to 16 inches of water, but need plenty of light. They provide security for some fishes; many *Lepomis* spp. (sunfish) build nests among them.

## Marsileaceae
*Marsilea quadrifolia*

This plant is one of the fern allies. It looks like a four-leaf clover, forming a mat across the bottom of either gravel or soil, or it may float on the surface. On the bottom, it provides good cover for fry, and on the surface, it provides restraint from jumping. It is unique and attractive and does well in poor light.

## Umbellifera
*Hydrocotyle americana*
*H. ranunculoides*
*H. umbellata*
*H. verticillata*

All species of *Hydrocotyle* are creeping stems with leaves arising on short petioles, differing in leaf attachment and shape among species. They form mats on the bottom or float. On the surface, they produce masses of roots. They need only gravel and will thrive in all temperatures and under all lighting conditions.

## Alismaceae
*Echinodorus cordifolius*
*E. radicans*
*E. tennellus*

*E. cordifolius* and *E. radicans* are the familiar Amazon sword plants ranging as far north as southern Missouri. They can be dug up entire from shallow streams, or seeds or plantlets formed on the flowering stalk can be harvested and gradually submersed. They need soil and plenty of light, but are hardy and do best at warm temperatures.

*E. tennellus* resembles a dwarf *Vallisnaria*. It forms dense mats on the bottom, does not do well over 12 inches deep, and needs intense light.

---

## Juncaceae
*Juncus militaris*
*J. repens*
*J. subtilis*

These are the true rushes. Like the sedges, they are wetland plants. See the comments for *Eleocharis obtusa* and *E. palustris*.

---

## Gentianaceae
*Nymphoides peltatum*
*N. cordatum*
*N. aquaticum*

All three species can be treated as miniature water lilies. They require good soil and strong light to flower, can be planted to depths of 2 feet, and provide cover and restraint for larger fishes.

# 6

# Foods and Feeding

BALANCED nutrition, exercise, and removal of pollutants are the keys to viability of eggs and fry, rapid growth, resistance to disease, and reproduction. Aquarists can reduce pollutant levels by changing water, and provide exercise by offering large quarters and supplementary currents with aeration and water pumps. As important as exercise and water changes, however, are live, frozen, and dried foods rich in proteins and fats.

Commercial preparations of dried foods are predominantly carbohydrate-rich grains and smaller amounts of proteinaceous fish meal, shrimp meal, blood, dried milk, fish oils, vitamins and minerals, and preservatives to extend shelf life. Select only dry products supplemented with *Spirulina* algae, which provides color-enhancing carotenoids.

The most frequently used frozen foods are adult brine shrimp and the larval chironomids known in the trade as bloodworms. Other commercially available frozen foods include mysid shrimp, euphausid shrimp (krill), penaeid shrimp, clam, mussel, kelp, fish, beef heart, and squid. Aquarists can make their own frozen foods, limited only by availability and imagination.

The sole recommended freeze-dried food is wax-rich euphausid shrimp, but all freeze-dried foods generate pollution from their waste dust. Freeze-dried tubificid worms have resulted in mass mortality in feeding experiments (Bouguenec 1992). The dried hemoglobin in dust of freeze-dried bloodworms (chironomid larvae) may cause allergic reactions (rhinitis, conjunctivitis, bronchial asthma, and urticaria) in the 20 percent of aquarists, perhaps genetically predisposed, that become sensitized after using the materials repeatedly.

Live foods have the best acceptability and nutritive value. Movement is the most important characteristic that draws predators to prey (Kaiser and Hughes 1993). Some live foods are collected or purchased. Others can be cultivated from starter cultures available through advertisements in aquarium magazines and the trade sections of specialty societies such as the American Killifish Association and the North American Fish Breeders Guild.

## Unicellular Organisms: Protozoa and Algae

**Infusoria.** Dating back to Antonie van Leeuwenhoek's writings describing "infusions" of tiny "animalcules" in pond water, "infusoria" has no biological meaning today. Methods of growing infusoria produce mostly ciliates.

*Paramecium.* Dried grass, lettuce leaf, or banana peel "infusoria" cultures induce growth of ciliated protozoans such as *Paramecium* from pond water or old aquarium water. Pure cultures of certain ciliates are available through magazine advertisements. The pure culture should be added to a jar containing diatomaceous earth-filtered water from an established aquarium. Add a single, dried, half split pea per quart. The peas slowly decay, and in time clouds of fine white specks (ciliates) will appear near the surface and cascade slowly to the bottom. They can be removed with a food baster. If the water smells foul or becomes translucent gray without discrete white specks, the culture should be discarded.

*Euglena.* Green water cultures frequently contain *Euglena,* a flagellated, chlorophyll-containing, one-celled organism that is an excellent first food more easily cultured than *Paramecium.* A culture may be purchased, or *Euglena* can be found outdoors. Filter the stagnant green water to remove other organisms and add it to dechlorinated tap water. Place the culture jar directly under a fluorescent lamp or on a window sill, and add dried yeast or liquid plant fertilizer. The water will turn deep green. Transfer *Euglena* to the fry tank with a food baster. Do not add water to replace what has been removed, because the change in water chemistry may shock and kill the culture. Begin additional cultures (subcultures) when the old culture is dark green. See instructions for culturing algae under the next category, rotifers.

## Rotifers

Rotifers are protozoan-sized, multicellular animals. Both marine and freshwater species are available. A healthy culture consists of females parthenogenetically producing eggs that hatch into more females. If water quality declines, a few males are produced. These mate with females which then produce resting eggs. The resting eggs sink to the bottom where they resist pollution and desiccation, and will not hatch until conditions are optimal. Resting eggs of both marine and freshwater rotifers, along with algal cultures, media, accessories, and instructional materials can be purchased commercially.

*Brachionus plicatilus.* This is the rotifer used worldwide to culture marine fishes. Food for growing rotifers include yeast, protozoa, or motile unicellular algae. *Dunaliella, Isochrysis, Chlorella, Monochrysis,* and other algae are grown in 7 tablespoons of marine salt per gallon of tap water with a small amount of plant fertilizer. The algal cultures are aerated and provided intense fluorescent light 24 hours a day. The green culture water is transferred into the rotifer culture. As the algal culture ages and becomes dark green, it is likely to die off (crash) due to high pH and high levels of waste products. Algal cultures should be regularly subcultured. The rotifers are also cultured at 7 tablespoons of salt per gallon and should receive light around the clock. They appear as fine white specks. Algal culture water is poured into the rotifer cultures for feeding. Rotifer culture water should be filtered through a coffee filter or handkerchief to avoid introducing wastes and fertilizers into the fry aquarium. Rotifers should, of course, also be subcultured. If the rotifers should crash, do not discard the culture; the vessel contains resting eggs. Decant to the last fraction of an inch, and add new algal culture water to the remainder. If resting eggs were in the old rotifer culture, the rotifers will regenerate.

*Brachionus calyciflorus.* This freshwater rotifer is also commercially available and fed algal culture. Use any freshwater algae or wild green water filtered through a handkerchief to prevent contamination. *Philodina* and *Asplanchia* are other rotifers readily cultured on yeast, algae, protozoa, or other foods and available from commercial suppliers.

## Nematodes

Nematodes, or roundworms (Nematoda), are the most abundant animals on earth. Two types are excellent food for larger fry.

**Microworms.** *Panagrillus silusiae* are nutritious foods for baby fishes that cannot rise up into the water column to feed on brine shrimp nauplii. Microworms are easily cultured. Mix 4 cups of dry flaked baby food to ¼ teaspoon of baker's yeast with tap water to make a paste. Spoon the paste into a plastic shoe box or a margarine container to a depth of one-half inch. Add microworm starter culture to the cereal surface and cover. The microworms eat the yeast, which in turn grows on the baby food and generates waste acids, liquids, and carbon dioxide that escapes through slits in the lid. Cultures contaminated with mold or maggots should be discarded. A good culture glistens with microworms swarming on the surface; the worms soon wriggle up the walls. Wipe your finger along the wall to collect pure worms for feeding the fry. At room temperature, the culture lasts only a week or two. One culture should be kept in the refrigerator, where it will last for months and remain available for making new cultures.

**Vinegar eels.** *Turbatrix aceti* are small nematodes living in acidic liquids. Mix brown apple cider vinegar with an equal amount of tap water in a gallon jar, and add starter culture and a slice of apple. Cover the jar with paper towels to keep out flies. As the culture matures, a white line (worms) will appear at the meniscus. To harvest worms, pour the liquid through a brine shrimp hatching net, and empty into tap water. Feed this to the fry with a baster. Vinegar eel cultures probably never die, but new cultures smell better.

## Annelids

The annelid (segmented) worms are divided into the polychaetes, leeches, and oligochaetes. Over 3,000 species of oligochaetes exist, among them the earthworms, red and black tubificid worms, whiteworms, and grindal worms.

**Common earthworms or nightcrawlers.** *Lumbricus terrestris* are excellent food for madtoms, sculpins, sunfish, and larger darters, whether whole or sliced. They can be collected by searching under leaves and rocks, or stimulated to come out of the ground by an electric current or by pouring salt water on the ground. Rake a pile of dried leaves onto a concrete sidewalk or driveway, mix in some garden dirt, water, and wait a few weeks. As the leaves decompose, worms migrate to the pile, multiply, and concentrate at the damp base. Each earthworm may produce 3–4 egg capsules a month, each hatching 2–20 worms that take two to three months to mature. For indoor culture, fill a wooden box with a damp, 50:50 potting soil and peat moss mixture, inoculate the culture with earthworms, and feed them vegetable scraps. Harvest the smaller worms, leaving the breeders to replenish the culture (Glascock 1994).

**Redworms or red wigglers.** *Eisenia* spp. are small earthworms living in mammal dung, and can be obtained from bait shops. The culture container should have a 50:50 peat moss and potting soil mixture and be moist. Feed every two weeks with cornmeal, flake food, or grain. The 4 to 5 mm egg cases are deposited on the surface, each case yielding 20 worms (< 0.5 mm) after seven to ten days at 70°F. The cases can be used to start new cultures or stored in the refrigerator. Place cases in small containers with a little water. They hatch at room temperature within three hours and the young can be fed to the smallest fishes or used to start new cultures.

**Aquatic earthworms.** *Lumbriculus variegatus* is a 1½- to 3½-inch-long aquatic earthworm used in toxicity studies. It reproduces mostly by budding. Set up a 10-gallon aquarium with less than ½ inch of sand, strong aeration, and trickle filtration or canister filtration. Feed every other day with sinking dry food. Harvest by swirling the worms from sand and collecting them with a net. They are available commercially or can be collected in the wild; look for mats of worms in shallow, muddy waters with their posteriors waving in the current (M. Rosenqvist 1994, pers. comm.).

**Tubifex.** Tubifex is a common name for members of the Oligochaete family, Tubificidae, which includes the genera *Tubifex, Nais, Aeolosoma,* and *Phallodrilus.* There are 60 species of tubificids in the fresh waters of the United States. Traditional red tubifex are a mixture of species collected from the effluents of sewage treatment plants where they thrive in the organically rich mud. Most of today's commercial supply is collected in Mexico. Tubificids carry some harmless tapeworms of primitive fishes, but there is no evidence that tubifex carry any major fish diseases. Keep tubificids in cold, slow running tap water. The small amount of chlorine in a dripping tap will not hurt them, and keeps them clean. The worms form a richly colored, active clump at the bottom that should be broken once a day to allow dead worms to wash free.

**Blackworms.** Blackworms are a mixture of tubificid species living in organically rich, highly oxygenated, cold water. They are dark purple, larger and thicker than red tubificids, and more vigorous. Whereas a clump of red tubifex worms forms a flaccid ball in your hand, a clump of black worms will disperse and escape between your fingers, not unlike trying to hold mercury. Black worms live in the sediments of settling ponds of trout hatcheries and food processing plants. One collector gathered 1,100 pounds of black worms a week from a trout hatchery with three settling basins and produced 750,000 to 800,000 pounds of trout a year. Be aware, however, that worm production depends on water flow and quality, food supply, space, weather, and other factors. Having access to a hatchery is no guarantee of a constant supply. When trout get sick, trout managers add chemicals to the water. One common treatment is salt, which will kill the black worms in the settling pond. A ketchup packer's pond produced a good crop of black worms but because the packing house only operated six months of the year, the supply of worms was seasonal.

Blackworms are sensitive to chlorine and cannot be maintained under running tap water. Store them damp, with a thin film of water, in an uncovered container in the refrigerator, where they may survive up to two weeks if washed in cold, dechlorinated water every day. Black worms are available commercially.

**Whiteworms, dwarf whiteworms, and grindal worms.** All are members of the Oligochaete family, Enchytraeidae, ½ to ¾ inch long, and as nutritious as earthworms. (Many older aquarium texts incorrectly state that excess worms in the diet can cause fatty degeneration of the liver.) Whiteworms *(Enchytraeus albidus)* are heat sensitive. Culture them in styrofoam fish shipping boxes with holes in the lid and bottom for air circulation and drainage. Fill the box two-thirds with potting soil and mix in one quart of sand. The medium should be damp, light, and loose. Spread starter over the surface, make a furrow in the middle, and press a small piece of fresh, white bread soaked in milk, or cornmeal mixed with sugar (5:1) to retard the growth of molds, into the hole. Place a pane of glass on the soil to retain moisture. The worms will congregate under the glass and may be removed with a toothpick. Stir the soil periodically to aerate. Eventually, mites or small black flies will infest the culture, which is then discarded.

Grindal worms *(Enchytraeus buchholtzi)* are smaller than whiteworms and should be fed bread or flaked baby food and milk. Their soil should be quite damp and the box kept at room temperature. Other whiteworms include *Enchytraeus variatus* and *E. bigeminus* (Bouguenec 1992).

## Arthropods

No foods are more important to freshwater fishes in nature than chironomids and cladocerans.

**Cladoceran crustaceans.** The most commonly cultured cladocerans are *Daphnia pulex, D. magna,* and *Ceriodaphnia dubia* (an important bioassay test animal). Reproduction occurs largely by parthenogenetic females producing large numbers of eggs in the brood chamber, a dorsal cavity. The few males produced become important only when food, photoperiod, or temperatures are reduced or pollutants increase (Taylor and Gabriel 1993). They fertilize females to make a different kind of egg within a brood chamber that thickens and darkens to become a black ephippium. The ephippium, which then drops off, contains drought- and freeze-resistant eggs that in nature, overwinter and hatch in spring to produce parthenogenetic females.

*Daphnia* may be grown indoors in jars or large aquariums with overhead fluorescent lights, and fed green water or yeast suspension. A culture requires continual feeding and harvest. Wild cladocerans, such as *Sida, Latona, Bosmina,* and *Scapholeberis,* live in open shallow waters, and can be collected from ponds with fine-mesh nets. *Holopedium* occurs in soft acid waters, while *Iliocryptus* lives in mud. *Leptodora* and *Polyphemus* are large and predators of other cladocerans, also attacking small fry. *Diaphanosoma* is a brine cladoceran.

**Anostracan crustaceans.** These are the distinctive fairy shrimp *(Streptocephalus, Polyartemiella, Branchinecta, Eubranchipus, Chirocephalus, Pristocephalus, Artemiopsis, Thamnocephalus)* and brine shrimp *(Artemia salina).* Males and females occur in every population. The females of different populations produce either fertilized or parthenogenetic eggs. Some are thin-walled and hatch immediately, and others are thick-walled for delayed development and cold and drought resistance. Brine shrimp are found in brine lakes and salt ponds. The fairy shrimps live in ephemeral freshwater ponds, ice-melt or prairie pothole pools, or pools in the floodplains of rivers.

*Artemia salina.* The best quality brine shrimp eggs are available in 15-ounce cans from mail-order suppliers. After opening, the can should be resealed and stored in the freezer. For optimal hatches use marine water, vigorous aeration, intense light, and room temperature. Gallon jars with strong aeration will keep all eggs in circulation until hatching; cones and upside-down jars are not necessary. The nauplii begin hatching in 24 hours, and hatching is complete in 48 hours. The smallest fry may require the smallest (youngest) nauplii. A 48-hour culture will contain nauplii twice the size of 24-hour nauplii.

To grow adults, place used marine aquarium or nauplii hatching water in large, shallow containers to evaporate and concentrate. Unadulterated rock salt may be used if marine fishes are not kept. Add nauplii (not eggs) to the water. After a few weeks, the increasing salinity will encourage growth of the nauplii to adulthood. A red alga that grows in brine is used by some commercial producers to feed adult brine shrimp raised in water with rock salt.

San Francisco and San Diego Bays provide less than one-third of the U.S. supply of live adult brine shrimp. The remainder is cultured by Sea Critters in Key Largo, Florida, whose 32 10,000-gallon tanks produce 1,200 pounds of shrimp a week. The shrimp are fed dry yeast, rice bran, spirulina, and vitamins and minerals. Cultured Florida brine shrimp should not be fed or chilled, but kept at 70°F; wild California brine shrimp should be maintained at 50 to 55°F.

*Streptocephalus, Branchinecta* spp. Fairy shrimp, available from mail-order suppliers, should be grown in large, flat containers under bright light, preferably outdoors. After the adults have matured and produced eggs, harvest all adults because they will eat newly hatched nauplii in the container. If no nauplii develop after harvest, dry the sediment on newspaper and store it for several months before submersing the paper to attempt another hatch of the cysts to produce nauplii.

**Amphipod crustaceans.** Amphipods are epibenthic detritivores (detritus feeders living on the bottom surface) collected from submersed vegetation and debris. Marine forms are common under shoreline rocks. Common genera are *Gammarus, Hyalella, Synurella,* and *Crangonyx. Hyalella azteca* is used in aquatic bioassay testing. Males frequently ride the backs of females. Females carry a dozen or more fertilized eggs in a marsupium where the young remain for days after hatching. *Gammarus* and *Hyalella* are cultured in shallow containers and fed presoaked and softened hardwood tree leaves, filamentous algae, cooked and macerated spinach, and finely ground dry fish food. They digest the bacteria and other microbes feeding on decaying vegetable matter.

Amphipods require gentle aeration, eight hours of darkness, and a refuge from overhead light, which is an added benefit of the hardwood leaves. There are eight juvenile and many adult stages, each marked by a molt, and each adult stage producing more young. The life cycle takes less than one month. They are prolific. Amphipods can be harvested from beneath sponge filters or sunken leaves with an aquarium net. They are excellent foods for darters and sunfish.

**Isopod crustaceans.** Isopods live in darkened refuges on land or water. Many are highly modified fish parasites bearing no resemblance to free-living forms. Many aquatic isopods are similar to *Sphaeroma,* the terrestrial pill bug or sow bug. The most common aquatic form is *Asellus,* which occupies the same habitats as amphipods and is cultured in the same way.

**Mysid crustaceans.** Mysids are freshwater, marine, and estuarine crustaceans that carry their young in a brood pouch, giving rise to the common name, opossum shrimp. *Mysis relicta* occurs in deep northern lakes, *Taphromysis louisianae* on the Gulf Coast, and *Acanthomysis awatchensis* on the Pacific Coast. *Mysidopsis almyra, M. bahia, M. bigelowi, Metamysidopsis elongata,* and *Neomysis americana* are used in toxicity testing.

*Mysidopsis bahia, M. bigelowi,* and *M. almyra* are kept at 25 parts per thousand (ppt) salinity or 75 percent sea water, utilizing an undergravel filter containing crushed oyster shell and an outside canister filter layered with oyster shell and activated carbon. Use a 20-gallon or larger aquarium with overhead fluorescent light for 12 hours per day. Strong aeration and high water quality are essential, the shrimp intolerant of nitrites above 0.05 milligrams per liter (mg/l).

The adults are fed live *Artemia* nauplii daily, and eat their own planktonic young if insufficiently fed. To protect juveniles, place a fine-mesh divider in the aquarium, or grow the adults in a large area of suspended netting. At two weeks of age, the females begin producing brood pouches containing 5 to 20 eggs that hatch within three weeks. A female can produce one brood a week.

Mysids are sensitive to salinity and temperature changes, and their aquaria should be managed so algae on the glass do not become excessive. Mysids feed on algae, including the diatoms *Nitschia, Amphora,* and *Cocconeis,* and the filamentous blue-green alga, *Spirulina subsalsa.* The pH should be maintained between 7.5 and 8.1 through water changes or the addition of calcium carbonate.

## Insects

Most native North American fishes are insectivores. Insects provide much higher returns of nutritive value for the energy spent capturing them than crustaceans. Adult and larval insects, and other invertebrates on the surface or in midwater, are called "drift" and are seasonally abundant. Those grazing on rocks, leaves, and logs are usually immature forms called nymphs. Few insects can be cultured, but many can be collected to provide live food, valuable in bringing fishes into spawning condition.

You don't need to be an entomologist to recognize the general types of aquatic insects. Some terms, however, should be explained. In some insects, the last in a series of larval stages goes into an encapsulated, nonfeeding stage (the pupa) that slowly undergoes a radical change, culminating in hatching of the sexually mature adult. This mode of life occurs in flies, mosquitos, and butterflies. Many aquatic insects do not have a pupa, but go to another immature stage that resembles the adult in form but is not sexually mature. This is called a nymph, and it is found in most aquatic groups. Unlike the single pupal stage, there may be many nymphal stages.

**Diptera.** This order encompasses the flies, which have a pupal stage during development. The aquatic types include mosquitos, bloodworms or midges, blackflies, and hover flies. The Diptera contain the only insects that are readily cultured.

Fruit flies. Wingless strains of *Drosophila melanogaster* are available through mail order or from a local school. Excellent for surface-feeding insectivorous fishes, they are cultured in jars using a wet mix of cornmeal, water, yeast, and corn syrup. A paper towel or a piece of cardboard provides the larvae with a dry surface on which to pupate. Cultures are subcultured with bits of pupa-laden paper in clean jars with fresh food. The flies are shaken from the jars directly into the aquaria.

Mosquito larvae are nutritious live foods for surface feeders. They are produced outdoors by placing meat scraps and vegetables into a shaded barrel or wading pool to rot and stagnate the water. The larvae and pupae are harvested by swirling an aquarium net through the surface. The aquaria receiving mosquito larvae should be covered to keep adults from escaping, although most mosquitos will not bite humans. In geographic regions where mosquito-borne diseases such as encephalitis of horses (and sometimes humans) are endemic, this technique should not be used. Contact a local veterinarian to determine risks.

Bloodworms are the larvae and pupae of chironomid flies, also called midges. Chironomids are the most important of all natural fish foods in North American waters, typically making up 90 percent or more of the diet of darters and sturgeons. Live bloodworms are sometimes sold in pet stores. Frozen bloodworms are always available and reasonably priced (about equal to frozen adult brine shrimp) when purchased in bulk. To culture midges, set a shallow tub of water outdoors, add a tablespoonful or more of manure, submerse a rolled up sheet of burlap, aerate vigorously, and in a few weeks the bottom, sides, and burlap should be covered in brown bloodworm casings. Washing the sludge through a window screen will leave clean worms ready to feed. Alternatively, if you withdraw aeration, the larvae will leave their cases and swarm at the surface seeking oxygen; best yields are after dark.

Hover flies have aquatic larvae known as rat-tailed maggots. These gigantic larvae occur in outdoor bloodworm, daphnia, and mosquito larvae ponds and barrels. The flexible air siphon ("tail") stretches to the surface and the flaccid, caterpillar-like body hangs below in the water or sludge. Medical records of people having ingested these maggots while drinking infested water report that the maggots survive in the stomach to produce a characteristically malodorous breath.

Glass worms, or phantom midges, are the half-inch, clear larvae of the insect family Chaoboridae. The most common species is *Chaoborus americanus*. Abundant in colder climes during the winter, glass worms are frequently sold in northern pet stores. To collect, look for farm ponds or ponds draining agricultural fields in winter. The landowner can advise if the ponds contain fish, in which case glass worms will not be present. Any fine-mesh net will suffice. Ponds covered with ice can be cut, and the net worked in a circle through the hole. Live glass worms can be stored in refrigerated tap water or frozen for later use. Methods for culturing are not known.

**Coleoptera** are the beetles. The aquatic forms of this order cannot be cultured, but terrestrial species grown for bird and reptile food are suitable as fish food.

Mealworms are inch-long larval beetles fed to reptiles, amphibians, birds, and large pet fishes. Keep them in cornmeal. At room temperature they become adults rapidly, and are too fast and too hard-shelled for many fishes. Keep them in a refrigerator to induce dormancy. Then once a week, warm them to 45°F, feed a slice of potato, and put them back in the refrigerator. With weekly warming and feeding, they will remain larvae for months.

Superworms (mighty meal worms, king meal worms) are South American beetle larvae that, at 2½ inches, are two to three times larger than mealworms. Their thinner shells are less chitinous, softer and more digestible than those of meal-worms. Refrigeration will kill these tropical larvae.

The remaining aquatic insects have nymphal stages and are collected by kick nets in riffles of streams. Some are large with mandibles that can seize fishes or fish collectors. Because of their preference for low nutrient, highly oxygenated water, several are used as biological indicators of water quality. Their absence indicates pollution from excessive nutrients, while their presence indicates clean, high quality water.

**Ephemeroptera,** the mayflies, are as important as the midges. Mayflies have wings that stand up vertically like a butterfly at rest. Mayfly nymphs have three tail filaments and gills protruding from the abdomen. The name reflects the spring emergence of adults. Mayfly nymphs cling to the underside of rocks and graze on diatoms and microbes. Others burrow in gravel or sand. All the members of a single generation (cohorts) emerge as adults simultaneously, and it is common for billions to cover the surface of the water, shorelines, bushes, and fish collectors. The phenomenon is called a hatch by trout anglers, although it really is an emergence. During an emergence, thousands can be collected in minutes with any kind of net and frozen for later feeding.

It is impractical to raise mayflies, but nymphs are easily collected year-round in riffles. A window screen stretched between two sticks should be placed on the bottom like a seine. The collector then kicks rocks and scrapes the gravel upstream to dislodge nymphs that drift downstream. Here they collect on the screen, from which they are picked with fingers or tweezers and stored in cold, aerated water or on ice. Mayflies quickly die if the dissolved oxygen level declines.

**Plecoptera,** the stoneflies, are similar to mayflies but the cohorts do not emerge all at once. The adults have wings held flat against the abdomen and an elongated body. Nymphs have two long filaments protruding from the rear (vs. three in mayflies), two large wing pads, and a sluggish reaction to capture. They cannot be cultivated, but the nymphs can be collected with kick screens.

**Trichoptera,** the caddisflies, resemble small moths as adults. The mealwormlike larvae may build protective cases from bits of leaves and litter or cemented sand grains or simply burrow, emerging to spin a web to catch drifting debris. The body is soft and has a hard exoskeleton on the head and chest, abdominal gills, large front legs, and prominent hooks at the rear. Collection is by kick screen.

**Odonata,** the dragonflies and damselflies, have nymphs that are useful to feed large fishes; however, they are predacious insects and should not be placed in tanks with small fishes. Nymphs are caught by dragging a net through vegetation or along the bottom.

**Megaloptera** includes the alderflies, dobsonflies, and fish flies. The larvae of this order, called hellgrammites, are large, predaceous, and can kill fishes and bite careless collectors. Diced large hellgrammites are good food for larger fishes, and smaller hellgrammites are treats for sunfish. Collection is by kick screen.

# 7

# The Order Acipenseriformes

*T*HE Acipenseriformes is an ancient order of primitive bony fishes. Their sharklike features include a spiral valvular intestine, cartilaginous endoskeleton, vertebral column extending into the upper lobe of the tail (heterocercal tail), and ventral mouth. The living families with representatives in North American waters are sturgeons (Acipenseridae) and paddlefish (Polyodontidae).

## Family Acipenseridae, the Sturgeons

Acipenseridae have large, protective bonelike plates, and sensory barbels used to explore bottom sediments for food. Their oily flesh takes well to smoking, and the roe is the premier caviar of connoisseurs. Not surprisingly, many are endangered or extinct (Birstein 1993b). Some 27 species of sturgeon occur in large rivers emptying into the sea throughout the northern hemisphere. The European sea sturgeon, *Acipenser sturio,* is probably the animal upon which the Loch Ness monster myth is based.

Sturgeons are in decline worldwide from: (1) fat-soluble pollutants that concentrate in eggs and adversely affect their viability; (2) dams on major rivers that block their migrations and expose the last remnants of populations to netters; and (3) a long juvenile stage and less-than-annual spawning habit (like sharks) that makes them especially vulnerable to depletion by overfishing. They are monitored by the U.S. Fish and Wildlife Service. The *Sturgeon Quarterly* newsletter disseminates information to researchers worldwide.

Sturgeons feed on aquatic insect larvae (mostly chironomids), snails, clams (including *Corbicula*), worms, crayfish and other invertebrates, fish eggs, small fishes, and some plant materials. They spawn in the spring, entering riffle areas of coastal rivers from the sea or inland rivers from large lakes. They scatter adhesive eggs on gravel, boulders, and rocks in strong currents, but the females typically spawn only once in five years.

### Genus *Acipenser*

*Acipenser* are large sturgeons with thick caudal peduncles. Two genera and eight species occur in North America.

### *Acipenser brevirostrum,* shortnose sturgeon

*A. brevirostrum* occurs in Atlantic Coast bays and rivers from New Brunswick to northeastern Florida (Scott and Crossman 1973; Kieffer and Kynard 1993). It spawns in rivers (Buckley and Kynard 1985a,b; Richmond and Kynard 1995; Kieffer and Kynard 1996).

This federally endangered species has been propagated in captivity (Buckley and Kynard 1985c).

| | |
|---|---|
| *Acipenser fulvescens,* lake sturgeon | *A. fulvescens* ranges from Alberta to Saskatchewan, from Hudson Bay and tributaries in the north southward to the St. Lawrence River, into the Great Lakes and Mississippi River drainages. |
| | The lake sturgeon migrates into rivers when water temperatures are 55–65.7°F, and spawns in riffles or rapids to 15 feet deep, its adhesive eggs scattered and adhering to rocks. Eggs hatch within eight days, and the 15 to 20 mm fry rely on yolk sacs for up to three weeks. Spawning locations are influenced by flow rate and temperature rather than bottom type (LaHaye et al. 1992). |
| *Acipenser medirostris,* green sturgeon | *A. medirostris,* an Asian fish, has been reported a few times from the Canadian Pacific south to central California (Birstein 1993a; Birstein et al. 1993). The young are beautiful, but grow too large for aquaria. |
| *Acipenser oxyrinchus,* Atlantic sturgeon | *A. oxyrinchus* is less beautiful and equally unsuitable at 6 to 12 feet. |
| | The major subspecies, *A. o. oxyrinchus,* ranges from the St. Lawrence River (rarely to Labrador) to Florida. The population from the Suwanee River, Florida through the Gulf Coast westward to Louisiana (rarely Texas) is a separate subspecies, *A. o. desotoi.* DNA analyses of Gulf Coast stocks indicate that as many as four distinct and nonoverlapping populations of *A. o. desotoi* exist (Stabile et al. 1996). |
| | The adults migrate into rivers to spawn, and the young remain in rivers for four years before leaving for the sea. |
| *Acipenser transmontanus,* white sturgeon | *A. transmontanus* ranges in rivers from Alaska to Monterey, California (Scott and Crossman 1973). In Canada, it occurs mostly in the Fraser River system, and is landlocked in the upper Columbia River. It attains 20 feet (Scott and Crossman 1973). Adults concentrated below dams are vulnerable to fishing (North et al. 1993). |
| | In the wild, juveniles feed on snails, *Corbicula* clams, tubificids, bloodworms, mysid shrimp, and amphipods (McCabe et al. 1993). White sturgeons are cultured and the young sold in the pet trade. |
| **Genus *Scaphirhynchus*** | *Scaphirhynchus* are the small sturgeons, rarely exceeding 3 feet, with thin caudal peduncles. They can be spawned in aquaria using fish over five years old and more than 16 inches long. |
| | Use at least a 100-gallon aquarium not less than 4 feet long. The aquarium should have an undergravel filter covered with pebbles, and a strong current provided by three or four undergravel filter-mounted powerheads. Add a diatomaceous earth–filled canister filter and two or three sponge filters for additional filtration and aeration. |
| | Feed heavily with chironomids until one fish appears rounded with roe and attended by other thinner fish. If spawning occurs, the eggs will appear adhering to the pebbles and hardware. Remove the parents, place a sponge prefilter over the intake of the canister filter, turn off the powerheads, and await hatching. Start the fry on *Artemia* nauplii. |
| *Scaphirhynchus albus,* pallid sturgeon | *S. albus* often has a filament extending from the upper lobe of the caudal fin, and a flattened, shovel-shaped head with middle barbels slightly in advance of side barbels (Pflieger 1975). The adult has small, scalelike plates on the belly. |

The pallid sturgeon occurs throughout the Mississippi and Missouri River systems, and into the Atchafalaya River.

*S. albus* occurs in strong currents of large, turbid rivers over sand or gravel. Sexual maturity occurs in 7 (male) to 12 (female) years, but females do not spawn until age 15 (Keenlyne and Jenkins 1993), when over 3 feet long. Declining populations have been associated with overfishing, with a failure of young to recruit to the adult population, and with low viability of the eggs or fry. It can hybridize with the shovelnose sturgeon (Henry and Ruelle 1992).

The U.S. Fish and Wildlife Service has detected high concentrations of selenium, cadmium, mercury, PCBs (polychlorinated biphenyls), chlordane, dieldrin, and DDT in fatty and ovarian tissues, suggesting accumulation may be related to reproductive failure (Ruelle and Keenlyne 1993).

The Pallid Sturgeon Recovery Team of the U.S. Fish and Wildlife Service calls for transport of these fish in a 1–3 percent salt solution. Note that 3 percent salt is 30 ppt or the salinity of sea water.

The endangered status of *S. albus* was recently reviewed (Clancey et al. 1993) and a recovery plan proposed (Dryer and Sandvol 1993). This federally endangered species cannot be collected or possessed.

| | |
|---|---|
| *Scaphirhychus platorynchus,* shovelnose sturgeon | *S. platorynchus* is smaller than *S. albus,* has no scalelike plates at any age, and its barbels are in a straight line from one side to the other (Pflieger 1975). It seldom exceeds 2 feet and is available to aquarists. |

The shovelnose sturgeon is common throughout the Mississippi basin but has been extirpated from a previously wider range to the west.

*S. platorynchus* occurs in deep, wide channels with hard sand or gravel in fast current and spawns on rocky or gravel bottoms in spring. Six weeks later, the young are 1 inch long. Maturity is reached in five to seven years (Pflieger 1975; Henry and Ruelle 1992).

Spawning in aquaria so far is unknown, but clean water, sponge filtration, and a diet of blackworms, *Artemia,* and bloodworms enable it to be kept easily. After injecting chorionic gonadotropin, gentle pressure will express milt from the males (J. Kahrs, pers. comm.). The females cannot be expressed and must be sacrificed for the roe. This is the smallest and most common sturgeon, and it is cultivated commercially for the pet trade.

| | |
|---|---|
| *Scaphirhynchus suttkusi,* Alabama sturgeon | *S. suttkusi* differs from the shovelnose sturgeon by lacking sharp, backward-pointing spines on the tip of the snout and in front of the eye (Williams and Clemmer 1991). |

Previously thought extinct, the Alabama sturgeon was rediscovered (Mayden and Kuhajda 1994) in large rivers of the Mobile River basin of Alabama and Mississippi.

*S. suttkusi* is protected as a federally endangered species.

| | |
|---|---|
| **Family Polyodontidae, the Paddlefish** | Only two species of paddlefish survive today, one in the United States and the other in China. The larger Chinese paddlefish is severely threatened by past habitat degradation and construction of the Three Gorges Dam on the Yangtze River. Scientists from China and Kentucky State University are working on techniques |

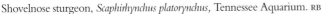

Shovelnose sturgeon, *Scaphirhynchus platorynchus*, Tennessee Aquarium. RB

American paddlefish, *Polyodon spathula*, Tennessee Aquarium. RB

for developing gynogenetic, all-female broodstock to restore the Chinese population.

**Genus *Polyodon***
*Polyodon spathula,* paddlefish

*P. spathula* is a large sharklike fish with an enormous flexible gill cover extending halfway back on the body and a distinctive oarlike snout that differs from marine sawfish (which enter large coastal rivers) in lacking lateral teeth. It is usually less than 4 feet long and 25 pounds, but reaches 5 feet and 184 pounds. Paddlefish breathe by ram ventilation, meaning they must move forward constantly (Burggren and Bemis 1992).

The paddlefish ranges from Mobile Bay, Alabama, westward into the Mississippi basin and northward to Montana, but has been extirpated from Texas and its historical range into the Lake Erie drainage. It is most common in the central and lower Mississippi and less common in other Gulf Coast rivers.

*P. spathula* inhabits backwaters of larger rivers. It feeds on plankton and other small organisms, and ascends smaller, faster rivers in April when the water is 60°F. It spawns over gravel bars, the eggs adhering to gravel and rocks. The nonfeeding prolarvae are swept downstream to pools (P. W. Smith 1979; Robison and Buchanan 1988). They reach maturity in seven to ten years.

Paddlefish have been overfished by the catfishing industry (landing it as a bycatch) to exploit the caviar market. A two-year moratorium in the late 1980s yielded the surprising information that natural mortality is a high 26 to 48 percent (Reed et al. 1992).

Paddlefish can be raised in captivity but are sensitive to their captive environments. Two-month-old paddlefish kept in 100-gallon aquaria with frequent water changes, continuous light, and fed ground trout food every hour grew slower than fish grown in outdoor ponds under natural light with less frequent feeding. Aquarium stock suffered snout damage from bumping into walls (Ottinger et al. 1992).

The Missouri Department of Conservation induced ovulation by injecting LHRH (luteinizing-hormone releasing hormone) and determined that 75°F was warm enough to kill (Kroll et al. 1992). The most recent technique is the injection of Luteinizing Hormone-Releasing Hormone Analog (LH-RHa). LH-RHa is the most potent spawning inducer to date, effective at 0.05–0.1 mg/kg body weight of the fish. It works best after priming the fish with carp pituitary extract (T. Otto, Argent Laboratories, pers. comm.).

Paddlefish are now commercially produced using second and third generation captive-bred brood stock. Most production is supplied to the Asian market as aquarium fishes and consumer caviar, but additional quantities for the North American pet trade are anticipated. Small paddlefish are on display at the Epcot Center in Florida and at the Tennessee Aquarium. Various laws restrict the harvest of adults, and the young are rare in nature.

# 8

# The Order Lepisosteiformes

## Family Lepisosteidae, the Gars

*T*HE gars are a single family of a single order. They are ancient and primitive bony fishes, with: (1) a sharklike spiral valvular intestine; (2) platelike scales composed of the unique material, ganoin; (3) a swim bladder doubling as an accessory breathing organ through its connection to the gut; and (4) a backbone extending slightly into the upper lobe of the tail fin (heterocercal tail). Their similarity to sharks extends to a physiological tolerance to marine water, in which they are equally at home. The roe of gars has been reported to be toxic.

Gars range from the Great Lakes to the Gulf of Mexico and offshore islands. Fossils from southern South America show that gars once had a much larger range in the New World. Fossils are also known from Africa to India, but gars apparently never extended into the Orient.

Capillaries in the swim bladder absorb oxygen and release carbon dioxide from the blood, enabling gars to survive in anoxic swamps using swallowed air. The elongate snout filled with myriad teeth makes them formidable predators of forage fishes.

Gars aggregate in the spring, many males attending each female. The eggs are scattered and adhere to vegetation, rocks, or debris. After the eggs hatch the large yolk-sac larvae remain motionless until the yolk is absorbed a week later. Upon swimming, they feed on zooplankton and mosquito larvae as their first food, later assuming a piscivorous habit.

Young gars are commonly taken by seine and dip net from dense shoreline vegetation of lakes and ponds; they are also available commercially. Two genera and five species occur in the continental United States. The two genera differentiated over 75 million years ago.

## Genus *Atractosteus*
### *Atractosteus spatula,* alligator gar

*A. spatula* is related to *A. tristoechus* of Cuba and *A. tropicus* of Central America (Page and Burr 1991). The young have a rough-edged dark stripe along the flank, and a white stripe bordered in black along the top. This is the largest North American gar at 6 to 10 feet and 300 pounds (Page and Burr 1991).

The alligator gar ranges from western Florida to Mexico, mostly in marine and brackish water. It ascends the Mississippi drainage to Ohio, Illinois, Indiana, and Missouri, but is common only in the extreme southern part of its range.

The adult eats fishes and blue crabs. In captivity, *A. spatula* thrives on minnows and goldfish and is not averse to engulfing smaller brethren.

Alligator gar, *Atractosteus spatula,* Tennessee Aquarium. RB

Spotted gar, *Lepisosteus oculatus,* Cypress Springs, Fla. WFR

Longnose gar, *Lepisosteus osseus,* Tennessee Aquarium. RB

---

**Genus *Lepisosteus***
*Lepisosteus oculatus,* spotted gar

*L. oculatus* has large dark spots. The juveniles have a wide dark band along the back and another along the midflank, often with a thin red line immediately above. The bands break into spots toward the rear.

The spotted gar ranges from the Coastal Plain of western Florida to central Texas. It occurs in the Mississippi drainage northward to southern Oklahoma, Kansas, and Tennessee, and then northward through Illinois. A disjunct population is found around Lake Erie and the eastern drainages of southern Lake Michigan.

*L. oculatus* persists in fresh to brackish, quiet, vegetated backwaters, lakes, and swamps, where it feeds on fishes, and to a lesser extent on crayfish, insects, and shrimp (Robison and Buchanan 1988). It breeds at age 3 or 4 and lives 18 years.

*Lepisosteus osseus,* longnose gar

*L. osseus* has a long snout resembling that of a needlefish *(Strongylura).* It is rusty brown above and on top of the tail and white along the lower body. The young have a black side band and a gold band just above.

The longnose gar ranges from the Delaware River to central Florida, westward to the Rio Grande in all Gulf Coast drainages, and northward within the Mississippi drainage to the Great Lakes and St. Lawrence River.

*L. osseus* occurs in vegetated lakes, swamps, and river backwaters, seldom in brackish habitats. After the planktivorous juvenile stage, it eats mostly shad and silversides. It spawns during spring in small tributaries when temperatures reach the

Shortnose gar, *Lepisosteus platostomus,* Black R., Mo. WFR

high 60s (°F). Maturity takes four to six years, and it lives up to 30 years (Robison and Buchanan 1988).

| | |
|---|---|
| *Lepisosteus platostomus,* shortnose gar | *L. platostomus* has prominent blotches on the unpaired fins, but none on the body, back, or upper jaw. The body is yellow-green, darker above, and white below. It generally grows to 2 feet and 5 pounds (Douglas 1974). |

The shortnose gar occurs in the Mississippi drainage from the Tennessee River in northern Alabama northward to Montana, and in the Lake Michigan drainage to Wisconsin.

*L. platostomus* occurs in turbid rivers and swamps over sand or mud, and near woody debris or vegetation, where it feeds mostly on fishes, but also on insects and crayfish. It spawns in shallows during spring when temperatures are in the 70s (°F) (Robison and Buchanan 1988).

A large aquarium (≥ 125 gal.) with a bed of *Vesicularia* or *Nitella* is required. Feed it fishes, meal worms, and crickets. *L. platosmus* is not spectacular and unlikely to breed in aquaria but worth the attempt.

| | |
|---|---|
| *Lepisosteus platyrhincus,* Florida gar | *L. platyrhincus* resembles the spotted gar with dark blotches everywhere but on top of the head. |

The Florida gar can be separated from the spotted gar by its distribution in southeastern Georgia and the entire Florida peninsula, westward to Panama City. The two species are difficult to separate in western Florida's panhandle.

The "mongrel gar" of Texas is a natural hybrid between the longnose and alligator gars. A hatchery hybrid between the Florida and the longnose gar was reported to be spectacular. Spotted and hybrid gars will be commercially available in pet stores as demand increases.

Gars are hatchery-produced by first injecting adults with hormones. The females are then sacrificed to obtain ripe eggs and the males are squeezed to acquire milt. The fertilized eggs are incubated in glass jars.

# 9 The Order Amiiformes

## Family Amiidae, the Bowfins

**Genus *Amia***

*Amia calva,* bowfin

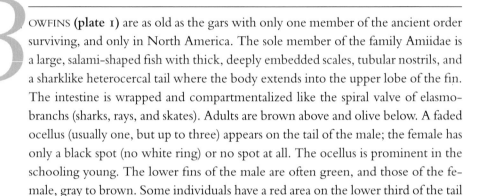

BOWFINS **(plate 1)** are as old as the gars with only one member of the ancient order surviving, and only in North America. The sole member of the family Amiidae is a large, salami-shaped fish with thick, deeply embedded scales, tubular nostrils, and a sharklike heterocercal tail where the body extends into the upper lobe of the fin. The intestine is wrapped and compartmentalized like the spiral valve of elasmobranchs (sharks, rays, and skates). Adults are brown above and olive below. A faded ocellus (usually one, but up to three) appears on the tail of the male; the female has only a black spot (no white ring) or no spot at all. The ocellus is prominent in the schooling young. The lower fins of the male are often green, and those of the female, gray to brown. Some individuals have a red area on the lower third of the tail fin. Adults are 1 to 2 feet long.

Bowfins occur in lowlands from southeastern Canada, Minnesota, and the Great Lakes to Florida, and in coastal drainages west to Texas and then northward to the Colorado River; on the Atlantic Coast they extend north to southern Pennsylvania, and have been introduced to Long Island, New York, but are absent from uplands and the mountain and western states.

Bowfins are common in weedy, muddy ponds, backwaters, ditches, or anywhere stagnant and vegetated. They survive anoxic waters by swallowing atmospheric air, passing it through a canal from the pharynx to a vascularized swim bladder for oxygen–carbon dioxide exchange. They may be capable of aestivating (i.e., hibernating in mud). Bowfins are active at night and often taken on trot lines baited with large shiners. Bowfins of all ages are predators on mostly flat, thin-bodied fishes and crayfish. The powerful gular plate in the lower jaw can crush small turtles.

From late spring to early summer, males nest in aggregations at lake margins, each fanning a clearing in the mud, plants, and woody debris down to a hard surface (often roots) and chewing the plants down to the nubs to make room for the nests. Over a thousand adhesive eggs are deposited by the female. The eggs hatch in eight days and the male defends the fry. He continues defending the young in a compact roving school until they are 3 to 4 inches long.

Adults are taken with hook-and-line but seldom eaten because of myriad small bones. Baited minnow traps sometimes produce young, but seining in deeper coves of small weedy lakes is more promising, as is collecting by dip net from holes in the ice during winter in the northern part of the range. The young aggregate into dense schools during spring, rewarding the collector who has a seine in the right place.

Juveniles are colorful, attractive, and social, tending to stack like cordwood in densely vegetated 40- to 55-gallon aquariums.

Bowfins do well in aquaria with water changes, water movement mostly at the surface, and a diet rich in freeze-dried tubificids, chopped earthworms, beef heart, beef liver, and ground beef. Older fish take live minnows. Adults kept as show predators have not yet bred in home aquaria, but might breed in small ponds or larger (125 gal.) aquaria.

The bowfin has a unique and ancient tapeworm, *Haplobothrium globuliforme,* the sole survivor of a primitive tapeworm order that resembles other strange tapeworms found exclusively in sharks, rays, and skates (elasmobranchs).

# IO    The Superorder Ostariophysi, Order Cypriniformes

*T*HE superorder Ostariophysi contains two lineages, the order Cypriniformes and the order Siluriformes. Ostariophysians are characterized by the presence of a Weberian apparatus, a structure connecting the gas bladder with the inner ear. They also have special club cells in the skin that leak an alarm substance when damaged, which is usually species specific and an adaptation to warn members of a school when one is attacked.

The order Cypriniformes contains over 30 families and 5,000 species, more than any other freshwater group. It is represented in North America by the suckers (Catostomidae) and minnows (Cyprinidae).

## Family Catostomidae, the Suckers

The suckers are stream, river, or lake fishes superficially similar to minnows, but more closely related to the Cobitidae (loaches) of Europe and Asia. Many suckers are tetraploid (i.e., have four sets of chromosomes), although the excess genetic material seems to be nonfunctional.

The primitive forms have smooth lips and feed in soft bottoms. The others have modified lips adapted to sensing and scouring hard bottoms for invertebrates. These lips are covered with tiny, pimpled projections (papillae), tightly folded into pleats (plicae), or some combination of the two.

Suckers are mostly North American, occurring from Mexico to the Arctic Circle. One North American catostomine species ranges into Siberia. The only non–North American sucker is *Myxocyprinus asiaticus,* native to China and a member of the Cycleptinae. The prettiest of the small suckers live in fast, shallow water with rocky bottoms. Because of their quick speed, they are best collected by large (12–20 ft.) seines. Larger suckers are not as attractive and are unsuitable as aquarium fishes.

The larger, primitive suckers inhabit large, slow rivers where they feed on algae, detritus, and small invertebrates. Several are sport fishes and some are harvested as food. The smaller suckers suitable for aquaria often occur in high gradient, clear, rocky streams where they feed on chironomids or diatoms coating the rocks.

Suckers are divided into three subfamilies, the Cycleptinae, Ictiobinae, and Catostominae. There are 12 genera and about 70 species. Smith (1992) evaluated over 150 characteristics of more than 60 species using a taxonomic procedure called parsimony analysis. Unlike traditional counts and measurements, this procedure allows interpretations of how species evolved in different habitats over geologic time. Important recent papers are Smith (1992) for relationships and Page and Johnston

Blue sucker, *Cycleptus elongatus,* Tennessee Aquarium. RB

(1990b) for spawning behaviors. Over 2,000 references to published and unpublished papers on suckers are provided in Bruner (1991).

Suckers are pair or trio spawners. In nonterritorial suckers, females may be larger than males. Nuptial males may develop spawning tubercles on the rays of the anal and lower lobe of the tail fins, and some species have tubercles on the body and head. Nuptial tubercles can wound competing males. They also help males maintain contact with females during spawning.

Typically, male and female suckers make separate short migrations (males first) upstream or to lake shores where males either aggregate with some space around each individual, or rigorously defend a territory using head butts and tail butts to chase competitors. The female remains upstream until ready to spawn, and then drifts downstream and signals a male that she is ready for spawning. The male (and often another nearby male) presses his caudal peduncle against the female; a second male may do the same from the other side. The male(s) then push down slightly, tail first and head up, into the loose bottom, quivering, the breeders releasing gametes to be covered by spraying gravel.

Other suckers scatter eggs high above the gravel (e.g., *Ictiobus*), and still others (e.g., *Erimyzon sucetta)* over plants, gravel, or even on the nests of largemouth bass. One *(Moxostoma carinatum)* constructs its own pit, and another *(Erimyzon oblongus)* may use the pits of minnows (Page and Johnston 1990b).

Some larger suckers have been propagated in hatcheries. The methods used to induce spawning may also work on smaller species.

## Subfamily Cycleptinae

The subfamily Cycleptinae (with 23 or more rays in a long-based dorsal fin) contains *Cycleptus elongatus* in North America and *Myxocyprinus asiaticus* in China; the latter is a popular aquarium fish.

## Genus *Cycleptus*
*Cycleptus elongatus,* blue sucker

*C. elongatus* can be distinguished from members of the Ictiobinae by its 50 or more lateral line scales. It attains 3 feet in length and is too large for aquaria.

The blue sucker occurs in large rivers that drain into the Gulf of Mexico.

Broodstock collected in March at 54°F were injected over a period of days with 1.2 to 10.8 mg of dried carp pituitary gland. Males leaked milt before injection, but females had to be stripped. The 3 to 4 mm eggs hatched in aerated jars in less than one week. The fry were transferred to a pond where they grew rapidly while oxy-

River carpsucker, *Carpiodes carpio,* Mississippi R. RB

Quillback, *Carpiodes cyprinus,* Tennessee R. RB

Smallmouth buffalo, *Ictiobus bubalus,* Brazos R., Tex. RJG

gen concentrations were high, dying off when the weather warmed and oxygen dropped below 2 ppm (Semmens 1985).

| Subfamily Ictiobinae | The subfamily Ictiobinae is characterized by 43 scales or fewer along the lateral line and 23 to 31 rays in a long, falcate dorsal fin. It contains *Carpiodes* and *Ictiobus*. The carpsuckers and quillback of the genus *Carpiodes* have an underslung mouth and silvery body. The buffalofish of the genus *Ictiobus* have a subterminal or terminal mouth and dark or purple body. Buffalofish are ecologically important for their consumption of the introduced Asian mussel, *Corbicula.* Consumption of buffalo, *Ictiobus cyprinellus,* may cause Haff disease, a sudden illness characterized by tender and painful muscles, dark brown urine, and often vomiting. Symptoms begin in less than a day. An unknown substance in some batches of fried or otherwise cooked buffalo fish damages human muscles (rhabdomyolysis) that then leak their cell contents into the blood stream. Diagnosis is supported by massively elevated levels of creatine kinase and elevated levels of other muscle enzymes (Anonymous 1998). No member of either genus is recommended for aquaria due to large size (18 in. to ≤ 2 ft.). |
|---|---|

## Subfamily Ictiobinae

The subfamily Ictiobinae is characterized by 43 scales or fewer along the lateral line and 23 to 31 rays in a long, falcate dorsal fin. It contains *Carpiodes* and *Ictiobus*. The carpsuckers and quillback of the genus *Carpiodes* have an underslung mouth and silvery body. The buffalofish of the genus *Ictiobus* have a subterminal or terminal mouth and dark or purple body. Buffalofish are ecologically important for their consumption of the introduced Asian mussel, *Corbicula.* Consumption of buffalo, *Ictiobus cyprinellus,* may cause Haff disease, a sudden illness characterized by tender and painful muscles, dark brown urine, and often vomiting. Symptoms begin in less than a day. An unknown substance in some batches of fried or otherwise cooked buffalo fish damages human muscles (rhabdomyolysis) that then leak their cell contents into the blood stream. Diagnosis is supported by massively elevated levels of creatine kinase and elevated levels of other muscle enzymes (Anonymous 1998). No member of either genus is recommended for aquaria due to large size (18 in. to ≤ 2 ft.).

## Subfamily Catostominae

The subfamily Catostominae is characterized by 17 or fewer dorsal fin rays. This subfamily contains two tribes.

Longnose sucker, *Catostomus catostomus,* Yellowstone R., Wyo. WFR

| | |
|---|---|
| Tribe Catostomini | The tribe Catostomini contains the genera *Catostomus, Chasmistes, Deltistes,* and *Xyrauchen.* |

**Genus *Catostomus***

*Catostomus* contains suckers with a ventral mouth, unbranched but knobby gill rakers, large but deeply cleft lower lip, and papillae on the upper and lower lips. They have more than 55 gill rakers, distinguishing them from *Moxostoma.*

*Catostomus ardens, C. fumeiventris, C. insignis, C. latipinnis, C. macrocheilus,* and *C. commersoni* are too large for aquaria and some are in serious decline due to impoundments on their native rivers (Chart and Bergersen 1992).

*Catostomus bernardini, C. microps, Castostomus* sp. from the Little Colorado River, and *C. warnerensis* are federally protected and may not be collected or possessed.

The Mexican *C. cahita, C. leopoldi,* and *C. wigginsi* are discussed in Rinne and Minckley (1991).

Subgenus *Catostomus (Catostomus)*

The subgenus *C. (Catostomus)* includes *C. (C.) catostomus* (longnose sucker), *C. (C.) commersoni* (white sucker), *C. (C.) occidentalis* (Sacramento sucker), *C. (C.) rimiculus* (Klamath smallscale sucker), *C. (C.) snyderi* (Klamath largescale sucker), and *C. (C.) tahoensis* (Tahoe sucker).

*Catostomus (Catostomus) catostomus,* longnose sucker

The nuptial male of *C. (C.) catostomus* is black above and the nuptial female is bronze; both sexes have a red stripe along the flank, yellow-orange chin and throat, and a white to pink belly. The longnose sucker matures at 5 inches (aquarium size) but attains 2 feet (Scott and Crossman 1973).

The longnose sucker is an arctic species ranging mostly from the Great Lakes to Labrador, but extends into Maryland, Colorado, and Siberia. It is omnivorous on plants, crustaceans, insects, clams, snails, and trout eggs.

When temperatures reach the low 40s (°F), *C. (C.) catostomus* migrates to tributaries or gravel lakeshores, where several males clasp one female and the 3 mm eggs are pushed into the gravel. The fry hatch in two weeks, remain in the gravel another one to two weeks, and are 11 mm long and swimming by four weeks after hatching (Scott and Crossman 1973).

*C. (C.) catostomus* may hybridize with the closely related *C. (C.) commersoni*

White sucker, *Catostomus commersoni,* Tennessee R. RB

(white sucker) in Canada (Dion 1994). Of the subspecies names *retropinnis, griseus, richardsoni, rostratus, nanomyzon, lacustris,* and *pocatello,* most are probably not valid.

---

*Catostomus (Catostomus) commersoni,* white sucker

The nuptial adult of *C. (C.) commersoni* is brassy with a wide red (eastern and southern forms), cream colored (Saskatchewan), or black (Ontario) stripe on the flank; the stripe may be absent (far north). It attains 2 feet in length.

The white sucker ranges from the Arctic Circle and Yukon Territory to Hudson Bay and Labrador, southward to Georgia and New Mexico, and occurs in most of the United States except the Gulf Coast and drainages west of the Rocky Mountains.

Also omnivorous, *C. (C.) commersoni* spawns much like *C. (C.) catostomus* on gravel riffles or sandy lake margins, several males to a female; the eggs hatch in one week or more at temperatures in the 50s (°F).

Although too large for aquaria at 2 feet long, the methods used by laboratories and bait dealers to breed *C. (C.) commersoni* may be applicable to other suckers. Wild, ripe fish are stripped of eggs into a dry dish, and milt is added up to five hours later. After five minutes river water is added. After one hour, the fertilized eggs are placed in cone-shaped hatching jars with flowing water to provide gentle rolling; small eggs of suckers tend to clump, requiring substantial agitation to break them up for oxygenation. Hatching takes two to three weeks at outdoor temperatures, and the fry are stocked into ponds to feed on bottom ooze and small animals (Kubista 1980; McMaster et al. 1992).

Hale (1970) placed ripe fish in 125-gallon aquaria at 61°F with a gravel bottom, and eggs were found within two days (injections were not necessary). Hatching indoors took one week. Three days after hatching, fry were given ground trout starter chow and live baby brine shrimp. Ludwig (1997) found injections effective in inducing egg ripening.

---

*Catostomus (Catostomus) occidentalis,* Sacramento sucker

*C. (C.) occidentalis* attains 8–20 inches, and the male has a red stripe on the side.

The Sacramento sucker ranges throughout northern California, the Sacramento–San Joaquin drainage northward to Goose Lake, with coastal and inland populations representing poorly defined subspecies.

*C. (C.) occidentalis* occurs in deep pools of clear streams where it feeds on small invertebrates, detritus, and algae, spawning over gravel riffles or along shorelines (Lee et al. 1980; Marshall 1992).

The Sacramento sucker is small enough for aquaria. Use a 55-gallon aquarium for two small fish or 125 gallons for adults; aquaria should have a gravel bottom, trickle filtration, and frequent water changes. A vegetable-based flake food should be offered several times a day.

C. (C.) occidentalis has not yet been bred in captivity, but has been stripped in hatcheries. Typically, the female is injected behind the pelvic fins with dried carp pituitary, but sometimes it is also necessary to inject the male. After 3 to 48 hours, females are stripped by applying slight pressure from the abdomen toward the vent and the expressed eggs collected in a dry bucket. Next, a male is stripped of sperm (milt) in the same manner, but only a drop is necessary. The milt is mixed with the eggs, and the eggs gently washed for several hours to prevent sticking; sometimes powdered clay is added to keep the eggs from clumping.

Hatching occurs in one week. Fry accept *Artemia* naupili and daphnia; pulverized flakes are taken within two weeks. Some subspecies (e.g., Goose Lake population) may be protected in the future under the Endangered Species Act.

| | |
|---|---|
| *Catostomus (Catostomus) rimiculus,* Klamath smallscale sucker | *C. (C.) rimiculus* is a small fish at 12 to 16 inches.<br><br>It occurs in pools of the Klamath River below Klamath Falls, Oregon, and in the Rogue and Trinity Rivers of southern Oregon and northern California (Lee et al. 1980). |
| *Catostomus (Catostomus) snyderi,* Klamath largescale sucker | *C. (C.) snyderi* attains 16 inches.<br><br>The Klamath largescale sucker is found in the upper tributaries above the Klamath River Falls, the Agency Lakes, Clear Lake, and Lost River of extreme southern Oregon, barely entering northern California.<br><br>*C. (C.) snyderi* occurs in larger creeks and rivers and feeds on bottom invertebrates. It spawns from March through April when temperatures exceed 42°F. |
| *Catostomus (Catostomus) tahoensis,* Tahoe sucker | *C. (C.) tahoensis* attains 12 inches. The nuptial male has a bright red stripe along the flank.<br><br>The Tahoe sucker occurs in streams and lakes throughout the Lahontan basin, including Lake Tahoe, Pyramid Lake, and Eagle Lake, California.<br><br>*C. (C.) tahoensis* is found over mixed sand, gravel, and silt where it eats benthic crustaceans and insects. It spawns May through June in riffles when temperatures reach the middle 50s (°F).<br><br>Tahoe suckers are sympatric (occur together) with *Chasmistes cujus* in Pyramid Lake, but do not hybridize with it (Lee et al. 1980; Page and Burr 1991; Buth et al. 1992; Marshall 1992; Bond 1994). |
| **Subgenus *Catostomus (Pantosteus)*** | The subgenus *C. (Pantosteus)* is characterized by a deep notch separating the lips (Smith 1966). Most have prominent cartilaginous jaw sheaths used for scraping mixed algal turfs and associated invertebrates (aufwuchs) from rocks.<br><br>All occur in Pacific drainages (Page and Burr 1991; Robins et al. 1991; Smith 1992). These mostly small fishes spawn on riffles, burying adhesive eggs at the bottom of a depression fanned by the female.<br><br>The predorsal scale counts are useful in separating the species: *C. (P.) clarki* (desert sucker); *C. (P.) columbianus* (bridgelip sucker); *C. (P.) discobolus* (bluehead sucker); *C. (P.) plebeius* (Rio Grande sucker); *C. (P.) platyrhynchus* (mountain sucker); and *C. (P.) santaanae* (Santa Ana sucker). |

**Catostomus (Pantosteus) clarki, desert sucker**

The desert sucker occurs in Colorado River tributaries below the Grand Canyon and into northern Mexico.

Adults are in mountain pools during the day and riffles at night, with juveniles in riffles scraping diatoms and encrusting algae from stones. The female fans a depression in riffles and, accompanied by two or more males, buries adhesive eggs under the gravel (Lee et al. 1980; Rinne and Minckley 1991).

*C. (P.) clarki* is aquarium size (6–12 in.). Small adults should be provided a 55- to 70-gallon covered aquarium with 2 inches of dolomite or aragonite over an undergravel filter driven by powerheads. Provide scattered rocks, trickle filtration, and plant-stimulating fluorescent lights to facilitate diatom growth. A 10- to 11-hour photoperiod mimics the spawning season. Supplement diatoms with cooked spinach, lettuce, squash, green beans, and *Spirulina*-based flake food before the lights go off at night. Ramshorn snails will control waste vegetable matter.

**Catostomus (Pantosteus) columbianus, bridgelip sucker**

*C. (P.) columbianus* is attractive, the nuptial male with a bright orange flank stripe. It is a good aquarium size at 5 to 10 inches.

The bridgelip sucker occurs in the Fraser River, British Columbia, ranging southward through the Columbia River to northern Nevada and eastward to Idaho.

*C. (P.) columbianus* lives in quiet parts of rivers with sand or mud bottoms, probably feeds on aufwuchs (diatoms, algae, other periphyton, and included invertebrates), and spawns in June (Wydoski and Whitney 1979).

**Catostomus (Pantosteus) discobolus, bluehead sucker**

*C. (P.) discobolus* attains a length of 10–16 inches. The nuptial male develops a spectacular blue head, contrasting with a deep brown to black body.

The bluehead sucker occurs in the upper Colorado River drainage and in the Bear and Weber Rivers of Idaho, Wyoming, Utah, Arizona, and New Mexico.

*C. (P.) discobolus* feeds in riffles on aufwuchs scraped from rocks and spawns in late spring at 60°F.

Provide a trio with a 125-gallon aquarium containing rocks and gravel with trickle filtration, plant-stimulating light to grow algae, vegetable foods, bloodworms, and brine shrimp. Include snails as scavengers.

**Catostomus (Pantosteus) plebeius, Rio Grande sucker**

*C. (P.) plebeius* is mottled black on tan above (tending to form bands) and white below. It is 3 to 4 inches long. The nuptial male has a distinctive red stripe along the entire flank.

The Rio Grande sucker occurs in the upper Rio Grande of Colorado and New Mexico, and in Pacific drainages of the Sierra Madre Occidental in northern Mexico. It has been introduced into the Gila River (Lee et al. 1980; Rinne and Minckley 1991).

*C. (P.) plebeius* often inhabits high elevation trout streams, but ranges lower. It spawns from February through April.

**Catostomus (Pantosteus) platyrhynchus, mountain sucker**

*C. (P.) platyrhynchus* attains a length of 5 to 9 inches. The juvenile has three dark vertical bars on the flank. The nuptial male is green to brown above, with an orange-red band immediately over a green-black band on the flank, and has dusky fins.

Rio Grande sucker, *Catostomus plebeius,* Mimbres R., N.Mex. WFR

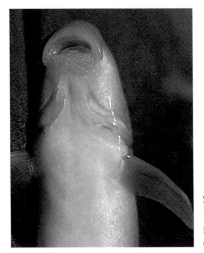

Santa Ana sucker, *Catostomus santaanae,* mouth, Sespe Cr., Ventura Co., Calif. RJG

Santa Ana sucker, *Catostomus santaanae,* Sespe Cr., Ventura Co., Calif. RJG

The mountain sucker ranges from the South Saskatchewan and Milk Rivers to the Columbia, Fraser, and Sacramento–San Joaquin Rivers, and eastward to the upper Missouri River. In the past, the upper Missouri River population was known as *P. jordani.*

*C. (P.) platyrhynchus* is found in upland rocky rivers, sometimes lakes, where it scrapes diatoms and aufwuchs, plants, and invertebrates from rocks. It spawns on riffles in June and July at 50 to 65°F, and has been known to hybridize with *C. (C.) tahoensis, C. (C.) ardens,* and *C. (P.) discobolus* (Scott and Crossman 1973; Wydoski and Whitney 1979; Lee et al. 1980). The mountain sucker matures in two years and lives up to nine.

*Catostomus (Pantosteus) santaanae,*
Santa Ana sucker

*C. (P.) santaanae* is the only gray sucker in its range with dark blotches or mottles. It is a small sucker attaining only 6 inches in length.

The Santa Ana sucker occurs in the San Gabriel and Santa Ana drainages and has been introduced into the Santa Clara drainage, all in California.

*C. (P.) santaanae* is common in creeks and small rivers.

**Genus *Chasmistes***

*Chasmistes* is a western genus with more than 35 branched gill rakers, 55–79 scales along the lateral line, weakly pleated or weakly papillose lips, and having a lower lip with a wide gap between the lobes.

*C. brevirostris* is in the Klamath basin, *C. cujus* in Pyramid Lake, and *C. liorus* in Utah Lake. *C. muriei,* known only from a specimen from the Snake River, is extinct. *C. brevirostris* may become extinct due to its continuing introgressive hybridization with both *Deltistes luxatus* and *Catostomus snyderi. C. liorus* underwent introgressive hybridization with *Catostomus ardens,* however, and the hybrids remained fertile. The original "pure" *C. liorus liorus* no longer exists, but a form in Utah Lake *(C. liorus mictus)* may be closest to the original *C. liorus liorus* (Miller and Smith 1981).

All are protected, and may not be collected or possessed by aquarists.

---

| | |
|---|---|
| *Chasmistes cujus,* cui-ui | The life history of *C. cujus* probably is typical of the genus. The cui-ui occurs in Pyramid Lake, Nevada, where it grazes on diatoms, algae, zooplankton and small benthic invertebrates. Each spring, cui-ui suckers migrate into the lower portions of the Truckee River to spawn on gravel. The eggs hatch in one to two weeks and larvae remain in the gravel another week before moving downstream to the lake. Spawning is successful two or three times every ten years, but the fish lives for 42 years. |

There were once so many fish in spawning runs that individuals were crowded onto the land and harvested as food by the Pauite Indians. Pyramid Lake has been tapped for human uses by 250,000 acre-feet a year, half the annual flow of the Truckee River. The lake has dropped 100 feet since 1900, affecting spawning runs; cui-ui populations have dropped to 300,000 individuals. It would require an additional 70,000 acre-feet (22.8 billion gal.) per year to enable the fish to recover (Emlen et al. 1993).

---

**Genus *Deltistes***
*Deltistes luxatus,* Lost River sucker

*D. luxatus* is the sole species in *Deltistes.* This fish has fewer than 35 branched gill rakers, and a distinctive hump on a blunt, superficially deformed snout. The upper lip is plicate, the lower lip papillose and deeply cleft with three rows of papillae at the narrowest point. It grows to 2 feet or more.

The Lost River sucker occurs in the upper Klamath and Lost Rivers, Agency Lakes, and Copco Reservoir on the Oregon-California border (Lee et al. 1980).

*D. luxatus* is an endangered species, and is not available.

---

**Genus *Xyrauchen***
*Xyrauchen texanus,*
razorback sucker

*X. texanus* is the only species of this genus. Bizarre and humpbacked, resembling the humpback chub *(Gila cypha),* it has rounded caudal fin lobes, sucker lips, and an inferior mouth. It is 15 to 20 inches long. The nuptial male is almost black above, with an orange flank band and yellow belly.

The razorback sucker occurs in lakes Mojave, Mead, and Havasu, but formerly ranged throughout the Colorado River from Wyoming to Mexico (Lee et al. 1980). Today it is confined to large lakes and the main stem of the lower Colorado River in quiet backwaters. Historically, it would spawn at age three on gravel in shallow water, shedding adhesive eggs among the intergravel spaces (Rinne and Minckley 1991).

Dam managers releasing cold, bottom water to protect recreational trout fisheries downstream were killing razorback sucker eggs which require 57 to 64°F water to hatch (Hamman 1985). In addition, exotic fishes introduced by fish and game departments also eat larval suckers and much of the reproductive failure is probably due to predation on the eggs by introduced *Tilapia.* The razorback sucker is

Creek chubsucker, *Erimyzon oblongus*, Obion R., Mississippi R. RB

protected by the states and proposed for listing under the federal Endangered Species Act.

The U.S. Fish and Wildlife Service has a recovery plan. At the Dexter National Fish Hatchery in New Mexico, three-year-old, hatchery-reared broodstock are injected intramuscularly with 220 units of chorionic gonadotropin per kilogram of body weight at 24-hour intervals, and maintained in holding tanks at 63°F with flow-through water. After the third injection, the females are stripped over a period of days. The fertilized eggs are mixed with the readily expressed sperm, then with bentonite clay dispersed in water to keep the eggs from clumping, and incubated in flow-through jars at 70°F.

The eggs hatch in two days and the fry swim up in another week. Some are stocked in rearing ponds and others into rivers, but the larvae are vulnerable (Hamman 1985; J. E. Johnson et al. 1993; Mueller et al. 1993). Only hatchery-reared fish maintain the species.

In the northern Grand Canyon, razorback suckers hybridize with flannelmouth suckers *(Catostomus latipinnis)* (Douglas and Marsh 1998).

| | |
|---|---|
| **Tribe Moxostomatini** | The second tribe of the subfamily Catostominae is the Moxostomatini, containing the genera *Erimyzon*, *Minytrema*, *Hypentelium*, *Thoburnia*, *Moxostoma*, and *Scartomyzon*. |
| **Genus *Erimyzon*** | The genus *Erimyzon* contains three Atlantic and Gulf Coast drainage species called chubsuckers. All have plicate lips, no lateral line, three or four large tubercles on the side of the snout in the nuptial male, and fewer than 13 rays in the short-based dorsal fin. In two species, the male has a bilobed anal fin, the rear shorter than the front. In the third species, the anal fin of the male is pointed. They spawn in gravel nests or vegetation, depending on species. |
| *Erimyzon oblongus,* creek chubsucker | *E. oblongus* has 9–10 rays in the dorsal fin, 39–41 unpored scales in a lateral series, and attains a length of 6 to 9 inches. A tinge of red flushes the fins of juveniles, and diffuse confluent blotches occur along the flank. The tubercles of the male are often recurved and form a triangle; his anal fin is bilobed. |

*E. o. oblongus* ranges from southern Maine and eastern Lake Ontario southward through the coastal states to Georgia, where it is replaced by *E. o. connectens*, a name that may represent intergrades. *E. o. claviformis* occurs in the central United

Lake chubsucker, *Erimyzon sucetta,* Cypress springs, Fla. WFR

States from the southern Lakes Michigan and Erie southward to the Gulf Coast, then east and west in minor drainages from Florida to Texas (Lee et al. 1980).

The creek chubsucker occurs in sluggish waters, often among vegetation, and feeds on small crustaceans, insects, and algae.

Spawning occurs from March through May at 53 to 75°F over gravel (Pflieger 1975). The male holds territory in or near nests of *Semotilus* or *Campostoma* minnows. The female pushes her snout in the gravel and moves pebbles as a signal of readiness, and occasionally spawns with two males (Page and Johnston 1990b; Etnier and Starnes 1993; Jenkins and Burkhead 1994).

In captivity, the creek chubsucker feeds on soft plants, tubificids, and daphnia, supplemented with frozen brine shrimp and bloodworms. Captive spawning has not been successful. Place three or four adults in a 40- to 55-gallon aquarium with gravel and large nesting minnows, or add minnow milt to the aquarium after males become territorial and females swell.

---

**Erimyzon sucetta, lake chubsucker**

*E. sucetta* has 11–12 rays in the dorsal fin, 35–37 scales in a lateral series, and attains a length of 4 to 12 inches. The dorsal fin is rounded in adults, pointed in juveniles. Juveniles sometimes have bold red fins, a black leading edge on the dorsal fin, and a broad black line along the flank. Groups of five to ten young are identifiable from above by the dark, black, longitudinal band.

The lake chubsucker occurs in Atlantic drainages from Virginia to Florida, and westward in Gulf of Mexico drainages to Texas. It ranges northward in the Mississippi basin to the Great Lakes (Lee et al. 1980) and Ontario, where it is rare (Scott and Crossman 1973).

*E. sucetta* inhabits sluggish, shallow waters, in which it browses on decaying vegetation. It feeds on algae, microcrustaceans, detritus, snails, and insects. It breeds in streams during two weeks in March or later, depending on latitude. In rearing ponds, it scatters eggs on vegetation (moss, masses of algae, grass stubs). The 2 mm, nonadhesive eggs hatch in one week at room temperature (Scott and Crossman 1973; Pflieger 1975).

---

**Erimyzon tenuis, sharpfin chubsucker**

*E. tenuis* is darker than the other *Erimyzon* spp., has 40–44 scales in a lateral series, and grows to 8 inches or more. The anal fin of the male is not bilobed, but longer, narrower, and pointed. In the other species, the dorsal is rounded in adults (but pointed in young of all three species). The young have a dark band from snout to

Spotted sucker, *Minytrema melanops,* Woods Reservoir, Franklin Co., Tenn. RB

caudal peduncle, and a narrower stripe above, converging on the snout to form a V. Schools of 10 to 20 young are identifiable from above by a broad stripe from snout to tail. It grows to 8 inches or more.

The sharpfin chubsucker is found in Alabama, Florida, Louisiana, and Mississippi in sluggish, stained backwaters among dense vegetation over sand or silt.

The breeding mode has not been observed, but they probably will spawn on plants over sand in captivity.

## Genus *Minytrema*

The monotypic genus *Minytrema* is closely related to *Erimyzon.* A lateral line, absent in the young, develops with age; in adults, the lateral line scales number 42–47.

### *Minytrema melanops,* spotted sucker

*M. melanops* has black spots forming horizontal rows on the body, orange lower fins, and a dorsal fin edged in black. The nuptial male has two dark flank stripes surrounding a pink stripe. The spotted sucker rarely attains 18 inches.

The spotted sucker is found in Gulf drainages from Florida to Texas and in Atlantic drainages from North Carolina to Florida.

*M. melanops* occurs in lowland rivers, in backwaters over soft bottoms with vegetation and slight current, but also upland streams and reservoirs. It feeds on detritus, small crustaceans, bloodworms, and diatoms.

The male defends a weak territory on gravel or rubble shoals in January. They spawn from March to May, two males usually attending a female. The males press and quiver against the female at the bottom, then drive her upward where eggs and milt are released near the surface in a burst. The sticky eggs sink, the fry hatching less than one week later at 65°F. A week following that, the fry will school (Robison and Buchanan 1988; Etnier and Starnes 1993).

Pond spawning has been induced with injections of human chorionic gonadotropin at the rate of 1,000 international units per kilogram of body weight per day for three to five days (Ludwig 1997). The HCG was injected just behind and to the side of the dorsal fin under anaesthesia. After a few days of injections, the females could be stripped of ripe eggs.

## Genus *Hypentelium*

In *Hypentelium,* the head is flat or concave on top between the eyes, the lips are large and inferior, and the body is marked with the camouflage pattern of dorsal saddles and lateral blotches found in many darters and sculpins. The three species

Northern hog sucker, *Hypentelium nigricans,* Sulphur Fork, Cumberland R., Tenn. RB

Alabama hog sucker, *Hypentelium etowanum,* Butler Cr., Etowah R., Cobb Co., Ga. RB

are *H. nigricans* (northern hog sucker), *H. etowanum* (Alabama hog sucker), and *H. roanokense* (Roanoke hog sucker).

| | |
|---|---|
| *Hypentelium nigricans,* northern hog sucker | *H. nigricans* has a concave area between the eyes, 11 dorsal fin rays, and 44–54 lateral line scales. It is brassy above and white below, with reddish lower fins and three to six black saddles and blotches including one between the head and dorsal fin. The lips are papillose, and the medial cleft extends halfway through the lower lip. It grows to 2 feet, but is usually less than 1 foot. It is the largest member of the genus and probably the least preferred as an aquarium fish. |

The most common species of its genus, it occurs from Ontario southward throughout much of the north-central and northeastern United States, in scattered populations near the mouth of the Mississippi River in Alabama and Mississippi, west of the Mississippi River in the Ozarks and central Arkansas, and on the Atlantic seaboard from North Carolina to New York.

*H. nigricans* occurs in mountain streams and Piedmont rivers, in riffles, runs, pools, and beneath rocks where it eats insect larvae, crustaceans, algae, snails, and fish eggs (by turning over rocks and invading minnow nests). Its plowing attracts other fishes to feed on dislodged foods.

It spawns in pools, riffles, and runs in April and May at 52 to 73°F. A female is attended by three or more males positioning alongside and above; gravel spawning is initiated by the quivering female (Etnier and Starnes 1993; Jenkins and Burkhead 1994).

| | |
|---|---|
| *Hypentelium etowanum,* Alabama hog sucker | *H. etowanum* has a flat area between the eyes and ten dorsal fin rays. It is much smaller (4–9 in.) than the northern hog sucker. |

The Alabama hog sucker occurs in north-central Alabama in the Mobile Bay drainage barely into Tennessee, the Chattahoochee system of Georgia, and the Tombigbee system in Mississippi.

*H. etowanum* typically inhabits fast-flowing riffles of small creeks to large rivers over gravel (Etnier and Starnes 1993).

The juveniles require a large aquarium, and growth is rapid.

| | |
|---|---|
| *Hypentelium roanokense,* Roanoke hog sucker | *H. roanokense* has its lips papillose on the outside only, and 39–44 lateral line scales. Of the four saddles, the first (between the head and dorsal fin) is weak or absent; |

Torrent sucker, *Thoburnia rhothoeca*, James R., Va. WFR

this can be diagnostic. Black speckles on the head and flank are pronounced, also distinguishing it from *H. nigricans*. The Roanoke hog sucker is a dwarf species at less than 4 inches long.

The Roanoke hog sucker is found in the upper and middle Roanoke River drainage (including the Dan River) of Virginia and North Carolina.

*H. roanokense* is found in fast, clear, headwater mountain and Piedmont streams. It feeds on insect larvae, detritus, and algae, and probably breeds during March and April (Jenkins and Burkhead 1994).

**Genus *Thoburnia***

*Thoburnia* species have 17 or fewer dorsal fin rays, plicate upper lips, and lower lips that are a mix of plicate and papillose. In Atlantic slope species, there is a pair of over-and-under white or gray blotches at the base of the tail fin as in *Hypentelium*, from which they differ by having a rounded head profile and a black peritoneum.

*Thoburnia* also differs from *Hypentelium, Scartomyzon,* and *Moxostoma* by having a gas bladder reduced to a single small round chamber, followed by a second wormlike and virtually vestigial chamber that does not extend halfway to the end of the pectoral fins. Like the jumprocks *(Scartomyzon),* species of *Thoburnia* can be identified by river basin as well as by morphology.

The species are *T. atripinne* (blackfin sucker), *T. hamiltoni* (rustyside sucker; both protected or likely to be), and *T. rhothoeca* (torrent sucker). Among all eastern suckers, only *T. hamiltoni* and *T. rhothoeca* have an orange flank stripe, making their identification easy.

*Thoburnia rhothoeca,* **torrent sucker**

*T. rhothoeca* has two white patches on the base of the caudal fin, a body with weak saddles and side blotches, and an orange-brown stripe along the flank that becomes bright orange in the nuptial male. The upper lip is plicate, the lower mostly plicate with elongate papillae.

The torrent sucker is found in the Potomac, Rappahannock, James, Chowan, and Roanoke (but not the Dan) drainages of Virginia.

*T. rhothoeca* is found mostly in upland streams, especially in runs and riffles of creeks and rivers on gravel, boulder, and bedrock. It feeds on algae, detritus, and small invertebrates, and probably breeds in April when temperatures are in the low 60s (°F) (Jenkins and Burkhead 1994).

See *Scartomyzon cervinum* for aquarium care.

Rustyside sucker, *Thoburnia hamiltoni*, Dan R., Va. WFR

Blackfin sucker, *Thoburnia atripinne*, Big Trace Cr., Clay Co., Tenn. RB

**Thoburnia hamiltoni,
rustyside sucker**

*T. hamiltoni* has two pale patches at the base of the caudal fin. The upper lip is plicate, the lower mostly papillose with only slightly developed elongate papillae, distinguishing it from the similar *T. rhothoeca* with longer papillae.

The rustyside sucker occurs in the upper Dan River (Roanoke drainage) in Patrick and Stokes Counties and on the North Carolina–Virginia border (Jenkins and Burkhead 1994; Rohde et al. 1994).

*T. hamiltoni* is found over rubble, gravel, or bedrock in riffles, runs, and heads of pools in clear, moderate to high gradient headwater creeks and smaller mountain rivers.

The rustyside sucker is state endangered in North Carolina and of state "special concern" in Virginia; it is not available to aquarists.

**Thoburnia atripinne, blackfin sucker**

*T. atripinne* is small and beautiful, with a black blotch in the dorsal fin and six or seven horizontal, bold black lines on a gray upper flank that contrasts with a white lower flank and belly. The adult male has tubercles over the entire body, the largest on the anal fin and lower part of the caudal fin. Similar to *Scartomyzon cervinum*, it has bolder black lines and a full blotch on the dorsal fin, rather than a thin tip. It attains 4–5 inches.

The blackfin sucker is found in the upper Barren River system in Tennessee and Kentucky.

*T. atripinne* inhabits headwater streams beneath slab rocks in pools and below undercut banks, where it feeds on insect larvae and small crustaceans. It probably breeds in April on riffles when the water is 55–65°F (Etnier and Starnes 1993).

It is protected in Kentucky and proposed for protection in Tennessee.

**Genus Moxostoma**

*Moxostoma* contains the redhorses, brass or silver colored suckers with orange or red fins and complete lateral lines. The mouth is large, the lips plicate or nearly so (semipapillose or papillose). There are 37–51 lateral line scales, and usually 12 scales around the caudal peduncle (16 in *M. valenciennesi* and *M. hubbsi*). The swim bladder has three chambers.

Most redhorses are too large (*M. anisurum, M. carinatum, M. collapsum, M. duquesnei, M. erythrurum, M. macrolepidotum, M. robustum, M. valenciennesi,* and the sicklefin redhorse) to be good aquarium fishes, but the literature on these species provides information useful on keeping and breeding others. The other species are

Silver redhorse, *Moxostoma anisurum*, Nolichucky R., Tenn. RB

River redhorse, *Moxostoma carinatum*, Nolichucky R., Tenn. RB

Black redhorse, *Moxostoma duquesnei*, Nolichucky R., Tenn. RB

Golden redhorse, *Moxostoma erythrurum*, White R., Mo. WFR

Smallfin redhorse, *Moxostoma robustum*, Oconee R., Ga. RB

*M. hubbsi* (copper redhorse), *M. breviceps* (hookfin redhorse), *M. macrolepidotum* (shorthead redhorse), *M. pappillosum* (shiner redhorse), *M. poecilurum* (blacktail redhorse), and the unnamed grayfin and sicklefin redhorses.

*Moxostoma hubbsi,* copper redhorse

*M. hubbsi* is a high-backed, large (18 inches) redhorse with a short, blunt snout, plicate lips, and a row of 20 massive pharyngeal teeth (subgenus *Megapharynx*) with 45 to 47 large scales along the lateral line.

The copper redhorse is found in Lac St. Louis, Lac St. Pierre, Lac de Deux-

Hookfin redhorse, *Moxostoma breviceps*, Nolichucky R., Tenn. RB

Montagnes, and the Ottawa, Richelieu, and Yamaska Rivers, St. Lawrence River system, entirely within southwestern Quebec.

It occurs in large rivers and lakes, where it feeds by crushing clams, snails, and other invertebrates. It has a long life span (12–15 years), high growth rate, high fecundity, and spawns later than other redhorses (Scott and Crossman 1973).

Branchaud and Gendron (1993) spawned wild fish held at 65 to 73°F and injected intramuscularly twice at 12-hour intervals with 15 mg/kg of carp pituitary extract. They used a 3 ml syringe and inserted a 23-gauge needle under a loosened scale in front of the dorsal fin.

Of four females injected, only one produced ripe eggs when gently pressed. Males injected with 6.6–8.6 mg/kg of pituitary extract readily expressed milt in 12–24 hours. Eggs and milt were mixed dry in a bowl, covered with water, stirred for five minutes, rinsed in clean water, and allowed to harden for one hour. Then the 2.8 mm, nonadhesive eggs were floated in a nitex net suspended in a 125-gallon aquarium and a stream of dechlorinated water played on them at 2.5 liters per minute (40 gal./hr.; the discharge from a small powerhead would suffice).

At two weeks, the fry were swimming up to the surface. They took ground trout chow and live *Artemia* nauplii as first foods, and sinking pellets afterward. At 1 inch long, they began eating small zebra mussels *(Dreissena polymorpha)*. Population enhancement with hatchery-reared stock may offer a good control of zebra mussels and *Corbicula* clams.

The copper redhorse is a rare fish that has been proposed for protection in Canada.

---

*Moxostoma breviceps,*
hookfin redhorse

*M. breviceps* was previously considered a synonym for the wide-ranging *M. macrolepidotum*. Its upper lip is plicate, the lower plicate adjacent to the mouth but segmented toward the rear (semipapillose); the rear of the lower lip is not indented. It matures at 9 to 12 inches, but attains 18 inches. Juveniles are attractive aquarium fish.

The hookfin redhorse occurs in the Ohio River basin and the Cumberland and Tennessee drainages to the south in large streams and rivers on rock-, sand-, or gravel-bottom riffles, runs, or pools. It eats mostly caddisflies and midges. It spawns during March, the male making large troughs or circular pits with sand at the edges and stones and pebbles in the middle (Burr and Morris 1977; Robison and Buchanan 1988).

Blacktail redhorse, *Moxostoma poecilurum,* Hatchie R., Tenn. RB

---

**Moxostoma macrolepidotum,**
**shorthead redhorse**

*M. macrolepidotum* has strongly plicate lips, the lower becoming segmented (subplicate) toward the rear. The dorsal fin is slightly concave but not falcate, usually with 13 rays. There are 9 pelvic fin rays and 40–46 large scales along the lateral line. It attains 20 inches.

The shorthead redhorse is found from Saskatchewan to Hudson Bay and the St. Lawrence drainage, southward through the Mississippi basin to Arkansas, and on the Atlantic slope from New York to South Carolina. The subspecies, *M. m. pisolabrum* (or pealip shorthead redhorse), occurs in the Ozarks of Arkansas and Missouri and surrounding areas. The newly recognized and revalidated *M. breviceps* of Kentucky, Tennessee, and Alabama was previously included within *M. macrolepidotum.*

*M. macrolepidotum* occurs in large rivers, lakes, and reservoirs, over sand, rubble, rock, and silt, and feeds on vegetation and small invertebrates. It spawns in rivers or ascends into gravel-bottom streams for spawning on runs during May at 55 to 60°F (Jenkins and Burkhead 1994).

Adults captured by electrofishing were stripped. The 3.3 mm eggs hatched in eight days at 60°F. Newly hatched, 10 mm fry rested on the bottom for the first five days before feeding, and reached the juvenile stage (all fins developed, mouth functional, yolk absorbed) when ¾-inch long (Buynak and Mohr 1979).

---

**Moxostoma pappillosum,**
**shiner redhorse**

*M. pappillosum* has a deeply indented (V-shaped) lower lip, and both lips are entirely papillose. The dorsal fin has 12–13 rays, the lower fins are orange, and it has 42–44 lateral line scales. At 9 or 10 inches, it is small enough to keep in large, covered aquaria.

The shiner redhorse is found in the Roanoke and Chowan drainages of Virginia and North Carolina, southward to the headwaters of the Santee River in South Carolina (Lee et al. 1980; Rohde et al. 1994).

*M. pappillosum* occurs in medium-sized streams and rivers, and sometimes in lakes, where it feeds on ostracods and plants on sand, gravel, or rubble of shallow pools and slow runs, often pushing aside stones. The shiner redhorse probably breeds during June and July (Jenkins and Burkhead 1994).

---

**Moxostoma poecilurum,**
**blacktail redhorse**

*M. poecilurum* has 41–44 large, lateral line scales and a bold black bar in the lower lobe of the caudal fin bordered below by two white lower rays. Adults are commonly 10–15 inches (see also the grayfin redhorse).

Bigeye jumprock, *Scartomyzon ariommus,* Dan R., N.C. FCR

The blacktail redhorse is in Gulf drainages from Texas to Florida, and northward in the Mississippi Valley to Kentucky, although it probably does not spawn north of the Obion River in Tennessee (Burr and Carney 1984).

*M. poecilurum* lives in medium- to large-sized streams over sand or rock bottoms (Lee et al. 1980), and can probably be maintained like *Catostomus occidentalis.*

*Moxostoma* sp., grayfin redhorse

The unnamed grayfin redhorse is similar to *M. poecilurum,* its closest relative, but lacks the black-and-white stripe on the lower lobe of the tail fin, at most having a pale gray bar.

The grayfin redhorse occurs in the Apalachicola drainage of Florida, Georgia, and Alabama, the river immediately east of *M. poecilurum*'s range. See Page and Burr (1991). It inhabits large, clear or turbid, sandy and rocky streams and rivers.

*Moxostoma* sp., sicklefin redhorse

The unnamed sicklefin redhorse has slightly molariform pharyngeal teeth, 13–14 dorsal fin rays, and usually 9 pelvic fin rays. The body is iridescent green to brassy, and the tail is red.

The sicklefin redhorse is known from the Little Tennessee and Hiwassee River systems on the western slope of the Appalachian highlands (B. Freeman, pers. comm.) in swift waters of creeks and medium-sized rivers. It is too large for aquaria.

**Genus *Scartomyzon***

*Scartomyzon* is a subgenus of *Moxostoma*. It is treated as a genus in this book in recognition of the common preferences for small streams, common ancestry, and contiguous ranges along the eastern and Gulf Coasts.

The jumprocks have 18 or fewer dorsal fin rays, 50 or fewer equally sized scales along a complete lateral line, 15 or 16 scales around the caudal peduncle, 3 or 4 chambers to the swim bladder, a silvery or speckled (but not black) peritoneum, and a lack of 2 pale areas at the base of the tail fin (Smith 1992; Jenkins and Burkhead 1994). Jumprock identifications can be approximated by the river system in which they are found, but identified with certainty only by morphology.

*Scartomyzon ariommus,* bigeye jumprock

*S. ariommus* has a large eye, slightly concave head, and flat, flaring, papillose lips. The fins are pale, dusky, yellow, orange, or red, and the fish reaches 9 inches.

The bigeye jumprock occurs in a small area of the upper and middle Roanoke drainage, including the upper Smith River and Dan River in Virginia and North Carolina.

S. *ariommus* occurs in mountains and foothills, in 30- to 75-foot-wide, clear streams of medium gradient, often under boulders in runs and pools. It feeds on aquatic insect larvae and mites, and spawns in February and early March at 40 to 50°F (Jenkins and Burkhead 1994).

Although not yet spawned in aquaria, it is a good candidate. Provide a 55- to 125-gallon covered aquarium with large rocks on a pea gravel base, strong current with submersed powerheads, and trickle filtration.

Feed frozen bloodworms and brine shrimp, supplemented with live blackworms, chopped shrimp, and earthworms. After conditioning, reduce the photoperiod to six hours of light and lower the temperature as much as possible. Then raise the temperature to 45°F and photoperiod to between eight and ten hours of light.

If spawning occurs, eggs will be visibly adhering to rocks. Remove the rocks to a sponge-filtered aquarium for hatching, and feed the fry after swim-up with *Artemia* nauplii and *Ceriodaphnia*.

| | |
|---|---|
| *Scartomyzon cervinus,* black jumprock | S. *cervinus,* the black jumprock, is elongate and has thick, plicate lips and seven or more dark horizontal stripes on the flank; the juveniles have four to six dark blotches. It matures at 4 to 5 inches and attains 7 inches. |

The black jumprock occurs along the Atlantic Coast, in the Chowan, Roanoke, Tar, and Neuse drainages, and has been introduced into the James and New drainages of Virginia and North Carolina.

S. *cervinus* is found mostly in mountain streams, less so in the Piedmont, and occasionally in the Coastal Plain. It prefers swift, high gradient creeks and small rivers (1 to 4 ft. deep), over rubble, rock, and bedrock. It feeds by scraping rocks for midges, mites, algae, and detritus. It spawns during May and June at 60 to 70°F (Jenkins and Burkhead 1994; Rohde et al. 1994).

Provide three or four adults with a 30- to 55-gallon aquarium equipped with trickle filtration, submersed powerheads for current, and scattered stones on a gravel base. Feed frozen bloodworms (chironomids) and adult brine shrimp, live blackworms, and chopped earthworms and shrimp.

| | |
|---|---|
| *Scartomyzon lachneri,* greater jumprock | S. *lachneri* has plicate lips, eight dark stripes above, a tail with the upper lobe pointed, lower lobe rounded, the lowest ray white, and the fins sometimes with an orange tint (Page and Burr 1991). The nuptial male is iridescent silvery black above, with fins primarily a rich, blue-gray. There are white tubercles on a single row in the anal fin and lower lobe of the tail fin. |

The greater jumprock occurs in small to medium tributaries of the Chattahoochee and Flint Rivers of the Apalachicola River drainage in Georgia and Alabama.

Spawning has been observed during June at 66°F in a 2-foot-deep rubble and gravel chute 30 feet long. Groups of three to seven adults were scattered through the chute facing upstream. Typically, two males pressed their bodies and rubbed their caudal regions against one female; then all three quivered and broke apart (Burr 1979a).

| | |
|---|---|
| *Scartomyzon rupiscartes,* striped jumprock | *S. rupiscartes* has 10–11 dorsal fin rays. The upper lobe of the caudal fin is pointed, and the lower lobe rounded. The body has brown horizontal lines wider than intervening white lines; the belly is white and the fins orange-red. The nuptial male has a yellow or brown stripe along midflank and orange fins. The dorsal and tail fins may be dusky at the edges, resembling *S. cervinus;* however, the two species occur in nonoverlapping areas (i.e., are allopatric). *S. rupiscartes* grows to 12 inches.

The striped jumprock is found in the Pee Dee and Santee Rivers of the Carolinas to the Altamaha River in Georgia on the Atlantic slope, and in the upper Chattahoochee River (Apalachicola drainage) on the Gulf slope in Georgia, probably by stream capture in the Blue Ridge.

*S. rupiscartes* occurs in mountain and upper Piedmont streams, over sand and rock, in riffles and runs. |
| *Scartomyzon* sp., brassy jumprock | The brassy jumprock is a slender fish, its back slightly elevated, with 12 rays in the dorsal fin and thick, plicate lips. It grows to 14 inches. Juveniles are stouter, dark horizontal lines alternating with wider white lines.

For 110 years this fish was known as the "smallfin redhorse, *Moxostoma robustum*" but is today considered an unnamed *Scartomyzon* species of the upper Cape Fear, Pee Dee (Yadkin), Santee, Savannah, and Altamaha drainages from Virginia to Georgia and is uncommon throughout its range.

The brassy jumprock lives in large creeks, rivers, and reservoirs, over sand, gravel, silt, or rubble. Adults are in pools and runs, the juveniles in backwaters. It feeds on aquatic insect larvae, and probably spawns in April, or later after migrating upstream (Jenkins and Burkhead 1994; Rohde et al. 1994).

A 55-gallon aquarium with small rocks on a gravel bottom and an outside power or canister filter is minimal for two or three 6- to 7-inch or larger individuals. Provide snails and madtoms as scavengers, and feed frozen bloodworms and adult brine shrimp, supplemented with live blackworms, crushed snails, and chopped earthworms and shrimp. |
| *Scartomyzon congestus,* gray jumprock | *S. congestus* has 42 or more scales along the lateral line and attains 2 feet.

The gray jumprock occurs in the Brazos River to the Rio Grande below the Big Bend in Texas and northeastern Mexico.

*S. congestus* is found in uplands (including the Edwards Plateau) and sometimes at lower elevations, in pools, deep runs, backwaters, and even lakes. |
| *Scartomyzon austrinus,* Mexico jumprock | *S. austrinus* has 42 or more scales along the lateral line, and fins more yellow-gold than orange. It grows to 18 inches.

The Mexico jumprock occurs in Pacific drainages in Mexico, and is now rare or extirpated from the Rio Conchos just above the Big Bend of the Rio Grande in Texas. It is found around rocks and boulders in seasonally torrential streams.

Check its status before attempting collection. |
| **Family Cyprinidae, the Minnows** | Typically fusiform, minnows are silvery fishes of less than 1 inch to over 6 feet long. They occur in Europe, North America, Africa, and Asia, making up one quarter of all freshwater fishes (Jenkins and Burkhead 1994). North America has 15 percent of the world's 2,100 cyprinids; indeed, minnows occur throughout the United States, Canada, and beyond. |

There are currently 49 genera and 291 described valid species in the United States, Canada, and Mexico (38 confined to Mexico). For information on Mexican species, see DeMarais (1991), Miller (1991), and Contreras-Balderas and Lozano (1994). Exotic minnows introduced into North America include the rudd and bitterling (from Europe), the goldfish, grass, bighead, and silver carps (from Asia), the common carp (from Asia via Europe), and a few others. Exotic species are not covered in this book.

Minnows typically occur in aggregations or schools consisting of many species. The best collection method is seining. Aggregations are found beneath undercut banks, over shallows, or in shaded pools. Some species are best taken by pulling the seine downstream, others by pulling the seine into corners. Some large minnows will take an artificial fly or a hook baited with dough or earthworm.

Most minnows scatter their eggs over vegetation or gravel, a few insert eggs into crevices or beneath rocks, and still others construct a nesting trough, pit, or hill. The preparation of the substratum for spawning is a recent or derived (apomorphic) character, whereas scattering eggs is the more primitive condition.

The reproductive behaviors of minnows are classified into seven types: (1) broadcasting or egg scattering (e.g., goldfish and many *Notropis*), (2) crevice spawning (e.g., *Cyprinella, Hesperoleucus*), (3) saucer building (e.g., *Agosia*), (4) pit building (e.g., *Campostoma*), (5) pit-ridge building (e.g., *Semotilus*), (6) gravel-mound building (e.g., *Nocomis, Exoglossum*), and (7) egg clustering (e.g., *Pimephales, Codoma, Opsopoeodus*) (Johnston and Page 1992).

## Broadcasters

Broadcasters with adhesive eggs, such as goldfish and golden shiners, are bred in ponds with Spanish moss, synthetic yarns, the roots of water hyacinths, or clumps of dense vegetation as the spawning substratum. Adhesion to plants protects eggs from being buried in silt in the absence of current. Some fast-water fishes also have adhesive eggs, which protects them from being swept from richly oxygenated water into stagnant pools.

Many broadcasting cyprinids with nonadhesive eggs deal with currents and predators by spawning near the bottom where eggs can fall into protective interstices between rocks and pebbles. Broadcasters may also produce nonadhesive eggs. The benefits of different strategies were discussed by Platania and Altenbach (1998).

## Genus *Notemigonus*

*Notemigonus* is a monotypic genus containing only *N. crysoleucas*.

## *Notemigonus crysoleucas*, golden shiner

*N. crysoleucas* naturally hybridizes with several American minnows, and may have affinities to the European rudd, *Scardinius erythrophthalmus*, with which it has been artificially hybridized. The golden shiner is an acutely snouted, angular minnow with a distinctive fleshy ridge or keel in front of the anal fin, which originates below the rear of the dorsal fin. It is variable throughout its vast range, but in general the young are silvery, and large adults are brassy with reddish highlights. It grows to 6 inches or more (twice this in Florida), but usually matures at 3 inches.

The golden shiner occurs throughout eastern Canada south of Hudson Bay from Saskatchewan to Nova Scotia, and the entire eastern United States. The most important of all largemouth bass bait fishes (fathead minnows are more important

Golden shiner, *Notemigonus crysoleucas,* Reelfoot Lake, Tenn. RB

for crappies), it has been transplanted through commercial bait sales everywhere except at high elevations.

*N. crysoleucas* originally consisted of three subspecies based on the number of anal rays (8–19): *N. c. crysoleucas* in the northeast, *N. c. auratus* from the Great Lakes to Arkansas and Oklahoma, and *N. c. bosci* from the Carolinas to the Gulf states. If ray counts are a genetic character indicating an isolated population, then subspecific status could be justified. It is now known, however, that ray counts are influenced by temperature during development of the embryo; thus higher counts would always occur in fish growing in the southern states, irrespective of their parentage. For this reason, the validity of these three subspecies is no longer accepted.

The golden shiner inhabits lower and middle elevation creeks, streams, rivers, ponds, and lakes, at low and high pH, warm and cold temperatures. It is most common in shallow, quiet, vegetated waters where it forms schools, but also occurs in mixed groups with other minnow species. It feeds on cladocerans, chironomids and other larval insects, snails, mites, and algae, mostly in midwater and at the surface. Golden shiner larvae and adults are saltatory-search or pause-travel foragers (i.e., they make short forward movements, scan the area, and then move on if there is nothing to attack) (Browman and O'Brien 1992).

*N. crysoleucas* is readily collected by seine or cast net, or can be purchased from a bait store. Large adults can be taken on small fish hooks baited with dough.

The golden shiner spawns at any time if provided a long photoperiod (16 hr. of light) and warm temperatures; either environmental alteration alone is insufficient (De Vlaming 1975).

In aquaria, *N. crysoleucas* spawns on sunken or floating spawning mops, floss bound into a mat, *Nitella, Vesicularia, Cabomba, Myriophyllum,* or even over gravel, the eggs numbering 100–300 in a 6-inch-square spawning mat (Stone and Ludwig 1993). It can also be spawned in outdoor wading pools using fiberglass furnace filters as the spawning medium (Buynak and Mohr 1980b).

The newly hatched larvae are 4 mm long, and differ from other minnow larvae by pigment pattern and fin ray counts (Snyder et al. 1977). Provide rotifers, green water, protozoa, or infusoria as first foods, and *Artemia* nauplii a week later.

**Genus *Notropis***

*Notropis,* as presently constituted, consists of several lines of evolution (Schmidt and Gold 1994). *Notropis* species lack barbels at the angle of the jaws, have eight dorsal rays, a dorsal fin origin over or behind the pelvic origin, an anal fin origin under the rear of the dorsal fin, and a 4–4 pattern of the major row of teeth in the throat (pharyngeal teeth). Most are silvery, with or without a black line along the middle of the flank, and some develop red or orange jaws, fins, or bodies during the spring breeding season. They are small, usually around 2 to 4 inches as adults.

*Notropis* are peaceful, and excellent in community aquaria. Breeding condition can be induced in aquaria by providing a long photoperiod (16 hr. light:8 hr. dark) and chilling followed by increased temperatures; thus nuptial coloration and spawning of many species is possible virtually year-round.

To spawn most species of *Notropis,* separate the sexes and provide live foods and high protein flakes at 60°F or less for two months. Then place the fish together into the spawning aquarium with large gravel or pebbles, and raise the temperature 5°F or more over five days. Spawning behavior usually commences within a few days, marked by flashing undulations by the males, fin erection, and operculum flaring. Females may also flash and undulate if ready to spawn.

Eggs are scattered a few inches above the gravel in the swiftest current, sometimes over plants. The eggs are not adhesive, drifting freely in the current before settling among the pebbles or gravel. After spawning, remove the adults for a second two month cycle of conditioning, and they may spawn again. The eggs hatch in three to five days, and the fry require microinvertebrates (e.g., vinegar eels, rotifers, ciliates) as first foods. Growth is rapid at first, and sexual maturity occurs in the second year.

The largest genus of the American Cyprinidae, *Notropis* today consists of three subgenera (*Alburnops, Notropis, Hydrophlox*) and species whose taxonomic allocation has not been agreed upon.

---

**Subgenus *Notropis* (Alburnops)**

Species of the subgenus *N. (Alburnops)* usually have eight or fewer anal rays, generally lack pretty colors, live in large rivers, and are mostly egg broadcasters. They are relatively easy to breed.

Members of *N. (Alburnops),* based on anal rays alone, would include *alborus, ammophilus, asperifrons, atrocaudalis, baileyi, bifrenatus, blennius, boops, braytoni, buccula, buchanani, cahabae, candidus, chalybaeus, chihuahua, chiliticus, chlorocephalus, dorsalis, edwardraneyi, girardi, greenei, harperi, heterodon, heterolepis, hudsonius, hypsilepis, longirostris, ludibundus, lutipinnis, maculatus, mekistocholas, orca, ozarcanus, petersoni, potteri, procne, rupestris, sabinae, shumardi, similus, spectrunculus, texanus, tristis, uranoscopus, volucellus,* and *xaenocephalus.*

---

*Notropis (Alburnops) anogenus,*
pugnose shiner

*N. (A.) anogenus* is a silvery to pale yellow minnow with a tiny upturned mouth, dark stripe along the flank to the snout, lips, and chin, and a black wedge on the tail fin. A dark line runs along the back and the back scales are dark edged. It is 1½ to 2 inches long.

The pugnose shiner occurs in the Lake Ontario drainage of Ontario and New York to the Red River of Minnesota and the Dakotas, but is rare.

*N. (A.) anogenus* is found in clear, slow moving, densely vegetated lakes and streams with sand or marl bottom, and is intolerant of turbidity. It spawns during June.

A 5-gallon aquarium is suitable for five individuals. Provide a filter pad-covered undergravel filter below 1 inch of mixed sand and dolomite gravel. The pugnose shiner is sensitive to water quality, and requires tiny foods such as *Cerio-*

*daphnia* and *Daphnia*. Include snails to maintain cleanliness, and abundant rooted *(Vallisneria)* and unrooted vegetation *(Nitella* or *Vesicularia)* that may be necessary to trigger spawning. Strong light is needed to maintain plant health; declining plants could pollute water and kill fish. Probably an egg broadcaster over plants.

| | |
|---|---|
| *Notropis (Alburnops) potteri,* chub shiner | *N. (A.) potteri* is dull yellow-olive above, silvery below, and has a finely black-spotted, silvery band along the flank. It averages 2 inches, but gets much larger.<br><br>The chub shiner occurs in the San Jacinto, Trinity, and Brazos Rivers of Texas and the Red River of Texas, Arkansas, and Oklahoma. It has recently extended into the Mississippi River downstream to Louisiana (Lee et al. 1980).<br><br>*N. (A.) potteri* lives close to the bottom in large, turbid rivers over sand and gravel close to shore. It feeds on bottom invertebrates (mostly chironomids), open-water invertebrates (mostly *Daphnia* and its relatives), and small fishes, also ingesting some sand apparently while digging midges from the bottom (Robison and Buchanan 1988). |
| *Notropis (Alburnops) bairdi,* Red River shiner | *N. (A.) bairdi* has a head similar to *N. (A.) potteri,* but has a rounded snout. The breast and the nape are partially unscaled. It has black specks on a silver flank concentrated in a large dusky patch in front, similar in configuration to the dark mark in emperor tetras. It is tan to yellow above, with a thin dusky stripe along the back. The nuptial male has a blue iridescence on the flank.<br><br>The Red River shiner occurs in the Red River from Arkansas and Oklahoma to Texas in the deeper channels of rivers and creeks. |
| *Notropis (Alburnops) buccula,* smalleye shiner | The related *N. (A.) buccula* once was considered a subspecies of *N. (A.) bairdi.* It is a rare fish with a slightly longer snout and smaller eyes.<br><br>The smalleye shiner occurs in the upper two-thirds of the adjacent and turbid Brazos River in Texas; it has also been introduced into the Colorado River.<br><br>*N. (A.) buccula* is found over shifting sand bottoms of deep channels. |
| *Notropis (Alburnops) girardi,* Arkansas River shiner | *N. (A.) girardi* is also a member of this species group, but its fins are larger and more scythe-shaped (i.e., pointed and concave).<br><br>The Arkansas River shiner occurs in Arkansas River drainages in western Arkansas, and in Kansas, Oklahoma, the Texas panhandle, northeastern New Mexico, and possibly southeastern Colorado.<br><br>*N. (A.) girardi* is found in broad, shallow, channels of turbid rivers, over silt and sand.<br><br>The Arkansas River shiner is an egg scatterer (broadcaster) that sheds its non-adhesive, semibuoyant eggs in July, the eggs then traveling with the current great distances downstream. Eggs hatch one day later and the yolk sac is absorbed by the third day (Lee et al. 1980; Platania and Altenbach 1998). |
| *Notropis (Alburnops) dorsalis,* bigmouth shiner | *N. (A.) dorsalis* has a flat head, long snout, large mouth, and upward oriented eyes. It is tan above with faintly edged scales and a dark stripe along the back; the flank is silver.<br><br>The bigmouth shiner occurs primarily in the Missouri-Mississippi drainage, Minnesota to Illinois and Missouri, and westward in the Platte River to South |

Longnose shiner, *Notropis longirostris,* Altahama R., Miss. WFR

Dakota and northeastern Colorado (Lee et al. 1980); it is occasionally found in the northeastern states of the Great Lakes basin.

*N. (A.) dorsalis* is found in open, broad expanses of shallow, prairielike streams with shifting sand bottoms, sometimes with a silt overlay. It schools just off the bottom, sometimes mixed with sand and red shiners. It feeds at the bottom, rapidly sucking up and emitting the sand from its mouth and gill openings, while consuming insects with some algae and bottom ooze (detritus and diatoms). It matures in two and lives three or four years. It spawns during May, June, and July (Pflieger 1975; P. W. Smith 1979; Lee et al. 1980).

---

*Notropis (Alburnops) ammophilus,*
orangefin shiner

*N. (A.) ammophilus* **(plate 2)** has an inferior mouth. The origin of the anal fin is below or behind the rear of the dorsal fin; the dorsal fin begins over the origin of the pelvic fins. The nuptial male has a rich flush of orange in all fins, but not extending to the clear edges. The body is translucent yellow.

The orangefin shiner occurs below the fall line in the Mobile Basin, the Hatchie system in Mississippi and Tennessee, Yellow Creek in Tennessee (Tennessee River drainage), and the upper Yazoo River system of Calhoun and Ponotoc Counties in Mississippi; the similar fish in the remainder of the Yazoo should be called *N. rafinesquei* (Suttkus 1991).

*N. (A.) ammophilus* is abundant in creeks and rivers of the Coastal Plain, in shallow, sandy areas with current. It probably feeds primarily on chironomids, the most abundant food source. It spawns after it is one year old, from April through September over sand and gravel, and lives up to two years.

---

*Notropis (Alburnops) longirostris,*
longnose shiner

*N. (A.) longirostris* resembles *N. (A.) ammophilus.* It is a stubby-nosed minnow with an inferior mouth, the snout projecting slightly above the jaw in a sharklike profile. It is sand colored, with a yellow band on the front of the flank becoming dusky gray to the rear. Nuptial fish develop bright lemon-yellow fins and grow to 2½ inches (Douglas 1974).

The longnose shiner occurs in lower Mississippi drainages, mostly east of the Mississippi River, except for a population in the lower Ouachita River in Catahoula Parish, Louisiana. Otherwise, it is found entirely north of Lake Pontarchrain in all drainages, and eastward to the Apalachicola River in Florida. Its range continues northward into the upper Altamaha River of Georgia. The populations in

Sabine shiner, *Notropis sabinae*, White R., Ark. WFR

western Florida through southeastern Alabama drainages may prove to be a separate taxon (C. Gilbert, pers. comm.).

*N. (A.) longirostris* is found in shallow streams with shifting sand bottoms, sometimes with *Ericymba buccata*. It feeds on midges and other insects. It spawns from March to October at the edges of flowing pools above shoals, over the sand bottom (Lee et al. 1980).

| | |
|---|---|
| *Notropis (Alburnops) sabinae,* Sabine shiner | *N. (A.) sabinae* also has a long snout on a flattened head and wide subterminal mouth, but the small upward-oriented eyes distinguish it from the closely related *N. (A.) longirostris*. It is olive on the back, but otherwise entirely silver with no dark markings or attractive colors on the body or fins at any time.<br><br>The Sabine shiner has a widely disjunct range. It occurs in the San Jacinto River of Texas along the lower Gulf Coast to small Mississippi River tributaries in eastern Louisiana, including the Red and Calcasieu Rivers. A separate population exists in the White, Black, Strawberry, and Current Rivers in the lowlands of Arkansas and Missouri, but the species may be extirpated from the St. Francis River (Lee et al. 1980).<br><br>*N. (A.) sabinae* inhabits clear, deep, slow-moving rivers over clean sand bottoms. Associates include blacktail and emerald shiners and silvery and bullhead minnows. It spawns during its first year from April through September, and lives less than two years (Pflieger 1975; Robison and Buchanan 1988). |
| *Notropis (Alburnops) asperifrons,* burrhead shiner | *N. (A.) asperifrons* has intensely dark-edged scales all along the back, a brown upper flank, a deep black line all along the flank from the upper jaw through the eye to a bold basicaudal spot, and a white belly, breast, and chin. It is small, averaging 2 inches.<br><br>The burrhead shiner occurs above the fall line in the Alabama and Black Warrior systems of Tennessee, Georgia, and Alabama.<br><br>*N. (A.) asperifrons* inhabits pools in sandy creeks and streams, and is sometimes found on gravel bars or among boulders in 3- to 6-foot depths in larger rivers. It spawns from April through June (Etnier and Starnes 1993). |
| *Notropis (Alburnops) hypsilepis,* highscale shiner | *N. (A.) hypsilepis* is closely related to *N. (A.) asperifrons*. It has large eyes situated high on the head. It is dark along the back and has a black stripe along the flank |

with a light (usually white) stripe along its upper margin. The basicaudal spot is black. It is light below, but has a dark line along the base of the anal fin. It is small at 1½ inches (average length).

The highscale shiner occurs in the Chattahoochee and Flint Rivers of the upper Apalachicola system in Georgia, and just into eastern Alabama. One location in the adjacent upper Savannah River of northeastern Georgia may be the result of a bait-minnow introduction (Lee et al. 1980; C. Gilbert, pers. comm.).

*N. (A.) hypsilepis* inhabits stream mouths, usually over sand. It spawns during March and June.

---

*Notropis (Alburnops) atrocaudalis,*
blackspot shiner

*N. (A.) atrocaudalis* has a black stripe from the tip of the snout along the flank to an oblong black basicaudal spot; a thin black line from this spot extends onto the tail fin. The area above the bold, black flank line has dark-edged scales that form four or five additional thin gray lines. It is robust, and has a small head (Robison and Buchanan 1988).

The blackspot shiner ranges from the Red, Little, and Calcasieu Rivers to the Brazos River, from Arkansas and Oklahoma to Louisiana and Texas.

*N. (A.) atrocaudalis* inhabits sandbars and rock riffles in flowing, clear water, and sometimes is found in springs.

The blackspot shiner is rare and should not be collected except by research biologists with a need for specimens.

---

*Notropis (Alburnops) bifrenatus,*
bridle shiner

*N. (A.) bifrenatus* has a black stripe on a silvery flank from the snout to the basicaudal spot, with a lighter stripe immediately above, and the scales on back black-edged. It grows to less than 2 inches.

The bridle shiner ranges from the St. Lawrence–Lake Ontario drainage of Quebec along the Atlantic slope to the Neuse River in North Carolina (Jenkins and Zorach 1970).

*N. (A.) bifrenatus* occurs in sluggish warm-water streams and rivers and in ponds and large lakes, typically in densely vegetated backwaters over silt, mud, or detritus. It occurs in low salinity (2 ppt) waters in the southern part of its range. It feeds on small invertebrates and some plant material. The bridle shiner spawns from May to August, depending on latitude, in quiet, vegetated shallows close to shore (Lee et al. 1980).

---

*Notropis (Alburnops) blennius,*
river shiner

*N. (A.) blennius* has a moderately pointed snout, the mouth extending to just under the front of the eye. A dark stripe along the back encircles the dorsal fin. It is a light golden color above, with barely outlined scales on the back. A faint, dusky stripe appears along the rear of a silvery flank. Adults average 4 inches.

The river shiner ranges from the Red River of southern Manitoba to Alberta, Canada, into the northern midwestern states south in the Mississippi and its Missouri, Arkansas, and Ohio River basins to Louisiana. Use the general distribution map in Page and Burr (1991) rather than the spot map in Lee et al. (1980), which contains errors for Illinois.

*N. (A.) blennius* occurs in deep main channels of large turbid rivers, over silt, sand, and gravel. It spawns during July and August in shallows on sand and gravel bars.

Mirror shiner, *Notropis spectrunculus,* Tennessee R., Tenn. WFR

| | |
|---|---|
| *Notropis (Alburnops) shumardi,* silverband shiner | *N. (A.) shumardi* resembles both *N. (A.) blennius* (with seven anal fin rays) and *Hybognathus hayi* (which has a coiled gut). It has a high, pointed dorsal fin with eight rays, eight or nine anal fin rays, and a deep, slab-sided, silvery body. It is olive above with a pale dusky stripe on the back. The fins are plain, and there are no dark markings or nuptial colors. Adults average 2 inches. |

The silverband shiner occurs in the Mississippi River and its larger tributaries, the Missouri, Illinois, Ohio, Red, and Arkansas Rivers. Disjunct populations exist in a few Texas streams from the Trinity westward to Lavaca Bay (Lee et al. 1980).

*N. (A.) shumardi* inhabits the open channels of large turbid rivers in current, over sand or fine gravel bars where it forms mixed schools with other shiners. It spawns from June through August at 80°F, over hard sand in 3 to 6 feet of water (Pflieger 1975; P. W. Smith 1979; Robison and Buchanan 1988).

| | |
|---|---|
| *Notropis (Alburnops) candidus,* silverside shiner | *N. (A.) candidus* resembles *N. (A.) shumardi,* but always has eight, never nine, anal rays. |

The silverside shiner occurs in the Alabama and Tombigbee systems of Alabama, and is more common below the fall line.

*N. (A.) candidus* occur in small groups on sand or gravel bars, in clear, flowing water. When alarmed, they flee to deeper water.

| | |
|---|---|
| *Notropis (Alburnops) spectrunculus,* mirror shiner | *N. (A.) spectrunculus* has a rounded head and snout on an elongate, slender body. It is olive above, lighter on the flank, and white below. The scales are dark-edged everywhere. It has a dark line on the rear half of the flank, and a bold black wedge in the tail fin. The nuptial male has a purple-blue iridescence on its flank. The fins are orange-red with clear or white margins. There is a tan-gold line on the back and a red-gold line on the upper side. It is closely related to the unnamed sawfin shiner of the North Fork Holston River (Jenkins and Burkhead 1994; Rohde et al. 1994). |

The mirror shiner occurs in high elevations in the Blue Ridge province of the upper Tennessee River drainage in North Carolina and Georgia (where common), and Virginia and Tennessee (where uncommon). It also is present in the Santee and Catawba Rivers of North Carolina, but is absent from the Watauga and the South Fork Holston River (Lee et al. 1980; Jenkins and Burkhead 1994).

*N. (A.) spectrunculus* inhabits clear, cool, bedrock or rubble bottom in small- to medium-sized mountain streams. Seldom in nuptial coloration, its spawning habits are unknown. It probably spawns from May through August.

The mirror shiner may be protected in Virginia, but is abundant in western North Carolina (Menhinick 1991).

| | |
|---|---|
| *Notropis (Alburnops) ozarcanus,* Ozark shiner | *N. (A.) ozarcanus* is a round-nosed, elongate minnow that is shaped like a tropical loach or a *Hybopsis* minnow. It has a yellow back marked with dark-edged scales, a silvery to black stripe (darkest to the rear) on the flank, and a white belly. The nuptial male has black fins and a thickened leading ray of the pectoral fin, similar to *Hoplosternum* catfish. Its closest relative appears to be *N. (A.) spectrunculus* of the Tennessee uplands (C. Gilbert, pers. comm.). |

The Ozark shiner occurs in the Current and North Fork Rivers (Black River system), and is now rare in the White River due to construction of Table Rock and Bull Shoals Reservoirs (Pflieger 1975). It may have been introduced by anglers into the Illinois River (all Arkansas River drainages) of Missouri and Arkansas (Burr et al. 1979).

*N. (A.) ozarcanus* inhabits large, clear, rocky streams with permanent strong flow, in midwater, near riffles over clean (silt-free) bottoms. It spawns from May through August (Pflieger 1975; Robison and Buchanan 1988).

The *procne,* or blackline shiner species group, includes *N. (A.) albizonatus, N. (A.) alborus, N. (A.) chihuahua, N. (A.) greenei, N. (A.) heterolepis, N. (A.) ludibundus, N. (A.) mekistocholas, N. (A.) procne, N. (A.) topeka,* and *N. (A.) uranoscopus* (Warren et al. 1994).

| | |
|---|---|
| *Notropis (Alburnops) albizonatus,* palezone shiner | *N. (A.) albizonatus* is yellow with a diffuse, broad dusky band along the flank from snout to tail, and a broad yellow band on the shoulder and upper flank. It has dark streaks on the proximal part of the upper and lower lobes of the tail fin. |

The Little South Fork Cumberland River and Paint Rock River hold the two remaining populations in Kentucky, Tennessee, and Alabama.

The palezone shiner occupies pools and runs of upland streams with permanent strong flow and bedrock, cobble, and gravel mixed with clean sand. It probably lives three years, and breeds at 1½ inches during June.

*N. (A.) albizonatus* is a protected species.

| | |
|---|---|
| *Notropis (Alburnops) alborus,* whitemouth shiner | *N. (A.) alborus* is yellow to olive above and white below. Scales along the back are edged in black. A narrow, jagged, iridescent blue-black stripe on the flank terminates in a black spot at the base of the tail. The pectoral fins are yellow at the base. The snout has a thin black stripe resembling a bridle in some individuals. The mouth is occasionally white. |

The whitemouth shiner occurs in Atlantic slope drainages from the Chowan River of Virginia to the Santee River of South Carolina, excluding the Neuse and Tar Rivers or North Carolina (Lee et al. 1980).

*N. (A.) alborus* is found in outer Piedmont creeks and streams along sand and rock shoals, often in groups of ten or more in larger pools. It also occurs in shallow pools, but not in riffles, and is not associated with vegetation.

Wedgespot shiner, *Notropis greenei,* White R., Ark. WFR

---

*Notropis (Alburnops) chihuahua,*
Chihuahua shiner

*N. (A.) chihuahua* is similar to the unrelated *N. (N.) perpallidus.* The head and upper and middle flank are peppered with black spots the size of scales. The spots overlay a diffuse, midlateral flank stripe, silvery in front and black toward the rear, ending in a basicaudal spot. The jaws and bases of fins are yellow to orange. The lateral line pores are edged in black.

The Chihuahua shiner occurs occasionally in Alamito Creek, near Presidio, and in Maravillas Creek in the Big Bend region of Texas. It is abundant in the Rio Conchos and Rio Durango (all Rio Grande tributaries) of the Chihuahuan Desert in the states of Durango and Chihuahua (northern Mexico).

*N. (A.) chihuahua* occurs in small to medium streams, in clear, cool water near springs, in pools or riffles. It usually occurs over sand and gravel near vegetation, but also over boulders, bedrock, and mud. It feeds on the bottom on midges, beetles, and stonefly larvae. Nematodes (roundworms) discovered in some intestines may have been food from the bottom or parasites transmitted by insects. It spawns six months of the year, from March to August (Burr and Mayden 1981).

---

*Notropis (Alburnops) greenei,*
wedgespot shiner

*N. (A.) greenei* is a slender silvery minnow with a black wedge-shaped spot on the caudal fin. Its large eye is oriented upward, and the front of the pupil has a nipple-like projection. It is gray to olive above, and the back scales are edged in black. A wide, dusky to dark predorsal stripe continues as a thin postdorsal stripe. There is a silver-black stripe along the flank, darker toward the rear.

The wedgespot shiner is common in Ozark upland tributaries of the Missouri, White, and Arkansas Rivers of southern Missouri, northern Arkansas, and northeastern Oklahoma (all western tributaries of the Mississippi River). Specifically, it occurs in the White, Black, Meramec, St. Francis, Gasconade, and lower Osage Rivers (Lee et al. 1980) where it occupies clear, permanently flowing streams and rivers, avoiding headwater creeks. It is usually near riffles over sand, gravel, or rubble, and schools in midwater with rosyface, bleeding, striped, telescope, and mimic shiners. It spawns from June through August over gravel riffles (Pflieger 1975). It is less attractive than its gorgeous associates.

---

*Notropis (Alburnops) scabriceps,*
New River shiner

*N. (A.) scabriceps* has iridescent purple or green reflections, somewhat darker on the back, but no colorful or bold black markings anywhere.

The New River shiner is fairly common in the upper Kanawha River (Blue Ridge portion of the New River drainage) of Virginia and North Carolina, and occasionally occurs in West Virginia (Lee et al. 1980).

*N. (A.) scabriceps* inhabits pools and backwaters near fast water in cool, small to medium mountain creeks and lower parts of trout rivers. It is found over rocks, gravel, and clean sand, usually in schools of 20 to 30. It is a bottom feeder on caddisfly larvae and leeches picked from rocks. It spawns from June through August (Lee et al. 1980; Jenkins and Burkhead 1994).

Phylogenetic relationships are unclear, but it is possibly close to *N. (A.) greenei,* and if so should be considered part of the *procne* group.

| | |
|---|---|
| *Notropis (Alburnops) heterolepis,*<br>blacknose shiner | *N. (A.) heterolepis* is silvery with light yellow highlights and dark-edged scales on the back. Upon death, an ephemeral dusky stripe on the flank darkens to a series of black crescents within a black stripe. The snout is round and slightly protuberant.<br><br>The blacknose shiner ranges from Hudson Bay and James Bay in Canada to New England, westward through the Great Lakes states to Iowa, then southward to Missouri and Tennessee. It occurs in Nova Scotia, Quebec, New Brunswick, Ontario, Manitoba, and Saskatchewan. In the United States, it is present in Missouri, Arkansas, Kansas, and north to the Dakotas, but is common only in Missouri and the Great Lakes states. It is sporadic and possibly declining elsewhere (Scott and Crossman 1973; Lee et al. 1980).<br><br>*N. (A.) heterolepis* inhabits clear embayments of glacial lakes and quiet streams, vegetated or not, usually over sand or gravel, but sometimes mud. It spawns during spring and summer over sand bottoms (Scott and Crossman 1973), and cannot survive turbidity, which may be causing its widespread decline (P. W. Smith 1979). |
| *Notropis (Alburnops) rupestris,*<br>bedrock shiner | *N. (A.) rupestris* has black coloration from the snout to the base of the tail and barely onto the fin, as in the closely related *N. (A.) heterolepis. N. (A.) rupestris* differs by being slightly rounder in front, having only a partial lateral line, having slightly fewer scales in front of the dorsal fin, and in habitat preference. A black line runs along the base of the dorsal fin. There are double thin lines along the upper flank. The bedrock shiner is clear iridescent green above and bright gold below. There is no nuptial coloration (Page and Beckham 1987).<br><br>The bedrock shiner occurs in the Cumberland, Stones, Caney Fork, and Duck (possibly introduced) Rivers of the central Cumberland drainage of Cannon, Rutherford, Smith, and Wilson Counties, Tennessee.<br><br>*N. (A.) rupestris* is found near emergent vegetation in limestone bedrock pools of clear, cool, low gradient, intermittent headwater streams where few other fishes occur. It is probably insectivorous. |
| *Notropis (Alburnops) heterodon,*<br>blackchin shiner | *N. (A.) heterodon* has a black stripe concentrated on the lateral line pores that produces a "zigzag" dip in the band. The jaws and chin are dusky to black. Nuptial fish develop a pale yellow tinge below. The average length of adults is 2 inches.<br><br>The blackchin shiner ranges throughout the upper St. Lawrence River of western Quebec, the Ottawa River, through Lakes Ontario, St. Clair, and Huron, and north to Sault Saint Marie. It also occurs in New York, Illinois, and recently has been reported in the Red River in Minnesota, but is most abundant in Canada |

and Michigan. It has recently been extirpated from Lake Erie, Iowa, Pennsylvania, and probably Ohio.

N. (A.) heterodon inhabits clear, cool, vegetated lakeshores and weedy pools of creeks and rivers. It feeds on copepods, cladocera (Chydorus, Daphnia, Bosmina), and flying insects (mostly small flies) at the surface. It spawns during May and June (Lee et al. 1980).

---

**Notropis (Alburnops) maculatus, taillight shiner**

N. (A.) maculatus (**plate 3**) is gray with dark-edged scales above and on the flanks, giving the appearance of a crosshatch. A dark band from the tip of the snout ends in a bold, black basicaudal spot. The nuptial male has a V-shaped, red-orange band on and along the head, gill covers, and flank; the fins are clear, distinctly black-edged, and red at the tips.

The taillight shiner occurs in the Atlantic slope Coastal Plain and Gulf Coast Mississippi embayment from Cape Fear River, North Carolina southward through all of Florida. It continues westward to northeastern Texas. It is found in the Mississippi embayment north to western Kentucky and in the bootheel of Missouri (Lee et al. 1980).

N. (A.) maculatus inhabits large, quiet, clear, and blackwater streams and lakes over mud or sand. It feeds on algae (Closterium) and diatoms (Navicula) in the warm months and invertebrates during colder months, especially cladocera (Bosmina, Chydorus, and Pleuroxus), ostracods, bryozoans (Plumatella), chironomids, and copepods. The taillight shiner spawns from March through September, scattering eggs; it also spawns in Micropterus nests. It has a one-year life cycle in Florida and lives to three years farther north (McLane 1955; Beach 1974; Johnston and Page 1992).

---

**Notropis (Alburnops) ludibundus, sand shiner**

N. (A.) ludibundus is almost colorless, tending toward translucent gray with black-edged scales above the midline, a hazy black line along the flank, and a white belly. Even nuptial individuals do not develop bright colors. It grows to 2½ inches.

The sand shiner is widespread, ranging from Quebec southward to New York, along the Gulf slope to Tennessee, and from Manitoba and Saskatchewan southward to the Rio Grande of Texas. In between, it ranges throughout the lower Great Lakes and northern Mississippi drainages, but is not common south of Missouri or Oklahoma (Lee et al. 1980). It has been known previously under the names N. deliciosus, N. stramineus, and N. blennius, and is included here in the procne group.

N. (A.) ludibundus is found in diverse habitats, from springs to large rivers, where it is common over sandbars, in open, clear moving water in groups of 10 to 20. It breeds from May through August.

---

**Notropis (Alburnops) mekistocholas, Cape Fear shiner**

N. (A.) mekistocholas has a wide black stripe from the snout to a basicaudal spot. The scales are dark-edged above; the back and upper flank are olive and the belly is white. The long, coiled black intestine is visible through the belly wall. The mouth is black inside. The nuptial male has orange-gold pelvics and pectorals, brightest at the bases of the fins.

The Cape Fear shiner occurs in scattered localities above the fall line in the Cape Fear River drainage (Deep, Haw, and Rocky Rivers) from Randolph to Harnett Counties, North Carolina.

Topeka shiner, *Notropis topeka,* Illinois Cr., Kansas R., Kans. GS

N. (A.) mekistocholas inhabits sand and rock pools and riffles, usually near or in aquatic vegetation (G. Pottern, pers. comm.). It is believed to feed on detritus and plant materials, consistent with the long, coiled gut.

The Cape Fear shiner is a federally endangered species. While doing a status survey for the U.S. Fish and Wildlife Service, which led to its protected status, Pottern (pers. comm.) accidentally raised one individual from an egg deposited in Java moss *(Vesicularia)* in a holding aquarium.

| | |
|---|---|
| *Notropis (Alburnops) procne,* swallowtail shiner | N. (A.) procne is an elongate minnow with an iridescent blue-black line along the entire flank from the jaws to the tail. It is olive above with dark-edged scales, and white below. Nuptial adults have an overall warm tan-yellow cast and yellow tint to the fins. |

The swallowtail shiner ranges from New York to South Carolina on both sides of the fall line of the Susquehanna and Santee Rivers (Lee et al. 1980). A few reports from Lake Ontario drainages are probably bait fish transfers, but could be stream captures.

N. (A.) procne is common in pools of large creeks or rivers over silt or sand/gravel bottoms. It sometimes occurs with plants, usually in warm water, and often in groups of mixed minnow species, numbering from dozens to hundreds of individuals. It forages mostly on aquatic insect larvae on sand bottoms, but feeds at all depths on algae, diatoms, small crustaceans, mites, worms, and aquatic and terrestrial insects.

The swallowtail shiner matures at age one or two, scattering adhesive eggs over sand and gravel during spring and early summer at 70 to 78°F. It is an opportunistic spawner, males establishing territories over shallow sand or gravel bottoms, and spawning either without benefit of a nest or, when available, on the nests of *Nocomis* sp. or *Lepomis auritus* (Jenkins and Burkhead 1994). It does well on flake food, supplemented with frozen brine shrimp and chironomids.

| | |
|---|---|
| *Notropis (Alburnops) topeka,* Topeka shiner | N. (A.) topeka is in the N. (A.) procne species group (Schmidt and Gold 1995). It resembles N. (A.) texanus, but without a clear area of undarkened scales above the black flank stripe. It also has seven anal rays. A dark stripe on the back is wide and distinct in front of the dorsal fin, but is thin and pale or absent behind. The nuptial male has orange-red fins (Pflieger 1975). |

Weed shiner, *Notropis texanus,* Black Warrior R., Ala. FCR

The Topeka shiner ranges from South Dakota and Minnesota to Iowa, Missouri, and Kansas in the Mississippi, Arkansas, and Missouri River drainages (Lee et al. 1980).

N. (A.) *topeka* occurs in quiet pools of clear, intermittent, headwater, upland streams with sand, gravel, or rock bottoms. It forms midwater and surface mixed schools with *Cyprinella lutrensis, Luxilus cornutus, Lythrurus umbratilis,* and *Notropis ludibundus.*

The Topeka shiner spawns from May to July over nests of *Lepomis cyanellus* and *L. humilus,* with males occupying territories at the edges of these sunfish nests (Pflieger 1975). It may be an obligatory parasite of sunfish nests.

*Notropis (Alburnops) uranoscopus,* skygazer shiner

N. (A.) *uranoscopus* has two black crescents between the nostrils. It is yellow above with dark-edged scales. The flank has a wide black stripe edged above with a thin gold stripe. The belly is white.

The skygazer shiner is restricted to Alabama, and common in the Cahaba River (including Little Cahaba River and Sixmile Creek). It also occurs in Uphapee Creek and the Alabama River, and all Mobile basin drainages of Dallas, Bibb, and Wilcox Counties in Alabama.

N. (A.) *uranoscopus* inhabits large creeks and rivers in strong current over sand and gravel. It feeds on filamentous algae and on bottom insects.

*Notropis (Alburnops) texanus,* weed shiner

N. (A.) *texanus* is olive-yellow above, silvery on the flank, and white below. The upper scales are dark-edged. A bold, black line runs from the jaws, through the eye, to a small basicaudal spot. A light colored zone, where scales are not dark-edged, is present immediately above the black flank band. Nuptial males have rose colored fins. There are seven anal rays, which are often diagnostic. It averages 2 inches (Pflieger 1975).

The weed shiner occurs in Minnesota and Michigan, including Lake Huron and Lake Michigan drainages, southward in the Mississippi basin to the Gulf Coast. It is found in Gulf drainages from Suwannee River in Florida and Georgia to the Nueces River in Texas (Lee et al. 1980).

N. (A.) *texanus* inhabits open, clear, sand or mud bottoms of small to large streams or river oxbows, often with aquatic vegetation. It forms schools near the bottom and feeds on algae, plant debris, and microinvertebrates. The weed shiner

Coastal shiner, *Notropis petersoni*, Savannah Branch, S.C. FCR

spawns from March through September. Life span is three years (Pflieger 1975; Robison and Buchanan 1988).

*Notropis (Alburnops) petersoni,*
coastal shiner

The related *N. (A.) petersoni* is elongate, and translucent olive-yellow above with dark-edged scales on the back. A broad, silvery black band runs from the jaws to the tail, ending in a small basicaudal spot. The belly is silvery. The lower edge of the anal fin and caudal peduncle are edged in black, and there are seven anal fin rays. *N. (A.) texanus,* with which it overlaps on the Gulf Coast, has pigment outlining the last four anal fin rays and pigment on the row of scales below the lateral line (pored scales) row.

The coastal shiner occurs on the Atlantic Coastal Plain from Cape Fear River, North Carolina to Dade County, Florida, and westward along the lower Gulf of Mexico drainages to Jordan River, Mississippi.

In Florida, *N. (A.) petersoni* occurs in swamp springs and creeks with: (1) limestone boulders, cobbles, and gravel riffles; (2) sandy or silted pools; (3) dense growths of *Vallisneria* and *Potamogeton* in currents; (4) *Egeria* in eddies; and (4) moss on rocks *(Fissidens deblilis)*. Where the bottom is muddy and sandy, *Ludwigia, Sagittaria, Polygonum,* and *Paspalum* occur along the shore. The breeding season is protracted throughout the warm months, and the life cycle abbreviated to one year, with the adults often dying after spawning at the end of the first year.

In North Carolina, the coastal shiner grows more slowly, lives three years, and occurs in rivers and lakes. It is found either in flowing waters or quiet backwaters, at all levels of the water column and usually over sand bottoms. It feeds on diatoms in springs, and elsewhere on insect larvae, filamentous algae, and aquatic crustaceans. *N. (A.) petersoni* spawns at 67 to 80°F from March to September (Carr and Goin 1959; Cowell and Resico 1975; Lee et al. 1980; Rohde et al. 1994).

The closely related and sometimes overlapping *volucellus* group contains *N. (A.) buchanani, N. (A.) cahabae, N. (A.) volucellus, N. (A.) wickliffi, N. (A.) saladonis* of Mexico (not covered in this book), and sometimes *N. (A.) procne, N. (A.) ludibundus,* and *N. (A.) heterolepis* (all three included herein with the *procne* group).

*Notropis (Alburnops) buchanani,*
ghost shiner

*N. (A.) buchanani* has extremely high and narrow lateral line scales (use a hand lens). Coloration is a translucent milky white, resembling a dead fish. The fins are enlarged and pointed compared to other *Notropis* species. It was once considered a subspecies of *N. (A.) volucellus*.

The ghost shiner occurs in Mexico and Texas, in the lower Rio Grande eastward in all other river drainages as far as the Mississippi River in Louisiana. It then ranges northward in the Mississippi and Ohio Rivers to West Virginia in the east. It is present farther north in the main stem of the Mississippi River to Minnesota and ranges westward in tributaries to Kansas and Nebraska (Lee et al. 1980).

*N. (A.) buchanani* inhabits large pools and protected backwaters of clear to turbid low gradient rivers. It breeds during August.

| | |
|---|---|
| *Notropis (Alburnops) cahabae,* Cahaba shiner | *N. (A.) cahabae* was once considered a variant of *N. (A.) volucellus*. It has a dark stripe on the flank that does not expand near the tail fin. |

The Cahaba shiner is endemic to the Cahaba River in deep, sandy main channels of Shelby and Bibb Counties in Alabama.

An endangered species, *N. (A.) cahabae* may not be captured or maintained.

| | |
|---|---|
| *Notropis (Alburnops) volucellus,* mimic shiner | *N. (A.) volucellus* may be a complex rather than a single species. Adults average 2 inches. The mimic shiner is green to olive above and white below, with dark-edged scales and a white flank. A silvery black line on the flank has a clear area (scales without dark edges) immediately above. There is a single line of tubercles on the first ray of the pectoral fin. |

The mimic shiner ranges from Quebec and New York westward to Saskatchewan, Manitoba, and Minnesota. It occurs in the St. Lawrence, Great Lakes, Ohio, and Mississippi drainages from New York along Gulf slope drainages southward to the Gulf of Mexico. It is present along the Gulf Coast from the Guadalupe and San Antonio Rivers eastward to Mobile Bay, Alabama (Lee et al. 1980). On the Atlantic slope, it is found only in the Roanoke and Neuse Rivers of North Carolina (Hubbs and Lagler 1958; Menhinick 1991).

*N. (A.) volucellus* schools in midwater or at the top in pools and backwaters of low to moderate gradient, medium to large streams and rivers; it occurs over sand or gravel in current. It feeds on chironomids and other aquatic and terrestrial insects, amphipods, cladocerans, mites, detritus, plant debris, and some algae. The mimic shiner spawns from May through September in riffles of streams, and broadcasts eggs in weed beds in deep water of lakes (Lee et al. 1980; Robison and Buchanan 1988; Menhinick 1991; Jenkins and Burkhead 1994).

| | |
|---|---|
| *Notropis (Alburnops) wickliffi,* channel shiner | *N. (A.) wickliffi* was until recently regarded as a subspecies of *N. (A.) volucellus*. It is often confused with *N. (A.) volucellus*. |

The channel shiner is abundant in the Wabash and Ohio Rivers, and common in the Mississippi River below the mouths of the Ohio and Missouri Rivers (P. W. Smith 1979).

*N. (A.) wickliffi* occurs in large rivers, and ascends into tributaries to spawn in spring. It also may occur in some lakes.

The *rubricroceus* species group of the subgenus *Notropis (Alburnops)* contains *N. (A.) baileyi, N. (A.) chiliticus, N. (A.) chlorocephalus,* and *N. (A.) lutipinnis*. These fishes are considered close to the subgenus *Notropis (Hydrophlox)*.

Rough shiner, *Notropis baileyi,* Tallapoosa R., Ala. WFR

---

*Notropis (Alburnops) baileyi,*
rough shiner

*N. (A.) baileyi* is red to brown above, usually red along the flank and at the fin bases, and has yellow fins. A straight dark line runs along the flank from the lower jaw to a basicaudal spot. During spawning season, the fins turn slightly orange-red to bright yellow, and a small hump develops behind the head of nuptial males (Page and Burr 1991).

The rough shiner occurs in Mobile Bay and the Pascagoula River drainages below the fall line in Alabama (mostly) and eastern Mississippi. It has been introduced into the Escambia and Chattahoochee Rivers of Georgia and Florida (Lee et al. 1980).

*N. (A.) baileyi* is found over unvegetated sand or gravel bottoms in moderate to high gradient, small (< 10 ft. wide), clear and blackwater streams in wooded areas. It feeds on aquatic and terrestrial insects (midges, mayflies, beetles, dragonflies, caddisflies, etc.), worms, amphipods, fish eggs, salamander larvae, diatoms, filamentous algae, and detritus (Mathur and Ramsey 1974).

The rough shiner spawns from May through September (peaking in June) in the nests of bluehead chub, *Nocomis leptocephalus* (Johnston and Kleiner 1994). It may hybridize, advertently or not, during spawning with *Notropis chrosomus.* It lives to two years (Lee et al. 1980).

---

*Notropis (Alburnops) chiliticus,*
redlip shiner

*N. (A.) chiliticus* **(plate 4)** is a beauty. Both sexes have brilliant red jaws (lips), a wide dusky silver band on the flank, a thin golden band along its upper margin, and red fins. The body is silvery with dark marks on the flank, and is not as curved as the much larger *Luxilus cerasinus,* with which it is sympatric. The nuptial male is scarlet with a golden head, a golden stripe on the flank, and yellow fins.

The redlip shiner occurs in the Piedmont and mountain foothills of the Dan and Pee Dee Rivers of Virginia and North Carolina.

*N. (A.) chiliticus* inhabits rocky, flowing headwater creeks, and often is found in groups of a dozen or more in the middle of the water column mixed with *Luxilus cerasinus* and other minnows.

The redlip shiner breeds at 52 to 63°F. Males aggregate over the nests of *Nocomis leptocephalus,* often with males of other minnow species. The female initiates spawning by moving over the nest until she is pursued. The male drives the female to the bottom of the small pit(s) atop the nest where clasping occurs. Artificial nests constructed in streams near active real nests were never used. This suggests that the presence of live *Nocomis* makes the nest attractive to *N. (A.) chiliticus,* an observation confirmed with other species of *Notropis* (Johnston 1991).

| | |
|---|---|
| *Notropis (Alburnops) chlorocephalus,* greenhead shiner | *N. (A.) chlorocephalus* **(plates 5 and 6)** is similar to *N. (A.) lutipinnis,* but the breeding male is scarlet red with a green head and brilliant white fins. |

*N. (A.) chlorocephalus* **(plates 5 and 6)** is similar to *N. (A.) lutipinnis,* but the breeding male is scarlet red with a green head and brilliant white fins.

The greenhead shiner occurs in the Santee-Catawba River system of North and South Carolina. The close relationship to *N. (A.) lutipinnis* was explained in the 1950s by a hypothesized northeastward flowing river from Old Fort, North Carolina to South Boston, Virginia that was destroyed by multiple stream captures. This was believed to have caused separation of the two closely related species (Wood and Mayden 1992).

*N. (A.) chlorocephalus* inhabits rocky, flowing pools. It breeds at 52 to 63°F. Males aggregate over the nests of *Nocomis leptocephalus,* often with males of other minnows, including *Hybopsis hypsinotus, Notropis (A.) chiliticus, Luxilus coccogenis, Campostoma anomalum,* and *Clinostomus funduloides.*

The female initiates spawning, and is driven to the bottom of the small pit(s) atop the nest where clasping occurs. As with *N. (A.) chiliticus,* artificial nests constructed in streams near active real nests were not used. This suggests that live *Nocomis* attract *N. (A.) chlorocephalus* to the nest, as confirmed with other species of *Notropis* (Johnston 1991).

*Notropis (Alburnops) lutipinnis,* yellowfin shiner

*N. (A.) lutipinnis* **(plate 7),** the yellowfin shiners, are olive above, white below. A wider than eye dark band on the flank is sharply margined by a gold band just above; the fins are slightly yellow. The nuptial male is spectacular. The body is entirely orange-red, the head and fins entirely yellow. A remnant of the flank band is barely perceptible toward the rear.

The yellowfin shiners range in Atlantic and Gulf rivers from the Santee River of North Carolina to the Altamaha (both are Atlantic slope drainages). They also occur in the upper Chattahoochee and upper Coosa of Georgia and the Little Tennessee (all Gulf slope drainages) in western North Carolina.

*N. (A.) lutipinnis* appears to be a species complex of five different taxa (species or subspecies). The unnamed form in the Santee-Broad and Pee Dee Rivers is distinct from the rest of the group, appearing more closely related to its evolutionary sister species, *N. (A.) chlorocephalus* (Menhinick 1991; Wood and Mayden 1992).

All yellowfin shiners occur in clear, flowing, rock and gravel pools and sandbars. They spawn in nests of the bluehead chub, *Nocomis leptocephalus,* at 61 to 70°F. They ignored artificial nests constructed nearby. When the shiners were isolated in the stream by enclosures that prevented them from reaching chub nests, they neither spawned nor displayed breeding coloration (Wallin 1992). This suggests that they are obligate parasites of chub nests.

Some *N. (Alburnops)* species, such as *N. (A.) chalybaeus,* bear a superficial resemblance to beautiful members of the genus *Pteronotropis.*

*Notropis (Alburnops) chalybaeus,* ironcolor shiner

*N. (A.) chalybaeus* has a broad, black stripe from the snout to a basicaudal spot. It is olive-yellow above and white below. The inside of the mouth is black, causing the jaws and throat to appear black. The nuptial male is orange-gold to rose red and has yellow fins.

The ironcolor shiner is disjunct in coastal and interior lowlands and widespread in the eastern and Gulf Coastal Plain, ranging northward into the south central states. It ranges from the Hudson River in New York to southern Florida, westward to Texas, and northward to the bootheel of Missouri. It occurs in the Red River of southeastern Oklahoma and another cluster persists in southern Lake Michigan drainages of Illinois, Indiana, Wisconsin, and Michigan.

In the South, N. (A.) chalybaeus occurs in sluggish, dark-tinted, acidic, Coastal Plain streams with abundant aquatic vegetation on clean sand bottoms. In the North, it is found in sandy, clear, heavily vegetated creeks, but also in swamps. It feeds on aquatic insects.

The ironcolor shiner breeds from April through September. An egg broadcaster, the male swims alongside the female, vents close together, and scatters 0.75 mm adhesive eggs in sand-bottom, quiet runs and pools. The eggs hatch in just over two days at 60°F; however, the fish spawns at a range of temperatures (P. W. Smith 1979; Robison and Buchanan 1988).

---

*Notropis (Alburnops) cummingsae,*
dusky shiner

N. (A.) cummingsae has a silvery flank and a wide black stripe extending from the jaws to a large basicaudal spot; streaks continue into the caudal fin and a thin gold stripe runs along its top margin. The body is yellow-brown above; the scales along the back are slightly edged in brown to yellow. Fins are usually clear, but tinted orange to red-yellow on some large males. N. (A.) cummingsae resembles N. (A.) chalybaeus, but has more anal rays (≥ 9 vs. 8). Its dark lateral stripe is wider, and N. (A.) chalybaeus lacks the adjacent golden stripe (Rohde et al. 1994).

Three populations of this oddly disjunct species are known. The largest group ranges from the Tar and Neuse Rivers of North Carolina all along the Piedmont and Coastal Plain to the Altamaha River of Georgia. It is absent from a group of rivers below the Altamaha and north of the St. Johns River of Florida. It then occurs only in the St. Johns, but not adjacent, drainages. A third population is found in the Florida panhandle from the Aucilla to the Chattahoochee and Choctawhatchee Rivers, ranging northward into Georgia and Alabama (Lee et al. 1980).

Adults usually are found in scour pools or eddies of black (tannin tinted) or slightly turbid (silty) water in the Coastal Plain. They occur in clear water (but are less common) in the Piedmont (Page and Burr 1991).

Schools of 15 to 100 dusky shiners will enter still pools briefly to feed on eggs and larvae and to spawn on nests of Lepomis auritus and L. punctatus while the sunfish are distracted. Normally, the sunfish try to drive away these voracious predators of its eggs and larvae. The shiners do not eat their own offspring, which occur in the same locale (Fletcher 1993; Fletcher et al. 1994).

It is not known if the dusky shiner can be spawned without a host nesting fish. It may be an obligate parasite; if so, some Central American cichlids may be acceptable substitute hosts.

---

*Notropis (Alburnops) harperi,*
redeye chub

N. (A.) harperi has a small barbel at the corner of its jaw and red eyes. Scales on the back are dark-edged. A broad black band extends from the snout and jaws to the

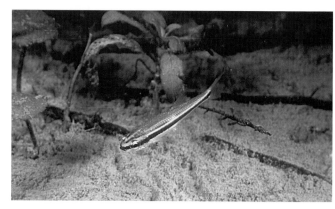

Redeye chub, *Notropis harperi,* Morrison Spring, Walton Co., Fla. GS

base of the caudal fin. The band is pink-purple above with a light yellow stripe immediately above the black band in the front part of the fish. The belly is white and the fins are colorless.

The redeye chub occurs in Atlantic drainages below the fall line in the Altamaha River of Georgia and the St. Johns River of Florida. It is found on the Gulf Coast in various Coastal Plain drainages from Tampa in peninsular Florida to the Escambia River in Alabama.

A cave form is restricted to spring heads and runs, underground streams in caves, and sinkholes not connected to rivers, typically at 68 to 73°F. It feeds on insects, crustaceans, and small fishes, and spawns year-round (Lee et al. 1980). The subspecies name *N. h. subterranea,* proposed for the cave form, is not generally accepted.

## Subgenus *Notropis (Notropis)*

Species of the subgenus *N. (Notropis)* have nine or more anal rays, generally lack pretty coloration, live in large streams and rivers, and are often egg broadcasters. This is the largest subgenus of the genus.

## *Notropis (Notropis) ariommus,* popeye shiner

*N. (N.) ariommus* has large eyes and nine anal rays. It is light brown above with dark-edged scales on the back and light silver to white below. A wide, dark silver stripe runs along the flank. There are no nuptial colors. The average adult length is almost 3 inches.

The popeye shiner occurs in the Ohio and Tennessee River drainages from Pennsylvania and Indiana southward to Georgia and Alabama; it is rare everywhere.

*N. (N.) ariommus* inhabits flowing pools of clear, gravel-bottom large streams and small rivers at depths of 3 feet or more. It feeds on a variety of adult insects and their aquatic larvae. It breeds from April through June.

## *Notropis (Notropis) telescopus,* telescope shiner

The related *N. (N.) telescopus* also has large eyes, but has ten anal rays and an oblique mouth. There are dark marks on the upper flank behind the dorsal fin, converging to form dark V-shapes when viewed from above; they are most apparent toward the rear. It has black-spotted lateral line pores, a white belly, and colorless fins. The average adult length is 2½ inches.

Telescope shiner, *Notropis telescopus,* Barren Fork, Cannon Co., Tenn. RB    Highfin shiner, *Notropis altipinnis,* Bolin Cr., N.C. FCR

The telescope shiner is disjunct on both sides of the Mississippi River. The western population ranges through the St. Francis, Little, White, and Black Rivers of the Ozark uplands in Missouri and Arkansas. The eastern population occurs in the Tennessee River basin of northern Georgia, Tennessee, and Virginia, and eastward to the Cumberland drainage of Virginia, North Carolina, and Tennessee. It has been introduced into the Kanawha River (New River drainage) of Virginia, North Carolina, and West Virginia (Pflieger 1975; Lee et al. 1980) to the east.

*N. (N.) telescopus* inhabits medium-sized, clear, flowing, upland creeks with gravel or rock bottoms near riffles, where it is abundant. It feeds on insects, mostly after dark. It spawns in April (Pflieger 1975; Robison and Buchanan 1988).

## *Notropis (Notropis) altipinnis,* highfin shiner

*N. (N.) altipinnis* also has large eyes. It has a rounded snout and terminal mouth. A dark stripe runs above the lateral line from the jaws to the caudal fin, with a golden-yellow stripe immediately above. Scales along the back are edged in black and the fins are usually colorless. Adults, especially males, are suffused with yellow around the head and snout.

The highfin shiner occurs mainly in the Atlantic slope Piedmont and in the Coastal Plain from the Roanoke River of Virginia to the northern (South Carolina) tributaries of the Savannah River.

*N. (N.) altipinnis* prefers pools, but occasionally is found along rock and sand shoals (usually away from vegetation) in small, shallow, clear creeks with moderate current.

## *Notropis (Alburnops) edwardraneyi,* fluvial shiner

*N. (A.) edwardraneyi* has an upward-oriented, large eye on a colorless body. The average adult length is 2 inches. A member of the subgenus *Alburnops,* it is placed in this section of the book with other *Notropis* that have large eyes.

The fluvial shiner occurs in the Mobile Bay drainage of Alabama and Mississippi, mostly below the fall line in the Tombigbee, Black Warrior, Cahaba, and Alabama Rivers (but not in the Coosa River).

*N. (A.) edwardraneyi* inhabits the main channels of these large, turbid rivers, in good current and over a sand-gravel-silt bottom.

The fluvial shiner spawns at depths of 1–2 feet, near banks over sand in June at 82°F (but also at other temperatures). It is easy to collect, but not very pretty.

Spottail shiner, *Notropis hudsonius*, Pee Dee R., N.C. FCR

*Notropis (Alburnops) hudsonius,* spottail shiner

The spottail shiner is another *Alburnops* with a large eye. It is olive above and white below. The flank is silvery with a gold tint, and has a pale dusky stripe. Inland populations have a large gray-to-black basicaudal spot that is prominent on juveniles and dead adults. The basicaudal spot is faint or absent and the body is more slender on Atlantic slope populations. The spottail shiner rarely grows to 5 inches.

It is abundant in the lower Mackenzie River of the Northwest Territories and ranges throughout Canada south of Hudson Bay (excluding British Columbia). It also occurs in the upper Mississippi basin, from Missouri northward in eastern (Ohio River) and western drainages. Eastern populations occur along the Atlantic slope from the St. Lawrence River in Quebec to the Altamaha and Savannah Rivers. It now occurs in the upper Chattahoochee River of Georgia (Lee et al. 1980). If more than a single taxon, the name *hudsonius* would apply to the Canadian and Mississippi drainage forms, but perhaps not to the Atlantic form.

*N. (A.) hudsonius* was previously considered a separate subspecies and named as follows: *N. h. hudsonius* for populations in the Mississippi valley north to, but excluding, the Great Lakes; *N. h. selene* for at least part of the Great Lakes population(s); *N. h. amorus* for populations in the Delaware and Potomac River basins; and *N. h. saludanus* for those in the Southeast from Virginia through Georgia (Hubbs and Lagler 1958; Scott and Crossman 1973).

All forms intergrade and may be only races, although DNA and other information may distinguish the Atlantic slope or eastern form(s) as a subspecies or higher (for which the epithet *saludanus* is available) (C. Gilbert, pers. comm.).

The spottail shiner is found from brackish (10 ppt), sluggish coastal streams to clear, strongly flowing mountain streams; it also is found in rivers and lakes, over sand or rock shallows, and is not associated with vegetation. It feeds 40 percent on mayfly and midge larvae and 40 percent on daphnia. It consumes smaller amounts of *Bosmina, Sida, Leptodora,* fish eggs, and fry, sometimes eating surprising amounts of filamentous algae. It is an egg broadcaster over algae on sandy shoals during June and July (Scott and Crossman 1973).

Provide them with *Nitella, Vesicularia,* or spawning mops over an open sand or gravel bottom.

Bigeye shiner, *Notropis boops,* White R., Mo. WFR

---

**Notropis (Notropis) semperasper,**
roughhead shiner

*N. (N.) semperasper* is olive above, silvery on the flank, and white below. A dark band becomes apparent in alcohol preservative.

The roughhead shiner is endemic to the upper James River of the valley and ridge provinces in western Virginia.

It occurs occasionally in riffles, but usually in runs and flowing pools of clear, warm, medium-sized streams and small rivers, over clean bottoms of various types. It feeds on aquatic insect larvae and may nest in the pits of other minnows. It is threatened by competition from the introduced *N. telescopus,* and by siltation and impoundments (Jenkins and Burkhead 1994).

---

**Notropis (Notropis) scepticus,**
sandbar shiner

*N. (N.) scepticus* is olive above and bright silver on the large eyes, gills, and flank; it is silver to white below. Large specimens in breeding condition are iridescent blue above.

The sandbar shiner occurs in the Cape Fear, Pee Dee, Santee, Edisto, and Savannah Rivers of the Carolinas and Georgia, mostly in foothill and Piedmont streams but occasionally below the fall line (Lee et al. 1980).

*N. (N.) scepticus* inhabits pools near riffles in streams and rivers (6 to 100 ft. wide) over sand bottoms, where it feeds on insect larvae. It spawns during May.

---

**Notropis boops,** bigeye shiner

*N. boops* has a small head with an eye width greater than the distance from the eye to the tip of the jaw. A broad black band runs along the entire flank bordered by a thin, silvery line above. It is yellow to olive above with dark-edged scales on the back. The average adult length is 2 inches.

The bigeye shiner was originally native to streams emptying into western Lake Erie. It occurs east of the main stem of the Mississippi River, from Ohio to Illinois to northern Alabama, and west of the Mississippi main stem in Missouri, Arkansas, Kansas, Oklahoma, and northern Louisiana (Lee et al. 1980).

*N. boops* inhabits clear upland streams over clean gravel or sand mixed with gravel. It also is found over rock, but most often in pools or at the edges of streams among abundant vegetation. It avoids strong currents and cold water, and thus favors springs. A schooling fish, it feeds on adult flying insects by jumping from the water and seizing them as they hover in the air. The bigeye shiner spawns from

June through August (Pflieger 1975; P. W. Smith 1979). Provide live *Drosophila* and freeze-dried Euphausid shrimp to accommodate its surface feeding habit.

| *Notropis xaenocephalus,* Coosa shiner | *N. xaenocephalus* has dark-edged scales above and on the flank, and a dark band from the jaws ending in a basicaudal mark. A light band of non-dark-edged scales appears immediately above the dark band. It is probably related to *N. boops* (Lee et al. 1980).

The Coosa shiner occurs above the fall line on the Coosa and Tallapoosa Rivers (Mobile basin) of Alabama and Georgia.

*N. xaenocephalus* inhabits clear, cool, spring-fed streams over rock, sand, or gravel, and sometimes near vegetation. It spawns from May through July. |

*Notropis (Notropis) melanostomus,* blackmouth shiner

*N. (N.) melanostomus* is a small (1½ in.), swamp-dwelling minnow with a strongly inclined mouth. It is gray above with dark-edged scales and white below, divided by an iridescent dusky band along the flank bordered by a light stripe along its upper margin.

The blackmouth shiner occurs in the Yellow and Blackwater Rivers draining into Pensacola Bay in the western Florida panhandle.

*N. (N.) melanostomus* inhabits lowland, mud-bottom backwaters of blackwater streams close to vegetation and around cypress tree aerial roots (knees). Its minute size and possible egg-scattering on plants are conducive to aquarium propagation.

The blackmouth shiner has long been known (Lee et al. 1980, p. 290), but was described as a new species only in 1989. It is closely related to the upland *N. ortenburgeri,* despite the distance separating the two species.

*Notropis (Notropis) ortenburgeri,* Kiamichi shiner

The closely related *N. (N.) ortenburgeri* is an upland version. It is slim, silvery, and has a small head, large eyes, dark-edged scales on the back and extreme upper flank, and a silvery black band along the flank. A clear or white band is immediately above, where the scales do not have dark edging. It is also small (2 in.).

The Kiamichi shiner occurs in the Arkansas and Ouachita drainages, and in the Kiamichi and Little River drainages of the Red River, all streams coming off the Ouachita Mountains in western Arkansas and eastern Oklahoma (Lee et al. 1980).

*N. (N.) ortenburgeri* inhabits gravel, boulder, or rubble pools in small or medium, clear, upland streams.

*Notropis (Notropis) amabilis,* Texas shiner

*N. (N.) amabilis* is readily recognized within its small range by the large eyes and black lips. A dark stripe runs along the back, and its scales are black-edged. Yellow tinted fins appear occasionally in breeding males.

The Texas shiner ranges from the Colorado to the Rio Grande (lower Pecos) Rivers of Texas, extending into the Rio San Juan and Rio Salado tributaries in Mexico.

*N. (N.) amabilis* prefers clear water, and schools in groups of 10 to 20 in runs, along sandbars or near rocky shoals.

A 30-gallon aquarium with moderate to swift current is suitable for 10 to 15 fish. The middle of the aquarium should be open, with room for schooling. The back and sides require plants for refuge at night. Flake foods are readily taken, but frequent feedings of live foods are recommended for spawning.

| | |
|---|---|
| *Notropis (Alburnops) braytoni,* Tamaulipas shiner | N. (A.) braytoni is straw colored above with black-edged scales on the back. The flank is silvery, with a strikingly broad, dark band from the operculum to the caudal peduncle that is separated from a large black basicaudal spot. The belly is white and the fins may be dark-edged.<br><br>The Tamaulipas shiner occurs in the Rio Grande drainage of Texas and Mexico, from the Pecos River in Texas to the Rio Conchos, Rio San Juan, and Rio Salado in Mexico.<br><br>N. (A.) braytoni inhabits weedless rock, gravel, and sand bottom (sometimes with a silt overlay) rivers, and large creeks (Lee et al. 1980). |
| *Notropis (Alburnops) orca,* phantom shiner | N. (A.) orca has a large blunt head, resembling a fathead minnow (Pimephales). The body is virtually colorless with scattered tiny black specks, and a hint of a stripe along the flank.<br><br>The phantom shiner occurs in the Rio Grande of New Mexico and Texas. It has not been seen since 1975 and is probably extinct (Hubbs et al. 1991), but is included here with optimism.<br><br>N. (A.) orca is found midchannel in turbid water, over sand. |
| *Notropis (Notropis) simus,* bluntnose shiner | N. (N.) simus has just a hint of a wide, dusky band that is not usually seen in live specimens. It has a variable anal fin ray count of 7 to 11.<br><br>N. s. simus of the upper Rio Grande of Texas and New Mexico has not been collected since 1964 and is probably extinct (Hubbs et al. 1991). N. s. pecosensis in the Pecos River of New Mexico is threatened, and thus unavailable for collection without permission to breed in captivity.<br><br>The bluntnose shiner occurs in main river channels below dams or other obstructions, over sand, silt, or gravel. |
| *Notropis (Notropis) perpallidus,* peppered shiner | N. (N.) perpallidus is translucent white, with scattered large black spots aggregating to form a horizontal line in the rear half of the flank; other spots appear along the dorsal and rear ventral midlines and on the jaws and head.<br><br>The peppered shiner occurs in the Ouachita (Saline, Ouachita, Little Missouri, and Caddo) and Red River (Little and Kiamichi) drainages of southern Arkansas and southeastern Oklahoma (Lee et al. 1980).<br><br>N. (N.) perpallidus is found above and below the fall line in moderately sized, warm, clear rivers in 2- to 4-foot-deep quiet pools and other still areas behind islands, logs, and other obstructions. It is present over various types of bottom, usually associated with Justicia (water willow). It feeds on insects and other larvae, mostly midges and other flies. The peppered shiner spawns during June and July (Robison and Buchanan 1988).<br><br>It is rare and should not be collected except by professional biologists for specific programs. |
| *Notropis (Notropis) atherinoides,* emerald shiner | N. (N.) atherinoides is slender, flattened from side to side, has a silver stripe, and resembles a silverside (Atherinidae). The mouth is large and terminal. The body is olive above with a narrow dusky stripe along the back. The silver stripe on the flank sometimes has a light green iridescence. The dorsal fin originates just behind the origin of the pelvic fin. The emerald shiner averages 4 inches as an adult.<br><br>It is widespread from the Arctic to the Gulf. Its range includes the Mackenzie |

River drainage and Northern Territory southward through the St. Lawrence, the Hudson River, and Great Lakes southward throughout the entire Mississippi basin to the Gulf of Mexico. On the Gulf Coast, it occurs from Mobile Bay, Alabama to Galveston Bay, Texas.

N. (N.) atherinoides usually is found in clear water over gravel and sand. It feeds in midwater (mostly) on zooplankton, aquatic insects, copepods, green and blue-green algae, and protozoans. In deep northern lakes, it follows zooplankton day-night vertical migrations.

The emerald shiner is a schooling egg broadcaster that spawns in deep water (> 6 ft. deep) over hard bottoms during summer nights. The peak of breeding activity occurs during June in the United States, but later in Canada, at around 75°F. A related species spawns in chub (Nocomis) nests. The larvae are 4 mm long at hatching, and start to feed four days later when they are 50 percent larger. The life span is three years (Scott and Crossman 1973; Etnier and Starnes 1993).

N. (N.) atherinoides is not attractive and not suitable for aquaria, preferring large spaces and depths.

| *Notropis (Notropis) amoenus,* comely shiner | N. (N.) amoenus is anything but comely and resembles N. (N.) atherinoides, but has smaller eyes and a less upwardly angled mouth. |

N. (N.) amoenus is anything but comely and resembles N. (N.) atherinoides, but has smaller eyes and a less upwardly angled mouth.

The comely shiner occurs in Atlantic slope drainages from the Hudson River in New York to the Cape Fear River in North Carolina.

N. (N.) amoenus is found in warm, low gradient streams and rivers over sand and gravel and cannot survive impoundment in lakes and ponds.

The comely shiner spawns in the nests of the river chub, Nocomis micropogon. The newly hatched larvae are 5.0 to 5.5 mm long, but feeding should be delayed until they are much larger (Buynak and Mohr 1980b). Jenkins and Burkhead (1994) speculated that it is a night spawner and may have been introduced into the Pee Dee River of North Carolina.

*Notropis (Notropis) jemezanus,*
Rio Grande shiner

N. (N.) jemezanus, the Rio Grande shiner, has black jaws and a black ridge of tissue supporting the caudal and anal fin bases. Its average adult length is 2 inches.

The Rio Grande shiner survives in the Pecos River of New Mexico, but since the report by Lee et al. (1980), it has probably been extirpated from the Rio Grande in New Mexico, Texas, and Mexico.

N. (N.) jemezanus is usually found in the main stems of large rivers, but also in large creeks. Its habitat is over sand, rubble, and rock bottoms, sometimes with silt overlay and without vegetation. It produces nonadhesive, semibuoyant eggs (Platania and Altenbach 1998).

*Notropis (Notropis) oxyrhynchus,*
sharpnose shiner

N. (N.) oxyrhynchus has a sharply pointed nose and a wide, dusky band on the flank that becomes darker to the rear.

The sharpnose shiner occurs throughout the Brazos River, and was introduced into the adjacent Colorado River above the Buchanan Reservoir in Texas.

N. (N.) oxyrhynchus is found in the main stem of turbid rivers over sand, clay, mud, and gravel bottoms. Reservoirs are giant settling basins, and clear water releases from reservoirs are associated with a decline of this fish immediately downstream, indicating a need for a turbid habitat (Hubbs et al. 1991).

The sharpnose shiner is threatened in Texas and should not be collected; in addition, the fish is not attractive.

---

**Notropis (Notropis) stilbius, silverstripe shiner**

*N. (N.) stilbius* has a long pointed head, a large mouth, and large eyes. The body is pale green with a wide, silvery band on the flank and a bold black basicaudal spot. Scales above the silver band have dark points. The jaws are dusky (Cook 1959).

The silverstripe shiner occurs mostly above the fall line in the Mobile Bay drainage throughout Alabama and ranges into northeastern Mississippi. It is found occasionally in northern Georgia and at one location in southeastern Tennessee (Lee et al. 1980).

*N. (N.) stilbius* inhabits flowing streams over gravel bottoms, but sometimes is present in slow water over sand, often associated with *Justicia* (water willow). It feeds mostly on insects and spawns from May through July.

---

**Notropis (Notropis) photogenis, silver shiner**

*N. (N.) photogenis* has a bright silvery coloration. It has a large mouth and lacks a dark band on the flank. The back is olive with a dark stripe; two black half-moons between the nostrils are diagnostic. It is large (≤ 5 in.) (Rohde et al. 1994).

The silver shiner is an occasional species in Lake Erie drainages. It is common in most Ohio River drainages to the Tennessee River in North Georgia, and most common in Ohio, Indiana, Kentucky, West Virginia, western Virginia, eastern Tennessee, and western North Carolina (Lee et al. 1980).

*N. (N.) photogenis* inhabits large, clear, unvegetated streams with high gradient, gravel, rock, or boulder bottoms. It is predaceous on insects.

---

**Subgenus Notropis (Hydrophlox)**

Species of the subgenus *N. (Hydrophlox)* typically have beautiful breeding coloration, and occur in smaller, often headwater, streams.

*N. (Hydrophlox)* generally spawn in the nests of other minnows *(Semotilus, Nocomis, Campostoma);* however, whether this nest parasitism is obligatory (required) or facultative (optional) is not clear for most species. Many behaviorists believe that this behavior protects all participating species, the chances of any individual egg or fry being taken by a predator decreasing as the number of eggs or fry at the nest increases. In predator-prey relationships, this is called the dilution effect.

In some *N. (Hydrophlox)*, spawning on the nest of a pit builder is known to be obligatory in the wild. It is not clear if these fish can be spawned in captivity in the absence of pit builders and their nests. Some minnows that are pit builders in nature may simply scatter eggs in aquaria, and it is possible that placing pit builders among nest-parasitizing *N. (Hydrophlox)* species may be sufficient to induce spawning in these colorful minnows.

Recently, one colorful *N. (Hydrophlox)* species was induced to spawn in captivity when *Nocomis* milt was added to the aquarium water. This lends support to the possibility that chemical, rather than visual, cues stimulate *Hydrophlox* spawning. The species within *N. (Hydrophlox)* probably include *N. (H.) chrosomus, N. (H.) leuciodus, N. (H.) micropteryx, N. (H.) nubilus, N. (H.) rubellus, N. (H.) suttkusi, and N. (H.) rubricroceus.*

---

**Notropis (Hydrophlox) chrosomus, rainbow shiner**

*N. (H.) chrosomus* **(plate 8)** is translucent pink to gold. Its back and upper flank are purple with the scales dark-edged. A silver-black stripe runs along the flank; the flank sometimes has a blue iridescence. The belly is gold to light blue and the fins are red at the base. The nuptial male has a purple head, a red nose and jaws, and powder blue ventral fins. Adults average 2½ inches long.

The rainbow shiner is common in the Coosa, Cahaba, Alabama, and portions of the upper Black Warrior systems of Alabama, extending into northwestern Georgia. It is rare in a few tributaries of the Conasauga River in southeastern Tennessee (Lee et al. 1980).

*N. (H.) chrosomus* is found in small, clear, spring-fed streams with moderate current, over sand and gravel. Associates include *N. asperifrons* and *N. xaenocephalus,* both of which have seven rather than eight anal rays. The rainbow shiner spawns from May through July in the nests of *Nocomis leptocephalus,* the bluehead chub, in the Alabama River drainage (Johnston and Kleiner 1994).

| | |
|---|---|
| *Notropis (Hydrophlox) leuciodus,* Tennessee shiner | *N. (H.) leuciodus* (**plate 9**) is spectacular in breeding dress. It is usually olive above with dark-edged scales. Wavy black lines appear on the back and upper side, meeting at the rear. A wide, silvery, blue-black band begins on the gill cover and runs along the entire flank, ending at a black basicaudal spot. Few nuptial males in a group reach peak coloration, with the head, flank, belly, and fins turning orange-red; however, other less brilliant males also spawn successfully (Etnier and Starnes 1993). It grows to 3 inches.

The Tennessee shiner ranges from the Green, lower and middle Cumberland, and Tennessee drainages of Virginia and Kentucky through North Carolina, Georgia, Tennessee, and Alabama. This includes Shoal Creek, the Hiwassee, Little, Clinch, Holston, and Powell Rivers. The Tennessee shiner has differentiated in all three major river systems, and may be a species complex; the Hiwassee River form is clearly distinct (Mayden and Matson 1992), and may be a separate taxon.

*N. (H.) leuciodus* is common in pools of clear, swift, highly oxygenated creeks and rivers, over gravel, bedrock, boulders, or rubble. The Tennessee shiner spawns over *Nocomis* mounds and *Campostoma* pits during May and June. |
| *Notropis (Hydrophlox) rubellus,* rosyface shiner | *N. (H.) rubellus* (**plate 10**) is a plain minnow outside the breeding season, with an olive back, a wide dusky band on the flank (thinly margined above in green), a pink flush to the dorsal fin base, and a silver to white belly. During the breeding season, the nuptial male is spectacular with a wide dusky band margined above with a thin, iridescent gold line. The entire head, lower flanks, and bases of fins are bright red. It grows to 3 inches.

The rosyface shiner ranges from Quebec westward to Manitoba, and southward to Alabama and Texas. It occurs in Great Lakes basins from New York westward to Montana. It ranges southward in the east to Virginia, and from Texas northward in western drainages of the Mississippi basin into Canada. Another subspecies (so far unnamed) may occur in the Red River of the North (e.g., Lee et al. 1980).

*N. (H.) rubellus* inhabits swift current in riffles and runs of clear, fast-flowing creeks and small rivers over sand, gravel, or rubble and retreats to pools during winter. It is found most often in schools at depths of 3 feet, where it feeds on drifting and bottom macroinvertebrates, aquatic and terrestrial insects (especially Simulidae or blackflies), spiders, fish larvae and eggs, algae, and diatoms.

The rosyface shiner spawns from May through July at 70 to 84°F. It breeds |

Ozark minnow, *Notropis nubilus*, White R., Mo. WFR

freely over gravel (nonparasitizing) or is parasitic on nests of longnose gar, chestnut lamprey, suckers, stoneroller *(Campostoma anomalum),* and chubs *(Semotilus* spp., *Nocomis biguttatus,* and *N. micropogon).* The nonadhesive eggs fall into crevices in the gravel and pebbles (Robison and Buchanan 1988; Jenkins and Burkhead 1994).

| | |
|---|---|
| *Notropis (Hydrophlox) micropteryx* | *N. (H.) micropteryx,* which has no common name, was previously considered a subspecies of *N. (H.) rubellus.* It reaches a smaller maximum size and has a shorter snout.<br><br>*N. (H.) micropteryx* occurs in the Tennessee and Cumberland River drainages below Cumberland Falls.<br><br>This fish inhabits upland, clear streams. More information appears in a book soon to be published on Alabama fishes by R. Mayden. See also Mettee et al. 1996. |
| *Notropis (Hydrophlox) suttkusi,* rocky shiner | *N. (H.) suttkusi* is similar and related to *N. (H.) rubellus,* but, in the latter, the lateral line is marked by melanophores, the dark lateral stripe is much thicker toward the rear (rather than even throughout), and the throat is unpigmented. In *N. (H.) suttkusi,* which is deeper-bodied and has a shorter snout, the lateral line is contained within a thick, even, continuous lateral band, and the throat is at least one-third pigmented. The nuptial male is a reddish purple (lilac), and orange on the head, flank, and belly. The eye is orange. The fins are light orange with a red-orange band at the base. The female is brightly but less intensely colored; of course, the female has no breeding tubercles on the head, while they are well developed in males (Humphries and Cashner 1994).<br><br>The rocky shiner occurs in the Blue, Muddy Boggy, Kiamichi, and Little Rivers (Red River drainage) emptying from the Ouachita Mountains. It also is found in a part of the interior highlands of southeastern Oklahoma and southwestern Arkansas.<br><br>*N. (H.) suttkusi* is found in clear, moderate to high gradient rivers and streams with gravel and rubble bottoms. |
| *Notropis nubilus,* Ozark minnow | *N. nubilus* may not be a *Hydrophlox* but has many similarities with that subgenus. It was previously placed in the genus *Dionda,* established for *Notropis*-like fish with long, coiled intestines.<br><br>The Ozark minnow has a prominent dark stripe on the midline of its back, dis- |

tinct and overlaid with golden spots. The back and upper flank are otherwise yellow-olive with dark-edged scales. A dusky stripe appears on the flank, ending in an indistinct basicaudal spot. The nuptial male is yellow with yellow-orange fins and breeding tubercles over most of its body. The average adult length is 2½ inches (Pflieger 1975; P. W. Smith 1979).

The distribution of the Ozark minnow has become disjunct, probably within the last 200 years, due to agricultural alterations of the prairies and their drainages. The major population occurs throughout the Ozark Plateau in Missouri, Arkansas, Kansas, and Oklahoma. Lesser populations are clustered to the north in Mississippi River tributaries below the Great Lakes in Wisconsin, Illinois, Iowa, and Minnesota (Lee et al. 1980).

*N. nubilus* schools near the bottom in streams with a permanent strong flow and gravel or rock bottoms, and in slack areas below riffles or in pools. Associates include the duskystripe, bleeding, rosyface, telescope, and wedgespot shiners. It spawns in May and June over the nests of *Nocomis biguttatus,* the hornyhead chub. It lives up to 2½ years (Glazier and Taber 1980).

*Notropis (Hydrophlox) rubricroceus,* saffron shiner

*N. (H.) rubricroceus* (**plate 11**) is considered either a member of the subgenus *Hydrophlox* or the related *rubricroceus* group of the subgenus *Alburnops.*

A pale black stripe originates behind the gills, becomes blacker in the rear, and is obscured in front by an overlying metallic pink line. A pale red tint appears on the snout and jaws. The nuptial male is spectacularly iridescent: dark gold above with a middorsal blue stripe; deep metallic red on the head, gills, flank, and belly; a gold stripe along the upper flank (above the lateral line) and around the head; a black stripe below is apparent only in the rear; and the fins are richly yellow. It is readily recognized when spawning by an elongate, U-shaped golden mark formed by the ends of the gold lines from both upper flanks meeting atop the head (Lee et al. 1980; Jenkins and Burkhead 1994).

The saffron shiner occurs in the upper Tennessee River drainage in the mountains of Tennessee, North Carolina, and Virginia. It invaded the upper tributaries of the Savannah and Santee Rivers in North Carolina by stream capture. It was recently introduced, probably by state game and fish agencies while stocking trout, to the New River drainage of North Carolina, where it is now abundant and widespread.

*N. (H.) rubricroceus* inhabits small, clear, high gradient, headwater mountain streams over gravel and rubble. It feeds on aquatic insect larvae (mostly mayflies, midges, and blackflies), worms, millipedes, spiders, and other benthic invertebrates, algae, and bits of plants.

Nuptial males awaiting females aggregate on the nests of *Nocomis micropogon, N. leptocephalus, Campostoma anomalum,* or *Luxilus chrysocephalus* from May through July at 61 to 85°F, but pairs have also been observed in breeding condition over gravel without nesting species present; thus, the saffron shiner may not be an obligate parasite on the nests of other fishes. When males were aggregated over chub nests, however, they were described as a "fiery spot in the stream . . . moving like colored waves" (Jenkins and Burkhead 1994).

**Genus *Pteronotropis***

*Pteronotropis* is a new genus for a group of spectacular Gulf Coast minnows previously placed in *Notropis,* and characterized by a broad, blue-black band on the flank

Bluenose shiner, *Pteronotropis welaka*. Photo by Dick Stober.

and brilliant yellow or blue colors in the males. Some of the names in use may represent more than one species; thus populations should be kept separate in aquaria.

| | |
|---|---|
| *Pteronotropis welaka,* bluenose shiner | *P. welaka* is the most popular of the *Pteronotropis*. The nuptial male has a large, black flaglike dorsal fin, a blue snout (not nape), and black bands on a yellow or orange, enlarged anal fin. A broad black stripe otherwise runs from the snout to the rear, expanding into a dark spot on the caudal fin. Scales are edged in black, and occasional silver-white spangles appear on the flank. The dorsal and anal fins are larger in nonnuptial males than in females. |

The bluenose shiner ranges from the St. Johns and Apalachicola drainages of Florida to the Pearl River drainage of Mississippi and Louisiana.

*P. welaka* is found in the quiet backwaters of deep vegetated pools, but moves into shallows during spawning season. Groups of 20 to 30 with males displaying are striking.

See *P. hubbsi* for instructions on care.

| | |
|---|---|
| *Pteronotropis hubbsi,* bluehead shiner | *P. hubbsi* (**plate 12**) has a bold double stripe from the jaws through the eye and entire flank. The upper stripe is narrower and bright red-gold above, and the lower stripe wider and deep black. The black stripe expands into a wide, black, triangular spot at the base of the tail fin. The dorsal and caudal fins have a thin black edge, and the dorsal and anal fin rays number nine or ten. |

There are two types of breeding males. The terminal male is much larger (usually > 2 in. long), deeper, and slab-sided than other males and females. He has an enlarged (flaglike) dorsal fin, enlarged anal and pelvic fins, a faded to obsolete patch of blue on the nape (never bright), a red tail, and lacks bright blue on the fins. The secondary male is smaller (usually < 2 in. long). His dorsal fin is not as large, and he is much more colorful with a bright blue patch on top of the head; all fins are bright blue (Fletcher and Burr 1992).

The bluehead shiner occurs in the southern third of Arkansas and north central Louisiana, and ranges into southeastern Oklahoma and eastern Texas in the Red, Ouachita, and Atchafalaya Rivers. It has been extirpated by pollution in southern Illinois.

*P. hubbsi* inhabits quiet backwater areas of blackwater swamp streams and oxbow lakes. It often is found in clumps of *Proserpinica palustris, Polygonum hy-*

*dropiperoides, Nelumbo pentapetala,* or *Ceratophyllum demersum* (hornwort), in 1½- to 4-foot-deep pools or in the deepest holes available, with scattered *Nuphar luteum* (lilies) and *Taxodium distichum* (bald cypress) around the margins, and a bottom of mud or sand and mud. It may be the dominant minnow in a population containing *N. (A.) maculatus, N. (A.) chalybaeus,* and *Notemigonus crysoleucas.* Adults feed at all levels, mostly on cladocerans (e.g., *Daphnia, Bosmina*) and copepods, and partly on chironomids and water mites.

The terminal male defends territories and spawns in nests of *Lepomis gulosus* (warmouth) among the roots of bald cypress trees or other plants not associated with sunfish nests. During nest defense, the terminal male may display vertical bars. Eggs are scattered on the nest litter on the bottom, on the sides of the cypress roots, and outside the cryptic nest at the rim of the depression. The more colorful secondary males (sneaky males) dart into the nest to spawn when the terminal male is distracted. Large schools are seen around structure or vegetation in open water, the males in full display. Mock battles take place among the terminal males, and spawning occurs from April through June (Robison and Buchanan 1988; Fletcher and Burr 1992). *P. hubbsi* lives three years in captivity versus two years in nature.

Seine in the deepest holes of creeks having dense vegetation, or collect eggs from warmouth nests by scooping up litter or rubbing the bark of the tree roots facing into the cavity (which will yield a mix of warmouth and bluehead shiner fry), or collect from minnow nests at the roots of buttonbush *(Cephalanthus occidentalis).* Larvae, distinctive for their bold, black caudal spot, occur at nests, among hornwort, and under lily pad leaves.

Dr. Brooks Burr at Southern Illinois University in Carbondale is participating in a captive breeding program to reintroduce this fish in Illinois. It was extirpated due to the loss of swamp habitat by gravel mining operations, and because of a toxic spill (P. W. Smith 1979).

Provide a 29-gallon, high aquarium for a group of 10 to 15 fish. The aquarium should have slight current, plants, or contain structure around the walls, leaving the middle unobstructed and the bottom covered with coarse gravel or pebbles. Feed live foods.

In eight weeks, lower the temperature to 65°F to induce the females to ripen; they should then be isolated from the males, and conditioned on increased feedings of live foods, especially *Daphnia* and ostracods or *Ceriodaphnia.* After eight weeks of conditioning, put them back into the aquarium with the males, and reduce the current slightly.

Spawning should commence within three to four hours. Males expand their fins and undulate their bodies, flaring their gill covers. Females spawn with selected males. Eggs are scattered in the current and drift into the plants or structure, or fall among the crevices in the large gravel, which will require all filters to be turned off.

Spawning may last several hours. The adults should then be removed and separated by sex for another round of conditioning and spawning, this procedure repeated several times a year. Eggs hatch in three to four days at 65°F, and in two to three days at 75°F. Fry take rotifers, infusoria, and green water *(Volvox* and *Euglena).* After two weeks, provide *Ceriodaphnia* and ostracods; *Artemia* nauplii are not readily accepted.

Other egg collection options include bottom spawning mops with mop removal to aerated gallon jars until hatching, or a pebble or marble filled spawning

Sailfin shiner, *Pteronotropis hypselopterus,* Black R., Fla. WFR

tray transferred to a 10- or 20-gallon aquarium for hatching. In all cases, there should be no turbulence in the fry aquarium, as it interferes with feeding.

*P. hubbsi* is protected in Arkansas, but not elsewhere.

| | |
|---|---|
| *Pteronotropis hypselopterus,*<br>sailfin shiner | *P. hypselopterus* is golden to coppery above and white below. A broad (three times the eye diameter), uniform, steel blue-black stripe runs along the flank, margined above in yellow and copper. The snout is gold to orange, the fins are generally yellow (except dorsal and pelvics which are dark), and there are small, bright red basicaudal spots (Bailey and Suttkus 1952). |

*Pteronotropis hypselopterus,*
sailfin shiner

*P. hypselopterus* is golden to coppery above and white below. A broad (three times the eye diameter), uniform, steel blue-black stripe runs along the flank, margined above in yellow and copper. The snout is gold to orange, the fins are generally yellow (except dorsal and pelvics which are dark), and there are small, bright red basicaudal spots (Bailey and Suttkus 1952).

The sailfin shiner occurs throughout most of the Florida peninsula above Lake Okeechobee, northward and all across the panhandle. It ranges from southern Alabama to Mobile Bay. In his Ph.D. dissertation in 1951, Suttkus (cited in Lee et al. 1980) suggested that the population in the Tampa Bay area and a population to the north in Georgia extending to the Pee Dee River of South Carolina might be a separate subspecies or full species *(stonei),* and that other subspecies could also exist. The genus needs further work to clarify the relationships of these many populations (C. Gilbert, pers. comm.).

*P. hypselopterus* occurs in the deeper parts of slow-moving, small, black or darkly stained headwater streams among vegetation.

Instructions for care are similar to those for *P. hubbsi,* with a few differences. Spawning occurs up to 75°F. Separate the sexes in the same aquarium with a glass partition, and condition heavily on live foods for weeks. When the females swell with roe, remove the partition.

It is impossible to judge when the group will spawn, but it often occurs within a few days and lasts several hours. When the females appear deflated, it can be assumed that spawning has occurred. The fish, or the mops, trays, etc., should be removed from the spawning tank. Sexes should be separated again, conditioned, and the process repeated several times a year.

*Pteronotropis euryzonus,*
broadstripe shiner

*P. euryzonus* is similar to *P. hypselopterus,* but the dorsal fin is rectangular and the stripe is much wider along the flank.

The broadstripe shiner occurs in the middle Chattahoochee drainage of Georgia and Alabama in flowing headwater streams.

Condition male and female broadstripe shiners in separate aquaria several

Flagfin shiner, *Pteronotropis signipinnis,* Fla. WFR

weeks, feeding frozen adult *Artemia* and chironomids, live tubificids, whiteworms, daphnia, and vegetable flake food (which protects against fin-clamping).

A 5- to 20-gallon aquarium is suitable for spawning, and should have subdued lighting, a pH of 7.0 to 7.8, a temperature of 74 to 78°F, and moderate water flow from a canister or box filter (Katula 1993b). Place the females in the aquarium one week prior to the males, and provide a 25 percent water change and a slight increase in temperature to trigger spawning.

The adults spawn in yarn mops, which can be removed and placed in aerated gallon jars with methylene blue until egg hatching five to seven days later. Alternatively, stock the aquarium densely with *Nitella* or *Vesicularia,* substitute sponge filters for the box or canister filters, and remove either plants or adults after spawning.

The eggs are sensitive to changes in water quality; use the parental tank water for incubation, with regular partial water changes. For the first five days, the fry are motionless, hanging or otherwise attached to vertical surfaces. At the free-swimming stage, they accept infusoria and microworms, and *Artemia* nauplii in ten days. Katula (1993b) found that maturity is reached at six months for females and at eight months for males.

| *Pteronotropis signipinnis,* flagfin shiner | *P. signipinnis* has a gold colored snout. The body is golden to coppery above and the flank is yellow above, with a broad, gunmetal, blue-black medial stripe and occasionally, vertical orange dashes. It is white below, and pale gold on the lower flank. The median fins are orange to yellow, edged in red-orange, and have a black line at the leading edge. The caudal fin has two large, bright yellow spots at the base, and a darker spot between them; the fin is yellow in the middle and orange at the edges. |

The flagfin shiner occurs in lower coastal rivers from the Chipola and Apalachicola Rivers in Florida westward across Alabama and Mississippi to the Pearl River of Mississippi and Louisiana.

*P. signipinnis* inhabits small (≤ 20 ft.), high gradient, flowing creeks and streams of darkly stained water that flow through tupelo and magnolia swamps mixed with maple and cypress. It is usually in the open. Look for *Orontium aquaticum* (golden club) as a good indicator of flagfin shiner habitat (Bailey and Suttkus 1952).

Care instructions are the same as for *P. hubbsi,* but the flagfin shiner breeds at 70 to 75°F.

**Genus Acrocheilus**

*Acrocheilus* is a monotypic genus of the western United States with a distinctive mouth structure and twiglike peduncle.

*Acrocheilus alutaceus,* chiselmouth

*A. alutaceus* is the sole species. It has a forked tail and a pinched caudal peduncle. The lower part of the blunt, wide head has a leatherlike cover and a chisel-like bony plate, rather than a typical jaw. It is dark above and lighter below, with black spots on the flank. The fins are dark, sometimes orange at the bases of paired fins. Its length is 6–7 inches.

The chiselmouth occurs in Columbia and Fraser River drainages from British Columbia across Washington and Oregon (including Malheur Lake) to Idaho and Nevada.

*A. alutaceus* inhabits lakes (especially in Canada), rivers, and creeks. Lake fish move into tributaries in June and July when temperatures reach the low 60s (°F).

It spawns by age four. Eggs are scattered on the bottom and sink among boulders. It scrapes rocks with the lower jaw, leading to speculation that green algae pass through and diatoms (golden algae) are digested (Scott and Crossman 1973). It lives six years or more.

The chiselmouth might be able to survive on cooked vegetables (e.g., zucchini, yellow squash, green beans); this has been successful with ecologically similar South American loricariid catfishes.

**Genus Couesius**

*Couesius,* a monotypic genus for a single but wide-ranging northern species, is sometimes included within *Hybopsis.* It resembles a *Semotilus* with red fins and, indeed, may be closely related to that genus. Both share a hidden barbel in the groove above the upper lip.

It is suitable for cold-water aquaria, and a good companion for freshwater sticklebacks which have similar requirements.

*Couesius plumbeus,* lake chub

*C. plumbeus* has a flattened head and small barbel at the angle of the jaw. The flank has a lateral dark band, and sometimes black spots. In some areas, both sexes are red-orange at the bases of pectorals, pelvics, or corners of the mouth. It may resemble *Semotilus atromaculatus* (creek chub), both having bright red fins. It grows to 4 inches.

The lake chub ranges from Labrador and Nova Scotia to British Columbia and the Yukon of Alaska. It is also present from New York and New England to Michigan, Idaho, Iowa, Wisconsin, Colorado, Montana, the Dakotas, and Colorado.

Three subspecies are recognized: *C. p. plumbeus,* ranging from the Yukon to the eastern slopes of the Rocky Mountains, east to the Great Lakes and the Atlantic coast of Canada; *C. p. greenei,* found in the Pacific slope of the Rocky Mountains; and an unnamed subspecies (previously referred to *C. p. dissimilis,* an unavailable name) in the upper Missouri system (Scott and Crossman 1973).

*C. plumbeus* inhabits lakes and streams. It feeds on chironomids, other insects, cladocerans, algae, and small fishes. It migrates from tributaries into lakes around April, spawning during late May or June at 57 to 66°F; the lake chub spawns during August in the North. It broadcasts eggs among large rocks in river shallows, and may die after spawning. It is an abundant food source for merganser ducks and kingfishers, lake trout, burbot, walleye, and northern pike (Scott and Crossman 1973).

Keep it cool, provide a pebble and rock bottom, and offer a diet of blood-worms and flake foods. Good filtration is important.

**Genus _Gila_**

_Gila_ contains western, riverine, egg-scattering chubs with fine scales, usually a complete lateral line, and sometimes oddly shaped heads. The species more closely resemble Asian minnows of the genus _Tribolodon_ than they do other North American minnows. Most are olive green above and sharply white below. They sometimes have a hazy black line along the flank that ends in a black basicaudal spot. The lower fins are pink or clear. The nuptial males, and some females, strongly contrast above and below, sometimes displaying very pretty golds, reds, or blues.

Most are too large, unattractive, or protected _(alvordensis, atraria, bicolor, borax-obius, coerulea, cypha, ditaenia, elegans, eremica, intermedia, nigrescens, orcutti, purpurea, robusta)_, and are not recommended for aquaria. Both _G. cypha_ and _G. elegans_ (the latter may be extinct) have spectacular nuchal humps, and the thin caudal peduncles are adapted to extremely strong currents and large habitat areas (Tyus 1998); they could probably be maintained in 150-gallon or larger aquaria with multiple power-heads for current, should they become available.

The smaller chubs, if handled gently during collection, may spawn in aquaria set up with a layer of rocks over a glass bottom. Chubs are omnivorous on small crustaceans, insects, small fish, and algae scraped from the bottom or picked from the water column. Many are rare, protected, or recently extinct due to loss of habitat. See DeMarais (1991), Rinne and Minckley (1991), Marshall (1992), Douglas (1993), Douglas and Marsh (1994), and Lynch et al. (1994) for species not covered here. Known as charalitos in Mexico, some species are interesting aquarium fishes.

_Gila copei,_ leatherside chub

_G. copei_ is olive with spotting. The nuptial males have red bases on the lower fins. It is usually 4 inches as an adult.

The leatherside chub occurs in the Snake and Sevier Rivers, and has been introduced into the Colorado River of Utah, Idaho, and Wyoming.

_G. copei_ is common in rocky pools and riffles of moderately flowing streams and small rivers.

See _Clinostomus_ for care and breeding instructions.

_Gila ditaenia,_ Sonora chub

_G. ditaenia_ is a robust chub with a black basicaudal spot and a green-gold iridescence on the gill cover that continues as a gold line above a dusky flank stripe. The nuptial male is red on the jaws, gill covers, bases of fins, and belly. It is typically an 8-inch chub (Rinne and Minckley 1991).

The Sonora chub is protected in Santa Cruz County, Arizona, but widespread and common in the Rio Conception basin of Mexico.

_G. ditaenia_ is found in shaded, headwater and flash-flood streams and arroyos, often beneath cliffs. When pools become reduced during the dry season, it is decimated by giant water bugs (Lee et al. 1980). It hybridizes near Cienega la Atascosa in Sonora, Mexico with an unnamed species of _Gila_ from seepage marshes of the Rio Yaqui (Rinne and Minckley 1991; DeMarais and Minckley 1992).

The Sonora chub may not be collected in the United States, but Mexican aquarists should have no difficulty keeping this omnivorous fish in 29- to 55-gallon aquaria with rocks on the bottom, good filtration, and frequent checking from below for eggs.

| | |
|---|---|
| *Gila orcutti,* arroyo chub | *G. orcutti* has a large eye, a short, rounded snout, and a thick (deep) caudal peduncle. Eight dorsal rays and seven anal rays distinguish the arroyo chub from most other common chubs within its range. Coloration is plain gray, sometimes with a darker stripe along the flank that ends in a dark spot at the rear. Superficially, it is similar to a fathead minnow. |

The arroyo chub occurs in coastal streams of California, but has been introduced into the Death Valley drainage by accident as a bait fish. Its habitat varies from pools and runs of headwater streams to small rivers over mud or sand (Page and Burr 1991).

*G. orcutti* is hardy, surviving even in small aquariums on frozen brine shrimp, flake food, cat food, and vegetables. Pittman (1987) described them as actively schooling midwater, much like danios, but not very colorful.

Pittman (1987) spawned them in a 10-gallon aquarium with rocks, gravel, and *Ceratophyllum.* The large, adhesive eggs were deposited among the plants and hatched in two to three days; the fry were slim and ¼-inch long. In one week the fry were free-swimming and started feeding on infusoria; they began taking live *Artemia* nauplii after another three to four days.

| | |
|---|---|
| *Gila pandora,* Rio Grande chub | *G. pandora,* the Rio Grande chub, has a short, second band ending at the anal fin (Page and Burr 1991). It rarely grows to 6 inches. Nuptial individuals have orange fins. |

It is common throughout the upper Rio Grande and Pecos Rivers of New Mexico. It has been introduced at Davis Mountain in Texas, into the Canadian River of New Mexico, and possibly into Colorado (Lee et al. 1980).

*G. pandora* inhabits the pools of small streams near riffles, undercuts, brush, and debris (Lee et al. 1980).

Keep and breed it like *Clinostomus* (see below); it hybridizes with *Rhinichthys cataractae.*

| | |
|---|---|
| **Genus *Richardsonius*** | *Richardsonius* contains two similar (almost identical) species of western minnows that are related to *Gila* and *Clinostomus.* Both have dark backs and upper flanks split by a white to gold zone, and silvery bellies. Both are egg broadcasters. |

| | |
|---|---|
| *Richardsonius balteatus,* redside shiner | *R. balteatus* has ten or more anal fin rays. It is steel blue to brown above and white below. Nuptial males darken further in the dark area, develop a yellow belly and lower fins, and display a bright red stripe in the yellow zone from the gill cover to just below the dorsal fin. Two subspecies, *R. b. balteatus* and *R. b. hydrophlox,* are based on anal ray counts and probably are not valid. |

The redside shiner occurs in the Nass River of British Columbia, extending southward to the Peace River in Alberta. It is found in coastal streams in the Columbia, Bonneville, Harney, and Malheur River basins of Oregon, Idaho, Montana, Nevada, and Utah. It has been introduced into the upper Missouri and upper Colorado Rivers (Scott and Crossman 1973; Lee et al. 1980).

*R. balteatus* inhabits springs, creeks, rivers, ponds, lakes, swamps, and ditches. It prefers slow current to none at all, where it occurs in the hundreds to thousands of individuals. It feeds on aquatic and terrestrial (beetles and ants) insects, fish eggs

Redside shiner, *Richardsonius balteatus*, Green R., Wyo. WFR

(including trout), algae, and mollusks. From May through July, groups of 30 to 40 move into their home streams when the temperature exceeds 50°F.

The redside shiner spawns over shallow (4 in.) riffles day and night, the female thrashed from side to side by one or two males. With each clasp, 10–20 adhesive 2.0 mm eggs fall and stick to the gravel where they hatch in 3 to 15 days. The 5 mm fry lie dormant, surviving on yolk sacs for the first week, then swim and feed when 9 mm long. It attains 4 inches in four years, but may live seven (Scott and Crossman 1973).

| | |
|---|---|
| *Richardsonius egregius,* Lahontan redside | *R. egregius* has eight or nine anal rays, but otherwise is similar to *R. balteatus*. It has an olive back, a silver belly, and a scarlet stripe on the flank. Adults average 5 inches.

The Lahontan redside occurs in the Lahontan basin of Nevada and California, including the Walker, Carson, Truckee, Susan, Reese, and Humboldt Rivers, Walker, Pyramid, and Tahoe lakes, and ponds and creeks within this region (Lee et al. 1980). Its range just enters Malheur County, Oregon (Marshall 1992).

*R. egregius* occurs in habitats that vary from mountain streams to deep lakes, where it often schools around structures such as logs and docks. It feeds on aquatic and terrestrial insects, crustaceans, and fish eggs. It matures in three to four years. The Lahontan redside spawns in June and July at 63°F over gravel and cobble, at a depth of 8 inches or more along lakeshores and in streams (Lee et al. 1980; Marshall 1992).

*R. egregius* and *R. balteatus* probably can be maintained and spawned in the manner described for *Luxilus cerasinus*. |
| **Genus *Clinostomus*** | *Clinostomus*, with just two species, is related to *Richardsonius* and, perhaps more distantly, to *Gila*. The snout is pointed, the eye and mouth large, and the jaws oblique. |
| *Clinostomus elongatus,* redside dace | *C. elongatus* **(plate 13)** has a large, deeply oblique mouth. The body is dark greenish black above, with blue, violet, purple, and green highlights. It has a dusky band and scattered dark crescents or slashes along the rear side, and is white below. The nuptial male has prickly tuberculate scales on its body, and an orange-red flush along the middle of its side. Adults average 4 inches (Etnier and Starnes 1993).

The redside dace occurs in the Great Lakes and upper Mississippi drainages from Lake Ontario tributaries of Canada into Wisconsin, Iowa, and Minnesota to the lower Mohawk River (Hudson River drainage) of New York. It ranges south- |

ward in the Susquehanna and Ohio River drainages through Pennsylvania barely into Kentucky.

C. elongatus inhabits pools within cool to cold, clear, high gradient, hard-bottom streams. It feeds mostly (95%) on terrestrial flies, mayflies, and dragonflies, but also eats aquatic insects, worms, crayfishes, and snails. The redside dace broadcasts eggs over gravel nests of *Nocomis, Semotilus,* and *Luxilus* (Scott and Crossman 1973; Johnston and Page 1992). It matures at age two and lives to 4 years (Etnier and Starnes 1993).

C. elongatus probably can be bred like the rosyside dace (see below).

| | |
|---|---|
| *Clinostomus funduloides,* rosyside dace | C. *funduloides* (**plate 14**) has a thicker body and a more rounded snout than the redside dace; its red coloration also is not as deep as in *C. elongatus.* The body has crescent marks similar to those of *Luxilus cerasinus.* |

The rosyside dace ranges from New Jersey to Kentucky, southward to the Savannah River on the Georgia–South Carolina border. It continues westward through Tennessee and northern Alabama, and just enters Mississippi.

Three subspecies are recognized: *C. f. funduloides,* ranging from the Delaware River to the Savannah River and parts of the upper Ohio River; *C. f. estor,* found in the Cumberland and Tennessee Rivers of the Highland Rim in Tennessee and Kentucky; and a third subspecies (possibly a full species) undescribed and unnamed, occurring in the Little Tennessee drainage of western North Carolina (Etnier and Starnes 1993).

C. *funduloides* inhabits pools of clear, rocky streams, where it feeds on drift insects and other invertebrates with its large mouth. The average temperature of its habitat in Alabama and Georgia streams is 50°F. The rosyside dace spawns from late spring to early summer when water temperatures average in the middle 60s (°F). It broadcasts eggs in the nests of *Nocomis* (chubs).

C. *funduloides* can be brought into spawning condition several times a year with an aquarium chiller. It breeds in small groups, scattering eggs over depressions in the gravel that are carried with the current. Place the males in a 30-gallon breeding aquarium with gravel, large rocks, and current from a powerhead; keep the females in a separate, bare aquarium.

Keep all fish at 55 to 58°F, and feed heavily on insect larvae. The females should be added to the aquarium with the males six weeks later, and the temperature slowly raised to 65°F. When spawning begins, usually within two weeks, turn off the filters. Afterward, remove the adults. Eggs hatch in 72 to 96 hours. The fry are small and require rotifers and ciliates.

| | |
|---|---|
| **Genus Relictus** | *Relictus* is a western genus related to *Gila* and *Rhinichthys* (Lee et al. 1980) and is monotypic. |

| | |
|---|---|
| *Relictus solitarius,* relict dace | R. *solitarius* is a short, fat minnow that superficially resembles an *Empetrichthys* in color, shape, and habitat preference. *R. solitarius* is gray-brown with iridescent highlights and dark spotting above, white below, and tiny yellow fins. It grows to almost 4 inches. |

The relict dace occurs in northeastern Nevada, in drainages to Lakes Franklin, Gale, Waring, Steptoe, and Spring.

R. *solitarius* inhabits pools, especially beneath undercut banks of springs and their outlets to nearby lakes. It is found over rock or silt bottom, usually near abundant vegetation; it dives into mud or vegetation when frightened. The relict dace spawns from June to September during its first year (Lee et al. 1980).

The relict dace is protected in Nevada, the only state in which it occurs. It if becomes available, it should be housed in a 10-gallon aquarium with a sand bottom, sponge filtration, and one side of the container filled with *Nitella* or *Vesicularia*. Feed flakes, supplemented with frozen adult and live baby brine shrimp, blackworms, and live daphnia. Eggs are probably scattered among the vegetation.

---

**Genus *Rhinichthys***

*Rhinichthys* contains the speckled daces, long-nosed, advanced minnows with a tiny barbel at the corner of the jaws, an inferior mouth below the elongate snout (the generic name means "nose fish"), small scales, and a bridge of tissue (a frenum) connecting the middle of the upper jaw to the head that prevents the jaw from protruding.

Most are dark olive to dusky above, silvery below, and have a prominent dark band in between. The body (usually upper) is often heavily marked with fine or coarse black dots.

Most are egg broadcasters; one species may use the nest of another minnow species as a spawning site, and at least one species is an egg clumper.

---

*Rhinichthys atratulus,*
blacknose dace

*R. atratulus* **(plate 15),** the blacknose dace, is plain with a bold black line from the upper jaw to the base of the tail, speckles over the entire body, and an eye diameter greater than the distance from the edge of the eye to the edge of the jaw (which distinguishes it from another sympatric species). The nuptial male of the three (or four) subspecies can be pretty, each developing bold black blotches and spots.

There are four subspecies (Matthews, Jenkins, and Styron 1982). *R. a. obtusus* and *R. a. meleagris* develop a rich, metallic pink-orange flush over the middle of the entire flank. *R. a. simus* may be identical to *R. a. obtusus* rather than a distinct subspecies. Only *R. a. atratulus* has a pink-orange flush limited to the pectoral fin area.

*R. altratulus* ranges from Nova Scotia to Hudson Bay, and southward along the Atlantic and Gulf slopes to Georgia and Alabama. It continues westward in Mississippi drainages from the Missouri River (outside the Ozarks) northward. The eastern blacknose dace, *R. a. atratulus,* occupies the Atlantic slope and is the least colorful; the northwestern form, *R. a. meleagris,* occurs in Canada and the northern and central United States, excluding the lower Ohio basin (Matthews, Jenkins, and Styron 1982). The "southern" blacknose dace, *R. a. obtusus,* is found in the lower Ohio River basin with its type locality in the Tennessee River drainage of Alabama. Many consider the Gulf blacknose dace, *R. a. simus,* of the Coosa River (Mobile basin) and other Gulf Coast drainages, as being identical to (and a synonym of) *R. a. obtusus,* but the types are from different drainages (C. Gilbert, pers. comm.).

Our aquarium breeding experience has been solely with *R. a. simus.* The geographically separated forms differ in breeding behavior. This subspecies occurs in springs and gently flowing, small upland headwater creeks over gravel, sand, and rubble bottoms, and in riffles, runs, and flowing pools with overhanging trees or banks. It feeds on drifting and bottom insects (mostly midge and blackfly larvae), amphipods, isopods, tubificid worms, and other invertebrates; it also eats algae,

Longnose dace, *Rhinichthys cataractae,* Cosby Cr., Cocke Co., Tenn. RB

both drifting and on the bottom, but cannot feed effectively in fast water (Etnier and Starnes 1993; Tyler 1993; Jenkins and Burkhead 1994).

*R. a. simus* is an egg-burying fish, males establishing territories in groups over gravel bottoms and clearing away silt by constantly wagging while suspended close to the bottom. It has been known to use *Nocomis* nests for spawning (Johnston and Page 1992), and has been reported (erroneously) to move pebbles with its mouth (P. W. Smith 1979); in fact, females move gravel with their snouts as a sign of willingness to spawn (Jenkins and Burkhead 1994). Some populations, and perhaps these are subspecific differences (Schwartz 1958), spawn midwater in a pool *(obtusus)* or close to the bottom in either a riffle or pool *(meleagris, atratulus).*

Keep in a 30-gallon aquarium with moderate current, sand or fine gravel, and plants and structure around the rear. The breeders should be conditioned as described for *Clinostomus funduloides.*

As the spawning season approaches, the male establishes a territory. Spawning occurs close to the bottom. The male makes small, tight circles in his territory and displays to the female by assuming a head-down, 45-degree angle with some fin and opercular flaring. The female approaches and is nudged around the vent. Eggs and sperm are expelled and the transparent, adhesive eggs fall to the gravel.

Spawning takes place from hours to days over a two-week period. Eggs hatch in five to eight days. Adults should be removed on the sixth day of spawning to prevent the newly hatched fry from being eaten. Fry need small live foods. Growth is rapid, but sexual maturity is reached in the second year.

*Rhinichthys cataractae,*
longnose dace

*R. cataractae* is similar in blotching to *R. atratulus* but lacks bright colors, and the distance from its eye to its jaw is much greater than the eye diameter. The adult has a reduced swim bladder. Eastern stream (but not lake) forms may develop a red-orange color at the corners of the jaws and bases of fins (but not on the flank); the western subspecies is colorless. In the east, dark stream forms have red on the mouths and fin bases, but fish from the turbulent pebbled shores of Lake Michigan are relatively faded and lack bright red colors.

The longnose dace occurs from the Arctic Circle to the Gulf of Mexico in Atlantic to Pacific drainages. The eastern subspecies, *R. c. cataractae,* ranges southward to the mountains of northern Georgia and is found in the Mississippi basin to the Gulf Coast; the western subspecies, *R. c. dulcis,* is restricted to Pacific drainages.

Loach minnow, *Rhinichthys (=Tiaroga) cobitis,* Gila R., N.Mex. WFR

The populations of this nominal species should be investigated with new DNA and electrophoretic analyses (C. Gilbert, pers. comm.).

*R. cataractae* inhabits fast, cold streams and rivers, in deep, swift water over rock bottoms, and turbulent shores of northern lakes. It occurs in both clear and turbid water. Its preference for swift water in larger streams, including trout streams, usually distinguishes it from *R. atratulus.* The longnose dace feeds mostly on midge, blackfly, and mayfly larvae, but also on small crustaceans, worms, and plant materials.

The longnose dace spawns during the early spring (depending on region) in fast currents over gravel, sometimes inadvertently fanning out a small, shallow depression while holding a territory (not a nest so much as an area of wagging activity close to the bottom); the western form (Lake Michigan) spawns at night.

The willing female (as in *R. atratulus*) pushes her nose into the gravel as a signal to the male. The eggs hatch in one week and the fry are pelagic. After several weeks, their swim bladders regress and they take up position close to the bottom (P. W. Smith 1979; Etnier and Starnes 1993; Jenkins and Burkhead 1994).

See *R. atratulus* for instructions on care.

---

*Rhinichthys cobitis,* loach minnow

*R. cobitis* is loach-shaped (similar to the loach genus *Cobitis*) with prominent scales. It is mottled black on a tan-silver body, with a dark mark at the base of its dorsal fin. The nuptial female has yellow on the body and fin bases. The nuptial male has bright red jaws, throat, and fins, and is sometimes red on the body; two white blotches separated by a dusky blotch appear just beyond the red base of its tail fin (J. E. Johnson 1987; Rinne and Minckley 1991). The average length is 2 inches. *Tiaroga cobitis* is a synonym.

The loach minnow has been extirpated, or nearly so, from the upper Gila River system of Arizona and New Mexico, but is found just into Sonora, Mexico, with a good population surviving in Aravaipa Creek, Arizona, a protected locality.

*R. cobitis* is secretive and darterlike (with a reduced swim bladder), and inhabits the bottom of swift, densely algae-covered rocky riffles (≤ 6 in. deep) in small to large streams. It feeds mostly on larvae of baetid mayflies and on midges.

The loach minnow spawns in the late winter from September through March and again in the spring during April and May, on the undersides of smooth stones on riffles, where it deposits an average of 80, but up to 250 eggs, in a single layer (which categorizes it as an egg clusterer). It has spawned in the Gila River of New Mexico when the water was in the 60s (°F) during the day.

R. cobitis has been almost extirpated in New Mexico because of water loss to human needs and competition from the introduced red shiner, *Cyprinella lutrensis* (Lee et al. 1980; Propst and Bestgen 1991; Rinne and Minckley 1991). It is protected in New Mexico and Arizona.

If state agencies provide spawning stock to a university or public aquarium, the following method could facilitate captive propagation: (1) use a half-filled, 10-gallon aquarium with strong current from powerheads; (2) provide algae-covered flat rocks over gravel; (3) illuminate with 6 to 8 hours of bright incandescent light and 12–14 hours of darkness to sustain the algae and provide a nuptial behavior–inducing photoperiod; (4) feed frozen bloodworms; (5) keep the water cool; and (6) periodically inspect the area below flat rocks for eggs, which should be removed to a gallon jar with aeration for hatching.

| | |
|---|---|
| *Rhinichthys evermanni,* Umpqua dace | R. evermanni is almost identical to R. cataractae, but with nine or ten dorsal fin rays rather than eight, and a narrow, sharply edged caudal peduncle (Page and Burr 1991).<br><br>The Umpqua dace is endemic to the Umpqua River drainage of Oregon, in habitat similar to that of *R. cataractae.* |
| *Rhinichthys falcatus,* leopard dace | The leopard dace was previously placed in *Agosia.* It is distinguished from *Rhinichthys umatilla* by the long barbel at the corner of the mouth. R. falcatus is dark on the back, creamy white on the flank, and has black blotches (up to eight scales in width) on the body. Some spotting extends onto the yellowish fins, the dorsal fin is slightly concave, and a prominent barbel is located at the corners of its jaws. The jaws and base of the pelvic fins in the nuptial male are bright orange-red; non-nuptial males show some red year-round (Scott and Crossman 1973).<br><br>The leopard dace occurs in the Fraser River of British Columbia and in the adjacent Columbia River of Washington and Oregon, east of the Cascade Mountains into Idaho (Lee et al. 1980). Its habitats are lakes and streams and rivers with slow currents. It feeds on mayfly, midge, and blackfly larvae, terrestrial insects, and on terrestrial earthworms during rains or floods. It spawns during July (Scott and Crossman 1973). |
| *Rhinichthys umatilla,* Umatilla dace | R. umatilla is also similar to R. falcatus, but has a short barbel at the corner of the mouth.<br><br>The Umatilla dace occurs in Columbia River drainages from British Columbia south to Idaho.<br><br>R. umatilla inhabits large, fast-flowing, rocky rivers. |
| *Rhinichthys osculus,* speckled dace | R. osculus is similar to R. falcatus, but has a faint, longitudinal band along the flank. Coloration is red (as in *R. falcatus*) in U.S. forms, but not in Canadian populations.<br><br>The speckled dace ranges from the Columbia River of British Columbia, south in most coastal drainages to the Colorado River of Arizona and New Mexico and just enters Sonora, Mexico. Page and Burr (1991) have reported R. o. nevadensis in Ash Meadows, Nevada, R. o. lethoporus in Independence Valley, Nevada, R. o. thermalis near Pinedale, Wyoming (in Kendall Warm Springs), and |

Speckled dace, *Rhinichthys osculus*, Mimbres R., N.Mex. WFR

Speckled dace, *Rhinichthys osculus nevadensis*, Ash Meadows, Nev. WFR

*R. o. oligoporus* in Clover Valley, Nevada. All are endangered. *R. o. yarrowi* occurs in Duck Creek, Green River, and Boulder Creek, is found both upstream and downstream from *R. o. thermalis,* and has been separated from that latter fish for thousands of years.

The subspecies *R. o. oligoporus, R. o. thermalis,* and *R. o. nevadensis* lack a minor row of pharyngeal teeth, a character present in the nonendangered *R. o. yarrowi* from nearby waters and in other forms (Gould and Kaya 1991). The genetics of 12 *R. osculus* populations from six major drainages have recently been analyzed (Oakey and Douglas 1994). The continuing evolution of this species complex resembles the history of desert pupfishes (Cyprinodontidae: *Cyprinodon*), which arose from a common ancestor as the Sierra Nevada range matured, desiccating the central basin (much of its original range).

Desiccation separated a once contiguous population into pockets of survivors, some in swift, cold mountain streams, others in sluggish, desert floor streams, and still others in other habitats. These small populations rapidly adapted to their different habitats once they were no longer mixing with other genetic populations. The phenomenon is not unique to American deserts, but occurs wherever a historically wide-ranging species is fragmented by changes in climate, hydrology, elevation, or other massive physical alterations, sometimes over only a few thousand years.

Their habitats vary considerably, indicating that the complex may consist of physiologically distinct subspecies or species. They occur in lakes, cool springs, desert springs, and both interior and coastal rivers, over rocks, sand, and silt. They feed mostly on insects, but to some extent on plant materials.

Burtson (1987) discovered fry feeding in algae at the top of a densely planted 55-gallon, high-sided aquarium supplied with a canister filter, but did not observe the adults spawning. The aquarium received daylight from a window and supplemental fluorescent lighting 12 hours a day. The water was soft with 1 teaspoon per gallon of rock salt added, 74–76°F, and pH 7.0. A sponge was placed over the intake of the canister filter, and the fry were fed live *Artemia* nauplii and microworms. The fry were allowed to stay with the parents until they showed nipped tails, at which time the parents were removed. The young were easily raised.

**Genus *Pararhinichthys***
*Pararhinichthys bowersi,*
cheat minnow

Finally, we have the odd occurrence of *P. bowersi*. It resembles *Rhinichthys cataractae* and was thought to be the occasional hybrid between *R. cataractae* and *Nocomis micropogon*. Although hybrids between species and even between genera are common in fishes, they typically are sterile or demonstrate reduced viability when crossed back to one of the parental species. Typical hybrids do not interbreed among themselves to sustain a perpetuating population. The cheat minnow is an exception. It is one of the few species that arose as a hybrid, but now is a self-perpetuating species.

The formation of a species from two different lines is termed introgressive hybridization. It is uncommon between species, and rare between genera. The cheat minnow is an evolutionary unit (i.e., species, or independent line of evolution) that did not arise solely from *Rhinichthys* or from *Nocomis,* but by introgressive hybridization between two species in widely separated genera.

How is one to represent its phylogenetic history? In fact, it is not a branch but an anastomosis (reticulation or webbing) of two separate branches that has provided a new line of evolution. Stauffer et al. (1997) has proposed the name *Pararhinichthys* for this species of hybrid origin to reflect its independence from either parental line; i.e., it is neither a new form of *Nocomis* nor of *Rhinichthys,* but a completely new and recent genus within the Cyprinidae. Stauffer et al. (1997) found ripe gonads in both sexes, but did not conduct tests to determine if the zygotes were viable. Whether the hybrids are self-sustaining has recently been questioned (Poly and Sabaj 1998).

The cheat minnow occurs in the Monongahela River system (Ohio River drainage) of West Virginia, Pennsylvania, and Maryland, in runs and pools of rocky rivers.

It can probably be cared for like *R. cataractae.*

| | |
|---|---|
| **Genus Eremichthys** | *Eremichthys* is a monotypic genus established for a pupfish-shaped desert minnow with a hard sheath on its jaws, not unlike that found in some suckers (Catostomidae). |

*Eremichthys acros,* desert dace

*E. acros* is a fat, squat fish with a blunt head and hard sheath on the jaws. It is brassy, and has a green stripe on the flank, black lips, and white fins (Page and Burr 1991).

The desert dace is found only at Soldier Meadows in Humboldt County, Nevada, where it is restricted to warm springs (≤ 100°F) and their runs. It feeds on small fishes and vegetation (Lee et al. 1980). Although locally abundant on private land, it is a protected species and may not be collected; no individuals (including ichthyologists) are allowed to trespass this land.

**Genus Orthodon**

*Orthodon* is a monotypic genus established for a large, distinctive *Gila* relative restricted to coastal drainages of California.

*Orthodon microlepidotus,*
Sacramento blackfish

*O. microlepidotus* is a very large (1–1½ ft.), fine-scaled, silvery minnow.

The Sacramento blackfish occurs in the Sacramento–San Joaquin drainage (including the Pajaro-Salinas and lower Russian Rivers), Clear Lake, and small coastal rivers of California (Lee et al. 1980).

*O. microlepidotus* inhabits warm river backwaters, sloughs, and lakes, where it is easily collected by seine. It feeds on detritus and phytoplankton, and is a good candidate for aquaculture production as a food fish. It hybridizes with *Gila bicolor* and *Lavinia exilicauda* (Lee et al. 1980).

The Sacramento blackfish is suitable for ponds, but not aquaria. Maintain on green water.

**Genus Ericymba**

*Ericymba* is also a monotypic genus, containing only *E. buccata.*

Streamline chub, *Erimystax dissimilis,* White R., Mo. WFR

**Ericymba buccata, silverjaw minnow**

*E. buccata* is plain with a silver stripe along the flank, and bright, pearlescent eruptions along the edge of the gill cover to the upper jaw. These eruptions are prominent, enlarged cavities surrounding the lateral line pores on the head, and appearing as a series of pearly swellings from the upper jaw to the upper part of the gill cover.

Silverjaw minnow populations are disjunct, with one of the strangest distributions of any North American fish. The northern population ranges from Illinois, Michigan, and New York south to Missouri in the west and to northern Virginia in the east. The southern population ranges through Gulf Coast drainages from Georgia and Florida to Louisiana. This distribution resembles that of *Ammocrypta pellucida* and *A. meridiana,* which occupy similar shifting sand habitat. This suggests that the same hydrogeological changes that split the ancestral silverjaw minnow group into two populations also may have divided the ancestral sand darter into populations that eventually became sibling species.

*E. buccata* inhabits creeks and rivers over shifting sand bottoms of riffles and raceways. It schools near the bottom and, when alarmed, it huddles in depressions. It feeds on crustaceans and aquatic insect larvae by sifting through the sediments for these benthic macroinvertebrates. The silverjaw minnow spawns at age one over fine gravel from April through June at 68 to 72°F, and usually dies after spawning in the third year (Pflieger 1975; P. W. Smith 1979; Etnier and Starnes 1993).

Provide a school of ten fish with a 20-gallon aquarium containing sand or gravel, moderate current, and no plants or structure. The sexes should be separated and conditioned on live foods for several weeks, then placed together. Raise the temperature over a 24-hour period to 75°F.

They aggregate tightly just above the gravel and scatter eggs that are dispersed by the current and settle into interstices. Spawning trays of gravel will collect large numbers of eggs. Remove the adults and let the eggs hatch in the aquarium, or remove the trays to a separate aquarium for hatching. Eggs hatch in three to seven days; the fry require the smallest of live foods. They grow quickly and mature in ten months.

**Genus *Erimystax***

*Erimystax* are slender, cigar-shaped chubs with seven rays in the anal fin, a protruding snout covering an underslung narrow mouth with corner barbels, and a species-specific pattern of dark markings on an otherwise colorless body. The average adult length is 3 to 5 inches.

Blotched chub, *Erimystax insignis*, Tennessee R., Tenn. WFR

Blotched chub, *Erimystax insignis*, Little R., Tenn. RB

Gravel chub, *Erimystax x-punctata*, Arkansas R., Mo. WFR

*Erimystax* live in deeper swift currents, feed on snails, attached algae, and aquatic insect larvae, and spawn over gravel during April and May at 60°F.

For the proposed status of some species, see Pflieger (1975) or Etnier and Starnes (1993). Protected species are *E. cahni* (federal protection), *E. insignis* (Georgia and Kentucky), and *E. x-punctatus* (New York and Pennsylvania; proposed in Kansas).

---

**Erimystax insignis, blotched chub**

*E. insignis* is dark above, with a green iridescent wash across the middle of the flank, and eight vertically elongate black blotches ending in a dark basicaudal spot. Dark scale edges form horizontal lines. Two subspecies, with intergrades, are known.

*E. i. insignis* in the Cumberland and lower Tennessee drainages has a normal upper jaw; *E. i. eristigma* has a swelling on the upper jaw and ranges from the upper Tennessee River to the Hiwassee River in Georgia; intergrades occur in the Clinch, Powell, and Holston Rivers (Etnier and Starnes 1993).

Blotched chubs occur in riffles and pools of small rivers and moderately sized creeks, over coarse gravel, rock, and cobble. The male settles on the female resting on the bottom and assumes a side-by-side position with rapid vibrations. Eggs are apparently pressed onto gravel (Etnier and Starnes 1993).

---

**Erimystax x-punctatus, gravel chub**

*E. x-punctatus* has scattered X-marks on the back and along the flank. The back is greenish yellow with a narrow dark stripe. The flank is silver, sometimes with a dusky stripe, and the basicaudal spot is black. Two subspecies are recognized.

Roundnose minnow, *Dionda episcopa,* San Solomon Springs, Tex. WFR

The gravel chub occurs in the Ohio drainage from Pennsylvania through Ohio, Kentucky, Indiana, and Illinois. A disjunct population in the Thames River of Ontario, Canada has been assigned to *E. x-punctata trautmani.* Populations in the Mississippi basin from Wisconsin and Minnesota to Oklahoma and Arkansas have been assigned to *E. x-punctata x-punctata.* Gravel chubs are found beneath rocks in deep riffles and raceways of large, gravel-bottom streams and small rivers, and feed on diatoms, algae, snails, and insects. Spawning is from March to May at the head of 2- to 4-foot-deep riffles on gravel (Pflieger 1975; Robison and Buchanan 1988).

**Genus *Dionda***

*Dionda* contains herbivorous chubs with affinities to *Nocomis* and *Campostoma.* They have a long, coiled intestine and a black peritoneum. *Dionda* is primarily a Mexican genus, with four species ranging into the southwestern United States. They are broadcasters, the heavy eggs falling into interstices in the substratum, a behavior that may have led to crevice spawning.

*D. episcopa, D. argentosa,* and *Dionda* sp. (Guadalupe drainage) of Texas and Mexico should be provided a 10-gallon aquarium with current, large pebbles on top of gravel laid over sand, and fed cooked vegetables and *Spirulina* flakes supplemented with *Daphnia* and *Artemia* nauplii. Change water frequently. The fish previously known as *Dionda nubilus* is a *Notropis,* and should never have been placed in *Dionda.*

*Dionda diaboli,*
Devils River minnow

*D. diaboli* is a plain, roundheaded minnow with a black line from the snout to the base of the tail, ending in a small, black triangular spot. The dorsal fin begins directly above the origin of the pelvic fins (Page and Burr 1991).

In the United States, the Devils River minnow has been extirpated from Kinney County, but survives in Val Verde County, Texas. It is rare in the Rio San Carlos and Rio Sabinas of Mexico (Garrett et al. 1992).

*D. diaboli* is an herbivore of fast moving, spring-fed streams over gravel with attached algae or other vegetation. Within the Devils River system, it tends to be found upstream of the more common *D. argentosa.* An egg broadcaster (Johnston and Page 1992), it is disappearing due to drawdown of the water table for human use and by the introduction of game fish (Garrett et al. 1992).

See care instructions for the genus. *D. diaboli* is protected in Texas, but the other species are available.

| | |
|---|---|
| **Genus *Hemitremia*** | *Hemitremia* is a monotypic genus found in the southeastern United States. The dorsal fin begins behind the origin of the pelvic fins. The lateral line is incomplete with only 10 to 15 pored scales. There are 7 or 8 dorsal fin rays, and up to 11 anal fin rays (Etnier and Starnes 1993). |

| | |
|---|---|
| *Hemitremia flammea,* flame chub | *H. flammea* (**plate 16**) is thick and dacelike, with a bold black line along the flank from the nose to the base of the tail that separates an olive back from a white belly. A gold line is adjacent immediately above the black line, and another black line runs along the back. The male displays some red year-round. The nuptial male is spectacular; the black flank band is faded, but coloration is orange-red on the belly and at the bases of all fins (mostly dorsal). The pectorals are dusky. The average adult length is 2½ inches. |

The flame chub occurs in Tennessee, northern Alabama, and just enters northwestern Georgia. It is found in streams of the middle Cumberland, upper Duck, and middle Tennessee Rivers, and in the Tennessee drainage from Knoxville downstream to Hardin County, Tennessee. It is also known from Kelley Creek, a tributary of Choccolocco Creek in the Coosa River system (Lee et al. 1980; Etnier and Starnes 1993). It is rare everywhere except in Cypress Creek in Wayne County, Tennessee and in Lauderdale County, Alabama.

*H. flammea* is always associated with densely vegetated springs or their runs. It feeds on chironomids, isopods, worms, bugs, snails, and some filamentous algae. The flame chub spawns from late December through early June, mostly in February and March (Lee et al. 1980; Etnier and Starnes 1993). It is probably a plant spawning egg broadcaster.

Water quality is likely to be critical, and a trickle filter on a large (29 gal.) aquarium is recommended for a group of two males and four or more females. Provide water sprite at the surface, and *Nitella,* hornwort, *Cabomba,* or *Vesicularia* on one side of the aquarium. Feed chironomids as the staple, supplemented with live blackworms and daphnia.

The flame chub is protected in Georgia, but not in Tennessee or Alabama.

| | |
|---|---|
| **Genus *Hybognathus*** | *Hybognathus* contains unmarked, silvery or brassy, slender, elongate herbivores/detritivores with eight anal fin rays, a rounded snout, and inferior mouth. All have a long, coiled intestine and a black peritoneum, readily determined by mashing one in the field. |

*Hybognathus* ranges from southern Canada to the Rio Grande, and from the Atlantic states to the Rocky Mountains. All species filter-feed in turbid backwaters of quiet rivers on bottom ooze, diatoms, and algae using highly modified rakers on the gill arches.

The identification of species often can be estimated by geography and drainage. For example, *H. nuchalis* is found throughout the Mississippi drainage; *H. regius* occurs along the Atlantic slope from Georgia to Quebec; *H. hankinsoni* overlaps with *H. regius* in New York and Canada, but is brassy yellow and has a pointed dorsal fin; *H. amarus* occurs only in the Rio Grande (Bestgen and Propst 1996); *H. argyritis* is primarily a Missouri River basin species; *H. placitus* overlaps through the Great Plains with *H. argyritis,* but extends farther south into Texas (possibly introduced into the Pecos River system where it overlaps with *H. amarus* but is not present throughout the Rio Grande, the main distribution of *H. amarus*); and darkly

Eastern silvery minnow, *Hybognathus regius,* Pee Dee R., S.C. FCR

outlined upper body scales point to *H. hayi* of the lower Mississippi cypress swamp region (Page and Burr 1991).

The species are so similar, however, that only an expert can tell them apart with confidence. None of the seven species *(amarus, argyritis, hankinsoni, hayi, nuchalis, placitus, regius)* is recommended for aquaria, but the techniques for handling *H. regius* offered below should be applicable to all.

The nonadhesive eggs are broadcast (Johnston and Page 1992) or scattered between April and August over the silt bottom near newly sprouting submersed vegetation, or on bare silt bottoms. The eggs hatch in one week (Pflieger 1975; P. W. Smith 1979; Robison and Buchanan 1988; Etnier and Starnes 1993). See also Burr and Mayden (1982a), Warren and Burr (1989), Cook et al. (1992), and Schmidt (1994).

The fish require free-flowing rivers for at least part of the life cycle, and disappear where impoundments replace their riverine habitat. It has been suggested that the larvae require current to feed in the water column, and cannot survive if they drift into lakes (C. Gilbert, pers. comm.).

*Hybognathus regius,* eastern silvery minnow

*H. regius* is similar to other members of the genus, but sometimes has a yellow cast on the flank. Males may be darker than females. It grows to an average of 4 inches.

The eastern silvery minnow occurs in Quebec and Ontario in the Great Lakes and in Atlantic slope rivers southward to the Altamaha River basin of Georgia.

*H. regius* is found in pools and backwaters of rivers and creeks. It scatters (broadcasts) eggs over mud and silt bottoms. Mud is used as a food source and to cover the eggs in nature.

Mud is not a necessary food in captivity; *Spirulina*-based flakes and paste foods may be used as substitutes, and fine-leaved plants will protect the eggs. Five females and ten males should be conditioned separately for several weeks, then placed together in a 30-gallon aquarium with one inch of fine sand, and *Myriophyllum, Cabomba, Nitella,* or *Vesicularia.* Keep the water shallow at 8 to 10 inches. Flashing males press against the females.

The nonadhesive eggs are scattered above the plants and fall to the bottom. Remove the adults after spawning. Eggs hatch in six to eight days, and the fry should be offered rotifers, vinegar eels, or protozoans. After four weeks, feed a suspension

Suckermouth minnow, *Phenacobius mirabilis,* Terrapin Cr., Ky. WFR

of *Spirulina* paste and add ramshorn snails to clean up excess food. Growth is rapid, and maturity is reached in one year.

**Genus *Phenacobius***

*Phenacobius* consists of the suckermouth minnows, bottom-adapted fishes sharing many features of suckers (Catostomidae); they are advanced minnows closely related to *Erimystax. Phenacobius* species have an elongate and flattened body, underslung and highly complex jaws with crushing pads of tough connective tissue, a reduced swim bladder and anal fin, and a characteristic short appendage at the base of the pelvic fin. They feed on aquatic insect larvae in riffles and runs, and spawn over gravel.

Keep suckermouth minnows in large aquaria set up as described for the orangethroat darter, *Etheostoma spectabile.* Spawning occurs in early spring, after which the parental fish should be removed. One species *(P. crassilabrum)* is a nest parasite that will be more difficult to spawn.

*Phenacobius mirabilis,*
suckermouth minnow

*P. mirabilis* is olive above with large, dark-edged scales. It is silvery on the flank and belly, with an ephemeral black line along the flank that ends in a black basicaudal spot. An indistinct gold line runs immediately above the black line. The average adult length is 3½ inches.

The suckermouth minnow occurs in the Mississippi and Great Lakes drainages from Lakes Erie and Michigan to the Gulf of Mexico, and is most abundant in Indiana and Kentucky. It ranges through non-Ozarkian Missouri, Iowa, Kansas, Nebraska, and New Mexico, continuing into Arkansas, Tennessee, Alabama, Mississippi, Minnesota, the Dakotas, Wyoming, and Colorado. It is found in Texas Gulf Coast rivers west of the Mississippi drainage, but not in any rivers east of the Mississippi (Lee et al. 1980).

*P. mirabilis* is the only Central Plains member of the genus, and the only one tolerant of turbid, low gradient streams. Its habitat is usually clear to moderately turbid, warm rivers, over sand or gravel riffles, or over mud in pools. Silt-tolerant and a frequent pioneer in disturbed rivers, it prefers clear water. It enters shallows after dark to feed, sucking up midges, caddisflies, and other aquatic insect larvae and crushing them with its jaw plates. It spawns on riffles from mid-April through August at 57 to 77°F; it is one of the few species remaining on riffles all winter

Riffle minnow, *Phenacobius catostomus*, Etowah R., Ga. RB

Stargazing minnow, *Phenacobius uranops*, Little R., Blount Co., Tenn. RB

(Pflieger 1975; P. W. Smith 1979; Robison and Buchanan 1988; Jenkins and Burkhead 1994).

| | |
|---|---|
| *Phenacobius catostomus,*<br>riffle minnow | *P. catostomus* is elongate, slender, and small-scaled. It is olive above and white below, with a black line along the entire flank. The average length is 3½ inches.<br><br>The riffle minnow occurs in the Black Warrior, Cahaba, Tallapoosa, and Coosa Rivers (Mobile River drainage) above the fall line in Alabama and northern Georgia, and barely enters southern Tennessee (Lee et al. 1980).<br><br>*P. catostomus* inhabits runs and riffles of warm, medium to large streams. It spawns during spring over gravel and rocky rubble. |
| *Phenacobius teretulus,*<br>Kanawha minnow | *P. teretulus* is an elongate, fine-scaled suckermouth minnow, with the upper lobe of the caudal fin slightly longer than the lower. It is usually olive above and white below, sometimes with a pretty iridescent green stripe along the side that obscures the wide, diffuse, black stripe. It sometimes has orange fins.<br><br>The Kanawha minnow occurs in the upper Kanawha River (New River drainage) in the Blue Ridge Mountains of North Carolina, Virginia, and West Virginia (Lee et al. 1980).<br><br>*P. teretulus* inhabitats riffles and runs of gravel, rock, and rubble mountain streams. It feeds on aquatic insects (mayflies, caddisflies, midges), snails, and tubificid worms. It spawns on gravel riffles during late April to mid-June at 67°F (Lee et al. 1980; Jenkins and Burkhead 1994).<br><br>The Kanawha minnow has been recommended for protection in North Carolina, but not Virginia. |
| *Phenacobius uranops,*<br>stargazing minnow | *P. uranops,* the stargazing minnow, is an elongate, large-scaled suckermouth minnow with upwardly directed eyes. It is dark gray above, milky white on the lower flank, and white to silvery below, with a distinctive bold black line from the snout to the base of the tail. Adults average 3½ inches.<br><br>The stargazing minnow occurs in the upper Tennessee River drainage, but also in the upper Cumberland and Green River tributaries of Alabama, Tennessee, North Carolina, Virginia, and Kentucky (Lee et al. 1980).<br><br>*P. uranops* inhabits gravel or rubble riffles and runs more than 6 inches deep in clear, warm streams and small rivers below the Blue Ridge range. Groups of 10 to 20 feed among or near groups of *Erimystax dissimilus* on midges, caddisflies, and |

other aquatic insect larvae. It spawns during May and June (Jenkins and Burkhead 1994).

| | |
|---|---|
| *Phenacobius crassilabrum,* fatlips minnow | *P. crassilabrum* is a small-scaled minnow. It is olive to tan above and silvery below with a dark spot on the gill cover and a diffuse, wide silvery gold band along the flank. The nuptial male is duskier than the female, with an orange tint to the upper body (marked on the pectoral fins). It is the only sexually dichromatic suckermouth minnow. |

The fatlips minnow occurs in the Little Tennessee system to the North Fork Holston system, all within the upper Tennessee River drainage. It also occurs in the Blue Ridge of North Carolina, and just enters southwestern Virginia and northeastern Georgia (Lee et al. 1980).

*P. crassilabrum* inhabits gravel and rubble runs and riffles of clear, rocky mountain streams. It feeds mostly on chironomids and craneflies, but also on beetles and caddisflies. It spawns during May or June at 60°F on the nests of *Nocomis micropogon* (Jenkins and Burkhead 1994), and is the only nest-parasitizing suckermouth minnow.

| | |
|---|---|
| **Genus *Phoxinus*** | *Phoxinus* contains seven fine-scaled North American fishes; more species occur overseas. An old name for the North American species was *Chrosomus,* but this name is no longer used in modern texts. |

*Phoxinus phoxinus* of Europe and Asia is a close Old World relative, suggesting that this genus formed early in the evolution of modern minnows. If the native *Notemigonus* (golden shiner) and the European *Scardinius* are determined to be congeneric, another example of minnows spreading to North America through an extinct land bridge from northeastern Asia will be established. No other North American minnow genera are known from Europe, suggesting that *Phoxinus* is the oldest survivor of the minnows existing when Europe, Asia, and North America were connected.

All native *Phoxinus* species are olive to brown above, white below, and have one or two bold, black elongate bands on the flank; the second is sometimes interrupted and offset, and sometimes broken into a series of blotches. Out of nuptial coloration, some resemble the blacknose dace, *Rhinichthys atratulus.* In nuptial coloration, they have brilliant red bellies, giving rise to the common name, redbelly daces.

Gynogenesis (all female reproduction), resulting from sperm of one species activating (but not fertilizing) the eggs of a second species to produce identical genetic copies (clones) of the mother (therefore all females), is known in this genus, but is aberrant behavior and no so-called "species" have resulted. Gynogenesis also occurs in the Poeciliidae, where males of *Poecilia mexicana* and others fertilize females of *P. latipinna* to produce an all female Texas-Mexico population known as the Amazon molly, *P. "formosa"* (chapter 14).

| | |
|---|---|
| *Phoxinus cumberlandensis,* blackside dace | *P. cumberlandensis* has a broad, diffuse, black flank band that tapers toward the rear. A second, thin and indistinct dark band appears above it, arching upward over the nape. The nuptial male has intensified dark bands and a dark stripe along the base of its dorsal fin; the belly and the lower part of the head is a brilliant red, the red extending up behind the gill cover to the top of the fish as an incomplete collar; the back is golden and the fins are light yellow. |

The blackside dace occurs above and immediately below Cumberland Falls in the Cumberland River of Kentucky and Tennessee.

*P. cumberlandensis* is found in small tributaries, in shale, sandstone, bedrock, or rubble pools shaded by large rocks, undercut banks, or overhanging riparian vegetation. It is a catholic feeder on detritus, diatom film on rocks, filamentous algae, and aquatic insect larvae. It spawns from April through July over open gravel riffles or on the nests of *Campostoma* species (Lee et al. 1980; Etnier and Starnes 1993).

Although the blackside dace spawns in chub nests in nature, it has spawned in aquaria on artificial (constructed) nests with a current played over the spawning area. Eggs were siphoned from the artificial nest and placed in nets suspended in the breeding aquarium, and the hatched larvae were then fed copepods, mosquito larvae, powdered dry food, and brine shrimp nauplii (Shute et al. 1993).

*P. cumberlandensis* is endangered in Tennessee and federally threatened throughout its range. A recovery plan is in effect, with a private firm conducting captive breeding.

*Phoxinus eos,*
northern redbelly dace

*P. eos* has two black lines, with a gold line beneath one or both. Its thinner upper black line runs from the top of the gill cover to the top of the caudal peduncle, and then to the top of the tail fin base. The wider lower black line extends from the snout through the eye to the middle of the caudal peduncle, but does not form a distinct basicaudal spot. The back and the upper flank have scattered black dots. The nuptial male is entirely red below from the chin to the base of the tail fin.

The northern redbelly dace occurs in the Northwest Territories, British Columbia, and northern Alberta (Hay, Peace, Athabasca, North Saskatchewan, Oldman, South Saskatchewan, and Milk River drainages) eastward to Nova Scotia. It ranges southward to New York, Pennsylvania, Michigan, Minnesota, Nebraska, Colorado, Montana, and Wyoming, mostly along the upper Missouri River basin (Scott and Crossman 1973; Lee et al. 1980; Inglis 1994).

*P. eos* inhabits marshy lakes, ponds, and feeder creeks, often in darkly stained, acidic bog water. Foods consist of diatoms, filamentous algae, zooplankton, and some aquatic insect larvae. It spawns during spring in the south and later in the north, scattering nonadhesive eggs over vegetation. It is also bred in bait production ponds with flowing water using mats of algae. Eggs hatch in nine days at 75°F (Scott and Crossman 1973).

The northern redbelly dace hybridizes with *P. neogaeus,* the finescale dace, throughout most of their overlapping range to form a self-perpetuating false species. The hybrids are normally diploid (one set of chromosomes from each parent). Eggs of hybrids are also diploid rather than haploid (as in normal eggs).

Sperm of either parental species can stimulate the diploid egg to divide and develop in either of two ways. First, the sperm may simply activate the diploid hybrid egg to develop into another diploid hybrid. Alternatively, the sperm chromosomes could fuse with the hybrid diploid egg chromosomes to produce a triploid individual. When the triploids reproduce and are activated by sperm again, they produce diploid hybrids. There are combinations that can result in mosaic individuals.

This suite of reproduction alternatives has resulted in populations of diploid, diploid-triploid, and mosaic individuals, all populations maintained by sperm activation from normal males of *P. eos* or *P. neogaeus* (Goddard and Schultz 1993). If these hybrids (at all or just some locations) qualify for species status as a distinct, genetically interbreeding population (an argument used to promote species status for *Rhinichthys bowersi*), they might be assigned the species name *Phoxinus milnerianus* (a name previously used for the hybrid Montana population); however, this name at present has no standing.

Sometimes found in feeder fish shipments, the northern redbelly dace should be given running room and areas of dense vegetation for spawning. It will feed on ground commercial koi pellets, flake food, and other dry feeds, having adapted to fish farm production. It spawns in ponds during mid-June. The male drives the female to plants (sometimes over soil or gravel), where the female stops. The male then forces the female downward, and both quiver for a few seconds. Upon hatching, the free swimming fry appear near the surface; either adults or fry should be removed (Inglis 1994).

If conditioned over winter in a 55-gallon aquarium and fed live foods and color enhancing and vegetable-based flake foods, the male will intensify in coloration and the female will swell with ripening roe in the spring. The fish may then be moved to smaller aquaria with dense vegetation and the temperature raised slightly to induce spawning. The parents are voracious egg eaters (Katula 1987a).

| | |
|---|---|
| *Phoxinus oreas,* mountain redbelly dace | *P. oreas* (plate 17) is one of two redbelly dace with an offset midlateral black band that breaks under the dorsal fin. Black blotches may appear on the upper flank. Black coloration of the nuptial male is intensified and surrounded by gold. Red appears on the entire belly and is scattered over portions of the head. |

The mountain redbelly dace occurs in Virginia, West Virginia, and North Carolina, from the Potomac River drainage southward to the Neuse River. Its range includes the Pee Dee (Yadkin in western North Carolina), New, and Tennessee Rivers. Multiple bait-bucket introductions have occurred.

*P. oreas* feeds mostly on algae and detritus, and somewhat on aquatic insect larvae. Groups of more than a dozen males take up station for spawning on the gravel nest of *Exoglossum, Nocomis leptocephalus,* or *Semotilus atromaculatus* from March into early July at 60 to 65°F. Placing *P. oreas* with spawning *Luxilus cerasinus* may induce spawning behavior in the dace. It does well on high protein paste foods, but declines above 65°F.

The mountain redbelly dace is apparently an obligate nest parasite in nature. It also hybridizes with *Nocomis leptocephalus, Luxilus cerasinus, L. cornutus, Clinostomus funduloides, Semotilus atromaculatus,* and probably other minnows that share the same nest sites (Maurakis and Woolcott 1992b; Jenkins and Burkhead 1994).

See care instructions for *P. erythrogaster* and *Clinostomus funduloides.*

| | |
|---|---|
| *Phoxinus erythrogaster,* southern redbelly dace | *P. erythrogaster* (plate 18) is virtually identical to *P. eos,* and identified in the field largely by geographic location and habitat. |

The southern redbelly dace ranges from the Great Lakes and Mississippi drainages south to Arkansas. It occurs in southern Oklahoma in the Blue River system of the Red River drainage and in northern Alabama (occasionally Louisiana). It ranges westward to Iowa and Kansas, and eastward to Pennsylvania (Lee et al. 1980).

*P. erythrogaster* inhabits cool, clear, upland (especially Ozark, Cumberland, and Highland Plateau), neutral to alkaline, tree-lined headwater or spring-fed streams with permanent strong flow, and gravel or rock bottoms (often in silt- or muck-bottom pools below undercut banks with exposed tree roots). The smallest juveniles feed mostly on diatoms *(Navicula, Cocconeis, Gomphonema, Nitzschia, Cymbella, Melosira)*, plankton, and intermediate-sized fish, then increasingly on filamentous algae *(Spirogyra)*, detritus, chironomids, and copepods and other small crustaceans. Adults feed on an increasing proportion of aquatic insect larvae (chironomids, caddisflies, mayflies, and stoneflies). It matures in one year and does not live much more than two years.

The southern redbelly dace spawns on gravel riffles, or on the nests of *Semotilus, Nocomis,* and other nesting minnows from April through June. Males do not establish territories, but individually segregate and divide the spawning area, maintaining space between them as they await females (Pflieger 1975; Settles and Hoyt 1976, 1978).

A bare 20- to 40-gallon aquarium is ideal for a group of 10 to 20 adults, preferably collected in winter. Include current and filtration from powerheads and/or outside power or canister filters. Feed mostly vegetable flake foods supplemented with live blackworms, frozen adult brine shrimp, and bloodworms. A plastic shoe box with gravel or pebbles serves as a spawning site; Sternburg (1986) used a sand bottom with live *Vallisneria* and current from powerhead pumps along the bottom.

Spawning behavior is indicated when increasingly, brightly colored males wag strongly when females approach. Both sexes become red, but the gravid females are swollen with roe. After a week, move the shoe box to a separate rearing aquarium where the eggs will hatch within eight days at 70°F, or remove the parents from the spawning aquarium.

Provide only sponge filtration after spawning and turn off the powerheads (the fry do not need current). The fry initially require green water, infusoria, a commercially prepared fry food suspension, or powdered fry food; they take *Artemia* nauplii at two weeks of age. Growth is rapid, fry attaining 6 mm at one week, 8 mm at two weeks, 12 mm at one month when they begin surface feeding, and 30–35 mm at seven months when the black and gold lines have appeared. The fish mature in one year, but seldom survive more than 18 months. Aquarium-raised nuptial males are not as colorful as wild fish.

---

*Phoxinus neogaeus,* finescale dace

*P. neogaeus* is black on the back and upper flank. The black extends down the flank to the upper edge of the gill cover and runs in a straight line rearward to the upper edge of the caudal fin. A single black stripe extends from the snout through the eye to a basicaudal spot. Between both black areas, the body is olive to gold. The belly is white. The black is intensified in the nuptial male; the entire lower region (from the throat to belly to tail) is metallic yellow to bright red. The finescale dace is distinguished in the field from *P. eos,* with which it hybridizes, by the single (rather than double) black stripe along the flank. The black back is also a good indicator of nuptial *P. neogaeus,* but hybrids might occur anywhere with various patterns.

The finescale dace ranges from the Arctic Circle (McKenzie River) southward to the Great Lakes and into the Mississippi basin. It continues southward to Nebraska in the west, from New England to New York in the east, and to Michigan and Wisconsin in the central states (Lee et al. 1980).

*P. neogaeus* is found in cool boggy lakes, large open lakes, and sluggish streams, often in acidic, tinted, neutral pH water. It feeds mostly on insects, crustaceans, snails, and small clams. It spawns under leaf litter and logs beginning in May, readily producing fertile hybrids when mixed with *P. eos.*

Feed mostly frozen brine shrimp and bloodworms, supplemented with a small amount of marine diet flake food. Its spawning mode in captivity is unknown, but it probably will spawn among sunken mops. It is sold in Canada as a bait-minnow (Scott and Crossman 1973; Lee et al. 1980).

See *P. eos* and *P. erythrogaster* for instructions on care.

| | |
|---|---|
| *Phoxinus tennesseensis,* Tennessee dace | *P. tennesseensis* (**plate 19**) is slimmer than *P. oreas,* and the series of large black blotches in the former is replaced in the Tennessee dace by a thin, black upper line with coarse edges that sometimes breaks into a line of spots. The nuptial male is brilliant, similar to *P. eos* in reds, but with a black throat and bright silver spots at the bases of fins (Etnier and Starnes 1993).

The Tennessee dace occurs in the upper Tennessee River system of eastern Tennessee, ranging southward to the Hiwassee River, and northward just into the Holston River of southwestern Virginia (Etnier and Starnes 1993; Jenkins and Burkhead 1994). A population from a part of Walden Ridge in eastern Tennessee represents an undescribed seventh species of the genus in North America (C. Gilbert, pers. comm.).

*P. tennesseensis* is found in small, upland forested or pasture streams less than 6 feet wide with gravel bottoms; it is usually at the bottom of debris-laden, gravel, silt, and rocky shallow pools below undercut banks. It feeds largely on decaying vegetation, diatoms, and algae, with minor amounts of small animal life (Etnier and Starnes 1993). It spawns during May at 61 to 62°F over spawning pits of *Campostoma anomalum* and *Luxilus cerasinus,* and on gravel runs outside the nests of other species (not an obligate nest parasite), together with nonnesting *Luxilus chrysocephalus* and *Notropis (H.) rubricroceus* (Jenkins and Burkhead 1994).

This species has been recommended for protection; consult state agency people for protection status before attempting collection. See also *P. erythrogaster.* |
| **Genus *Hybopsis*** | *Hybopsis* are silvery, chublike minnows. All but *H. amnis* have barbels at the corner of the jaws and a long rounded snout with an underslung mouth. They have eight anal rays, eyes wider than they are high, and pointed fins.

The group has a tortuous taxonomic history, although there is no doubt that its species (the *amblops* group) form a natural assemblage. Robins et al. (1991) have argued that *Hybopsis* cannot be used as a generic name under the rules of nomenclature, and relegated the *amblops* group of species to *Notropis.* We agree with Jenkins and Burkhead (1994) and Etnier and Starnes (1993) that this cure is worse than the disease, and herein retain *Hybopsis,* leaving the selection of a final generic name to others.

These 3-inch fishes occur in clear upland streams with sand, rock, or rubble bottoms and moderate flows. They feed on aquatic insect larvae, spiders, snails, and other small invertebrates among rocks and aquatic vegetation. They scatter eggs in vegetation from March through June. See also Pflieger (1975), P. W. Smith (1979), Robison and Buchanan (1988), and Jenkins and Burkhead (1994). |
| *Hybopsis hypsinotus,* highback chub | *H. hypsinotus* has a wide purple-black band along the flank that separates a dark olive dorsum from a white belly. The fins may be tinged with pink. The nuptial |

Highback chub, *Hybopsis hypsinotus,* Pee Dee R., N.C. WFR

Lined chub, *Hybopsis lineapunctata,* Beech Cr., Haralson Co., Ga. RB

male is dark green to black above; the flank is dusky with a purple iridescence; the belly is light red; the upper jaw and nose are red; the fins are dark red to the edges; a gold line appears just above the flank stripe and at the base of the dorsal fin (Jenkins and Burkhead 1994).

The highback chub occurs only in the upper Pee Dee and Santee drainages in Atlantic slope streams of Virginia and the Carolinas. Between the Blue Ridge and the fall line, its habitats vary from small creeks to medium-sized rivers.

*H. hypsinotus* is found over bedrock and sand, around logs, beneath undercut banks, and sometimes in pools. It is not a schooling species. It spawns over the nests of *Nocomis leptocephalus* (Johnston 1991; Jenkins and Burkhead 1994). This egg broadcaster may require an active *Nocomis* nest for spawning.

| | |
|---|---|
| *Hybopsis rubrifrons,* rosyface chub | The closely related *H. rubrifrons* apparently spawns over nests or freely over gravel. It is red only in the front third of the body. Synonyms are *Notropis rubescens* and *Nocomis rubrifrons.* |

The rosyface chub occurs in the headwaters of the Altamaha River in Georgia through the main stem of the Savannah River, even below the fall line, to the headwaters of the Santee River in South Carolina (Lee et al. 1980).

*H. rubrifrons* is found in small streams, near banks or in pools, over sand or gravel (but not silt). It spawns from mid-April through June at 70°F over clean gravel in riffles, or over *Nocomis* nests, but is not an obligate nest parasite.

Provide a sand, gravel, and rock bottom, some current, and a diet rich in invertebrates (brine shrimp, bloodworms, blackworms). Separate sexes in the spring for two weeks before bringing them together to spawn. Other species *(amblops, amnis, lineapunctata, winchelli)* have no attractive colors and are not recommended for aquaria.

**Genus *Platygobio***

The monotypic *Platygobio* was established for a wide-ranging chub with a compressed head, long considered a member of *Hybopsis.* Revisions to *Hybopsis* and its relatives left the flathead chub by itself with nowhere else to go.

*Platygobio gracilis,* flathead chub

*P. gracilis* is an elongate minnow with a flat head and pointed snout, a prominent barbel at the corner of the jaws, and the lower lobe of the tail fin darker than the upper lobe. It is dusky above, and abruptly becomes silvery on the midside and belly.

The flathead chub ranges from the Arctic Circle (McKenzie River to the Arctic Ocean) southward through Alberta and Saskatchewan into northwestern tributaries of the Mississippi River. It continues southward to the Gulf Coast and occurs in the upper Rio Grande of New Mexico (Lee et al. 1980). The northern large river form is the subspecies *P. g. gracilis,* and the southern small creek form is *P. g. gulonellus;* the subspecies are based on the number of scales above the lateral line and slight differences in head shape. Both forms and their intergrades occur together in the Mississippi drainage.

The subspecies are found in large, swift, turbid rivers over shifting sand bottoms *(P. g. gracilis),* or in rocky pools of small creeks *(P. g. gulonellus).* They feed mostly on water boatmen, ants, beetles, flies, and some aquatic crustaceans. They may attain 12 inches, but mature at less than 4 inches (Scott and Crossman 1973; Pflieger 1975; Lee et al. 1980). They spawn in the summer during seasonal low water. They probably scatter eggs over vegetation; in captivity, eggs are broadcast in vegetation or sunken yarn mops.

| | |
|---|---|
| **Genus *Oregonichthys*** | *Oregonichthys* contains two species previously placed in *Hybopsis.* This western genus has small barbels at the angle of the jaw, and fewer than 40 pored scales in the lateral line. Members are usually less than 2 inches long. |

| | |
|---|---|
| *Oregonichthys crameri,* Oregon chub | *O. crameri* has a scaled breast and is generally silver colored with a green-yellow sheen along the midshoulder to the flank. Fine black spots provide a lightly peppered appearance and the fins are clear to yellow. |

The Oregon chub occurs in the Willamette River (Columbia River drainage) and the adjacent Umpqua River in western Oregon.

*O. crameri* inhabits vegetated pools, ponds, and backwater sloughs over detritus or vegetation and avoids currents. It feeds mostly in the open water on cladocerans and copepods, and eats chironomids on the bottom.

The Oregon chub is in danger of extirpation through loss of habitat and introduction of largemouth bass into its remaining habitats (Markle et al. 1991; Marshall 1992). It spawns among plants in quiet water during early spring, with the female selecting the spawning site.

Provide a 5- to 10-gallon aquarium with a sand bottom, sponge filter, abundant *Vesicularia* or *Nitella,* and feed chironomids, adult brine shrimp, and live blackworms and daphnia. It is a good candidate for captive breeding and reintroduction into bass-free reserves.

| | |
|---|---|
| *Oregonichthys kalawatseti,* Umpqua chub | *O. kalawatseti* has few or no scales on the breast, and can be defined by enzymatic LDH gel electrophoresis migration. |

The Umpqua chub occurs throughout the Umpqua River in western Oregon.

*O. kalawatseti* inhabits runs, sloughs, and pools where flow is slow (sometimes behind structures in runs) and daytime temperatures average from 62 to 78°F. It is found over bedrock or beneath undercut vegetated banks, usually over hard bottom. In nature, the female selects the spawning site among rocks.

In the laboratory, Umpqua chubs were exposed to luteinizing hormone-releasing hormone ethylamide (LH-RHa), absorbed through the skin. Apparent spawning motions were observed, with the female approaching rocks and the male

Speckled chub, *Macrhybopsis aestivalis,* Etowah R., Cherokee Co., Ga. RB

approaching the female for contact. No eggs were released, but the authors concluded a real spawning behavior had occurred (Markle et al. 1991).

Provide a 5- to 10-gallon aquarium with a pebble and flat rock bottom, a sponge filter, *Vesicularia* or *Nitella,* and feed chironomids, adult brine shrimp, and live blackworms and daphnia.

See the discussion on *Hybopsis* species.

**Genus *Macrhybopsis***

*Macrhybopsis* was elevated from a subgenus of *Hybopsis.* The group is characterized by protruding snouts over underslung mouths, one or two barbels at the angle of the jaw, eight anal fin rays, markedly concave dorsal fins, and the dorsal fin origin over the origin of the pelvic fins.

*Macrhybopsis* species are egg broadcasters over gravel; the eggs drift for days, much like those of striped bass. Collect by seining at night on riffles.

If spawning occurs in captivity, the eggs should be collected by swirling a net through the water and transferred to a gallon jar with vigorous aeration to keep them in suspension. Provide the adults with a strong current using a powerhead, and feed them bloodworms and adult brine shrimp.

*Macrhybopsis aestivalis,*
speckled chub

*M. aestivalis* is a complex of species, previously included in the monotypic *Extrarius* and prior to that in *Hybopsis.*

They range along the Gulf Coast, from the Rio Grande eastward to the Florida panhandle, and northward to Minnesota, Wisconsin, Indiana, and Ohio. The eastern forms are being studied by Rick Mayden and Carter Gilbert, the western forms by David Eisenhour, a student of Brooks Burr. Some members of the complex will be given species rank, according to Page and Burr (1991) who have discussed this fish under *Extrarius.* Etnier and Starnes (1993) have offered another version of the species complex. The group includes as many as ten distinct species, of which about half have not yet been described (C. Gilbert, pers. comm.).

All live in large rivers over sand or fine gravel and probably feed at night on chironomids and other insect larvae. They spawn from May through August, the eggs drifting a day or two in the current.

The other three species of *Macrhybopsis* are all in the Missouri and Mississippi River systems. The genus ultimately will be found to consist of at least a dozen valid species.

Sturgeon chub, *Macrhybopsis gelida*, Missouri R. RB

Sicklefin chub, *Macrhybopsis meeki*, Missouri R. RB

Silver chub, *Macrhybopsis storeriana*, Tennessee R., Hardin Co., Tenn. RB

| | |
|---|---|
| *Macrhybopsis gelida,* sturgeon chub | *M. gelida* is probably a sensory feeder, having taste buds scattered all over the body and fins. |
| *Macrhybopsis meeki,* sicklefin chub | *M. meeki* is rare south of the Ohio River. |
| *Macrhybopsis storeriana,* silver chub | *M. storeriana* also occurs in lakes in the northern part of its range. It apparently feeds near shore at night on caddisflies, burrowing mayflies, chironomids, beetles, *Corbicula* clams, worms, and amphipods. It spawns in May and June when the water is in the upper 60s to low 70s (°F) (Robison and Buchanan 1988; Etnier and Starnes 1993). |
| **Genus Iotichthys** | *Iotichthys* is a monotypic western genus of uncertain affinities surviving today in a harsh, disappearing habitat. |
| *Iotichthys phlegethontis,* least chub | *I. phlegethontis* is a stubby, *Gila*-like minnow with a short snout and terminal mouth. It has fine black speckles on a silvery to sky blue body, a gold line along the flank, and gold to yellow fins. The nuptial male has a copper flush to the lower flank, golden fins, and an iridescent gold eye. It grows to an average of 2 inches (Page and Burr 1991). |
| | The least chub occurs only in the Bonneville basin of northern Utah in streams, ponds, and swamps around the Great Salt, Utah, and Sevier Lakes, Provo and Beaver Rivers, and Parowan and Clear Creeks. |

*I. phlegethontis* is found in vegetation over mud, muck, clay, or peat bottoms at depths of 4 inches to 3 feet. It feeds on mosquito larvae and small crustaceans. It breeds during June at 61 to 75°F, the males developing breeding tubercles (Lee et al. 1980).

The least chub can probably be fed brine shrimp, bloodworms, and daphnia, and spawned in a 10-gallon aquarium with hard water and dense vegetation.

| | |
|---|---|
| **Genus *Lepidomeda*** | *Lepidomeda* species *(L. albivallis, L. mollispinis, L. vittata)* are the spinedaces, 3- to 5-inch silvery minnows with dark marks on the gill cover and flank. Coloration is red, yellow, or orange at the bases of the paired fins. |

They occupy small areas in the Arizona-Nevada desert, ranging into Utah. They live in cool (65–70°F) streams on riffles, runs, pools, and eddies, foraging on aquatic invertebrates. All are egg broadcasters over gravel, spawning from March through July (Rinne and Minckley 1991; Johnston and Page 1992).

All are protected and unavailable to aquarists. *L. altivelis* is extinct.

*Lepidomeda vittata,*
Little Colorado spinedance

Now restricted to northward-flowing streams emptying into the Little Colorado River in Apache, Coconino, and Navajo Counties in Arizona, it was probably more widespread in the past, extending into Mexico. Predation by rainbow trout is suspected in its decline. Blinn, White, Pradetto, and O'Brien (1998) observed spawning in a stream and pond at Northern Arizona University. During May, small schools ascended the stream, where about a dozen males hovered around a single female over the gravel. Both sexes had developed bright orange-red patches at the bases of the paired fins, the males more intensely colored. Spawning occurred on the gravel in the stream, but not in the pond. Eggs spawned above trays of gravel hatched within five days. The 6 to 7 mm long larvae moved to the protection of shallow shoreline vegetation and grew rapidly.

**Genus *Meda***

*Meda* is a monotypic southwestern genus, probably derived from *Lepidomeda.*

*Meda fulgida,* spikedace

*M. fulgida* is olive with dusky mottling above, silvery on the flank, and white below. The mouth is terminal, the snout not markedly overlapping. The nuptial male is brassy to gold above and on the flank.

The spikedace occurs in the Gila River system of Arizona, New Mexico, and Sonora, Mexico. The spikedace has declined dramatically as a result of competition by the introduced red shiner, *Cyprinella lutrensis.* The red shiner has forced the spikedace into swift water, to which it is not well adapted (Douglas et al. 1994).

*M. fulgida* is a stream fish that prefers runs, pools, and eddies less than 3 feet deep, and usually occurs in midwater where it feeds on drifting aquatic and terrestrial insects. Adults aggregate at the edge of currents in broad shallows, upstream of gravel sandbars and downstream of riffles in eddies. They spawn during spring and summer (Rinne and Minckley 1991) as egg broadcasters (Johnston and Page 1992).

The spikedace is a threatened species, and cannot be collected.

**Genus *Plagopterus***

The monotypic *Plagopterus* contains a relict species that has evolved adaptations to life on the bottom, much like certain catfishes. These include the loss of scales on a naked skin, a dorsal fin modified into a stout spine (hence the common name), and a flat belly.

| | |
|---|---|
| *Plagopterus argentissimus,* woundfin | *P. argentissimus* is silvery and flat-headed with tiny barbels at the corner of the jaws, scales on the body reduced to a series of tiny ridges, and the leading rays of the dorsal fin modified into a stout spine that can wound a predator or the careless handler. The nuptial male has a pink flush on the lower flank. It is adapted to its habitat by an elongate, streamlined body, large sickle-shaped fins, and a flat belly area. It is closely related to *Meda* and *Lepidomeda* of the tribe Plagopterini. The average adult length is 2½ inches (Lee et al. 1980; Rinne and Minckley 1991).<br><br>The woundfin was originally distributed in the Virgin, Gila, and Salt Rivers (lower Colorado River) during the 1880s, but now survives only in the Virgin River of Arizona, Nevada, and Utah.<br><br>*P. argentissimus* is found in the main stem of turbid, warm rivers subject to flash flooding, over unstable sand bottoms. It spawns at 77°F on rocky bottoms, and the fry reach 1 inch within one month (Rinne and Minckley 1991).<br><br>This rare fish is endangered and under federal protection. |
| **Genus *Pogonichthys*** | *Pogonichthys* is a monotypic western genus, so bizarre in shape that it cannot be confused with any other fish. Its only close relative recently became extinct. |
| *Pogonichthys macrolepidotus,* splittail | *P. macrolepidotus* is elongate, rounded, and silvery with a deeply forked, massive tail fin, the upper lobe longer and larger than the lower. It is olive above and silver to gold on the flank. The nuptial male has orange lower and caudal fins and a fatty hump on the nape. It grows to over 15 inches (Page and Burr 1991).<br><br>Historically, the splittail occurred in rivers and lakes of the Sacramento–San Juan delta system of California; today it is only around San Francisco Bay and in the Sacramento River, upstream to the Red Bluff Dam (Lee et al. 1980; Page and Burr 1991). *P. ciscoides,* the only relative of the splittail, was once endemic to Clear Lake, California and its tributaries; abundant less than 40 years ago, it has since become extinct.<br><br>*P. macrolepidotus* inhabits lakes, sluggish river backwaters, and upper coastal bays with slightly brackish water. It feeds on bottom invertebrates. |
| **Genus *Luxilus*** | *Luxilus* contains nine species that were until recently placed in *Notropis*. Members are characterized by large, elongated scales in the front of the body, the dorsal fin beginning directly over the origin of the pelvic fins, nine anal fin rays, and the nuptial male having prominent hooked tubercles on the snout. These mostly large minnows average 3–6 inches. Most are broadcasters, some spawning over the pits of *Nocomis* and *Semotilus*.<br><br>Three groups are distinguishable: (a) striped, common, white, and crescent shiners are silver with pink overtones, and characteristic of moderate slope, medium-sized, sand-bottom rivers of Piedmont and foothill regions; (b) warpaint and bandfin shiners have vertical black bands behind the gill cover and on the dorsal fin, and prefer upper Piedmont slopes with stronger flows; (c) bleeding, cardinal, and dusky-stripe shiners have horizontal black stripes on the flank and red heads and tails, and occur in small, upland headwater streams with rocky or gravel bottoms. |

Two modes of breeding behavior occur in the genus (Maurakis and Woolcott 1993). *Luxilus cerasinus, L. coccogenis,* and *Luxilus zonistius* scatter eggs on the surface of a *Nocomis* or *Semotilus* nest (Johnston and Birkhead 1988); of this group, *L. cerasinus,* at least, will scatter eggs in aquaria without benefit of a host fish nest and is therefore a facultative nest parasite. A second group consisting of *L. albeolus, L. cardinalis, L. chrysocephalus, L. cornutus, L. pilsbryi,* and *L. zonatus* do not scatter eggs on the surface of a nest, but within a furrow (about 2 cm deep and as long as the male) excavated by the territorial male on the upstream slope of a parasitized *Nocomis* or *Semotilus* nest.

A 30-gallon aquarium will provide space for six fish. Supply one inch of pebbles or large gravel on the bottom (but no rocks or plants), vigorous aeration, and moderate current. Cool water is important for conditioning. They spawn when the temperature is gradually increased from 60 to 70°F over 30 days. Note that some species spawn in furrows constructed by pit building minnow species and others do not. In captivity, *L. cerasinus* at least will broadcast eggs over pea gravel or pebbles. They spawn a few inches above the bottom, spawning lasting several hours over a few days. Adults should be removed after either spawning or several days of bright nuptial coloration and flashing are observed.

Insufficient information is available to advise whether the furrowing group of *Luxilus* are obligate or facultative nest parasites. The eggs of *L. cerasinus* in the gravel and pebble spaces hatch in five to eight days. The early fry are thin, and should be fed rotifers, ciliates, motile algae, dry food dust, or other fine foods. After a week, the fry hover in small, tight aggregations just above the bottom. Growth is rapid, and sexual maturity is reached in the second year.

*Luxilus* is divided into taxonomic groups that do not reflect the spawning behavior of the species.

| | |
|---|---|
| **Group a**<br>*Luxilus cerasinus,* crescent shiner | *L. cerasinus* (**plate 20**) occurs in the James, Roanoke, Cape Fear, and New River (through introduction) drainages of Virginia, West Virginia, and North Carolina. |
| *Luxilus albeolus,* white shiner | *L. albeolus* ranges from the James and Roanoke Rivers of Virginia to the Cape Fear River in North Carolina; evidence exists that it originated as a hybrid between *L. cornutus* and *L. cerasinus* (Meagher and Dowling 1991), but this has been questioned (Gleason and Berra 1993) because the two species are allopatric and are less closely related than *L. cornutus* is to *L. chrysocephalus,* two species that are more closely related and sympatric. |
| *Luxilus chrysocephalus,*<br>striped shiner | *L. chrysocephalus* is described as two subspecies: *L. c. chrysocephalus* ranges from the Great Lakes to northern Arkansas in the White, St. Francis, and Arkansas Rivers, and has crooked lines on its back; *L. c. isolepis* ranges from southern Arkansas (Red and Ouachita drainages) southward, and has straight lines on its back, as noted in the text but mislabeled in the black and white illustration in Page and Burr (1991). |
| *Luxilus cornutus,* common shiner | *L. cornutus* ranges from Nova Scotia to Saskatchewan and from Hudson Bay to the Great Lakes. It continues southward along the Atlantic slope to Virginia, and ranges westward to Wyoming and southward to Missouri. Species in this group may be either furrowers or surface egg scatterers. |

Striped shiner, *Luxilus chrysocephalus isolepis,* Ouachita R., Ark. RB

Common shiner, *Luxilus cornutus,* spawning in nest of Semotilus atromaculatus. GS

Warpaint shiner, *Luxilus coccogenis,* Hiwasee R., Tenn. RB

| | |
|---|---|
| **Group b** | Each has a black band in the dorsal fin, but the warpaint also has a black band on the tail fin and red mark on the gill cover. Species in this group may be either furrowers or surface egg scatterers. |
| *Luxilus coccogenis,* warpaint shiner | *L. coccogenis* (**plate 21**) occurs in the upper Tennessee, Savannah, Santee, and New River drainages of the mountain regions in Tennessee, Georgia, North and South Carolina, Virginia, and Alabama. |
| *Luxilus zonistius,* bandfin shiner | *L. zonistius* ranges throughout northern and western Alabama (Mathur 1977), just entering eastern Mississippi and the Florida panhandle in the Apalachicola, Altamaha, Coosa, Tallapoosa, and Savannah Rivers (Page and Burr 1991). |
| **Group c** | All members of this group are furrowers. All three species are closely related, and have red heads in nuptial coloration. The bleeding shiner is the only one of the three with a black band or slash behind the gill cover. The cardinal shiner gradually develops a striking, completely red belly, but a white or partially red belly is not a reliable indication that the fish is a duskystripe or bleeding shiner; banding and striping should be considered.<br><br>For a recent review of species groups relationships in *Luxilus,* see Dowling and Naylor (1997). |

| | |
|---|---|
| *Luxilus zonatus,* bleeding shiner | *L. zonatus* (**plate 22**) is similar to *L. cardinalis* and *L. pilsbryi.* The bleeding shiner occurs in the St. Francis, Black, Little, Meramec, Osage, Big Piney, and Gasconade Rivers of the Ozark Plateau. |
| *Luxilus cardinalis,* cardinal shiner | *L. cardinalis* (**plate 23**), the cardinal shiner, is nearby in the lower Arkansas River drainage (including the upper Neosho River) and tributaries of the Red River drainage. |
| *Luxilus pilsbryi,* duskystripe shiner | *L. pilsbryi* (**plate 24**) has a bold black horizontal stripe that extends to the lateral line (it extends below the lateral line in the cardinal shiner). The duskystripe shiner is also in the Ozark uplands of Missouri and Arkansas, but restricted to the White and Little Red Rivers (Mayden 1988). A report of it as a pit builder is probably erroneous. |
| **Genus *Lythrurus*** | *Lythrurus* was also elevated recently from a subgenus of *Notropis,* and can be distinguished from the similar *Luxilus* by smaller nape and upper body scales, a dorsal fin origin well behind the pelvic fin origin, and usually 10 or 11 anal fin rays rather than 9. Molecular studies have recently placed doubt on the traditional groupings in this genus (Schmidt, Bielawski, and Gold 1998). Some *(L. fumeus, L. umbratilis)* are lowland fishes of oxbows, sluggish rivers, and even blackwater streams; a few *(L. bellus, L. atrapiculus, L. matutinus, L. roseipinnis)* are found in gently flowing coastal plain habitats; but most *(L. ardens, L. fasciolaris, L. alegnotus, L. lirus, L. snelsoni)* are upland fishes of clear, strongly flowing streams. Some *Lythrurus* species have distinctive coloration. They feed at all levels, including the surface, on insects, crustaceans, and some vegetation. Some are reported to use the nests of minnows or sunfish; in general, however, they are typical broadcasters over gravel, spawning from May to August at 55 to 80°F in different regions of the country. See also Etnier and Starnes (1993). |
| *Lythrurus ardens,* (Atlantic slope) rosefin shiner | *L. ardens* has reddish fins and a rosy flush to the body. *L. ardens* occurs from the York River in Virginia to the Cape Fear River in North Carolina, and above Kanawha Falls in the New River of Virginia. |
| *Lythrurus fasciolarus,* (Ohio basin) rosefin shiner | *L. fasciolarus* is almost identical to the Atlantic slope species and occurs in the Ohio basin from the Scioto River in Ohio southwestward to extreme southeastern Illinois. It ranges southward to the Tennessee drainage of Alabama, and is present in the upper Black Warrior River of Alabama. *L. fasciolarus* spawns over the nests of chubs or sunfish. |
| *Lythrurus matutinus,* pinewoods shiner | *L. matutinus* has a distinctive red head. The pinewoods shiner occurs in the Tar and Neuse Rivers of North Carolina. Dimmick et al. (1996) confirmed the validity of *L. fasciolaris* and *L. matutinus.* Recent DNA analyses at Texas A&M University revealed the entire sequence of the mitochondrial cytochrome *b* gene, the first time it had been accomplished in higher (neopterygian) fishes (Schmidt and Gold 1993). |
| *Lythrurus roseipinnis,* cherryfin shiner | *L. roseipinnis* has a prominent leading black mark in front of the reddish dorsal and anal fins, but otherwise little body or fin color. |

Rosefin shiner, *Lythrurus fasciolaris,* Green R., Ky. WFR

*Lythrurus fasciolaris* is often considered a subspecies of the rosefin shiner, and called *Lythrurus ardens fasciolaris,* shown here from the Tennessee River. RB

Cherryfin shiner, *Lythrurus roseipinnis,* Yazoo R., Miss. WFR

The cherryfin shiner occurs in Gulf drainages from Mobile Bay, Alabama to Lake Pontchartrain, Louisiana, and in the Mississippi, Yazoo, Big Black River, and Bayou Pierre drainages of Mississippi.

| | |
|---|---|
| *Lythrurus atrapiculus,* blacktip shiner | *L. atrapiculus* is similar to the cherryfin shiner but the breeding male has light red, orange, or yellow fins.<br>The blacktip shiner occurs in the Apalachicola, Choctawhatchee, Yellow, and Escambia drainages of Georgia, Alabama, and Florida. |
| *Lythrurus bellus,* (lower) pretty shiner | *L. bellus* has yellow or light orange (but not red) fins.<br>This fish occurs below the fall line in the Black Warrior system of Alabama, and elsewhere in the Mobile Bay drainage of Alabama and Mississippi. The name, pretty shiner, has referred to this and the following species. |
| *Lythrurus alegnotus,* (upper) pretty shiner | *L. alegnotus* is closely related to *L. bellus* and occurs above the fall line in the same systems. It has, as yet, no officially recognized common name. It was previously considered a subspecies of *L. bellus.* |
| *Lythrurus fumeus,* ribbon shiner | Nuptial males of *L. fumeus* may be yellowish, but both sexes are otherwise plain.<br>The ribbon shiner occurs in the Mississippi basin from Illinois and Indiana |

Ozark redfin shiner, *Lythrurus umbratilis,* Ouachita R., Ark. RB

to Oklahoma and Kentucky southward to the Gulf states, and in other Gulf drainages from Lake Pontchartrain, Louisiana to Navidad, Texas, mostly below the fall line.

| | |
|---|---|
| *Lythrurus lirus,* mountain shiner | *L. lirus* is plain, although the nuptial male develops pink fins and a slightly yellow head.<br><br>    The mountain shiner occurs mostly in the Coosa River of Alabama and Georgia above the fall line, but historically had a wider distribution. |
| *Lythrurus snelsoni,* Ouachita shiner | The nuptial male of *L. snelsoni* has a red head, snout, throat, and dorsal fin.<br><br>    The Ouachita shiner occurs in the upper Mountain Fork and Cossatot Rivers above the fall line in Arkansas. |
| *Lythrurus umbratilis,* (Ozark) redfin shiner | *L. umbratilis* is olive to steel blue above with a stripe along the back, a few black specks above, and a dark blotch at the origin of the dorsal fin; the breeding male develops a blue head, dark vertical stripes on the front half of the body, and dark or red fins.<br><br>    This pretty minnow occurs in the Missouri, Arkansas, and upper Salt Rivers of the Ozark region.<br><br>    *L. umbratilis* prefers sluggish gravel or sand-bottom pools lined with *Justicia* (water willow), where it spawns over the nests of green, orangespotted, and longear sunfish (Robison and Buchanan 1988; Snelson 1990; Page and Burr 1991; Etnier and Starnes 1993; Jenkins and Burkhead 1994). |
| *Lythrurus cyanocephalus,* redfin shiner | *L. cyanocephalus* has similar coloration but is more heavily spotted.<br><br>    It occurs in the Great Lakes and Mississippi and Gulf Coast basins. It ranges from New York and Ontario westward to Minnesota and southward to Louisiana, continuing westward to the San Jacinto River of Texas. It is usually considered a subspecies of *L. umbratilis.* |
| **Genus *Margariscus*** | *Margariscus* is a monotypic genus often included within *Semotilus,* but modern workers think it more likely related to *Phoxinus, Couesius,* or *Hemitremia.* In fact, its red lower body, white throat, and fine scales make it look much like a *Phoxinus,* and it does not construct a nest. |

### Margariscus margarita, pearl dace

*M. margarita* is a roundheaded dace with small scales. It is dusky to black above and often densely speckled. The nuptial male is white between the head and anal fin and has an orange-red lower flank and belly. It averages 5 to 6 inches long.

The pearl dace occurs throughout virtually all of Canada from Nova Scotia to Hudson Bay to eastern British Columbia. In the United States, it ranges southward to northern Virginia, the Great Lakes, and Montana, with disjunct populations in South Dakota, Nebraska, and Iowa.

*M. m. margarita,* the Allegheny pearl dace, ranges from Vermont to Virginia and may have as few as 50 large lateral line scales. The subspecies *M. m. nachtriebi,* with up to 75 smaller lateral line scales, occupies the remainder of the range throughout most of Canada and all of the United States. Two other nominal subspecies, *M. m. koelzi* (an isolated lake population on Isle Royale in Lake Superior) and *M. m. athabascae* (a population from the Jasper region of Alberta, Canada) (Scott and Crossman 1973), may not be valid (C. Gilbert, pers. comm.).

*M. margarita* inhabits cool, clear, headwater streams in the south, and lakes, ponds, and creeks draining stained peat bogs and beaver ponds in the north; relict populations south of its normal range occur in cool springs. It appears to be limited to temperatures no higher than the 60s (°F). It feeds on copepods, daphnia, chironomids, and some beetles and algae.

The pearl dace spawns during spring when water temperatures are in the low 60s (°F). The red-marked male maintains a territory 8 inches in diameter and 6 feet from the nearest competitor, but does not excavate or build a nest. Pairs join in a spawning clasp and broadcast the fertilized eggs over sand or gravel in 1½ to 2 feet of water.

It requires colder water and is not demanding in diet. Set up for spawning like *Luxilus,* except use only one male and two to four females in a 10-gallon aquarium or no more than two males in a 29-gallon aquarium. It often can be purchased as a bait minnow.

### Genus *Mylocheilus*

The ancient *Mylocheilus* contains a single, widespread, salt-tolerant species of Pacific Coast drainages.

### Mylocheilus caurinus, peamouth

*M. caurinus* is elongate with characteristic molariform pharyngeal teeth. The juvenile has two dark stripes on the flank, the upper from the gill cover to the tail, and the lower only to the level of the anal fin origin. The adult male has a green back; the female's back is brown. Nuptial males and females have red stripes on their flanks, and red on their gill covers and lower jaws. Adults average 5 inches, but grow to 1 foot long.

The peamouth occurs in Alberta, British Columbia, Vancouver Island, Washington, Oregon, Idaho, and Montana. It is found in the Athabasca, Peace, and Columbia River drainages, but is present elsewhere in rivers and lakes of the region and on offshore islands; it has even been taken at sea (Scott and Crossman 1973).

*M. caurinus* inhabits the weedy shallows of lakes and slow rivers, where it feeds on insects, crustaceans, mollusks, small sculpins, and other fishes. It spawns during May or June, when the water temperature is in the middle 50s (°F). Densely packed aggregations of 50 to 400 adults approach shallow lakeshores, separated from other aggregations by 25 to 100 feet. A female is swarmed by two or more males and the eggs are broadcast in 1 or 2 inches of water. The gray-green adhesive eggs stick to rocks and rubble until hatching, and the fry remain in the shallows until late summer (Scott and Crossman 1973).

A 55-gallon chilled aquarium with a sand bottom and strong filtration is suitable for 10 to 20 fish. Feed flake foods supplemented with bloodworms and earthworms, and keep madtoms in the aquarium for cleaning uneaten food from the bottom. For spawning, condition on meaty foods (no flakes) until the females are heavy with roe and both sexes have bright red lines. Deep water and a bare bottom should retard spawning. Move the group outdoors during late winter into a shallow wading pool, raising one side and supporting it with a rock or tree stump; lay pea gravel in the shallowest portion. The eggs are large and readily observed. After spawning, remove the parents and begin feeding live *Daphnia* and *Ceriodaphnia.*

**Genus *Ptychocheilus***

*Ptychocheilus* contains four (possibly five) species of squawfish, the largest American minnows at 2 to 6 feet long, clearly unsuitable for home aquaria.

The squawfish can be identified by locality; their ranges do not overlap. *Ptychocheilus,* together with *Mylopharodon* and *Lavinia,* constitute an evolutionary group known as the western clade of North American minnows, all derived from a common ancestor (Gold and Li 1994). Squawfish have eight or nine dorsal and anal rays, whereas *Lavinia* has ten or more. Squawfish are broadcasters (Johnston and Page 1992).

*P. lucius* is endangered due to habitat degradation and thus unavailable, and *P. oregonensis* and perhaps others are predators of trout and at risk from sportfishing enthusiasts who consider them nuisances. Squawfishes are regarded with ambivalence by state agencies sworn to protect legally protected species but supported by fishing license fees.

*Ptychocheilus grandis,*
Sacramento squawfish

*P. grandis* has 38–48 scales from the head to the dorsal fin origin, 12–15 scales above the lateral line, 8 dorsal rays, and 8 anal rays. It resembles the closely related hardhead *(Mylopharodon conocephalus),* which occurs in the same waters and eats mollusks. The upper lip of the Sacramento squawfish is entirely separated from the snout by a deep groove; the groove is bridged on top by a thin strip of tissue in the hardhead. It probably attains 4 feet in length (Carney and Page 1990), but historically is known to have grown larger.

The Sacramento squawfish occurs in Clear Lake and in the Sacramento–San Joaquin, Russian, upper Pit, and Eel Rivers of California.

*P. grandis* is found in pools and runs, over rock or sand.

*Ptychocheilus lucius,*
Colorado squawfish

*P. lucius* has 18–23 scales above the lateral line, 9 dorsal rays, and 9 anal rays. It is torpedo-shaped, brassy metallic blue-black above, and creamy white below. The nuptial male is silvery above and creamy yellow below, with bright gold flecks on the upper flank (Rinne and Minckley 1991). It probably grows to 3 feet, but historically has been twice as long (Carney and Page 1990).

The Colorado squawfish occurs in the Colorado River drainage of Colorado, Utah, New Mexico, Arizona (Carney and Page 1990), and Wyoming (Marsh et al. 1991), and just enters Baja California (Page and Burr 1991).

*P. lucius* is found in deep rock and gravel pools, eddies, riffles, sloughs, backwaters, swift runs, and shallow shorelines, usually in large rivers but also in creeks. Young eat mostly insects and crustaceans; older fish feed on any kind of fish, including trout. They spawn over gravel bars in channels when temperatures exceed 68°F.

This endangered species may not be possessed.

| | |
|---|---|
| *Ptychocheilus oregonensis,* northern squawfish | *P. oregonensis* has 50–60 scales from the head to the dorsal fin origin, 12–20 scales above the lateral line, 9 dorsal rays, and 8 anal rays. It is dark green-brown above, and cream or white below. The nuptial male is brighter, with the lower fins entirely yellow or yellow-orange. In preservative, the juvenile has a black spot at the base of the tail. Northern squawfish can attain a length of up to 2 feet but are usually half this size (Carney and Page 1990). |

The only squawfish in Canada, the northern squawfish occurs in British Columbia throughout the Fraser, Columbia, Skeena, Klinaklini, and Dean River systems northward to the Nass River system and Meziadin Lake. It ranges across the Continental Divide, occurring in the Peace River system as far as Alberta, and in Summit and McLeod Lakes (Scott and Crossman 1973). In the United States, it ranges throughout the Columbia River system from Oregon to Nevada, and in the Harney River basin of Oregon (Carney and Page 1990).

*P. oregonensis* inhabits lakes and occasionally large, slow-moving rivers. It feeds on *Richardsonius* (shiners), *Gasterosteus* (sticklebacks), juvenile salmon *(Oncorhynchus),* crayfish, insects, spiders, worms, clams, and plankton. The smallest fish eat mostly bloodworms and copepods.

Spawning sites must have a bottom of gravel and rock, be free of sand, and have a bottom current of less than 1 foot per second. During June and July at 54 to 64°F, hundreds to thousands fish (more males than females) aggregate at these sites for spawning. Slow-moving females are ignored; rapidly moving females are quickly joined by excited males, and eggs and sperm are broadcast in seconds near the bottom. The adhesive eggs fall between crevices in rocks and gravel, and stick to the bottom (Beamesderfer 1992).

Juveniles are easily taken by seine; adults will take an artificial fly. They are not recommended for aquaria, however, due to large size and the lack of unusual behaviors or attractive colors. Cool water is required.

| | |
|---|---|
| *Ptychocheilus umpquae,* Umpqua squawfish | *P. umpquae* has 60–80 scales from the head to the dorsal fin origin, 9 dorsal rays, and 8 anal rays. The maximum length 1½ feet (Page and Burr 1991), but half this size is typical. |

The Umpqua squawfish occurs in the Umpqua and Siuslaw River drainages of Oregon. Chromosomal evidence indicates that the fishes in these two rivers should be considered different species (Gold and Li 1994).

*P. umpquae* inhabits pools of small rivers and lakes and requires cool water.

| | |
|---|---|
| **Genus *Mylopharodon*** | The monotypic *Mylopharodon* should probably be merged into *Ptychocheilus* because it is a squawfish in most characters. |

| | |
|---|---|
| *Mylopharodon conocephalus,* hardhead | *M. conocephalus* is brown above and silvery on the flank and below; it is similar to *Ptychocheilus grandis,* with which it coexists. The hardhead, however, has a premaxillary frenum, a bridge of tissue from the snout to the upper jaw that is visible when the upper jaw is pulled forward. To confirm identification, look down the throat to see the molar-shaped pharyngeal (throat) teeth it uses to crush mollusks |

(its favorite prey). No squawfish has molariform pharyngeal teeth. It attains 3 feet long.

The hardhead occurs in the San Joaquin, Russian, and Pit Rivers of northern California, in larger, lowland to mid-elevation streams.

Although not protected, it is too large for aquaria.

| | |
|---|---|
| **Genus _Lavinia_** | _Lavinia_ is a monotypic California genus related to the squawfish _(Ptychocheilus)_ and to the California roach _(Hesperoleucas)._ |

_Lavinia exilicauda,_ hitch

_L. exilicauda,_ the hitch, resembles the unrelated _Notemigonus crysoleucas_ (golden shiner) in shape, but with ten or more dorsal rays rather than eight and no keel on the belly; it is brown above and white below (Page and Burr 1991). It also resembles the closely related _Hesperoleucas symmetricus,_ with which it hybridizes in the wild.

The hitch inhabits northern California. _L. e. chi_ is found in Clear Lake, _L. e. exilicauda_ in the Sacramento and San Joaquin drainage, and _L. e. harengus_ in the Parajar and Salinas drainages (Lee et al. 1980).

All occur in low elevation warm lakes, ponds, and backwaters, and feed on pelagic zooplankton. They spawn during spring in streams and on lakeshores, and are believed to be egg broadcasters. They hybridize with _Orthodon microlepidotus, Hesperoleucas symmetricus,_ and _Gila crassicauda_ (Lee et al. 1980). _Hesperoleucas_ is suspected of crevice spawning. Captive breeding and hybridization of these two species should be conducted to confirm spawning behaviors.

No information is available on aquarium care, but they should thrive on daphnia and brine shrimp, and be maintained in vegetated aquaria with clear water and little turbulence.

Saucer Nesters
**Genus _Agosia_**

_Agosia_ is monotypic, containing only _A. chrysogaster._

_Agosia chrysogaster,_ longfin dace

The front of the anal fin is elongate in the female of _A. chrysogaster,_ giving rise to the common name. The snout overhangs the inferior mouth. The longfin dace is silvery brown above and white below, with a lateral band that ends in a black spot at the base of the tail fin. The nuptial male is dark with small white breeding tubercles and yellow from the throat to the belly and at the bases of the fins.

The longfin dace occurs in the Colorado and Rio Yaqui River systems of Arizona, New Mexico, and Mexico. It is the most widely distributed of desert fishes, among the first to invade a new stream, and tolerates heat and low oxygen concentrations in pools or damp algae of dried-up streams. It is omnivorous.

The only confirmed saucer-spawning minnow, _A. chrysogaster_ breeds year-round. Nuptial males swirl out pits on soft bottoms but do not move gravel or sand in their lips or remain with the pits after spawning. These pits average 1 to 2 inches deep, 8 inches in diameter, have a ½-inch-high rim all around the edge (the "saucer"), and are clustered so tightly as to touch or overlap at their rims.

When the female enters a pit, one or two males move alongside and clasp while pushing downward, forcing the female partly into the sand. Eggs are buried ½-inch deep in the pit and its walls and are not guarded. The fry hatch in a few days and

Longfin dace, *Agosia chrysogaster,* Mimbres R., N.Mex. WFR

initially remain in the pit. They move to stream margins and then to open sandy runs with the adults (Rinne and Minckley 1991; Johnston and Page 1992).

Provide a large, low aquarium with a sand bottom for a group of a dozen fish. Feed flakes, cooked vegetables, bloodworms, and brine shrimp. Aquarium breeding has not yet been reported; it probably has not been attempted because the fish is common and not brilliantly colored.

**Genus *Moapa***

*Moapa* is a monotypic southwestern genus probably related to *Agosia* and derived from a *Gila*-like ancestor.

*Moapa coriacea,* Moapa dace

*M. coriacea* is a velvety, *Gila*-like dace with a barely discernible dusky stripe below a light iridescent gold light stripe along the flank, a dusky mark at the base of the dorsal fin, and a bold black mark at the center of the tail fin. It is small, averaging 2½ inches.

The Moapa dace is native to thermal springs and their runs in a short section of the upper Moapa River in northern Clark County of Nevada; it may be persisting in Spring Valley, where it was transplanted in 1972.

*M. coriacea* tolerates a temperature range of at least 68 to 93°F, but is rarely found below 86°F and prefers warmer water (Lee et al. 1980; Rinne and Minckley 1991). It may be a saucer builder like *Agosia,* both fish apparently derived from a common ancestor (Lee et al. 1980).

It is endangered due to its limited range.

## Pit Builders
**Genus *Campostoma***

*Campostoma,* appropriately called stonerollers, are the only pit-building minnows. Stonerollers have an overhanging snout with the mouth well underneath the nose. The lower jaw is armed with a bony ridge for scraping algae from rocks. Nest builders that push pebbles or stones have keratinized epithelium on the jaws, while those that pick up and carry stones have keratinized epithelium inside their cheeks (McGuire et al. 1996).

The nuptial male has a characteristic pattern of tubercles on the snout and a red eye. The male digs a 4- to 8-inch circular depression in a run just above a pool; it pushes gravel with its snout and picks up pebbles and small stones with its mouth, moving them to the outside of the pit. Males may build, take over, and defend more

Central stoneroller, *Campostoma anomalum*, Kansas R., Kans. GS

than one pit, chasing away conspecific males but ignoring other species of minnows that also use the pits for spawning.

Stonerollers spawn above the pit, the fertilized eggs sinking into the gravel and pebble interstices; there, they are prevented from washing downstream and protected from predation, but are near enough to the surface to receive oxygenation (Jenkins and Burkhead 1994). *Campostoma* will also spawn in the nests of *Nocomis, Exoglossum,* and *Semotilus* (Johnston and Page 1992).

Provide a large (long and ≥ 40 gal.) aquarium with gravel, pebbles, and small rocks to a depth of 2 inches, current from a submersed powerhead, canister and/or trickle filtration, and activated carbon to maintain high quality water. *Campostoma* will generally ignore cooked vegetables; it adapts to *Spirulina* algae-based flake foods and frozen adult *Artemia,* but tends to decline in health due to a lack of food volume or important nutrients. Constant replenishment with algae-covered stream rocks may provide a good food source.

Stonerollers have not yet been spawned in captivity. Success with any of the stonerollers should bring about breeding of nest-parasitizing minnows, although the latter might be induced to breed by cichlid pits or stoneroller gonadal extracts.

---

*Campostoma anomalum,*
central stoneroller

*C. anomalum* has a black band within an orange dorsal fin, an orange anal fin, 55 or fewer lateral scales, and 36 or more scales around the body immediately in front of the dorsal fin.

The central stoneroller occurs in the uplands of the Ohio and Mississippi basins, from New York to Minnesota and North Dakota. It ranges southward along the Appalachian chain to the mountains of North and South Carolina, westward through Colorado and New Mexico, and southward through the central states to Texas and northern Mexico.

The central stoneroller consists of at least three subspecies. *C. a. anomalum* ranges from the Ohio River to the eastern states, except for the Santee and Savannah Rivers of South Carolina and Georgia, respectively, where it is replaced by *C. a. michauxi. C. a. pullum* ranges throughout the Mississippi basin from southern Minnesota and North Dakota southward to New Mexico, Oklahoma, and Arkansas, through central (but not northern) Texas southward into northern Mexico (Page and Burr 1991). The identity of populations in the Mobile basin and in the Tennessee River drainage of Tennessee are being investigated by Et-

Largescale stoneroller, *Campostoma oligolepis,* Duck R., Tenn. RB

nier and Boschung, building on clarification of the genus by Burr (C. Gilbert, pers. comm.).

*C. anomalum* is found in clear, rocky upland streams with strong flow, but also in lower gradient streams. It grazes on diatoms (golden algae), green and blue-green algae, and microbe-coated plant detritus (Fowler and Taber 1985). The central stoneroller also takes earthworms on hook-and-line. It matures at age one and may live to age six.

It nests from mid–March to May, adjacent to deep water (where it retreats if threatened). Males are social pit builders (many pits occur together) and steal pits of others; they do not hold permanent territories (Pflieger 1975). Females ready to spawn enter a pit and are rushed by males in a frenzy (Jenkins and Burkhead 1994). The adhesive 2.7 mm eggs are abandoned in the gravel. The newly hatched yolk-sac larvae are 6 mm long and unable to feed until more than 8 mm (Buynak and Mohr 1980a).

*Campostoma oligolepis,*
largescale stoneroller

*C. oligolepis* is darker and less orange on the flank than *C. anomalum;* it also lacks a distinct black mark on the anal fin and the dorsal fin is white at the base. It can be separated from all but the bluescale stoneroller by its 43–47 lateral scales and 36 or fewer scales around the body just in front of the dorsal fin. There are 20 tubercles on the head and none between the nostrils (Pflieger 1975; Etnier and Starnes 1993).

Three populations occur in the Mississippi basin, but subspecies are not recognized. The northern group is sympatric (occurs together) with *C. anomalum* in Wisconsin, Illinois, Minnesota, and Iowa. An Ozark population also occurs with *C. anomalum* in Missouri, Arkansas, and Oklahoma. The southeastern group in Kentucky, Tennessee, Alabama and northern Georgia is allopatric (nonoverlapping in distribution); its range is adjacent to but does not overlap with *C. pauciradii,* the bluefin stoneroller.

The largescale stoneroller usually occurs in higher quality waters and larger rivers than the central stoneroller. Reservoir construction and other habitat alterations may soon extirpate this species from the Arkansas River, its only stream in Oklahoma (Burr, Cashner, and Pflieger 1979).

It is not recommended for aquaria because of its requirement for diatoms, but *Spirulina*-based foods may make captivity feasible. Fry reared in ponds reached 4½ inches in one year (Pflieger 1975).

| | |
|---|---|
| *Campostoma ornatum,* Mexican stoneroller | *C. ornatum* has intense black banding in the dorsal and anal fins, a diffuse wide dark slash behind the gill cover, and a black-spotted body. Its breeding tubercles are not as extensive as in *C. anomalum*. It has 58 or more lateral scales, the most in the genus. It grows to 6 inches.

The Mexican stoneroller occurs in the desert Southwest, mostly in the central highlands of Mexico, but extends into Brewster and Presidio Counties of south Texas and near the town of Douglas in Arizona.

Adults inhabit pools during most of the year, and runs during spawning season; juveniles occupy riffles and runs year-round (Rinne and Minckley 1991).

It is rare and of special concern in the United States, but common in Mexico. |
| *Campostoma pauciradii,* bluefin stoneroller | *C. pauciradii* is very attractive. The nuptial male is bright blue-green in the dorsal, anal, and pelvic fins, whereas other stonerollers have orange fins. The bluefin stoneroller has 11–17 gill rakers on the first arch, while *C. anomalum* and *C. oligolepis* have 19 or more (Burr and Cashner 1983; Etnier and Starnes 1993).

The bluefin stoneroller occurs in Georgia and Alabama, in streams of the Chattahoochee River bordering the two states, and extends into the Altamaha, Tennessee, and Apalachicola basins. Its range is east of *C. oligolepis* in higher elevations; their ranges apparently do not overlap (Page and Burr 1991). Seek it in small streams at intermediate elevations. |
| Egg Clusterers | The adhesive, demersal eggs are clustered in a single layer on the undersurface of a cave roof and guarded by the territorial male. *Pimephales* is closely related to *Codoma* and *Opsopoeodus*. |
| **Genus *Pimephales*** | *Pimephales* contains four species of fathead minnows characterized by tightly crowded scales on the back in front of the dorsal fin smaller than the scales on the remainder of the body.

The nuptial male has a vertical black and white pattern that provides excellent shadow and light camouflage in caves. Nuptial tubercles (enlarged, modified sensory scales) on the snout and chin are used to excite the female and a modification of the nape scales forms a cushionlike pad (giving rise to the term *fathead*) with which to brush eggs in his care. The male defends his nest vigorously.

More than one species may occur in the same stream, apparently based on different feeding habits in nature (resource partitioning) that are not maintained in captivity. All four species can hybridize in captivity, but seldom do in nature. |
| *Pimephales promelas,* fathead minnow | *P. promelas* (**plate 25**) is deep bodied, broad in the chest, and slim behind the anal fin. The nuptial male has a black dorsal fin, a black expanded head with a broad white area immediately behind and a broad pale area on the midside, a cushionlike pad on the nape, and breeding tubercles on the snout.

The fathead minnow is widely distributed east of the Rocky Mountains throughout the United States and Canada, its range extended by commercial bait fish sales.

*P. promelas* occurs in clear to turbid water of lakes, rivers, and streams. It is omnivorous.

During spring, nuptial males establish territories under structures in shallows, vigorously defend them, and emit chemical sex attractants (pheromones) that the |

females use to locate males; the substance is probably a prostaglandin or a steroid glucuronoid, the most common pheromones in fishes (Cole and Smith 1992).

The male displays in figure eights as the female nears. The female turns on her side with the male closely apposed, and both bend into an S-shape. A single egg is emitted during clasping, which adheres to the cave roof after the female swats it there with her tail (Page and Ceas 1989). Several females may spawn in one nest. The male scrubs the eggs with his snout and nape, protecting them from infection, and defends them from predation.

Seine wild fish, or purchase bait fish (tuffys) from bait-and-tackle shops or the domestic orange strain (ruby reds) from pet stores, where they are sold as feeder fish. Ruby reds also develop black heads and a black dorsal fin. Fathead minnows are among the most widely used of all laboratory fishes, the adults (Schultz et al. 1978) and fry recommended by the Environmental Protection Agency (EPA) for aquatic toxicity bioassays to test the quality of effluents from wastewater treatment plants.

A bare 10-gallon aquarium with an outside floss filter and inside sponge filter is suitable for one male and four females. The EPA recommends 6-inch-long halves of 4-inch-diameter PVC pipe as spawning caves, but flat rocks (slate) work fine in the wild and in aquaria. At least 16 hours of light are needed. Flake food is adequate, but spawning is more likely on a diet of frozen bloodworms and brine shrimp, live daphnia, *Artemia* nauplii, and blackworms.

Most spawning occurs in the morning. Examine the cave daily; eggs can hatch in three days. Eggs removed with fingers are incubated in a 1-gallon jar with aeration. If large numbers are found, remove the plastic or rock cave and incubate the entire cluster under aeration. Fry are easily raised on *Artemia* nauplii and powdered flake food.

| | |
|---|---|
| *Pimephales notatus,* bluntnose minnow | *P. notatus* (plate 26) is slimmer than the fathead minnow, and its body is as high as it is wide (square in cross section). A black line along the middle of the flank ends in a basicaudal spot. The fins are short and rounded, the dorsal with a black blotch in front. The nuptial male has more than 12 tubercles on the snout.<br><br>The bluntnose minnow ranges from southern Saskatchewan and Manitoba eastward to Quebec and southward to Louisiana. It occurs from the Mississippi basin to the western slopes of the Appalachians.<br><br>*P. notatus* is found in small rocky creeks and rivers that flow into lakes. It is present in clear water over various bottoms, but not among plants. It is omnivorous, feeding on detritus, plants, aquatic insects, fish eggs, worms, and small crustaceans. It probably consumes more vegetation than other members of the genus (based on the black peritoneum and long intestine). It is a prolific egg clusterer, with 40 to 400 eggs per spawning, and a nest sometimes containing up to 5,000 eggs (Rohde et al. 1994). |
| *Pimephales tenellus,* slim minnow | *P. tenellus* is similar in shape to *P. notatus*. The nuptial male has 12 tubercles in three rows, his unpaired fins often are tinged orange, and his pectoral fins become black with a white leading edge (Pflieger 1975).<br><br>The slim minnow generally occurs in the Ozarks of Missouri, Arkansas, Oklahoma, and Kansas. Disjunct populations, however, have been given subspecies status based on whether the upper lip is terminal (*P. t. tenellus,* the common west- |

Bullhead minnow, *Pimephales vigilax*, Brazos R., Tex. RJG

ern form found in the Spring River of southwestern Missouri and adjacent states) or inferior (*P. t. parviceps,* the rare eastern form found only in the Black, St. Francis, and Castor Rivers of eastern Missouri). *P. tenellus* was originally placed in the genus *Ceratichthys,* a name no longer in use (Lee et al. 1980; Eschmeyer 1990).

*P. tenellus* is found in mostly clear but warm water of quiet or moving streams and small rivers, over sand, gravel, or rock bottoms.

---

**Pimephales vigilax,**
bullhead minnow

*P. vigilax* resembles *P. notatus,* but the nuptial male has fewer than ten tubercles in two rows on the snout. The pectoral fin of the nuptial male is mostly white, with a black leading edge (Pflieger 1975).

The bullhead minnow occurs in the Mississippi and Ohio drainages northward to Minnesota and Wisconsin, and along the Gulf Coast westward to Texas. It ranges eastward to Mobile Bay and northward to Pennsylvania.

*P. vigilax* is found in sluggish backwaters and slow-moving runs of medium-sized streams with rocky bottoms, in clear to slightly turbid water where it feeds on everything from detritus and diatoms to insects, clams, plants, and worms. It may be more carnivorous than other members of the genus, based on the silvery peritoneum and relatively short intestine.

---

**Genus Opsopoeodus**

*Opsopoeodus* was recently derived from *Notropis* to describe a single species that breeds in a manner similar to *Pimephales.*

---

**Opsopoeodus emiliae,**
pugnose minnow

*O. emiliae* is dusky olive above and white below, with a black horizontal line along the flank. It consists of two subspecies. The nuptial male of the northern subspecies *(O. e. emiliae)* becomes dark silver-blue with white tips on the anal and pelvic fins. The dorsal fin becomes dark with a broad white vertical band through the center, and the first three rays develop white knobs at the tips (Page and Johnston 1990a). *O. e. emiliae* ranges from Minnesota and Wisconsin westward to Michigan and Ontario, and southward to the Gulf Coast. It continues along the Gulf Coast from the Nueces River of Texas to the Edisto River of South Carolina on the Atlantic slope.

*O. e. peninsularis* is restricted to peninsular Florida on both coasts from the St. Johns River southward to Lake Okeechobee. The nuptial male of this southern form *(O. e. peninsularis)* becomes straw colored, tinged with pink (McLane 1955).

Intergrades occur from the Tallahassee to rivers north of the St. Johns and south of the Edisto (Lee et al. 1980).

The pugnose minnow is common in clear, sluggish rivers and large lakes over sand bottoms. It occurs in the St. Johns River in association with *Vallisneria, Naias, Potamogeton,* and *Panicum,* and is found on sandy shoals by the thousands with *Menidia beryllina.* It feeds on chironomids and other aquatic insect larvae, filamentous algae, copepods, cladocerans, water mites, and some fish eggs.

The peninsular subspecies breeds from March through September, and the northern form during June (McLane 1955). The male displays in front of its cave territory by flaring the fins and gill covers to drive the female inside. The female enters and the pair aligns laterally, invert, and instantly (one second) deposit 1 to 5 eggs until 30 to 120 are spawned. Several females may spawn in one nest.

The best yields are accrued by moving the egg-laden structure to a separate aquarium with aeration. Eggs hatch in three to six days, and fry require rotifers, ciliates, small copepods, ostracods, vinegar eels, or microworms, later graduating to *Artemia* nauplii, and *Ceriodaphnia.* Growth is rapid, and maturity is reached in one year.

| | |
|---|---|
| **Genus Codoma** | *Codoma* was recently separated from *Notropis* to describe a small group of Mexican species with eggs that adhere beneath rocks. |

| | |
|---|---|
| *Codoma ornata,* ornate minnow | *C. ornata* has a broken black line along the flank. The nuptial male has tubercles on a swollen nape, his body is blue-black on silver, and his fins are black with white edges (Rinne and Minckley 1991). Adults average 2 inches in length. |

The ornate minnow is widespread in several Mexico basins, and may be a complex of species.

*C. ornata* is an egg clusterer (Johnston and Page 1992). The defending male is strongly territorial and seldom leaves the nest. Mayden (1989) considered *C. ornata* a member of *Cyprinella,* but that genus is characterized by crevice spawning and differs in morphology.

The ornate minnow is desirable trading material from Mexican aquarists; specimens can be obtained by trading eggs through the mail. It is probably as easy to spawn as the fathead and bullhead minnows.

| | |
|---|---|
| Crevice Spawners | North American crevice spawners are *Cyprinella* and, presumably, *Hesperoleucas.* Crevice spawners seek tight locations into which they insert eggs, the crevices affording protection from siltation and predation. Crevice spawning is more advanced than broadcasting but less than nesting. Crevice spawners neither construct nor defend nests, using whatever cracks are available. |

| | |
|---|---|
| **Genus Cyprinella** | *Cyprinella* contains 24 U.S. and 9 Mexican species (with some overlap) recently removed from *Notropis.* All have silvery flank scales that are higher than wide and a dark mark on the chin. Barbels on the chin occur in three species, apparently an adaptation to bottom foraging; this character sometimes is used to place them in *Hybopsis.* Mayden's (1989) "Phylogenetic Studies of North American Minnows, with Emphasis on the Genus *Cypinella*" is recommended for students of the genus. |

The nuptial male has breeding tubercles on the snout and top of the head, white tips on the unpaired fins, and rich suffusions of red, orange, yellow, blue, or green on the body (and sometimes the fins); males produce sounds during nuptial activity.

*Cyprinella* are found over pebbles and rocks in runs, riffles, pools, and sometimes lakes. They spawn several times during the warm months (fractional spawning) rather than all at once.

Keep *Cyprinella* species in pairs or groups in 10-gallon or larger aquaria. Maintain on flakes, but condition for spawning with live blackworms and frozen adult brine shrimp. In aquaria they spawn year-round on spawning mops, over marbles on a bare bottom, or in the cracks among piled stones. The pleated filter cartridge used in some commercial canister filters is an excellent substratum (Goldstein 1997a).

Adhesive eggs are deposited inside crevices. Adults should be removed if the fish spawn on stacked rocks or among plants. If mops are used, pick the yellow to colorless eggs with your fingers for incubation in shallow dishes with a drop of acriflavine. If a filter cartridge is used, move it to a 1-gallon jar with strong aeration and acriflavine. The elongate, glasslike fry hatch in three to four days at 68°F.

The majority of species have small fry that require rotifers, protozoa, green water (motile algae), or infusoria for two to three weeks; offer *Artemia* nauplii or vinegar eels after one week. A few species have large fry that can take *Artemia* nauplii at once. Growth is slow even on live baby brine shrimp, but accelerates after reaching 1 inch when they start feeding heavily on live daphnia. They will take powdered flake food at ½ inch, but whole flakes should be deferred until they are 1 inch long.

## *Cyprinella lutrensis,* red shiner

*C. lutrensis* (**plate 27**) is the only member of the genus widespread in both the aquarium hobby and bait fish production. The nuptial male is iridescent sky blue and is bright orange on the head, cheek, lower body, and middle flank. A bright blue slash appears behind his gill cover, the dorsal fin is clear to metallic blue, and the other fins are yellow to bright orange, depending on locality. The maximum length is about 3 inches.

The red shiner occurs in the Mississippi basin from Minnesota, South Dakota, and Illinois southward to Louisiana and Texas. It also occurs west of the Mississippi in other Gulf Coast drainages throughout Texas and southward into Mexico. *C. l. blairi,* the Maravillas red shiner from the Big Bend region of Texas, is believed extinct (Hubbs et al. 1991).

*C. lutrensis* is a popular aquarium fish in Europe. It became popular in the United States under the commercial name, African fire barb. It has been widely introduced as a bait fish into rivers of the middle Atlantic Coast states and waters of the western states. In low elevation streams of the Colorado River system in Arizona and New Mexico, it has been implicated as having caused the decline and incipient extinction of *Meda fulgida,* the spikedace (Douglas et al. 1994).

The red shiner inhabits runs and pools of creeks and small rivers over sand, rock, and gravel. It spawns in rock and log crevices, at the bases of plants, and among algal masses. This plasticity in spawning site acceptance, the catholic feeding habits, and great tolerance of water conditions (turbid to clear, fast or slow, warm to cold), account in part for its wide distribution.

*C. lutrensis* was one of the first fish to recover following a massive kill in the Pecos River of Texas caused by the toxic golden alga, *Prymnesium parvum.* It comprised 75 percent of all fishes in the river one year after the kill (Rhodes and Hubbs 1992). Adaptability and competitiveness make it a threat to other native fishes. It is

Beautiful shiner, *Cyprinella formosa*, Mimbres R., N.Mex. WFR

propagated by bait dealers and distributed throughout the United States where releases have reduced or obliterated native minnows that were unable to compete.

The red shiner has been spawned in aquaria in clumps of Java moss (Lambinon 1994), among stones resting on a saucer to provide crevices (Hellwig 1994), in sunken spawning mops, and in the pleats of canister filter cartridges. A 10-gallon aquarium is sufficient for five or six fish. Provide good aeration and filtration, clean cool water, and privacy. Feed flakes sparingly to provide a small vegetable component, but the diet should be predominantly frozen bloodworms and brine shrimp, live daphnia, tubificids, and blackworms or whiteworms.

*C. lutrensis* is spawned readily with canister filter cartridges. The eggs hatch in one week and the fry congregate on the bottom. After hatching, pour the fry into a 2- to 5-gallon aquarium with good aeration. The fry should be provided green water, rotifers, infusoria, ciliates, vinegar eels, *Spirulina* powder, a commercially prepared suspension, or APR (artificial plankton rotifer) dry food scattered on the surface. After two weeks, feed *Artemia* nauplii.

*C. formosa* and *C. bocagrande* of the Guzman Basin in northern Mexico represent an evolutionary line related to *C. lutrensis.*

Another line related to *C. lutrensis* includes *C. lepida, C. rutila, C. xanthicara, C. panarcys, C. garmani,* and *C. proserpina,* several of them Mexican (Mayden and Hillis 1990), and thus not included in this book.

These species comprise the *lepida* group: *C. rutila* occurs in the Rio San Juan of Mexico; *C. proserpina* is in the Rio Pecos of northeastern Coahuila; *C. xanthicara* is from the Cutra Cienegas basin; *C. panarcys* is in the Rio Conchos; and an unnamed form occurs in the Rio Salado. These rivers are all in different subbasins of the Rio Grande.

*Cyprinella formosa,* beautiful shiner

*C. formosa* is similar to *C. lutrensis,* but has an orange or yellow back, a silver flank, and an orange tail and lower fins. It grows to 3 inches.

The beautiful shiner occurs in San Bernardino Creek of New Mexico and Arizona, and ranges into Mexico. It is found in sand and rock pools, and sometimes in slower portions of streams.

It is listed as a threatened species in the United States, and not available to aquarists.

**Cyprinella lepida,**
Edward's Plateau shiner

*C. lepida* looks much like *C. lutrensis.* The nuptial male has a yellow and purple iridescence on the flank and orange to yellow fins. It grows to 3 inches. Two species currently share this name. Both are found in spring-fed creeks in clear water over gravel.

The true Edward's Plateau shiner occurs in the Frio and Sabinal Rivers (Nueces River basin; Gulf Coast drainage just north of the Rio Grande) on the Edward's Plateau of Texas. A second species from the Neuces River, previously believed to be *C. lepida,* has been detected by DNA analyses and is undescribed. Both species are disappearing due to habitat loss, attributable to groundwater removal for agriculture (Richardson and Gold 1995).

**Cyprinella alvarezdelvillari,**
Rio Nazas shiner

*C. alvarezdelvillari,* although Mexican, is included because of the excellent information available from Contreras-Balderas and Lozano (1994) that is presented below. The female is a drab, dark green above and light below. During the breeding season the nuptial male is covered in tubercles and is bright orange-bronze on the body and fins, brighter below; his breast is black at the peak of spawning, and his lower fins have a wide, white border. It is a pygmy member of the *lepida* group (< 1½ in. long).

The Rio Nazas shiner occurs in headwaters of the Rio Nazas in Durango, Mexico close to the source, but generally is parapatric with *C. garmani,* which occupies the same river but is farther downstream.

*C. alvarezdelvillari* inhabits a headwater creek with a gravel and boulder bottom fed by hot thermal springs; it is sympatric with *Cyprinodon nazas* and the introduced *Oreochromis mossambicus* where the water is warmer than 84°F. It does not occur where the water cools to below 77°F and the stream is occupied by *Codoma ornata, Gila conspersa,* and *Astyanax.*

Provide a 5-gallon aquarium at 80°F, good current from a powerhead or outside power filter, and a diet rich in bloodworms, daphnia, and *Artemia.*

**Cyprinella pyrrhomelas,**
fieryblack shiner

*C. pyrrhomelas* (**plate 28**) has a black-edged, light orange caudal fin in both sexes, a dark basicaudal spot, and a faint, oblique dusky bar behind the head. The nuptial male has a blue hue, a reddish mouth, and a bright orange-and-white caudal fin edged in black. Adults average 4 inches.

The spectacular fieryblack shiner occurs above the fall line in the Yadkin–Pee Dee and Santee River drainages of North and South Carolina.

*C. pyrrhomelas* inhabits rocky runs in clear, cool, foothill streams, behind (downcurrent) or among large rocks. When alarmed, the groups of five to ten individuals flee to faster open water.

A 40-gallon, long aquarium is recommended for six fish, but after spawning begins they will continue in smaller quarters. Provide a bare aquarium that is strongly aerated and well filtered, with no structures except one or two pleated canister filter cartridges. Feed heavily on frozen adult *Artemia,* supplemented with other meats and some flake food.

Spawning begins after two weeks, with bursts of activity separated by days of inactivity. Eggs are deposited within the pleats of the filter cartridges. Periodically, remove an egg-laden cartridge and place it in a widemouthed gallon jar with clean aquarium water and vigorous aeration.

The fry, large for *Cyprinella,* hatch in ten days and rise into the water column

Tricolor shiner, *Cyprinella trichroistia*, Conasauga R., Tenn. RB    Tallapoosa shiner, *Cyprinella gibbsi*, Haralson Co., Ga. RB

at once. Feed APR or vinegar eels for one or two days in the gallon jar, then pour the contents and cartridge into a 10-gallon or larger aquarium with a sponge filter and begin feeding *Artemia* nauplii.

| | |
|---|---|
| *Cyprinella trichroistia,* tricolor shiner | *C. trichroistia* has a diffuse horizontal band ending in a basicaudal spot and a black spot on the rear of the dorsal fin. The breeding male has orange and white fins, a blue flank, and one row of tubercles on the lower jaw. The tricolor shiner is 3 inches average adult size.<br><br>The tricolor shiner occurs in the Alabama River drainage of the Coosa and Tallapoosa River systems in Alabama, in sand and gravel runs of cool streams. |
| *Cyprinella gibbsi,* Tallapoosa shiner | *C. gibbsi* resembles *C. trichroistia,* but has a longer, more protruding snout overhanging a subterminal mouth, and two rows of tubercles on the lower jaw. Adults average 3 inches.<br><br>The Tallapoosa shiner occurs in the Tallapoosa and Alabama Rivers of Alabama and Georgia.<br><br>*C. gibbsi* inhabits gravel and rocky runs in moving water. It is solitary or found in small schools, and occasionally in groups of five to ten in slow moving pools. |
| *Cyprinella leedsi,* bannerfin shiner | *C. leedsi* has a small black blotch on the front of the dorsal fin and a blue–black stripe along the flank. The dorsal fin of the nuptial male is enlarged and black (Page and Burr 1991; Rohde et al. 1994). The bannerfin shiner grows to 4 inches.<br><br>*C. leedsi* occurs in Atlantic rivers from the Edisto in South Carolina to the Altamaha in Georgia, and in the Suwannee and Ochlockonee drainages of Georgia and western Florida (Page and Burr 1991; Rohde et al. 1994).<br><br>It inhabits sandy and moderately vegetated runs of medium- to large-sized rivers. |
| *Cyprinella analostana,* satinfin shiner | The nuptial male of *C. analostana* has a white slash behind the gill cover, a cluster of tiny dusky marks at the rear of the enlarged dorsal fin, and white-edged fins. His tail is suffused with yellow, and his other fins are also sometimes yellow. The average adult length is 3 inches.<br><br>The satinfin shiner occurs in the Atlantic slope from Lake Ontario drainages southward, just entering South Carolina between U.S. 1 and U.S. 621 (Rohde et al. 1994). |

Satinfin shiner, *Cyprinella analostana,* Potomac R., Fairfax Co., Va. RB    Greenfin shiner, *Cyprinella chloristia,* Santee R., S.C. WFR

*C. analostana* is found in gravel runs and riffles of creeks and rivers, and sometimes in lakes. Schools of six to ten fish forage in current close to the bottom on small insects and crustaceans. The satinfin shiner matures in one year and lives to age four. It breeds mostly during June and July at 65 to 85°F (Jenkins and Burkhead 1994).

| | |
|---|---|
| *Cyprinella chloristia,* greenfin shiner | *C. chloristia* is similar to *C. analostana* and *C. whipplei,* but has eight anal fin rays rather than nine and a more prominent stripe on the flank. Adults average 3 inches.<br><br>The greenfin shiner occurs above the fall line in the Santee River drainage of the Carolinas and hybridizes with *C. analostana* in part of the Pee Dee drainage.<br><br>*C. chloristia* is found in deeper rock, sand, or gravel pools in slow water adjacent to swift flows. When disturbed, the group may flee to the faster water. |
| *Cyprinella nivea,* whitefin shiner | *C. nivea* has a rounded snout and eight anal fin rays. A dark blue-black stripe along the flank becomes darker to the rear, and a dark stripe is present on the back. The rear half of the dorsal fin has black blotches. The nuptial male is large with white fins (Page and Burr 1991). Adult *C. nivea* grow to 5 inches.<br><br>The whitefin shiner occurs in the Atlantic slope from the Neuse River in North Carolina to the Savannah River in Georgia.<br><br>*C. nivea* is found in deep riffles in moving, clear water of moderately sized rivers. It is a prolific spawner on canister filter cartridges. The fry are small, requiring APR dry food, rotifers, or infusoria as a first food, but grow rapidly and some can take *Artemia* nauplii after two weeks. Faster growing fry will starve out or eat their siblings. |
| *Cyprinella spiloptera,* spotfin shiner | *C. spiloptera* has blue iridescence on the back and flank, and a diffuse horizontal band that terminates in a large basicaudal spot. It has eight anal fin rays and grows to 4 inches, on average. The nuptial male is steel blue with a dusky stripe to the rear; his dorsal fin is black, and lower fins are yellow and edged in white (Page and Burr 1991).<br><br>The spotfin shiner occurs in Canada north to Hudson Bay and in Atlantic drainages from the St. Lawrence of Quebec to the Potomac of Virginia. It is present in the Great Lakes (except Lake Superior) and the Mississippi basin from On- |

Spotfin shiner, *Cyprinella spiloptera,* Arkansas R., Mo. WFR　　　Steelcolor shiner, *Cyprinella whipplei,* Little Red R., Ark. WFR

tario to New York. It ranges to southeastern North Dakota, southward to Alabama and westward to Oklahoma (Lee et al. 1980; Page and Burr 1991).

*C. spiloptera* inhabits medium-sized creeks to rivers, where it schools over sand, gravel, or rocky bars in groups of 10 to 20.

It was bred in captivity at 70 to 75°F (Snyder et al. 1977); the method was not described. The eggs were 1.2 to 1.5 mm in diameter, and the fry hatched in five to seven days and were 4 mm long; they did not feed until 50 percent larger when the jaws became functional.

---

*Cyprinella whipplei,*
steelcolor shiner

*C. whipplei* is similar to *C. spiloptera.* It is steel blue to purple above, with purple to blue cheeks and opercula. It has a dark, middorsal stripe and scales edged in black. Nine anal fin rays are present. It grows to an average of 3 inches. The nuptial male is blue above with a red snout, yellow fins, and an enlarged dorsal fin (Page and Burr 1991; Rohde et al. 1994).

The steelcolor shiner occurs in the Mississippi basin from Ohio and West Virginia to Illinois and Missouri. It ranges eastward to Oklahoma and southward to western North Carolina, central Alabama, and Louisiana. It is also present in the Mobile Bay drainage of the Black Warrior River system of Alabama (Page and Burr 1991). It is similar in appearance to *C. camura,* possibly sympatric with it only at the northern border of Oklahoma and Arkansas; the two are otherwise geographically separated.

*C. whipplei* inhabits quiet rock, sand, and gravel pools of medium to large rivers.

---

*Cyprinella camura,* bluntface shiner

*C. camura* has a blunt snout and small eyes. A dark line along the back and dark-edged scales on the flank create an appearance of crosshatching. The caudal fin is cream colored at the base (in large specimens, a creamy bar; indistinct in juveniles) and then becomes dusky; the pectorals are dusky on the upper margins. The nuptial male has orange, pink, or red fins and snout (Page and Burr 1991). Adult *C. camura* grow to an average of 4 inches.

The bluntface shiner occurs in the Mississippi and Tennessee River drainages of Kentucky, Tennessee, Mississippi, and Louisiana, in the Arkansas River drainages of Missouri and Kansas, and in the Neosho River drainages of Missouri and Oklahoma.

Bluntface shiner, *Cyprinella camura,* Spring Cr., Hatchie R., Hardemon Co., Tenn. RB

Blacktail shiner, *Cyprinella venusta,* Conasauga R., Tenn. WFR

*C. camura* is found in headwaters of lowland rivers in swift current over sand bottoms (Etnier and Starnes 1993).

| | |
|---|---|
| *Cyprinella galactura,* whitetail shiner | *C. galactura* (**plate 29**) has two large, clear to white outer areas on the base of the caudal fin, diffuse black blotches on the rear of the dorsal fin, and nine anal fin rays. The nuptial male is mostly blue-black above, the fins suffused with yellow or orange and edged in white. Adult *C. galactura* are about 3 inches.<br><br>The whitetail shiner occurs in the Cumberland and Tennessee River drainages and was introduced into the upper New River from Virginia through Kentucky and Tennessee. It ranges southward to Georgia, Alabama, and Mississippi on the western slopes of the Appalachians and is present in the Savannah and Santee Rivers of the Atlantic slope. West of the Mississippi, it inhabits the St. Francis and White Rivers of Missouri and Arkansas (Page and Burr 1991; Etnier and Starnes 1993).<br><br>*C. galactura* is found in deep, swift, rocky runs and pools of upland creeks and rivers. It feeds on surface and midwater insects; large adults are sometimes caught using artificial flies (Etnier and Starnes 1993). |
| *Cyprinella venusta,* blacktail shiner(s) | *C. venusta,* the blacktail shiner, appears to be a complex of several closely related but yet unrecognized species with lightly spotted scales and a large basicaudal spot. The nuptial male typically has orange to yellow fins, and individuals generally attain 3 inches.<br><br>*C. venusta* occurs in Gulf drainages from the Suwannee of Georgia and Florida to the Rio Grande of Texas. The subspecies are: *C. v. venusta* in Mississippi and other Gulf Coast drainages to the west; *C. v. cercostigma* in several Gulf drainages (excluding Mobile Bay) east of the Mississippi; *C. v. eurystoma* in the Apalachicola, Ochlockonee, and Suwannee drainages of northern Florida and southern Georgia; *C. v. stigmatura* in the upper Alabama and Tombigbee Rivers of Alabama; and an undescribed species in streams currently thought to hold only *C. v. cercostigma.* See Page and Burr (1991) for morphological differences. DNA analyses indicate that many of these subspecies, and perhaps other populations, may warrant full species status (Kristmundsdottir and Gold 1996).<br><br>Blacktail shiners are found in sand, rock, or gravel runs of moderately sized, swift streams, usually in the swiftest areas. A school typically has four or five individuals; solitary individuals are common. |

Alabama shiner, *Cyprinella callistia*, Conasauga R., Tenn. RB

| | |
|---|---|
| *Cyprinella caerulea,* blue shiner | *C. caerulea* (**plate 30**) has a dark band from the snout to the base of the tail. It grows to 3 inches. The nuptial male is dark blue from the head to the tail fin, and darker and more intense to the rear; it has yellow to orange fins, occasionally with white edging. |

*C. caerulea* (**plate 30**) has a dark band from the snout to the base of the tail. It grows to 3 inches. The nuptial male is dark blue from the head to the tail fin, and darker and more intense to the rear; it has yellow to orange fins, occasionally with white edging.

The blue shiner is known from the Coosa and Cahaba River drainages of Alabama and Georgia and in the Conasauga River of Tennessee. It may have been extirpated in the Cahaba.

*C. caerulea* inhabits the rocky runs and gravel bars of medium to large streams. It is uncommon, but persists in schools of ten or more well above the bottom.

This federally threatened species may not be collected or possessed. It is a good candidate for captive breeding to enhance populations.

**Cyprinella proserpina, proserpine shiner**

*C. proserpina* has a black stripe on the chin and throat and grows up to 3 inches. The nuptial male is blue with orange fins edged in yellow or white.

The proserpine shiner occurs in the Devils and lower Pecos Rivers and in their confluences with the Rio Grande in Texas, and in the Rio San Carlos, another tributary of the Rio Grande in Coahuila, Mexico.

*C. proserpina* is common in rock or gravel runs in clear streams. It spawns over shallow rock bottoms.

**Cyprinella callistia, Alabama shiner**

*C. callistia* has a blunt snout, large eyes, and usually a large, black basicaudal spot. It grows to 3 inches. The dorsal fin of the nuptial male is dusky, the tail fin is suffused with pink to red, and the body is dark silver above.

The Alabama shiner occurs in the Mobile Bay drainage of the Alabama River system.

*C. callistia* inhabits clear, boulder-strewn runs in habitats ranging from small creeks to rivers, mostly at the fringes of vegetated areas near swift currents. It is a bottom feeder on aquatic insect larvae and mites. It breeds at least from May through early November (Etnier and Starnes 1993).

**Cyprinella xaenura, Altamaha shiner**

*C. xaenura* has a dark stripe along the back and a silver-black stripe on the rear of the flank. It grows to 3 inches. The nuptial male has a blue flank and white fins and sometimes a yellow or orange caudal fin.

The Altamaha shiner occurs in the upper Altamaha drainage of Georgia (Page and Burr 1991) in sand and gravel pools.

Thicklip chub, *Cyprinella labrosa*, Pee Dee R., N.C. WFR

| | |
|---|---|
| *Cyprinella callisema,* Ocmulgee shiner | *C. callisema* has a blue stripe (darker toward the rear) from the head to the caudal fin and grows to 3 inches. The nuptial male has orange to yellow dorsal and caudal fins, with white edging on all lower fins.<br><br>The Ocmulgee shiner occurs in the Altamaha and Ogeechee River drainages of Georgia in sandy and rocky runs of clear streams. It schools close to the bottom in groups of five to ten. |
| *Cyprinella callitaenia,* bluestripe shiner | *C. callitaenia* is similar to *C. callisema,* but is distinguished by its crescent-shaped line of black specks from the eye to the mouth and by its pharyngeal tooth arrangement in preserved specimens (Page and Burr 1991). It grows to 3 inches.<br><br>The bluestripe shiner occurs in the Apalachicola River drainages of Georgia, Alabama, and Florida in sandy runs (in the open) near submersed vegetation.<br><br>Three *Cyprinella* species have barbels. |
| *Cyprinella labrosa,* thicklip chub | *C. labrosa* is colorless with an arched back, underslung (inferior) mouth, long barbels at the angle of the jaws, a black line through the flank, and brown blotching on the side.<br><br>The thicklip chub occurs in the Pee Dee and Santee Rivers of North and South Carolina in sand, gravel, rock and boulder runs and riffles in high gradient streams. It feeds on aquatic mites and insects (Jenkins and Burkhead 1994).<br><br>*C. labrosa* was previously included in *Hybopsis.* It has not been confirmed as a crevice spawner. |
| *Cyprinella monacha,* spotfin chub | *C. monacha* **(plate 31)** has small barbels at the corners of the mouth. The snout is long, and the eyes are pointed slightly upward. A dark stripe along the silver flank expands into a large black caudal spot. It grows to 4 inches. The nuptial male has two large white bars on a blue flank and white edges on blue fins.<br><br>Historically, the spotfin chub was collected in the Tennessee River drainage from Virginia southward through Alabama. Recently, however, its presence has been confirmed only in the Little Tennessee River of North Carolina, the Duck and Emory Rivers of Tennessee, and the North Fork Holston River of Virginia and Tennessee (Page and Burr 1991).<br><br>*C. monacha* is found around rocks and in clear streams. |

Santee chub, *Cyprinella zanema*, Black R., N.C. FCR

It is being propagated for reintroduction in Tennessee by Conservation Fisheries, Inc. of Knoxville under contract to the Tennessee Wildlife Resources Agency. Groups are spawned in 100-gallon aquariums with water pumps to provide current and stacked rocks to provide crevices (Shute et al. 1993).

The spotfin chub is a federally threatened species and is not available for collection.

---

**Cyprinella zanema, Santee chub**

*C. zanema* resembles *C. labrosa* in its long snout, underslung mouth, moderately sized barbels, and absence of color, but it lacks the small brown blotches on the flank. The nuptial male has yellow fins and black streaks in the dorsal fin (Rohde et al. 1994).

The Santee chub occurs in the Pee Dee and Santee drainages of the Carolinas, in mountain and foothill streams. Disjunct populations in the Coastal Plain in both states may be an undescribed species (Rohde et al. 1994).

*C. zanema* inhabits small creeks to medium-sized rivers of high gradient, over rock, sand, and gravel. It was previously in *Hybopsis*.

It is protected in North Carolina, and not common anywhere.

---

**Genus *Hesperoleucas***

The monotypic *Hesperoleucas* was previously combined with the similar and geographically overlapping genus *Lavinia*. It is a member of a western evolutionary line that gave rise to the successful genus *Gila*. *Hesperoleucas* is believed to be the only western crevice spawner, but the mode of spawning has not yet been confirmed. Crevice spawning in this primitive line of minnows would be unrelated to its development in *Cyprinella*, a separate evolutionary line of minnows.

---

**Hesperoleucas symmetricus, California roach**

*H. symmetricus* is a chunky *Gila*-like minnow with small scales and an underslung mouth. It is steel blue to dusky gray above, and silvery on the sides and belly. Both sexes develop orange-red blotches on the chin, gill cover, and base of the anal fin. The male develops tubercles on the head. The California roach is often less than 2 inches, but some populations average 4 inches.

The California roach is native to the Sacramento–San Joaquin drainage basin and was presumably introduced into the Cuyama River in San Luis Obispo and Santa Barbara Counties.

*H. symmetricus* has been divided by some into subspecies: *H. s. subditus* in streams emptying into Monterey Bay; *H. s. venustus* in the Russian River and streams in San Francisco Bay; *H. s. parvipinnis* in the Gualala River of Sonoma County; *H. s. mitrulus* from tributaries of the Pit River and Goose Lake in Modoc County (also in Lake County, Oregon); and *H. s. symmetricus* everywhere else (Moyle 1976).

It is found in small tributaries, sometimes in warm alkaline streams, in streams polluted by sewage, and often is abundant in hot coastal streams if the salinity does not exceed 10 percent sea water or 3 parts per thousand (it is killed by 30 percent sea water or 10 ppt). It tolerates up to 100°F and crowded conditions in which dissolved oxygen concentrations fall to 1 or 2 ppm. It is mostly omnivorous, eating filamentous algae and detritus during the winter and feeding heavily on crustaceans and aquatic insect larvae during the summer; it even eats baby lampreys. It spawns from March through June in flowing, shallow, rock-bottom areas, laying adhesive eggs in rock crevices or even among plants (Moyle 1976; Marshall 1992). It is being considered for federal protection.

## Gravel-Mound Builders

This group of nesters includes *Exoglossum* and *Nocomis*. Thick lips and highly modified, distinctly lobed lower jaws with bony plates identify the two members of the small minnow genus *Exoglossum*. At first glance, the modified jaws suggest the extreme lip development found in some suckers.

*Exoglossum* are mound builders, although their mounds are less complicated than those of *Nocomis* (Johnston and Page 1992). The dark colored male uses his unusual mouthparts to build a mound of pebbles near a bank or sunken log in an area of slow but perceptible current. The pebbles are 2.5–6.0 mm, some stolen from other minnow mounds, and the finished nest might even be topped with snail shells. Mounds are as large as 12 to 18 inches wide, 3 to 6 inches high, and flat on top. The male does not dig a pit or furrow in the mound.

Spawning occurs on the side of the mound facing into the current, the male and female clasping close to the gravel, and the 2 mm yellow eggs drifting back into the mound where they are covered by the male with more gravel to a depth up to 3 inches (Scott and Crossman 1973; Maurakis et al. 1991b; Jenkins and Burkhead 1994). Newly spawned eggs are nonadhesive and sink into interstices among the pebbles. Older eggs become adhesive and form clumps. The young hatch from the gravel in a few days and remain with the mound a few more days before dispersing.

## *Exoglossum maxillingua,* cutlips minnow

*E. maxillingua* is a thick, stout minnow with fine scales and an inferior and complex mouth with the upper part of the lower jaw divided into three lobes; the outer lobes have a large gap in between, a central lobe resembling a tongue above and between these two lobes, and the entire three-lobed structure rests atop enlargements similar to turkey wattles on each side of the throat. No distinct lip is apparent. The inside of the lower jaw is divided into bony plates. The cutlips minnow is olive on top, gray on the flank, and white below. The fins are dusky with a basicaudal spot in the young. It is large, averaging 4 inches or more.

The cutlips minnow occurs in the St. Lawrence River drainage to Lake Ontario and the Saint-Francois River of Lac St. Pierre in Quebec. It also occurs from the Lake Champlain drainage of Ontario to the Roanoke River of Virginia along the Atlantic slope of the Appalachians (Scott and Crossman 1973).

*E. maxillingua* is found in medium-sized, clear, slow-moving streams free of silt

Cutlips minnow, *Exoglossum maxillingua*, Potomac R., Fairfax Co., Va. RB

Cutlips minnow, *Exoglossum maxillingua*, Dan R., N.C. FCR

and plants, preferring gravel runs and rock and boulder pools. It forages under and around rocks on aquatic insect larvae (e.g., chironomids and caddisflies), snails, clams, worms, mites, lamprey larvae, and fish eggs (Jenkins and Burkhead 1994), and has been reported to pluck out the eyes of fishes (Page and Burr 1991). Throughout its range, breeding takes place from May through July and lasts only a few days.

Cutlips minnows have been spawned in captivity by collecting adults during the breeding season and placing them in a 6-foot-long by 1½-foot-wide by 1½-foot-deep trough loaded with 3 inches of pea gravel, and providing a good current (Buynak and Mohr 1980a). A half-filled, 125-gallon aquarium with 3 inches or more of pea gravel or pebbles is suitable to induce nesting. Use a trickle filter or canister filter to maintain good water quality and at least one 1,000-gph powerhead for current. The parents should be removed after spawning and the filter turned off. After the eggs hatch, the young can be reared in the same aquarium.

## *Exoglossum laurae,* tonguetied minnow

*E. laurae* has two lobes but no distinct lip on the lower jaw and bony plates inside; outside, a tiny barbel is usually present at each corner of the jaw; the upper lip is thick. Otherwise, the tonguetied minnow is similar to *E. maxillingua,* but lacks the central lobe in the lower jaw.

The tonguetied minnow is widespread but disjunct in the Ohio River basin. It occurs in the upper Allegheny and Genessee drainages of New York and Pennsylvania, the Great and Little Miami Rivers of Ohio, and the New River drainage of North Carolina (Jenkins and Burkhead 1994).

*E. laurae* inhabits clear, cool, moderately flowing rocky creeks and small rivers with abundant riffles and pools, usually where *Nocomis* does not occur.

## Genus *Nocomis*

The river chubs of *Nocomis* contain seven species of large, big-headed minnows with dark-edged scales on the back and upper flank and prominent breeding tubercles on the head of the nuptial male. Most have olive to bronze bodies and reddish fins. They all have a barbel at the angle of the jaws, eight dorsal fin rays, seven anal fin rays, and a dorsal fin origin slightly ahead of the pelvic fin origin.

Because the taxonomy is based in part on the head tubercles of nuptial males, juveniles can be difficult to identify and ichthyologists typically inspect the pharyngeal (throat) teeth. In *Nocomis,* a cluster of four throat teeth on each side of the

Redspot chub, *Nocomis asper,* Spring R., Mo. WFR

gullet may have an extra tooth to the outside of each cluster *(biguttatus, asper)* or not *(effusus, micropogon, raneyi, leptocephalus).* The number of myomeres (muscle blocks) in larvae matches the number in adults, enabling identification of species from plankton collections (Maurakis, Woolcott, Radice, and McGuire 1992).

The larger territorial males construct a pit in gravel or sand, and fill it with carefully selected pebbles or gravel to create a mound. A spawning pit or trough (or more than one) is then constructed atop the mound. After the spawning clasp and release of eggs into this high pit, the eggs are covered with a mound of gravel, and the mound is fanned.

This mound-building behavior is unique among minnows (Johnston and Page 1992), and ecologically important because many other kinds of parasitic or cuckoo-like minnows use *Nocomis* nests as their adopted spawning sites, a few species having no nest-making behavior of their own.

*Nocomis* is the only minnow genus in which the male builds a complex nest (a constructed platform upon a constructed depression with constructed rims), defends the nest by swimming head to tail with competing males in a continuous circle about the nest, and uses the anal fin to fan the eggs in the pit or trough (Maurakis, Woolcott, and Sabaj 1991a).

## *Nocomis asper,* redspot chub

*N. asper* is olive above, brassy on the flank, and white below. It has a large red spot behind the eye in both sexes, and yellow to pink fins. The barbel is difficult to see. The juvenile has reddish fins and a black stripe along the entire flank that ends in a dark basicaudal spot. The average length is 6 inches, but it gets much larger. The red coloration of the fins and belly is intensified in the nuptial male; the breeding tubercles on the head extend well back onto the nape and forward part of the flank (three per scale).

The redspot chub is common in the Elk and Spring River systems in the Ozark uplands of the Arkansas River drainage in Missouri, Arkansas, Kansas, and Oklahoma. Disjunct populations also are found in the Illinois River and in the South Fork and Little Missouri Rivers of the Ouachita River system.

*N. asper* is found in clear, rock and gravel bottom, small- to medium-sized, moderately to swiftly flowing spring-fed streams. It feeds on insects, crustaceans, and some algae, mostly in midwater and at the surface.

The redspot chub spawns during May and June at 70°F. The male constructs a spawning mound of pebbles or stones 6–12 inches high and up to 1 yard wide. The mound is also used as a spawning site by other minnows, including the southern redbelly dace, duskystripe shiner, and the Ozark minnow (Pflieger 1975; Robison and Buchanan 1988).

Provide at least a 55-gallon aquarium for one male and one or two females. The bottom should be covered in 2 to 3 inches of large pea gravel mixed with river stones. Then top with closely spaced, large flat rocks, leaving a clearing of 1 foot where the male can construct a pit (and subsequent mound). Use canister or trickle filtration, and supplement the current with one or two submersed powerheads. Feed heavily on frozen brine shrimp and bloodworms supplemented with chopped earthworms.

---

**Nocomis biguttatus, hornyhead chub**

N. *biguttatus* is similar to N. *asper,* but the tubercles are restricted to the top of the head (absent on the body) and the red spot behind the eye is not as large and bright. Locality is a better guide to these two similar species, as their ranges do not overlap.

The hornyhead chub occurs in the Great Lakes and Mississippi drainages from New York through the Ohio basin, ranging southward to Arkansas and the Ozark uplands, northward to the Dakotas, and westward into Wyoming and Colorado. In Canada, its distribution is restricted to Ontario and Manitoba streams of the Great Lakes drainages (Lee et al. 1980). Even in the Ozarks, it occupies different streams than N. *asper.*

N. *biguttatus* inhabits clear, slow-moving gravel streams and small rivers, usually in tributaries, where it occurs in mixed schools with other minnows. Its catholic eating habits include filamentous algae, higher plants, cladocerans, chironomids, caddisflies, snails, worms, crayfish, and small fishes, with the diet consisting of about half plants and half animals.

It spawns from April through June when temperatures reach 65°F. The male builds a nest of stones and pebbles in shallow water, often below a riffle, and the mound eventually may reach upward until the nest is ½–1½ feet below the surface. Stones, sometimes as large as the male's head, are carried in the jaws or pushed with the powerful blunt snout. The height of the nest is determined by the number of spawnings. Early spawnings occur while the nest is relatively flat. Later spawnings result in layers of eggs placed on the ever higher mound. Many other minnow species swarm over and spawn on the chub nest, and darters and sunfish may snatch eggs of the various spawners.

The hornyhead chub matures at age two or three, and lives up to four years with males getting larger than females (Scott and Crossman 1973; Pflieger 1975; Robison and Buchanan 1988).

---

**Nocomis effusus, redtail chub**

N. *effusus* is similar to N. *biguttatus,* but the red spot behind its eye is not as prominent. The spot is developed only in the adult male, and the head is not as large. The fins are a brighter red-orange, especially in the black-lined juveniles. The nuptial male's tubercles extend from the head onto the nape and upper flank, but only one or two tubercles per scale rather than three as in N. *asper* (Etnier and Starnes 1993). The redtail chub is allopatric with the other two closely related species.

It is restricted to the Highland Rim of the Mississippi basin in Tennessee and Kentucky. It occurs in the Duck River of the Tennessee drainage, in the Cumber-

Redtail chub, *Nocomis effusus,* Cumberland R., Dickson Co., Tenn. RB     Bluehead chub, *Nocomis leptocephalus,* James R., Mo. WFR

land drainage below the falls, and in the Barren and Green Rivers of the Green River drainage (Lee et al. 1980).

N. *effusus* is found in clear, moderate gradient, small- to medium-sized, usually first- and second-order streams with rock and gravel bottoms, usually in pools and runs.

*Nocomis leptocephalus,*
bluehead chub

N. *leptocephalus* is brassy and has no red spot behind the eye. It is olive above with an orange, yellow or gold stripe on the back. The flanks are brassy and the belly white. The fins are typically light orange to pink, sometimes with a white edge and sometimes with blue rays (Jenkins and Burkhead 1994). The nuptial male becomes sky blue, the head a darker blue, and a prominent hump develops atop the head (larger in the largest males). Two forms occur in different locations (not related to the number of breeding tubercles on the head or to the three subspecies): those with and those without a bold orange stripe on the front of the blue flank.

The bluehead chub ranges in Atlantic slope rivers from the Shenandoah and Potomac Rivers of Virginia to the Altamaha River of Georgia. Gulf slope rivers include the Apalachicola, Mobile, Pascagoula, and Pearl River drainages westward to Alabama. It also occurs in the New and Tennessee drainages of the Ohio system and in other lower Mississippi tributaries in Mississippi and Louisiana (Lee et al. 1980).

The subspecies (*N. l. interocularis, N. l. bellicus, N. l. leptocephalus*) are identified by the number of breeding tubercles and each group's distribution; however, subspecies are not consistent with the presence or absence of the orange banded versus the all-blue color types.

N. *l. bellicus* was previously considered a full species. It is abundant in headwater streams at pools, runs, and riffles with gravel, rock, and bedrock and less common in larger streams and over finer substrata. It is omnivorous, feeding on plants, insects, and especially algae. It matures in the second or third year, spawning once or twice, and lives three years. It builds gravel mound nests during May and June when temperatures reach 65 to 70°F.

Breeding occurs over midslope of the nest where water currents are slow to moderate (Maurakis, Woolcott, and Sabaj 1992), during both day and night (Maurakis and Woolcott 1996). Unique among *Nocomis,* up to five males may occupy and build one nest. The nests of the bluehead chub are used by cuckoo-spawning minnows (as many as 13 species in Virginia) as breeding sites. Some minnows, such as *Notropis lutipinnis*, will not spawn unless chub nests guarded by nuptial males are present; they reject artificial or abandoned nests (Johnston 1991; Wallin 1992).

The bluehead chub will hybridize with *N. platyrhynchus, N. micropogon, Campostoma anomalum, Clinostomus funduloides, Luxilus albeolus, L. cerasinus, L. coccogenis, L. cornutus,* and *Phoxinus oreas* (Jenkins and Burkhead 1994).

---

*Nocomis micropogon,* river chub

*N. micropogon* (**plate 32**) is similar to *N. biguttatus,* but has a distinct basicaudal spot; the adult lacks a red spot behind the eye and the juvenile does not have a red tail (P. W. Smith 1979). The nuptial male has a swollen head and abundant tubercles, but the head is olive, not blue as illustrated in Page and Burr (1991). Overall, it is olive above, brassy on the flank, and white below; the fins are yellow-olive, sometimes with orange toward the outside, and edged in white. The nuptial male is rosy below, with a fading lateral band shimmering dusky to green.

The river chub occurs in the Great Lakes, Ohio River, and Atlantic slope drainages from New York to Indiana and southward to Virginia on the Atlantic coast and to northern Alabama and Georgia on the Gulf slope (Lee et al. 1980). It is present in Canada (Scott and Crossman 1973) in the Lake Ontario drainage from the Humber River westward, and in tributaries of Lake Erie (Grand River, Catfish Creek), Lake St. Clair (Thames River, Medway Creek), and southern Lake Huron (Ausable, Maitland, and Saugeen Rivers).

*N. micropogon* inhabits clear, large tributaries and main stem rivers with moderate to high gradient and gravel and rock bottoms, in pools, runs, and riffles. It feeds on drifting aquatic insects, worms, crustaceans, mites, snails, and small fishes. It matures when it reaches 5 inches at three years of age, sometimes earlier.

The river chub spawns in pools and runs during April and May at 65°F, during the day or night (Maurakis and Woolcott 1996). When ready to spawn, the male digs a trough at the top of the mound, tossing stones to either side. The female enters, and the male sidles up; they clasp, break apart, and the male proceeds to bury the eggs with stones and eventually build a new trough over the covered area (the mound growing with increased spawning).

One biologist calculated the pit plus mound could consist of 7,050 stones in a volume of 17½ gallons. River chub eggs are 2.6 mm in diameter, and the newly hatched fry are 6 mm long (but do not feed until they are 9 to 10 mm long). River chub larvae can be diagnosed from mixed assemblages of minnow fry (but not reliably) by evaluating both the number of muscle segments and pigment patterns at various sizes (Buynak and Mohr 1980a).

*N. micropogon* hybridizes with *Campostoma anomalum, Clinostomus funduloides, Luxilus chrysocephalus,* and *L. cornutus,* frequent nest associates (Jenkins and Burkhead 1994). In fact, the original species name was based on the description of a hybrid, which should invalidate the name *N. micropogon,* but no new name has been proposed to the international agency charged with resolving these taxonomic issues (C. Gilbert, pers. comm.).

---

*Nocomis platyrhynchus,* bigmouth chub

*N. platyrhynchus* is often regarded to be only a subspecies of *N. micropogon,* but recent authors have elevated it to full species rank. It differs from *N. micropogon* in the number of scales around the body (which resembles *N. raneyi*), the head tubercles extending past the eyes (but only up to the front of the eyes in *N. micropogon*), and primarily in its geographic range.

The bigmouth chub is restricted to the New River drainage of Virginia, West Virginia, and North Carolina. It occurs in runs and riffles, often over bedrock, in the main stem of the river and pools of its tributaries.

*N. platyrhynchus* hybridizes with nest associates *Campostoma anomalum, Luxilus albeolus, L. chrysocephalus, Nocomis leptocephalus,* and *Rhinichthys cataractae.* Spawning occurs during May at 68°F (Jenkins and Burkhead 1994).

---

**Nocomis raneyi, bull chub**

*N. raneyi* resembles both *N. platyrhynchus* and *N. micropogon,* but is deeper-bodied, and has a smaller mouth, a larger tail, and a shorter head and snout. Otherwise, the nuptial male is rosy below with white-edged fins. It is the largest of the *Nocomis* chubs, with the males averaging 10 inches but attaining 1 foot in length (Jenkins and Burkhead 1994).

The bull chub occurs in the Atlantic slope streams of Virginia and North Carolina, from the James and Roanoke to the Tar, Chowan, and Neuse Rivers.

*N. raneyi* is found mostly well above the fall line over rock and gravel, and sometimes sand, but it sometimes occurs below the fall line on gravel bottoms. It feeds on bottom and drifting insects, snails, crayfish, algae, and small fishes.

The bull chub breeds during May at 70°F, building the largest nests of any *Nocomis,* up to 40 inches in diameter and 16 inches in height. It clears its spawning pit area by pulling or pushing flat stones as large as 4 inches across. It may live up to five years (Jenkins and Burkhead 1994).

---

**Pit-Ridge Builders**
**Genus *Semotilus***

*Semotilus* contains the creek chubs, which are large and husky minnows as adults and relatively nondescript (olive above, white below, with a black line along the flank) as juveniles.

*Semotilus* is unique in having a small, flaplike barbel located distinctly forward from the angle of the jaws; here it depends down into or slightly beyond the groove between the head and upper jaw. The barbel is best seen when the mouth is held open and the groove of the upper jaw is inspected under a magnifier. The barbel of *Semotilus* differs from that of *Hybopsis* and *Nocomis,* in which it is located at or behind the angle of the jaws.

In addition to barbel differences, the dorsal fin origin of *Semotilus* is slightly to the rear of the pelvic fin origin rather than above it. The anal fin usually has eight rays (seven in *Nocomis* and *Campostoma*), and adult males can be large (up to 1 ft. long) and decorative with brassy coloration and well-developed nuptial tubercles on the snout. Of the four species, two are widespread and two have limited ranges.

Among American minnows that construct nests, only *Semotilus* are pit-ridge builders (Johnston and Page 1992). The dominant male excavates a small pit in the gravel and places the stones or large pebbles on the upstream edge (creating a rim to start).

Spawning can be a complex U-clasp as in *Betta splendens,* or a rapid and simple near-clasp, but in either case, the eggs fall into the pit. The male then takes pebbles from just downstream of the pit (which creates another pit) to cover the spawned eggs (which creates a small hill). As the male continues to spawn, taking stones from downstream and placing them in the newly created pits, a continuous ridge of stones is formed over the previous spawning sites, sometimes extending several feet. Other species of minnows, both nest builders and nest parasites, often spawn in the pits of *Semotilus* species.

Creek chub, *Semotilus atromaculatus,* Rock Castle R., Ky. RB

Larvae of some of these closely related nesting minnows can be distinguished to the species level by their myomere counts under the microscope (Maurakis, Woolcott, Radice, and McGuire 1992). For details on the spawning behavior of *Semotilus* see Maurakis and Woolcott (1992a), Maurakis, Woolcott, and Magee (1990), and Maurakis, Woolcott, and McGuire (1995).

*Semotilus atromaculatus,* creek chub

*S. atromaculatus* has a large mouth reaching back beyond the front rim of the eye; the dorsal fin origin is over the pelvic fin origin or slightly behind, and there are eight dorsal fin rays. The juvenile has a black spot at the base of the dorsal fin and a basicaudal spot at the end of a black flank line. The nuptial male has a dorsal fin spot and loses the flank line; the body is greenish above and brassy (sometimes with an orange tint) below; the fins are orange-pink; three or more prominent hooked tubercles occur in a single row from in front of the nostrils to just behind the upper rim of the eye; other smaller tubercles are on the top edges of fins and on the head and body. Nuptial males may grow to 1 foot long.

The creek chub occurs from Prince Edward Island to Manitoba (and some locations as far north as Hudson Bay), southward to the fall line along the Atlantic seaboard and then all the way to the Gulf Coast. It continues westward in many drainages to Texas, with an isolated population in New Mexico. It ranges into most of the tributaries on both sides of the Mississippi River. Its range is bordered on the west by Montana and on the southwest by Kansas. It is not found in the Atlantic Coastal Plain, most of Georgia, or in Florida outside the panhandle (Lee et al. 1980).

*S. atromaculatus* inhabits upland or hill streams, brooks, and creeks, usually in small, clear to turbid, gravel-bottom, headwater streams of moderate flow without vegetation. In northern areas, it also occurs along the shores of small lakes. It is a catholic feeder on insects (e.g., mayflies, midges, caddisflies, beetles), crayfish and other crustaceans, snails, clams, worms, small fishes, plant materials, diatoms, and sometimes frogs.

The creek chub spawns in April or later when temperatures reach 55°F; spawning occurs in current, day and night. Spawning after dark prevents the female from observing the intense spawning colors of the male, and it is likely that touch, sound, or olfactory senses are more important stimuli for the female (Maurakis, Woolcott, and McGuire 1995).

A single dominant male begins nest construction. The female backs into the nest tail first from upstream. The male clasps the female, whose head is pointing upward, in a rapid, *Betta*-like clasp (which takes only a fraction of a second) and 50 eggs are released. Upon release from the clasp, the female is tossed violently to the side or upward. The female drifts belly-up momentarily (again, very *Betta*-like), as the male covers the nest with pebbles from downstream of the pit.

The male thus extends the trench or pit for new spawning, creating an elongate ridge over the old trench as the spawning season progresses during the next two to three weeks. The fry hatch in several days, work their way up through the pebbles to the surface, and initially pursue plankton. The life span can be six to eight years, but is usually three to four. Larger females produce larger eggs (Scott and Crossman 1973; Robison and Buchanan 1988; Maurakis, Woolcott, and Magee 1990; Etnier and Starnes 1993; Jenkins and Burkhead 1994).

Spawning in captivity requires not less than a long 40-gallon aquarium with powerheads for current and a pea gravel bottom. At the beginning of the breeding season, collect two nuptial males and two to four females. Feed heavily on blackworms, adult brine shrimp, flake food, and crushed snails. Eggs are covered by the male and the nest is sometimes abandoned. Remove the adults after spawning. Fry hatch in four to six days. Only the smallest live foods should be offered. Growth is fast and sexual maturity is reached in ten months.

---

*Semotilus corporalis,* fallfish

Juveniles of *S. corporalis* are similar to *S. atromaculatus,* but the dorsal fin spot is indistinct. The adult is the largest minnow in eastern North America (≤ 18 in.). Coloration is olive to dusky above, silvery with a purple sheen on the flank, and white below, with no dark line on the flank and no colors on the fins. The scales of adults are darkly pigmented in front, creating the illusion of being inserted backwards.

In Canada, the fallfish ranges from New Brunswick through Quebec and Ontario to Hudson Bay. It also occurs in Great Lakes drainages and southward along the Appalachian highlands to Virginia.

*S. corporalis* is found in clear, gently flowing, cool, gravel, sand, or rubble streams and rivers, usually in pools or wide runs with little current. It occasionally is present in lakes. It avoids temperatures above the high 70s (°F) and feeds on terrestrial and aquatic insects, crayfish, fish (including smelt and other forage fish), algae, and detritus.

The fallfish begins nest construction during April or May when temperatures reach 50°F. The nest may be built in one day, is often in line with or perpendicular to the flow in gravel runs; it also may be in pools or on the shores of lakes, and is the largest of all minnow nests (≤ 6 ft. diam. with a ridge 3 ft. high).

The male is highly territorial, aggressively chasing or displaying to competitors over a great distance. The female backs downcurrent onto the nest for spawning. There is no clasp, only a brief side-to-side contact without quivering. After one or more spawning acts, the eggs are buried under stones or pebbles by the male.

Eggs hatch in two days and fry swim away (when 12 mm) two days later. The fallfish attains 1½ inches the first year, and matures at 7 inches when age two or three; it lives up to nine years (Scott and Crossman 1973; Jenkins and Burkhead 1994). Ross and Reed (1978) described what they interpreted as communal nesting in fallfish, but ten hours of videotaping by Maurakis and Woolcott (1992a) never verified such behavior.

Sandhills chub, *Semotilus lumbee,* Drowning Cr., N.C. FCR

## Semotilus lumbee, sandhills chub

*S. lumbee* is similar to *S. atromaculatus,* but has nine rays in the dorsal fin rather than eight, and no dark mark in the dorsal fin. The nuptial male is olive above, with a rosy orange side becoming bright orange near the head, and has pink-orange pectoral fins. This is a small chub, not known to exceed 8 inches; males mature at 6 inches, females at a lesser length.

The sandhills chub occurs in the Sandhills of North and South Carolina, from the Cape Fear to the Wateree Rivers, and encompassing the Lumber, Little Pee Dee, Pee Dee, and Lynches Rivers (Rohde and Arndt 1991).

*S. lumbee* is found in clear, cool, medium-current streams with sand or gravel on the bottom and little or no vegetation. It prefers narrow (5 to 10 ft. wide), shallow (< 1 ft. deep), headwater creeks with slightly acidic to neutral pH (5.0–7.2), and clear or slightly stained water. It frequently occurs with other species, especially *Aphredoderus sayanus* and *Notropis cummingsae* (Rohde and Arndt 1991). The nest of the sandhills chub is longer than that of *S. atromaculatus,* and is constructed by a dominant male in first- or second-order streams, in pools midstream or nearshore with a nearby hiding place such as an undercut bank.

Spawning begins when the temperature reaches 57°F. The female presses her vent and caudal peduncle against the bottom at the pit-ridge interface. The male wraps his pectoral under the female breast and his caudal peduncle over her back. The female is momentarily pinned to the bottom, head up and tail down, at which time the eggs are expelled. The male will spawn with multiple females over time. Small females tend to be thrown to the surface, while larger ones are thrown to the side (Woolcott and Maurakis 1988; Maurakis et al. 1990). There are no nest associates (nest parasites) in waters occupied by *S. lumbee.*

This is a federally protected species, and not available to aquarists.

## Semotilus thoreauianus, dixie chub

*S. thoreauianus* has eight dorsal fin rays; the dorsal fin origin is well behind that of the pelvic fin. The fins of the nuptial male are yellow; the belly is pink or orange; a prominent stripe along the flank is wide and dark, but not sharply outlined. The smallest of the chubs, it does not exceed 6 inches (Page and Burr 1991).

The Dixie chub occurs above and below the fall line from the Ochlockonee River drainage of Georgia and Florida westward to the Tombigbee or the Pearl River drainage of Alabama and Mississippi. Any chub in nuptial coloration at a size well under 6 inches is likely to be this species; *S. atromaculatus,* with which it overlaps in central Alabama and northwestern Georgia, matures at a much larger size. *S. thoreauianus* inhabits creeks and small rivers in sand and gravel pools.

Pit-ridge nests are constructed in first- or second-order streams, in pools nearshore or midstream, with a nearby place to hide (e.g., an undercut bank). Spawning begins when the temperature reaches 63°F, and the behavior is identical to that of *S. lumbee*. Pit-ridge construction is the same as for *S. atromaculatus,* but fine sand usually forms the downstream rim of the pit (Woolcott and Maurakis 1988; Maurakis, Woolcott, and Magee 1990; Maurakis et al. 1993).

# II    The Order Siluriformes

THE order Siluriformes consists of 31 families of fishes worldwide, encompassing 400 genera and more than 2,200 species, with 1,300 in the Americas (Burgess 1989). In the United States, native catfish families are the freshwater Ictaluridae (39 species) and the coastal Ariidae (3 species); the latter are mouthbrooders with huge eggs, but not covered in this book as they are too large for aquaria.

## Family Ictaluridae, the Bullhead Catfishes

*Ameiurus* (plate 33), *Ictalurus,* and *Pylodictis* species are mostly regulated game fish species too large for aquaria. Baby *Ameiurus* species are often captured in seines, and attractive with their black coloration and great activity. They grow fast, fade to gray-brown before even 2 inches long, and eat other tank inhabitants at night; they should not be taken.

### Genus *Noturus*

Most of the known species of *Noturus* (madtoms) are small enough for aquaria, but 18 are federally or state protected due to depletion associated with habitat degradation. Many are more sensitive to water quality than even the darters.

The adipose fin continues into the caudal fin and may resemble a keel, sometimes set apart by a notch or a lobe. The caudal fin is square or rounded, never forked.

Madtoms range from the St. Lawrence River and Hudson Bay to Florida and Texas. Sexes are similar, but nuptial males have enlarged heads. All madtoms can inflict pain when their spines puncture human skin, but the toxin (from the skin around the spine rather than from glands below it) is not lethal.

Most madtoms are shallow sand-, gravel-, or rock-bottom stream fishes, active at night, and often under flat rocks or, in sandy streams, among branches and debris or even within discarded aluminum drink cans. Most prefer riffles or quiet backwaters of clear, high gradient streams, but a few occur in low gradient waters. During the late spring or early summer, males develop vastly enlarged and flattened heads. Spawning occurs under a large flat rock, the territory, eggs, and fry defended by the male.

Madtoms are best collected by seine on riffles, by examining sunken cans, and by kicking over rocks and woody debris anywhere with the seine butted up against the disrupted material. Madtoms that bury in gravel when disturbed have been collected by shoveling small rocks and gravel onto the bank. Madtoms are also taken in baited minnow traps at night.

Most madtoms require clean, cool water with current provided by a power-

Black bullhead, *Ameiurus melas,* Mississippi R. RB

Blue catfish, *Ictalurus furcatus,* Tennessee Aquarium. RB

Yellow bullhead, *Ictalurus natalis,* White R., Mo. WFR

Channel catfish, *Ictalurus punctatus,* Mississippi R. RB

Flathead catfish, *Pylodictis olivaris,* Tennessee Aquarium. RB

head and good filtration, a sand or gravel bottom, and large, flat rocks. Those from low gradient streams do better without a powerhead-driven current. Madtoms should be fed bloodworms supplemented infrequently with raw fish, shrimp, and crawfish (from a supermarket) cut into fragments. They do not thrive on tubificid worms or earthworms, which they engorge and have difficulty digesting.

To attempt breeding madtoms, place four to six fish in a 20- to 40-gallon long aquarium with a pebble and stone layer over gravel, and a large, flat rock for spawning. Use a 14- to 16-hour photoperiod, vigorous aeration and filtration, and a current provided by powerheads for most of the species. Feed mostly frozen blood-worms and brine shrimp, supplemented with some live blackworms, small earth-worms, and freeze-dried plankton after soaking.

Watch for one fish to develop a flattened and enlarged head and another to swell around the abdomen. Keep them in the aquarium and remove the other fishes. The male will usually guard the eggs, but for better survival move the egg clump to a separate aquarium with strong aeration and sufficient acriflavine to tint the water light green; maintain the eggs in darkness until hatching. Start the young on crushed pellets and *Artemia* nauplii in a strongly aerated and sponge-filtered aquarium, and change water daily.

To date, madtoms have rarely been reported to spawn in captivity, although attempts have commonly yielded females swelling with roe and males developing enlarged heads associated with nesting. Stimulants such as massive water changes, a sudden drop and then rise in temperature, and ad libidum feedings with insect larvae (chironomids or "bloodworms") followed by withholding of food, may provide stimuli necessary to trigger spawning.

Taylor (1969) defined three subgenera: *Noturus, Schilbeodes,* and *Rabida.*

---

**Subgenus *Noturus (Noturus)***
*Noturus (Noturus) flavus,* **stonecat**

*N. (Noturus) flavus* is the only member of its subgenus. It is unmottled and tan with a white margin on the upper edge of the caudal fin and light marks immediately before and behind the dorsal fin. In the Cumberland River population, the predorsal light mark is a pair of narrow white bands rather than the large light blotch found elsewhere. The stonecat is the largest madtom at 12 inches maximum size.

It is the most widely distributed madtom, ranging from Quebec and New York westward through the Great Lakes states and northward into Manitoba. It continues southward into Mississippi drainages to Missouri, Illinois, and Tennessee (occasionally into Arkansas and northern Alabama), and northwestward into Colorado, Wyoming, Montana, and Alberta.

*N. (Noturus) flavus* inhabits hard bottoms of rivers and fast-flowing, riverine sections of large lakes (segments with sufficiently strong flow to support, for example, greenside, fantail, and rainbow darters). It matures at three or four years and 4 or 5 inches. The eggs are 2.6–4.0 mm in diameter and number 100–300. Adults eat insects and crayfish (Walsh and Burr 1984b).

The largest individuals have been collected from western Lake Erie where their unusual size was thought to be associated with an abundant food base of mayfly larvae (typically associated with an oxygen-rich, nutrient-poor, high gradient stream environment). Changes in the ecosystem of western Lake Erie in recent decades may have altered the mayfly population and perhaps the maximum size of madtoms (C. Gilbert, pers. comm.).

A fishing license is required to collect stonecats in some states. It can be collected by hook-and-line, especially at dusk. It is among the least desirable madtoms due to large size and lack of coloration.

---

**Subgenus *Noturus (Schilbeodes)***

*N. (Schilbeodes)* contains species that are generally dull or dark, without blotches or saddles, and have straight pectoral spines without serrations on the leading edge; they are further defined by the shape of the patch of teeth on the roof of the mouth.

Margined madtom, *Noturus insignis,* Roanoke R., Va. WFR    Slender madtom, *Noturus exilis,* Kansas R., Kans. GS

---

*Noturus (Schilbeodes) insignis,*
margined madtom

*N. (S.) insignis* has dark margins on the dorsal, anal, and caudal fins, an overhanging snout, and no light blotches surrounding the dorsal fin. A narrow bridge of pigment on the belly in front of the pelvic fins may be absent in larger specimens.

The margined madtom occurs in the Atlantic slope above the fall line from New York to Georgia, and was introduced into the Lake Ontario drainage, the upper Tennessee River system, and tributaries of the Ohio River in Maryland, Pennsylvania, and West Virginia (Taylor 1969).

*N. (S.) insignis* inhabits high gradient streams with rocky bottoms. Its associates include *N. leptacanthus, N. gilberti,* and *N. furiosus* (Taylor 1969).

---

*Noturus (Schilbeodes) exilis,*
slender madtom

*N. (S.) exilis* has a long slender body, a low keeled adipose fin without a flap, and distinctive dark edging on the dorsal, anal, and tail fins. Slender madtoms are unmarked, with a hint of yellow blotching on the back just before and behind the dorsal fin; these light marks, and the equal upper and lower jaws, distinguish it from the margined madtom, *N. (S.) insignis.* It attains 4 inches.

The slender madtom occurs on both sides of the Mississippi drainage. In the west, it is most abundant in the Ozark Plateau of Missouri and Arkansas and adjacent states, but also extends in isolated areas in states far to the north. In the east, it occurs on uplands in Georgia, Tennessee, and Kentucky.

*N. (S.) exilis* inhabits spring-fed streams with strong flow over gravel and rock bottoms (Pflieger 1975; Mayden and Burr 1981). Adults prefer pools except during the breeding season when they move to riffles. The slender madtom feeds on insect larvae, snails, and crustaceans. They mature at 3 inches and two years of age.

The slender madtom spawns from May through July when the water warms to the high 70s and low 80s (°F). Nests are excavated under flat rocks and guarded by the male. The 25–125 eggs in the nest (Burr and Mayden 1984) hatch in eight to nine days at 77°F. The slender madtom matures in two years and lives to four (Robison and Buchanan 1988).

Although normally nocturnal, *N. (S.) exilis* adapts well to captivity, feeding during the day on any meaty foods, sunken pellets, worms, and even flake foods at the surface. The female swells with eggs and the male develops a greatly enlarged head during late spring or early summer; however, spawning has not been reported by aquarists and is cryptic if it occurs at all in captivity. Check under flat rocks at least weekly for the large eggs.

Tadpole madtom, *Noturus gyrinus,* Paw Paw Cr., Obion Co., Tenn. RB

---

*Noturus (Schilbeodes) gyrinus,* tadpole madtom

*N. (S.) gyrinus* has a thin dark line along the flank and radiating upper and lower lines that approximate the borders of muscle segments. Otherwise, it is olive, yellow, or gray, with no spots or blotches. It is usually under 3 inches.

The tadpole madtom ranges from Ontario, Saskatchewan, Manitoba, Quebec, and New York to North Dakota, continuing southward to Florida and Texas. It is absent from uplands, except where introduced in parts of New Hampshire and Massachusetts.

A lowland, backwater species, *N. (S.) gyrinus* is found below the fall line in lakes, swamps, ponds, and river oxbows, usually with dense vegetation and a sandy mud or mud bottom. It eats insect larvae, and spawns in cavities (Taylor 1969).

The tadpole madtom does not require strong currents or a gravel bottom. Provide a bottom of sand mixed with peat moss, cavities (PVC pipe), flat rocks, vegetation, floss and activated carbon filtration, gentle aeration, and a diet of frozen bloodworms and brine shrimp, live blackworms, and freeze-dried euphausiid plankton. Tadpole madtoms from locales as distant as Canada and southern Florida probably have different temperature tolerances.

---

*Noturus (Schilbeodes) lachneri,* Ouachita madtom

*N. (S.) lachneri* is distinguished from *N. (S.) gyrinus* and *N. (S.) exilis* by characters requiring examination under a microscope.

The Ouachita madtom is restricted to the upper Saline River, a tributary of the Ouachita River of central Arkansas in sand, gravel, and rubble bottom high gradient streams, in quiet pools or backwaters. It is a rare fish that depends on pools as refuges. From these pools it is able to recolonize streams that periodically dry out, killing all the fishes (Gagen, Standage, and Stoeckal 1998). Because of its limited distribution and dependence on these pools, the Ouachita madtom's specialized refuges should be protected.

---

*Noturus (Schilbeodes) funebris,* black madtom

*N. (S.) funebris* is gunmetal blue to dark brownish black with large black spots on the lighter chin and belly that become diffuse with age. The pectoral spine is smooth along the leading edge and barely irregular (but not serrated) along the trailing edge. The black madtom attains 6 inches.

It ranges from the Lower Pearl River of Mississippi and Louisiana to Econfina Creek of Florida, and continues northward into the Alabama and Tombigbee River systems (Thomerson 1966a; Taylor 1969; Douglas 1974).

Brown madtom, *Noturus phaeus,* Terrapin Cr., Tenn. FCR

Broadtail madtom, *Noturus* sp., Lake Waccamaw, N.C. FCR

N. *(S.) funebris* inhabits permanent springs and streams, often under vegetation, in fast, clear water over gravel or coarse sand. It attains 1 inch the first year, 2 inches the second, and probably lives three to four years (Thomerson 1966a; Taylor 1969).

**Noturus (Schilbeodes) phaeus,**
**brown madtom**

N. *(S.) phaeus* is similar to the black madtom, but the rear edge of its pelvic spine is slightly serrated (Taylor 1969; Douglas 1974). The chin and belly are heavily spotted, the spots becoming diffuse to obliterated with age. The unpaired fins may be unpigmented.

The brown madtom occurs in lower Mississippi drainages of Kentucky, Tennessee, Mississippi, and Louisiana; it now is present in the Sabine River of Louisiana. Its occurrence in the Bayou Teche in Louisiana is a result of diverting the Red River.

N. *(S.) phaeus* inhabits permanent springs and small streams and creeks, frequently under vegetation in moderate to fast, clear water over small gravel and coarse sand.

**Noturus (Schilbeodes) leptacanthus,**
**speckled madtom**

N. *(S.) leptacanthus* has a slender body and is dark brown above and on the flank, white below, and richly decorated with large black or brown spots on the fins, head, and side (with finer spots below), the spotting most vivid in smaller fish. The adipose fin and tail fin sometimes have a light margin. Adults average 2½ inches (Douglas 1974).

The speckled madtom ranges from the Edisto River of South Carolina and the Suwannee and St. Johns Rivers of Florida to the Gulf Coast, and through Georgia, Alabama, Mississippi, and Louisiana (Taylor 1969; Douglas 1974).

N. *(S.) leptacanthus* inhabits swift creeks with abundant vegetation, on riffles of coarse sand, rocks, or large gravel. It often is associated with the darter, *Percina nigrofasciata.*

**Noturus (Schilbeodes) sp.,**
**broadtail madtom**

This *Noturus (S.)* sp. is similar to the speckled madtom but stubbier, with a rounded tail fin, and no dark body specks (Rohde et al. 1994). It is tan and unmarked.

The broadtail madtom occurs in Lake Waccamaw of North Carolina and the lower Cape Fear and Pee Dee drainages of North and South Carolina.

It inhabits sand-bottom pools, runs, and lakes. At 4 to 5 inches, it is probably easy to maintain, but more attractive madtoms occur in rivers to the north and west.

| | |
|---|---|
| *Noturus (Schilbeodes) gilberti,* orangefin madtom | *N. (S.) gilberti* has an unmarked belly. The dorsal fin is dusky at the base; otherwise, the unpaired fins are orange to yellow with wide, light margins. The tail fin has an especially broad white to orange border that is wider above than below. The body and flank are dark, and the belly is light and unmarked. |

The orangefin madtom occurs in headwaters of the James, Roanoke, and Mayo Rivers of Virginia (state listed as threatened) and North Carolina (state listed as endangered) beneath large stones and debris in riffles, often in association with *Percina roanoka.* It is absent from streams containing *Nocomis* spp., *Luxilus cerasinus, Clinostomus funduloides, Phoxinus oreas,* and crayfish (*Cambarus* spp.). Nests have not been found. It is believed to spawn at age two from April through June when the water temperature is 68°F, and to die after spawning (Simonson and Neves 1992).

It is a rare fish with a restricted range and state protected.

| | |
|---|---|
| *Noturus (Schilbeodes) nocturnus,* freckled madtom | *N. (S.) nocturnus* has a caudal fin darker than the other fins; the anal fin often has a dark marginal or submarginal band with a clear outer edge. The source of its common name is not apparent. |

The freckled madtom occurs from Illinois and Missouri to the Gulf Coast. It is found in the lower and central Mississippi drainage and other tributaries from Alabama to Texas to the Gulf of Mexico in the Ohio, Tennessee, Illinois, Osage, Arkansas, and Red River systems.

*N. (S.) nocturnus* inhabits streams and rivers with swift current over rock, boulder, and gravel bottoms (Taylor 1969). Females may mature at age one, males at age two. It nests on shaded riffles with reduced flow during June and in aluminum cans where available; the 3.6 to 4.5 mm eggs number 50–150 and hatch in 150 hours. Insect larvae, isopods, and small crayfish are the principal foods (Burr and Mayden 1982b).

Not demanding, it should have a diet rich in chitinous invertebrates.

| | |
|---|---|
| **Subgenus *Noturus (Rabida)*** | Members of *Noturus (Rabida)* have serrations on the leading edge of the strongly curved pectoral spine, and a color pattern of dark blotches or saddles on the back over a light background; this subgenus has the prettiest species. |

Most should have a 20-gallon aquarium as described in the introduction to the group, but the three dwarf species described next will do fine in half that space.

| | |
|---|---|
| *Noturus (Rabida) miurus,* brindled madtom | *N. (R.) miurus* is characterized by a black blotch in the adipose fin extending to the margin, a dark blotch on the outer third of the dorsal fin, and a dark, submarginal band on the rounded or lanceolate tail fin. The top and the flank have blotches; the belly and lower fins are not marked; it has no black bar across the caudal peduncle. |

The brindled madtom occurs in the Ohio River and nearby drainages of the Mississippi basin. It has invaded (with bait or game fish introductions) Great Lakes drainages, and drainages of the lower Mississippi (Taylor 1969).

*N. (R.) miurus* is found in the lower reaches of rivers and streams, in pools, lakes, backwaters, over sticks, leaves, and debris, often over a mud bottom (Taylor 1969). It is one of the few madtoms to inhabit low gradient streams.

Brindled madtom, *Noturus miurus,* Mill Cr., Ill. FCR

Carolina madtom, *Noturus furiosus,* N.C. RJG

The male matures at age two and some females by age one. The 3.5 mm eggs, numbering 65, were found in cans and under flat rocks in pools, and hatched in nine days. Insects and isopods make up the bulk of the diet (Burr and Mayden 1982c).

As with the other low gradient stream madtoms, *N. (R.) funebris, N. (R.) gyrinus,* and *N. (R.) phaseus,* they should be fed daphnia, frozen *Artemia* and blood-worms, and freeze-dried euphausiid plankton; they do best in low flow aquariums.

## *Noturus (Rabida) furiosus,* Carolina madtom

*N. (R.) furiosus* has a short, wide body, a crescent of brown pigment in the middle of the tail fin and another near the edge, an intense dark blotch in the adipose fin (not reaching the margin), a dark head, an unspotted belly, and an irregular but horizontal concentration of brown pigment along the middle of the flank that is not sharply delineated enough to be a band.

The Carolina madtom occurs in the Neuse and Tar Rivers of North Carolina (and probably the Roanoke River before the dam was constructed at Roanoke Rapids, North Carolina), at and just below the fall line.

*N. (R.) furiosus* inhabits riffles and runs in clear water, over gravel, rocks and rubble at the fall line, and on the Coastal Plain over sandy bottoms, typically hiding among mussel shells and debris during the day. Below the fall line, it nests in cans and bottles in pools and runs. Guarding males were three to four years old, and 2½ to 4 inches long. Each clutch contained 150 eggs just over 3 mm in diameter. It feeds on insect larvae (Burr et al. 1989).

Its closest relatives *(N. (R.) placidus, N. (R.) stigmosus)* occur on the other side of the Appalachians, evidence that the historic Roanoke River was once connected to the present-day Ohio River before the Appalachians reached their current elevation.

## *Noturus (Rabida) stigmosus,* northern madtom

*N. (R.) stigmosus* has two dark lines through the tail fin, a dark blotch in the adipose fin (not extending to the edge), a light spot in front of the dorsal fin, and a dark blotch in the front of the dorsal fin that extends as a saddle and band on the flank.

The northern madtom is a pretty fish of the Mississippi River tributaries of Tennessee and the Ohio River system, from the Shenango River in Pennsylvania through Ohio to the Wabash River in Indiana and the Green River in Kentucky. It also occurs in the western Lake Erie basin in the Detroit, Huron, and Maumee Rivers (Taylor 1969).

N. (R.) stigmosus inhabits small rivers and creeks in Tennessee over sand and mud, with moderate current and little cover except for branches, logs, and debris. In larger streams of the Ohio Valley and Michigan, it occurs over sand, gravel, rock, and marl, most commonly over riffles with large stones, near vegetation, in moderate to strong current (Taylor 1969).

## Noturus (Rabida) placidus, Neosho madtom

N. (R.) placidus is brown with indistinct blotches and saddles, irregular brown markings on the flank, an unmarked belly, a tail fin with two brown bands, and an adipose fin with a dark mark not extending to the edge. It lacks a notch before the tail fin and is small at much less than 3 inches average length.

The Neosho madtom occurs in the Cottonwood River, throughout the Neosho River below Emporia in Kansas, the Spring River of Kansas and extreme western Missouri, and the lower few miles of the Illinois River in Oklahoma (Taylor 1969).

N. (R.) placidus inhabits large rivers, in riffles, among and under large rocks and gravel.

To collect this fish, remove large rocks from gravel riffles, and then shovel the gravel onto the bank and look for the madtoms; alternatively, kick over rocks with a seine immediately downstream, and continue to kick up the exposed gravel to chase the fish out. A small fish from large rivers, it is intolerant of pollution.

## Noturus (Rabida) hildebrandi, least madtom

N. (R.) hildebrandi consists of two subspecies. The southern subspecies N. h. hildebrandi has prominent dorsal saddles extending all around the flank to the belly and a dark blotch extending into the adipose fin, sometimes to the margin. In N. h. lautus (the northern subspecies), the color intensity and pattern are subdued. It attains just under 2 inches.

The least madtom ranges in the southeastern branches of the Mississippi basin from northern Mississippi to western Tennessee in slow to moderate streams over sand, silt, and debris; the northern subspecies is often in turbid water.

N. (R.) hildebrandi spawns at 1 year and just over 1 inch long, but does not live more than 18 months. It feeds on insect larvae, and breeds during June and July of the second summer. Females produce 30 large (2.3 mm) eggs to a spawn. The larvae are 6.3 mm when they hatch eight days later at 77°F (Mayden and Walsh 1984).

## Noturus (Rabida) stanauli, pygmy madtom

N. (R.) stanauli is distinguished from the least madtom by its white snout and three marks at the base of the tail fin (Page and Burr 1991). It is even smaller than the least madtom at 1½ inches.

The two populations are widely separated in the lower Duck and upper Tennessee River drainages in Hancock and Humphries Counties (at opposite ends of Tennessee). The disjunct distributions of several Noturus are in part due to stream course alterations that have left surviving populations geographically far apart.

The pygmy madtom inhabits moderate to fast gravel runs of medium-sized, clear rivers.

**Noturus (Rabida) baileyi,**
smoky madtom

*N. (R.) baileyi* is brown with four yellow saddles.

The smoky madtom occurs in the Little Tennessee River drainage of Monroe and Blount Counties in Tennessee in strongly flowing clear, cool to cold streams over riffles and pools in a high gradient area (44 ft./mi. at the type locality) of Great Smoky Mountains National Park.

Do not collect madtoms in Monroe and Blount Counties of Tennessee to avoid inadvertently taking this protected fish. It is endangered due to destruction of its habitat by an impoundment of Abrams Creek in Chilhowee, Tennessee built for sportfishing.

After the fish was found in a second, unimpacted creek, John Tulloch and J. R. Shute of Conservation Fisheries, Inc. in Knoxville (under contract to the U.S. Fish and Wildlife Service) successfully reintroduced this fish back into Abrams Creek.

**Noturus (Rabida) flavater,**
checkered madtom

*N. (R.) flavater* (**plate 34**) is spectacular with a wide black bar at the base of the tail, a bold black edge in the tail fin, a bold black mark on the dorsal fin, and four bold black saddles on a yellow body, the last one extending through the center of the adipose fin to its margin. It is at the other size extreme ($\leq$ 7 in. long).

The checkered madtom occurs in the upper White River system of the Ozark Plateau in Missouri and Arkansas, but is absent from the St. Francis, Black, and Strawberry Rivers (Pflieger 1975; Robison and Buchanan 1988).

In these clear, high gradient and permanently strong-flowing rivers, *N. (R.) flavater* occurs mostly in quiet backwaters and silt-free pools having large chert and limestone rocks, boulders, and gravel.

In the summer, when the water heats to 80°F, the male guards a nest under 12- to 16-inch-wide, thick, flat rocks in pools or raceways. One nest may contain up to 300 eggs (Burr and Mayden 1984). The 3.5 mm eggs hatch in 10 to 12 days and the 10 to 13 mm larvae remain under the care of the male for some time. It matures at age three and lives five years (Robison and Buchanan 1988).

This large madtom should have no less than a 40-gallon aquarium. Most of the remaining *N. (Rabida)* are 4 to 6 inches long and do well in a 20-gallon aquarium.

**Noturus (Rabida) albater,**
Ozark madtom

*N. (R.) albater* has a large, dark adipose bar (a black blotch on the keel-like adipose fin), dark blotches above and below the base of the tail fin (basicaudal bar), and is creamy white on the upper margin of the tail fin (Taylor 1969). The body is yellow with four dark saddles or blotches on the back that extend to the flank; the belly is yellow to white.

The Ozark madtom occurs in the Ozark Plateau of Missouri and Arkansas, in the upper White and St. Francis River systems. Specimens from the Black River may be a new species, based on differences in chromosome numbers and other characters (Robison and Buchanan 1988).

*N. (R.) albater* inhabits clear streams with strong flow and rock-gravel bottoms. It prefers the swiftest water of the shallowest riffles and feeds on aquatic insect larvae. During the day it buries in coarse gravel. Maturity is attained at 2½ inches after one year.

The Ozark madtom spawns during June and July. The nonfeeding male guards a mass of 3.5 to 4.0 mm eggs numbering 40–100 in a 4- to 8-inch-deep cavern under a 1-square-foot flat rock at the head of a riffle or in a rocky pool. The fry hatch

Elegant madtom, *Noturus elegans,* Trammel Cr., Ky. FCR

in 12 days and begin feeding when the yolk sac resorbs 4 days later; eggs and fry are eaten by darters and bleeding shiners. The Ozark madtom probably lives three years (Pflieger 1975; Mayden et al. 1980; Robison and Buchanan 1988).

*Noturus (Rabida) elegans,*
elegant madtom (or saddled madtom, Chucky madtom)

*N. (R.) elegans,* the elegant madtom (or the saddled madtom or Chucky madtom), has a pink flush and four yellow saddles on a dark back, the first saddle on top of the head, and the second beginning before and extending up onto the leading edge of the dorsal fin; concentric dark bands appear on the tail fin.

Page and Burr (1991) illustrated patterns of different populations which, it now seems, may be different species. Taylor (1969) described *N. (R.) elegans* from the Duck, Green, and Barren Rivers and noted that Green and Barren River specimens were similar, but Duck River fish were more distinctly banded with less background pigmentation. Other differences were noted, but Taylor did not think the variation warranted recognition of a Duck River species.

Etnier and Jenkins (1980) noted variation between specimens taken from the upper main river channel of the Duck River and those from the lower Duck River tributaries. Other reports of conspicuous differences in isolated populations suggested that the name was being applied either to several variable, isolated populations or to several species.

Grady (1988) and Grady and LeGrande (1992) reported genetic differences between the Green/Barren and Duck River tributary populations. A new population was recently discovered in Little Chucky Creek, a tributary to the Nolichucky River. Allozyme comparisons revealed that Little Chucky Creek, Green/Barren River, and Duck River populations are genetically distinct, with no evidence of recent interbreeding.

Based on genetic and morphological data, *N. (R.) elegans* includes three species: (1) the elegant madtom in the Green and Barren Rivers, (2) the undescribed saddled madtom found in the lower Duck River and its tributaries, and (3) the undescribed Chucky madtom in Little Chucky Creek (J. Grady, pers. comm.).

In general, all these fishes occupy riffles of clear, gravel- or rubble-bottom streams, creeks, and medium-sized rivers. At least one population (Barren River) nests in June under flat rocks above riffles, producing a brood of 25 eggs that are 4 mm in diameter and adhere in a mass like sculpin eggs. The male does not feed while incubating. The fry hatch in 12 days and may be eaten by fantail darters (Burr and Dimmick 1981).

| | |
|---|---|
| *Noturus (Rabida) eleutherus,* mountain madtom | *N. (R.) eleutherus* has a dark bar across the base of the tail just before the fin (not always apparent), a well-developed adipose fin that is separated from the caudal fin by a deep notch producing a small flap at its rear, and an intense dark blotch on the lower half of the adipose fin (Taylor 1969).

The mountain madtom consists of disjunct populations, one group in the Ouachita River system of Arkansas and Oklahoma, and a much larger group widespread in the Ohio and Tennessee basins from Pennsylvania, Ohio, and Indiana to North Carolina, Kentucky, and Tennessee (Clay 1975).

*N. (R.) eleutherus* inhabits strongly flowing rivers in sand, gravel, or rubble riffles; it occurs mainly among dense algae or *Podostemum,* under large rocks or within mussel shells during the day. One nest site was reported during early summer in a pool at 75°F; the bottom was fine gravel under an 8-inch-wide flat rock; 70 eggs were guarded by the male (Robison and Buchanan 1988). |
| *Noturus (Rabida) flavipinnis,* yellowfin madtom | *N. (R.) flavipinnis* has a yellow dorsal fin with submarginal brown spots, a brown vertical band across the caudal peduncle, a dark blotch on the adipose fin extending to the edge, and the tail fin does not have a black edge (Taylor 1969).

The yellowfin madtom is rare, restricted to just three mountain tributaries of the upper Tennessee River system in Tennessee, Georgia, and Virginia, and has been extirpated from part of its range by dam construction. It is known from another Tennessee River locality, but probably has been eliminated from the North Fork Holston River in Virginia (Page and Burr 1991).

*N. (R.) flavipinnis* inhabits quiet backwaters and depressions around rocks and boulders in small, clear streams.

The yellowfin madtom is a protected species; do not collect any madtoms from Copper Creek in the Clinch River system or Citico Creek in the Little Tennessee River system to avoid inadvertently taking yellowfin madtoms. |
| *Noturus (Rabida) taylori,* Caddo madtom | *N. (R.) taylori* is white with intense dark saddles, two dark bands through the tail fin, a dark blotch on the outer part of the dorsal fin, and a black blotch in the adipose fin that does not extend to the edge.

The Caddo madtom occurs in the Caddo, upper Ouachita, and Little Missouri Rivers of the Ouachita River drainage (Robison and Buchanan 1988).

*N. (R.) taylori* inhabits shallow, gravel bottom pools of clear upland streams, among rocks and below the gravel downstream of riffles. It eats snails, insects, and isopods, but mostly mayfly and fly larvae. It probably spawns during April and May, producing up to 48 eggs.

The Caddo madtom is rare and should be protected, so determine its status before collecting. |
| *Noturus (Rabida) trautmani,* Scioto madtom | *N. (R.) trautmani* has a clear adipose fin, is speckled above, white below, has three bands in the tail fin, and the dorsal and anal fins are clear.

The Scioto madtom was last reported in Big Darby Creek, near Fox, Ohio, but has not been seen since 1956; although still legally protected, it is probably extinct. |

*N. (R.) trautmani* inhabits riffles with a sand, gravel, silt, and boulder bottom, in fast to moderate current near vegetation, and has been found with *Etheostoma tippecanoe*.

The Ictaluridae contains four blind cave-dwelling species, two each from Texas and Mexico. All four species are either protected or proposed for protected status by one or both governments. The threats to cave-dwelling species are not from aquarists (who are inefficient at collecting in these inaccessible habitats), but from groundwater depletion attributable to agricultural and industrial water withdrawal, and groundwater contamination caused by leaking, underground fuel storage tanks and agricultural chemicals that migrate through the soil to the water table.

Methods to care for cave catfish (troglodytes) are unknown, but they are probably sensitive to light, and would require cool water and small invertebrates for food. True troglodytic cave fishes (as opposed to cave populations of surface fishes) are typically slow growers that take years to mature.

| | |
|---|---|
| **Genus *Trogloglanis***<br>*Trogloglanis pattersoni,*<br>toothless blindcat | *T. pattersoni* is white or pink, and without teeth or eyes.<br>    The toothless blindcat occurs 1,000–2,000 feet below San Antonio, Texas in subterranean waters. *Trogloglanis* is probably related to *Ictalurus* of the United States and Canada. |
| **Genus *Satan***<br>*Satan eurystomus,*<br>widemouth blindcat | *S. eurystomus* is white or pink, with well-developed teeth and without eyes.<br>    The widemouth blindcat occurs in subterranean waters 1,000–2,000 feet below San Antonio, Texas.<br>    Because it is abundant, it may be unprotected at present; however, contact Texas Parks and Wildlife before offering well drillers a reward for either fish. *Satan* is probably related to *Pylodictis* of Mexico. |
| **Genus *Prietella*** | *Prietella* is a Mexican blindcat genus with two species most likely related to *Noturus* (Walsh and Gilbert 1995). *Prietella lundbergi* and *P. phreatophila* from Mexico are unlikely to be available for collection unless propagated by an agency under contract to Mexico.<br>    Mexico also has three blindcats in the family Pimelodidae (Weber and Wilkens 1998). *Rhamdia macuspanensis* was recently described from a cave in Tabasco. *R. reddelli* is found in caves in Oaxaca and *R. zongolicensis* occurs in caves in Veracruz. |

# 12

## The Order Esociformes

*T*he order Esociformes contains the families Esocidae (pikes and pickerels) and Umbridae (mudminnows).

## Family Esocidae, the Pikes

The Esocidae consist of sport fishes ranging from the small pickerels to the giant muskellunge. The body is elongate to tubular, and the lower jaw projects from a ducklike mouth armed with prominent teeth. Pikes and pickerels are top predators wherever they occur. The dorsal and anal fins are far back, single, and unspined with soft rays only; the tail fin is forked. The body is typically green with a broken pattern, which facilitates hiding in vegetation to await prey. They range worldwide in the north temperate climes of the northern hemisphere (holarctic distribution).

Of the four species in American waters, only *Esox niger* and the two subspecies of *Esox americanus* are suitable aquarium fishes. The muskellunge, northern pike, and their popular hybrid are large and unsuitable for aquaria, and will not be discussed here.

Pickerels are game fish that require a fishing license to collect in most states. These fishes occur in eastern and central North America from Alaska to the Gulf of Mexico. Pickerels are taken by seining and dipnetting in dense shoreline vegetation.

## Genus *Esox*
### *Esox americanus,* redfin and grass pickerels

The redfin and grass pickerels have an oblique black bar below the eye that extends past the angle of the jaws to the throat. The similar chain pickerel (another species) has a vertical bar. In all other members of the family, the black bar does not extend past the angle of the jaws. The redfin pickerel has pink to red fins and the grass pickerel has clear fins. Both have a series of off-vertical dark bands on a green body, the bands usually indistinct.

The redfin or bulldog pickerel (because of its short snout), *E. a. americanus,* is restricted to the Atlantic slope from Maine to Florida along the Coastal Plain.

The grass pickerel, *E. a. vermiculatus,* has a longer snout. It ranges along the Gulf Coast from Florida to Texas, and northward in the Mississippi drainage. It continues westward to Iowa, eastward through the Ohio Valley, and northward into the Great Lakes and Canada.

Both subspecies occur in densely vegetated edges of shallow, quiet lakes, river backwaters, ponds, and slow-moving streams. They spawn from fall through spring, with the eggs scattered over vegetation in shallows. They feed mostly on small fishes but also eat crayfish and large insects they attack by darting from hid-

Grass pickerel, *Esox americanus vermiculatus,* Cypress Springs, Fla. GS

ing places. In Florida, they feed on sunfish, minnows, pirate perch, pygmy sunfish, livebearers, killifish, shrimp, crayfish, and insect nymphs (McLane 1955).

A large aquarium (≥ 29 gal.) is needed; pickerels may attain 1 foot in length. The redfin and grass pickerels adapt quickly to captivity and do not require vegetation or hiding places. Spawning in captivity is unlikely, but could be attempted in a 4-foot-long tank (≥ 100 gal.) densely planted with *Ceratophyllum* (hornwort), *Myriophyllum,* or *Elodea.* Pickerels are jumpers and should be covered. They are predaceous on any smaller fishes.

## *Esox niger,* chain pickerel

*E. niger* has a black bar behind the eye that passes straight downward past the angle of the jaws. The green body is crossed by a broken network or chainlike pattern of dusky markings. All fins are clear. It grows to 18 inches, but 1 foot is average size.

The chain pickerel occurs on the Coastal Plain, ranging from Nova Scotia and New Brunswick southward through Florida and westward to the Texas border. It continues northward in the Mississippi River valley to the southeast corner of Missouri, and into Illinois and western Kentucky.

*E. niger* most often inhabits lowland quiet waters, and may ascend streams in uplands. Typically, it is found in densely vegetated lakes, ponds, and edges of slow-moving rivers. In habits, it resembles the redfin and grass pickerels, but is more common in lakes and other larger water bodies, the redfin more often in smaller sloughs and ponds.

It spawns from fall to spring when water temperatures are 48°F. Eggs are scattered over vegetation or detritus (Robison and Buchanan 1988). Although lacking the rich, red pigment of the eastern redfin pickerel, the body pattern of the adult chain pickerel is attractive. The chain pickerel has been crossed experimentally with the northern pike (Schwartz 1962).

## Family Umbridae, the Mudminnows

Umbridae occur in North America and southeastern Europe. They are cylindrical, with a single dorsal fin set far back, and similar in shape to *Rivulus* of the Rivulidae.

Three genera with four species occur in North America and another species in Europe. The European mudminnow is included in this book in order to complete coverage of the family. American aquarists may wish to exchange mudminnow species with European aquarists through the mails. All are plant spawners and often occupy habitats deficient in oxygen, which they can obtain from atmospheric air. When frightened, they dive into the mud; this characteristic has led to their common names. Larval development indicates relationships to the Esocidae (Kendall and Mearns 1996).

Collect mudminnows by dip net or seine in dense vegetation along banks of ponds and lakes.

---

**Genus *Umbra***
*Umbra krameri,*
European mudminnow

*U. krameri* of Europe lives two years, and has habits similar to American species of the family (Makara and Stranai 1980). The presence of *Umbra* in both North America and Europe suggests that the genus spread eastward to this continent across an ancient land bridge from northeastern Asia, and westward from Asia to Europe. The genus could not have spread directly between North America and Europe because the Atlantic Ocean was already formed by that time, having originated more than 75 million years ago in the Cenozoic era (well before the families had evolved).

A similar distribution of species on both sides of the Atlantic is seen in the Percidae and Cyprinidae, families that also originated long after the formation of the Atlantic Ocean.

---

**Genus *Dallia***
*Dallia pectoralis,* Alaska blackfish

*D. pectoralis* is an elongate mudminnow with a large head and minute pelvic fins set far back just before the anal fin. It is olive, with five dark blotches, bars, or spots on the flank. The unpaired fins are clear to white-edged, but red in the nuptial male. The fins are speckled red-brown.

The Alaska blackfish occurs in western Alaska, inland to the Fairbanks area, islands in the Bering Sea, and the tip of Siberia.

*D. pectoralis* inhabits swamps, ponds, lakes, and river backwaters, in heavily vegetated, quiet waters with mud bottoms, often in enormous numbers. In the spring, when the water increases 10–15°F and the ice breaks in May, the fish migrate upstream to swampy potholes.

Spawning occurs from May to August and is probably protracted due to the large number (200) of large, 2 mm eggs found in mature females. Eggs adhere to vegetation; at 54°F, they hatch in nine days. Normal life expectancy is up to eight years, with maturity reached in the third year. The maximum size is 8 inches. The major foods are fly larvae, snails, ostracods, and cladocerans. The only other fishes in the same habitat are sticklebacks (Gasterosteidae) (Scott and Crossman 1973).

The Alaska blackfish is probably not suitable for aquaria because of its adaptation to cold temperatures, but the effort may be worthwhile. It is tolerant of low, dissolved oxygen concentrations in cold water, but is probably intolerant of heat.

---

**Genus *Novumbra***
*Novumbra hubbsi,*
Olympic mudminnow

*N. hubbsi* is killifish-like with vertical bars on a brown body. There is no dark bar on the base of the tail fin. The nuptial male is black with a dozen or more thin vertical bars. His body is an iridescent green, white, or blue, and his dorsal and anal fins have a thin white, blue, or yellow border. The female is olive, lighter below, and has a few faint vertical bars.

The Olympic mudminnow occurs in the Chehalis River and vicinity, the Olympic Peninsula, and Washington (northwestern United States). All North American mudminnows can be identified by locality; their ranges do not overlap.

*N. hubbsi* inhabits standing or gently flowing water with dense aquatic vegeta-

Central mudminnow, *Umbra limi,* Reelfoot Lake, Obion Co., Tenn. RB

tion over a thick mud bottom; it also is found in shallow, overflow areas adjacent to streams in clear to darkly stained water.

During courtship, the male becomes dark and flares (expands) the gill covers in threat displays to other males and other fishes. Spawning occurs in dense vegetation, and the territory is defended by the male with flaring and charging. Courtship is marked by wagging and intense color development, flaring of the fins, and circling of the female. The female enters the vegetation and presses against the side of the male while vibrating; they then snap apart as one or two eggs are released.

The 1.9 mm amber eggs adhere to vegetation. They hatch after an incubation period of two weeks at 50°F; the helpless fry are heavily pigmented and 5 mm in length. When Olympic mudminnows occur together with sticklebacks, the normally red breeding color of the latter is replaced with a black breeding color (Hagen et al. 1972; Kendall and Mearns 1996).

Provide live daphnia, blackworms, and other living foods. The mudminnow will adapt to dry or frozen foods with difficulty. Males are highly territorial and may divide a 20-gallon aquarium into two territories, but one male per aquarium is better, especially with up to three females.

Supply a dense clump of *Myriophyllum, Nitella,* or *Vesicularia* as the nesting material. After spawning, which may take an hour, move the vegetation to a hatching tank and replace it with another clump for additional spawning. Eggs hatch in nine days; fry are light brown and generally motionless, attached to the vegetation by adhesive glands on the head. Feed the fry *Artemia* nauplii or microworms, supplemented with *Daphnia* or *Ceriodaphnia*. Because mudminnows are difficult to identify out of breeding color, different species should not be mixed in aquaria.

**Genus *Umbra***
*Umbra limi,* central mudminnow

*U. limi* has a dark vertical bar on the base of the caudal fin; otherwise, it is olive brown above and white below. Darker mottling and marbling along the flank may coalesce into vertical bands or a horizontal band. The male in nuptial coloration may have iridescent green highlights.

The central mudminnow ranges from Manitoba, Ontario, and Quebec southward to Ohio, Arkansas, and the northwestern corner of Tennessee (Reelfoot Lake).

*U. limi* occurs in still waters, often low in dissolved oxygen and always densely

Eastern mudminnow, *Umbra pygmaea.* WFR

vegetated and over a mud bottom. It normally uses its gills to extract oxygen from the water, but under high temperature conditions switches to aerial respiration; it gulps air from the surface and swallows it. The air then leaves the gut through a connecting channel and enters the vascularized (rich in blood vessels) swim bladder (Gee 1980).

Spawning occurs during early spring at 55°F. Eggs are spawned in dense vegetation. Eggs hatch in six days and the 5 mm fry appear primitive with a retained notochord.

These carnivorous bottom feeders eat snails, ostracods, amphipods, copepods, isopods, spiders, and insect larvae. They only rarely eat fish (Scott and Crossman 1973).

Mudminnows can be used to bioassay the quality of lakes that do not differ in physical parameters by placing captive fish in enclosures within the lakes and measuring weight loss/gain and survival over a protracted period. Not surprisingly, the greatest densities of mudminnows are in high-quality lakes (although they are tolerant of low oxygen concentrations) lacking predators and competitors for food (Paszkowski and Tonn 1992).

---

*Umbra pygmaea,*
eastern mudminnow

*U. pygmaea* is similar to the central mudminnow but has a dozen horizontal, thin, dark lines along the flank.

The eastern mudminnow occurs in the Atlantic Coastal Plain from New York to northern Florida, but is common to abundant only in Virginia and the Carolinas.

*U. pygmaea* is found in dense vegetation over mud bottoms in ponds, lakes, river backwaters, and ditches. Its principal foods are aquatic invertebrates picked from vegetation and the bottom. It spawns in dense vegetation.

Fish that overwintered in cold water, below 40°F at times, began nuptial activity in March with two smaller males courting a clearly gravid female (Eccleston 1982). The trio was transferred to another aquarium where spawning occurred the following day at 55°F and pH 6.7. Offered gravel, rocks, a flowerpot, and a nylon spawning mop on the bottom, the fish spawned over the nylon mop.

The 1.5 mm diameter eggs were transparent and adhesive, and protected by the female which provided only weak, occasional fanning. The eggs hatched in two weeks and the fry became free-swimming with absorbed yolk sacs about two weeks later.

The fry took live *Artemia* nauplii as a first food after rejecting frozen nauplii. At two weeks of age, 80 fry were counted, and the author estimated clutch size at about 100. At less than three months of age, the fry had attained 2 cm in length, a dark band had developed on the caudal peduncle, and dark pigmentation had begun to appear on the larger fish.

# 13       The Order Percopsiformes

THE ancient order Percopsiformes contains three primitive families (Percopsidae, Aphredoderidae, Amblyopsidae) with few species. All are small carnivores with large heads and tiny teeth, fused bones supporting the tail, distinctive pelvic fin structures, and sometimes an anal opening migrating forward during development.

Dark adaptation is widespread throughout the order. Pirate perches and trout-perches have large eyes for low light vision, and are most active at night (or in dark depths or dense vegetation in lakes). Cavefishes have carried dark adaptation to its extreme, losing their vision and compensating with a highly developed acoustic and tactile sensory system covering the body. This dark adaptation indicates maintenance in dark or dimly lit aquaria, and observation with red (darkroom) lights. When plant materials are important for hiding places, use java moss *(Vesicularia),* which has a low light requirement.

## Family Percopsidae, the Trout-Perches

The Percopsidae is largely extinct, its two surviving species distributed from the Atlantic to the Pacific Coasts, from New York and the Great Lakes to the Bering Straits, in lakes and rivers.

They can be collected by night seining sandy shores, or by day seining or dip-netting undercut banks and other dark or shaded refuges. Include stress-relieving chemicals in the transport water to retard skin infections resulting from abrasions.

## Genus *Percopsis*
### *Percopsis transmontana,* sand roller

*P. transmontana* is diamond-shaped with a stubby body, highly arched, blue-green back, prominent dorsal and anal fin spines, and a robust adipose fin. It grows to 5 inches. The male tends to be blackish, especially at night, and develops black banding on the fins.

The sand roller ranges from the lower Snake River in western Idaho to the Columbia River drainage of Washington, Idaho, and Oregon and is present in the Willamette River of Oregon.

*P. transmontana* occurs most often in quiet, weedy margins of lakes and backwaters of rivers, usually over rubble and sandy bottoms with *Elodea* or other aquatic vegetation. It is usually found beneath shady undercut banks or behind bridge stanchions, logs, and other obstructions and away from the light. It spawns from April through July.

A 40-gallon aquarium is recommended for six adults. Use an undergravel filter, powerhead, and sand and gravel bottom with rock caves and rooted or potted

Sand roller, *Percopsis transmontana*. RJG

plants. The water should be aerated and filtered, neutral, and not allowed to warm above the high 70s (°F). Provide frozen brine shrimp and bloodworms, live adult brine shrimp, mosquito larvae, small fishes, and earthworms.

The dominant male will take over the best cave. The male becomes blacker, including black banding on the fins at night, and the female plumper prior to spawning. The 2 mm diameter, strongly adhesive eggs are laid on rocks and gravel in the cave or at its mouth when the temperature is in the 60s and 70s (°F) (Katula 1992b).

## *Percopsis omiscomaycus,* trout–perch

*P. omiscomaycus* is silvery, and has two rows of gray marks along the flank, the lower along the lateral line. It has a prominent adipose fin, a forked tail, a large dorsal fin, and dorsal and anal fin spines not as prominent as in *P. montana*. It is usually 4 inches or slightly larger.

The trout-perch ranges from the Great Lakes and New York through northern West Virginia and northern Missouri. It ranges northward into Canada through central and western Quebec, Ontario, Manitoba, Saskatchewan, Alberta, British Columbia, the Yukon, and the Porcupine and Yukon Rivers in Alaska to the Arctic Circle.

*P. omiscomaycus* inhabits mostly large lakes, but also rivers. It resides in deep waters during the day, probably inactive, and is a valuable forage fish for many cold water game fishes. At night, it moves to shoal waters where it feeds mostly on insect larvae and occasionally on darters and minnows.

Spawning occurs from May through August, depending on latitude and temperature. The large eggs, 1.25 mm in diameter and numbering 200, have been lauded for use as laboratory tools to observe both normal development and, in poor water quality, pathological development. The preferred spawning sites are gravel- and sand-bottom shallows of lakes and tributaries of rivers (Scott and Crossman 1973). A 12-hour photoperiod is recommended, along with a diet of blackworms, frozen adult *Artemia,* and bloodworms (chironomids).

Provide at least a 20-gallon aquarium for a group (sexes cannot be distinguished except when the female enlarges with roe), with cool to cold water and a sand or gravel substratum. Periodically stir the bottom with the handle of an aquarium net and, if eggs are swirled up into the water column, net them out. Eggs hatch in 20 days, and the fry take *Artemia* nauplii soon thereafter.

Pirate perch, *Aphredoderus sayanus,* Haywood Co., Tenn. RB

## Family Aphredoderidae, the Pirate Perches

The Aphredoderidae is an ancient family represented by a fossil genus *(Trichophanes)* from western North America and a single living species distributed widely in lowland waters of the eastern half of the continent.

The pirate perch is characterized by a large mouth, smooth skin with fine, deeply embedded ctenate scales, no adipose fin, and an awkward, front-heavy appearance. During development the anus migrates forward, reaching the throat region in adults.

### Genus *Aphredoderus*
*Aphredoderus sayanus,* pirate perch

*A. sayanus* is blackish brown with lavender highlights on the side or an orange tint on the pale belly. Normal length is 2 inches, rarely attaining 4.

The subspecies *A. s. sayanus* is abundant on the Atlantic Coastal Plain from Long Island, New York through Georgia, becoming less common in northern and central Florida. The inland group of the Mississippi River Valley and Great Lakes is *A. s. gibbosus* (Lee et al. 1980). The two subspecies intergrade along the eastern Gulf slope in a manner similar to that of the redfin and grass pickerels.

The pirate perch occurs in densely vegetated edges and debris of mud-, sand-, or silt-bottom ponds, lakes, and slow-moving streams, and is as common in acidic blackwater habitats as in clear or even calcareous alkaline waters. It is a nocturnal carnivore on insects, crustaceans, and an occasional small fish. Pirate perch are readily collected by dip net or seine in dense vegetation at the edges of quiet waters. Collect in winter as pirate perch are spring spawners.

A 10-gallon aquarium is suitable for a small group. Provide sand and gravel, with an overlay of sphagnum peat moss, and rock caves for security. The male is larger and darker with purple highlights, while the female has a smaller head and plumper body. Feed live *Daphnia, Ceriodaphnia, Artemia,* mosquito larvae, blackworms, earthworms, whiteworms and/or grindle worms, and small fishes *(Gambusia, Heterandria).* Pirate perch are nocturnally active, and can be seen feeding at night when illuminated with a red darkroom light.

Ichthyologists had reported as far back as 1943 that the pirate perch spawned in a nest on the bottom with both parents guarding the eggs. Subsequently, it was suggested that the fish is a branchial brooder, based on the finding of eggs in the gill chamber of a preserved specimen (Boltz and Stauffer 1986) and the relationship of the Aphredoderidae to the branchial brooding cavefishes (Amblyopsidae). Both observations were misleading.

Katula (1992a) confirmed that the pirate perch is neither an oral nor branchial brooder but a substratum brooder. Normally, each individual fish occupies its own cave in an aquarium. Spawning is imminent during early spring (48–55°F) when a pair jointly inhabits a cave, and the male becomes unusually active, swimming up and down the glass (perhaps equivalent to patrolling territory in the wild).

The female excavates a shallow, 2-inch-wide pit inside the cave and near its entrance, apparently by fanning (mouthing was not observed). The pair aligns side by side and moves backwards over the pit, occasionally angling slightly vent to vent followed by a quick vibration. By April, many large, clear eggs were seen scattered 1–2 inches outside the cave in the peat moss, and a few eggs were within the pit inside the cave. No oral or branchial brooding was observed.

On the third day after spawning, 38 eggs were removed for incubation with strong aeration and methylene blue in a nursery aquarium. The eggs began to hatch in two weeks, the fry ungainly with enormous yolk sacs. Fry congregated on the bottom for the first few days. Upon yolk resorption they consumed microworms; *Artemia* nauplii might have sufficed but was not offered until one week of age. By three weeks, pigmentation was initiated with a gray head and gray midlateral stripe appearing; the remainder of the body was clear. The spawnings by Katula (1992a) and others numbered 125–160 2 mm diameter eggs, and no branchial or oral brooding was observed.

## Family Amblyopsidae, the Cavefishes

The Amblyopsidae are adapted to a dark (aphotic) environment. The head is flattened and the nostrils protrude on stalks. The skin appears smooth due to deeply embedded fine scales. Pelvic fins are reduced or absent. The anus migrates forward to a position under the throat during development. Egg size increases, egg production decreases, and age to maturity increases with cave adaptation. The female of the cave species is a gill cavity egg brooder (Poulson 1963).

Four species are subterranean (troglodytic) with distributions determined by underground channels through limestone formations. One species occurs around cave mouths (troglophilic), while still another is not tied to caves at all, but lives on the surface (epigean). The epigean swampfish is fully pigmented, the troglophilic species partially so, and the remaining aphotic species all unpigmented. Correspondingly, their eyes may be completely absent, present but covered with skin, or uncovered but degenerate. Tactile sensory structures associated with the lateral line cover the body.

The epigean swampfish is not protected, and can be taken in ⅛-inch or finer mesh nets from shallow shorelines of forested swamp streams where it is associated with plant roots, leaf litter pack, and debris. Unprotected cavefishes might be dip-netted from beneath overturned rocks. Care differs depending on their normal habitat.

Most cavefishes are state protected and may not be collected. When in doubt, check with state agencies.

## Genus *Chologaster*
*Chologaster cornuta,* swampfish

*C. cornuta* is a thin, cylindrical surface fish with tiny black spots for eyes. A black line on either side of a peach-orange, wormlike body mimics a small, 2- to 3-inch salamander. The male has sensory structures in front and a white belly; the female is swollen with roe in the spring.

The swampfish occurs along the Atlantic coastal plain from southern Virginia to Georgia, and is most abundant in North Carolina.

Swampfish, *Chologaster cornuta,* Carteret Co., N.C. FCR

Spring cavefish, *Forbesella agassizi,* Duck R. system, Tenn. RB

Seek *C. cornuta* in slow-flowing, sand-bottom, blackwater streams, in shore-line root mats or sunken woody debris, where it feeds on amphipods, ostracods, and copepods. It lives little more than one year, and breeds during April, producing less than 100 eggs per female (Poulson 1963; Lee et al. 1980).

Provide a 2- to 5-gallon dimly lit aquarium having a sand bottom with a thin sprinkling of peat moss, a clump of java moss, carbon filtration, and regular water changes (to keep the peat moss from acidifying the aquarium). Feed live foods only, including *Daphnia pulex, Artemia,* amphipods, baby snails, blackworms, and baby *Heterandria.*

The mode of breeding is unknown, but relatives are all branchial brooders. Begin with a long, dark photoperiod (14 hr.) and cooler water, and gradually change to 10 hours of darkness and a few degrees warmer to mimic the change from winter to spring. The temperature change can be accomplished by moving the small aquarium from the floor to a higher level. Inspect regularly for fry or for swollen gill covers, and remove all other fishes if brooding is suspected. The fry are likely to be large and readily detected.

**Genus *Forbesella***
*Forbesella agassizi,* spring cavefish

*F. agassizi* is a salamander-shaped fish that attains a length of 2 inches or slightly larger. It is brown above and lighter below, with stripes on the sides. The small eyes are overgrown by skin. It has a dark tail fin and no pelvic fins. It is similar to and was previously placed in *Chologaster,* to which it should probably be returned.

The spring cavefish is distributed east of the Mississippi from southern Illinois to Kentucky and Tennessee and west of the Mississippi in just a single locality in Missouri.

*F. agassizi* occurs beneath stones in springs outside caves, especially during high water; otherwise, it is found within caves in streams and pools. It lives four years, spawning from January through March at two years of age. It has a wide temperature tolerance, but retreats from light. It feeds mostly on amphipods *(Gammarus)* in nature, and on its own young (Poulson 1963; P. W. Smith 1979).

The remaining cavefishes are true troglodytes.

**Genus *Amblyopsis***
*Amblyopsis rosae,* Ozark cavefish

*A. rosae* is translucent pink, with a flattened, eyeless head. The dorsal fin is directly over the anal fin (both fins spineless) and pelvic fins are absent; four to six rows of sensory papillae appear on the rays of the tail fin. It may attain 2 inches long.

The Ozark cavefish is known from 25 caves and their streams, springs, and wells in honeycombed limestone uplands of southwestern Missouri, northern Arkansas, and eastern Oklahoma.

*A. rosae* lives in complete darkness, on a chert rubble or silt-sand bottom; the groundwater is 55–60°F year-round. The Ozark cavefish has been pumped from wells at a goldfish hatchery near Lebanon, Missouri on the Ozark Plateau.

What does it eat? The caves often are occupied by colonies of gray bats *(Myotis grisescens),* whose guano supports the growth of fungi that form the base of the invertebrate food chain. The food available includes cave copepods, isopods, amphipods, ostracods, crayfish, its own young, and salamanders. See also the discussion of the Alabama cavefish.

The Ozark cavefish probably matures after 15 years of age and breeds during spring high water from February through April. Only one in five fish breed in any year, with 25 eggs brooded in the gill cavity (Poulson 1963; Pflieger 1975; Robison and Buchanan 1988).

*A. rosae* has disappeared from caves around Springfield, Missouri, possibly because of leaking underground gasoline storage tanks or surface agricultural chemicals seeping down to groundwater. The Ozark cavefish is protected under the federal Endangered Species Act and may not be collected or possessed.

| | |
|---|---|
| *Amblyopsis spelaea,* northern cavefish | *A. spelaea* is similar to the Ozark cavefish but has minute pelvic fins, one or two rows of sensory papillae on the rays of the tail fin, and prominent sensory canals and pits on the head. It is also larger at 4 to 5 inches long. |

The northern cavefish occurs in caves in the Pennroyal and Mitchell limestone plateaus from southern Indiana southward to the Mammoth Cave area of Kentucky (Lee et al. 1980).

*A. spelaea* is entirely subterranean, inhabiting limestone cave streams most often on silt-sand bottoms. It feeds on cave crustaceans and surface invertebrates carried down from above.

The northern cavefish breeds during high water from February through April, and the females carry the eggs and fry in the gill cavities for four to five months until the yolk sac is absorbed (Poulson 1963). It is a slowly maturing fish with low reproductive capacity.

Although it is not federally protected, do not attempt collection before consulting state agencies. If available, maintain the northern cavefish in a chiller-equipped aquarium at 55 to 60°F in the dark with a red light for observation, filtration over limestone or aragonite, and daily water changes with hard water. Feed live *Daphnia magna,* amphipods, baby guppies, small snails, and live tubifex or blackworms. Do not add plants; they will not survive without light. A brooding female should be isolated until the young are released, and then separated from the fry.

**Genus *Speoplatyrhinus***
*Speoplatyrhinus poulsoni,*
Alabama cavefish

*S. poulsoni* has a long, flat head with a spatulate snout; it is eyeless, colorless, and lacks pelvic fins; four rows of sensory papillae occur on the tail fin. It grows to just over 2 inches in length.

The Alabama cavefish is known from a single cave in the Highland Rim of the Tennessee River drainage in Lauderdale County, northwestern Alabama, and is the rarest (described from just 9 specimens) and most cave-adapted fish.

*S. poulsoni* is assumed to grow, mature, and propagate slowly. Its cave is occupied by the gray bat, *Myotis grisescens,* which provides quantities of guano. The guano supports a rich cave fauna of mites, nematodes, spiders, heliomyzid and mycetophilid flies, dermestid beetles, millipedes, and other small animals. The cave is shared with white crayfish *(Cambarus jonesi* and *Procambarus pecki),* amphipods, and isopods (Cooper and Kuehne 1974). The Alabama cavefish probably feeds on any small animals detected with its well-developed lateral line and caudal sensory systems.

**Genus *Typhlichthys***

*Typhlichthys subterraneus,* southern cavefish

*T. subterraneus* is eyeless, colorless, lacks pelvic fins, and has two rows of sensory papillae on the tail fin. It attains just over 3 inches.

The southern cavefish is found in two separate populations. West of the Mississippi River it occurs in caves of Missouri, Arkansas, and Oklahoma on the Ozark Plateau (Jones and Taber 1985). The population east of the Mississippi occurs on the Cumberland and interior low plateaus of Alabama, Georgia, Tennessee, Kentucky, and Indiana (Lee et al. 1980).

*T. subterraneus* inhabits springs, pools, and streams in limestone caves, and has been found in wells. It feeds on copepods, isopods, and other crustaceans. Its most common associates are copepods and the cave crayfish, *Orconectes pellucidus.*

The southern cavefish probably is a branchial brooder that spawns during the late spring when water table levels rise (Poulson 1963). Spawning is completed and young are abundant by June or July (Pflieger 1975), but the incubation period is unknown.

It is not federally protected, but could be protected in some states.

*Color Plates*

1. Bowfin, *Amia calva,* Fifteen Mile Cr., Candler Co., Ga. RB

2. Orangefin shiner, *Notropis ammophilus,* Hatchie R., Tenn. RB

3. Taillight shiner, *Notropis maculatus,* Bear Branch, N.C. FCR

4. Redlip shiner, *Notropis chiliticus,* Pee Dee R., N.C. WFR

5. Greenhead shiner, *Notropis chlorocephalus,* day prior to spawning, Catawba R., N.C. WFR

6. Greenhead shiner, *Notropis chlorocephalus,* day of spawning, Catawba R., N.C. WFR

7. Yellowfin shiner, *Notropis lutipinnis,* N.C. WFR

8. Rainbow shiner, *Notropis chrosomus,* Cahaba R., Ala. RB

9. Tennessee shiner, *Notropis leuciodus*, Duck R., Tenn. WFR

10. Rosyface shiner, *Notropis rubellus*, Verdigris R., Kans. GS

11. Saffron shiner, *Notropis rubricroceus*, Tennessee R., Tenn. WFR

12. Bluehead shiner, *Pteronotropis hubbsi*, secondary male, Locust Bayou, Ark. WFR

13. Redside dace, *Clinostomus elongatus*, Clear Fork R., Ohio. WFR

14. Rosyside dace, *Clinostomus funduloides*, Tennessee R., Tenn. WFR

15. Blacknose dace, *Rhinichthys atratulus*, Tallulah R., Towns Co., Ga. RB

16. Flame chub, *Hemitremia flammea*, Tennessee R. RB

17. Mountain redbelly dace, *Phoxinus oreas*, James R., Va. WFR

18. Southern redbelly dace, *Phoxinus erythrogaster*, White R., Mo. WFR

19. Tennessee dace, *Phoxinus tennesseensis*, Pinhooke Cr., Roane Co., Tenn. RB

20. Crescent shiner, *Luxilus cerasinus*, Roanoke R., Va. WFR

21. Warpaint shiner, *Luxilus coccogenis*, head, Little R., Tenn. WFR

22. Bleeding shiner, *Luxilus zonatus*, spawning aggregation, Osage R., Mo. WFR

23. Cardinal shiner, *Luxilus cardinalis*, Jenkins Cr., Mo. WFR

24. Duskystripe shiner, *Luxilus pilsbryi*, White R., Mo. WFR

25. Fathead minnow, *Pimephales promelas,* White R., Mo. WFR

26. Bluntnose minnow, *Pimephales notatus,* Kansas R., Kans. GS

27. Red shiner, *Cyprinella lutrensis,* Osage R., Mo. WFR

28. Fieryblack shiner, *Cyprinella pyrrhomelas,* Pee Dee R., S.C. WFR

29. Whitetail shiner, *Cyprinella galactura,* White R., Mo. WFR

30. Blue shiner, *Cyprinella caerulea,* Conasauga R., Tenn. WFR

31. Spotfin chub, *Cyprinella monacha,* Emory R., Morgan Co., Tenn. RB

32. River chub, *Nocomis micropogon,* French Broad R., N.C. FCR

33. Spotted bullhead, *Ameirus serracanthus,* Walton Co., Fla. GS

34. Checkered madtom, *Noturus flavater,* White R., Mo. WFR

35. Golden topminnow, *Fundulus chrysotus,* Cypress Springs, Fla. WFR

36. Northern studfish, *Fundulus catenatus,* White R., Mo. WFR

37. Pygmy killifish, *Leptolucania ommata,* Indian R., Fla. WFR

38. Bluefin killifish, *Lucania goodei,* Cypress Springs, Fla. WFR

39. Comanche Springs pupfish, *Cyprinodon elegans,* Reeves Co., Tex. GS

40. Owens pupfish, *Cyprinodon radiosus,* Owens R., Calif. WFR

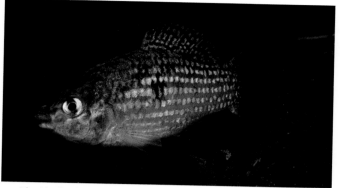

41. Florida flagfish, *Jordanella floridae,* St. Johns R., Fla. WFR

42. Brook silverside, *Labidesthes sicculus,* White R., Mo. WFR

43. Everglades pygmy sunfish, *Elassoma evergladei,* Cypress Springs, Fla. WFR

44. Okefenokee pygmy sunfish, *Elassoma okefenokee,* River Styx, Fla. FCR

45. Carolina pygmy sunfish, *Elassoma boehlkei,* Juniper Cr., Brunswick Co., N.C. FCR

46. Banded sculpin, *Cottus carolinae,* White R., Missouri. WFR

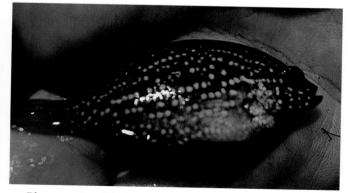

47. Bluespotted sunfish, *Enneacanthus gloriosus,* N.C. RJG

48. Banded sunfish, *Enneacanthus obesus,* St. Johns R., Fla. WFR

49. Warmouth, *Chaenobryttus gulosus,* Black R., Mo. WFR

50. Pumpkinseed, *Lepomis gibbosus,* Potomac R., Montgomery Co., Md. RB

51. Green sunfish, *Lepomis cyanellus,* Verdigris R., Kans. GS

52. Redbreast sunfish, *Lepomis auritus,* San Marcos R., Tex. WFR

53. Orangespotted sunfish, *Lepomis humilis,* Mississippi R. RB

54. Spotted sunfish, *Lepomis punctatus,* Tennessee Aquarium. RB

55. Longear sunfish, *Lepomis megalotis,* Tennessee Aquarium. RB

56. Dollar sunfish, *Lepomis marginatus,* Jackson, Miss. RB

57. Dollar sunfish, *Lepomis marginatus,* habitat, Cypress Springs, Fla. GS

58. Gilt darter, *Percina evides,* Current R., Mo. WFR

59. Bronze darter, *Percina palmaris,* Beech Cr., Tallapoosa R., Ga. RB

60. Tangerine darter, *Percina aurantiaca,* Little R., Tenn. WFR

61. Amber darter, *Percina antesella,* Conasauga R., Tenn. WFR

62. Blueside darter, *Etheostoma jessiae,* Little R., Blount Co., Tenn. RB

63. Speckled darter, *Etheostoma stigmaeum,* Black Warrior R., Ala. FCR

64. Arrow darter, *Etheostoma sagitta,* Hickory Cr., Cumberland R., Campbell Co., Tenn. RB

65. Niangua darter, *Etheostoma nianguae,* Pomme de Terre R., Mo. WFR

66. Variegate darter, *Etheostoma variatum,* Hocking R., Ohio. WFR

67. Kanawha darter, *Etheostoma kanawhae,* New R., N.C. RJG

68. Candy darter, *Etheostoma osburni,* Stoney Cr., New R., Va. WFR

69. Missouri saddled darter, *Etheostoma tetrazonum,* Gasconade R., Mo. WFR

70. Arkansas saddled darter, *Etheostoma euzonum,* Beaver Cr., Mo. WFR

71. Turquoise darter, *Etheostoma inscriptum,* S. Fork Edisto R., Aiken Co., S.C. FCR

72. Greenside darter, *Etheostoma blennioides,* White R., Mo. WFR

73. Banded darter, *Etheostoma zonale,* habitat, Elk R., Mo. GS

74. Slough darter, *Etheostoma gracile,* Ohio R. WFR

75. Cypress darter, *Etheostoma proeliare,* Saline R., Ark. WFR

76. Yoke darter, *Etheostoma juliae,* White R., Mo. WFR

77. Tippecanoe darter, *Etheostoma tippecanoe,* Ohio R. WFR

78. Greenfin darter, *Etheostoma chlorobranchium,* Little Pigeon R., Sevier Co., Tenn. RB

79. Spotted darter, *Etheostoma maculatum,* Big South Fork, Tenn. WFR

80. Wounded darter, *Etheostoma vulneratum,* Nolichucky R., Tenn. RB

81. Yellowcheek darter, *Etheostoma moorei,* Little Red R., Ark. WFR

82. Greenbreast darter, *Etheostoma jordani,* Conasauga R., Tenn. WFR

83. Sharphead darter, *Etheostoma acuticeps,* Nolichucky R., Tenn. RB

84. Redline darter, *Etheostoma rufilineatum,* Buffalo R., Tenn. WFR

85. Coldwater darter, *Etheostoma ditrema,* Conasauga R., Tenn. RB

86. Greenthroat darter, *Etheostoma lepidum,* Comal R., Tex. WFR

87. Redband darter, *Etheostoma luteovinctum,* Barren Fork, Tenn. RB

88. Redband darter, *Etheostoma luteovinctum,* Duck R., Tenn. WFR

89. Watercress darter, *Etheostoma nuchale*, spring, Birmingham, Ala. WFR

90. Rainbow darter, *Etheostoma caeruleum*, Tennessee R., Tenn. RB

91. Rainbow darter, *Etheostoma caeruleum*, White R., Mo. WFR

92. Rainbow darter, *Etheostoma caeruleum*, Little Red R., Ark. WFR

93. Orangethroat darter, *Etheostoma spectabile*, upper Cumberland R., Ky. WFR

94. Orangethroat darter, *Etheostoma spectabile*, lower Strawberry R., Ark. WFR

95. Orangethroat darter, *Etheostoma spectabile,* Niangua R., Mo. WFR

96. Orangethroat darter, *Etheostoma spectabile,* two males spawning with one female, Kansas R., Kans. GS

97. Highland Rim darter, *Etheostoma kantuckeense*, Little Salt Lick Cr., Tenn. RB

98. Creole darter, *Etheostoma collettei*, Saline R., Ark. WFR

99. Gulf darter, *Etheostoma swaini*, Cypress Springs, Fla. WFR

100. Christmas darter, *Etheostoma hopkinsi*, Beaverdam Cr., Edgefield Co., S.C. FCR

101. Redfin darter, *Etheostoma whipplei*, Saline R., Ark. WFR

102. Orangebelly darter, *Etheostoma radiosum*, Ouachita R., Ark. WFR

103. Trispot darter, *Etheostoma trisella*, Conasauga R., Tenn. RB

104. Paleback darter, *Etheostoma pallididorsum*, Ouachita R., Ark. WFR

105. Sunburst darter, *Etheostoma* cf. *punctulatum*, White R., Mo. WFR

106. Arkansas darter, *Etheostoma cragini*, Spring R., Mo. WFR

107. Tennessee snubnose darter, *Etheostoma simoterum*, Pigeon R., Cocke Co., Tenn. RB

108. Cumberland snubnose darter, *Etheostoma simoterum atripinne*, Duck R., Tenn. WFR

109. Blackside snubnose darter, *Etheostoma duryi*, Little Swan Cr., Lincoln Co., Tenn. RB

110. Coosa darter, *Etheostoma coosae*, Conasauga R., Tenn. WFR

111. Tallapoosa darter, *Etheostoma tallapoosae*, Tallapoosa R., Ga. WFR

112. Kentucky snubnose darter, *Etheostoma rafinesquei*, Green R., Ky. WFR

113. Emerald darter, *Etheostoma baileyi*, Kentucky R., Ky. WFR

114. Splendid darter, *Etheostoma barrenense*, Barren R., Ky. WFR

115. Cherry darter, *Etheostoma etnieri*, Barren Fork, Warren Co., Tenn. RB

116. Firebelly darter, *Etheostoma pyrrhogaster*, Obion R., Tenn. RB

117. Bandfin darter, *Etheostoma zonistium*, Terrapin Cr., Tennessee R. WFR

118. Brown darter, *Etheostoma edwini*, Cypress Springs, Fla. WFR

# 14

# The Order Cyprinodontiformes

TRADITIONALLY, the order Cyprinodontiformes was considered to contain seven families in North America, namely the flyingfishes (Exocoetidae), needlefishes (Belonidae), sauries (Scomberesocidae), silversides (Atherinidae), livebearers (Poeciliidae), rivulins (Rivulidae), and killifishes (Cyprinodontidae). The group was recently rearranged with the needlefishes, flyingfishes, and sauries moved into a new order (Beloniformes), and the silversides and livebearers into the order Atheriniformes.

Aquarium literature for years has placed all the North American, South American, Asian, and African killifishes and topminnows in the Cyprinodontidae. More recent work (Parenti 1981; Parker and Kornfield 1995; Murphy and Collier 1997) divides the order Cyprinodontiformes into two subgroups, the Aplocheiloidei and the Cyprinodontoidei. The Aplocheiloidei contains the Old World Aplocheilidae and the New World Rivulidae.

## Family Rivulidae, the Rivulins

The Rivulidae is represented in the United States by just one species, the mangrove rivulus. Other species occur in the Caribbean and Mexico and into South America.

### Genus *Rivulus*
*Rivulus marmoratus,* mangrove rivulus

*R. marmoratus* is a salamander-shaped fish with a rounded head and rounded cross section. It has an entirely gray-brown (sometimes mottled) body and a distinctive ocellus at the base of the tail. It is 2 to 3 inches long.

The mangrove rivulus is a member of a predominantly Central and South American genus. In Florida, the mangrove rivulus occurs from Vero Beach on the Atlantic side to southern Dade County (at least), south to the Florida Keys, and northward along the Gulf Coast to the limits of the mangrove communities. It also occurs in the Bahamas, Lesser and Greater Antilles, Turks and Caicos Islands, Mexico, and even Brazil where it has been reported under the (now invalid) name *R. ocellatus.*

*R. marmoratus* occurs in vegetated tidal flats, ditches, estuarine marsh ditches and pools, inside peat bank burrows of land and mangrove crabs (e.g., *Cardisoma, Ucides*), and in shallow saline flats vegetated with marsh grasses or mangroves. It is associated with cord grass, and red, black, and white mangroves (all salinities). It is sometimes seined in pools and ditches while collecting other killifish, but is more likely to be found in mangrove crab burrows lining tidal creeks (Davis et al. 1990;

Mangrove rivulus, *Rivulus marmoratus,* Dade Co., Fla. RJG

Turner et al. 1992), termite burrows in fallen or drifting mangrove logs (B. Turner, pers. comm.), and resting on mangrove leaves above the water.

The mangrove rivulus has been captured from crab burrows using miniature minnow traps constructed of plastic cups and funnels, and by tiny number 12 to number 15 fish hooks baited with earthworms. In tidal ponds, kick the bottom to release marsh gas, and this may cause the mangrove rivulus to come out from under detritus and become vulnerable to a seine. Split mangrove logs and search the exposed termite burrows. The American Killifish Association is a good source of mangrove killifish; its thousands of members trade domestic and exotic species through the mails.

*R. marmoratus* has two kinds of specialized cells in the skin that allow it to survive high concentrations of salt (e.g., in crab holes during prolonged low tide) and to extract oxygen from the air, thus enabling survival in hypoxic waters toxic to other fishes. It cannot tolerate elevated levels of hydrogen sulfide (marsh gas), and will emerge from stirred up salt marsh mud to escape the gas.

The mangrove rivulus is a synchronous, internally self-fertilizing hermaphrodite, a mode of reproduction unique among vertebrates. Each individual has an ovotestis producing both eggs and sperm. The cavity of this organ is frequently filled with sperm, so most eggs produced by the ovarian tissue are immediately self-fertilized (Thomerson 1966b; Harrington 1967, 1968; Harrington and Kallman 1968; Hastings 1969; Vrijenhoek 1985). Each fish is capable of being the origin of a genetically identical fish (clone), providing a powerful tool for biological investigations.

Low temperatures (and sometimes high ones) may induce development of individuals without ovarian tissue, and these rare *primary males* are brightly colored with orange pigment and capable of producing sperm. The term *secondary male* is used for fish that have lost the ovarian tissue in the ovotestis, and thus have changed from hermaphrodite to male. On mangrove islands off the coast of Belize, Central America, the mangrove rivulus population may contain 10 to 24 percent *precocious secondary males* (i.e., those having lost their ovarian tissue at an early age) (B. Turner, pers. comm.).

What role do these males play? They can probably inhibit self-fertilization in normal mangrove rivulus and fertilize any nonfertile eggs released by them. Perhaps they emit huge amounts of sperm in the burrows that chemically inhibit sperm production by normal rivulus, resulting in the release of unfertilized eggs. That explanation, if true, would account for the existence of so many known clones.

Maintain in warm, 25 to 100 percent synthetic sea water, and do not trade through the mail during winter months; this subtropical fish can be killed if the temperature drops below 60°F. Ship during the warm months in a plastic bag with a clump of damp cotton instead of water. It has been stored in Dr. Bruce Turner's laboratory in nothing but wet leaves for over two months. A 1-gallon jar is sufficient for a single specimen. Keep it covered; this fish is a jumper that adheres to the side or lid. Feed *Artemia* (nauplii and adults), crickets, and even cockroaches. Provide aeration and a top-to-bottom synthetic yarn spawning mop (they are egg eaters).

The eggs are large (2 mm) and clear. Place them in a jar of saline water with aeration, or in shallow covered dishes without aeration. Developed eggs sometimes require forced hatching, accomplished by breathing carbon dioxide into the water through a soda straw, or by fouling the water with powdered milk and replacing the fouled water in a couple of hours. Elevated carbon dioxide stimulates the embryo to release the enzyme chorionase, which dissolves the inner layers of the egg envelope, causing it to swell and weaken so the larva can escape. The fry take *Artemia* nauplii or microworms as a first food. Determine its protected status in Florida prior to attempting collection, or acquire a breeding population (one individual) through the American Killifish Association.

*R. marmoratus* has been proposed in Florida to be classified as threatened; however, there is no biological basis for this action because no minimal population size is required to maintain a self-fertilizing fish, and extensive habitat exists both in the state (where it is not subject to development degradation) and throughout its vast range.

The Cyprinodontoidei contains the families Cyprinodontidae, Goodeidae, Fundulidae, and Empetrichthyidae. In her monumental revision of the Cyprinodontiforme fishes, Parenti (1981) transferred *Crenichthys* and *Empetrichthys* to the Goodeidae, based on many similarities in structure. Miller and Smith (1986) proposed placing these two genera in their own family, Empetrichthyidae.

More recently, Grant and Riddle (1995) found that 5-million-year-old fossils from California assignable to the *Empetrichthys-Crenichthys* group indicated an early divergence. Their DNA analyses supported a closer relationship of the modern genera with the Goodeidae than with other killifish groups, but they did not address whether these fishes should be placed within a separate family, Empetrichthyidae. In this book, *Crenichthys* and *Empetrichthys* are placed in the Empetrichthyidae based in part on the above evidence and in part on the goodeids having unique trophotaeniae that nourish developing embryos; no such organs occur in the Empetrichthyidae.

## Family Empetrichthyidae, the Springfish and Poolfish

The springfish and poolfish resemble pupfishes *(Cyprinodon)*, but have bicuspid *(Crenichthys)* or conical *(Empetrichthys)*, teeth, and lack pelvic fins.

### Genus *Crenichthys*
*Crenichthys baileyi*,
White River springfish

*C. baileyi* is heavy-bodied and rounded in front, abruptly narrower in the rear. It has no pelvic fins. Two dark bands appear on the flank, the upper one longer.

The White River springfish occurs in the White and Moapa River drainages of southeastern Nevada (Lee et al. 1980).

*C. baileyi* inhabits springs and spring runs at temperatures up to 98°F and dissolved oxygen concentrations as low as 0.7 ppm. Introduced convict cichlids *(Cichlasoma nigrofasciatum)*, largemouth bass *(Micropterus salmoides)*, shortfin mollies *(Poecilia mexicana)*, sailfin mollies *(P. latipinna)*, and mosquitofish *(Gambusia affinis)* have depressed or extirpated populations of *C. baileyi* (Tippie et al. 1991). It will probably survive in thermal pools where high temperatures and low dissolved oxygen concentrations are intolerable to exotic species (Rinne and Minckley 1991). It feeds mostly on small invertebrates, despite its elongate, coiled intestine (usually indicative of a vegetable diet).

An endangered species, it may not be collected or possessed.

---

*Crenichthys nevadae,*
Railroad Valley springfish

*C. nevadae* has no pelvic fins. It is shaped like its cogener, but has horizontal blotches rather than bands along the flank. The nuptial male is dark gray with a golden yellow stripe down the back.

The Railroad Valley springfish occurs at Lockes Ranch and Duckwater in Nye County, Nevada, and was introduced at Sodaville in Mineral County, Nevada.

*C. nevadae* inhabits warm springs at 90 to 95°F, with a dissolved oxygen concentration down to less than 1 ppm. Its teeth and long, coiled intestine suggest herbivory, but see the previous species.

Tom Baugh collected 18 springfish under a Nevada state permit and held them at 85°F, with gravel, undergravel filtration, aeration, artificial plants, flake food, and frozen brine shrimp. When one male and two females were placed in a separate 10-gallon aquarium, courtship began almost immediately. The male pursued the females, nipping at their vents. When a female stopped, indicating receptivity, the male pressed the female against the gravel, the pair S-shaped and vibrating. Eggs are 1.5 mm in diameter and clear, and hatch in eight to ten days at 85°F. The 3 mm fry take live *Artemia* nauplii at hatching, and attain 8 mm at 30 days.

This threatened species is not available to aquarists.

---

**Genus *Empetrichthys***
*Empetrichthys latos,*
Pahrump poolfish

*E. latos* resembles *Crenichthys* in lacking pelvic fins and the black mottling on the flank. The breeding male has an iridescent blue flank, orange fins, and an orange eye (Page and Burr 1991).

The Pahrump poolfish occurred originally near the Pahrump Ranch in Nye County, Nevada, but perhaps has been extirpated from its native habitats. It was transplanted to Spring Valley, but its survival is tenuous.

*E. latos* lives in deep, clear, silt-bottom springs at 75 to 80°F.

Because it is endangered, it may not be collected. The closely related Ash Meadows poolfish, *E. merriami,* is now extinct. Attempts to save it did not make use of the volunteered expertise of the American Killifish Association.

---

Family Fundulidae,
the Topminnows

Fundulidae contains the best known American killifishes (from the Dutch *kill* for small stream). The New World *Fundulus, Adinia, Lucania,* and *Leptolucania* were removed from the old family Cyprinodontidae (in the broad sense) and placed into a newly erected family (Fundulidae) by Parenti (1981). The current family Cyprinodontidae is much more restricted.

These are small fishes of shallow waters that feed mostly on small invertebrates (some species on algae), and in turn provide important forage for larger piscivores. Characteristics include no spines in the fins, a single dorsal fin, usually an upturned mouth, and a taxonomically useful pattern of scales and pores on the lateral line of the head. All North American species deposit adhesive eggs in vegetation, sand, or gravel. Most are placed in the genus *Fundulus,* known commonly as topminnows, killifishes, or studfishes.

Fundulids use bright colors, sound production, and sensitive contact organs in sexual encounters. By also shifting from all-at-once spawning to daily and (usually) one-egg-at-a-clasp spawning behavior, there is more prenuptial activity per egg, and the evolutionary selection for brighter colors and more complex behaviors in successful males (Foster 1967).

| | |
|---|---|
| **Genus *Fundulus*** | *Fundulus heteroclitus,* the mummichog, is a classic animal for studying pituitary control of salt balance. Several *Fundulus* normally found in fresh water can tolerate salinities up to 29 ppt (sea water is 36 ppt). If the pituitary gland is removed, estuarine species of *Fundulus* will not survive transfer to fresh water (Griffin 1974a,b), but fish with the gland intact can tolerate enormous salinity differentials. |

Dip nets work best in shoreline vegetation. Seining is effective where vegetation is sparse. The open water surface species are vulnerable to cast nets. Minnow traps are effective in tidal marshes. The bucket trap, also effective in coastal zones, is a 5-gallon bucket sunk into a hole in a grassy marsh during low tide. At high tide it is covered with water, and on the receding tide becomes a refuge for many fishes and invertebrates.

*Fundulus* do well in a 5- or 10-gallon aquarium; provide larger quarters for larger or aggressive species. They feed on insects, crustaceans, and snails, usually at the surface of quiet waters with dense vegetation. They should be fed flake food, daphnia, adult brine shrimp, mosquito larvae, tubificid worms, and vestigial-winged fruit flies. Larger species also take chopped earthworms.

Most lay adhesive eggs in plants. *Nitella* is a good, natural spawning substratum; periodically transfer the *Nitella* to another aquarium for hatching. Most species readily accept spawning mops as a substitute. The eggs average 1–2 mm in diameter, can be picked from the mops with fingers for incubation in shallow dishes of water (with or without acriflavine), and take two to four weeks to hatch. Fry take *Artemia* nauplii at once. Bad (white or fungus-covered) eggs should be removed with an eyedropper and the bottom cleaned of biofilm, a complex slime of fungi and bacteria.

Hatching may require assistance; foul the incubation water with flake food to raise the concentration of dissolved carbon dioxide, or expel breath into the water through a soda straw or air-line tubing. When carbon dioxide concentrations rise, hatching glands in the throat of the fry release chorionase, an enzyme that dissolves the inner layers of the egg shell or chorion and allows the egg to swell with water and weaken its wall. This subsequently permits the thrashing fry to escape by puncturing the now-weakened chorion.

The genus has several clearly identifiable groups.

| | |
|---|---|
| 1. *chrysotus-seminolis-* *"cingulatus"* group. *Fundulus chrysotus,* golden topminnow | *F. chrysotus* (plate 35) is a classic aquarium fish from the United States. It has a golden body with brassy spots and eight vertical bars on the flank, more easily seen on the male. The male has scattered red spots and, occasionally, black spots. |
| | The golden topminnow ranges in Gulf Coast lowlands from Florida to Texas, |

Golden topminnow, *Fundulus chrysotus*, black-spotted male, Fla. RJG

northward in the Mississippi valley to southeastern Missouri, and on the Atlantic Coastal Plain from Florida to Wilmington, North Carolina.

*F. chrysotus* occurs in vegetated, clear backwaters. It is not a schooling fish, individuals dispersed in *Cabomba, Elodea, Myriophyllum,* and algae along steep banks.

The golden topminnow is spawned easily in vegetation or synthetic yarn mops with or without floats. The eggs are picked from the yarn strands with the fingers and transferred to a covered dish of shallow water tinted with acriflavine, methylene blue, malachite green, or nothing at all (but stored in the dark). The fry hatch in less than two weeks. They may be force-hatched by increasing the carbon dioxide content of the water with breath blown through a straw, by adding rotting milk solids, or sometimes simply by strong agitation. The large fry take brine shrimp nauplii at once and grow quickly.

---

**Fundulus auroguttatus,**
banded topminnow

*F. auroguttatus* has horizontal rows of small red spots that contrast with a dozen thin, green-gray vertical bands. The fins are red to pink and the head is pink to a flesh color.

The banded topminnow occurs in the Florida panhandle, ranging eastward to the peninsula on the Gulf Coast side of the state. This western Florida fish has for years been combined with an eastern relative as *Fundulus "cingulatus,"* a name that will probably be suppressed (Gilbert et al. 1992).

Seek *F. auroguttatus* in hot, shallow, clear waters in ditches and swamps among dense aquatic vegetation, often in the open (no stream canopy).

Care is typical for the genus. It is spawned easily on mops, and the fry are raised on *Artemia* nauplii, microworms, and dry foods (Thomerson 1966b).

---

**Fundulus rubrifrons,**
redface topminnow

*F. rubrifrons* is the so-called *"cingulatus"* of the Florida peninsula, but not the panhandle. It has a gray body. The male has a bright orange-red head, jaws, and snout. Bars are prominent in the male but faint in the female. The fins are pink to red. Dark red-brown spots occur in six or more regular rows on the flank in the male (in male *F. chrysotus,* these spots are irregular and not in rows), and the body is golden. The female lacks both spots and color.

The redface topminnow is found in extreme southeastern Georgia and all of the Florida peninsula north of the Miami-Tampa region (Gilbert et al. 1992).

| | |
|---|---|
| *Fundulus seminolis,*<br>Seminole killifish | *F. seminolis* has horizontal rows of fine black spots that contrast with thin, dusky vertical bars on a green body. The male has a bright, brassy operculum, a bright pink-red anal fin, and the anal and pelvic fins have black borders. At 6 inches, it is among the largest freshwater members of the genus. |

*F. seminolis* has horizontal rows of fine black spots that contrast with thin, dusky vertical bars on a green body. The male has a bright, brassy operculum, a bright pink-red anal fin, and the anal and pelvic fins have black borders. At 6 inches, it is among the largest freshwater members of the genus.

The Seminole killifish occurs only in Florida, from Lake Okeechobee northward to Jacksonville and westward to the Suwannee drainage.

A fish of shallow lakes, the nuptial male occupies territories marked by *Vallisneria, Naias,* or other vegetation and awaits females; at other times it is gregarious. Schools feed at the bottom on insect larvae, crustaceans, and snails, crushing them with pharyngeal teeth. Smaller fish feed on cladocera and ostracods, shifting with age toward chironomids. They spawn during April and May, grow rapidly, mature the first year, and live up to two years (McLane 1955; DuRant et al. 1979).

Purchase them from bait-and-tackle shops near lakes. Provide a 12-hour photoperiod, a sand bottom, and spawning mops. Feed frozen bloodworms to enhance red color. It is a bottom feeder; do not pollute the aquarium with floating flake foods.

**2. studfish group**

*Fundulus catenatus, F. julisia, F. stellifer, F. rathbuni,* and a fourth relative, *F. albolineatus,* recently extinct, were placed in the subgenus *Xenisma* by Williams and Etnier (1982).

**Genus *Fundulus***
Subgenus *Fundulus (Xenisma)*
*Fundulus (Xenisma) catenatus,*
northern studfish

*F. (X.) catenatus* (**plate 36**) is an attractive fish that is difficult to keep in good health and grows to 7 inches. The nuptial male is aggressive. He is iridescent blue overall with a yellow margin on the tail fin and has rows of red dots in front and red lines on the flank. The female and young are gray with dark red to black spots.

The northern studfish occurs in uplands from Alabama to Kentucky and Indiana, and on the Ozark Plateau (Missouri, Arkansas, eastern Kansas, eastern Oklahoma).

*F. (X.) catenatus* inhabits shallow sand or gravel backwaters of clear, high gradient streams with rock bottoms on limestone beds. Adults feed in the early morning and late afternoon on mosquito and blackfly larvae and adults from the bottom and the water column. Early juveniles eat rotifers, crustaceans, nematodes, snails, and insect larvae, later shifting mostly to larval flies and mosquitoes. It breeds from April through August, the eggs buried in sand or gravel (McCaskill et al. 1972; Fisher 1981).

Provide a large, open, aerated aquarium with a gravel bottom. It spawns in pebbles or gravel. The abundant, large eggs can be swirled out of the substratum, netted, and removed for incubation. Alternatively, the parents can be moved, the filters disconnected, and the eggs allowed to develop in the gravel.

*Fundulus (Xenisma) stellifer,*
southern studfish

*F. (X.) stellifer* is about 4 inches long. The nuptial male is iridescent blue-green, heavily spotted with red, with a bold black margin on the dorsal and caudal fins (Williams and Etnier 1982).

According to the late George S. Myers, writing about the southern studfish in the old *Aquarium Journal,* "There are many other of our Southern fishes which are brilliantly colored and probably good aquarium fishes. Trouble is, some aquarists are afraid to get their feet wet looking for them."

Barrens topminnow, *Fundulus julisia,* Barren Fork, Cannon Co., Tenn. RB

The southern studfish occurs in Mobile Bay and in the Alabama, Chatta-hoochee, Coosa, and Tallapoosa River systems of Georgia and Alabama. It may have been introduced into Chickamauga Creek (Tennessee River drainage) in Walker County, Georgia as bait (Dahlberg and Scott 1971; Lee et al. 1980).

*F. (X.) stellifer* inhabits backwaters and edges of clear, high gradient streams with sand and gravel bottoms and feeds mostly on snails.

Care as for *F. catenatus,* but provide crushed snails as the major food.

| | |
|---|---|
| *Fundulus (Xenisma) rathbuni,* speckled killifish | *F. (X.) rathbuni* has a husky golden brown to gray body with black speckles. The male has a black line from the corner of the jaw to the bottom of the eye, black speckles on the cheek below the black line, and a lighter margin on the tail. |

The speckled killifish occurs in the lower Piedmont and upper Coastal Plain of North Carolina and southern Virginia in the Roanoke, Neuse, Pee Dee, Cape Fear, and Santee River drainages, but is absent from the Tar (between the Roanoke and Neuse). The isolated distribution of this and related studfish is similar to that of *Noturus furiosus* and related madtoms, probably for the same historical reasons (C. Gilbert, pers. comm.).

*F. (X.) rathbuni* inhabits shallow pools of moderately sized rivers over mud or sand near rubble. It picks water boatmen from the surface, chironomids and other insect larvae from the bottom, and occasionally eats small minnows *(Notropis).*

| | |
|---|---|
| *Fundulus (Xenisma) julisia,* Barrens topminnow | *F. (X.) julisia* has an iridescent white line from the head to the origin of the dorsal fin. The nuptial male is light blue-green to yellow-green above and white below, has scattered orange to dark red spots, a light-edged tail, and orange anal and paired fins. The female and young are brown-gray with scattered dark spots (Williams and Etnier 1982). |

The Barrens topminnow is known from six locales in the upper Caney Fork and Duck Rivers of Tennessee. The specific epithet, *julisia,* is derived from the Cherokee words for watercress and fish.

*F. (X.) julisia* is found in springs with lush watercress *(Nasturtium officinale)* growth over chert and gravel. It spawns during early spring.

The Barrens topminnow has been spawned off-season in aquaria at 70 to 72°F,

Plains topminnow, *Fundulus sciadicus*, Spring R., Mo. WFR

with the photoperiod manipulated to simulate spring and a mat of vegetation at the surface for security. Males will readily kill each other, females, and other species. Twenty-five eggs/female/day are laid in a floating spawning mop.

It is not federally or state protected, but should be; it is a vulnerable species existing in only a few small habitats.

The remaining two species of studfish are not members of the subgenus *Xenisma*.

| | |
|---|---|
| *Fundulus bifax,* stippled studfish | *F. bifax* has short rows of red dots on a plain tan flank, no iridescence, and no black edge on the tail fin. Until recently, it was considered a variant of *F. stellifer,* but the electrophoretic differences are considerable, and consistent with the pigmentary differences previously thought unreliable.<br><br>The stippled studfish occurs in the Tallapoosa and lower Coosa systems of Georgia and Alabama.<br><br>*F. bifax* inhabits silty or sandy backwaters in clear, large, high gradient streams. It is intolerant of nutrient enrichment and pollution. |
| *Fundulus sciadicus,*<br>plains topminnow | *F. sciadicus* is olive with bronze highlights, faint blue-green crosshatching (Pflieger 1975), a narrow light gold line on the forward back, and yellow fins with a wide orange-red marginal or submarginal band in the nuptial male.<br><br>Two separate (disjunct) populations are known: one throughout Nebraska and extending into adjacent states and another in central Missouri on the south side of the Missouri River. The scattered populations are difficult to locate in pools and backwaters near submersed vegetation. They spawn during spring in vegetation, the eggs hatching in eight to ten days at 70°F (Pflieger 1975). |
| 3. starhead topminnows | Starhead topminnows have a gold spot on the head, another on the back just before the dorsal fin, and a dark teardrop (inverted triangle) through the eye. Horizontal rows of black dots and scattered red dots on the flank characterize a species group that includes *F. dispar, F. notti, F. lineolatus,* and *F. escambiae.* The species can be identified by the rivers in which they are captured and by the number and arrangement of the sensory pores just above each eye (supraorbital pores). Most are gregarious at the surface of densely vegetated backwaters, where they feed on in- |

Starhead topminnow, *Fundulus dispar*, Mississippi R., Lake Co., Tenn. RB    Russetfin topminnow, *Fundulus escambiae*. WFR

sects, crustaceans, snails, and other small invertebrates. Relationships were recently reviewed by Ghedotti and Grose (1997).

| | |
|---|---|
| *Fundulus dispar,* starhead topminnow | The starhead topminnow ranges from the Great Lakes to Alabama. |

The northern subspecies, *F. d. dispar,* has prominent dark green bars. Bars are absent in the southern/western subspecies, *F. d. blairi,* and intergrades occur in Alabama.

*F. d. blairae* occurs in lowlands from western Florida to Texas. *F. d. dispar* ranges from Mississippi above the fall line to the Great Lakes, and is replaced on the Coastal Plain by *F. d. blairae.* Page and Burr (1991) and Robison and Buchanan (1988) considered *Fundulus blairae* a full species, but there are no consistent differences between the subspecies other than the bars.

*Fundulus escambiae,* russetfin or eastern starhead topminnow

*F. escambiae* also occurs in western Florida near *F. dispar.* To confirm an identification requires a dissecting microscope to examine the supraorbital pores. Both *F. escambiae* and *F. nottii* have pores 4a and 4b (Wiley 1977) joined with just a single opening to the surface; *F. lineolatus* has these same pores very close together but still separated; and *F. dispar* has these pores widely separated (Gilbert et al. 1992).

The russetfin occurs in vegetated backwaters of the Florida panhandle, southwestern Georgia, and southern Alabama, from the Suwannee River westward to the Perdido River in lowland drainages. It cannot tolerate cold. The red spots and pink fins fade without live daphnia or frozen bloodworms in the diet.

*Fundulus lineolatus,* lined topminnow

*F. lineolatus* is the only starhead with a half dozen or more dark black horizontal lines characterizing the female, whereas the male has a dozen dark vertical bars on the flank. Both sexes have a dark vertical bar under the eye (teardrop mark); the snout and gill cover are often orange to red.

The lined topminnow occurs in Atlantic slope drainages from southern Virginia to Lake Okeechobee in Florida, and westward to the Gulf Coast Ocklockonee drainage in peninsular Florida and southern Georgia.

*F. lineolatus* inhabits ponds, sandhill lakes, and backwaters, in clear water with abundant vegetation, and is always at the surface. In Florida it is found near *Nuphar, Nymphoides,* and *Sagittaria* (McLane 1955).

Lined topminnow, *Fundulus lineolatus*, male, Juniper Cr., Brunswick Co., N.C. FC

Lined topminnow, *Fundulus lineolatus*, female, Wake Co., N.C. RJG

Blackstripe topminnow, *Fundulus notatus*, Hatchie R., Tenn. RB

| *Fundulus notti,* bayou topminnow | *F. notti* is similar to *F. escambiae* in supraorbital pores. The male has 12 thin, vertical bars and the female has spots that form horizontal lines. The male also has spots between the bars. |

*F. notti* is similar to *F. escambiae* in supraorbital pores. The male has 12 thin, vertical bars and the female has spots that form horizontal lines. The male also has spots between the bars.

The bayou topminnow is found on the lower Gulf Coast from the Mobile Bay drainage in southwestern Alabama to the Lake Pontchartrain tributaries in southern Louisiana backwaters.

*F. notti* often is found away from vegetation in the open and at the surface (Lee et al. 1980).

---

**4. *olivaceus-notatus-euryzonus* group**

These three similar species have a prominent band along the flank (as opposed to bars in the starhead group), but are today separated primarily by their chromosome numbers.

---

**Fundulus notatus, blackstripe topminnow**

*F. notatus* is typical of the group. It is tan above and white below, with spotted fins and lacking a teardrop below the eye. It sometimes has scattered, small, diffuse or indistinct spots above the band, the spots never bold and intense as in the closely related blackspotted topminnow. A thick horizontal, blue-black line from the snout to the base of the tail is jagged-edged in the male and straight-edged in the female. *F. notatus* attains 3 inches and differs from *F. olivaceus* in the number of chro-

Blackspotted topminnow, *Fundulus olivaceus,* Hatchie R., Tenn. RB

mosomes (40 in this species), yet can interbreed and produce viable offspring. Hybridization in nature is rare, in part because the two species often occupy different habitats in their common range (Thomerson 1966c, 1967).

The blackstripe topminnow occurs from the Great Lakes to the Gulf of Mexico, continuing eastward in Mississippi drainages and westward to Texas, Kansas, and Oklahoma; it is absent from the Ozark Plateau.

*F. notatus* inhabits backwaters of smaller rivers, typically in somewhat turbid water (P. W. Smith 1979; Robison and Buchanan 1988). It feeds during morning and late afternoon on surface ants, spiders, and flies, and on snails and small crustaceans picked from the algae that passes through the gut undigested (Atmar and Stewart 1972). It spawns on plants or leaf litter, producing up to 30 eggs a day.

| | |
|---|---|
| *Fundulus olivaceus,* blackspotted topminnow | *F. olivaceus* is similar to *F. notatus,* but has bold, dark spots above the horizontal band, 48 chromosomes, and attains a larger (almost 4 in.) maximum size. |

*F. olivaceus* is similar to *F. notatus,* but has bold, dark spots above the horizontal band, 48 chromosomes, and attains a larger (almost 4 in.) maximum size.

The blackspotted topminnow occurs in several Gulf Coast drainages from eastern Texas to the Florida panhandle, and northward to the Ozark Plateau, Shawnee Hills of Southern Illinois, and West Virginia.

*F. olivaceus* inhabits vegetated backwaters of clear, high gradient, upland streams above the fall line over gravel bottoms. It enters lakes with sand bottoms below the fall line. It feeds mostly on surface aquatic insects, and typically on larger food than *F. notatus.*

*Fundulus euryzonus,* broadstripe topminnow

*F. euryzonus* is speckled black above and in the fins. A broad black stripe with iridescent highlights, a third to a fourth the height of the fish, runs from the tip of the snout to the base of the tail, and has no crosshatching. The stripe is so wide as to extend halfway down the depth of the pectoral fin.

The broadstripe topminnow occurs only in Lake Pontchartrain and its tributaries in Louisiana and Mississippi, and is not common. There is some slight overlap in range with *F. notatus* and *F. olivaceus,* but in those species the stripe is narrower, not extending below the top margin of the pectoral fin.

A small aquarium is sufficient. *F. euryzonus* accepts live, frozen, and flake food, and spawns in bottom mops; the eggs hatch in 14 days at 70 to 75°F. The fry reach maturity in six to eight months, at which time the males become territorial. *F. euryzonus* will hybridize with *F. olivaceous* (B. G. Granier, *American Currents,* undated).

Mummichog, *Fundulus heteroclitus,* rigged as flounder bait, N.C. RJG    Gulf killifish, *Fundulus grandis,* Rio Grande R., Tex. WFR

5. salt-marsh group
*Fundulus heteroclitus,* mummichog

*F. heteroclitus* is large (2–4 in.) and gray, with thin, dark vertical lines on the flank of the female. The male is smaller, but in nuptial color is deep dark green above, brilliant yellow below, and with numerous vertical rows of silver spots and alternating light and dark bars.

The mummichog ranges from Newfoundland to the mouth of the St. Johns River at Jacksonville, Florida.

*F. heteroclitus* is the most abundant killifish in low-salinity salt marshes over silt, mud, sometimes sand, and is often associated with vegetation and with *Cyprinodon variegatus.* It is tolerant of temperatures from near freezing to the high 90s (°F). It usually spawns in algae, but will spawn in sand on a high spring tide, where the eggs remain damp and well-oxygenated until they hatch on becoming wet during the next high spring tide, not unlike California grunion.

The mummichog is an abundant and vital member of the ecological community wherever it occurs, an important forage fish for piscivores, a commercially important bait fish, and among the most important of fishes used in biological and biomedical research. The most abundant east coast *Fundulus,* it can be purchased from bait-and-tackle shops or taken by seine or minnow trap.

*F. heteroclitus* does best in 15 to 20 percent sea water at 70 to 74°F; raise the temperature between 78 to 80°F to induce breeding. It spawns in sunken spawning mops. It is one of the most studied of all fishes (Kaighn 1964; Brummett 1966; Pickford et al. 1966; Copeland 1969; McNabb and Pickford 1970; Umminger 1970; Jean and Garside 1974; Prinslow and Valiela 1974; Kuchnow and Foster 1976; Mitten and Koehn 1976; Kneib and Stiven 1978; Taylor et al. 1979; DiMichele and Taylor 1981).

*Fundulus grandis,* Gulf killifish

*F. grandis* replaces *F. heteroclitus* below Jacksonville, Florida and is larger (usually about 5 in.) and darker above with black cheeks in the male and a more upturned mouth.

The Gulf killifish ranges southward along the Florida coast from the St. Johns River and westward along the Gulf Coast to Texas and the Gulf Coast of Mexico. It is replaced on the Yucatan coast by the similar and even larger *F. grandissimus.*

All three species are derived from common ancestral stock and all three have silvery bars interspersed with dark vertical bars. Whereas the mummichog can tolerate extreme cold in parts of its range, *F. grandis* cannot; it responds to cold with a decrease in serum Na (sodium) and chloride, and an accumulation of organic substances in the serum while the K (potassium) level remains unchanged. For survival, the serum K and Na levels must maintain osmotic balance, which cold temperatures inhibit in this fish, but not the mummichog (Umminger 1971).

| | |
|---|---|
| *Fundulus confluentus*, marsh killifish | *F. confluentus* is easily distinguished from the mummichog. The male has an ocellus in the dorsal fin and 10–20 thin dark vertical bars, but no silvery bars. The female has black spots and sometimes a horizontal line on the shoulder. |

*Fundulus confluentus*, marsh killifish

*F. confluentus* is easily distinguished from the mummichog. The male has an ocellus in the dorsal fin and 10–20 thin dark vertical bars, but no silvery bars. The female has black spots and sometimes a horizontal line on the shoulder.

Ken Relyea (1965) considered *F. pulvereus* of peninsular Florida to the Florida Keys to be a subspecies of *F. confluentus*. Robins et al. (1991) treats them as separate species, but I follow Relyea (1965) herein. Based on a similar disjunct distribution of similar blennies *(Chasmodes bosquianus* and *C. saburrae)*, gobies *(Gobiosoma ginsburgi* and *G. bosci)*, and killifish *(Fundulus grandis* and *F. heteroclitus)*, all breaking at about the same locations, it appears that historic events isolated peninsular Florida populations of several estuarine fishes long enough to produce speciation, only to have the isolation subsequently disappear. A rise in sea level that submersed at least northern peninsular Florida for a time would explain the disjunct distribution, but there is no evidence for that hypothetical event.

The marsh killifish probably ranges from lower Chesapeake Bay to the Florida Keys and westward on the Gulf Coast to Texas. Further study may result in *F. c. pulvereus* being elevated to full species rank (following Robins et al. 1991) with a range restricted to peninsular Florida. The range of *F. confluentus* would then be disjunct, with an East Coast population and a Gulf Coast population separated by *F. pulvereus*.

Marsh killifish occur in hard, calcium-rich fresh water, artesian wells, brackish marshes, and coastal black or white mangrove swamps, from 0 to 20 ppt (Dahlberg and Scott 1971; Lee et al. 1980), and in full sea water (30 ppt) near Jacksonville, Florida (B. Turner, pers. comm.).

*F. confluentus*, like *F. heteroclitus*, lays eggs high on the beach during the spring tides, where they remain in damp sand until they hatch when inundated at the next spring tide. Delayed hatching of *F. confluentus* eggs was described by Harrington (1959). A diapause period in killifish eggs associated with temporary drought (as in eggs laid in sand during the spring high tide) is also known in *F. heteroclitus* (see above) and reaches its extreme in the annual freshwater killifishes of eastern South America and eastern Africa.

*Fundulus jenkinsi*, saltmarsh topminnow

*F. jenkinsi* is not easy to recognize. This plain gray killifish has scattered black blotches on the flank that tend to fuse vertically, but the marks are so similar to blackspot infection with larval trematodes *(Neascus)*, that they might not be recognized as taxonomic indicators. The male and female are similar, differing slightly in fin size.

The saltmarsh topminnow is rare to locally common from the extreme western panhandle of Florida to western Galveston Bay. The Texas and Louisiana populations are geographically isolated from one another.

*F. jenkinsi* occurs in low-salinity (1–4 ppt) *Spartina* salt marshes (Hoese and Moore 1977; Lee et al. 1980). As salinity increases, it becomes less common and is not seen beyond 20 ppt.

Spotfin killifish, *Fundulus luciae,* Carteret Co., N.C. FCR

---

**Fundulus luciae, spotfin killifish**

*F. luciae* is the smallest member of the salt-marsh group, at up to 2 inches maximum length. The male has bold, dark lines on an olive body and a prominent dark spot in the dorsal fin. The female is plain, unmarked, larger, and rounder.

The spotfin killifish has an erratic distribution, with isolated collections known from Massachusetts to Georgia, but none from South Carolina.

*F. luciae* is often found in small, shallow (1–6 in., seldom to 18 in.) mud holes, ditches, and rivulets, over mud-detritus and surrounded by dense *Spartina alterniflora,* at a salinity around 12 ppt. It tolerates low dissolved oxygen concentrations, allowing it to take refuge in the mud when pursued (Richards and Bailey 1967; Byrne 1978).

The spotfin killifish adapts well to aquaria, and has been bred at 75°F and specific gravity 1.020 (McDonnell 1993), but will breed in 5 to 50 percent sea water at any room temperature. Its 2 mm diameter eggs are laid mostly near the bottom strands of spawning mops and hatch in two to four weeks. The fry are raised easily on *Artemia* nauplii, microworms, or powdered flake food.

A single member of the salt-marsh group is native to the West Coast.

---

**Fundulus parvipinnis, California killifish**

*F. parvipinnis* is olive above, yellow below, with indistinct vertical bars on the side. The nuptial male is black-brown, darker above.

The California killifish ranges from Morro Bay in central California southward to Magdalena Bay in northern Baja California, Mexico (Lee et al. 1980; Eschmeyer and Herald 1983).

*F. parvipinnis* occurs in coastal fresh water, salt marshes, lagoons, and embayments, always near shore. It feeds on shellfish, worms, and snails, and tolerates salinities from fresh water (mostly in the south) up to 128 ppt (3–4 times sea water) in salt drying ponds.

The California killifish also tolerates hydrogen sulfide concentrations that would kill other fishes. The sulfide comes from decomposition of vegetation in anaerobic salt marsh sediments. In most fishes, sulfide is converted to sulfhemoglobin, which interferes with the oxygen-carrying capacity of the red blood cells. This results in a shift to an anaerobic pathway for burning carbohydrates and a buildup of lactic acid in the blood that eventually kills most fish. The California killifish is adapted to high sulfide levels by having a detoxifying enzyme (one of the detoxifying cytochrome C enzymes in liver cell mitochondria) that converts sulfide to nontoxic thiosulfate. Thiosulfate accumulates harmlessly in the blood until it reaches 2–3 times the lethal level in other fishes, at which time it becomes lethal to this killifish (Bagarinao and Vetter 1993).

| | |
|---|---|
| *Fundulus diaphanus,* banded killifish | *F. diaphanus* is a mostly freshwater member of this group that extends into coastal marshes of an intermediate salinity of 15 to 20 ppt. It has an elongate body and a long, flattened head. It is silvery with 15 thin vertical bars on the flank, olive above, and white below. |

The banded killifish ranges from South Carolina northward to Newfoundland, and westward in the northern part of its range to the Great Lakes and Montana. South of Virginia, it is coastal, whereas in the north it is primarily a freshwater fish extending to the coast.

Two subspecies are recognized. *F. d. diaphanus* occurs along the Atlantic seaboard and westward to Lake Ontario, and *F. d. menona* occurs from Lake Ontario westward. (According to Dr. Bruce Turner, a unisexual *Fundulus* reported from Newfoundland is a permanent F, hybrid of *F. heteroclitus* and *F. diaphanus.* This phenomenon is similar to *Poecilia formosa,* the Amazon molly, being maintained by the eggs in *P. latipinna* females that are activated by sperm from other *Poecilia* species.)

| | |
|---|---|
| *Fundulus waccamensis,* Waccamaw killifish | *F. waccamensis* is more slender, slightly thinner, and derived from *F. diaphanus* through isolation over thousands of years. |

The Waccamaw killifish is endemic to Lake Waccamaw and was introduced as bait into nearby Lake Phelps, North Carolina.

*F. waccamensis* inhabits the shallow margins of two sand-bottom, shallow, clear water lakes with emergent vegetation. It is a surface schooling fish, feeding on the top and the bottom primarily on crustaceans and insects. It is protected in North Carolina, although abundant, and is taken in minnow traps for bait by local residents.

Maintain in fresh water with a small amount of sea water (one 8 oz. cup/10 gal.) to increase hardness. Use both vigorously aerated sponge filtration and an outside power filter with carbon to maintain good water quality. Large adhesive eggs from spawning mops should be moved to a shallow dish for incubation and hatching two to four weeks later.

| | |
|---|---|
| *Fundulus majalis,* striped killifish | *F. majalis* is the largest killifish of the Atlantic coast of the United States. It is gray above and white on the flank and below. The male shares the juvenile pattern (vertically striped), and has a dorsal fin ocellus (usually a female characteristic). The female has a small number of bold horizontal lines along the flank. Fins of both sexes become yellow during the summer breeding season. The female commonly grows to 5 or 6 inches, the male somewhat less. |

The striped killifish occurs along the Atlantic and Gulf coasts of the United States.

*F. majalis* is a marine killifish inhabiting high-salinity outer sounds and ocean-front beaches on shallow sand bottoms, often with sparse vegetation. It sometimes occurs with mummichogs where salinities are above 10 ppt (Richards and McBean

Waccamaw killifish, *Fundulus waccamensis,* Lake Waccamaw, N.C. RJG

Striped killifish, *Fundulus majalis,* males and females, N.C. RJG

1966), but more often separately and at much higher salinities. Not easily acclimated or spawned, the striped killifish requires high quality water and a high dissolved oxygen concentration. Wild fish may be parasitized by *Swingleus* sp., a monogenetic trematode on the skin. *Cyprinodon variegatus* may be a cleaner fish, picking those parasites from the striped killifish (Able 1976).

---

*Fundulus similis,* longnose killifish

*F. similis* has an elongate head profile and numerous dark vertical lines. The male is much smaller than the female, and becomes completely black during spawning.

The longnose killifish occurs along the Gulf Coast from Florida to Texas, in salt marshes and ocean beaches at 0.09 to 35.35 ppt and 40 to 85°F.

A burrower, *F. similis* is found on open beaches with soft bottoms free of vegetation. It avoids bottoms into which it cannot burrow (e.g., shell hash). It breeds in the spring, stops during summer, and resumes in fall.

The correct name of the Florida Keys population is in question, partly because the Keys population has characteristics of a distinct species and partly because the name *F. similis* was originally used for a fish from Texas (Robins and Ray 1986; C. Gilbert, pers. comm.).

Provide a large (30 gal.) aquarium with 75 percent sea water and a sand bottom. Eggs can be swirled from the sand, collected in an aquarium net, and removed to a 1-gallon jar of strongly aerated 50 percent sea water for hatching. Feed *Artemia* nauplii upon hatching (Martin and Finucane 1968). It hybridizes with *F. majalis* along the northeastern Florida coast (Duggans et al. 1995).

---

6. *plancterus* group
*Fundulus zebrinus,* plains killifish

*F. zebrinus* is sometimes placed in the monotypic genus *Plancterus.* It attains 3 or 4 inches. About 15–20 vertical lines are faint in the female and bold in the male. The nuptial male is reddish above and creamy white below, with bright yellow to orange-red dorsal, anal, pelvic, and pectoral fins, and a light blue caudal fin.

The plains killifish occurs in the Great Plains of the United States from Montana to Missouri and Texas. It was introduced into Utah, Arizona, and the Rio Grande River basin, and now occupies the Trinity, Colorado, and Brazos systems of New Mexico and Texas (Lee et al. 1980).

Diamond killifish, *Adinia xenica,* Manatee Co., Fla. RB

The subspecies *F. z. zebrinus* of Texas and New Mexico has red fins and larger scales (thus a smaller number) in the lateral line; *F. z. kansae* to the north has yellow fins and smaller scales (thus more of them) in the lateral line (Page and Burr 1991).

*F. zebrinus* occurs on sandy bottoms in low gradient or even still waters of low or high salinity and from neutral pH to highly alkaline, typically in desert plains where temperatures often approach 90°F. It buries in the sand, possibly to escape predators or to remain cool. In saline and in alkaline waters, it may be the only species present. It has been recommended for mosquito abatement (Nelson and Keenan 1992).

An interesting distinction in osmotic balance was demonstrated between this fish from inland, often hard, saline waters, and the mummichog, which occurs in low-salinity brackish waters but never inland in hard, alkaline water. If the pituitary glands are removed, the plains killifish survives deionized water with calcium added, but the mummichog does not (Pickford et al. 1966).

Parasites include monogenetic trematodes on the gills *(Salsuginus thalkeni, Gyrodactylus bulacanthus)* and body *(Gyrodactylus stableri),* gill protozoans (*Myxosoma funduli* and *Trichodina* sp.), and encysted larval digenetic trematodes that cause "blackspot" *(Neascus)* in the eyes and body cavity (Janovy et al. 1991). The encysted trematodes are harmless, and the others can be eliminated with formalin.

Seek it in the first, fast, haul of the seine. Otherwise, use a dip net to dig into sand or kick them out of sand during subsequent seining of the same bottom.

Care as for other members of the genus. Water need not be saline, alkaline, or hot, but must not be cold. If maintained in ponds, it should be brought indoors for the winter. Breed with spawning mops. One can also hold fish in a net and gently squeeze out the gametes into a dish, then incubate in dishes or test tubes (Wilson and Hubbs 1972). The large fry grow fast and can be sexed in four months.

---

**Genus *Adinia***

*Adinia* is monotypic, with affinities to *Fundulus.*

---

*Adinia xenica,* diamond killifish

*A. xenica* is thin and laterally compressed, with a pointed snout and high back. The body is gray with thin, dark vertical bars on the flank, and the fins are yellow.

The diamond killifish ranges from southern Florida to Texas.

*A. xenica* mostly inhabits red mangrove salt flats and grassy marshes, usually at

20 to 30 ppt; it is widespread in 1 foot of water amid dense vegetation on a silty substratum and is sometimes concentrated in pools by the receding tide (Koenig and Livingston 1976). It is tolerant of salinities from 1 to 54 ppt and temperatures from near freezing to 95°F.

A 10-gallon tank is adequate for one male and three females. For best results, use 75 percent sea water, a sponge filter with vigorous aeration, and spawning mops. Feed vegetable flakes, frozen adult and live *Artemia* nauplii, and macerated edible shrimp.

The eggs, 2 mm in diameter, are large for a fish barely 2 inches long. The eggs should be removed from the mops with fingers and placed in a 1-gallon jar containing 75 percent sea water and supplied vigorous aeration. Incubation is ten days and the fry consume *Artemia* nauplii at hatching. *Adinia* is a poor competitor and should not be mixed with other killifishes.

| | |
|---|---|
| **Genus *Leptolucania*** | *Leptolucania* is monotypic and restricted to dense shoreline vegetation in ponds and lakes of Florida and Georgia. It ranges from north of Lake Okeechobee into Georgia along the Coastal Plain, and into the entire Florida panhandle; there has been one report from Alabama and one from Mississippi. |
| *Leptolucania ommata,* pygmy killifish | *L. ommata* (plate 37) is a golden medaka-like killifish with a yellow eye, yellow fins, and a large black blotch at the base of the tail. A dusky horizontal line runs through the lower flank and indistinct vertical bars appear in the rear of some individuals. It seldom exceeds 1 inch. |
| | The primary foods year-round are aquatic insect larvae, cladocera, and mites (Oliver 1991). |
| | One pair is maintained easily in a 1-gallon jar. Feed live *Artemia* nauplii supplemented with live daphnia. It breeds in vegetation or mops and is peaceful. |
| **Genus *Lucania*** | *Lucania* is represented in the United States by *L. goodei* and *L. parva,* in Mexico by *L. interioris,* and by *L. pengelleyi* (formerly *Chriopeoides*) in Jamaica. Of the two species in the United States, one is strictly fresh water in habitat and the other is almost always in brackish coastal water, occasionally in hard water springs. |
| *Lucania goodei,* bluefin killifish | *L. goodei* (plate 38) is silvery with a bold black horizontal stripe along the flank. The nuptial male has a red blotch at the base of the pink tail fin and iridescent blue dorsal and anal fins; the fins are colorless in the female. |
| | The bluefin killifish inhabits inland peninsular Florida, but not the Keys, and only rarely occurs west of the Apalachicola River in the panhandle. It is uncommon in scattered Coastal Plain populations northward through South Carolina. |
| | *L. goodei* spawns among vegetation in clear ponds and backwaters of spring-fed streams. It feeds on small invertebrates among the plants and grazes epiphytic algae. It can survive waters of low dissolved oxygen concentrations using its small, upturned mouth to capture the oxygen layer adjacent to the surface film on the water; this is a technique also used by *Gambusia holbrooki* under the same conditions (Lewis 1970 cited in Lee et al. 1980). |
| | A 2-gallon aquarium is adequate for a pair. Maintain scrupulously clean conditions with carbon filtration, live snails for sanitation control, frequent water |

changes, and a 12- to 18-hour photoperiod to stimulate spawning in mops or vegetation. Remove eggs from mops for water incubation at warm temperatures (not less than 72°F).

| | |
|---|---|
| *Lucania parva*, rainwater killifish | *L. parva* is gray and deeper bodied, with dark-edged scales that make it appear similar to *Gambusia holbrooki* (with which it often occurs in brackish coastal waters) in the field. The male has red or orange flushes and a black edge on the fins and may have a clear or yellow tail and a black spot in the front of the dorsal fin. The rainwater killifish averages about an inch. |

It ranges along the Atlantic and Gulf coasts from Cape Cod to the Rio Grande and inland only in New Mexico. It has been introduced into California.

*L. parva* is found in salt marshes at all salinities, in vegetation or debris and on silt-mud bottoms, always in shallows. It is abundant and omnivorous.

A 1-gallon jar is adequate for a pair. Maintain in 25 to 50 percent sea water, and feed *Artemia* nauplii supplemented with flake food. Eggs from spawning mops should be incubated in shallow dishes. Eggs are small, but fry take *Artemia* nauplii upon hatching.

## Family Cyprinodontidae, the Pupfishes and Their Relatives

At present, the family Cyprinodontidae is restricted to the New World *Cyprinodon, Jordanella, Garmanella, Floridichthys, Megupsilon, Cualac* (North America), and *Orestias* (South America), and the Old World *Aphanius* and *Kosswigichthys*. The largest genus is *Cyprinodon,* with tricuspid teeth (same as *Floridichthys*), and pelvic fins in all but one species *(C. diabolis).*

### Genus *Cyprinodon*

*Cyprinodon* appears to have a Caribbean marine origin. Today only one species ranges along the Atlantic Coast of North America. A large species complex is centered in the western United States, often in highly saline and alkaline waters.

Those of the Death Valley system of California evolved as an inland sea was cut off from the Pacific Coast, caused by an uplifting and tilting toward the east of a deeply sunken valley far below sea level. As a result, groundwater recharge from mineral springs of these increasingly isolated habitats, combined with lack of rain and continuous evaporation at desert high temperatures, increased salinities to two times or more that of sea water.

Today, major threats to survival are the lowering of the water table by human demands on groundwater, and the introduction of species with which they cannot compete. The American Killifish Association has a specialized division, the *Cyprinodon* and Related Genera Study Group, that is attempting to preserve rare species through captive breeding and occasionally is permitted to handle a protected species. Those interested in the protected desert *Cyprinodon* species should contact the Desert Fishes Council in Bishop, California. The discussion herein is expanded to include species that range well outside the United States.

| | |
|---|---|
| *Cyprinodon variegatus,* sheepshead pupfish | *C. variegatus* has a thick and short body, with a marbled pattern on a silvery flank that is most pronounced in the female and juvenile. The male has a brilliant iridescent blue (equivalent to the neon tetra) nape from the origin of the dorsal fin to the snout; the unpaired fins are pink to yellow, often with a black margin. |

The sheepshead pupfish is called (erroneously) in all the aquarium and technical literature the sheepshead minnow; it is not a minnow. One of the most studied

Sheepshead pupfish, *Cyprinodon variegatus,* Fla. WFR

Lake Eustis pupfish, *Cyprinodon variegatus hubbsi,* Fla. RJG

of all fishes (Bengston 1980), it is used in aquatic toxicity bioassays of treated sewage effluent under EPA guidelines.

*C. variegatus* ranges from Cape Cod to the mouth of the Rio Tuxpan in Mexico along the Atlantic Coast; it is the only pupfish on the Atlantic and Gulf Coasts of the United States. It is divided into subspecies from north to south. Page and Burr (1991) relegated the Lake Eustis pupfish *(Cyprinodon hubbsi* or *C. variegatus hubbsi)* to synonymy with *C. variegatus.*

*C. variegatus* is found in low-salinity estuarine marshes. Jordan et al. (1993) noted that the Lake Eustis pupfish, although long isolated in a freshwater lake and a "species of special concern" in Florida, retains the remarkable capability of the genus to tolerate wide ranges in salinity; experiments showed *C. v. hubbsi* could tolerate double strength sea water.

The sheepshead pupfish typically inhabits a tidal pool or stream with sand bottom and sand slopes or oyster and mussel peat muck banks. It occurs within a well-developed shoreline seagrass habitat, but also appears in disturbed habitats with little vegetation. Its most frequent associates are *Fundulus heteroclitus* in the northeastern states and *F. grandis* in the South. It inhabits full-strength ocean water along the shoreline at Key West, Florida, where it associates with *Poecilia latipinna.* It is excluded from fresh waters, mostly by centrarchid fishes and competition from other species, but can survive in fresh water supplemented with calcium or other hardening minerals (Martin 1972). Wild specimens may be infested with fish lice, *Argulus funduli* (Yeatman 1966). Its reproductive behavior has been thoroughly investigated (Raney et al. 1953; Fanara 1964; Itzkowitz 1974).

*C. variegatus* is maintained easily in brackish or marine water, and an excellent community fish that gets along well with gobies, blennies, and *Fundulus.* For breeding, a bare 5-gallon aquarium with 25 percent sea water is suitable for one male and three or four females.

Provide a spawning mop, and feed flake foods, frozen adult *Artemia,* and blackworms. The egg-laden mop should be removed to a 1-gallon jar with 25 percent sea water and vigorously aerated. The eggs hatch in one week, and the fry take *Artemia* nauplii on the second day. Growth is slow. Rearing the fry and juveniles in varying salinities will expand the salinity tolerance of the adults (Martin 1968). Note: males fight and sometimes kill one another.

| | |
|---|---|
| *Cyprinodon artifrons,*<br>Yucatan pupfish | *C. artifrons* is sometimes considered a subspecies of *C. variegatus,* but is darker with yellow fins.<br><br>The Yucatan pupfish ranges from the coast of Yucatan to southern Belize and possibly south to Nicaragua (not confirmed).<br><br>*C. artifrons* occurs in vegetated ditches and beaches, from fresh water to sea water, and usually over soft, gray muck bottoms. It becomes black in full-strength sea water. Inland populations referred to as *C. variegatus baconi* are minute and dark, but their offspring assume normal *C. artifrons* size and color in captivity. |
| *Cyprinodon dearborni,*<br>Dearborn's pupfish | *C. dearborni* occurs on the Venezuelan coast inland to Lake Maracaibo, and offshore on Bonaire, Aruba, and Curacao in the southern Caribbean.<br><br>Dearborn's pupfish is found in fresh water, coastal estuaries, and hypersaline salt ponds (salinas), among dense vegetation over soft gray muck bottoms. Vast schools look like tiny, dark, charcoal colored tadpoles, their small, thick bodies capable of great speed. Almost all the islands of the Caribbean contain isolated populations of pupfish, but their genetics have not been investigated. Further studies may indicate more species than currently recognized.<br><br>The remaining members of the genus are restricted to southwestern North America. They can be divided into wide-ranging and isolated species. The wide-ranging species include *C. macularius, C. pecosensis, C. eximius,* and *C. rubrofluviatilis. C. nevadensis* is intermediate. |
| *Cyprinodon rubrofluviatilis,*<br>Red River pupfish | *C. rubrofluviatilis* has thick blocklike blotches on the side of the male; the female has dark but ventrally reduced blotches, and is mostly silvery below. The nuptial male is light iridescent blue overall.<br><br>The Red River pupfish occurs in headwaters of the Red River and Brazos River drainages of Texas and Oklahoma, where it endures extremes of temperature (freezing to 100°F) caused by the salt having eliminated shade vegetation at the shallows, and by its geographic location in western Texas, which suffers from excessive summer heat, flash flooding (when saline trickles become roaring freshwater rivers), and frigid winters (Echelle, Hubbs, and Echelle 1972).<br><br>*C. rubrofluviatilis* usually is found in saline waters (10–20 ppt), but it tolerates conditions from fresh water to full-strength marine water (Renfro and Hill 1971). It readily hybridizes with other species of *Cyprinodon.* Its most common associates are *Fundulus zebrinus, Hybognathus placitus,* and *Notropis bairdi* (Echelle, Echelle, and Hill 1972). |
| *Cyprinodon macularius,*<br>desert pupfish | *C. macularius* is blue with a yellow or orange caudal peduncle. The male has a thin black margin on the anal, dorsal, and caudal fins.<br><br>The desert pupfish is widespread in the lower Colorado and Gila Rivers of Arizona and California and in the Salton Sea and in some rivers of Mexico and Baja California.<br><br>Page and Burr (1991) indicate two subspecies, *C. m. eremus* from Organ Pipe Cactus National Monument and *C. m. macularius* for those occurring elsewhere.<br><br>*C. macularius* inhabits ephemeral rivers, springs, pools, the Salton Sea, and desert saline marshes, over mud or sand bottoms where it grazes on algae, |

Desert pupfish, *Cyprinodon macularius,* Rio San Pedro, Ariz. WFR

cyanobacteria, tiny snails, ostracods, amphipods, and other small animals. It tolerates unusual temperatures, salinities, and dissolved oxygen concentrations (Sweet and Kinne 1964; Lowe et al. 1967; Lowe and Heath 1969).

Crear and Haydock (1971) demonstrated that the fish is reared easily in captivity, obviating the need to collect wild stock after a brood stock is established. Fish were fed tubifex and whiteworms, brine shrimp, beef liver, lettuce, spinach, and commercial fish food, and given a 16-hour photoperiod (8 hr. dark).

Spawning occurred on a green plastic mat or on white cheesecloth held down by glass rods, but those on the mat were exposed and usually eaten. Best results were obtained in 50 percent sea water. It tolerates 0–70 ppt and temperatures from near freezing to over 100°F, and survives reduced dissolved oxygen concentrations that would kill other fishes.

It is uncommon and protected.

---

### *Cyprinodon nevadensis,* Amargosa pupfish

The male of *C. nevadensis* is mottled gray overlaid with a sky blue iridescence, and has black-edged dorsal, anal, and caudal fins. The dorsal fin originates slightly more than half way back. It is a large (often up to 2½ in.) desert pupfish.

The Amargosa pupfish is found in springs and streams of the Amargosa River basin on the California-Nevada border, where it is had been differentiating into six subspecies. *C. n. nevadensis* occurs in Saratoga Springs; *C. n. calidae* from Tecopa Hot Springs is extinct; *C. n. shoshone* from Shoshone Springs barely survives; *C. n. pectoralis* occurs near Devils Hole; *C. n. amargosae* is known from an artesian well (Tecopa Bore) and other waters in the area; and *C. n. mionectes* occurs in Ash Meadows.

*C. nevadensis* survives in saline waters ranging from freezing to over 100°F, with constant temperature refuges at spring mouths. It feeds mostly on blue-green cyanobacterial mats and their invertebrate fauna (aufwuchs). The Amargosa pupfish is among the most studied of all pupfishes (Brown and Feldmeth 1971; Feldmeth et al. 1974; Naiman 1976; Lee et al. 1980; Page and Burr 1991).

If available, provide 50 percent or more sea water, warmth, and both meat and vegetation to supplement a diet of flake foods.

Joy Shrode (Developmental temperature tolerance of a Death Valley pupfish: pp. 378–89; date and journal unknown) described spawning in captivity. A male took position over an orlon mop, and females came into the mop for spawning.

Eggs were placed in temperature controlled waters with methylene blue to retard fungus, and the eggs given 16 hours of light and 8 hours dark. A great range of temperatures was tested, and normal hatching was attained mostly at 70 to 85°F; fry survival plunged when the temperature exceeded 90°F.

A permit from the state or the federal Bureau of Land Management is required to collect this fish. *C. n. mionectes* and *C. n. pectoralis* are protected. The best place to collect *C. n. amargosae* is Tecopa, where it is abundant; Tecopa Bore is not a good place to collect, as it is mucky.

---

*Cyprinodon pecosensis,*
Pecos pupfish

*C. pecosensis* has a marbled body. Blotches are larger on the upper flank than on the lower in the female and juvenile. The male has a blue iridescent nape, a white belly and cheeks, yellow pectoral fins, distinctive black dorsal and anal fins, and a narrow black band on the dusky tail fin (Echelle and Echelle 1978).

The Pecos pupfish occurs in the Pecos River drainage from Independence Creek in Terrel County, Texas, to Roswell in Chaves County, New Mexico. In Texas, most populations are hybrids with introduced *Cyprinodon variegatus*, whereas New Mexico populations are mostly pure (Wilde and Echelle 1992).

*C. pecosensis* inhabits saline springs, gypsum sinkholes, and desert streams, usually in highly saline waters with few other species (although it can tolerate lower salinities). Frequent associates are *Fundulus zebrinus, Lucania parva, Gambusia affinis,* and *Cyprinella lutrensis*. In the Bitter Lake National Wildlife Refuge, it occurs with *Gambusia nobilis* and *Etheostoma lepidum* (Echelle and Echelle 1978). It chases *F. zebrinus* from its spawning territory, this behavior and intense blue coloration of the males stronger in saline waters (close to its 30 ppt salinity tolerance limit), and less marked at 20 ppt (Kodric-Brown and Mazzolini 1992).

The Pecos pupfish is available for breeding. Use a sand bottom with scattered rocks, hard and saline water, and bottom spawning mops. Use Malawi salts or two-thirds strength synthetic sea water.

---

*Cyprinodon eximius,*
Conchos pupfish

*C. eximius,* the Conchos pupfish, apparently consists of four species and many other related forms. The best-known form does not have prominent blue coloration. The robust male has dark bars on the side, a black-edged and speckled tail fin and an orange dorsal fin.

Locally abundant in the Rio Conchos drainage (tributary to the Rio Grande) of the Chihuahuan desert in northern Mexico, and northeastward to Val Verde County, Texas (Lee et al. 1980).

*C. eximius* inhabits quiet backwaters of larger streams and creeks, where it feeds on small organisms that collect in pits the fish construct in the soft bottom, a food-gathering behavior also occurring in the detritus-feeding mullet *(Mugil cephalus)* of Atlantic and Gulf estuaries. Mexican stock is preferred, for the fish are common there, but uncommon in Texas. The fish is a member of a group of a dozen similar species found primarily on the Mexican Plateau. In addition to four nominal *C. eximius,* there are three nominal *C. nazas,* plus *C. macrolepis, C. pachycephalus, C. atrorus, C. meeki, C. alvarezi,* and *C. ceciliae*. The relationships were recently discussed by Echelle and Echelle (1998).

The remaining pupfish occur in limited, often isolated, habitats and are almost all protected.

*Cyprinodon alvarezi* of Mexico is a member of the *C. eximius* complex. RJG

---

**Cyprinodon diabolis,**
Devils Hole pupfish

*C. diabolis* is the pupfish best known to the public. It is slimmer than other pupfishes and the only one without pelvic fins (a characteristic of springfishes). It has no bars or blotches. The male is iridescent blue with golden median fins with black margins. It is the smallest desert pupfish at barely 1 inch long maximum size.

*C. diabolis* is native only to Devils Hole, a single limestone spring in Ash Meadows (Death Valley) in Nye County, Nevada.

The U.S. Fish and Wildlife Service has established another limestone spring refugium where it is reproducing. Propagation in captivity is difficult due to its evolutionary adaptations to the unusual water chemistry of Devils Hole. Interestingly, laboratory-propagated fish are much larger than wild fish and resemble *C. nevadensis* in color, suggesting that the Devils Hole pupfish is derived from one of the large pupfishes in the area.

Dr. Richard Haas of the American Killifish Association has attempted to persuade the U.S. Department of the Interior, National Park Service, and U.S. Fish and Wildlife Service to allow distribution of eggs propagated in his laboratory to selected expert aquarists, but was unsuccessful. The fish is endangered nearly to extinction by water table drawdown many miles from Death Valley.

---

**Cyprinodon bovinus,**
Leon Springs pupfish

*C. bovinus* is silvery with brown blotches, large in the male but large and small (especially on the lower side) in the female. The male has a yellow edge on his dorsal fin, and a black edge on the partially yellow tail fin.

The Leon Springs pupfish occurs in Pecos County, Texas, at Leon Creek and Diamond-Y Spring (Pecos River system).

*C. bovinus* is found on the edges of algae-free clearings in pools and springs, where the water has high concentrations of sulfates, silica, and chlorides. Where it coexists with the introduced *C. variegatus,* introgressive hybrids have been eliminating the original species (Echelle and Echelle 1994).

The Leon Springs pupfish is an endangered species that may not be collected or possessed.

---

**Cyprinodon elegans,**
Comanche Springs pupfish

Large males of *C. elegans* (**plate 39**) have a series of indistinct indigo blotches along the midline and a black-edged caudal fin.

The Comanche Springs pupfish occurs only in San Solomon Spring, Phantom Cave Spring and irrigation canals, Toyah Creek (fed by Griffin Spring) and adjacent marshes, and in Lake Balmorhea of Reeves County, Texas (Echelle 1975; Lee et al. 1980; Echelle and Echelle 1994). It is now rare in Toyah Creek since invasion by *Lepomis cyanellus, Dionda episcopa, Astyanax mexicanus, Fundulus zebrinus, Gambusia geiseri, G. affinis,* and *Cyprinella lutrensis* (Echelle 1975).

The populations are different, reflecting thousands of years of isolation. It has been extirpated from Comanche Springs (which has dried from water demands for irrigation) in Pecos County, Texas, and has been outcompeted by invading *C. variegatus* (with no evidence of hybridization). It inhabits flowing waters, over mud and vegetation *(Chara).*

*C. elegans* is an endangered species and cannot be collected.

| | |
|---|---|
| *Cyprinodon radiosus,*<br>Owens pupfish | *C. radiosus* **(plate 40)** has horizontal and vertical dark markings reminiscent of *Heterandria formosa.* The breeding male is much larger than the female and is bright blue with orange edges on the fins.<br><br>The Owens pupfish originally occurred in the Owens River basin in Inyo and Mono Counties of California, but now is restricted to three locales near Bishop, California (Lee et al. 1980; Page and Burr 1991).<br><br>*C. radiosus* is found in clear, warm marshes, backwaters, and other stagnant habitats.<br><br>An endangered species, it cannot be collected. Should it become available, which is not likely, propagation would probably be easy; the fish does not require high temperatures or unusual water chemistry. |
| *Cyprinodon salinus,*<br>Salt Creek pupfish | The male of *C. salinus* is iridescent sky blue with gray bars on the body, and the tail fin is black-edged. The female is similar to other desert pupfishes.<br><br>The Salt Creek pupfish occurs in McLean's Spring, which feeds into a 2-mile segment of Salt Creek in northern Death Valley. It has since been transplanted to River Springs in Mono County, California (Lee et al. 1980). The Salt Creek population is periodically extirpated by droughts, but is reintroduced by flooding from McLean's Spring during rainy seasons. Populations once became so large that the Shoshone tribal people would bake them in massive pies.<br><br>*Cyprinodon s. milleri* differs slightly in pores, rays, and proportions, and occupies adjacent Cottonball Marsh (LaBounty and Deacon 1972). Although capable of withstanding over 100°F (Otto and Gerking 1973) and salinities twice that of sea water, its normal habitat is best illustrated by conditions in Cottonball Marsh in Death Valley (250 ft. below sea level).<br><br>Throughout this extensive marsh, salinities range from 14 to 160 ppt (sea water is 36 ppt), and the ground is encrusted with gypsum and sodium sulfate. Emergent vegetation consists of *Ruppia maritima, Juncus,* and algae. The algae is grazed by *Tryonia* (a snail in the marine family Hyabrobiidae), *Hyalella* (an amphipod), and ostracods (LaBounty and Deacon 1972).<br><br>Despite a population in the millions, this fish may not be taken from the area. |
| *Cyprinodon tularosa,*<br>White Sands pupfish | *C. tularosa* is a silvery pupfish that rarely attains 2 inches. The male has an orange outer dorsal fin and a black-edged tail fin; the female has dark vertical bands that coalesce along the lower flank. |

The White Sands pupfish is abundant in Malpais Spring, Salt Creek, and other springs and runs in Tularosa Valley of Otero County, New Mexico.

*C. tularosa* inhabits clear saline water with vegetation, over mud, silt, gravel or sand. Because of its limited range, it is vulnerable to extinction. Before collecting, confirm its availability with state agencies.

## Genus *Megupsilon*

*Megupsilon aporus* is a *Cyprinodon* in almost all respects. It has a single row of tricuspid teeth and occurs in a single, spring-fed pond on a high, arid plateau in Nuevo Leon, Mexico. It was placed in its own genus (Miller and Walters 1972) because it has unequal numbers of chromosomes in the sexes (n = 47 in the male; n = 48 in the female), and the male also has a huge Y-chromosome. It did not hybridize with any *Cyprinodon* species in laboratory-forced matings.

Males are iridescent blue on the nape and front of the flanks and black between the dorsal and anal fins. The head and caudal peduncle also have a bronze sheen. The base of the dorsal is orange, the remainder of the fin opaque bluish white. The anal fin is also bluish white, and the caudal fin is light orange and has no contrasting marginal color. Females are golden. Neither sex nor the juveniles possess an ocellus in the dorsal fin, a common mark in *Cyprinodon* species. Maximum size is 2 inches for a large female, and males are smaller.

The predominant vegetation is *Ceratophyllum* (hornwort), but *Potamogeton* and *Nasturtium* are also present. The water in the pond was pH 7.2–7.4, and DH 11–15 or 197–269 ppm as CaO.

*Megupsilon* feeds on chironomids and shares the pond with an omnivorous *Cyprinodon*, perhaps *C. cf. eximius*, and introduced goldfish. Its protected status is not known.

## Genus *Floridichthys*

*Floridichthys* contains two species, *F. carpio* and *F. polyommus*. Both are adapted to excessively hot and hypersaline water but tolerate normal sea water. They are much larger and deeper-bodied but not as plumply rounded as *Cyprinodon*, or as laterally compressed as *Adinia*.

## *Floridichthys carpio*, Florida goldspotted killifish

*F. carpio* has yellow to orange spots on a silvery side, mixed with indistinct dashes above and stripes on the flank (the female and most males). The occasional dominant male (only one of hundreds) has brilliant red-orange to golden yellow spots on the body and margins of the unpaired fins. The male may attain 3 inches, but 2 inches is normal adult size.

The Florida goldspotted killifish occurs in Dade County, Florida and is the only killifish abundant in the hypersaline cooling canal system at the Turkey Point nuclear power plant site. Outside the canals in nearby Card Sound, it is abundant in red mangrove forests in hypersaline (from solar evaporation), hot shallows. Schools contain hundreds of individuals.

## *Floridichthys polyommus*, Yucatan goldspotted killifish

*F. polyommus* occurs at Cancun on the Atlantic Coast of Mexico. It occupies hot, hypersaline red mangrove shallows in open pools and deep inside the cooler shaded forest.

The Yucatan goldspotted killifish is aggressive, usually occurring in schools of fish all the same size, with no other fish species present. Roving schools presum-

Florida goldspotted killifish, *Floridichthys carpio,* Dade Co., Fla. RJG

Yucatan goldspotted killifish, *Floridichthys polyommus,* Cancun, Q. R., Mexico. RJG

ably feed on young mollies, gobies, and other inshore fishes, young of their own species, grass shrimp, amphipods, other crustaceans, and algae. *Floridichthys* are voracious on flake foods, frozen brine shrimp, and meat.

A 10-gallon aquarium with 100 percent sea water is minimum size for a trio, but a larger tank would be better. Use strong aeration, sponge filtration, frequent water changes, and sunken spawning mops.

The eggs are colorless, clear, unusually small for a killifish at less than 1 mm, and may be too numerous to pick. Remove the egg-laden mop to a 1-gallon jar of sea water with strong aeration, and allow the eggs to hatch directly from the mops. The fry take *Artemia* nauplii in a day or so, and are strongly attracted to the bottom, where they resemble tiny sand colored amphipods. They do not ascend into the water column for some weeks.

---

**Genus *Jordanella***

*Jordanella* contains two species having a diagnostic single spine in the dorsal fin and tricuspid teeth.

---

*Jordanella floridae,* Florida flagfish

*J. floridae* (**plate 41**) is a chunky killifish with a prominent dark mark and characteristic horizontal thin green lines on the flank. A larger male has intervening red lines that extend into the enlarged dorsal fin. Its nearest relative is the Yucatan *Jordanella pulchra* from low-salinity water (Parker and Kornfield 1995), a fish previously placed in *Garmanella.*

The Florida flagfish occurs in southern peninsular Florida, and is the most southerly of American killifishes.

The male occupies a territory in dense vegetation of ponds and lakes over mud or silt, and fans the silt to uncover benthic animals upon which it feeds. With maturity, this behavior develops into territorial spawning behavior, as the male attempts embraces with females entering his feeding territory (Foster 1966).

*J. floridae* is maintained easily in fresh water, with or without salt, and spawned in bare aquariums with spawning mops (Smith 1973), especially on the bottom (Isgro 1982). The fish does better in a larger aquarium with *Nitella* or *Ceratophyllum* and strong light with a 14-hour photoperiod.

Best egg production will result with one fish per gallon in large (50 gal.) tanks. The vegetation can be transferred to another tank for hatching, or fry can be re-

Yucatan flagfish, *Jordanella pulchra,* Cancun, Q. R., Mexico. RJG

moved when seen at the surface. The Florida flagfish requires heat. Its fecundity, ease of breeding, and complex behavior make it a good animal for aquatic toxicity studies (Foster 1969).

*Jordanella pulchra,* Yucatan flagfish

The Yucatan flagfish was previously placed in the monotypic genus *Garmanella,* but recent DNA studies and morphology support merging *Garmanella* into (previously monotypic) *Jordanella.*

Smaller and less sexually dimorphic or dichromic than *J. floridae, J. pulchra* averages 1 inch, probably does not attain 2 inches, and is principally golden white with brownish black blotches and green iridescence. It occurs in coastal ditches and ponds of the Yucatan peninsula in brackish and fresh waters, always associated with dense vegetation.

Like *Megupsilon, J. pulchra* has 47 chromosome pairs in the male and 48 in the female, and a giant male Y-chromosome (Levin and Foster 1972).

The Yucatan flagfish is intolerant of pollution and requires clean water, dense vegetation or spawning mops, and live foods such as *Artemia* adults and nauplii. It is not prolific. The young also require good water quality, maintained by siphoning decaying, uneaten food from the bottom.

# 15     The Order Atheriniformes

*T*HE order Atheriniformes was recently split out of the Cyprinodontiformes. It includes the families Poeciliidae and Atherinidae.

## Family Poeciliidae, the Livebearers

The Poeciliidae are small, insectivorous or omnivorous fishes that produce living young by ovoviviparity. There is no lateral line, and only a single dorsal fin. The anal fin of the male is modified into an intromittent organ (the gonopodium) with taxonomically diagnostic hooks and spines. The gonopodium delivers sperm packets inside the female.

The female, in many but not all species, can store sperm for several rounds of pregnancy and births. The eggs are fertilized internally, but no nourishment is provided from any source other than the egg itself; the fish is thereby classified as ovoviviparous. There is no placenta-like nutrient contribution by the mother, as there is in the related Mexican livebearer family Goodiidae. There is no cannibalism by and of the embryos prior to birth as in some other fishes.

In the process known as gynogenesis, eggs are activated by the sperm of another species, resulting in the egg developing into an embryo entirely with the chromosomes of the mother (i.e., all offspring are identical copies of the mother, or clones). This occurs in the Poeciliidae of southern Texas; the sperm of *Poecilia mexicana* stimulates the eggs of *P. latipinna* to develop, without contributing any genetic material. This has produced an all female Texas population known as the Amazon molly, *P. "formosa."*

The Poeciliidae range throughout the United States and Central America, including the entire Caribbean. All livebearers can be collected by dip net or seine. There are 4 genera and 14 species in the continental United States.

Students of this family should read Meffe and Snelson's (1989) *Ecology and Evolution of Livebearing Fishes.*

## Genus *Heterandria*
*Heterandria formosa,* least killifish

*H. formosa* is the only member of its genus in the United States. It is minute (females are seldom more than 1 in.; males seldom attain 1 inch), dark olive above, bright white below, with a thick horizontal dark stripe and numerous thinner dark vertical bands that suggest a checkerboard pattern. The male may have a spot of red in the dorsal fin. Misnamed, a more appropriate name would be least livebearer.

The least killifish ranges along the Atlantic Coastal Plain from southern North Carolina to all of Florida, and continues westward to Louisiana on the Gulf Coast.

Least killifish, *Heterandria formosa,* Manatee Co., Fla. RB

Sailfin molly, *Poecilia latipinna,* Ginny Springs, Fla. WFR

*H. formosa* occurs in dense floating and shoreline vegetation of fresh water or slightly brackish ponds, lakes, sluggish swamp streams, and in roadside ditches, feeding on small crustaceans, insect larvae, and filamentous algae (McLane 1955).

A fine-mesh (⅛ in.) dip net or an aquarium net will yield both sexes, whereas a normal ¼-inch seine will yield only the larger, pregnant females.

A delightful livebearer, peaceful and prolific, it should be kept in a densely vegetated aquarium with snails and small fishes such as pygmy sunfishes *(Elassoma)* and swampfish *(Chologaster cornuta).* It thrives on flake food, but its health declines in the presence of decaying food or vegetation. The young are birthed only one or two a day until the brood is completely expelled. A forage fish for many other types of fishes, it will not survive with dwarf sunfishes *(Enneacanthus)* or in open habitats.

**Genus *Poecilia***
*Poecilia latipinna,* sailfin molly

*P. latipinna* was previously in the large genus, now relegated to subgenus, *Mollienesia.* (New DNA studies may clarify the complex and unwieldy genus *Poecilia* and lead to restoration of some older subgeneric names to full generic ranking.)

The sailfin molly has thickened, upward facing jaws, horizontal rows of black spots along a green-gray flank and, in older males, a spectacular, flaglike, spotted dorsal fin originating in advance of the pelvic fin origin. A rich golden breast and gold edging on the dorsal fin are common in males of many populations. The sailfin molly attains 3–5 inches.

Populations in the northern part of the range consist of small individuals with poorly developed dorsal fins; to the south, especially in marine environments, they are larger, the males are more colorful, and they have immense dorsal fins. Some populations have blotched individuals.

*P. latipinna* ranges from southern coastal North Carolina through Florida and the Gulf Coast to western Yucatan, and is replaced on the northern Yucatan peninsula by the strictly Mexican *P. velifera.*

The sailfin molly occurs in fresh, brackish, and marine water, in weed-choked shallows (polluted or not), but inland in clear, hard water rivers. It is uncommon in turbid waters. The sailfin molly grazes on algae, detritus, floating insects, small crustaceans, and zooplankton.

*P. latipinna* does well in fresh water, better if the water is hard or brackish. It is an excellent community fish in both freshwater and marine aquariums. It thrives

Gila topminnow, *Poeciliopsis occidentalis,* Santa Cruz R., Ariz. WFR

on flake food supplemented with filamentous algae and other vegetation (including cooked vegetables). The female should be provided a private, densely vegetated aquarium for birthing her young, which may number more than 100.

| | |
|---|---|
| *Poecilia mexicana,* shortfin molly | *P. mexicana* has a normal dorsal fin that begins behind the origin of the pelvic fins. The body may be dark above, with rows or orange spots on the side and an orange border on the caudal (and sometimes the dorsal) fin. It averages 2 to 3 inches long.<br><br>The shortfin molly may be a species complex in the United States, consisting of *P. mexicana, P. "sphenops"* (of aquarium origin), or a hybrid swarm of species. *P. mexicana* originated in Mexico, and the scientific name may refer to more than one biological species. Isolated populations occur to the north in Arizona, California, Florida (aquarium origin), and elsewhere in warm, heavily vegetated springs, spring runs, and ditches.<br><br>Mollies should never be released into natural waters, particularly in the western United States, as they have a record of competing with and displacing desert pupfishes with similar habitat and feeding requirements. |
| *Poecilia "formosa,"* Amazon molly | *P. "formosa"* is a name applied to a population of parthenogenetic females of sailfin mollies, *P. latipinna,* whose eggs are activated by the sperm of shortfin mollies, *P. mexicana,* and other species of Poeciliidae. Males of Amazon mollies, therefore, cannot exist.<br><br>This population is confined to coastal extreme southern Texas and northern Mexico. |
| *Poeciliopsis occidentalis,* Gila topminnow | A large male of *P. occidentalis* becomes black, with orange at the bases of the fins; smaller males are light, with gradually developing dark spots and a horizontal stripe on the flank. The female has a dark stripe along the flank on a gray body.<br><br>The Gila topminnow is a livebearer in the Gila River system of Arizona (where it is a protected species); it ranges southward into Mexico.<br><br>*Poeciliopsis o. occidentalis* has been mostly extirpated, but survives in isolated locales in Arizona and New Mexico, mostly in streams, springs, and cienegas (marshes); *P. o. sonoriensis* ranges northward from Sonora, Mexico, into the Rio Yaqui drainage of southeastern Arizona, occurring mostly in narrow streams susceptible to flash floods. |

Throughout most of its range, the Gila topminnow has been eliminated by competition from introduced *Gambusia affinis,* but appears to survive competition in the southern part of its range where it has adapted to episodes of flash flooding by hugging the banks; the introduced *Gambusia* is washed away by flash flooding (Galat and Robertson 1992).

| | |
|---|---|
| **Genus *Gambusia*** | The large genus *Gambusia* occurs throughout North and Central America. In the United States, it contains about a dozen species, including a few wide-ranging eastern and central species; the rest are western, almost all protected and nearly or actually extinct. |

*Gambusia affinis,*
central mosquitofish

*G. affinis* is an important public health tool, transplanted everywhere to control the mosquitoes that carry malaria, yellow fever, and a host of other human and livestock diseases.

The central mosquitofish is gray to olive with iridescent metallic highlights, occasionally with fine black speckles, and identified by its gonopodial hook pattern and geographic distribution in the United States. It usually has six dorsal and nine anal rays.

In its native range, *G. affinis* occurs in the central and coastal states in Gulf Coast drainages from Mobile, Alabama, to Vera Cruz, Mexico, ranging northward to Indiana and Illinois (Lee et al. 1980; Lydeard et al. 1991). Suspected transplants or stream capture populations are found in the Savannah and Chattahoochee drainages of Georgia. It occurs elsewhere in the United States due to bait bucket introductions.

The central mosquitofish is abundant in the margins of lakes, rivers, streams, ponds, and roadside ditches, usually in shallow clearings among shoreline vegetation, on mud, silt, or leaf-litter bottoms.

Maintained easily in small (5 gal.) aquaria, the central mosquitofish does better in larger quarters with abundant vegetation. It is cannibalistic on its young. Top feeders engorging on flake foods, they will take anything offered, from live blackworms and fruit flies to crushed snails and macerated meats.

Newly captured females near term tend to drop young prematurely with unabsorbed yolk sacs (they seldom survive). Females only slightly swollen with developing young should be isolated in densely vegetated aquaria, and removed after birthing.

Mosquitofish released in western aquatic habitats for mosquito control or as bait bucket introductions have overpopulated these waters and have eliminated or threaten to eliminate endangered native species. Excess aquarium stock should be fed to predatory fishes or destroyed, but never released.

*Gambusia holbrooki,*
eastern mosquitofish

*G. holbrooki* is similar to the central mosquitofish, but usually has seven dorsal and ten anal rays. Melanistic (dark spotted) males are common in coastal populations in the southern part of the range, but melanistic females are rare.

The eastern mosquitofish occurs in Atlantic coastal states from the Delmarva Peninsula to peninsular Florida, and along the Gulf Coast to Pensacola or slightly westward.

*G. holbrooki* is found in roadside ditches, lake margins, quiet streams, ponds, and river shallows, among clearings in shoreline vegetation.

Eastern mosquitofish, *Gambusia holbrooki,* pair, N.C. RJG

Eastern mosquitofish, *Gambusia holbrooki,* melanistic male, N.C. RJG

The melanistic males are readily spotted in surface schools of these abundant fishes and are most common near the coast. Melanistic males begin life with fine black spots that enlarge and coalesce with age. Continued crossing of these males to sisters may result in melanism on females, but no such aquarium strain exists.

In the related G. *yucatana,* the Yucatan mosquitofish, melanistic females are common, and melanistic males and females also may have yellow patches. Because yellow, red, and black are all part of the same biochemical pathway to melanin production, combinations should not be surprising.

| *Gambusia rhizophorae,*<br>mangrove gambusia | G. *rhizophorae* is a large, hot water marine mosquitofish with fine black spotting.<br><br>The mangrove gambusia ranges from coastal southern Florida to the north shore of Cuba (Lee et al. 1980).<br><br>G. *rhizophorae* is found in red mangrove flats at high temperatures and seawater salinity (sp. gr. 1.025 or 35 ppt) or higher (hypersaline) due to intense solar evaporation of the shallows. It extends slightly inland to lower salinities dominated by black or white mangroves, but its distribution is also limited by temperature (Getter 1982). Its major foods in the mangrove forests are spiders and ants, and its principal associates are marine fishes.<br><br>Traps and small seines work best in these vegetated shallows, but a small boat will be needed when entering from the sea to penetrate the vast, dense grass flats and mangrove forests. The mangrove gambusia is suitable for marine aquaria; its young will provide food for predatory fishes, but it is not attractive.<br><br>The remaining members of the genus are western. |
| :--- | :--- |
| *Gambusia senilis,*<br>blotched gambusia | G. *senilis* has a few large, black spots distributed randomly on the flank below the lateral line, a dusky horizontal stripe, and no spotting of the fins. Its diagnosis is based on the gonopodial hook pattern.<br><br>The blotched gambusia is known from Devils River, Texas, from which it may have been extirpated.<br><br>G. *senilis* probably survives in tributaries of the Rio Conchos in Mexico, in densely vegetated shallows.<br><br>Collecting in Mexico requires a permit, not readily obtained. |

Pecos gambusia, *Gambusia nobilis,* female, Reeves Co., Tex. GS

Pecos gambusia, *Gambusia nobilis,* male, Reeves Co., Tex. GS

---

**Gambusia geiseri,**
**largespring gambusia**

*G. geiseri* has a row of black spots at the base of the dorsal, anal, and caudal fins, and another row vertically in the middle of the caudal fin; no red appears in the fins. Otherwise, its taxonomy is based on gonopodial spines.

The largespring gambusia occurs in the San Marcos Spring and River, Comal Spring and Creek, Bear Creek, Devils River, South Fork Guadalupe River, Concho River, Tunis Springs (Lee et al. 1980), and in the Colorado and Pecos drainages (Page and Burr 1991) of Texas and Mexico.

*G. geiseri* inhabits clear, cold, high volume springs pouring from limestone aquifers. Keep it in cold, clear water. Although not a protected species, it occurs in the same waters as other protected mosquitofish and with the protected fountain darter, *Etheostoma fonticola.*

Collection in habitats of protected species *will be* construed as interference with those protected species, and thus violate the federal Endangered Species Act. The consequences are considerable.

---

**Gambusia nobilis,** Pecos gambusia

*G. nobilis* is a slim mosquitofish with slightly dark edging on the unpaired fins, a dusky horizontal band along the flank, and a diagnostic gonopodial hook pattern.

The Pecos gambusia occurs in western tributaries of the Pecos River system in Texas and New Mexico (Lee et al. 1980). In New Mexico, it is found at Blue Springs and at Bitter Lake National Wildlife Refuge. It is known from three times as many locales in western Texas, but is still rare and localized.

*G. nobilis* prefers limestone-rich sink holes and springs in the shallow, dense, edge vegetation.

The Pecos gambusia is a protected species and cannot be collected or possessed.

The remaining members of the genus are near extinction or may already be extinct.

---

**Gambusia amistadensis,**
**Amistad gambusia**

*G. amistadensis* is a typical gray mosquitofish with black spots and crescents on the upper sides, most similar to the Big Bend mosquitofish (Page and Burr 1991), but with a more elongate body and different gonopodial hook pattern. It probably no longer exists.

Big Bend gambusia, *Gambusia gaigei,* Rio Grande R., Tex. WFR

The Amistad gambusia has been extirpated from its natural habitat, the large, fast-flowing, warm Goodenough Spring and its runs, tributaries to the Rio Grande. Goodenough Spring was a flooded area and the unique habitat of the fish was eliminated by construction of Amistad Reservoir. The captive population brought in to reintroduce the species became contaminated with *G. affinis;* unless another wild population is found, the Amistad gambusia must now be considered extinct.

Stock of this species was maintained at the U.S. Fish and Wildlife Service's Dexter Fish Hatchery and at the University of Texas at Austin (Lee et al. 1980). Johnson (1987) stated that it was protected but Page and Burr (1991) reported it extinct.

Care would be as for the central mosquitofish, but the Amistad gambusia should have warmer water and moderate current. If rediscovered, coordination between the State of Texas and the U.S. Fish and Wildlife Service to once more attempt protection of this fish is strongly urged, as is the cooperation of these agencies with hobby aquarists whose husbandry skills often exceed those of fish hatchery workers. Skilled breeders are abundant in the American Livebearer Association, the Breeders Guild, the North American Native Fishes Association, and the American Killifish Association.

*Gambusia gaigei,*
Big Bend gambusia

*G. gaigei* is a large, husky mosquitofish, built like a pupfish *(Cyprinodon).* It has black spots and crescents above, and an indistinct line along the flank. Orange stripes and fins and an orange nose appear in good specimens, but it is not known if this coloration is induced by algal foods. Otherwise, its taxonomy is based on the hook arrangement of the gonopodium.

The Big Bend gambusia has been extirpated from vegetated warm springs and ponds in its native Boquillas Spring and Graham Ranch Warm Springs in Brewster County, Texas, but is maintained in one pond at Big Bend National Park, Texas. All extant individuals were derived from three captive fish held in Clark Hubbs' laboratory at the University of Texas (Guillory in Lee et al. 1980; p. 540). It is the only fish species known to have been reduced to three individuals and yet survive.

*G. gaigei* is a federally endangered species and may not be kept in captivity.

*Gambusia georgei,*
San Marcos gambusia

*G. georgei* is elongate and delicately silvery. It has yellow fins with dark edges, and a vertical line of spots through the center of the tail fin; no lines of spots occur at the bases of the unpaired fins.

The San Marcos gambusia is known from San Marcos Spring and River in

Texas, but may be extinct (Lee et al. 1980; Page and Burr 1991); it is nonetheless listed as protected (Johnson 1987).

G. *georgei* has been found in shallow, quiet, mud-bottom shaded areas of its only known river.

Because of its status as a protected species, the San Marcos gambusia cannot be collected or possessed.

| | |
|---|---|
| *Gambusia heterochir,*<br>Clear Creek gambusia | G. *heterochir* is lightly spotted, uncolored, and has a notch on the upper margin of the pectoral fin. It is sometimes difficult to identify, especially when it hybridizes with G. *affinis*.<br><br>The Clear Creek gambusia is probably extinct due to impoundment of its densely vegetated habitat, Clear Creek, in Menard County, Texas. It is a rare fish and hybridizes with other *Gambusia*. |

## Family Atherinidae, the Silversides

The silversides are a second family of small, elongate fishes of the order Atheriniformes. They possess two separate dorsal fins, scaled heads, a small number of spines in all fins but the caudal, no lateral line, and a swim bladder not connected by a duct to the intestine. Silversides can be distinguished from the similar coastal anchovies (Engraulidae) in having protrusible jaws that can be pulled slightly away from the head; a fingernail hooked onto the jaw of an anchovy and pulled forward will cause the head and gill plates to expand like a basket.

The best-known close relatives of silversides in the aquarium hobby are the Australian and Indonesian dwarf "rainbowfishes" of the genera *Pompondetta, Bedotia, Pseudomugil,* and *Telmatherina*. Most silversides are marine or estuarine.

Collect them with a cast net, seine, or dip net in open, shallow waters near shore. In coastal areas, immediately place captives in a bucket of full-strength sea water; in fresh waters, add salt to the water. Four drops per gallon of a quinaldine solution will enhance survival.

North American atherinids are sensitive to water quality and not usually maintained by aquarists; however, the tidewater silverside is readily propagated in brackish or marine water with spawning mops, and therefore is recommended by the EPA to monitor the toxicity of wastewater effluents discharged to coastal waters.

In the United States, one coastal species extends from New England to the Rio Grande and well up the Mississippi River; one strictly freshwater species occurs in disjunct populations from Canada to the Midwest and Gulf Coast, and throughout Florida. There are additional coastal species.

**Genus *Labidesthes***
*Labidesthes sicculus,* brook silverside

*L. sicculus* (plate 42) is the only freshwater North American silverside. It is elongate, metallic to silvery, flattened side to side, and has a long snout and upwardly turned mouth. The breeding male has a black mark on the front of the dorsal fin. Adults are 3 to 4 inches long.

The brook silverside occurs from Quebec in the St. Lawrence River system through the eastern and central Great Lakes and continues southward into most Gulf Coast drainages from Florida to eastern Texas; on the eastern seaboard, it ranges northward to South Carolina.

*L. sicculus* prefers the shallows of lakes, reservoirs, rivers, and large streams, where the water is clear and rich in zooplankton. It feeds on surface insects, daphnia, ostracods, copepods, amphipods, isopods, and other small aquatic or semi-

Tidewater silverside, *Menidia beryllina,* Mississippi R. RB

aquatic planktonic animals. It often is found in large surface schools in lakes and reservoirs, but singly or in small groups in streams.

The brook silverside spawns among vegetation or debris, with the large, adhesive eggs sticking to gravel, sticks, or (most often) vegetation. Hatching occurs in one week, and the young attain sexual maturity early in their first and typically only year of life. There is no nest, and no protection of territory, fry, or eggs.

A large, shallow, well-lighted aquarium will show a group at its best, but for breeding, a 10-gallon tank with sponge filtration is adequate for a pair or a half dozen. Provide floating spawning mops and feed with live *Artemia* nauplii and blackworms, *Ceriodaphnia* (if available), and frozen bloodworms. The eggs should be picked from the mop, incubated in water with good aeration, and the fry fed on *Artemia* nauplii upon hatching.

**Genus *Menidia***

*Menidia beryllina,*
tidewater silverside

*M. beryllina* is the most widespread and abundant of all coastal silversides, and is likely to confused with anchovies. It is elongate, gray to white with a silvery band on the side, and has an upwardly turned mouth. It has a thicker body than the brook silverside, and larger scales and shorter jaws. The sexes are similar. Adults are 2 to 3 inches long.

The tidewater silverside ranges in coastal waters from Maine to the Rio Grande, throughout hard waters of Florida, and continues northward in the Mississippi basin to the bootheel of southeastern Missouri. It also occurs along the Gulf Coast westward to the Rio Grande.

*M. beryllina* is found in large subsurface schools in bays, estuaries, and near-shore oceanic waters where it may be mixed with anchovies. It invades some hard water rivers well inland. Its habitats are over open sand bottom or near rooted vegetation; it avoids deep waters. It feeds on zooplankton of all types.

Spawning occurs among shoreline vegetation, with the moderately large eggs adhering to vegetation or drifting debris. Hatching takes place in days, and the young grow rapidly. The fry of the tidewater silverside are used in laboratory aquatic toxicity studies at wastewater treatment facilities using brackish receiving waters for effluent. There is no nest, and no protection of territory, fry, or eggs.

A 5-gallon tank will support four to six fish. Water should be 25 to 50 percent sea water for optimal health and egg survival. Provide a floating spawning mop for the eggs, and feed heavily on live *Artemia* adults and nauplii. Silversides in good condition will spawn daily. Transfer the egg-laden mop to a 1-gallon jar with vigorous aeration until hatching. Fry take *Artemia* nauplii as a first food and are easily raised.

# 16

# The Order Gasterosteiformes

THE order Gasterosteiformes (referring to bonelike plates covering the belly) contains six families in American waters; the marine trumpetfishes (Aulostomidae), cornetfishes (Fistulariidae), and snipefishes (Centriscidae); the mostly marine pipefishes (Syngnathidae); the coastal and freshwater sticklebacks (Gasterosteidae); and the freshwater pygmy sunfishes (Elassomatidae) (Johnson and Springer 1997).

## Family Gasterosteidae, the Sticklebacks

The sticklebacks lack scales, but have varying degrees of development of the bony plates covering the body, from none to heavily encased. They vary in body depth, head length, and in the development of a supporting plate for the tail fin. Some lack pelvic fins but retain the internal skeletal structure that supports them, and some lack even the supporting skeletal structure.

Sticklebacks include the European and/or Asian *Spinachia spinachia, Pungitius platygaster, P. pungitius, P. hellenicus* (proposed for protection and known only from Greece), and others (Keivany et al. 1997). Some of the classification is based on behavior, an unusual criterion among fish taxonomists, but accepted for this group (McLennan 1993). The most important references on the sticklebacks are Wootton (1976, 1984) and Bell and Foster (1994).

Six species occur in North American waters. The tube-snout of the Pacific is strictly marine and will not be covered. The others occur in fresh to marine habitats and one, *Culaea,* is restricted to fresh water. Sticklebacks are coldwater fishes of the northern hemisphere with circumglobal distributions. They occur in North America, Europe, Asia, and portions of the Arctic.

The male builds a nest on or above the bottom and develops red or black threat colors to enhance his threat displays. The female enters the nests for spawning, then leaves; the male alone defends the eggs. Sticklebacks are a favorite of ethologists (animal behaviorists), and literature on sticklebacks is among the most extensive for any group of fishes. All are predaceous on small aquatic crustaceans and insect larvae. The sticklebacks are models for understanding the relationships between predators and prey (Ohguchi 1981).

Europeans may offer to trade *Spinachia* for North American sticklebacks. Should the opportunity arise, the European 15-spined stickleback should be fed adult brine shrimp and amphipods in aquaria. In nature it feeds on copepods, mysids, amphipods, and isopods, and will take anything that moves when hungry; however, it becomes selective for the most frequently consumed item when well-fed (Kaiser et al. 1992; Kaiser and Hughes 1993).

Sticklebacks readily enter baited minnow traps, and are also easily collected with cast nets, seines, and dip nets from shallow, vegetated, sand-bottom, low-salinity tidal areas in early spring. Carry a hydrometer to determine the salinity at which the vegetation is growing, and take vegetation as well as fish.

**Genus *Apeltes***
*Apeltes quadracus,*
fourspine stickleback

*A. quadracus* is a stiff, metallic-brassy fish with an elongate, bullet-shaped body, a sharp nose, four hard spines where a first dorsal fin should be, and a thin and delicate caudal peduncle. It is small (often up to 2 in.). The nuptial male becomes black with red pelvic fins.

The fourspine stickleback ranges from the Gulf of St. Lawrence to New York (rarely as far as North Carolina), in marine or estuarine coastal streams.

*A. quadracus* occasionally enters fresh water and is associated with dense bank and bottom vegetation over sandy tidal runs, but is not restricted to these areas. It feeds on small aquatic animals, mostly amphipods and isopods, and bits of vegetation.

The male constructs a nest above the bottom by biting off bits of vegetation and cementing them into a cup-shaped nest using an adhesive substance emitted by the kidneys. The nest could be attached to rooted plants or even to air-line tubing. When the nest is finished, the male does a spectacular dance before the female, dashing in circles and flicking the pelvic fins, the red of the fins contrasting with a black body.

The female enters the nest and deposits 40 sticky 1.5 mm diameter eggs. The male then fertilizes the eggs, drives the female away, and completes the nest by constructing a cover, leaving a small opening on each side. Upon completion, the male aerates the eggs by inserting his snout in one opening and drawing water out of the nest through the other opening.

The male may spawn again, constructing a second nest on top of the original. This may result in as many as four nests, one atop the other, and a busy male aerating all the eggs, defending territory, and paying dearly for youthful excesses (Scott and Crossman 1973). The young are guarded until they disperse.

A 5-gallon aquarium is sufficient for one male and one to three females. Outside the spawning season, the sexes are similar, but the male tends to be darker, thinner, and more aggressive. The fourspine stickleback is so thin it often slips through ¼-inch mesh seines.

The aquarium should contain brackish water with the salinity measured in the field during collection. Sticklebacks do not accept spawning mops. To provide spawning construction materials, bring back some vegetation from the fish collection area, or substitute other aquatic plants able to tolerate some salinity (e.g., *Vesicularia* or coastal species of *Myriophyllum*). Feed live adult *Artemia* and *Artemia* nauplii, live daphnia, and live blackworms to start; sticklebacks quickly learn to accept frozen *Artemia*. The fourspine stickleback lives only two years, and requires abundant food.

**Genus *Culaea***
*Culaea inconstans,*
brook stickleback

*C. inconstans* is brown to bronze with a mosaic of light spots. The nuptial male is blackish green with the light spots sometimes replaced by wavy, vertical light lines on the flank. During spawning, the male's fins may blacken with a pink tinge on the pelvics, but some populations lack pelvic fins. The nuptial female is dusky.

The brook stickleback occurs primarily in Canada, from Nova Scotia and New Brunswick westward to Hudson and James Bays. It continues to Quebec, Mani-

Brook stickleback, *Culaea inconstans,* N.Y. RJG

toba, and Ontario and northward to the Great Slave Lake. It ranges southward into New York, Pennsylvania, Iowa, and Montana (Scott and Crossman 1973). A disjunct population in New Mexico probably represents an accidental introduction. The history of *Culaea* dispersion throughout central North America, despite its absence from both coasts, has been explained by Gach (1996).

C. *inconstans* prefers cool, clear, densely vegetated small streams, spring-fed ponds, and the margins, bays, and coves of lakes. It normally is not found in brackish or marine water, but is tolerant of salinities up to 50 percent in cold (but not warm) water.

The brook stickleback has been taken by trawl at depths to 30 fathoms (180 ft.) in Lake Huron, and also in oxygen-depleted, stagnant water. It is known to migrate in streams, but the cause for the migrations is not understood; it may be an attempt to escape warming water during the summer. It feeds on aquatic crustaceans, insects, fish larvae and eggs, snails, worms, and algae. One study reported stomach contents of midge (bloodworm) and caddisfly larvae and ostracods.

The male builds a nest on a rock or attached to a stem of a reed or grass, cementing fragments of plant debris and algae with a kidney secretion. The nest is less than 1 inch in diameter and round, with one opening.

The male now becomes dark, with an intense vertical dark band through the eye. The male entices the female to enter the nest for spawning. The willing female creates a second opening upon exiting the nest.

Eggs are 1 mm in diameter and adhesive. Hatching occurs in eight or nine days at 65°F. The male defends eggs and larvae until they disperse. The male continues to protect his territory against intruders with an elaborate threat display (McKenzie 1969). Maturity is reached in one year, the life span is probably two years, and the maximum size is 3 inches (Reisman and Cade 1967; Scott and Crossman 1973).

A 10-gallon aquarium is sufficient for a small group (six to eight fish). Include some salt (5% sea water). The temperature should not exceed 65°F; higher temperatures inhibit reproductive behavior. The photoperiod should be 14–16 hours of light. Provide abundant live plant material, such as *Elodea, Anacharis,* and algae, and some structure, such as rocks or driftwood. The newly hatched fry take *Artemia* nauplii as a first food, and are easily raised in cold water. The brook stickleback declines in warm water.

Care as for the fourspine stickleback.

Threespine stickleback, *Gasterosteus aculeatus,* male, N.H. RJG

Threespine stickleback, *Gasterosteus aculeatus,* males and females, N.H. RJG

**Genus *Gasterosteus***

*Gasterosteus aculeatus,*
threespine stickleback

*G. aculeatus* is silver, green, brown or olive above and silvery below. The nuptial male has a red belly and flank and blue eyes; the female has a pink tint on the fins. In different parts of its range, the threespine stickleback may be fully armored with bony plates along the flank, partially armored (mostly toward the front), or naked (unarmored).

Populations also differ in the lengths of the pelvic and dorsal spines, and some populations lack pelvic fins. With its wide distribution and great variation, it has been regarded as a superspecies, composed of many different units called semi-species (Bell 1976). It resembles the blackspotted stickleback, but distinguishable by the structure of the pelvic fin.

The threespine stickleback occurs in North America, Europe, and eastern Asia. In Europe, it ranges from Greenland to Spain and the Mediterranean and Black Seas. In North America, it is present from Chesapeake Bay to Hudson Bay in the east, and from Baja California, Mexico northward to British Columbia and western Alaska.

*G. aculeatus* is a complex of populations differing in many biological criteria separating traditional species. For example, most populations consist of 2- to 3-inch fish living two or three years, sometimes only one; however, a population of giants (up to 4 in.) from Drizzle Lake in the Queen Charlotte Islands on the Pacific Coast live up to eight years (Reimchen 1992).

Two life history modes are known. The best known is anadromous with marine populations from a mile offshore migrating upstream in coastal waters to fresh water (North America) or brackish water (Europe) for spawning, with the young then returning to the sea at the end of the warm season. Anadromous fish typically are fully armored. The subspecies *G. a. microcephalus* is naked (without armor), and strictly fresh water in distribution, restricted to the upper reaches of the Santa Clara River basin of Los Angeles County, California. Other freshwater populations vary considerably in armature. It has been suggested that armature has been lost in populations that do not have predators.

In all populations, the male establishes a territory, usually near other males, in shallow fresh or brackish water with a sandy or rocky bottom and a great deal of vegetation. Males are aggressive, threatening other males entering their territories. This behavior probably wanes during the breeding season; males presented with other males as threats in the laboratory gradually became less aggressive (Peeke 1969). Males also threaten and attack egg and fry predators such as sculpins, at great risk to themselves (Pressley 1981).

The adaptability of these fishes to environmental conditions seems limitless. In one study, predator pressure from lake trout appears to have been the stimulus that induced development of a giant strain (population), too large for trout to ingest (Reimchen 1991).

Vegetation is necessary to induce spawning behavior (Cleveland 1994). The nuptial male, normally drab olive, becomes richly colored with a red belly and iridescent blue eyes. Using bits of vegetation cemented together with a secretion from the kidneys, the male may construct an ovoid nest or the nest may be just a simple depression in the sand beneath a cover of vegetation. The nest site is in slightly flowing (not stagnant) water on the bottom, near but not among submersed plants.

In some populations, after the clump of vegetation is constructed, the male pushes through to form a cavity with holes at each end. As a ripe female approaches the territory, the male does a zigzag dance to entice the female who responds by tilting her head upward. (Behavior of both sexes is different from *G. wheatlandi,* which spawns slightly later in the season, but may occur in the same waters in eastern North America.)

The female threespine stickleback enters the nest to deposit a mass of adhesive, yellow 1.5 mm eggs, and leaves. The male then enters the nest to fertilize the eggs. The egg clumps of several females may be deposited in a single nest and may total as many as 600 eggs.

The eggs hatch in one week at 66°F, and the male continues guarding until the fry disperse. The male will continue to spawn and guard all summer. Evidence obtained through DNA fingerprinting indicates that the male guarding the eggs and fry is the father, i.e., males do not take over the nests of other males. Sticklebacks normally live three years, maturing after the first year, and normally attain a maximum size of 3 inches (Scott and Crossman 1973).

A 10-gallon tank with a sand bottom and abundant vegetation is suitable for not more than two males and four to six females. Determine the salinity where the fish are collected, and duplicate using synthetic sea salts. In the United States and Canada, they are often found in zero salinity water. A small addition of marine salts will aid in the survival of *Artemia* nauplii, the staple food for adults and fry. Feed live adult *Artemia* if available, but simultaneously wean them onto frozen adult *Artemia* or freeze-dried plankton (euphausiid shrimp).

When fry are obtained, it is wise to expose them to a wide range of temperatures. They can acclimate as adults to a large temperature range if exposed when young, but lose the ability to thermally acclimate if initially exposed to a wide temperature range at a later age (Jordan and Garside 1972). Sticklebacks will not breed at high temperatures, and can be killed by warm water. Sticklebacks eat small insects, aquatic crustaceans, and algae.

---

**Gasterosteus wheatlandi,**
**blackspotted stickleback**

*G. wheatlandi* is similar to *G. aculeatus,* but its pelvic fin has two sharp cusps at the base of the single spine, and two supplemental soft rays. In the threespine stickleback, the single spine of the pelvic fin is smooth, without cusps, and there is one supplemental ray. *G. wheatlandi* is greenish yellow with dark spots or blotches on the caudal peduncle. The nuptial male is gold to bright green above and on the flank, with a white belly and orange pelvic fins. In general, the male of blackspotted sticklebacks is smaller than that of threespine sticklebacks (1¼ in. vs. 2 in.).

The blackspotted stickleback occurs from Newfoundland to southern New York, in coastal brackish and marine habitats (rarely fresh water). Adults presumably migrate from the sea to the heads of estuaries and smaller tributary streams to spawn in low-salinity water. In Long Island Sound, it occurs in 3 feet of water with drifting seaweed (*Zostera, Enteromorpha, Fucus* spp.).

The male builds a nest on the bottom, similar to that of the threespine stickleback, usually in a much more vegetated area, but will also nest on bare sand when no vegetation is available (Cleveland 1994). The male displays before the female with the head down and quivering, while the female assumes a head-up posture, the snout of the female at the pelvic fin base of the male.

Spawning begins a bit later than in the threespine stickleback. It is pushed away from the most vegetated sites by the larger and more aggressive threespines. The larger than 1 mm eggs number 170–270. The male is usually 1¼ inches, and the female rarely attains 3 inches maximum (McInerney 1969; Scott and Crossman 1973; Cleveland 1994).

In aquaria, males and females of *G. wheatlandi* from different populations produce more and larger broods than when bred with members of their own populations (Ayvazian 1993). *G. wheatlandi* will not hybridize with *G. aculeatus* due to behavioral differences in nuptial displays between the two species.

Care as for the threespine stickleback.

---

**Genus *Pungitius***
*Pungitius occidentalis,*
ninespine stickleback

*P. occidentalis* has a series of nine low spines along the back, constituting a remnant of the spiny dorsal fin. A keel on the caudal peduncle may be strongly developed or reduced. The abdominal bony plates vary from heavily armored in coastal populations to virtually naked in inland stocks (Ayvazian and Krueger 1992). It is olive with dark blotches or vertical bars on the flank, and silver below.

The ninespine stickleback occurs in coastal and inland waters of Canada and the coast of Alaska. On the Atlantic Coast, it ranges southward to New Jersey on occasion, but is largely a Canadian species.

The ninespine stickleback spawns in fresh water. The nuptial male becomes black with white pelvic fins and a pink tint around the head. The nest, constructed of plant debris and attached above the bottom, has two openings.

The female is enticed inside with an elaborate dance, and deposits a clump of 20 adhesive eggs, after which she leaves and the male enters the nest to fertilize them. The male may build and use two nests simultaneously, and each nest may have multiple spawns. The fry leave the care of the male two weeks after hatching. The maximum size is 2 inches, and the average maximum age is three years (Scott and Crossman 1973).

In most literature, the American ninespine stickleback is called *Pungitius pungitius,* and that name will probably be retained in the next edition of *Common and Scientific Names of Fishes.* Consistent with that view, Keivany et al. (1997) suggested that *P. occidentalis* of North America and *P. sinensis* of Japan should be considered junior synonyms of *P. pungitius.* I follow Hagland et al. (1992), who suggested that *P. occidentalis* represents the North American ninespine stickleback, *P. pungitius* be restricted to the European ninespine stickleback, and *P. sinensis* be applied to the Asian ninespine stickleback.

Care as for the threespine stickleback. This is a coldwater fish that does not tolerate heat and must be kept cool to induce spawning.

## Family Elassomatidae, the Pygmy Sunfishes

Species of the family Elassomatidae are superficially similar to the sunfishes (Centrarchidae), but are now believed to be related to the sticklebacks (Johnson and Springer 1997). Generally, they do not exceed 2 inches in total length, the caudal fin is rounded, and a lateral line is absent. The nuptial male resembles *Badis badis* or *Cynolebias nigripinnis* in size and coloration; it has iridescent spots on a black background and larger fins than the brownish female.

Their pectoral locomotion and nesting with vegetation are reminiscent of the sticklebacks, and unlike the peduncle-driven locomotion and sand depression nesting behavior of sunfishes. Where different species occur in the same water body, they often occur in separate locations. Whether this is resource partitioning or social interaction is not known.

Pygmy sunfishes are characteristic of quiet lowland ponds and small lakes over mud or silt, but they sometimes occur over sand in dense shoreline vegetation ranging from *Myriophyllum* and filamentous algae to the pink roots of willow trees.

Pygmy sunfishes are best collected by ⅛-inch mesh seine, dip net, or Goin dredge; they may slip through normal ¼-inch mesh nets. Transport them from the field in tap water containing a small amount of sea salt or rock salt, a commercial tranquilizer, and oxygen or air inside plastic bags. Fish transported in open containers with soft, acidic water not containing salts or tranquilizer often develop fulminating (rapidly fatal) skin infections within 48 hours.

They can all be propagated in the same way. One-gallon widemouthed jars are ideal for a pair or a trio. The aquarium should be filled with dechlorinated tap water at neutral pH, half filled with *Nitella* or *Vesicularia,* placed near a window for natural daylight, and provided with gentle aeration. Feed living foods *only,* including *Artemia* nauplii, mosquito larvae, and *Ceriodaphniae* or *Daphnia.*

Pond or ramshorn snails are added for two reasons. First, the snails consume dead *Artemia* nauplii, protecting water quality. Second, the baby snails are an important natural pygmy sunfish food. In nature, pygmy sunfishes eat copepods, cladocerans, snails, bloodworms, amphipods, and insect larvae. When the black-eyed, glasslike fry appear in the breeding jar, move the parents to another jar for continued breeding, and begin feeding the fry lightly on *Artemia* nauplii. Too heavy a feeding risks promoting a bloom of *Chlorohydra,* which will then eat most of the fry. (Outbreaks of *Chlorohydra* can be eliminated with the veterinary anthelminthic drugs fenbendazol or flubendazol sprinkled on the water surface.)

The young attain ½ inch by three months of age, and mature and breed at one year. Pygmy sunfishes cannot tolerate degraded water quality from dead *Artemia* or dying plants, and will quickly succumb to bacterial infection (indicated by massive swelling, pale coloration, and failure to swim). Death rapidly follows the appearance of symptoms. Frequent 20 percent water changes with chlorinated tap water helps maintain water quality.

---

**Genus *Elassoma***

*Elassoma evergladei,*
Everglades pygmy sunfish

*E. evergladei* (**plate 43**) is the best-known member of the group in the aquarium hobby. It is the only pygmy sunfish with scales on the top of the head, but a microscope is needed to see them. The female has no markings and a reddish brown body. The male has black fins, with or without brown dots; his body is black, brown, or dark green and blotched, spotted, or with a few indistinct dark bars; no black mark appears on the shoulder. Brassy to blue-green iridescent scales are lightly to densely scattered over the body, not forming bars, and two distinct light blotches occur at the root of the caudal fin.

The Everglades pygmy sunfish ranges along the Coastal Plain from southern North Carolina (Cape Fear River basin) southward to Lake Okeechobee, Florida, and westward to the Mobile area of western Alabama, usually less than a hundred miles inland from the coast.

*E. evergladei* occurs in the margins of both stagnant and spring waters and sinkholes over mud, sand, or limestone, among woody debris, algae, submerse vegetation, and the pink roots of willows in banks. It is also found in ponds and lakes among roots of water hyacinth, water lettuce, and other surface plants.

According to Rubenstein (1981a,b), males establish territories when food is centrally located, with the dominant male closest to the source. When food is distributed evenly, the fish range freely without territories.

---

*Elassoma okefenokee,*
Okefenokee pygmy sunfish

*E. okefenokee* (**plate 44**) can be identified by the depigmented (white) central portion of the lower lip in juveniles and subadults. The nuptial male is black with scattered iridescent blue speckles that tend to form weak lines. *E. okefenokee* has 11–12 dorsal and 7 anal rays (and the white region of the mouth), whereas the otherwise similar *E. evergladei* has 9–10 dorsal and 5–6 anal rays.

There are two populations differing consistently in the number of pores on the head in front of the preopercular bone. The "true" *E. okefenokee* occupies the eastern portion of the range in the Santa Fe River system, a major tributary entering the Suwannee River from the east. The generally western form (which may represent an unnamed species) occurs in springs and backwaters of the Suwannee River main stem, and in the Waccasassa River drainage. Although found in different sections of the same (Suwannee River) drainage, the two forms do not occur together.

The distribution of the Okefenokee pygmy sunfish resembles that of the species pair *Fundulus rubifrons* and *F. auroguttatus,* and supports the view that the present Waccasassa River was once the lower Suwannee, which has since changed its route to enter the Gulf of Mexico farther north (C. Gilbert, pers. comm.).

The Okefenokee pygmy sunfish is generally distributed from the lower Altamaha River basin in southern Georgia and the Florida panhandle southward to Lake Okeechobee (Kissimmee River drainage) in the middle of the peninsula, but only to Fort Pierce on the east coast and the Hillsborough River drainage (Tampa area) on the west coast of the peninsula.

The first known specimens were collected from Kettle Creek, a tributary of the Satilla River near Waycross, Georgia, near the northern edge of the Okefeno-

Banded pygmy sunfish, *Elassoma zonatum,* Juniper Cr., Brunswick Co., N.C. FCR

kee Swamp in 1956, and described by Dr. Jim Bohlke of the Academy of Natural Sciences of Philadelphia. The site was a ditch at a culvert where streamside vegetation had been removed and grass grew to the edge. The bottom was sand and silt, leaves, roots, and woody debris, and the water was black with a pH of 5.0 to 6.0. In other locations, *E. okefenokee* occurred with *Leptolucania ommata* in soft, acidic water among rootlets and plants overhanging deep water.

The adults breed at pond and lake edges, in ditches, sinkholes, and backwaters, in clear or stained water, over mud and silt, among submersed, emersed, and floating vegetation (including algal masses).

Whereas the Everglades and Okefenokee pygmy sunfishes are easily confused in the field, that is not the case with the markedly different *E. zonatum.*

## *Elassoma zonatum,* banded pygmy sunfish

*E. zonatum* is the only pygmy sunfish with a prominent dark oblique stripe through the eye. One or more bold, dark shoulder marks behind the gill cover and under or just in front of the dorsal fin are not always visible in live fish. There are nine wide, dark bars interrupted in the male by green or brassy lines of iridescent scales, and another brassy mark under the eye. Both sexes are generally olive-green to gold, and dark-banded with many black speckles around and under the head. The breeding male has a blacker body. It is the largest pygmy sunfish at 2 inches maximum size.

The banded pygmy sunfish is widely distributed in the Piedmont and Coastal Plain from North Carolina to Texas, ranging northward along the Mississippi River drainages to southeastern Missouri, southern Illinois, western West Virginia, western Tennessee, eastern Arkansas, southern Georgia, southern Alabama, and all of Mississippi and Louisiana. It is the only pygmy sunfish of the Gulf Coast and the only one in inland states.

As with others of the genus, *E. zonatum* is found in backwaters, ponds, lakes, and ditches. Even in springs, the banded pygmy sunfish occupies dense vegetation such as *Ludwigia, Nasturtium,* and *Naias.* Stomach analyses have yielded rotifers, amphipods, snails, copepods, daphnia and other crustaceans, and midge and other insect larvae.

In a study in Kentucky, banded pygmy sunfish were in breeding condition

Bluebarred pygmy sunfish, *Elassoma okatie,* Jasper Co., S.C. FCR

from February to June, with peak spawning during March and April. They spawned in dense vegetation near the bottom where a male held territory. Eggs were scattered, adhering to vegetation, hatched in 100 hours, and the fry had yolk sacs for a week. Half grown at eight weeks, most lived one year, spawning at ten months or so, while a few lived to two years (Walsh and Burr 1984a).

Three other species have been discovered and named in recent years.

| | |
|---|---|
| *Elassoma boehlkei,*<br>Carolina pygmy sunfish | The nuptial male of *E. boehlkei* has black fins and 13 thin black bars alternating with 13 thin, brilliant blue-green vertical lines on the flank (Rohde and Arndt 1987). |

The Carolina pygmy sunfish **(plate 45)** is limited to a few counties in the Coastal Plain of the Waccamaw River drainage in southern North Carolina and the Santee River drainage of northern South Carolina.

*E. boehlkei* inhabits darkly stained, slow-moving, acidic (pH 4.0–6.1), moderately deep, blackwater creeks and old rice fields over mud and sand with plant debris. This pygmy sunfish is common at the edges of creeks with dense vegetation, including *Myriophyllum, Egeria,* algae, and bank willow roots.

Following the instructions of F. C. (Fritz) Rohde, we seined and dip netted Juniper Creek in Brunswick County, North Carolina during winter, collecting large numbers of Carolina pygmy sunfish and a few blackbanded and bluespotted sunfish from vegetation. On summer trips, we typically found the water level 2 feet below normal, little vegetation remaining, and only small juvenile pygmy sunfish of indeterminate species.

*E. boehlkei* is easily propagated. If several females are used with one male in the spawning jar during the spring spawning season, proportionally more fry are produced, suggesting little or no cannibalism.

| | |
|---|---|
| *Elassoma okatie,*<br>bluebarred pygmy sunfish | The nuptial male of *E. okatie* has 11 dark bars that are three times wider than intervening lines of bright blue-green iridescent scales (Rohde and Arndt 1987). The blue-green bars extend from top to bottom. The male usually has a bright spot on the lower front edge of the eye. Otherwise, it is similar to the Carolina pygmy sunfish, which has much narrower dark bars and often incomplete blue-green lines, and not at all similar to the banded pygmy sunfish. |

The bluebarred pygmy sunfish occurs in Bamberg, Allendale, and Jasper

Spring pygmy sunfish, *Elassoma alabamae*, male, Tennessee R., Ala. FCR

Spring pygmy sunfish, *Elassoma alabamae*, female, Tennessee R., Ala. FCR

Counties in the New, Savannah, and Edisto River drainages of southern South Carolina, and near Augusta (in Richmond County), Georgia.

*E. okatie* is found in ditches, ponds, and backwaters in darkly stained water, with a substratum of mud, sand, plant debris, and instream vegetation comprised of *Myriophyllum, Ceratophyllum, Utricularia, Lemna, Potamogeton, Nymphaea, Nuphar, Brassenia,* and *Juncus* (rushes), *Carex* (sedges), or Poaceae (grasses). One location is a broad floodplain where the water is only 2 inches deep over submersed vegetation. Temperature and pH from the literature range from 50 to 89°F and 4.5 to 7.5. To date, no stomach analyses have been performed, but it probably feeds on small macroinvertebrates.

Determine its status in South Carolina before attempting collection.

---

**Elassoma alabamae, spring pygmy sunfish**

*E. alabamae* is the most recently described species. Both sexes have 5–6 block-shaped, wide brown to black bars interrupted by widely spaced, thin, brassy to blue-green, indistinct lines, three dorsal fin spines, and no scales on top of the head. The male is more intensely colored, darker, has brighter iridescent lines, and is smaller with larger dorsal and anal fins than the female. The rear of the dorsal and anal fins both have a clear area (a window) and a dark blotch. It is the smallest (seldom 1 in.) and least colorful of all *Elassoma* species.

The spring pygmy sunfish was previously known from three springs and their flows in Lauderdale and Limestone Counties of northern Alabama; today a remnant population occurs in just one remaining spring.

The natural habitat of *E. alabamae* is clear, spring-fed pools and their runs into marshes with dense hardwoods, shrubs, grasses and weeds around the margins, and a bottom of fine sand, limestone, clay, and mud. They have been found just above submersed *Ceratophyllum, Myriophyllum, Elodea,* and *Utricularia* (Mayden 1993).

The spring pygmy sunfish is in danger of extinction, and already extirpated from two of its previously known sites. It is a good candidate for home aquarium breeding. Its natural habitat of spring-fed pools indicates an intolerance of pollution. Other springs in the area may be suitable transplantation sites. Although it has been recommended for protection under the Endangered Species Act, it may be available. Feed only live foods and provide abundant snails.

Do not attempt collection before determining its status from the U.S. Fish and Wildlife Service and the Alabama Department of Fish and Game.

# 17

# The Order Scorpaeniformes

THE Scorpaeniformes, or scorpionfishes, are represented by six families in North America (scorpionfishes, sea robins, sculpins, sablefishes, poachers, snailfishes). All are strictly marine except for the family Cottidae, or sculpins, which contains both marine and freshwater species.

## Family Cottidae, the Sculpins

Cottidae are large-mouthed, spiny headed, bottom dwelling predators with 70 genera and approximately 300 species, including an unclear number of *Cottus* species. Sculpins are mostly cold and cool water marine fishes of the northern hemisphere, with a few deepwater marine species in the southern hemisphere off New Zealand, Australia, and New Guinea.

In North America, a few species enter fresh water along the coast, and many species have adapted entirely to fresh water. Sculpins often have precise habitat preferences, seen most clearly in marine species in which many kinds of sculpins divide or partition the resources of each habitat type.

Sculpins demonstrate two main methods of feeding, ram and suction, although many species fall somewhere in between. In ram feeding, the fish opens its mouth and charges the prey, surrounding it with its jaws; this is also known as grasping. In suction feeding, the fish opens its mouth widely, and the prey is drawn inside with inrushing water (Norton 1991a, b).

Sculpins are readily collected by dip net or seine in shallow, rocky bottom streams year-round. In aquaria, they prefer live foods and regard smaller fish as snacks. Many mature at only 2 inches long but continue to grow with age. Because their potential size of 6 inches or more has been interpreted as normal size, they have been incorrectly regarded as too large for home aquaria.

There are 38 genera of strictly marine sculpins on the Atlantic and Pacific Coasts; the relationships of the principal genera have been recently examined (Strauss 1993). Two genera and 24 species occur in the fresh waters of North America. One genus *(Cottus)* has two species living in fresh and salt water; a large number are restricted to the rivers and lakes of the United States and Canada. North American freshwater sculpins occur from the southern Appalachians and Ozark uplands northward through Canada and Alaska to the Aleutians. They also occur throughout Europe and northern Asia.

Sculpins are difficult to sex out of the breeding season; use a large tank and several fish to improve chances of having a pair. A 20- to 29-gallon aquarium is usually sufficient for four to six fish. Provide undergravel filtration and current from one or two powerheads. A coarse gravel or pebble substratum, rooted plants, and one or two large, flat rocks completes the breeding aquarium.

Blackworms and small earthworms are taken with gusto, and snails seem to disappear. Frozen brine shrimp and bloodworms are accepted if living foods also are provided, and if other fishes, such as madtoms, are in the aquarium to set an example. Once adapted to the feeding regimen of the aquarist, they quickly learn to take bits of shrimp and even pellet foods.

Eggs should be removed and hatched under aeration in a separate aquarium. The fry are large but do not feed until the yolk is absorbed some days later.

---

**Genus *Myoxocephalus***
*Myoxocephalus quadricornis,*
shorthorn sculpin

*M. quadricornis* has a large gap between the first (spiny) and second (soft) dorsal fins, distinguishing this genus from *Cottus;* the four large spines on the head identify it as a shorthorn sculpin. It is dark brown above, golden on the flank, and white below. It grows to 10 inches.

The shorthorn sculpin occurs along the Bering Sea coast of Alaska, ranging to Greenland and Eurasia (Leim and Scott 1966), but not along the Pacific Coast of southern Alaska or in Canada (Hart 1973).

*M. quadricornis* is found in the ocean, estuaries, and well into coastal rivers, but not lakes. Although it attains over 1 foot in length, it probably spawns at a smaller size and in marine waters.

The shorthorn sculpin is capable of outgrowing most aquaria, and will eat many of the other inhabitants.

---

*Myoxocephalus thompsoni,*
deepwater sculpin

*M. thompsoni* differs from the shorthorn by lacking spines on the head. It is gray-brown above and light below, with speckling, mottling, and seven saddles that taper down the side, not reaching the belly. It grows to 5 inches, but is usually 2 inches long.

The deepwater sculpin ranges from the Great Lakes northwestward to the Arctic lakes of Canada in a narrow band that marks the glacial line determining its present distribution and that of its associated glacial relict food source, *Mysis relicta* and *Pontoporeia affinis* (both crustaceans) (Scott and Crossman 1973).

*M. thompsoni* occurs in deep lakes, usually at depths of over 200 feet. It feeds on relict crustaceans and on chironomid larvae in cold, deep proglacial lakes in Canada, and on many other crustaceans and chironomids in the Great Lakes.

Little is known of its biology. Presumably, the deepwater sculpin spawns beneath flat rocks in deep water. An egg mass found in the mouth of a trawled specimen from Lake Ontario is of interest, but no other instance of egg clumps in mouths of this fish are known. The deepwater sculpin is discussed in detail in Scott and Crossman (1973) under the name *M. quadricornis thompsoni.*

*M. thompsoni* is a protected species in Canada.

---

**Genus *Cottus***
*Cottus bairdi,* mottled sculpin

*C. bairdi* has an incomplete lateral line that ends on the caudal peduncle, and a pair of pore openings appear at the tip of the chin. The body is indistinctly banded and overlaid with many small white spots. The two dorsal fins are connected with no gap between them. Adults average 3 to 4 inches. The spiny (first) dorsal fin of the male has an orange edge, a black mark at its front, and another black mark at its rear.

The mottled sculpin is common, abundant, and widespread. It is also disjunct.

Mottled sculpin, *Cottus bairdi,* Current R., Mo. GS

In the east, it ranges from Manitoba to Quebec, and southward to northern Georgia and Alabama. In the western United States, it ranges from Colorado northward to Washington, Idaho, and Montana. The population in the Colorado River drainage of southwestern Colorado and northwestern New Mexico is strongly isolated and may represent a distinct species (C. Gilbert, pers. comm.). The fish in Harney County, Oregon may be a separate subspecies or even species (Marshall 1992). In eastern North America, the occurrence of *C. bairdi* in divergent drainages has been attributed to stream capture (Howard and Morgan 1993). (Stream capture is the process in which erosion in the headwaters of one stream eventually cuts into the drainage of another, capturing its flow and allowing fishes from the captured stream to invade a different drainage.)

The mottled sculpin is found in springs, creeks, rivers, runs, riffles, and edges of rocky or gravelly lakes, where temperature seldom exceeds the low 60s (°F). It feeds on aquatic insects, mostly bloodworms and stonefly, dragonfly, and mayfly nymphs, beetle larvae, and to a lesser extent on crayfish and occasionally other fishes.

*C. bairdi* is vulnerable to death from ionic imbalance in acidic Appalachian streams, in which the streams have low buffering capacity (i.e., have little calcium) and high concentrations of inorganic aluminum (> 200 µg/L) from old mining operations; the free aluminum apparently enhances the effects of low pH by stimulating the loss of sodium from the gills (Gagen et al. 1993).

First spawning is usually at age two or three. The breeding season in most of its range is from April through June, when the male takes up spawning territories, either a burrow or the undersurface of a rock or log. Females visit the sites before selecting a mate. Upon selection, a mass of 200 eggs is deposited on the roof of the burrow or grotto and the female departs while the male guards the eggs and fry for the next few weeks.

The fry then disperse, selecting bottom materials in accordance with their size (i.e., larger fry will settle on cobble or rocks, while smaller ones settle over gravel). As the fish grow, cannibalism alters the population which then consists mostly of large males and few small ones (Scott and Crossman 1973; Downhower and Brown 1979). This cannibalism-driven population structure may occur widely in Cottidae.

An Atlantic Coastal Plain population from Delaware differs from the norm; the fish are smaller, mature by the end of the first year, seldom live beyond age two, and breed earlier during February and March (Rohde et al. 1994) beneath (not within) cans and bottles in gravel-bottom streams devoid of rocks. The larvae are not planktonic but benthic, hiding on the gravel for the first 12 days, although capable of strong swimming.

## Cottus cognatus, slimy sculpin

*C. cognatus* is another widespread and common species. It is smooth-skinned and elongate, with one spine and three rays in the pelvic fin; its lateral line is short, extending only half way back on the body; and its pattern is mottled, with only two fairly distinct saddles (not well-developed on the flank). It grows to 4 inches.

In the United States, the slimy sculpin occurs from Virginia to Maine, in the Great Lakes states, and from Idaho northward. It occurs from coast to coast in Canada, entering every Canadian province, all of Alaska, and even Siberia. The northern group has been considered by some Americans to be a distinct subspecies, *C. c. cognatus,* and the southern and eastern form as another subspecies, *C. c. gracilis,* but Canadian workers do not accept this division (P. W. Smith 1979).

*C. cognatus* is found in coldwater streams, springs, and lakes, on riffles or rocky bottoms, both at great depths and on shorelines. The male becomes black with an orange edge to the first (spiny) dorsal fin when nesting under a rock. It prefers a temperature of 46 to 57°F, and is killed by temperatures in the 70s (°F) (Symons et al. 1976). It feeds mostly on aquatic insect larvae and nymphs, especially mayflies, caddisflies, stoneflies, bloodworms, blackflies, and dragonflies, with bigger sculpins eating bigger insect larvae (Scott and Crossman 1973). It also feeds on fish eggs, and competes with crayfish *(Orconectes virilis)* for both habitat and this food source (Miller et al. 1992).

Slimy sculpins are vulnerable to death from ionic imbalance in acidic Appalachian streams for the same reasons given previously for the mottled sculpin. A temperature of just under 60°F is recommended; 10°F higher is lethal.

## Cottus ricei, spoonhead sculpin

*C. ricei* has a long, slender, and prickly body and a flattened, triangular head with sharp spines curving upward at the rear angle of the gill cover. Four indistinct blotches appear on the back (sometimes absent in Great Lakes specimens) and the fish is mottled overall. The juvenile has a dark bar on the caudal peduncle. The lateral line is complete. The spoonhead sculpin averages less than 3 inches but can attain 5 inches.

It occurs from Lake Superior northward to Hudson and James Bays and into all the Canadian provinces. It ranges from the St. Lawrence River in the east to the Mackenzie River in the northwest, but is absent from Pacific Coast drainages. It is rare to absent in the other Great Lakes following the invasion of alewives *(Alosa pseudoharengus)* in the 1960s, and only recently is recovering in Lake Michigan (Potter and Fleischer 1992).

*C. ricei* habitats vary from swift clear creeks to turbid rivers to lakes, from shore to depths of 400 feet; it is always found in cold water on rocky bottoms where it is presumed to feed on crustaceans and insect larvae.

Spawning occurs during late summer or fall when water temperatures are 40°F (Scott and Crossman 1973). The pelagic larvae are vulnerable to predation by planktonic feeders such as the alewife, and this sculpin declines where filter feeders are introduced. Sculpins without planktonic larvae are unaffected.

The remaining species of *Cottus* fall into two groups, those from the eastern/central part of North America and those exclusively western. We will begin with the eastern and central species.

| | |
|---|---|
| *Cottus girardi,* Potomac sculpin | *C. girardi* is similar to *C. bairdi,* but has a single pore opening at the tip of the chin, the lateral line is incomplete, and the bands are not sharply defined. The chin is mottled. |

*C. girardi* is similar to *C. bairdi,* but has a single pore opening at the tip of the chin, the lateral line is incomplete, and the bands are not sharply defined. The chin is mottled.

The Potomac sculpin occurs in the Blue Ridge Mountains and foothills of the Potomac River drainage in Virginia, West Virginia, Maryland, and Pennsylvania, and in the Cowpasture River of the James River system in Virginia, where it may have been introduced as a bait fish.

*C. girardi* inhabits rocky streams and medium-sized rivers with strong to moderate current, sometimes with a mildly silted bottom, and usually among dense vegetation (especially beds of *Elodea*). It feeds on aquatic larval mayflies (Ephemeroptera), caddisflies (Trichoptera), and bloodworms (Diptera), and on copepods and sometimes fishes. It is probably a winter or early spring breeder (Lee et al. 1980).

*Cottus carolinae,* banded sculpin

*C. carolinae* (plate 46) has spiny and soft dorsal fins that are barely separated, forming a notch on the surface of the fish. The lateral line is complete, and the unspotted body is crossed by distinct, sharply defined black saddles and bands on a gray to rusty brown body; the bands contrast strongly in juveniles, but less so in adults. There are no dark smudges on the spiny dorsal fin. It grows to 6 inches or more.

The banded sculpin occurs on the western slopes of the Appalachians through West Virginia, western Kentucky, Tennessee, and eastern Georgia, and ranges westward through limestone uplands across southern Illinois to all of the Ozark Plateau (southern Missouri, northern Arkansas, and extreme southeastern Kansas and northeastern Oklahoma).

*C. carolinae* is common in coldwater springs, including those in caves, in creeks and high gradient rivers, on gravel or rock rubble riffles, and in cool lowland streams with strong flow and high dissolved oxygen concentrations. It feeds on fishes, crayfish, and insects. This fish will eat every darter in the same aquarium and all the minnows it can catch. Dr. C. Richard Robins has suggested that it may not build a nest under a rock, but instead scatter its eggs.

Three subspecies are recognized at present: *C. c. carolinae* through most of the range, *C. c. zopherus* in the Coosa, Tallapoosa, and Black Warrior Rivers (Mobile Bay drainage), and *C. c. infernatus* deep into the Coastal Plain of Alabama, almost to the Gulf of Mexico (Williams and Robins 1970; Lee et al. 1980; Page and Burr 1991).

*Cottus hypselurus,* Ozark sculpin

The breeding male *C. hypselurus* has a yellow, orange, or red margin and a black submargin in the spiny dorsal fin and has a greenish head. During nesting, almost the entire spiny dorsal fin becomes black below the red rim. The chin and belly are green at this time, but it fades out of breeding season. Fins and body are otherwise dusky.

The Ozark sculpin occurs in the Ozark uplands of Missouri south of the Missouri River and in northern Arkansas.

*C. hypselurus* inhabits cool, clear brooks and moderate to large streams and rivers with rapid flow and gravel or rock bottoms (most often on shallow, gravel-bottom riffles or shoals). It feeds on *Orconectes* crayfish, members of the family Hydropsychidae of the Trichoptera, members of Plecoptera, Ephemeroptera, and Diptera (*Chironomus*, or bloodworms, and *Simulium*, the blackfly), snails, beetles of the family Elmidae, and other fishes, including its own species (Robins and Robison 1985).

The Ozark sculpin nests from winter through spring, usually under the largest flat rock in fast-moving water. Eggs are 2–3 mm in diameter and number from 100 to 1,000 (Burr and Warren 1988), and one nesting male may have clutches from multiple females. The eggs are clustered, similar to madtoms, rather than in a single layer as in the cave-breeding species of darters.

## *Cottus baileyi,* black sculpin

*C. baileyi* is virtually indistinguishable from the mottled sculpin and is not black. It is usually about 1½ inches, but can attain twice that length.

The black sculpin occurs in the Upper Fork, Middle Fork, and South Fork, and in the Watauga River of the upper Holston system, and in the upper Clinch River of the Tennessee River drainage in the mountains of West Virginia and Tennessee (Lee et al. 1980).

*C. baileyi* is common in riffles of small rocky streams and springs, where it feeds on insect larvae and spawns during April.

## *Cottus "pygmaeus,"* unnamed pygmy sculpin

*C. "pygmaeus"* has a bold black top of the head that contrasts with its white nape and white chin. The jaws are green, and dark lines radiate from the eye. The fins are heavily spotted and the bold dark saddles on the back extend onto the flanks as vertical bands in males. Females are more evenly colored. Juveniles have black heads on light bodies. The nuptial male develops an intense dark band below a reddish orange margin in the spiny dorsal fin (Williams 1968). It is a small sculpin, rarely exceeding 2 inches at any age.

*C. "pygmaeus"* is found in one tributary spring to the Coosa River in Calhoun County, Alabama. In this spring and spring run, adults are in the current and juveniles in vegetation (*Ceratophyllum, Myriophyllum,* and *Nasturtium*) out of the current. The water is cool and slightly alkaline and hard from the underlying limestone spring. The bottom is sand and gravel, with some rocks overgrown with *Fontinalis* and another moss, and occasional sprigs of *Potamogeton* in the run. Spawning occurs year-round, with sexual maturity reached at just over 1 inch, excluding the tail fin. Eggs number 2–4 dozen.

Other fish in this spring run are less abundant than the sculpin, but include *Lampetra aepyptera* (the least brook lamprey), *Esox niger, Hypentelium etowanum, Campostoma anomalum, Notropis chrosomus, Gambusia affinis, Micropterus salmoides, Lepomis cyanellus, L. macrochirus, L. microlophus, Etheostoma ditrema,* and *Cottus carolinae zopherus* at the edge of the spring (Williams 1968).

Because the specific epithet *pygmaeus* was in use for a species of *Cottus* from Russia at the same time the North American species was named, the name of the North American species will have to be changed (C. Gilbert, pers. comm.).

A threatened species, it cannot be collected.

The remaining species are all western sculpins.

**Cottus gulosus, riffle sculpin**

In *C. gulosus* the caudal peduncle is flattened from side to side, the body is vaguely mottled, and the back has weak saddles. There is a large black spot at the rear of the spiny dorsal fin but none in front. It grows to 3 inches. The breeding male is dark overall; the spiny dorsal fin has an orange margin and a black submargin.

The riffle sculpin occurs in the lower Columbia River of Washington and Oregon, southward in coastal streams to Morro Bay in California, but is absent from a long stretch of coastline including the Trinity, Klamath, and Rogue Rivers.

*C. gulosus* inhabits small, gravel- or sand-bottom creeks, often in quiet waters. It eats aquatic insect larvae, amphipods, isopods, and snails. It breeds in riffles under rocks during spring (Lee et al. 1980).

Some populations may be taxonomically distinct and aquarists are advised not to mix fish collected from different rivers.

**Cottus perplexus, reticulate sculpin**

*C. perplexus* resembles the riffle sculpin. It is usually 2 inches, but attains twice that length.

The reticulate sculpin ranges in the Rogue River northward to Puget Sound and Oregon, and is most common in coastal streams on the southern side of the Columbia River (Lee et al. 1980).

Where *C. perplexus* has no competitors, it occupies riffles. Where it shares rivers with torrent and coastrange sculpins, it is displaced to pools and runs (Page and Burr 1991). In Oregon, it has been found with northern and Umpqua squawfish, sandrollers, redside minnows, *Rhinichthys,* and suckers. It is abundant and widespread.

A male and several females were placed in a 10-gallon aquarium with rock caves and vigorous aeration and fed generously with live adult *Artemia,* tubificids, and earthworms; they rejected *Phoxinus* fry offered as food (Katula 1991b).

Around March, the head and nape of the cave-dwelling male darkened while the three females retained normal coloration and swelled with ripening eggs. Ripening females would approach the cave but were chased away by the male. Spawning commenced in mid-March, one adult inverting at a time to the ceiling of the cave where eggs were deposited over a period of several hours.

Water conditions were pH 7.8 and 53°F. Only a single female spawned, depositing about 75 greenish eggs which were protected by the male. Two attempts to remove all the females may have disturbed the male sufficiently to induce him to eat the eggs, which disappeared on day four (postspawning). Katula (1991b) concluded that it would have been better to remove the eggs for hatching under aeration.

**Cottus aleuticus, coastrange sculpin**

*C. aleuticus* has long pelvic fins reaching back to the vent; an orange band appears on the dark spiny dorsal fin of the duskier male. It is usually 3–4 inches but attains 6 inches.

The coastrange sculpin ranges from San Luis Obispo County, California, northward to Kiska Island in the Aleutians. A disjunct population 500 miles to the north occurs in the Kobuk River of the Chuchki Sea drainage within the Arctic Circle (Scott and Crossman 1973).

*C. aleuticus* is found on gravel bottoms in fast water of coastal streams and rivers, but also in mud-bottom, deep inland lakes not far from the Pacific Coast, and sometimes even in estuaries. It feeds mostly at night on insects, snails, bloodworms, daphnia, ostracods, fish eggs and fry, and on each other.

Spawning occurs between February and June. An egg mass contains up to 800 eggs, and up to 7,000 eggs have been found in multiple masses in a single nest (Scott and Crossman 1973). The fry are planktonic for one month after hatching, suggesting a recent marine origin. The planktonic requirement of the larvae makes this an undesirable aquarium sculpin. Although temperature tolerance has not been studied in this fish, it is likely to have similar requirements as the slimy sculpin.

## Cottus asper, prickly sculpin

*C. asper* has prickles over most of the body in inland populations, but is less prickly in coastal populations. It has five dark saddles that break into diffuse mottles on the flanks (rather than bands). Both sexes have a thin orange band in the spiny dorsal fin; the male has a black blotch at the rear of this fin. Usually 4 inches, it attains 7 inches.

The prickly sculpin occurs from the Ventura River of California northward to Seward, Alaska. In Canada, it is widespread throughout British Columbia but does not reach Alberta. It is present in coastal and inland rivers and lakes of the Sitkin, Nass, Skeena, Dean, Fraser, and Columbia River systems, and on Queen Charlotte and Vancouver islands (Scott and Crossman 1973).

*C. asper* inhabits quiet waters and feeds on bloodworms and caddisflies (and other insect larvae), snails, and other invertebrates.

Breeding occurs from February through July, usually in fresh water but sometimes in brackish, typically in flowing streams with a gravel to rock bottom. The male establishes a nest under boulders or flat rocks. After the male secures a territory, females arrive and court near the nest before egg-laying.

The jelly-enclosed egg mass of 700 to 4,000 eggs is deposited on the ceiling. Multiple spawnings may result in 25,000 or more eggs in a single nest. The eggs are small for sculpins (1 mm), and guarded by the male until hatching, when they become planktonic for the next 30 days (Scott and Crossman 1973). The planktonic larvae, small eggs, tolerance of marine water, and distribution all point to a recent derivation from a marine environment.

## Cottus princeps, Klamath Lake sculpin

*C. princeps* is prickly and elongate with a short lateral line, boldly marked with blotches (but not bands) above and on the side, and white below. Its average length is 1½–2 inches.

The Klamath Lake sculpin occurs in the upper Klamath River and Agency Lakes in Oregon, and in adjacent irrigation canals (Lee et al. 1980). It has been extirpated from Lost River, Oregon.

*C. princeps* is strictly a lake species, where it is abundant and probably a winter spawner. It is probably not difficult to keep, but also not competitive with other fishes.

## Cottus extensus, Bear Lake sculpin

*C. extensus* is elongate and prickly except on the belly, has no saddles, is mildly mottled, and has an incomplete lateral line. The average length is about 2 inches, but it attains 4 inches.

The Bear Lake sculpin is restricted to Bear Lake, on the border of Idaho and Utah just a few miles west of Wyoming.

This sculpin is found on the rocky bottom of Bear Lake from shore to a depth of over 150 feet. Occurring in this single habitat, it is at risk from careless sportfishing activities. Bait fish introductions have seriously altered the species mix of

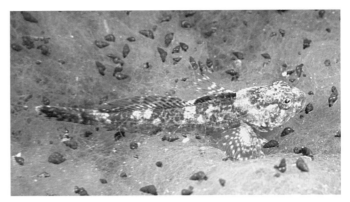

Paiute sculpin, *Cottus beldingi*, Snake R., Idaho. GS

many habitats, and those with endemic species have no backup populations should the species be extirpated from its sole locale.

*C. extensus* breeds during April close to shore, but little else regarding spawning habits has been studied. It is a forage fish for trout and other sport fish (Lee et al. 1980).

| | |
|---|---|
| *Cottus beldingi,* Paiute sculpin | *C. beldingi* is similar to the mottled sculpin, including the black blotches and orange margin in the first dorsal; however, its dorsal fins are separated by a notch on the back, and its body is slimmer. |

The Paiute sculpin is common and widespread from Wyoming westward through Idaho and Oregon, with a few localities in California and Nevada. Isolated locales also exist in Colorado and Washington (Lee et al. 1980).

*C. beldingi* inhabits lakes, is especially common in Lake Tahoe, but is most common in swift riffles over rubble or large gravel.

The Paiute sculpin spawns during May and June under rocks, with eggs guarded by the male. Stomach contents have included insects, crustaceans, detritus, and algae, the latter probably inadvertently consumed while preying on insects in detritus and attached algae.

| | |
|---|---|
| *Cottus marginatus,* margined sculpin | *C. marginatus* is similar to the Paiute sculpin, with dark blotches at the front and rear of a spiny dorsal fin. It is usually less than 3 inches long. It is best identified by locality, or use the key provided by Bond (1994). |

The margined sculpin occurs in the Umatilla River of Oregon and the Walla Walla River of Oregon and Washington, both part of the Columbia River system (Lee et al. 1980).

*C. marginatus* is found in moderate to rapid currents over gravel or rubble, but is adaptable to all types of bottoms (Lee et al. 1980; Marshall 1992).

| | |
|---|---|
| *Cottus confusus,* shorthead sculpin | *C. confusus* resembles the mottled sculpin, but the male has a black smudge at the front and back of its orange-edged spiny dorsal fin. Saddles are indistinct, and the body is slightly more slender than in the mottled sculpin and differs in the pattern of spines. Its length is about 2 inches but it attains 4 inches. |

The shorthead sculpin occurs in Puget Sound tributaries of Washington, and in Columbia River drainages from Washington and Oregon eastward to Idaho; an-

Shoshone sculpin, *Cottus greenei,* Snake R., Idaho. GS

other group is located on the Montana-Alberta border. It is present in the lower Columbia and Snake Rivers of Oregon and Idaho, the Boise, Salmon, and Clearwater Rivers of Idaho, the Little Blackfoot River in Montana, and the Flathead River of Montana and Alberta (Lee et al. 1980).

*C. confusus* inhabits riffles of streams and rivers where it feeds on insect larvae, crustaceans, and fishes, depending on opportunities. It breeds in rubble-boulder riffles beneath rocks during the spring. It should not be mixed with other sculpins having black marks and an orange edge in the spiny dorsal fin.

Do not collect or keep this fish in Canada, where it is a protected species.

---

*Cottus greenei,* Shoshone sculpin

*C. greenei* is short and stocky, with an abbreviated caudal peduncle, and dark (especially juveniles), and adults have saddles on the back and a single dark smudge at the rear of the spiny dorsal fin. The average length is 2 inches.

The Shoshone sculpin is restricted to small, spring-fed, clear, rocky streams in Hagerman Valley, Idaho.

Determine if it is protected before attempting collection.

---

*Cottus klamathensis,*
marbled sculpin

*C. klamathensis* is stubby with an incomplete lateral line, a single dark smudge at the rear of the spiny dorsal fin, and marbled, with no clear pattern of saddles or bands. The male becomes dark brown when nesting (Page and Burr 1991). It is usually under 2 inches, but attains much more.

The marbled sculpin inhabits rivers, lakes, and reservoirs of southern Oregon and northern California, usually over soft bottoms. The northern population occurs in the Klamath River (including Lost River and Agency Lakes) of California and Oregon, and a southern form is present in the Pit River (including the Fall River and Hat Creek) which flows far to the south. Because fish from the two river systems have some inconsistencies in coloration and perhaps taxonomic differences, it would be best to keep them separated.

It spawns during spring, with a female capable of producing over 1,000 eggs in a clutch (Lee et al. 1980). It tolerates a wide temperature range from 50 to 75°F.

---

*Cottus leiopomus,*
Wood River sculpin

*C. leiopomus* has an incomplete lateral line, blotches at both the front and rear of the spiny dorsal fin, and a reticulate pattern. It is usually under 2 inches, but attains 4 inches.

The Wood River sculpin occurs in the Little Wood River and the Big Wood River, and adjacent tributaries of the Snake River located immediately north of Magic Reservoir in Blaine County, Idaho. It was probably more widespread in the past, but its distribution has been reduced by reservoir construction.

*C. leiopomus* inhabits gravel and rubble riffles of small to medium rivers with cool, clear waters and a strong current (Lee et al. 1980).

---

*Cottus pitensis,* pit sculpin

*C. pitensis* has indistinct saddles on the back, distinct wormlike markings on the flanks, and a blotch at the rear of the spiny dorsal fin. The lateral line is complete. The usual length is 1½–4 inches. For more complete characterizations, see Bond (1994).

The Pit sculpin occurs throughout the Pit River in the upper part of the Sacramento River system, including tributaries to Goose Lake. It ranges from Oregon southward to Squaw Valley Creek in Shasta County, California; it is also in the upper Sacramento River (Lee et al. 1980).

*C. pitensis* inhabits rocky riffles of small streams, where it feeds mostly on aquatic insect larvae (Marshall 1992).

---

*Cottus rhotheus,* torrent sculpin

*C. rhotheus* has a narrow caudal peduncle, two bold bands beneath the second dorsal fin, a complete lateral line, and no blotches in the spiny dorsal fin. It attains 2–3 inches.

The torrent sculpin is widespread in both coastal and inland streams. It occurs in the Fraser River and Columbia River drainages from British Columbia southward through Puget Sound tributaries into Oregon and Washington, and ranges westward into Idaho and Montana (Lee et al. 1980).

*C. rhotheus* inhabits deeper water of rivers and large streams (also lakes), usually over gravel and rubble, and prefers fast water. It eats aquatic insect larvae, switching mostly to fish when fully grown (probably an adaptation to the most abundant food source midriver and in lakes).

The torrent sculpin breeds during May and June. Provide feeder minnows as the staple food. Becoming black in captivity, it often rests well off the bottom on filter parts or plants to ambush small prey fishes.

---

*Cottus tenuis,* slender sculpin

*C. tenuis* has a metallic white or yellow belly that contrasts sharply with the brown body. It is mottled but not banded, and its spiny dorsal fin lacks blotches (Page and Burr 1991). It is usually less than 2 inches, and does not reach 3 inches.

The slender sculpin occurs in the upper Klamath River and Agency Lakes (and their tributaries) and in the Klamath irrigation canal in Oregon (Lee et al. 1980).

*C. tenuis* is found in lakes and their tributaries, over various bottoms in still and moving water.

Care protocol is unknown, but it is probably tolerant of lower dissolved oxygen concentrations than other sculpins.

Despite its small range, it is abundant and not protected.

---

*Cottus asperrimus,* rough sculpin

*C. asperrimus* is similar to the slender sculpin *(C. tenuis),* but has many speckles on the belly. The incomplete lateral line extends to the middle of the second dorsal fin, whereas it extends to the end of the fin in the slender sculpin. It is usually 2 inches and attains less than 4 inches.

The rough sculpin occurs in the Fall River system, lower Hat Creek, and sections of the Pit River, in Shasta and Lassen Counties of California (Lee et al. 1980).

*C. asperrimus* inhabits soft bottoms with beds of vegetation at depths of 3 to 6 feet, and is abundant. It feeds on bloodworms and mayfly larvae.

# 18

# The Order Perciformes

THE Perciformes constitute the largest and most modern order of bony fishes. They are represented in North America by some 70 families. Those not covered in this book include the snooks, temperate basses, sea basses, basslets, bigeyes, cardinalfishes, tilefishes, bluefish, cobia, remoras, jacks, roosterfish, pomphrets, dolphins, rover, snappers, tripletail, mojarras, grunts, bonnetmouths, porgies, drums, goatfishes, sweeper, sea chubs, spadefishes, butterflyfishes, angelfishes, armorhead, surfperches, damselfishes, hawkfish, mullets, barracudas, threadfins, wrasses, parrotfishes, ronquils, eelpouts, pricklebacks, wrymouths, gunnels, wolffishes, quillfish, prowfish, graveldiver, jawfishes, sandfishes, flatheads, triplefins, stargazers, sand stargazers, clinids, ragfish, sand lances, dragonets, wormfishes, surgeonfishes, louvar, snake mackerels, mackerels, swordfish, marlins, and butterfishes.

Families that are covered include the sunfishes (Centrarchidae), perches (Percidae), cichlids (Cichlidae), combtooth blennies (Blenniidae), gobies (Gobiidae), and sleepers (Eleotridae).

## Family Centrarchidae, the Basses and Sunfishes

Centrarchidae are deep-bodied, typically have ctenoid scales, and their pelvic fins are situated under the pectoral fins. There are 8 genera and 30 species. Centrarchids spawn in sandy depressions constructed by the males, these nests often in proximity. The species are almost all native to the eastern and central United States and eastern Canada. The largemouth bass, bluegill, and green sunfish are among the most widely transplanted sport fishes in the world, and might be found anywhere in North America or abroad.

For the smaller species, dip net and seine in dense vegetation, around roots and logs close to shore in lakes and ponds, and around boulders and beneath undercut banks in streams. When nesting, the larger sunfishes can also be taken by hook-and-line or cast net.

Young centrarchids adapt well, are easily cared for and raised, but larger adults adapt with difficulty, unaccustomed to confinement and having developed strong feeding preferences. Smaller centrarchids are good aquarium fishes.

### Genus *Micropterus,* Black Basses

*Micropterus,* at 1 to 2 feet, are too large for home breeding, but popular in public aquariums. *Micropterus* are heavy-bodied predators, shaped like the South American *Cichla ocellaris.* They eat fishes, amphibians, snakes, crayfish, and aquatic insects. They breed in sandy depressions over 2 feet in diameter, in deep, clear water. Nests may contain 1,500 or so 2 mm eggs. All black basses are game fish or protected as threatened species.

Largemouth bass, *Micropterus salmoides,* Bull Shoals Lake, Mo. WFR

Spotted bass, *Micropterus punctulatus,* Bull Shoals Lake, Mo. WFR

White crappie, *Pomoxis annularis,* Reelfoot Lake, Obion Co., Tenn. RB

Black crappie, *Pomoxis nigromaculatus,* Bull Shoals Lake, Mo. WFR

The largemouth bass is the only lacustrine (lake) member of the genus; the others are all riverine. The largemouth is the most sought after game fish in the United States, the subject of hundreds of tournaments in which tens of thousands of dollars are at stake. The smallmouth bass is less popular because river fishing is less popular than lake fishing. All the other black basses resemble the smallmouth, differing in spots on the lower flanks, banding, teeth on the tongue, and colors of the caudal fin. Subspecies of black bass have been obscured by transplantations that have also endangered the continued existence of the Guadalupe bass in Texas.

For distributions and distinguishing marks, see Lee et al. (1980) and Page and Burr (1991). See also Robison and Buchanan (1988) for *M. coosae,* Cofer (1995) for *M. punctulatus,* Ongarato and Snucins (1993) and Snyder et al. (1996) for *M. dolomieui,* and Boyer et al. (1977) for *M. treculi.*

**Genus *Pomoxis***

*Pomoxis* contains the two crappie species, both popular small game fish of lakes, ponds, and river backwaters. They are too large for home aquaria. Their distribution is widespread from Mexico to the Canadian border and beyond. See also Smeltzer and Flickinger (1991).

**Genus *Enneacanthus***

*Enneacanthus,* the dwarf sunfishes, are among the best of all native fishes for the home aquarium. Usually less than 3 inches long, they mature at half this size, and can be spawned in 20-gallon or even smaller tanks.

A pair or trio should have a well-lit 20-gallon aquarium with a 1- or 2-inch

Blackbanded sunfish, *Enneacanthus chaetodon*, N.C. RJG

deep sand bottom thickly planted with rooted *Vallisneria, Sagittaria,* dwarf Amazon sword plants, or native rooted plants. Provide neutral to slightly alkaline water, tinted tan with peat moss. Soften the water by placing clinoptilolite (zeolite) inside the cartridge of a filter until the calcium hardness is below the detection limits of a standard aquarium hardness kit.

Live blackworms, mosquito larvae, *Artemia, Daphnia,* or live adult brine shrimp are required for newly captured fish, but they quickly learn to eat frozen brine shrimp and bloodworms. The eggs vary from much less than 1 mm in the blackbanded sunfish to twice as large in the other species. The fry should be provided infusoria (rotifers, protozoans, motile algae) as a first food for a week or two before graduating to brine shrimp nauplii and microworms.

---

**Enneacanthus chaetodon, blackbanded sunfish**

*E. chaetodon* is the "angelfish" of native fishes. It has 4–6 intense black vertical bands crossing a round, silver body. The fins are clear except for possible black or orange leading spines. It lives 4 years, and attains 1–1½ inches the first year; it reaches 2–4 inches maximum, with most of its growth by the end of age two.

*E. chaetodon* was originally placed in the now defunct genus (sometimes subgenus) *Mesogonistius.* Earlier divisions into northern *[E. (Mesogonistius) c. chaetodon]* and southern *[E. (M.) c. elizabethae]* subspecies are no longer recognized (Bailey 1941a). Popular in Europe, where they are supplied by Far East commercial breeders.

The blackbanded sunfish is found below the fall line from the New Jersey Pine Barrens southward in many Atlantic Coast Sandhills and upper/inner Coastal Plain drainages (Wicomico Terrace elevation of a Pleistocene feature in Florida), in small, isolated (disjunct) populations that extend westward along the Gulf Coast to the Aucilla River of northern Florida (Jenkins et al. 1975; Lee et al. 1980). *E. chaetodon* is usually uncommon, but occasionally abundant.

The blackbanded sunfish inhabits stained ponds, lakes, and slow-moving streams, occurring in dense shoreline vegetation in or near the Sandhills (longleaf pine forests) of the South and Pine Barrens of the North. It is always in water with a sandy bottom and an overlay of silt or mud. It often occurs with pygmy sunfishes, bluespotted sunfish, pirate perch, and other swamp fishes. It feeds on cladocerans, amphipods, copepods, bloodworms, dragonfly and caddisfly larvae, and other invertebrates (McLane 1955; Schwartz 1961).

Smith (1907) reported March spawning in North Carolina based on ripe eggs, but I have collected 1- to 3-month-old juveniles during January in the state. McLane (1955) suggested late winter or early spring spawning in Florida, based on the failure to find ripe gonads in July and October. In my fish room, breeding occurred from August through October, and probably will occur year-round in captivity if live food is abundant and 12 hours of daylight provided.

The bars on the male fade and his body changes from silver to muddy gray as he defends a shallow depression in the sand. The clear eggs and tiny, newly hatched fry are virtually invisible; fry more than one week old are as small as gourami or tetra fry. They stick to plants at first, and shoal when free-swimming. See also Sternburg (1991).

| | |
|---|---|
| *Enneacanthus gloriosus,* bluespotted sunfish | *E. gloriosus* (**plate 47**) sometimes has banding in the juveniles, but not in adults. Many blue-green to gold body spangles extend into orange-tinted dorsal and anal fins. The dark spot on the gill cover may be less than half the eye diameter. The bluespotted sunfish has a thinner and flatter forehead than the banded sunfish, with usually 17 (15–19) scales around the caudal peduncle. |

*E. gloriosus* occurs near the fall line and throughout the Coastal Plain from New York through Florida, and is frequently abundant (Lee et al. 1980) in the vegetated edges of stained ponds, lakes, and slow-moving streams.

The bluespotted sunfish is found over sand, silt, or mud, often with fliers and pirate perch. It eats copepods, cladocerans, ostracods, chironomids, amphipods, shrimp, and snails.

McLane (1955) discovered gravid females during April, May, August, September, and October, indicating a protracted breeding season in Florida. The great north-south range (and associated temperature differences) of *E. gloriosus* have been addressed in a study of its thermoregulation (Casterlin and Reynolds 1979). Typically, it does not occur together with *E. obesus,* but often does with *E. chaetodon.*

In captivity, do not feed flake foods, which remain uneaten and degrade water quality. Bluespots prefer dark hiding places and are not aggressive toward other fishes. They spawn in densely vegetated aquaria, and will probably spawn year-round.

The most delicate species of the genus, they should be transported with salt added to their water to control stress-induced, delayed bacterial septicemia that often follows collection in the wild.

| | |
|---|---|
| *Enneacanthus obesus,* banded sunfish | *E. obesus* (**plate 48**) is light gray with sparse blue-green to gold spangles that do not extend onto the clear dorsal and anal fins. Distinct vertical bands are common in adults. A dark opercular spot may be more than half the eye diameter. The forehead is rounded and the body is thicker than that of *E. gloriosus.* The number of scales around the caudal peduncle is usually 19 (18–22). |

The banded sunfish ranges along the Atlantic Coast from just above the fall line throughout the Coastal Plain from Massachusetts to northern Florida.

*E. obesus* is often common and sometimes abundant (Lee et al. 1980) in densely vegetated edges of stained ponds and slow-moving streams, over sand covered with leaf litter. It eats ostracods, snails, copepods, cladocerans, amphipods, chironomids, and other aquatic insect larvae. It does not appear to occur in the same habitat with *E. gloriosus* or with *E. chaetodon,* although the latter two species often occur to-

Flier, *Centrarchus macropterus,* Juniper Cr., Brunswick Co., N.C. FCR

gether. The spawning season in Florida is March through November (McLane 1955).

The banded sunfish is a hardy, often aggressive fish that readily adapts to frozen foods.

Wild New Jersey fish developed nuptial colors after tap water was acidified and softened with a rechargable ion exchange softening pillow (probably clinoptilolite) and commercial "blackwater tonic" (peat moss extract). The final pH was 6.0 and hardness was below the detection limits of a commercial aquarium hardness kit.

In November, females swelled with eggs. One male subsequently intensified in color and spawned with several females on a shallow, circular depression nest. The fish were removed, the power filters stopped, and the tank provided with gentle, air-driven sponge filtration.

Eggs hatched in three days at 65°F and pH 6.0; the fry became free-swimming three to five days later. They began to consume *Artemia* nauplii and microworms two days later, but aeration was discontinued during feeding for the fry to capture prey. With growth, larger cohorts did not eat the smaller ones.

**Genus *Centrarchus***
*Centrarchus macropterus,* flier

*C. macropterus* is the only species in its genus. It is laterally compressed (thin) and deep-bodied to circular. It has a small mouth and a metallic green or gold body with a small black spot on each scale forming horizontal rows. It has a black bar below the eye, and indistinct vertical dark bands. The dorsal fin is inserted in advance of the anal; it has 11–12 dorsal spines; and the body is thinner and more metallic than any other centrarchid. The juvenile has a prominent red and black ocellus in the soft dorsal fin. It matures at 3 inches in one year, and may attain 8 inches.

The flier is restricted to the Atlantic Coastal Plain from Virginia through central Florida to eastern Texas. It also extends up the Mississippi drainage to lowlands of Illinois and Missouri.

*C. macropterus* prefers heavily vegetated, sluggish, mud-, silt-, and sand-bottom creeks, ponds, backwaters, swamps, and other darkly stained acidic waters that are hostile to other centrarchids except for *Enneacanthus* spp. and warmouth (*Chaenobryttus gulosus*). It is frequently associated with pygmy sunfishes, pirate perch, and other swamp-inhabiting species. The flier spawns from February or March through May in colonies, the young protected by the parents. It consumes copepods and other crustaceans and aquatic insects, and later will eat young bluegills and other fishes (Pflieger 1975).

Maintain in large (70–125 gallons), densely planted aquaria, with a sand/gravel bottom, at least 12 hours light, and trickle filtration for high water quality. The flier takes small feeder minnows and quickly learns to eat frozen brine shrimp and bloodworms. It has not yet been spawned in captivity, but is a good candidate. Grow juveniles together and let them pair off.

## Genus *Archoplites*
*Archoplites interruptus,* Sacramento perch

*A. interruptus* is the most primitive of the centrarchids and the only one native to the West Coast. The single living member of its genus is related to fossils from Idaho and Washington (Lee et al. 1980). With 6 to 7 anal fin spines, it resembles a rock bass, but the eye is not red and the vertically banded body is thin (Page and Burr 1991). It reaches 2 feet in length.

The Sacramento perch was originally found in the vegetated backwaters and mud-bottom sloughs of the San Joaquin–Sacramento drainages in California but has been greatly depleted in its native range. It has been widely introduced in highly alkaline reservoirs and farm ponds throughout California, Nevada, Utah, the Dakotas, and Colorado (Lee et al. 1980).

*A. interruptus* is noncompetitive with other centrarchids, and is not a nest guarder according to Page and Burr (1991). Additional information can be found in Moyle (1976). Its distribution in alkaline waters may indicate either a tolerance or a requirement; the answer has not been resolved. It is likely to breed in hard water, alkaline fish ponds, but not aquaria.

## Genus *Acantharchus*
*Acantharchus pomotis,* mud sunfish

*A. pomotis* the only member of its genus and the only centrarchid with cycloid (smooth-edged) scales. It is golden brown with broad dark horizontal bands on a light background; black bands appear on the cheek when stressed. It has a blunt head, rounded tail fin, thick body, and three anal fin spines. The purported subspecies *A. p. mizelli* from the Suwannee River is not valid (Cashner et al. 1989). It grows to 6 inches.

The mud sunfish occurs in the lower Piedmont and throughout the Coastal Plain of the Atlantic Coast from the Hudson River in southern New York to the St. Johns River in northern Florida; it continues westward from the Suwannee River to the St. Marks River (Cashner et al. 1989).

*A. pomotis* prefers darkly stained, frequently muddy, oxygen-poor, slow-moving, densely vegetated streams, lakes, and ponds, occurring over organic mud and silt (Smith 1907; Bennett and McFarlane 1983) and sometimes sand. The mud sunfish may be more active at night (Smith 1907), and is nowhere abundant. The mud sunfish is a catholic predator on crustaceans, insects, and fishes.

The sexes are similar in coloration. They breed from late winter through spring when temperatures are rising and may be the first sunfishes to spawn, but nesting has not been observed (Pardue 1993). People who love oscars *(Astronotus ocellatus)* might like the mud sunfish, which it resembles.

Provide a 15- or 20-gallon aquarium with clean, neutral water, a sand bottom, and dense *Nitella, Vesicularia, Vallisneria, Myriophyllum,* or water sprite. Feed live adult brine shrimp, earthworms, blackworms, mosquito larvae, daphnia, crushed snails, and frozen foods. Despite its habitat in the wild, the mud sunfish cannot tol-

Rock bass, *Ambloplites rupestris,* day, Little R., Blount Co., Tenn. RB    Rock bass, *Ambloplites rupestris,* night, Clear Fork R., Ohio. WFR

erate low oxygen and acidic decomposition in the confines of an aquarium. Provide a short (8 hr. light) photoperiod and cold temperatures (≤ 50°F). Gradually increase the temperature (55–60°F) and photoperiod (10 hr. light) to mimic the spring spawning period.

**Genus *Ambloplites***

*Ambloplites* are the rock basses, characterized by six anal fin spines, red eyes, a thick body, and dark and silver markings (often in a marble pattern). The genus was revised by Cashner (1974), with one additional species described since (Cashner and Suttkus 1977). The sexes are similar in coloration.

Most rock basses occur in flowing, clear, upland streams with sand or rubble bottom and high dissolved oxygen content, but two species inhabit lowlands.

Provide a 55-gallon or larger (not < 29 gal.) aquarium for a pair collected in late fall or early winter before the breeding season. Add sand to the bottom and refuges of plants and rockwork. Feed live minnows or goldfish, snails, earthworms, blackworms, and adult brine shrimp; provide meal worms and crickets for the larger species. Keep cold, and gradually increase the temperature to 55–60°F and the photoperiod to 10-hour light to simulate the spring spawning period.

*Ambloplites rupestris,* rock bass

*A. rupestris* has rows of indistinct spots along the sides, and its mottling is most evident at night. It matures at 7 to 11 inches in length.

*A. rupestris* is the most northerly and widespread of the rock basses, ranging from Canada to the Great Lakes and the Dakotas. It continues southward through Missouri, Arkansas, and Oklahoma, and ranges in the east from Maine to northern Georgia and Alabama. It is replaced by related rock basses mostly in the Ozark Plateau and along the Gulf Coast (Lee et al. 1980).

*A. rupestris* occurs over most of its range in clear, cool, vegetated lakes and streams with a rock, sand or gravel bottom, but is also found in lakes and swamps. Rock bass nest in groups, competing for clean, sandy bottom, around June at 60 to 70°F.

The saucer-shaped nest, up to 2 feet in diameter, is constructed and defended by the male. A female, enticed by the displaying male, enters the nest and slides on her side (with her head opposite the tail of the male). After spawning, the female is dismissed, sometimes replaced by another.

The male guards the 800–11,000 eggs until the fry have dispersed. During protection of eggs and fry, the male loses body mass. Larger males lose more mass,

Ozark bass, *Ambloplites constellatus,* White R., Mo. WFR

but larger males get more eggs to brood, and the survival rate of their broods is higher than that of broods belonging to smaller males. Late in the season, when the larger males have spawned and lost considerable mass, the remaining females spawn with the largest of the smaller males not yet having lost body mass. Those larger males having had the most breeding success during the year (and also having lost the most body mass) are unlikely to spawn the following season (Sabat 1994a,b). Growth of juveniles is rapid, some attaining 2 inches the first year (Scott and Crossman 1973).

Large and not especially colorful, the rock bass may be a ready breeder. The aquarium should be at least 55 gallons, and the female(s) should be removed after spawning. Rock bass may be prolific. The excess young should be released solely in the location where the parents were caught, or be destroyed to avoid their introduction into a habitat supporting another rock bass species that is incapable of competing.

---

*Ambloplites constellatus,* Ozark bass

*A. constellatus* has prominent, irregular black speckles all over the body not arranged in rows, and its anal fin lacks a black margin. It matures at 6 to 7 inches.

The Ozark bass is abundant in higher elevations (Ozark Plateau) of the White River in southern Missouri and northern Arkansas. It is occasionally found in the Osage River of Missouri where it was probably introduced by state agencies while stocking other fishes (Cashner and Suttkus 1977).

*A. constellatus* is one of the most common centrarchids in pools of clear, small to moderately sized streams having rock or cobble and considerable aquatic vegetation.

Pflieger (1975), who did not distinguish between *A. constellatus* and *A. rupestris* (but probably observed *A. constellatus* more), reported that breeding was triggered by temperatures of 55 to 60°F from early April to early June in Missouri.

The male prepares the isolated 8- to 10-inch, saucer-shaped nest in sand or gravel (near large objects) in 1 to 5 feet of water in the current. The female visits only to spawn, and the male guards the nest until the fry disperse.

*A. constellatus* is the best rock bass for aquarium breeding due to its small size, good looks, and catholic carnivorous habits. A group of juveniles should be raised together in a 29- to 55-gallon aquarium with a gravel or sand bottom, filtration, water changes, and a varied diet. Eventually, a pair will establish a territory.

Shadow bass, *Ambloplites ariommus,* Conasauga R., Tenn. RB

Warmouth, *Chaenobryttus gulosus,* Tennessee R. RB

| | |
|---|---|
| *Ambloplites cavifrons,* Roanoke bass | *A. cavifrons* has dark fins, a slightly indented tail fin, and a light colored, heavily built, almost square body with the suggestion of horizontal rows of dots (Cashner and Jenkins 1982). It attains 1 foot in length.

The Roanoke bass is restricted to the Piedmont of North Carolina and southern Virginia.

*A. cavifrons* usually occurs above the fall line in clear rivers, pools, and some lakes. It is found over sand, rock, rubble, or gravel, and avoids even slightly silty habitats.

The Roanoke bass has been hatchery bred at two years of age between mid-May and mid-June; it spawned in sand or gravel shallows, and the nests were guarded by the male. |
| *Ambloplites ariommus,* shadow bass | *A. ariommus* has a high contrast marbling pattern. It attains 8 inches.

This lowland species ranges from the Apalachicola River of the Florida panhandle westward to Lake Pontchartrain, and continues up the Mississippi River's tributaries to just enter southeastern Missouri.

The shadow bass inhabits pools, riffles, open areas, and vegetation under banks. It breeds from April through mid-August. It is more tolerant of warmer water than other rock basses.

No aquarium breeding reports are available. |
| **Genus *Chaenobryttus***
*Chaenobryttus gulosus,* warmouth | *C. gulosus* **(plate 49)** is, at 8 inches or more, an impressive large-headed, large-mouthed sunfish that is often placed in *Lepomis.* The young are deep yellow and overlaid with dark vertical wavy bands; the bands are replaced by dense, dark mottling in the yellow breasted adults. Brown horizontal streaks on the face extend into the opercle, but no distinct opercular flap is present. The warmouth is similar to some rock basses, but can be identified by its three anal spines and a rough patch on the tongue that can be felt with the finger tip.

The warmouth occurs along the Atlantic slope from Pennsylvania to southern Florida. It ranges along the entire Gulf Coast into northern Mexico, and continues northward to the Great Lakes area (Lee et al. 1980).

*C. gulosus* is found in ponds, lakes, and quiet backwaters with dense vegetation or woody debris over mud and silt bottoms. It is a game fish within most of its range, and a predator on crayfish, isopods, insect larvae, and small fishes.

The warmouth breeds (at 5 inches) over silty rubble next to a large structure |

(e.g., rock, driftwood); the nest is constructed and guarded by the male. Eggs hatch in less than two days and the schooling fry are free-swimming five or six days later. Fry grow rapidly on baby brine shrimp, feeding later on live daphnia and then each other. *C. gulosus* is predatory on small tankmates of all kinds (not just fishes). It avoids open space and bright light.

## Genus *Lepomis*

*Lepomis* contains the familiar colorful sunfishes of lakes, ponds, streams, and rivers. They are most often identified in the field by the colors of the gill cover extension ("flap" or "ear") and whether the margin on the remainder of the gill cover is stiff *(cyanellus, gibbosus, punctatus, symmetricus)* or flexible *(auritus, humilus, macrochirus, marginatus, megalotis, microlophus).*

Sunfishes can be caught in seines or dip nets, and a few are large enough to be taken by hook-and-line. They adapt well to captivity, and include species that are popular as aquarium fishes in Europe and as food fishes in Asia.

Provide a 20- to 70-gallon aquarium based on aggressiveness and adult size (2–8 inches). The aquarium should be densely planted on 2 inches of sand, with rocks or flowerpots for refuges, and have 12–15 hours (80–100 watts) of light. Most sunfishes do well in captivity when fed adult brine shrimp, bloodworms, blackworms, daphnia, crushed snails, chopped earthworms, the occasional small feeder minnow, and cricket or meal worm larvae. Many adapt to flake food and a meat mixture (fish, beef heart, liver, etc.).

### *Lepomis gibbosus,* pumpkinseed

*L. gibbosus* (**plate 50**), a prized aquarium fish in Europe, has wavy blue-green streaks on the face and a black opercular flap with a red spot in the rear and blue margins above and below. The soft dorsal fin has rows of spots and the caudal fin has a blue margin. It normally grows to 8 inches or more.

The pumpkinseed is ubiquitous in the East but spotty in the West where it was introduced. It originally ranged from southern Canada through South Carolina, and from the Great Lakes (except Lake Superior drainages) through the northern Mississippi basin. It has been widely transplanted as a sport fish and now occurs westward to Oregon, Washington, and northern California; it even occurs in Europe.

*L. gibbosus* inhabits shallow, cool lakes and river backwaters, preferring more cover than the bluegills with which it frequently occurs. It feeds on insects, small fish, clams, and snails, crushing them with powerful jaws and pharyngeal teeth. Pairs usually nest alone but occasionally in colonies with the nests 3–4 inches apart. The pumpkinseed prefers a bottom of flat rocks and gravel, barren of plants, for its saucer-shaped nest. The male protects the eggs from the most important egg predators, snails and bullhead catfishes, until the fry are free-swimming about seven days later (Carter 1963; Miller 1967).

Readily bred, a 15-hour photoperiod will stimulate sexual activity, whereas constant light deters it. The pumpkinseed declines at elevated temperatures. Bockstael (1984) recommends large aquaria with open spaces, a bottom of fine gravel or sand with a few (not many) rocks, and a diet of chopped earthworms plus a prepared mix of beef heart, flake food, and oatmeal bound with gelatin and frozen until use, fed several times daily.

Pumpkinseeds should be overwintered outdoors (chilled) and spawn at 6 to 8 inches. The male turns a brighter orange on the belly and becomes territorial; thereafter remove all fish except one pair or a trio. When spawning is imminent, turn off the undergravel (and other) filtration and supply filtration only through a sponge filter.

The pair or trio spawns side by side in a pit prepared by the male. Females should then be removed. The male does not eat while it guards, fans, and mouths the 300–500 eggs until hatching three days later, after which he should be removed. The fry take live *Artemia* nauplii upon swim-up, microworms one week later, and blended prepared food thereafter. They grow rapidly with little mortality.

*L. gibbosus,* a game fish in many states, usually requires a license to collect.

---

*Lepomis cyanellus,* green sunfish

*L. cyanellus* (**plate 51**) is large, thick, and yellowish green. It has indistinct vertical bands and scattered iridescent spots. The opercular flap is dark with a light margin. A black blotch appears on the rear of the dorsal and anal fins. The breeding male has white-edged dorsal, anal, and caudal fins.

The green sunfish is native to Gulf drainages from the Great Lakes to Mexico and occurs throughout the central United States. It has been transplanted to most Atlantic slope drainages.

*L. cyanellus* is ubiquitous, inhabiting headwater streams to big rivers, lakes, and ponds. It feeds on fishes, insects, and crayfish. The green sunfish spawns from spring through summer in backwaters less than 1 foot deep on a gravel or rock bottom, occasionally on twigs and leaves (Pflieger 1975).

*L. cyanellus* is not usually colonial except where habitat is sparse. The breeding females are banded. Several females may spawn at the nest of one male. The male guards the eggs until they hatch, and the fry are free-swimming in one week.

Rollo (1994) successfully bred *L. cyanellus* in a gravel-bottom, 20-gallon aquarium during November by providing live foods and canister filtration and raising the temperature 8°F in a short period (usually 15–30 days). A group of fish was housed together. The male excavated and guarded the nest, keeping the spent female and supernumerary fish at bay.

Eggs were described as adhesive, ¹⁄₁₆-inch (about 2 mm) in diameter, and numbering in the hundreds. All fish but the male were removed, the canister filter was turned off and replaced with a sponge filter, and 25 percent of the water was changed. When the male was seen eating eggs kicked up by current, he too was removed. Eggs hatched in three days at 65°F and pH 7.0. With daily 25 percent water changes, the fry became free-swimming in one week, but it was another two days before they would feed on *Artemia* nauplii. Survival was less than 100 percent because the hundreds of fry were crowded in a 20-gallon aquarium.

The green sunfish is a game fish in many states, requiring a fishing license for collection.

---

*Lepomis auritus,* redbreast sunfish

*L. auritus* (**plate 52**) is elongate with light yellow medial fins, a bright red-orange belly in the breeding male, olive sides with tiny red-orange dots, blue facial streaks, and an elongate, solid black opercular flap. It rarely attains 9 inches.

The redbreast sunfish was once restricted to streams on the Atlantic slope of the Appalachians and south of the Appalachians westward to the Apalachicola River (emptying into the eastern Gulf of Mexico). It has been widely stocked and now occurs in Atlantic and Gulf slope states from Maine to Louisiana (Lee et al. 1980).

*L. auritus* is a riverine sunfish inhabiting mountain headwaters to coastal embayments; it is usually not found in lakes or ponds. It is predatory on smaller fishes.

Nesting adults are difficult to approach with a cast net or seine. The young, distinguished by a dusky blotch in the dorsal fin, can be dipnetted from woody debris and rooted vegetation along stream banks. Adults can be caught on fine (No. 18–22) long-shank hooks baited with grasshoppers or worms. Supplement the diet with feeder minnows.

The redbreast sunfish requires 100 gallons or more of space, and is thus not suitable for most aquaria. It is a game fish, and in many states cannot be taken without a fishing license.

| | |
|---|---|
| *Lepomis humilis,* orangespotted sunfish | *L. humilis* (**plate 53**) has a blue body with brown to orange spots extending onto the face, the dark opercular spot is completely edged in white, no streaks appear on the face, and the fins are unspotted. All sunfishes have two pores on the head between the eyes, but in this species, they are in large depressions and separated by one depression width (Pflieger 1975). When breeding, the spots, belly, and fins of the male become brilliant orange, and the paired fins are edged in black. It matures at 2–3 inches in its third year and commonly attains 4 inches. |

The orangespotted sunfish occurs in Gulf Coast drainages from Alabama to Texas, and ranges northward in the Mississippi to the Great Lakes in Ohio and North Dakota (Lee et al. 1980).

*L. humilis* is found in lowland backwaters, ponds, oxbows, and overgrown lakes with a silt or mud bottom, avoiding currents. As expected from its long, thin gill rakers, it feeds mostly on insects and crustaceans, but not snails; it also takes small fishes.

The orangespotted sunfish is a group spawner with peak activity during June. The 2-inch-deep, 1-foot-diameter nests are constructed on a sandy bottom, in sheltered water 16 inches deep, among plants, and behind logs or boulders or below an overhanging bank. The eggs are tiny, colorless, and adhesive, and hatch in five days at 80°F (Pflieger 1975; Robison and Buchanan 1988). *L. humilis* is a slow grower and not competitive with larger sunfishes.

| | |
|---|---|
| *Lepomis punctatus,* spotted sunfish | *L. punctatus* (**plate 54**) is dark with a metallic sheen; the face and fins are dusky; three indistinct dusky bands appear on the cheek; and the belly is light. The short opercular flap is black and may or may not have a thin white to yellow margin; a red flush or blotch appears just above the opercular flap; and the opercle edge is exceptionally stiff. Horizontal rows of tiny red-orange (male) or yellow (female) spots appear on the scales along the flank. The row of pored lateral line scales is unbroken in the middle of the body. It grows to 8 inches but 5 inches is average. |

Warren (1992) proposed that the subspecies be elevated to species rank. *L. p. punctatus* has sharply defined black spots on the body and dark outer edges on the dorsal and anal fins in the nuptial male; it ranges from southern North Carolina to Florida. *L. p. miniatus* has more diffuse black spotting; the nuptial male has orange edges on the dorsal and anal fins; it occurs in Gulf slope drainages from western Florida to Texas and ranges up the Mississippi River to Illinois (Lee et al., 1980), intergrading in western Florida.

The spotted sunfish occurs in shallow, sluggish swamp waters with silt or mud bottoms and dense vegetation or woody debris, mostly in oxbow lakes, backwaters, and the pools of springs or rivers, and also occurring over rock, boulder, sand, or gravel, in clear or stained water. Stomach contents included mostly insects, some

Bantam sunfish, *Lepomis symmetricus*, Saline R., Ark. WFR

Bluegill, *Lepomis macrochirus*, Tennessee R., Tenn. RB

spiders, mussels, snails, detritus, vegetation, and fragments of fish (Robison and Buchanan 1988).

The spotted sunfish is a solitary nester, breeding at 3 inches in shallows at the edge of a silty, vegetated shoreline in late spring. The nuptial male displays bold black pelvic fins. The eggs hatch in two days at 68 to 75°F and the fry swim up and begin feeding ten days later (Pflieger 1975).

The aquarium bottom should contain a small amount of peat moss. Use a canister filter with activated carbon to limit staining by tannins. *L. punctatus* is a gentle fish that prefers solitude, shallow water, and an invertebrate diet; it will not thrive in a community tank with other sunfishes.

## *Lepomis symmetricus,* bantam sunfish

*L. symmetricus* is a pale version of the spotted sunfish. It has a prominent black blotch at the base of the dorsal fin (faded in adults), and a sharp break midbody in the row of lateral line scales. It has rows of both dark- and light-colored spots on the side, no red or pink patch above the opercular flap, and only one indistinct stripe on the face (Robison and Buchanan 1988). The young have a red flush in the fins and a vivid black dorsal spot. The breeding male is black with bright red irises. At 3 inches maximum, *L. symmetricus* is the smallest species of *Lepomis*.

The bantam sunfish occurs in Coastal Plain and other lowland streams northward to Illinois in the Mississippi River drainage and in other rivers westward through Texas.

*L. symmetricus* inhabits sluggish streams, oxbows, swamps, and wherever else the lack of current combines with a shallow mud bottom and dense woody debris or shoreline vegetation. It eats snails, crustaceans, spiders, and insects.

The bantam sunfish breeds at one year in a nest constructed of leaf litter and debris, with the female producing 200–1,600 eggs. It lives to 3 years (Burr 1977; P. W. Smith 1979).

Although it lacks striking coloration, *L. symmetricus* will become popular because of its easy propagation. It is not known if the bantam will hybridize with the spotted sunfish, and the two species should be kept apart.

## *Lepomis macrochirus,* bluegill

*L. macrochirus* is a large (average 6–9 in.) sunfish with a small mouth. Its long pointed pectoral fin is a character also found in *L. microlophus*. Juveniles have a chainlike pattern of double vertically squiggly lines on the flank. Adults have a dusky blotch on the soft dorsal fin and a black opercular flap.

The native distribution of the bluegill includes the Great Lakes east of Lake Superior westward just into South Dakota and Nebraska, then southward through most of Oklahoma and Texas to southeastern New Mexico, just entering Mexico. It occurs from the Rio Grande eastward to the Atlantic slope, northward to the Cape Fear River in North Carolina, and continues northward inland along the Appalachians to the St. Lawrence River.

The bluegill has been introduced widely elsewhere. Most populations are *L. m. macrochirus*. North Carolina has *L. m. purpurescens;* and *L. m. mystacalis* (with beautiful lavender highlights) occurs in peninsular Florida.

*L. macrochirus* is most abundant in large lakes and farm ponds and least abundant in fast rivers. Typically, it is found at the edges of steeply sloping recreational lakes over sand, often near but not within vegetation except when young. It is primarily a surface feeder on insects and algae, its weak teeth precluding it from eating hard-shelled snails, to which the eggs are vulnerable in the nest.

The bluegill is a synchronous colonial spawner, with males breeding at the same time and the nests close together. This mass spawning overwhelms egg predators (mostly snails, which account for half of all egg predation, and bullhead catfishes). Outside nests bear the brunt of predation, but mass spawning enables the many defending males to provide overlapping protection, giving the masses of newly hatched fry the same protection as in schools of other forage fishes (e.g., in terms of confusing predators and in sacrificing outside members of the school). It also appears to select for the fittest in the Darwinian sense, as the best and strongest males tend to nest in the center of the colony (Gross and MacMillan 1981).

*L. macrochirus* will spawn in a 30- to 50-gallon aquarium with a sand or gravel bottom when the temperature climbs above 70°F and day length is 12–15 hours. The nest diameter is twice the length of the adult fish. The small white eggs hatch in 2½ days and the fry are free-swimming 3 days later. The fry aggregate toward light, on the surface or adherent to the tank sides or other structures, and will take *Artemia* nauplii as a first food. After one week, they lose their phototropism and swim everywhere. Feed frozen brine shrimp, daphnia, blackworms, small earthworms, or meal worms.

---

*Lepomis microlophus,* redear, red ear, or shellcracker sunfish

*L. microlophus* has long, pointed pectoral fins, a character shared only with *L. macrochirus*. It has prominent pharyngeal (throat) teeth and a red rear edge on the black opercular flap. It is a thin fish with a slightly orange belly, a small mouth, and stubby gill rakers. Juveniles often do not develop a red opercular edge. It grows up to 10 inches.

Historically, the redear consisted of two subspecies with a zone of intergradation in the Florida panhandle. The eastern form, *L. m. microlophus,* ranged from North Carolina southward through the Georgia-Alabama border (Apalachicola River drainage) into the Florida panhandle and continued eastward and southward through all of peninsular Florida. The western, and still unnamed, subspecies ranged from the Florida panhandle west of the Apalachicola drainage to the Rio Grande, and northward in the Mississippi valley to southern Indiana and Illinois (earlier even to Iowa).

Redear sunfish, *Lepomis microlophus,* White R., Mo. WFR

Today, the subspecific populations have been mixed by transplantations. The redear is most abundant in Florida and western Gulf drainages, but has been introduced as far north as New Jersey and Pennsylvania and points west, and westward of Texas.

*L. microlophus* inhabits heavily vegetated quiet waters of southern swamps, forested ponds, backwaters, and sluggish lowland lakes with a mud, sand, or clay bottom. The cold intolerant redear has been transplanted to clear reservoirs, and might occur anywhere in the South one finds bluegills; it prefers a soft bottom, submersed woody debris, and dense vegetation. A bottom feeder with strong pharyngeal teeth with which it cracks the shells of mussels and snails, the redear also eats aquatic insects and many other invertebrates. Not a fish eater, it sometimes nests among colonial spawning territories of bluegills and will eat the eggs from their nests (McLane 1955).

The redear is a game fish in many states. It is suitable for southern ponds or aquaria larger than 55 gallons.

**Subgenus *Lepomis (Icthelis)***
*Lepomis (Icthelis) megalotis,*
longear sunfish

*L. (I.) megalotis* (**plate 55**) has two small pits between the eyes, the pits separated by a distance much greater than the width of a pit; the gill rakers are short and stubby; and the long black opercular flap is surrounded completely by a blue-white margin. The breeding male intensifies with a brilliant orange chest and belly, a reddish nuchal crest (lumpy nape) in some populations, columns of bright orange spots on the flank, and orange streaks on the face; all appear against an iridescent sky blue background with the colors extending into the fins. The 6 rows of scales on the cheek and 13 pectoral fin rays distinguish it from the similar but smaller *L. (I.) marginatus*. It frequently exceeds 6 inches in length.

The longear sunfish occurs in Gulf drainages northward to Canada (rarely), and is most abundant in the southernmost and middle part of its distribution. It generally ranges from northern Mexico to Alabama and northward to the Great Lakes (Lee et al. 1980). *L. m. peltastes* is the smallest of its four to six subspecies in Great Lakes drainages.

*L. (I.) megalotis* inhabits quiet pools of upland clear streams with gravel, sand, or rock bottoms, but also is found in clear reservoirs and farm ponds. It eats insects, bryozoans, fish eggs, crayfishes and other crustaceans, and small fishes. *L. (I.) megalotis* readily hybridizes with other members of the genus.

The longear sunfish breeds when the temperature reaches the middle 70s (°F). Males associate and fan out 18-inch-diameter nests on sloping gravel bottoms away from vegetation. A temperature in the 70s (°F) may induce breeding. Provide not less than a 20-gallon aquarium with a 2- to 3-inch sloping layer of coarse gravel. A frequently cleaned canister filter will help maintain water quality.

| | |
|---|---|
| *Lepomis (Icthelis) marginatus,* dollar sunfish | *L. (I.) marginatus* (**plates 56 and 57**) has stubby gill rakers and a large opercular spot that is edged entirely in greenish white. Short and fat with a tiny mouth, the usually dull dollar sunfish becomes brighter when breeding, developing wavy blue streaks on the face, scattered orange spots on the flanks, and an orange belly. *L. (I.) marginatus* is a smaller version of *L. (I.) megalotis* (about half the size), from which it can be distinguished by 12 pectoral fin rays and 4 rows of scales on the cheek. The dollar sunfish may consist of more than one species (Lee et al. 1980; Lee and Burr 1985). |

*L. (I.) marginatus* ranges in coastal drainages from North Carolina through Florida, continuing westward to Texas and northward in the Mississippi drainage to Arkansas, Tennessee, and the southwestern tip of Kentucky (Lee et al. 1980).

The dollar sunfish prefers clear, sluggish, creek or swamp waters, a mud, silt, or detritus bottom not far from sand, and moderate to heavy vegetation (Robison and Buchanan 1988). In Florida, it inhabits pools of sluggish, darkly stained swamp streams, and occurs along the margins of lakes and sluggish rivers. It is found in dense beds of *Vallisneria* and other vegetation, over mud and sand bottoms. It eats mostly chironomids and other aquatic insects, ostracods, copepods, amphipods, a few small snails, and, in the brackish coastal portions of its range, even polychaete worms and small shrimp (McLane 1955).

*L. (I.) marginatus* matures at 2½ inches and breeds from May through August in North Carolina. It spawns in densely aggregated nests in shallow, hard sandy bottoms free of vegetation. The females develop dark bands that inhibit aggression by the males, which fight among themselves constantly. A successful male may guard two spawns simultaneously, with up to 200 fry per spawning. The fish breed in their second year and live six years (Lee and Burr 1985).

The dollar sunfish is an ideal community aquarium fish except when spawning. It will not develop breeding coloration without warmth, isolation, and a diet of invertebrates. Frozen bloodworms appear necessary to develop the orange breast coloration of breeding males.

## Family Percidae, the Perches and Darters

The percids are mostly North American, with just a few species in Eurasia and Europe. Arguments for dividing the family Percidae into various higher groupings (subfamilies and tribes) were given by Hubbs (1971) and Collette and Banarescu (1977).

The Percidae contains two subfamilies, each with two tribes. These are the subfamily Percinae (tribes Percini and Etheostomini) and subfamily Luciopercinae (tribes Romanichthyini and Luciopercini). That species of *Stizostedion* and *Perca* occur today in both Europe and North America is evidence that the Percidae spread westward from Asia to Europe and eastward across a now extinct land bridge to North America.

## Subfamily Luciopercinae Tribe Luciopercini

The North American walleye and sauger (*Stizostedion*) are in the tribe Luciopercini and are egg scatterers whose eggs fall into crevices on the bottom (McElman and Balon 1979); they look like giant darters. In fact, they are game fishes.

Yellow perch, *Perca flavescens*, Tennessee R., Tenn. RB

| | |
|---|---|
| Tribe Romanichthyini | *Zingel* and *Romanichthys* of Eurasia are in the Romanichthyini. These three genera constituting the subfamily Luciopercinae are not suitable for aquaria and are not discussed further. |
| **Subfamily Percinae**<br>Tribe Percini | The North American yellow perch *(Perca flavescens)* is placed in the Percini, a tribe that also includes *Percarina* and *Gymnocephalus* of Europe. They all release eggs in a large jellylike mass, like many frogs and the marine sargassum frogfish, *Histrio*. The ruffe *(Gymnocephalus cernuus)* recently invaded the Great Lakes from shipping ballast water (Pratt et al. 1992). These three genera are not suitable for aquaria and are not discussed further. |
| Tribe Etheostomini | The darters *(Etheostoma, Percina, Ammocrypta, Crystallaria)* constitute the Etheostomini of the subfamily Percinae. They are bottom-dwelling stream fishes that seldom attain 6 inches in length. |

Many state fish books have extensive chapters on the darters. In addition, you will need three other books to become a darter aficionado: Page and Burr's (1991) *A Field Guide to Freshwater Fishes, North America North of Mexico*, Page's (1983) *Handbook of Darters*, and Kuehne and Barbour's (1983) *The American Darters*.

Darters are restricted to eastern and central North America, from Canada to northern Mexico. They are most numerous in streams of the Mississippi River and adjacent Gulf drainages westward to the Platte and Missouri River drainages, also occurring on both sides of the Appalachian slopes. Because only a few darters are found in Mexico and are close to the Texas border, they are included in this book.

Most darters are present in moderate- to fast-flowing streams and rivers with rocky or rubble bottoms. Many are difficult to capture because they occur in third order or larger streams in waist-high water (e.g., *Percina, Nothonotus*, rainbows, *variatum* group of *Etheostoma*). Others are common in first order streams only 1 or 2 inches deep, and are easily collected (e.g., *Ozarka, punctulatum* group of *Etheostoma*, orangethroats, fantails, greensides). Most can be collected by two persons holding a 10- to 20-foot seine and a third person kicking over rubble from less than 10 feet away toward the net.

Darters that associate with attached algae often occur where clumps of algae stream out from rocks in fast water. Several darters are nesters: the male guards a territory under a flat rock and the eggs are placed in a large patch on its underside, the roof of this cave. When a nest is found by turning over a flat rock, put the rock back and wait ten minutes; often the male will return and can be captured with his own nest. Alternatively, harvest the rock and aerate just as you would angelfish eggs. If the male is not taken with his nest, he will find another flat rock and perhaps nest again.

Some darters occur beneath undercut banks, where a long-handled D-net (a type of dip net with a straight leading edge) is useful. Swamp darters can be dip-netted from dense vegetation along the edges of ponds. The habitat of the darter should determine collection technique, but seines will be used most often, dip nets occasionally, and removal of an entire flat rock only rarely.

Finally, some darters occur in such deep, fast water that they remain uncollectible by aquarists without specialized equipment (e.g., electroshock devices used by professional biologists). The juveniles, however, may occur in quiet pools or shoreline backwaters and are vulnerable to fine-mesh dip nets; the species identification of juveniles is often difficult.

Unlike larger percids, which spawn their ripe egg complement all at once (total spawners), darter spawning can be protracted over days or weeks (fractional spawners). Darters that will not spawn can be hand-stripped with gentle pressure or chemically induced by a single injection of 50 international units of human chorionic gonadotropin (50 IU of HCG), or with 0.05–0.1 mg/kg LH-RHa (see Polyodontidae).

Breeding behaviors fall into four types: (1) **burying** eggs in gravel and abandoning them; (2) **egg-attachment** to plants, wood or leaf debris, or rocks; (3) **egg-clumping** under rocks, wherein the *mass* of eggs laid by the female adheres both to the overlying rock and the underlying gravel (also found in madtoms, sculpins, and one minnow); and (4) **egg-clustering,** in which a *single layer* of eggs is laid on the undersurface of a flat rock, as in cave-spawning cichlids (Page and Swofford 1984).

The four genera of darters are *Crystallaria, Ammocrypta, Percina,* and *Etheostoma.* There are 35 subgenera, 150 species, and several subspecies. Many well-known darter species have not yet been described and named in the scientific literature.

## Genus *Crystallaria*

*Crystallaria* was previously considered a subgenus within *Ammocrypta,* but recent DNA studies validate it as an early offshoot and distinct line of evolution. The work included a statistical analysis computer program that compared large numbers of characters in many different species. The program, called Phylogenetic Analysis Using Parsimony (PAUP), revealed that the genus arose early from a branch that later gave rise to *Percina* and *Etheostoma* (Simons 1991).

## *Crystallaria asprella,* crystal darter

*C. asprella* is elongate, mostly translucent and flesh colored, and differs from *Ammocrypta* by having three or four dark wide saddles on the back that angle backward and downward to become contiguous with lateral blotches. The nuptial male has slightly longer soft dorsal and anal fins, and is larger than the female (George et al. 1996).

The crystal darter occurs in the Mississippi and Ohio River basins, from Minnesota southward to the Gulf Coast, and in Gulf Coast drainages from western Florida to possibly eastern Texas. Its historical range was much larger.

*C. asprella* occupies fast-flowing (1½–3 ft./sec.) rivers at depths of 4 to 6 feet on mostly gravel, sand, and some cobble. It also is found on shallower, quieter shoals

Crystal darter, *Crystallaria asprella,* St. Francis R., Mo. WFR

where it is more easily collected. It feeds from cover, darting out to grasp passing food and then returning under the sand. Live foods are taken eagerly, but the fish learns to feed on frozen daphnia, mosquito larvae, and chironomids.

The male defends a territory with zeal; his activities form a depression or shallow pit. The crystal darter spawns when one year old, from late January through April, over gravel without constructing a nest; the 1.0 mm eggs are dispersed by current shifting the fine gravel and sand (George 1994).

Collect wild fish in early spring and condition for months with live foods. A gradual (over 30 days) lowering of water temperature to 65°F often triggers breeding. A 30-gallon aquarium is suitable for a spawning group. A moderate current should be supplied by an external power filter or an undergravel filter with a powerhead. The substratum should be coarse sand mixed with small amounts of gravel. The crystal darter will usually bury itself only slightly, but sometimes deep enough that only the eyes are exposed at the surface.

The female visits the male and engages in mock spawning for days. When a pair actually spawns, the eggs are deposited into the pit and the male covers them with flicks of its caudal fin. After spawning, adults should be removed from the aquarium. Fry appear in seven to ten days at 65°F. First foods should be freshwater rotifers, ciliates, or infusoria. After three weeks, the fry take other foods. See also Johnston (1989).

## Genus *Ammocrypta*

*Ammocrypta* contains the sand darters, elongate, peach or flesh colored, translucent fishes inhabiting deep water on shifting sand bottoms of moderate to large, fast-flowing rivers. They typically bury themselves in sand with only their eyes above the surface, and pluck drifting invertebrates out of the passing water.

All the species of *Ammocrypta* are included within *Etheostoma* in Page and Burr (1991). However, analyses of darter DNA sequences indicate that *Ammocrypta* is a distinct line of evolution, and not a specialized group of *Etheostoma.* The more primitive *pellucida* group *(A. pellucida, A. meridiana,* and *A. vivax)* is mostly scaled and the rear edge of the gill cover is saw-toothed. The more advanced *beani* group *(A. beani, A. clara,* and *A. bifascia)* is mostly naked, its few scales restricted to the lateral line and the base of the tail; the rear edge of the gill cover is smooth (Williams 1975).

Members of the mostly scaled *pellucida* group are discussed first. All should be handled as described for *Crystallaria*.

| | |
|---|---|
| *Ammocrypta meridiana,*<br>southern sand darter | *A. meridiana* is strongly scaled, but has dark markings similar to those of *A. clara*. It has 8–13 small dark blotches along the flank and 10–15 along the back. The translucent body, top of the head, and vertebral column are yellow-orange. It is iridescent yellow-green on the cheeks and along the lateral line and has a blue-green lower head and blue chin. The unpaired fins are orange, more intense toward the base; the pelvic fins are dark at the base. Coloration of the male and female is similar, but the male is brighter. *A. meridiana* grows to 2 inches.

The southern sand darter occurs in the Alabama, Tombigbee, Warrior, Cahaba, and Tallapoosa River drainages of the Mobile River basin below the fall line. *A. meridiana* and *A. pellucida* are most closely related within the genus and separated by the Tennessee River drainage in which neither occurs. They resemble *Ericymba buccata* (silverjaw minnow) with which they share the same shifting sand habitat.

*A. meridiana* is found from 6 inches to 5 feet deep in moderate to large creeks and rivers with sufficient current to provide clean sandy bottoms.

The southern sand darter breeds during June and July (Williams 1975). |
| *Ammocrypta pellucida,*<br>eastern sand darter | *A. pellucida* is well-scaled, with 9 to 15 small, dark, and often elongate marks (dashes) on the flank and 11 to 19 small dark marks on the back. It is yellowish above to silvery below, translucent overall, and a band of bright yellow runs along the lateral line. *A. pellucida* differs from *A. clara* by lacking a sharp opercular spine (Linder 1959).

The eastern sand darter ranges from southern Quebec and Ontario to the St. Lawrence River and Great Lakes shores and tributaries. It continues to the Ohio River drainage and downstream to the Wabash and Cumberland Rivers in Illinois, Indiana, and Kentucky.

*A. pellucida* is widespread in small creeks, large rivers, and sandy lakeshores, occurring on riffles, limestone terraces, and in silty pools (wherever a sand bottom persists). Velocity, depth, distance from shore, or the presence or absence of other species are not important, as sand is the overriding factor in its distribution. Sand darters aggregate on sand beds (Daniels 1993) and spawn during June and July (Williams 1975; Johnston 1989).

The eastern sand darter has been taken at pH 8.2 to 8.6 in Canada at 76°F, and in Lake Erie at depths up to 48 feet (Scott and Crossman 1973). It eats mostly chironomid larvae (to 90% by stomach volume). |
| *Ammocrypta vivax,* scaly sand darter | *A. vivax* has 10–15 yellow-green lateral blotches on the flank (about 2 or 3 vertebrae wide and vertically elongate) that extend toward a similar number of wide saddles. Otherwise, it is a rich, translucent yellow-orange above and lighter below. The head and snout are bright orange and the gill covers and sides of the head are yellow-green. The fins are yellow-orange, the unpaired fins with black edges and black medial bands. It grows to over 2 inches.

The scaly sand darter occurs on the Coastal Plain of the Gulf of Mexico and up the Mississippi River embayment from the bootheel of Missouri rarely to the |

Scaly sand darter, *Ammocrypta vivax*, St. Francis R., Mo. WFR

Florida sand darter, *Ammocrypta bifascia*, Perdido R., Ala. WFR

Hatchie River system of western Tennessee in the north. It is more common southward through southeastern Oklahoma, all but northwestern Arkansas, most of Louisiana, and all of Mississippi, ranging along the Gulf Coast from Pascagoula Bay in Mississippi to the San Jacinto River of eastern Texas.

*A. vivax* inhabits sandy rivers with moderate currents, often occurring in the main channel (Etnier and Starnes 1993). The scaly sand darter burrows vertically into the sand, usually head down, and then rises so only the eyes show above the surface. It darts out of the sand to feed on drifting prey, then back. Because the sandy, shifting bottom in which it occurs has few other animals and virtually no predators, the behavior is thought to provide shelter from the current and energy conservation in addition to camouflage (Williams 1975).

Members of the mostly unscaled *beani* group have similar requirements.

| | |
|---|---|
| *Ammocrypta beani,* naked sand darter | *A. beani* has an iridescent greenish yellow lateral line and a blue-green head, dark pigment in a broad dark band through the middle of all the unpaired fins, and yellowish to milky white paired fins. Its maximum length is about 2½ inches. |

The naked sand darter occurs in the lower Mississippi and Mobile (below the fall line) drainages of the Gulf Coast in Alabama, Mississippi, and Louisiana; a disjunct population is in western Tennessee (Starnes et al. 1977).

*A. beani* occurs in waters from small creeks (occasionally) to large streams and rivers (commonly) that are 6 inches to 4 feet deep, usually in moderate current on sand and gravel bottoms. The 1 mm diameter golden eggs are spawned during July and August (Williams 1975).

Maintain as for *Crystallaria asprella*. A spawning group of three males and at least ten females is recommended.

| | |
|---|---|
| *Ammocrypta bifascia,* Florida sand darter | *A. bifascia* is translucent yellow and slightly larger than *A. beani,* with an orange snout, no blue-green pigment along the lateral line or on the head, and its unpaired fins have dark edges. |

The Florida sand darter occurs along the Gulf Coast from the Perdido River of southern Alabama to the Choctawhatchee River drainage of western Florida. It inhabits moderate to large, fast-flowing streams and rivers, over shifting sand bottoms at depths of 2 to 4 feet. It breeds during late May and early June (Williams 1975).

**Ammocrypta clara,
western sand darter**

*A. clara* has scales along the rear of the body and a spine on the angle of the gill cover. It is translucent yellow with iridescent green on the gill covers. There are 16 small dark marks (not saddles) on the back and another 12 along the lateral line.

The western sand darter is native to the Neches and Sabine Rivers of Texas, ranging eastward to the Mississippi River and then northward (although absent from some rivers) to Minnesota and Wisconsin; it also occurs from Indiana to Oklahoma (Linder 1959). It is also found in one small area in the extreme upper portion of the Tennessee River system (Powell River).

*A. clara* inhabits moderate to large rivers over cleanly swept sand and gravel at depths to 5 feet, both in and out of the main current. In the northern part of its range, it may occur with *Notropis dorsalis* on barren sand or may be the only small fish species there. It breeds during July and early August (Williams 1975).

**Genus *Percina***

*Percina* has 9 subgenera with 35 mostly noncolorful species, with one well-known species (the snail darter) and one exceptionally gorgeous fish too large for aquaria (the tangerine darter). *Percina* have a typically elongate shape and pointed snout and a better developed swim bladder compared with other darters, adaptations for living and feeding both on the bottom and up in midwater in gravel and sand riffles, raceways, and pools with strong currents. All *Percina* species bury eggs in sand or gravel or spawn above it, the eggs drifting downstream.

Darters of this genus have a unique allele at the $B_4$ lactate dehydrogenase locus, the enzyme in all species migrating at the same fast rate. Where the enzyme occurs in other percid fishes, it has a slightly slower [*Etheostoma (A.) cinereum*] to much slower (other *Etheostoma, Crystallaria, Stizostedion*) electrophoretic mobility (Dimmick and Page 1992). The unique specific mobility of the $B_4$ lactic dehydrogenase isozyme in *Percina* (Page and Whitt 1973) and, more recently, DNA analyses support the origin of all *Percina* to be a single evolutionary group that arose early in the descent of darters from the earliest percids.

*Percina* differs from *Etheostoma* most importantly in the enlarged, highly pronged scales between the pelvic fins and along the midline of the belly in males. These scales appear to play a stimulatory role when the male mounts the female for spawning, much like the contact organs of killifishes (Page 1976).

*Percina* species spawn in, on, and above the gravel, and should have deep, large aquaria not less than 20 to 29 gallons. Important breeding stimulants are strong currents and overwintering, or providing a period of chilled water with reduced feeding. After this period of chilling and starvation, the fish should be brought indoors (or temperatures elevated) and provided abundant food; spawning condition will be reached in three to six weeks. Species that spawn in sand or gravel are handled by removing the adults or the substratum, which is contained in a tray. Species that produce drifting eggs should be removed after spawning, the power filter disconnected, and aeration provided by a sponge filter.

Page (1974a) recognized or established the subgenera *Percina, Hadropterus, Swainia, Alvordius, Ericosma, Odontopholis, Hypohomus, Cottogaster,* and *Imostoma.* Many characters of these subgenera are too small to observe without a microscope,

Logperch, *Percina caprodes,* French Broad R., N.C. RB

or too subtle to interpret without training. Still others are negative characters (i.e., the absence of). Some useful indicators for aquarists are provided below, but these are not complete definitions; for more technical or complete darter literature, see Page (1974a, 1983) and Kuehne and Barbour (1983).

| | |
|---|---|
| **Subgenus *Percina (Percina)*** | *P. (Percina)* is characterized by a conical and projecting snout, a black teardrop mark, and a prominent dark spot (basicaudal spot) at the base of the tail. |
| *Percina (Percina) caprodes,* logperch | *P. (P.) caprodes* has 10–12 thin and elongate vertical bars on the flank that alternate with an equal number of thin, shorter bars; the bars are contiguous over the back with those on the other side. The log perch attains 6 inches. |

There are 3 subspecies. *P. (P.) c. fulvitaenia* has a broad, submarginal yellow to orange band in the first dorsal fin of the male (sometimes the female); *P. (P.) c. caprodes* has a thin orange marginal band in the first dorsal fin and a scaled nape; and *P. (P.) c. semifasciata* has no orange in the first dorsal fin and no scales on the nape.

The logperch is widespread from southeastern New Mexico to northwestern Florida, ranging northward to Hudson Bay. It occurs mostly in Mississippi River drainages from Minnesota, Wisconsin, and Iowa. *P. (P.) c. semifasciata* occurs southward to the fall line in Mississippi; *P. (P.) c. fulvitaenia* is western, found mostly in the Meramec and southern tributaries of the Missouri River in the Ozark uplands of Arkansas, Missouri, Oklahoma, and Kansas; *P. (P.) c. caprodes* occurs in southern and eastern drainages; and intergrades are present everywhere between ranges (Morris and Page 1981). Atlantic slope reports are scattered, few, or the result of bait introductions.

*P. (P.) caprodes* occurs on hard bottoms (large gravel and rubble) in slower and deeper riffles and throughout fast runs and pools with strong current. It inhabits medium-sized rivers and large streams.

The logperch spawns during spring in riffles and runs. The eggs hatch in six days, and the larvae begin feeding on small planktonic animals even before the yolk sac is resorbed. During this time, they rest on the bottom or swim up into the current, which sustains them in the horizontal as they feed in midwater or at the surface. By six weeks they transform and go to the bottom; the stomach develops and they initiate feeding on small crustaceans, graduating to insect larvae (Grizzle and Curd 1978). Adults feed on a wide variety of aquatic insect larvae, including mayflies, stoneflies, chironomids, beetles, and dragonflies. Maximum age is four years. The logperch is often parasitized by the leech, *Illinobdella moorei* (Thomas 1970).

In captivity, this midwater forager will adapt to a sandy bottom with little or no structure. The males do not fight, and several can be kept in a single aquarium. For spawning, provide a 55-gallon aquarium with a strong current on one end supplied by a power filter or powerhead. The bottom should contain trays of fine sand and little structure.

To induce spawning, the fish should be chilled for a month (if not collected from the wild during early spring). If the fish are collected after the spring spawning season, house them in unheated quarters the following winter and reduce the amount of food offered. If possible, they should be left outdoors in wading pools or large aquariums, taking precautions not to let the water freeze, but again providing minimal food. Specimens collected in southern Alabama and central Mississippi required four weeks of chilling temperatures. Canadian logperch colored up within one-half hour of capture in the wild during the spring spawning season.

When the fish are brought indoors to room temperature and provided increased quantities of bloodworms, frozen *Artemia*, glass worms, crushed snails, and blackworms, spawning should begin within three weeks. Females fill with roe to the point of appearing as if they had swallowed golf balls. The males gather near the center of the aquarium; they briefly display and stir the sand to attract a gravid female. When the female approaches, the male quickly mounts and presses the cloacal region of the female into the sand.

The thrashing pair release eggs and sperm against the sand; most eggs are buried and others are scattered everywhere, adhering to whatever they contact. Bockstael (1983) provided fine sand on the bottom, rocks, and large, black PVC pipe. She reported thrashing during spawning with the white eggs scattered everywhere, and noted that sand was important as gravel would surely damage the delicate eggs. The female emits about a dozen eggs per clasp, with more than 150 over a few days. There is no parental care by either parent. Remove all adult fish when spawning has ceased. The trays of sand can be removed and placed into wading pools outdoors, where microscopic foods should be abundant if the pool has been established at least three weeks.

The eggs hatch in seven to ten days at 60 to 70°F. The fry are small and require rotifers, green water, or infusoria (usually ciliates) as a first food. The fry appear to get most of their food from the surfaces of structures, but may do well indoors on a mixed diet of microworms, crushed snails, crushed worms, and prepared foods that will support protozoan and rotifer blooms as they decay. After ten days, the young browse along the bottom, and now small foods such as *Ceriodaphnia*, ostracods, *Artemia* nauplii, and even pulverized flake foods will be accepted. After four weeks, the fry can be weaned to flake foods and small live foods. After ten weeks, even chopped meats are accepted.

| | |
|---|---|
| *Percina (Percina) carbonaria,*<br>Texas logperch | *P. (P.) carbonaria* can be identified by its longer bars being narrow in the middle and expanded above and below (but not enough to be called blotches). It is similar to the logperch subspecies, *P. (P.) caprodes fulvitaenia,* but the side bands are not uniform and the broad orange band in the first dorsal fin of the male has a black margin above and a black base below. The throat, lower cheeks, breast, and lower fins |

Blotchside darter, *Percina burtoni*, Little R., Tenn. WFR

of the nuptial male are black; the sides are dusky, obscuring the bands; the orange and black portions of the first dorsal fin become intensified. It grows to more than 4½ inches (Morris and Page 1981).

The Texas logperch occurs in streams of the Brazos, Colorado, Guadalupe, and San Antonio Rivers on the Edwards Plateau of Texas, usually at rocky riffles and runs in small to medium streams.

| | |
|---|---|
| *Percina (Percina) burtoni,* blotchside darter | *P. (P.) burtoni* is a typical logperch in shape, but not in markings. The flank is marked with a dozen oval blotches (not vertical lines); a teardrop mark is present below the eye. The spiny dorsal fin has an orange margin and a distinctive black blotch in the rear. It attains 4 inches.

The blotchside darter occurs in the Little River of Tennessee and Copper Creek in Virginia (upper Tennessee River system). It has been extirpated from the Cumberland River drainage of Tennessee and Kentucky.

*P. (P.) burtoni* inhabits medium to large rivers with permanent strong flow on gravel runs and riffles.

The blotchside darter is rare and likely to be protected. |
| *Percina (Percina) jenkinsi,* Conasauga logperch | *P. (P.) jenkinsi* lacks an orange band in the spiny dorsal fin, and is distinguished mostly by a black spot at the root of the pectoral fin (Page and Burr 1991). It grows to more than 4 inches.

This logperch occurs in the Conasauga River of Georgia and Tennessee and in part of the Alabama River system (in rocky runs and pools with current in a single, fast-flowing, small river).

If collecting in the Conasauga River, be alert to any logperch with a black spot at the base of the pectoral fin and release it immediately. *P. (P.) jenkinsi* is endangered and not available to collectors. |
| *Percina (Percina) macrolepida,* bigscale logperch | *P. (P.) macrolepida* has 25 elongate, thin, dark bars on the flank, with those extending below the lateral line alternating with those that do not. The body is pale; the teardrop mark below the eye is diffuse or absent. The nuptial male is tinged with yellow-green and has dull yellow spots in the spiny dorsal fin, but no orange band. It grows to just over 3 inches (small for a logperch).

The bigscale logperch ranges from the Red River in Oklahoma southward to |

Roanoke logperch, *Percina rex*, Roanoke R., Va. WFR

Shield darter, *Percina peltata*, James R., Va. WFR

the Sabine River in Texas; it continues westward to the Rio Grande and southward to the Rio San Carlos in Coahuila, Mexico, ranging northward to the Pecos River in New Mexico. It has been transplanted as a bait fish into California and perhaps elsewhere (Kuehne and Barbour 1983; Page 1983).

*P. (P.) macrolepida* inhabits lakes and medium to large rivers, in deep, nonturbulent fast flows in rubble and gravel raceways, but not in riffles. The 1.4 mm eggs number only a few hundred.

| | |
|---|---|
| *Percina (Percina) rex,* Roanoke logperch | *P. (P.) rex* has ten short, linear blotches on the side that are not connected to blotches on the back, with intermediate blotching in between. The spiny dorsal fin is black at the edge with an orange or yellow submarginal band and dark below. The second dorsal and tail fins are heavily spotted. The female has the same colors but not as bright. *P. (P.) rex* grows to 4 inches. |

*Percina (Percina) rex,*
Roanoke logperch

*P. (P.) rex* has ten short, linear blotches on the side that are not connected to blotches on the back, with intermediate blotching in between. The spiny dorsal fin is black at the edge with an orange or yellow submarginal band and dark below. The second dorsal and tail fins are heavily spotted. The female has the same colors but not as bright. *P. (P.) rex* grows to 4 inches.

This logperch is found in the Roanoke River basin (upper Roanoke, Dan, and Chowan Rivers) of Virginia in riffles of rubble, sand, and gravel in medium to large rivers, but is rare. It probably spawns during early spring or late winter (Kuehne and Barbour 1983).

*P. (P.) rex* is an endangered species that cannot be possessed. It has been spawned in captivity.

**Subgenus *Percina (Alvordius)***

A protuberant or conical snout and bands crossing to the other side are absent; there is no keel and the anal fin is not elongated. Males of *P. (Alvordius)* have an incomplete row of highly modified scales on the midline of the belly and usually lack breeding tubercles and bright colors.

*Percina (Alvordius) peltata,*
shield darter

*P. (A.) peltata* has a distinctive row of bold dark spots throughout the base of the first dorsal fin, a line of dark pigment at the edge, often a dusky patch at the midline of the chin, and sometimes a black spot is on the breast (Mayden and Page 1979). A gold area along the upper sides and the back is much reduced and surrounded by black saddles (Raney and Hubbs 1948; Page and Burr 1991). Blotches on the sides are square-shaped. The male and female are marked identically, but the male is easily identified by the modified enlarged scales above the vent (the female lacks such scales). The dorsal fin and dark teardrop pigmentation intensify during spawning, especially in the male.

The shield darter is widespread along the Atlantic Coastal Plain from the Neuse River in North Carolina northward to the Susquehanna and Hudson Rivers of New York.

*P. (A.) peltata* is found in small rivers and tributary streams not less than 10 feet wide, in or just above riffles, on fine gravel and rock bottoms with rich growths of aquatic vegetation. During late summer, the vegetation provides postspawning cover and foraging habitat for juveniles and adults.

The shield darter occurs year-round in the same habitat. Gravel alone is insufficient as a spawning substratum, and must be mixed with sand. Rocks, ranging from cobble to boulders, are important as hiding places. Shield darters spawn from mid-April through May, sometimes for only a two-week period when temperatures are in the 50s (°F). The male mounts the female, who works her way forward and down into the gravel-sand mixture while the male remains above the surface (New 1966).

Groups were placed in 40-gallon, long aquariums with 2 inches of coarse sand and aquarium gravel with a few flat rocks for shelter, with current and filtration provided by an air release and an outside power filter. No plants were provided, and the fish were fed exclusively whiteworms, *Enchytraeus albidus.* The temperature was elevated into (but not above) the 50s (°F).

Spawning often involved more than one male mounting a female. Eggs were buried, but sometimes uncovered and on the surface, but never eaten by the adults (New 1966). A more diverse diet, including chopped earthworms (Loos and Woolcott 1969) should be given for long-term health. Smaller aquaria (10–20 gal.) are probably adequate for one or two pairs. Shield darters will hybridize with *P. (A.) notogramma* (Loos and Woolcott 1969).

---

*Percina (Alvordius) notogramma,* stripeback darter

*P. (A.) notogramma* is similar to *P. (A.) peltata,* but with six to eight large blotches on the flank connected by a dark line and a teardrop mark below the eye. Its principal diagnostic pattern is the pale golden streak on the upper flank (not reaching the midline of the back) that extends from the tail to the eye and is interrupted by a wavy black line; the illusion can be viewed as an irregular yellow line, bordered in black, along the level of the high shoulder from front to back. From above, the back appears yellow, broken by a series of small, elongate black blotches along the midline, not as extensive nor as bold as saddles; this pattern is not diagnostic in the female, which appears mottled from above. The first dorsal fin is dusky at the base. During spawning, a dark blotch appears at the base of the front of the first dorsal fin, decreasing in size into smaller spots toward the rear (Loos and Woolcott 1969). There are no black marks on the midline of the chin or the breast. During spawning, the body becomes light colored (sometimes green, when fish are collected from vegetation), and the lateral markings, which range from vertical bands to round blotches, stand out in sharp contrast to the light olive back and silvery belly (Loos and Woolcott 1969). It grows to 2½ inches (Raney and Hubbs 1948; Mayden and Page 1979).

The stripeback darter occurs in the Patuxent, Potomac, Rappahannock, James, and Appomattox Rivers, which are all Maryland, Virginia, and West Virginia tributaries to the Chesapeake Bay. *P. n. montuosa,* distinguished by more scales, occurs in the Upper James River; *P. n. notogramma* occurs in the remaining drainages (Page and Burr 1991).

Roanoke darter, *Percina roanoka*, Roanoke R., Va. WFR

Blackside darter, *Percina maculata*, Clear Fork R., Ohio. WFR

*P. (A.) notogramma* inhabits small and medium streams most of the year, but ascends small brooks during a spring spawning migration. Its typical habitat is pools near riffles during the summer and among boulder strewn riffles in spring, usually associated with vegetation.

A 10-gallon or larger aquarium with an outside power filter, aeration, and 1 or 2 inches of gravel mixed with sand is sufficient; rocks are not necessary as the fish does not hide. The temperature should be 59–68°F. Chopped earthworms suffice as a diet. Specimens from the upper James River should be separated from those originating in other Chesapeake Bay drainages; furthermore, different *Alvordius* species should never be mixed because they hybridize in nature.

## *Percina (Alvordius) roanoka,* Roanoke darter

*P. (A.) roanoka* is dark olive brown above, with 7 dark saddles connecting on the side to 12 dark vertical bars (tending to blotches that are diffuse in the nuptial male). The nuptial male is blue-green on the flank and yellow-orange below. The spiny dorsal fin of both sexes has a thin black edge (submargined in red) and a broad diffuse dark band below the red band. The chin and breast lack black markings. The Roanoke darter commonly grows to 2 inches or more.

A Piedmont-mountain population occurs in the Roanoke, James, and New Rivers of West Virginia, Virginia, and northern North Carolina; a Coastal Plain population in the Neuse, Tar, and Chowan Rivers of North Carolina extends into southern Virginia (Mayden and Page 1979).

*P. (A.) roanoka* inhabits pebble and cobble riffles (often only 1 or 2 inches deep) of small to medium streams. It is more common in uplands than in the Coastal Plain. As streams become turbid from nearby land-disturbing activity, the Roanoke darter disappears.

A 10-gallon aquarium is sufficient for one male and two or three females. Provide a gravel bottom, rocks for hiding places, some vegetation, and undergravel filtration driven by a powerhead for strong current and clean gravel. Feed live blackworms and frozen *Artemia* and chironomids.

Do not confuse the Roanoke darter *(P. roanoka)* with the Roanoke logperch *(P. rex).*

## *Percina (Alvordius) maculata,* blackside darter

*P. (A.) maculata* has 8–9 dark blotches on the back that run into wavy lines on the upper side. Six oval to elongate blotches on the flank are connected by a horizontal black band. It has a black basicaudal spot and teardrop and averages 2½ inches long.

The blackside darter ranges from Hudson Bay to the Great Lakes, and occurs in Mississippi and Ohio drainages from Manitoba, Saskatchewan, and Ontario southward to Alabama, Mississippi, and Louisiana on the Gulf Coast. In Canada, it ranges from the western part of the Lake Ontario drainage (but not the lake itself) in Ontario westward (but not in the drainage of Lake Superior) to Manitoba (Winnipeg, Red, and Assiniboine River drainages and near Swan Lake) and Saskatchewan (Qu'Appelle drainage and Souris River) (Scott and Crossman, 1973).

*P. (A.) maculata* is abundant in small to medium rivers throughout its range; it prefers low gradient streams and pools, avoiding strong currents. It often feeds in midwater using its well-developed air bladder for buoyancy. It may occur in sand and gravel riffles and runs during spring, and in mud-bottom pools during summer, sometimes among brush and logs.

The blackside darter spawns when the water temperature reaches 60°F during April and May, in sand and gravel runs 12 inches or more deep. The male mounts the female and the female buries the eggs; over a thousand 2 mm eggs are produced per female during a season. The eggs hatch in six days and the larvae are 6 mm long. Juveniles feed on small crustaceans; adults feed mostly on chironomids, blackflies, and mayflies; beetles and caddisflies round out the insectivorous diet. The life span is four years (Thomas 1970; Scott and Crossman 1973; Kuehne and Barbour 1983).

Captive spawning procedures are the same as those for *P. (P.) caprodes,* except use fine gravel instead of sand, and spawning is usually over in just two days. *P. (A.) maculata* hybridizes readily in nature with other darters (Page 1976) and in aquaria (Katula 1987b).

| | |
|---|---|
| *Percina (Alvordius) macrocephala,* longhead darter | *P. (A.) macrocephala* has an elongate head and snout, but the snout is not upturned and the flank lacks bars. The back has one or two black lines or a series of blotches (variable); the upper side has wavy lines. The entire middle of the flank has a broad, black, scalloped band that obscures ten blotches; the black band extends from the base of the tail fin (all along the flank) through the eye to the tip of the snout. The band is developed best in the southern (more elongate) forms; the northern forms are more robust and more likely to have the lateral blotches remain distinct below the less-developed lateral stripe. The lateral line appears as a light thin line within the black band. The teardrop is present and the black bar appears below the basicaudal spot. It occasionally grows to 4 inches (Kuehne and Barbour 1983). |

The longhead darter is rare in the Ohio River drainage from Ohio, New York, and Pennsylvania to Kentucky, West Virginia, and Tennessee; it may occur in western North Carolina. See Page and Burr (1991) for a discussion on the distinct races from different river systems.

*P. (A.) macrocephala* inhabits pools and runs of medium-sized streams, away from riffles and over various clean bottoms ranging from rock and gravel to bedrock or vegetation.

| | |
|---|---|
| *Percina (Alvordius) crassa,* Piedmont darter | *P. (A.) crassa* has seven or eight dark blotches on the side connected by a dark stripe; a teardrop is present. Large males have a dark spot at the midline of the chin, another at the midline of the breast, and a bright yellow band in the first dorsal fin |

surrounded by a dusky band outside and a series of black spots inside. The Piedmont darter otherwise has no bright colors and grows to 3 inches (Mayden and Page 1979).

The Piedmont darter occurs in the Cape Fear, Pee Dee, and Santee Rivers of North and South Carolina, among large rocks and gravel in deep riffles and fast raceways of large streams; it is more common on the Piedmont than on the Coastal Plain.

A 20-gallon aquarium is suitable for one male and up to three females.

---

*Percina (Alvordius) gymnocephala,*
Appalachia darter

*P. (A.) gymnocephala* has no obvious sexual dichromatism or dimorphism. It resembles *P. (A.) notogramma* and *P. (A.) peltata* but has six or seven square saddles on the back separated by wavy bands on the upper flank and six or seven ovoid black blotches on the side fused into a horizontal band; ovoid black marks appear in the membranes of the spiny dorsal fin, rather than crescents as in *P. (A.) peltata;* no dark bar occurs on the chin. It grows to 3 inches (Kuehne and Barbour 1983; Page 1983; Page and Burr 1991).

The Appalachia darter is common in the New River system of North Carolina, Virginia, and West Virginia (including the Gauley and Greenbrier Rivers) and above Kanawha Falls, mostly in the Blue Ridge Mountains.

*P. (A.) gymnocephala* inhabits riffles early in the year and retreats to pools during late summer and winter (Kuehne and Barbour 1983). During spring, it forages along rocks and gravel in swift riffles. *P. (A.) gymnocephala* occupies *Etheostoma*-type riffle habitats, and acclimates well to captivity.

Place six or more adults in a 55-gallon aquarium with gravel on the bottom and rocks at both ends. Spawning habits of the Appalachia darter are consistent with those of other *Percina;* it moves away from the rocks and spawns over open gravel. The eggs are seldom buried and mostly drift in the water column. Both the spawning and nonspawning adults should be removed from the tank to prevent their eating the drifting eggs. The addition of *Cabomba, Ceratophyllum,* or *Vesicularia* will aid in catching the eggs and protect them from the voracious adults.

---

*Percina (Alvordius) pantherina,*
leopard darter

*P. (A.) pantherina* is olive above and yellowish white below. A row of 12 distinct, round black spots run along the midline, with one principal and up to two minor rows of less distinct and smaller spots on the upper flank (leopard spots); 12 blotch-like dorsal saddles are present. It has a dark teardrop and dark bands from the eyes through the nostrils. A central, vertically elongate spot appears at the midpoint of the base of the tail.

The leopard darter is restricted to a small geographic area at the juncture of southwestern Arkansas with southeastern Oklahoma just north of Texas. It occurs in four of six branches of the Little River system (part of the Red River drainage): the Glover, Mountain Fork, Cossatot, and main stem of the Little River, but not in the Saline River or Rolling Fork. The Glover River has the largest population of this rare fish.

*P. (A.) pantherina* is found in moderate to large rivers, inhabiting swift riffles over gravel or cobble bottoms 1–3 feet deep, and sometimes occurs above riffles at the edges of vegetated areas *(Dianthera, Potamogeton).* It feeds mostly on blackfly and mayfly larvae.

The panther darter has suffered habitat loss due to impoundments constructed by the U.S. Army Corps of Engineers, gravel mining of the rivers, and watershed degradation due to agriculture, road building, and industrial development. Minor fish kills and one major fish kill occurred when a creosote waste pond from a lumber treating plant was flushed, destroying fishes and invertebrates for several miles downstream (Robison 1978).

Although *P. (A.) pantherina* is a threatened species and not available as an aquarium fish at present, it can be kept by researchers under permit. Provide strong current, food primarily in the water column, and anticipate spawning as for *P. (S.) phoxocephala*.

| | |
|---|---|
| **Subgenus *Percina (Cottogaster)*** | Members of *P. (Cottogaster)* are often less than 2 inches long. The male has almost a complete row of modified scales on the midline of the belly, a black basicaudal spot, and a group of negative characters (no orange in the dorsal fin, no caudal keel, and the snout neither conical nor projecting). |
| ***Percina (Cottogaster) aurora*, Pearl darter** | *P. (C.) aurora* occurs in the Pascagoula and Pearl Rivers of southern Mississippi and in the Black Warrior, Cahaba, and Coosa Rivers of central Alabama (Suttkus et al. 1994). |
| ***Percina (Cottogaster) brevicauda*, coal darter** | *P. (C.) brevicauda* is a Mobile River basin species only recently split out of *P. (C.) copelandi*. It occupies large rivers, which suggests that it may be too sensitive for home aquaria. |
| ***Percina (Cottogaster) copelandi*, channel darter** | *P. (C.) copelandi* has a blunt snout and a delicate body. The juvenile is not well marked, and easily confused with the johnny darter *(Etheostoma (Boleosoma) nigrum)*. The back is sand colored with brown speckles and 6 or more indistinct blotches and zigzag markings (not saddles); the belly is white; the sides have weak, dusky markings, including a dozen weak blotches fused into a narrow horizontal line; the basicaudal spot is indistinct; and the teardrop is distinct. The breeding male is dusky, especially around the head (further resembling *E. (Boleosoma) nigrum)*. It is usually less than 2 inches long. |

The channel darter is widespread, but in separate populations. It is rare in Canada, but occurs in Quebec from the upper St. Lawrence River eastward to the Nicolet and St. Francis Rivers into Lac St. Pierre, Lachine Rapids, and the Châteauguay River; it occurs in Ontario around Lake Erie. In the United States, *P. (C.) copelandi* ranges from drainages surrounding the eastern Great Lakes (Ontario, Erie, and Huron) southward into the Ohio River drainage (Indiana, Ohio, Kentucky, West Virginia, western Pennsylvania, western New York, to northern Tennessee). Another population from southwestern Missouri and southeastern Kansas extends southward into eastern Oklahoma and central Arkansas and continues southward into northern Louisiana (Arkansas, Ouachita, and Red Rivers).

The channel darter inhabits rivers, creeks, and lakeshores, over nearshore sand and gravel bottoms and on sandbars. It prefers deeper channels ($\geq$ 3 ft.) during the day and shallows at night. It feeds on chironomids, mayflies, caddisflies, and small crustaceans, but also ingests debris from the bottom. It moves to streams with moderate current at the edges of channels or the lower end of riffles to spawn. The female burrows into gravel, with the male mounting to spawn in typical *Percina* fashion. Spawning occurs from May through July at 69 to 72°F, but populations probably differ by latitude. The 1.4 mm eggs are few; the larvae are 6 mm long (Scott and Crossman 1973).

## Subgenus *Percina* (Ericosma)

Males of *P. (Ericosma)* have a row of modified scales on the midline of the belly, broad vertical bands crossing the back to join the bands on the other side, a bright orange spiny dorsal fin, ridges of sensory breeding tubercles in the lower fins, and contiguous (side-top-side) broad vertical bands.

## *Percina (Ericosma) evides*, gilt darter

*P. (E.) evides* (**plate 58**) is one of two named species in this subgenus, and consists of three (so far unnamed) subspecies. Generally, flank bars are very wide and dusky blue-green to blue-black on a yellow to orange-yellow body; the lower fins are often dusky. The spiny dorsal fin has an orange edge (most places) or is entirely orange-red; the second dorsal and tail fins have bands. The female is smaller and less intensely colored than the male and has shorter dorsal and anal fins.

The Ozark subspecies is red-orange on the throat. The Blue Ridge Mountain subspecies is red-orange on the entire belly and has bands on the second dorsal and tail fins. The gilt darter may be red-orange on the entire belly but lacks bands on the second dorsal and tail fins. It lives to four years and attains 2½ inches (Kuehne and Barbour 1983; Page 1983).

The distribution of the gilt darter is disjunct. It was originally widespread throughout the upper Mississippi and Ohio basins, but today is most common in Minnesota and has been extirpated from Iowa. It occurs in the eastern and central Ozarks of Missouri and northern Arkansas and in the upper Ohio River basin of New York and Pennsylvania, ranging southward through Kentucky to northern Alabama and the mountains of Tennessee and North Carolina. It probably has been extirpated from Ohio and Illinois.

*P. (E.) evides* is found in gravel and rubble riffles of small to medium, clear rivers with permanent strong flow. It feeds primarily on bloodworms supplemented with other insect larvae and snails. The gilt darter spawns during May when the water is in the 60s (°F).

## *Percina (Ericosma) palmaris*, bronze darter

*P. (E.) palmaris* (**plate 59**) has a yellow-brown body and 8–10 brown saddle bands that become greenish brown during the breeding season. In the female, the bands do not cross the back, and her fin ray and scale counts differ slightly from the male (as well as among populations) (Denoncourt 1976). Bright colors are lacking, although they do have iridescent highlights (Kuehne and Barbour 1983). Bronze darters grow to 3 inches.

The bronze darter occurs above the fall line of the Coosa and Tallapoosa Rivers (Mobile River drainage) in northwestern Georgia and eastern Alabama.

*P. (E.) palmaris* is often found beneath deeply undercut banks that extend to midstream and in small to large, clear rocky rivers with permanent, strong flow over gravel and sand. It feeds on blackfly, midge, mayfly, stonefly, and caddisfly larvae, and on snails (Kuehne and Barbour, 1983).

## Subgenus *Percina* (Hadropterus)

Members of *P. (Hadropterus)* have a vertical row of three black spots on the base of the tail. The male has nearly a complete row of modified scales on the midline of the belly.

## *Percina (Hadropterus) nigrofasciata*, blackbanded darter

*P. (Hadropterus) nigrofasciata* is the most common *Percina* in the southeastern states, readily recognized by the high number (12–15) of vertical dark bars on the flank, the last three expanded into blotches. A dark spot appears on the tail at the center of the base and other slightly lighter spots are at the top and the bottom of the tail

Blackbanded darter, *Percina nigrofasciata,* Conasauga R., Tenn. WFR

Dusky darter, *Percina sciera.* WFR

base (all three in vertical alignment). The nuptial male has a greenish tint on the flanks, but is overall dusky. The female often has spots or blotches between the dark vertical bands on the flank.

Two subspecies have differing numbers of scales along the lateral line (Crawford 1956; Suttkus and Ramsey 1967). *P. n. nigrofasciata* of the west and Coastal Plain usually has 50–61 scales and *P. n. raneyi* (eastern and above the fall line) usually has 60–67 scales along the lateral line (Crawford 1956; Keuhne and Barbour 1983). Intergrades occur.

The blackbanded darter ranges from the Edisto River in South Carolina southward to the Suwannee and St. Johns Rivers in Florida. It continues northward to the Chattahoochee and Savannah River headwaters in Georgia and South Carolina and extends westward to the Mississippi River. Throughout most of Florida, it is the only species of *Percina.*

*P. (Hadropterus) nigrofasciata* inhabits streams and rivers throughout the Coastal Plain and Piedmont, occurring over sand, rock, or rubble in uplands, and over sand and silt in lowland streams. It has a preference for moderate to swift current, gravel, bedrock, and boulder, and submersed aquatic vegetation (e.g. *Podostemum, Justicia*). It sometimes is found over sand with woody debris. It is an opportunistic feeder, consuming mostly mayfly nymphs, and chironomid and caddisfly larvae in the morning and evening (Mathur 1973a,b).

Care as for *P. (A.) maculata,* but provide more structure and a sand and gravel bottom, but not in a tray. Spawning occurs close to roots or structure, above or on the gravel bottom. Some eggs are buried, but many are not and drift in the water column where they may be eaten by the adults. Remove the adults from the spawning aquarium and turn off the power filtration to prevent drifting eggs from being pulled into the filter. Allow the eggs to hatch in the aquarium, and feed as for other *Percina.*

---

*Percina (Hadropterus) sciera,*
dusky darter

*P. (Hadropterus) sciera* is dusky green, with 8 to 12 large (often fused) dark blotches on the flank, 8 small saddles just above (first 2 small with wavy lines or crosshatching between the side blotches), and dorsal saddles; there is no teardrop. The nuptial male is iridescent blue-green above and yellowish below; it is duskier above and below and on the fins; the blotches progress to black at the height of the spawning season.

There are two subspecies. The spiny dorsal fin has a faint orange marginal band in the Guadalupe River form, and a dusky blotch in the rear; the soft dorsal fin has a dusky submarginal band; fins otherwise have rows of spots (Page and Smith 1970; Kuehne and Barbour 1983). It also has bands rather than blocks of pigment, and often lacks an interconnecting horizontal band (Hubbs 1954).

The dusky darter is widespread from Mobile, Alabama to Port Aransas, Texas along the Gulf Coast, and ranges northward in the lower Mississippi River basin to the lower Ohio River (Illinois, Indiana, and Ohio). It occurs in Mississippi, Arkansas, Tennessee, northern Alabama, southeastern Oklahoma, and eastern Texas to the Guadalupe River. It attains 4 inches or more. The form in the Guadalupe River (including the San Marcos, Comal, and Blanco Rivers) is *P. s. apristis,* with *P. s. sciera* occupying the remainder of the range (Hubbs 1954; Hubbs and Black 1954; Page and Smith 1970).

*P. (Hadropterus) sciera* inhabits quiet backwaters and waters of medium to large, slow moving but clear rivers, both above and below the fall line. It occurs in the deeper riffles of tributary streams during spring and in pools and channels of the main river during the remainder of the year, and is not necessarily associated with debris or aquatic vegetation. It feeds mostly on chironomid and blackfly larvae, but also on mayfly and caddisfly larvae.

The dusky darter breeds at age one during May or June, and lives to three or four years. When large enough, it can be stripped of eggs and sperm, and the gametes mixed in a dish and incubated in water. Hatching occurs in about five days. It is not certain whether it buries eggs in gravel or is a broadcast spawner (Page and Smith 1970), or if it could do both. *P. (Hadropterus) sciera* hybridizes with other species of *Percina,* and has even hybridized with an *Etheostoma* species.

| *Percina (Hadropterus) aurolineata,* goldline darter | Males of *P. (Hadropterus) aurolineata* have yellow to orange spots and blotches on the head and snout, a yellow iris, and blue chin and throat. A bright yellow stripe that shades to olive and then to blue-olive appears below the marginal dark line on the upper flank. A dark midlateral band composed of eight blotches connected to each other and to a dark stripe through the eye extends to the snout. The unpaired fins are dusky with a submarginal yellow band; the caudal fin is yellow at the base. The upper fins are dark-edged; the lower fins are light-edged. The female also has dark marks, but the body is mostly yellow with yellow to clear fins. *P. (Hadropterus) aurolineata* attains 2½–3 inches. |

The goldline darter occurs in the Cahaba and Coosawatee Rivers (Alabama River drainage) of northern Georgia and central Alabama. Populations are apparently disjunct, with different associates at different elevations and differences in counts and meristics among the populations.

*P. (Hadropterus) aurolineata* inhabits moderate to wide rivers (50–200 ft. across) in white water rapids of the main channel. It typically is found 4–36 inches deep, over bedrock, boulder, rubble and gravel, and associated with aquatic vegetation (e.g., *Podostemum* and sometimes *Justicia*) growing on the boulders. It has many associates (Suttkus and Ramsey 1967).

| *Percina (Hadropterus) lenticula,* freckled darter | *P. (Hadropterus) lenticula* has a discrete upper spot on the tail (almost an ocellus), and two lower spots fused into a blotch. The lower front of the spiny and soft dorsal fins each has a prominent dark spot. Eight saddles above are separated by wavy lines from eight blotches on the flank; the rear side blotches are vertically elongated into |

bands. The chest and the pectoral fin base are spotted (freckled), with the spotting extending to the head, cheeks, and chin, but not to the belly, which may have a central dark stripe. A teardrop is present. The fins have many rows of black spots (Richards and Knapp 1964). The freckled darter is the largest (often 6–7 in.) member of its subgenus.

*P. (Hadropterus) lenticula* occurs above and below the fall line in the lower Pascagoula, Pearl, and upper Mobile (Etowah and Cahaba) drainages of northwestern Georgia, Alabama, and Mississippi.

The freckled darter is found in swift, deep riffles and runs of medium to large rivers, but little else is known as few specimens have been collected. Its large size may preclude normal breeding attempts, but stripping of gametes to fertilize in dishes may be feasible. This fish is likely to produce drifting eggs.

State or university ichthyologists with access to electrofishing gear could provide live adults to aquarists willing to assist in collections, maintain records for scientific personnel, and preserve old specimens.

Determine the protected status of *P. (Hadropterus) lenticula* before attempting collection.

| | |
|---|---|
| **Subgenus *Percina (Hypohomus)*** | Males of *P. (Hypohomus)* have no modified scales on the midline of the belly and no basicaudal spot or teardrop. They are large and have bright colors. |

| | |
|---|---|
| *Percina (Hypohomus) aurantiaca,*<br>tangerine darter | *P. (Hypohomus) aurantiaca* (**plate 60**) is the only species in this subgenus. It is a big darter (often more than 6 in.). A thin dark line along the back breaks up into spots toward the rear. A dozen large black blotches on the flank are obscured by a horizontal black band; there is a distinctive horizontal row of small dark spots on the upper flank. The belly is light (female) to deep orange (male). The spiny dorsal fin has an orange submarginal band. |

The tangerine darter occurs in small- to medium-sized tributaries of the Tennessee River, ranging from southwestern Virginia through the mountains of North Carolina and Tennessee; it continues southward just into northern Georgia.

*P. (Hypohomus) aurantiaca* inhabits swift, deep, rocky riffles and pools and overwinters in pools. It feeds on caddisfly, mayfly, and chironomid larvae from beneath rocks and within clumps of riverweed (*Podostemum ceratophyllum*). It spawns from May through June or July on clean gravel in shallows. Associates include *Percina (E.) evides, P. (P.) caprodes, P. (P.) burtoni, Etheostoma (N.) acuticeps, E. (N.) chlorobranchium, E. (E.) swannanoa, E. (U.) simoterum,* and *E. (N.) rufilineatum* (Kuehne and Barbour 1983; Page 1983). The male matures at age one and the female at age two; the tangerine darter lives to age four.

*P. (Hypohomus) aurantiaca* is too lovely and valuable to risk mixing with other fishes.

| | |
|---|---|
| **Subgenus *Percina (Imostoma)*** | *P. (Imostoma)* is defined in part by an elongate body. The breast and belly is mostly unscaled, and the male lacks modified stimulatory scales on the midline of the belly but has abundant breeding tubercles. The soft dorsal and anal fins are fanlike and elongated. |

| | |
|---|---|
| *Percina (Imostoma) shumardi,*<br>river darter | *P. (I.) shumardi* has a large black blotch at the base and rear of the spiny dorsal fin, and another smaller and less intense spot in the front base of the fin. A prominent |

River darter, *Percina shumardi,* St. Francis R., Mo. WFR

basicaudal spot and teardrop occur, and the flank and top both have indistinct dark markings, diffuse at the edges, that fade into vermiculations and mottling in between. It attains 2½ inches.

The river darter is widespread from central Ontario and Manitoba (Hudson Bay drainage) southward through the southern part of the Lake Huron and eastern Lake Erie drainages, ranging into the Mississippi, Tennessee, and Ohio Rivers (but not the Missouri River). It continues all the way to the Gulf Coast, from the Guadalupe River in Texas eastward to the Mobile basin of Alabama. It is uncommon in Canada, but occurs from the Lake Winnipeg drainage in Manitoba northward to Sipiwesk Lake and westward to Lake Dauphin and the Red Deer River; in Ontario, the river darter occurs from the Kenora District northward to Lake Attawapiskat and Sandy Lake (Scott and Crossman 1973).

*P. (I.) shumardi* is found in deep waters of large, wide rivers, over the deeper, lower end of boulder-strewn riffles, over rocks and gravel, and on rock-strewn bedrock where moderate current, and sometimes turbidity, exist. In the north, it also occurs in deep water of lakes. It feeds on chironomid, blackfly, mayfly, and caddisfly larvae, but not on stoneflies, beetles, bugs, or snails (despite its relationship to the snail darter and its allies in *Imostoma*) (Thomas 1970). It spawns during April or earlier in the southern United States and as late as July in Canada (Kuehne and Barbour 1983).

Katula (1987b) placed a single female river darter in a 55-gallon community aquarium containing several male blackside darters *(Percina (Alvordius) maculata),* western sand darters *(Ammocrypta clara),* troutperch *(Percopsis omiscomaycus),* gizzard shad *(Dorosoma cepedianum),* and orangespotted sunfish *(Lepomis humilis).* The substratum was gravel; structure was provided by a large mound of rocks in the center and a large piece of driftwood alongside. The water had vigorous aeration and turbulence from powerheads mounted on the undergravel filter outlet tubes. Fish were fed frozen brine shrimp, live tubificids, and occasionally frozen chironomids.

The addition of glassworms to the diet seemed to induce nuptial coloration in the males and ripening of eggs as the lone female swelled. Spawning occurred from late January through March, with a single male displaying to the female with erect fins, and contacting the female with its head ("head-bopping," according to Katula). The female buried in the gravel, and the male mounted and vibrated. At each spawning, three to seven eggs were laid, based on samples recovered from gravel.

Spawning occurred many times a day over several days. The eggs were not saved for incubation.

| | |
|---|---|
| *Percina (Imostoma) antesella,* amber darter | *P. (I.) antesella* (**plate 61**) is golden brown from the dorsum to just above the lateral line and cream colored below with an occasional black spot. The back has four black saddles (the first saddle before the first dorsal fin) that are narrow on top, expanding and opening as they extend toward the flanks. A teardrop is present. The anal and pelvic fins are clear, the other fins lightly pigmented. It grows to 2½ inches. |

The amber darter occurs in the Conasauga River of Murray County in northwestern Georgia and Polk and Bradley Counties in southeastern Tennessee. A habitat in Cherokee County of Georgia was destroyed when the U.S. Army Corps of Engineers constructed the Altoona Reservoir on Shoal Creek (Etowah River) in the 1950s. Both the Etowah, from which the fish has been extirpated, and the Conasauga, where populations are healthy, are headwater tributaries of the Coosa River (Williams and Etnier 1977).

*P. (I.) antesella* is associated with riffles up to 2 feet deep, and moderate current on a bottom of fine gravel, cobble, and silt-free sand.

Determine the protected status of the amber darter from state agencies before attempting collection.

| | |
|---|---|
| *Percina (Imostoma) vigil,* saddleback darter | *P. (I.) vigil* was previously known as *Percina ouachitae.* The top of the body is tan with five widely separated saddles (the first pale); ten small, square blotches appear on the flank; a network of lines and streaks occur between the top and side markings; the lower flank and belly are silvery; there is a small black basicaudal spot and a prominent teardrop. It commonly reaches 2 inches. |

The saddleback darter ranges from the southeastern bootheel of Missouri and surrounding areas in Illinois, Kentucky, Arkansas and Tennessee southward into Alabama, Mississippi, eastern Louisiana, and extreme western Florida. The same fish is discussed in Pflieger (1975) under the name *P. uranidea* (an upland species).

*P. (I.) vigil* is a Coastal Plain species of small to large, low gradient rivers, occurring over sand or sand-gravel, often in turbid water. It also is found along shallow shores or at the foot of a riffle or snag where the moderately increased flow washes the bottom clean of silt. It feeds on snails and other small aquatic invertebrates. It apparently spawns during winter.

| | |
|---|---|
| *Percina (Imostoma) uranidea,* stargazing darter | *P. (I.) uranidea* resembles the saddleback, snail, and amber darters. It has four dorsal saddles. The top of the head is dark and the lower part stippled; the teardrop is prominent. It is distinguished from *P. (I.) vigil* by its generally upland location, larger head, one less saddle, and the lack of a medial spot on the base of the tail. It is distinguished from the snail darter in lacking pigment at the base and edge of the first dorsal fin. It attains 2½ inches. |

The stargazing darter occurs in the St. Francis, Ouachita, and White Rivers of Arkansas, extending just into southern Missouri and northern Louisiana. Populations in Indiana and Illinois (Wabash River) have been extirpated.

*P. (I.) uranidea* inhabits medium to large upland rivers with a permanent, strong flow, often in riffles and gravel runs (especially if vegetated). It feeds mostly on snails and other small invertebrates.

Stargazing darter, *Percina uranidea,* Current R., Mo. wfr

Snail darter, *Percina tanasi,* Holston R., Tenn. rb

*Percina (Imostoma) tanasi,*
snail darter

*P. (I.) tanasi* is similar to *P. (I.) uranidea* in the number of saddles and large head, but it has a dusky thin line at the base and at the edge of the spiny dorsal fin and is slightly larger at 3 inches (Page and Burr 1991).

The snail darter occurs in the Tennessee, Little Tennessee, Chickamauga, and Sequatchie Rivers of Tennessee and northern Georgia, and has been introduced into the Hiwassee River in Tennessee (Kuehne and Barbour 1983).

*P. (I.) tanasi* inhabits the deeper portions of medium to large rivers, on sand and gravel shoals up to 3 feet deep. It eats mostly snails, supplemented with caddisfly and other insect larvae. It spawns during winter (February and March) at 53°F and lives two years (Kuehne and Barbour 1983).

The snail darter is not available to aquarists, but is not attractively colored. It formerly was classified as federally endangered but has been downgraded to threatened status, based on new populations and a successful transplantation to the Hiwassee River where it is now established.

**Subgenus *Percina (Odontopholis)***

The two members of *P. (Odontopholis)* have a keel covered with long-spined scales on the lower edge of the caudal peduncle.

*Percina (Odontopholis) stictogaster,*
frecklebelly darter

*P. (O.) stictogaster* has a narrow, uninterrupted light stripe above an uninterrupted broad and scalloped dark stripe on the flank. A teardrop is present and a black bar appears on the throat of the male. A light lateral line bisects the middle of a dark lateral stripe. The spiny dorsal fin has two rows of prominent black spots (one marginal and one medial) and the other fins are spotted. The belly is white and densely spotted (freckled). The nuptial male has green iridescence (Burr and Page 1993).

The frecklebelly darter occurs in the upper Green, Barren, and Kentucky Rivers of Kentucky and Tennessee (Cumberland Plateau and Highland Rim). It is most common in the Kentucky River, but is not found or collected easily.

*P. (O.) stictogaster* inhabits creeks and small, clear, rocky rivers among tree roots, below undercut banks, around woody debris, or among water willow *(Justicia).* It is a midwater feeder that behaves more like a sauger than a darter; it rests on tree roots and may occur in dead leaf accumulations during winter. It spawns during March and April.

This recently recognized species may soon be protected, although its abun-

Bluestripe darter, *Percina cymatotaenia*, Gasconade R., Mo. WFR

dance has probably not changed in the past two decades. Do not confuse it with the freckled darter *(P. lenticula)*.

| | |
|---|---|
| *Percina (Odontopholis) cymatotaenia,* bluestripe darter | *P. (O.) cymatotaenia* is the other member of the subgenus. Similar to *P. (O.) stictogaster,* the pigment on the base of its tail is reduced to a single medial spot, and pigment is absent from the fins. The lateral stripe is blue-black in the nuptial male. |

The bluestripe darter is rare in the Osage and Gasconade Rivers of the Missouri River system in south-central Missouri.

*P. (O.) cymatotaenia* inhabits quiet, vegetated backwaters of small to medium rivers with permanent strong flow; it avoids strong currents except when spawning and often occurs over sand or mud.

The bluestripe darter spawns below and at the edge of riffles during May, but spawning has not been observed. Because the belly in this subgenus lacks modified scales, but such scales appear on the caudal peduncle, it is assumed that the peduncle plays a tactile role in stimulating the female (Kuehne and Barbour 1983). It has a strongly developed swim bladder and is a midwater swimmer. It may spawn in open water.

For both species of *P. (Odontopholis)*, provide large, sand-bottom quarters (≥ 20 gal./pair) with dense vegetation for resting and hiding and only moderate current. Live adult *Artemia, Daphnia magna,* and blackworms should be supplemented with frozen *Artemia* and bloodworms.

| | |
|---|---|
| Subgenus *Percina (Swainia)* | Members of *P. (Swainia)* have a dozen small blotches on the flank but no bands, a mottled or zigzag pattern of dusky markings on the back, a prominent spot at the base of the tail fin, and an orange submarginal band in the spiny dorsal fin surrounded by dark pigment above and below. |

| | |
|---|---|
| *Percina (Swainia) phoxocephala,* slenderhead darter | *P. (S.) phoxocephala* is yellow-tan above and white below. It attains 2–3 inches. |

The slenderhead darter is widespread in the Mississippi River drainage from Wisconsin, Minnesota, and South Dakota to Pennsylvania and Ohio in the upper Mississippi basin, ranging southward to eastern Oklahoma and western Arkansas in the west, and erratically to northwestern Alabama and northern Mississippi in the east.

*P. (S.) phoxocephala* occurs virtually everywhere, but is most abundant in shallow, gravel runs and raceways of medium-sized rivers during most of the year. Its winter habitat is not known. From spring through fall, it occurs in sand-bottom pools, in small streams, on large rocky riffles with boulders, and on bedrock littered with stones. It spawns above the gravel at depths of 6 to 24 inches during June. The most common food items are blackfly, mayfly, and caddisfly larvae; it appears to avoid stonefly and beetle larvae (Page and Smith 1971).

Provide a large, deep aquarium (29–55 gal.) with a strong current from a powerhead or power filter. The spawning techniques are as described for *P. (P.) caprodes*. This fish releases more eggs into the current than it deposits in sand. The adults should be removed from the aquarium after spawning.

---

*Percina (Swainia) nasuta,*
longnose darter

*P. (S.) nasuta* has a long, narrow snout that is one-third the length of the head, and a head that is a third of the body length (excluding the tail). Twelve to 15 bands across the back extend slightly downward along the upper side; an equal number of bands on the flank are offset from the top bands, tending to drop between them. The body is dull yellow-orange above, and a bright orange submarginal band decorates the spiny dorsal fin (Bailey 1941b).

The longnose darter occurs in the Ozark uplands of Arkansas, and extends into southern Missouri and eastern Oklahoma in the Ouachita, White, St. Francis, and Arkansas Rivers (Page and Burr 1991). (A population south of the Arkansas River will be described as a new species by Bruce Thompson.)

*P. (S.) nasuta* inhabits small to medium rivers in clear water over gravel and rubble, often in swift riffles, but also in vegetated (*Potamogeton,* pond lily, algae), quiet backwaters over silty sand (Bailey 1941b). It may be a sand spawner.

---

*Percina (Swainia) oxyrhynchus,*
sharpnose darter

*P. (S.) oxyrhynchus* has ten dark blotches that sometimes expand into bars along the middle of the flank. Just above on the upper flank, continuous, dark, wormlike markings (vermiculations) are present. The back has 12–15 blotches, and the spiny dorsal fin has an orange submarginal band. The fins of specimens from vegetated areas are light orange-yellow and the body is greenish; the fins of fish from boulders are dusky and the body is slate gray (Hubbs and Raney 1939). It attains 3½ inches.

The sharpnose darter occurs in the Monongahela, Kentucky, New, Kanawha, Little Kanawha, Big Sandy, and Licking Rivers of western Virginia, West Virginia, northwestern North Carolina, Kentucky, and Pennsylvania (Kuehne and Barbour 1983; Page and Burr 1991).

Adults inhabit fast, turbulent riffles and runs up to 3 feet deep, on sandstone bedrock covered by rubble and boulders. Juveniles are everywhere, including in vegetation and on sand (Denoncourt, Hocutt, and Stauffer 1977; Kuehne and Barbour 1983).

---

*Percina (Swainia) squamata,*
olive darter

*P. (S.) squamata* has 10–15 saddles and lateral blotches that are distinct in juveniles but change in adults to a reticulate top and a continuous band on the flank. The spiny dorsal fin is dark-edged with a broad orange submargin (brighter in the male) and a dusky base. The head is dark and a teardrop is present. It grows to 3½ inches.

The olive darter occurs in the Rockcastle and Big South Fork of the Cumberland River. It also is present in the Tennessee basin in the French Broad, Watauga, Hiwassee, Nolichucky, and Emory Rivers (all along the Appalachian ridge of

North Carolina and Tennessee) and ranges into northern Georgia, continuing from western Tennessee northward into Kentucky (Kuehne and Barbour 1983). Although it occurs in low concentrations, its range is widespread through an area not yet excessively developed.

*P. (S.) squamata* inhabits deep, rocky, boulder-strewn chutes and riffles and gravel runs of medium-sized, high gradient mountain rivers. It is uncommon and often in areas where the force of rushing water is too strong to wade with a seine. Juveniles could be taken from pools in these rivers, but would be difficult to identify; the snout does not elongate until adulthood when the pattern also changes.

| |
|---|
| **Genus *Etheostoma*** |

*Etheostoma* is the largest, most advanced, diverse, and beautiful darter genus, with 100 species and 20 subgenera. The belly scales are ordinary, neither enlarged nor modified. *Etheostoma* are not translucent or exceptionally elongate, and they rarely bury in sand. They are generally smaller than *Percina,* with shorter bodies and blunter heads.

*Etheostoma* tend to prefer shallow, fast, rocky riffles, while *Percina* tend to occur in quiet pools or backwaters, and *Ammocrypta* in deep sandy runs. There are many exceptions, for there are many more species of *Etheostoma* and they have exploited more habitats. *Etheostoma,* lacking a swim bladder, are typically bottom dwellers, whereas *Percina* often have swim bladders that enable them to feed in the water column and at the surface.

Recent statistical interpretations of comparative analyses for a number of enzymes (Wood and Mayden 1997) and of DNA sequences (Turner 1997) have provided quite different interpretations of the relationships within *Etheostoma.*

*Etheostoma* have diverse breeding habits, ranging from egg burying in sand and gravel (as in *Percina*) to adhering eggs onto twigs and vegetation, and even laying single-layer clusters of sticky eggs on the underside of flat rocks (sculpins and madtoms produce multilayered clusters) that are protected by the male.

In the cave nesters, sexes are dimorphic and dichromatic, and eggs are placed on the underside of a flat rock and protected by the male. Hiding eggs in a cave would suggest light sensitivity, but that has not been found in darters. Subgenera with this behavior are *Boleosoma* and *Catonotus.* DNA analyses, however, while aligning species within each of these groups, does not align the groups with each other. Generally, the cave nesters are fishes of small creeks and rivers, occurring in shallow riffles and runs. If adults cannot be collected, the nest sometimes can. The flat rock with its covering of eggs is carried in a large styrofoam box to an outdoor barrel or cool aquarium filled with clean water. The rock is tipped at 45 degrees with the eggs facing downward, and aerated with the stream of bubbles playing directly on the eggs.

The snubnosed darters have a different association with rocks. They select vertical surfaces in deep pools for egg deposition, and the eggs are apparently not light sensitive.

Gravel spawners are set up with a shallow aquarium and a bottom of coarse gravel, and an outside filter cascading return water over an area of turbulence that is reserved by the dominant male. In many darters, this area is selected for spawning, while in others the eggs might be deposited anywhere in the tank.

After spawning has been observed (or a reasonable time has passed), either the parental fish are removed to allow the eggs to hatch from the gravel (all filters are

Ashy darter, *Etheostoma cinereum,* Little R., Tenn. WFR

turned off but aeration is continued), or the eggs are stirred out of the gravel and swirled up with an aquarium hand net and subsequently removed to a shallow dish for incubation.

A modification is gravel deposition of egg clumps, often just under the edge of a large rock. Darters practicing this spawning technique often occur in large, swift rivers, and do not spawn readily in captivity.

Plant spawners are of two types. One group deposits eggs in the green vegetation of swift, clear streams, while the other group tends to select dense vegetation in swampy, stagnant waters.

Upon hatching, almost all darter fry take *Artemia* nauplii at once and are easily raised.

---

**Subgenus *Etheostoma (Allohistium)***

*E. (Allohistium)* contains a single species.

---

*Etheostoma (Allohistium) cinereum,* ashy darter

The brightly colored male of *E. (A.) cinereum* has a long snout with an underslung mouth, an elevated second dorsal fin, and breeding tubercles (sensory contact organs) on the lower fins. It has thick lips (red-orange in the Cumberland River population), a dozen horizontally elongated black rectangles in a row along the lateral line, and four rows of thin red dots, clustered to form dashes and stripes above the lateral line. Coloration of the nuptial male is pronounced; a red margin appears on the first dorsal fin; the fanlike second dorsal fin has red blotches and bands throughout; the lower fins and the body are iridescent blue-green to black; and the pelvic and anal fins have a few small, white, rounded tubercles. The female and the non-nuptial male are yellow above and white below. It is a large darter (4 in.) that lives up to five years (Shepard and Burr 1984) and matures at 2 inches.

At one time its $B_4$ LDH enzyme was thought to relegate *E. (A.) cinereum* to a basal position in *Etheostoma,* perhaps to a stem ancestor that also gave rise to *Percina* because all species of the latter genus have this isozyme. The enzyme, however, occurs in other *Etheostoma, Crystallaria,* and even *Stizostedion* (Dimmick and Page 1992).

*E. (A.) cinereum* is known from Buck Creek and the Rockcastle, Big South Fork, Roaring, Red, Upper Duck, Buffalo, Obey, Clinch, Emory, Elk, and Little Rivers of the Cumberland and Tennessee River drainages in Kentucky and Tennessee. It has been extirpated from Virginia, Alabama, and probably Georgia and

Savannah darter, *Etheostoma fricksium*, male, Orangeburg Co., S.C. FCR     Savannah darter, *Etheostoma fricksium*, female, Colleton Co., S.C. FCR

is rare in most places, but more frequent in the Rockcastle, Big South Fork (Cumberland) and Little Rivers (Tennessee River) of Tennessee (Page 1983).

*E. (A.) cinereum* inhabits clear pools and sluggish backwaters of medium to large upland rivers, close to shore near tributary streams that it may enter to spawn (Kuehne and Barbour 1983). It is usually found among boulders, fallen trees, or water willow *(Justicia)* on sand or gravel (not silt) and is not found in riffles. Its pool habitat is reflected in its diet of burrowing mayflies *(Ephemera),* oligochaete worms (tubificids), and midges (chironomids or bloodworms); this diet is supplemented with smaller numbers of other insects that it digs from the bottom with its long snout and thick, papillose (probably sensory) lips. It matures at one year (males) or two years (females) and breeds during March.

In captivity, the diet should consist mostly of frozen bloodworms and adult *Artemia,* with treats of small earthworms, whiteworms, and blackworms. *E. (A.) cinereum* probably is not difficult to propagate; one can strip gametes if necessary.

---

**Subgenus *Etheostoma (Belophlox)***

The two members of *E. (Belophlox)* have a marginal broad orange band in the spiny dorsal fin; the lateral line is complete (i.e., all scales in the series have pores) or partially complete; the lateral line scales are light colored within a broad dark stripe along the middle of the side; and there are two anal fin spines.

The subgenus is restricted to small ranges in Atlantic and Gulf Coastal Plain drainages of Georgia and the Carolinas. Bailey and Etnier (1988) limited the subgenus to include only *E. (Belophlox) mariae* and *E. (Belophlox) fricksium.*

---

*Etheostoma (Belophlox) fricksium,*
Savannah darter

The nuptial male of *E. (Belophlox) fricksium* has bright green and red bars expanding to a red patch on the lower flank (unusual in southeastern Coastal Plain darters), a green to black breast and a green belly, a dark band across the head and upper flank, a lighter brown dorsum, and a broad red submarginal band in the spiny dorsal fin. The female is mostly black on the flank, with a white belly and tan back (Rohde et al. 1994).

The Savannah darter occurs in streams of the Savannah, Broad, Combahaee, and Edisto Rivers below the fall line in the Sandhills and upper Coastal Plain of Georgia and South Carolina.

Layman (1993) found the Savannah darter in medium currents among logs, sticks, and leaves over sand or sand-gravel, beneath undercut banks, and in beds of

Pinewoods darter, *Etheostoma mariae,* Naked Cr., Richmond Co., N.C. FCR

*Vallisneria;* it was not usually over open sand or in silt, mud, or fine detritus. One typical stream was clear, but tinted from tannins, 20 feet wide and up to 6 feet deep, and consisted of runs and pools with no riffles. A canopy of hardwood trees shaded the water, limiting in-stream vegetation to woody debris, leaf litter, and occasional patches of *Vallisneria americana* and other rooted plants where the canopy opened to the sun. The diet of mostly chironomid larvae and mayflies includes caddisflies, many other insects, and crustaceans.

Breeding occurs continuously from February through May at water temperatures of 52 to 73°F (Layman 1993). The Savannah darter is a gravel spawner with a preference for sticks, detritus, and other cover. Eggs are 1.7 mm and hatch in less than 2 weeks at 70°F (Layman 1993).

*Etheostoma (Belophlox) mariae,* pinewoods darter

*E. (Belophlox) mariae* is reddish brown to black above with many dark saddles. Dark blotches on the flank may fuse to form a dark stripe. The spiny dorsal fin is clear at the edge with a broad reddish black submarginal band and another wide dark band just below. The soft dorsal fin is dusky and lightly spotted, a bold, black vertical bar appears behind the pectoral fin, and the pelvic and anal fins are black (Rohde et al. 1994).

The pinewoods darter occurs below the fall line in the Sandhills of the Lumber and Little Pee Dee Rivers (Little Pee Dee drainage system) of southeastern North Carolina; it has been extirpated from South Carolina and some localities in North Carolina due to habitat destruction by humans and beavers (Rohde and Arndt 1991).

The Sandhills are an area of dry sandy hillocks 200–450 feet above sea level that extend from the Carolinas to Mississippi; the area is vegetated by longleaf pine, turkey oak, post oak, holly, tag alder, and other xeric (drought-tolerant) plants in an ecosystem dependent on renewal by periodic fires started by lightning. The fires clear the underbrush of competing plants, stimulating seed germination of native vegetation and allowing the ecosystem to sustain itself. This habitat is disappearing through commercial forestry conversion to loblolly pine (faster growing and more valuable) which requires fire elimination.

The pinewoods darter occurs on sand-gravel and gravel riffles in clear, cold creeks 15 feet wide and less than 2 feet deep, usually near filamentous algae, *Fonti-*

Johnny darter, *Etheostoma nigrum*, Kansas R., Kans. GS

*nalis, Potamogeton diversifolius, Vallisneria americana, Orontium aquaticum, Sparganium americanum, Juncus,* and *Nuphar luteum* (Rohde and Ross 1987). It is probably a gravel spawner in riffles but its care is not known.

The pinewoods darter has been proposed for listing under the Endangered Species Act, and may be protected as well by the state of North Carolina.

*Boleosoma, Ioa,* and *Vaillantia* constitute a line of evolution known as the *Boleosoma* group of subgenera (Cole 1967, 1971).

| | |
|---|---|
| **Subgenus *Etheostoma (Boleosoma)*** | The johnny darter of *E. (Boleosoma)* nest in caves, laying a single layer of eggs on the roof below a flat rock; the eggs are guarded by the male. The female has a bilobed genital papilla (breeding tube or ovipositor), and the male has a conical breeding tube (sometimes with a small slit at the tip) and lacks breeding tubercles on the body. Members of *E. (Boleosoma)* have black heads when nesting; this group of species has no bright colors. The premaxilla (upper lip) is protractile, enabling the fish to extend its lip and lower jaw into crevices for feeding. |
| *Etheostoma (Boleosoma) nigrum,* johnny darter | *E. (Boleosoma) nigrum* is the best known cave-spawning darter. One anal spine, a blunt and rounded snout, and bilobed ovipositor identify this gray darter. A mixture of X-, V-, or W-shaped lateral blotches on a gray body, subdued dorsal saddles, and dark lower fins in the dark-headed male (when spawning) are diagnostic. The head and lower fins of the nuptial male are black. It attains 2 inches. |

The johnny darter is widespread throughout eastern North America, from eastern Saskatchewan through Hudson Bay to Montreal and the Great Lakes. It ranges southward along the Piedmont to North Carolina, and continues southward on the western slopes of the Appalachians to the upper Mobile Bay drainage of the Gulf Coast. It occurs westward along the Mississippi drainage to Arkansas and Oklahoma, with a population extending just into Colorado and Wyoming along the Platte River.

Of three nominal subspecies, only two are valid. *E. n. susanae* has fewer scales on the head and belly and occurs in the upper Cumberland River in Kentucky and Tennessee. *E. n. eulepis* (the scaly johnny darter), recognized most recently by Cole (1971), is not valid (Bruner 1976). *E. n. nigrum* occupies most of the johnny darter range, which may be the largest distribution of any darter species.

Tesselated darter, *Etheostoma olmstedi*, Curtis Cr., N.C. WFR

*E. (Boleosoma) nigrum* inhabits quiet, sand or sand-gravel streams and sandy or weedy lake edges, sometimes occurring over mud and often to considerable depths in northern lakes. It avoids large rivers and fast waters, but may occur on or near riffles in small, low gradient streams. In one western study, it avoided riffles, remaining in slow-moving runs and deeper pools even where the surface velocity was swift. It prefers depressions, stones, or other structures for cover (but not cobble bottoms) and sunlight to shade (Leidy 1992). It can tolerate heat up to 86°F, and prefers 68–72°F (Ingersoll and Claussen 1984).

The johnny darter spawns during spring, with the male selecting sloping flat rocks and vigorously cleaning the undersurface upside down with his tail and pectoral and pelvic fins to remove debris. When another male approaches, the defending male erects his fins in threat. When a female approaches, the erect fins are quickly relaxed, and the male enters his cave, swimming upside down on the roof.

The female enters and turns upside down, laying one egg at a time (sometimes two or three), either alongside or preceding the male; most of the eggs are laid on the side sloping closest to the bottom. Eggs number from 30 to over 1,000, and are fanned by his pectoral fins while the male is upside down (Winn 1958). If a johnny darter is injured, it emits an alarm substance (R.J.F. Smith 1979) that warns conspecifics.

A 5- to 10-gallon aquarium is suitable for one male and two or three females. The bottom should be sand, with a single large flat rock set at an angle, beneath which the male can excavate a cave. Provide an undergravel filter (protected with fiber floss to prevent sand from entering the pores of the filter plate), sponge filter, or outside filter with low flow, but no strong water movements. Feed frozen adult *Artemia* and bloodworms (chironomids), and live blackworms, whiteworms, and daphnia. After spawning, all fish but the guarding male should be removed, allowing him to fan the eggs until hatching about ten days later. The fry take brine shrimp nauplii as a first food. Alternatively, the rock can be removed and placed in a bucket with aeration until the eggs hatch. Johnny darters will spawn repeatedly at one to three week intervals in captivity and do not require an overwintering period (Katula 1990b).

*Etheostoma (Boleosoma) olmstedi,* tesselated darter

*E. (Boleosoma) olmstedi* has a much larger second dorsal fin in both sexes that becomes peach colored with dark lines. The head of the nuptial male is not dark. The tesselated darter usually has 12–15 rays in the second dorsal fin while the johnny darter has 10–12; the tesselated usually has 12–13 rays in the pectoral fin while the johnny darter has 11–12 (Cole 1965).

The tessellated darter ranges from Quebec and the southern shores of Lakes Erie and Ontario southward through all of New York and New England. It continues through eastern Pennsylvania and below the fall line to the St. Johns River in northern Florida. The ranges of the johnny and tesselated darters overlap only in the Genesee River and Lake Ontario drainages in New York.

Subspecies are based on having one or two anal spines and the number of pored scales in the lateral line. *E. o. maculaticeps* ranges from Wilmington, North Carolina to Florida and has two anal spines. *E. o. vexillare* is a dwarf species restricted to the upper Rappahannock River in Virginia and has one anal spine and no more than 42 pored scales along the lateral line. *E. o. olmstedi* occupies the remainder of the range and has one anal spine and more than 42 pored scales along the lateral line (Kuehne and Barbour 1983; Page and Burr 1991). *E. o. atromaculatum,* recognized by Cole (1967, 1971), is no longer valid because the characters used to define it are not consistently associated with geographic distribution, but are variable within populations (Zorach 1971). Xanthic (yellow bodies lacking black pigment) specimens have been collected in Mill Creek (south of New Holland) in Lancaster County, Pennsylvania (Denoncourt, Robbins, and Stauffer 1976).

The tessellated darter occurs in low gradient, small, shallow stream runs and pools with sand, mud, or silt bottoms. The habitat may be vegetated or not, polluted or not, and on or below riffles. *E. (Boleosoma) olmstedi* is usually associated with little structure or undercut banks; it is not found on extensive cobble or rock bottoms or in swift or deep water. It feeds mostly on midge (chironomid or bloodworm) larvae (Tsai 1972; Layzer and Reed 1978).

Spawning similar to *E. (Boleosoma) nigrum,* but different males may spawn under common rocks, cleaning and protecting eggs fertilized by other males while cleaning the remaining available surfaces for themselves (Constantz 1979).

---

*Etheostoma (Boleosoma) perlongum,*
Waccamaw darter

*E. (Boleosoma) perlongum* is probably derived from *E. (Boleosoma) olmstedi,* but is more elongate, with square to triangular blotches on the midside and zigzag lines on the upper flank below the vague and numerous saddles. The nuptial male becomes pink and charcoal, the bars and triangles of the side disappearing under a velvetlike dusky hue; the top of the head from the eyes to the tip of the snout becomes golden pink with dark edges; the fanlike fins become golden with black margins and rows of black spots. It attains almost 3 inches.

The Waccamaw darter is endemic to Lake Waccamaw, North Carolina, a vast, shallow, sunlit lake on the Coastal Plain isolated from other bodies of water, and derived from the burned out cavity of a giant peat bog fire during the last Ice Age or perhaps from a meteorite strike. It is among the most important waterfowl overwintering grounds on the Atlantic flyway, and bird-watchers gather here every fall to view millions of swans, geese, ducks, herons, and other birds overwintering or resting on their way south.

Other fishes endemic to the lake and derived from regional fauna include *Fundulus waccamensis* (a derivative of *F. diaphanus*) and the silverside or atherinid fish *Menidia extensa* (a derivative of *M. beryllina*). Nonendemics in the lake include *Noturus gyrinus* and *Etheostoma (Hololepis) fusiforme.*

Riverweed darter, *Etheostoma podostemone,* Dan R., N.C. FCR

Longfin darter, *Etheostoma longimanum,* James R., Va. WFR

The spawning season of the Waccamaw darter is from March through June when the male leaves the deeper water in the middle of the lake to nest in warm water (72–84°F) near shore. The male excavates a depression in the soft sand beneath woody debris and the female arrives soon after. The pair spawns upside down on the undersurface of a twig, branch, or other debris. The single layer of eggs may number 150 to 4,700, with a mean of 1,400. The eggs hatch in five to seven days (Lindquist et al. 1981, 1984). *E. (Boleosoma) perlongum* may hybridize with *E. (Boleosoma) olmstedi* in the Waccamaw River; *E. (Boleosoma) olmstedi* does not enter Lake Waccamaw.

The Waccamaw darter is undemanding in captivity. Provide a large, shallow aquarium (e.g., a 20- to 40-gallon long) with a sand bottom and pieces of wood or root. This fish does not like current; only sponge filters should be used. A male will perch on any structure. Approaching females are treated to displays. If the female is interested, she approaches the underside of the perch. The male nudges the female in the ventral area. Both invert and a single egg is attached and instantly fertilized. Spawning takes one hour. The male returns to his perch and ignores the eggs, occasionally abandoning them to search for a new spawning site. The egg-laden wood or root should be removed and incubated in a separate aquarium. See *E. (E.) euzonum* for instructions on the care of fry.

*Etheostoma (Boleosoma) podostemone,* riverweed darter

The nuptial male of *E. (Boleosoma) podostemone* is robust, with a dark velvety body and expansive dark orange finnage. Out of the spawning season it has six or more saddles and a series of pronounced zigzag dark marks on the flank, with those on the upper flank tending to form horizontal lines toward the rear.

The riverweed darter is common in the upper Roanoke River of Virginia and northern North Carolina in small- to medium-sized, clear, rocky streams above the fall line, on rocky, sandy, and rubble riffles. It is usually not far from riverweed *(Podostemum),* in which it may forage outside the May–June breeding season (Kuehne and Barbour 1983; Matthews, Bek, and Surat 1982).

*Etheostoma (Boleosoma) longimanum,* longfin darter

The male of *E. (Boleosoma) longimanum* changes dramatically during the spring breeding season, becoming charcoal black with the enlarged fins richly blotched and spotted in orange.

The longfin darter occurs in the upper James River of Virginia and just enters West Virginia.

*E. (Boleosoma) longimanum* is found in small to medium, swiftly flowing clear streams over gravel, rubble, and rocky riffles in the mountains and Piedmont. If adults cannot be collected, try to find their 50–150 eggs in a single layer beneath flat rocks in medium-sized fast-flowing streams.

Egg-laden rocks can be transported home in a styrofoam box, eggs upward, and then tipped downward on a 45 degree angle beneath vigorous aeration until hatching.

| Subgenus *Etheostoma (Ioa)* | Members of *E. (Ioa)* resemble *Ammocrypta* in translucence and sand habitat; the snout is long, and the anus is surrounded by fleshy papillae. The body is elongate, the pectorals elongate, and nuptial tubercles occur on the paired fins in both sexes (Bailey and Etnier 1988). The single species is sometimes placed in *Boleosoma,* but it is retained here in *Ioa* in part because of its unique form of reproduction. |

| *Etheostoma (Ioa) vitreum,* glassy darter | *E. (I.) vitreum,* the glassy darter, has a long snout and translucent body with dark saddles, spots, and lateral dashes. The male becomes darker than the female, and the female develops fingerlike projections on the genital papilla during the spring.<br><br>The glassy darter occurs from the Patuxent River in Maryland to the Neuse River of North Carolina in sand-bottom rivers and streams above and below the fall line, in moderate to fast current.<br><br>*E. (I.) vitreum* is a communal spawner during March and April when the water is 50–64°F. Males and females spawn *en masse* over a day or more on a single structure, which may be a rock, log, concrete culvert, or bridge footing that faces into the current. This shared nest may contain 50,000 eggs. No other darter has this mode of reproduction. DNA sequences suggest a close relationship to *E. (Boleosoma) nigrum* which would put it in the *Boleosoma* group (Turner 1997), but its reproductive behavior is quite different from *E. (Boleosoma)* species.<br><br>The glassy darter does best in large aggregations; provide a 20-gallon long aquarium with a sand bottom, strong current from one end, and a few high profile rocks along the midline of the aquarium. Feed bloodworms and brine shrimp, supplemented with blackworms. |

| Subgenus *Etheostoma (Vaillantia)* | Members of *E. (Vaillantia)* have a stubby and blunt head and a slim body. Neither sex has bright colors. Two dark bars in front of the eyes are fused to look like the bridle on the head of a horse; a suborbital bar (teardrop) is present; the back and sides are speckled; and the side has lateral blotches. The male has a diffuse black band in the spiny dorsal fin that is most prominent in front where it appears as a dark blotch. The genital papilla of the female is large, flat, and pimply. These are generally plant spawners. |

| *Etheostoma (Vaillantia) chlorosoma,* bluntnose darter | *E. (V.) chlorosoma* has a blunt head, slim trunk, and dense speckles on a yellow body not attaining over 2 inches. It has one anal spine. The male may darken during spring spawning.<br><br>The bluntnose darter occupies lowland Gulf drainages from the Mobile to the Guadalupe Rivers, and ranges northward in the Mississippi basin to the southern border between Minnesota and Wisconsin. It is widespread throughout central Alabama and ranges westward through Louisiana and Mississippi to east Texas and much of Arkansas. It continues into Oklahoma, eastern Kansas, and western Missouri. |

*E. (V.) chlorosoma* inhabits silt-, mud-, and sand-bottom oxbows and sluggish pools of rivers.

A 29-gallon aquarium with broad-leaved plants, such as *Echinodorus cordifolius* in pots, should be provided for spawning. The eggs are attached to the undersides of leaves and stems. The male does not guard the eggs but stays in their vicinity for several days. Remove the breeders or remove the egg-laden plant for incubation separately. Eggs hatch in eight days at 68°F and fry can take brine shrimp nauplii at once.

| | |
|---|---|
| *Etheostoma (Vaillantia) davisoni,* Choctawhatchee darter | *E. (V.) davisoni* has a darkly speckled yellow body with a dark patch at the rear of the cheek and two anal spines. The nuptial male becomes dark with a thin pink line in the colorful and flaglike spiny dorsal fin. It attains less than 2 inches. |

The Choctawhatchee darter ranges from the Escambia to Choctowatchee Rivers in the western Florida panhandle around Pensacola, and continues northward into southern Alabama.

*E. (V.) davisoni* is common and widespread in sand-bottom pools and runs in shallow streams and backwaters of small rivers over leaf litter and submersed vegetation. It spawns in February and March at 63–65°F.

Wild fish captured during the spawning season were placed in a 15-gallon aquarium at 63°F with substrata of sand or gravel on separate sides of the aquarium; leaves, wood, *Vallisneria americana,* and a rock were added.

Spawning occurred the day after capture with one male taking over a sand territory and spawning with any female that entered; it remained in the territory longer than five seconds. Males mounted numerous females during the day, each female depositing about two eggs per clasp, and as many as nine eggs per female per day. Eggs were laid on leaves, twigs, the side of the aquarium, and on apparently any solid substratum, but were not buried. Eggs were 1.16 mm in diameter and hatched in 11 to 14 days at 61°F. The fry were not raised (Bart 1992).

| | |
|---|---|
| **Subgenus *Etheostoma (Doration)*** | *E. (D.) stigmaeum* and *E. (D.) jessiae* were previously listed in *Boleosoma,* but are now set apart in this subgenus (Cole 1967; Page 1981; Bailey and Etnier 1988; Simon 1997). Members are distinguished by the blue band over a red-orange band in the spiny dorsal fin, the long ovipositor, and the two anal spines. |
| *Etheostoma (Doration) jessiae,* blueside darter | The female of *E. (D.) jessiae* has six brown saddles and up to ten dark squares or W-shaped markings on the flank, plus numerous spots and dashes above and on the flank. The male has striking blue bands on the flank, a blue patch on the cheek, a blue anal fin, and blue margins on the upper and lower edges of the tail fin base. The spiny dorsal fin has a thin blue edge, a wide orange submarginal band, and a dark sub-submarginal blue-black band a third of the distance out into the fin. A thin row of dark speckles appears near the outer edge of the soft dorsal fin. *E. (D.) jessiae* (plate 62) differs from *E. (D.) stigmaeum* by having one less dark blotch on the flank, a longer snout and a thin frenum, and blue rather than turquoise bands. It averages almost 2 inches. |

The blueside darter occurs at middle elevations in eastern and southern Tennessee and northern Alabama. It is present in the middle and upper Tennessee River basin from Bear Creek in Alabama northward (but not in the Clinch and Powell Rivers), possibly in the Stones River in the Cumberland River basin, and is rare in Henderson County in North Carolina.

*E. (D.) jessiae* occurs in deeper gravel riffles and adjacent pools of medium to high gradient, small rivers to large streams. It is an egg-burier that spawns in the spring. Larval development and identification have been described by Simon (1997).

| | |
|---|---|
| *Etheostoma (Doration) stigmaeum,* speckled darter | *E. (D.) stigmaeum* **(plate 63)** has a blunter snout, no frenum, and turquoise rather than blue bands in the male. The turquoise blotches or bands on the flank complement the turquoise on the cheek and at the base of the anal fin. The spiny dorsal fin has a submarginal orange-red band surrounded above and below by blue. It is a small darter, seldom 2 inches. |

The speckled darter occurs in West Virginia in the Green and Cumberland Rivers southward through most of middle Tennessee, northwest Georgia, Alabama, Mississippi, western Florida, and Louisiana to the Gulf Coast. It ranges northwestward into Arkansas, southwestern Missouri, and just enters Kansas and Oklahoma.

This darter is probably a complex of about four species, all represented today under the name *E. stigmaeum*. The fish in the Clinch and Powell Rivers of Tennessee and Virginia is considered by Lee et al. (1980) to be a distinct species, *E. meadiae;* the fish in the upper Cumberland is probably another species (Kuehne and Barbour 1983); the bluemask darter of the Caney Fork in the Cumberland system will be described as a new species by Steve Layman.

Populations on both sides of the Mississippi River are likely to be different species, as in the case of Alabama and Arkansas populations (Simon 1997). Fish from the Escambia and adjacent drainages in Florida and Alabama seem to be smaller than others and should be investigated (C. Gilbert, pers. comm.). More studies are needed to clarify this species group. Recent studies of larval development (Simon 1997) support the separation of *stigmaeum* from *jessiae,* and that *stigmaeum* consists of more than one taxon.

The speckled darter occurs in medium to large streams and small rivers, usually over gravel and sand riffles and in adjacent rocky and sandy pools. It presumably feeds on chironomids and other aquatic insect larvae. The female stops over gravel but does not bury herself; the male then mounts the female. Four or five small eggs are laid at a time in the gravel (Winn 1958).

A 10-gallon or larger aquarium will accommodate two males and four females. Include sand and gravel, with rocks to mark territorial boundaries, and current provided by an outside power filter that cascades onto the spawning area. Eggs can be swept and swirled from the gravel and incubated in shallow dishes. Stocks from the Clinch and Powell Rivers should be kept separate from other stocks because they are probably a different species, as noted by Lee et al. (1980).

| | |
|---|---|
| Subgenus *Etheostoma (Litocara)* | Members of *E. (Litocara)* have an elongate head and a large body shaped like a *Percina.* The lateral line is straight and completely or incompletely pored; scales on the gill covers occur near the top or not at all. There are many (11–12) anal fin rays and two basicaudal spots that may be fused. The male has sensory breeding tubercles on the lower body. |

This subgenus of arrow-shaped darters is represented by *E. (L.) sagitta* in the Appalachian uplands (Cumberland Plateau drainages) and *E. (L.) nianguae* in the Ozark uplands (Missouri River drainage), on the opposite side of the Mississippi

River. *E. (Litocara)* provides evidence, also found among other species groups, that these regions and their faunas were historically connected.

---

*Etheostoma (Litocara) sagitta,*
arrow darter

*E. (L.) sagitta* (**plate 64**) has an incompletely pored lateral line. It is similar to *E. (L.) nianguae,* but the two black basicaudal spots are virtually fused into a vertical bar. It grows to 3½ inches.

The arrow darter ranges from Kentucky to northern Tennessee (Clay 1975). Two subspecies differ in scale counts and the number of pores in the lateral line. The southern form, *E. s. sagitta* of the upper Cumberland River system above Cumberland Falls, Kentucky (possibly ranging southward into Tennessee) appears to be the older, original form. The northern and probably younger form, *E. s. spilotum,* occurs in the upper Kentucky River system of Kentucky.

The geological and biological evidence suggests that erosion upstream from the Kentucky River cut into the upper Cumberland drainage and diverted some of its streams into the Kentucky River, capturing the flow and acquiring several species, among them *E. (L.) sagitta.* After only a few thousand years, the captured population in the Kentucky River system changed sufficiently to become distinguishable as *E. s. spilotum,* quite different (using a microscope) from the ancestral Cumberland *E. s. sagitta* (Kuehne and Bailey 1961).

The original collection was made by David Starr Jordan on one of his walking trips. He stopped at Wolf Creek and other tributaries on the Clear Fork of the Cumberland River in Kentucky, where he found a single specimen of what he considered a new species. He published the name *Poecilichthys sagitta* in 1883. The fish was again collected and the habitat described by Bailey (1948) who worked out its phylogenetic relationships.

Little Wolf Creek, near the original locality, is a pool and riffle stream 10 to 15 feet wide and up to 2 feet deep. The bottom is bedrock, gravel, and rubble. *E. (L.) sagitta* was found beneath flat stones on the deepest and fastest riffles of small, gently flowing brooks. Throughout its range, the arrow darter occurs in pools and undercut banks of first- and second-order streams, often among large, flat stones. It feeds mostly on mayflies and midges, but also on stoneflies, caddisflies, crayfish, and crustaceans.

The arrow darter enters riffles to spawn from March through May, with a peak in April. Associates include *E. (C.) kennicotti, E. (Oligocephalus) caeruleum, E. (C.) flabellare, E. (Boleosoma) nigrum, Semotilus atromaculatus, Phoxinus cumberlandensis,* crayfish, and the two-lined salamander, *Eurycea bislineata.* The largest arrow darters are the males; the life span is three years (Kuehne and Barbour 1983; Page 1983). The arrow darter is probably as easy a gravel spawner as *E. (Oligocephalus) spectabile* or *E. (Ozarka) punctulatum.*

---

*Etheostoma (Litocara) nianguae,*
Niangua darter

*Etheostoma (L.) nianguae* (**plate 65**) is an exceptional member of its genus that lives in pools resembling *Percina* habitat. In an example of convergent evolution, *E. (L.) nianguae* has adopted the typical *Percina* form; it is large and elongate with a pointy snout (Page 1973) and a barred pattern. Even more striking is the pattern of the female *E. (L.) nianguae,* which when combined with its shape and lack of bright colors, mimics a *Percina.*

*E. (L.) nianguae* has a completely pored lateral line and is elongate, with a long, low snout (as in many *Percina* species); the similarity is especially notable in the darkly marked female. It attains 3–4 inches. Two small, black basicaudal spots on both sexes and on juveniles are diagnostic of the species within its range. The male is light above and red-orange below; eight to ten gray-green saddles become bands on the back and sides; red coloration on the belly extends up the sides between bands toward the rear (or as spots on the sides) from the nape to the caudal fin base. The margins of the first dorsal and the caudal fins are red, there are red spots at the base of the first and second dorsal fins, and there is a red blotch on the rear of the second dorsal fin; the anal fin and caudal fin base are blue. The female has a dark zigzag pattern (or dark bands with light centers) along the midline of the flank, often aligned with the dark saddles above.

The Niangua darter occurs in the lower Osage River system (rarely in the Sac River) on the Ozark Plateau of Missouri.

*E. (L.) nianguae* inhabits small, shallow, clear creeks with a permanent moderate flow, on rubble or rock-gravel bottoms among boulders in chutes, pools, backwaters, sometimes riffles, and disturbed areas downstream of concrete-slab road crossings. It probably feeds on aquatic insect larvae, crustaceans, and worms located in the gravel and under rocks with its elongate snout.

The Niangua darter spawns at age 2 in riffles during April when water temperatures suddenly rise into the mid-60s (°F). The male displays with vertical head-bobbing. The female buries in gravel with her head and tail exposed; the male mounts, vibrates, and eggs are released and fertilized and left in the gravel. The female and male continue mating with other individuals (Pflieger 1975).

*E. (L.) nianguae* is state-protected because it is thought to be rare; however, it escapes predation (and seines) by burying in gravel, and we have found it to be more abundant than generally recognized in the literature.

---

**Subgenus *Etheostoma (Catonotus)***

The males of some *E. (Catonotus)* species have swellings on either the dorsal spines or the soft dorsal fin ray tips that are thought to mimic eggs (Page and Bart 1989). The absence of antibiotic activity in the knob tissue supports the idea that they have no role in preventing infection (Bart and Page 1991), leaving only the egg-mimic hypothesis, which is supported by the apparent preference of females for nests containing eggs. Other characters of the subgenus are a frenum (wide band of tissue) connecting the upper lip to the snout, and an incomplete (only partially pored), straight lateral line. The female has a wide, flat and undivided genital papilla (ovipositor). The subgenus is divided into three groups (Page 1975a; Wolf and Branson 1979; Wolf et al. 1979).

The *virgatum* group (with nine dorsal spines) contains *virgatum, smithi, striatulum, barbouri,* and *obeyense.*

---

*Etheostoma (Catonotus) obeyense,* barcheek darter

*E. (C.) obeyense* has vertically elongated dark marks on the flank. It grows to 3 inches.

The barcheek darter occurs in the Cumberland River drainage. In Kentucky, it has been reported from Indian, Spring, and Smith Creeks, and from the Albany Branch in Clinton County. It occurs in Crocus and Marrowbone Creeks in Cumberland County, Beaver Creek in Wayne County, and Fishing Creek in Pulaski County. In Pickett County, Tennessee, it occupies Pitman and Rock Creeks. It is

Barcheek darter, *Etheostoma obeyense*, Big South Fork, Ky. WFR

Striated darter, *Etheostoma striatulum*, Hurricane Cr., Duck R., Bedford Co., Tenn. RB

also present in the Obey, Wolf, and Little South Fork Rivers of south-central Kentucky and north-central Tennessee (Page and Braasch 1976).

*E. (C.) obeyense* inhabits pools of second-, third-, and fourth-order streams, commonly over sand in shallow water, but also in bedrock and in slabrock pools.

| | |
|---|---|
| *Etheostoma (Catonotus) barbouri*, teardrop darter | *E. (C.) barbouri* is another member of the *virgatum* group. The nuptial male is yellow-orange with vertically elongate dark blotches; the head and paired fins are black; the spiny dorsal fin has a black smudge at the origin and an orange margin; other fins are orange-spotted (or blotched) near the body and clear toward the edge; the anal fin and the lower edge of the tail fin may have a black edge. In both sexes, an intensely dark teardrop and a parallel bold black line appear behind the gill cover; a thinner black line runs horizontally through the eye from the nose to the edge of the gill cover. He has a brilliant opalescent patch behind the eye between the horizontal and vertical black lines. The female is otherwise black-spotted without the red or blue-black fin margins, and other body colors are subdued (Kuehne and Small 1971; Kuehne and Barbour 1983; Page 1983; Page and Burr 1991). |

The teardrop darter occurs in the Green, Nolin, and Barren Rivers (upper Green River drainage) of Kentucky, ranging southward slightly into Tennessee.

*E. (C.) barbouri* inhabits rocky or vegetated pools along the edges of small to medium upland streams, under leaf litter or amid vegetation below overhanging sandy banks and rarely in riffles. Its major foods are chironomids, copepods, blackfly and mayfly larvae, and cladocerans (*Daphnia* and relatives). It lives two years, breeding during its first in pools under stones during April and May at 55 to 60°F (Flynn and Hoyt 1979; Kuehne and Barbour 1983).

Dipnet, seine, or remove the entire flat, egg-laden rock from a leaf litter pool below undercut banks in small creeks. The egg patch should be aerated until the fry hatch; fry take *Artemia* nauplii as a first food, and are then easily raised. Wild adults do well in a sponge-filtered, 10-gallon aquarium on live *Daphnia* and frozen bloodworms, and should have a flat rock for possible spawning.

| | |
|---|---|
| *Etheostoma (Catonotus) striatulum*, striated darter | *E. (C.) striatulum* has eight dorsal spines. A dark bar occurs just behind and parallel to the upper edge of the gill cover (barcheek group); there are saddles on the back |

Striped darter, *Etheostoma virgatum,* Rock Castle R., Ky. WFR

and ten dark blotches along the side. Dark pigment along the horizontal plane on the center of each scale form up to eight distinct lines. The female is plain, barely or not at all lined; her fins are spotted but not colored; and a dark blotch appears in her spiny dorsal fin. The male is peach-yellow with a dark head and black pelvic fins, a dark blotch appears in his spiny dorsal fin, and his other fins are orange with black edges.

The striated darter occurs in streams of the upper Duck River system in Bedford, Marshall, and Maury Counties of Tennessee (Page and Braasch 1977).

*E. (C.) striatulum* is found beneath slab rocks in pools of slow-moving, small to medium streams, usually on bedrock but sometimes on gravel. It spawns at age one during April at 60 to 72°F, on the lower surface of flat stones in 4- to 20-inch-deep pools. Look for a single compact layer of 150 (25–325) 2 mm eggs (Page 1980).

The striated darter is rare; determine protection status prior to collection. If available, seek nests under flat rocks in pools. Then remove a portion of the eggs with a razor blade, and return the rock to the nesting male (in exactly the same location and position in which it was found). Eggs removed from a nest should be aerated in shallow water until hatching.

| | |
|---|---|
| *Etheostoma (Catonotus) virgatum,* striped darter | *E. (C.) virgatum* is similar to *E. (C.) striatulum,* but has nine dorsal spines (eight in the Collins River population), ten or more horizontal lines (less prominent in female), and blue-black on the pelvic fins and lower portions of the red anal and tail fins. Otherwise, the red in the spiny dorsal fin is restricted to the margin, and limited to rows of spots in the soft dorsal fin. It has a bicolored bar on the cheek, a dark shoulder spot, and ten midlateral blotches (Page and Braasch 1977; Page and Burr 1991).

The striped darter is found in the Rockcastle River and the Buck and Beaver Creek systems, all in the upper Cumberland River system. In the middle and lower Cumberland, it occurs only in the upper Caney Fork and tributaries from the Red to the Stones Rivers (Page and Braasch 1977).

*E. (C.) virgatum* inhabits slab-rock pools of small to large creeks. |
| *Etheostoma (Catonotus) smithi,* slabrock darter | *E. (C.) smithi* is a dusky member of the barcheek darter group, similar to *E. (C.) virgatum* in the dark edging of the lower tail and anal fins, but with ten prominent vertical bars rather than ten or more horizontal lines. The pectoral fins have a wide |

Fantail darter, *Etheostoma flabellare,* White R., Mo. WFR

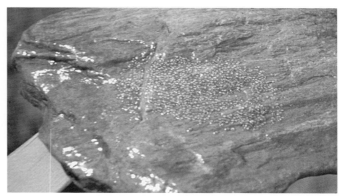

Fantail darter, *Etheostoma flabellare,* eggs on underside of flat rock, N.C. RJG

black margin. It is most similar to *E. (C.) obeyense,* but differs in the number of head pores (Page and Braasch 1976). It is usually less than 2 inches long.

The slabrock darter occurs in the lower Cumberland River (from near its mouth upstream to the Caney Fork) and in tributaries of the lower Tennessee River in Tennessee and Kentucky.

*E. (C.) smithi* inhabits slab-rock pools of slowly flowing headwater creeks or small rivers and lakes with slab-rock shores. The principal foods of adults are mayfly and chironomid larvae and some isopods, but the smallest juveniles feed mostly on copepods. The diet reflects the typical invertebrate populations of slab rocks in slow moving but unpolluted water.

Breeding is at its maximum during May at 59 to 68°F in fish over one year of age; few attain age two. Typical of the subgenus, 300 (175–600) 2 mm eggs are laid in a single compact layer on the flat roof of a rock cave and guarded by the male. At 70°F, eggs hatch in less than two weeks; eggs die at 40 or 80°F (Page and Burr 1976).

The *flabellare* group has knobs on the tips of its seven or eight dorsal spines and contains *flabellare, kennicotti,* and *percnurum.* Species in the *flabellare* and *virgatum* groups are further related by shared swollen ridges on the scales of the lower body (Mayden 1985).

---

*Etheostoma (Catonotus) flabellare,* fantail darter

*E. (C.) flabellare* has knobs on the dorsal spines and no red or blue colors. It is elongate and varies from dark green with horizontal black lines to light yellow with vertical dark bars. The caudal fin has concentric rows of black spots. The head of the nuptial male is black.

The fantail darter is widespread throughout the north-central region, ranging from southern Quebec southward along the Ohio and Mississippi drainages to northern Alabama. It extends eastward into Atlantic slope drainages of Virginia and the Carolinas, but does not reach the coast. It ranges westward from Quebec to Minnesota, and continues southward to Arkansas, Oklahoma, and Kansas. Throughout its range, it is among the most common darters of small streams.

The southeastern North Carolina and the South Carolina populations are *E. f. brevispina,* with a yellow body, dark vertical bars, and no horizontal lines on the flank. Just to the north, populations from the Cape Fear River to the Susquehanna River drainage basin are *E. f. humerale,* with black lower fins and dark bars on a yellow body as in the southern group. Populations in generally flat terrain northwest of the Mississippi River are usually dark green with horizontal black lines, and are *E. f. lineolata.* Finally, a variable population with bars and lines and in various shades of green occupies the remainder of the range east of the Mississippi River in the north and extending west of the Mississippi River only in the Ozark Plateau, and is referred to as *E. f. flabellare.* Most experts agree this arrangement is temporary, and future changes will occur in the taxonomy of this variable and widespread complex (probably a species group) we currently call *E. (C.) flabellare.*

The fantail darter is a typical and common occupant of small to large, clear, rocky streams. It usually occurs in swift, shallow riffles in larger streams, and in any riffle at all in small creeks. It is an opportunistic feeder, mostly on chironomid and some blackfly larvae, but also seasonally abundant mayfly, stonefly, caddisfly, and other insect larvae, and ostracods that live among the cracks in stones. It does not forage in mud, sand, or gravel for buried fare (Strange 1993). Its wide gape enables it to eat insect larvae too massive for the small mouths of other darters sharing the same habitat, and allows it to exploit small tributaries where the food supply may be specialized or size-limited (Matthews, Bek, and Surat 1982).

The fantail darter is a year-round resident of riffles and does not make a spawning migration (Ingersoll et al. 1984). The male occupies a nesting site beneath flat rocks on gravel and uses its spiny dorsal fin knobs to brush the roof of the flat rock cave to clear adhering debris, an activity most cavity nesting fishes accomplish with their mouths and lower fins. Breeding occurs from March through June when the water is in the mid-60s to mid-70s (°F). Each female may produce up to 200 eggs to a nest, with the egg patch extending more than 6 inches in diameter. The eggs are 2 mm and yellow at first, but gradually darken during the 10 to 12 days of development. The male fans the eggs and guards the nest until the 6.0 to 6.5 mm non-feeding, yolk-sac larvae hatch and disperse. The yolk sac is absorbed in one week, when the larva has attained 9 mm in length (Cooper 1979), but feeding probably begins well before.

A 10-gallon aquarium is suitable for one male and two or three females. Provide a flat rock on sand or gravel, and current from a cascading outside power filter or a submersed powerhead or water pump. Feed frozen bloodworms and adult brine shrimp, and some live tubifex or blackworms; fantail darters are not fussy. After spawning, the females or the egg-laden rock can be removed.

Winn (1958) and others accepted that egg rubbing by the spiny dorsal knobs of the male prevented infection of the eggs, but the knob tissue does not have antimicrobial activity (Bart and Page 1991). It is more likely that rubbing merely cleans the eggs of debris and perhaps grazing protozoa. The egg-laden rock can be removed and the eggs bathed in a stream of air bubbles until hatching. The fry should be offered *Artemia* nauplii and green water (motile algae) as first foods, but will survive on the nauplii alone.

*Etheostoma (Catonotus) kennicotti,*
stripetail darter

*E. (C.) kennicotti* has knobs on the dorsal spines of the male, three basicaudal spots (not readily seen), and no red or blue colors. The nuptial male develops a darkened head, brilliant orange knobs on the tips of the spiny dorsal fin, an orange belly, and white pelvic and anal fins; the concentric rows of black spots on the fins may be-

Stripetail darter, *Etheostoma kennicotti*, Big South Fork R., Tenn. WFR

come intense; and the head and nape become swollen as has been described for male *Noturus* madtoms. It resembles *E. flabellare humerale*, but is easily distinguished from all *E. (C.) flabellare* by the black submargin of the spiny dorsal fin, geographic location, and the high number (ten) of vertical dark bars on the flank. Other subtle characters include the occasional rows of dark spots on the barred flank [not present in barred *E. (C.) flabellare*] and head pore pattern characteristics cited in Page and Burr (1991), Kuehne and Barbour (1983), and Page (1983) that require microscopic examination.

The stripetail darter occurs primarily in Tennessee and Kentucky and just enters surrounding states. It is restricted to the Tennessee, upper Cumberland, Green, and portions of the Ohio River systems. It is absent from the Kentucky River system and much of the Tennessee system. Its distribution is influenced by the presence of other species within the subgenus *E. (Catonotus)* and within its own *flabellare* group. If no other *E. (Catonotus)* are present, it attains large size (> 3 in.). As more *E. (Catonotus)* species of the *virgatum* group occur, its numbers decline as well as its maximum size, and it may be the smallest *E. (Catonotus)* present under these circumstances. It does not occur where its closest relative and competitor, *E. (C.) flabellare* of the *flabellare* group, occurs (Page and Smith 1976).

*E. (C.) kennicotti* is found on slab rock, in shallow pools of small rivers and headwater creeks where there is little current. It is not usually a riffle species, but may enter riffles during spring and fall to feed on seasonally abundant insect larvae. The largest adults feed on chironomids, caddisflies, and alder flies (Megaloptera); smaller fish take mayflies, isopods, copepods, and other small animals. It lives more than two years but less than three, spawning during its first year; older and larger males are more successful than younger and smaller males. *E. (C.) kennicotti* is a derivative of *E. (C.) flabellare*, spawning sooner with eggs hatching sooner. It lives a shorter life and is restricted in geographic distribution and to pools rather than riffles.

The stripetail darter spawns on the roof of a cave between the gravel bottom of the shallow pool and a flat slab rock; spawning often occurs during April and May at 58 to 68°F. The female inverts on her side to spawn, and may hold the inverted position for a long time, while the male quickly assumes an upright position after each spawning clasp (probably to defend the nest). Eggs in a nest stimulate selection by subsequent females for the same nest (Page 1975b). Eggs held at 66 to

73°F in aquaria hatched in six days (Page 1975b). The yolk-sac fry are less than 5 mm at hatching, begin to develop pigment on the midline at 7 mm, and have the full complement of fins and considerable body pigment at 12 mm (Simon 1987).

| | |
|---|---|
| *Etheostoma (Catonotus) percnurum,* duskytail darter | *E. (C.) percnurum* males have knobs on the dorsal spines, three basicaudal spots (not readily seen), and no red or blue colors. A dozen dark vertical bars on the side, densely black-spotted cheeks, sharply black-edged anal and pectoral fins, and locality distinguish this species from other members of its group. The describer, Jenkins (in Jenkins and Burkhead 1994) called it "the most drab darter in Virginia." |

The duskytail darter occurs in Copper Creek and the Clinch River of Virginia, and has been mostly extirpated from Citico Creek, Abrams Creek, South Fork Holston River, and Big South Fork Cumberland River in Tennessee (Jenkins and Burkhead 1994). A good population remains upstream of the SR 33 bridge on the Little River.

Downstream (reverse) seining and kicking in shallow, rocky pools is more effective than the normal stationary seine method, in which kickers work from an upstream location down to the fixed net. It is the only *E. (Catonotus)* restricted to larger streams and major rivers.

*E. (C.) percnurum* inhabits shallow, slab-rock pools with moderate to slow current. Spawning occurs under flat rocks during May and June. About 90 (40–200) 3 mm eggs occur in each nest.

If state agencies will permit captive breeding, use the method employed by Layman (1984). A 15-gallon aquarium with gravel and flat rocks accommodated two males and a female collected during early March. They spawned one month later at 55 to 75°F after being maintained on a diet of chopped earthworms and mosquito larvae. The female remained inverted [see *E. (C.) kennicotti*] for three to five hours during spawning. The huge, brilliant yellow-orange knobs on the tips of the spiny dorsal fin of the nuptial male are indistinguishable from eggs on the roof of the nest.

Jenkins and Burkhead (1994) reported that this rare fish is protected in Tennessee and Virginia and is a good candidate for federal protection.

The spottail darter or *squamiceps* group *(corona, chienense, crossopterum, forbesi, neopterum, nigripinne, olivaceum, oophylax, pseudovulatum,* and *squamiceps)* have three basicaudal spots (not always distinct), no red and blue pigmentation or bicolored bar on the cheek, and no knobs on the eight or nine dorsal spines. There are two subgroups, one with knobs (egg mimics) and the other with a fringe (brushy branching) on the rays of the second (soft) dorsal fin.

Spawning occurs either in slab pools or riffles above the gravel on the undersurface of a flat rock (cave roof), the nest defended by the male. Species spawning in slab pools typically occur with no other kinds of *E. (Catonotus);* those spawning in riffles tend to share this habitat with other *E. (Catonotus)* species (Page and Schemske 1978).

| | |
|---|---|
| *Etheostoma (Catonotus) squamiceps,* spottail darter | *E. (C.) squamiceps* has three branches on each ray of the second dorsal fin, the second and third adnate (adhering to one another) and ending in a small white knob at the tip in the nuptial male. The head of the nuptial male is black.<br><br>The spottail darter occurs in the lower Ohio River system, including the |

Spottail darter, *Etheostoma squamiceps,* Green R., Ky. WFR

Spottail darter, *Etheostoma squamiceps,* Cumberland R., Tenn. WFR

Cache River in Illinois, both the Green and Red Rivers in Kentucky and Tennessee, and the Wabash in Indiana (Page et al. 1992).

*E. (C.) squamiceps* inhabits clean, permanent small streams with abundant slab rocks. Silt, agricultural pollution, oil spills, and the periodic drying of portions of streams (due to lowering of the water table) all degrade habitat sufficiently to eliminate this species (Page et al. 1976). Adults occupy riffles in July and quiet pools during the rest of the year, wherever slab rocks occur. Juveniles frequently occupy slab-rock areas on riffles. A catholic and opportunistic feeder at all ages, the diet consists mostly of chironomid larvae supplemented with seasonally available mayflies, other aquatic insect larvae, and crustaceans.

The male sweeps silt and sand from beneath the flat rocks to create caves as nesting sites. The male is aggressive and will even drive off crayfishes. *E. (C.) squamiceps* spawns during April and May at 56 to 66°F. The male leaves its cave to court females in the area, and displays with color changes, erect fins, and tail beating. The female enters the cave, and picks a deposition site on the roof with her snout, rolls over, and deposits two to five eggs. As the female rolls, the male inverts alongside and ejaculates sperm simultaneously with oviposition by the female. Both then turn upright until the next egg-laying 15 minutes later.

Several females may spawn with one male, and the 2 mm eggs in the nest may number 450 (100–1500). At 68°F, the eggs hatch in 12 days; hatching takes half the time at 75°F. Soon after hatching, the 6 mm larvae hide in gravel (Page 1974b). By the time they reach 14 mm, all the fins have developed and pigment covers most of the body (Simon 1987).

Care as for *E. (C.) flabellare* and *E. (Boleosoma) olmstedi.* A 10-gallon aquarium is suitable for two males and four females. Include a flat rock, a gravel substratum, and sponge filtration. Feed frozen bloodworms supplemented with frozen adult and live baby brine shrimp. The rock with eggs can be removed to another aquarium for hatching over aeration and another rock substituted, or the adults can be moved to another aquarium after the eggs hatch. The fry take *Artemia* nauplii as a first food.

---

*Etheostoma (Catonotus) corona,*
crown darter

In *E. (C.) corona,* the tips of alternating rays in the second dorsal fin have two and three long yellow branches. The yellow branches have been likened to the teeth of a king's golden crown. Its caudal fin is dark with yellow bands, and all other fins are black. It grows to 3 inches (Page et al. 1992).

The crown darter occurs in the Cypress Creek system of northwestern Alabama and extends into southern Tennessee.

*E. (C.) corona* inhabits slab-rock pools of small creeks.

| | |
|---|---|
| *Etheostoma (Catonotus) chienense*, relict darter | *E. (C.) chienense* has a small white knob at the tip of each double-branched ray in the second dorsal fin. The fins are generally black, but concentric yellow bands appear in the tail fin (Page et al. 1992).<br><br>The relict darter is known from just a few sites within the Bayou de Chien, a sandy Coastal Plain–type drainage in Kentucky.<br><br>*E. (C.) chienense* is at risk due to water quality impacts from stream damming, siltation, other pollutants attributable to poor land and farm management, and construction in the watershed.<br><br>The relict darter is a federally protected species and is not available. A group under a U.S. Fish and Wildlife Service permit is attempting to propagate this fish for reintroduction to historic streams from which it has disappeared. |
| *Etheostoma (Catonotus) crossopterum*, fringed darter | *E. (C.) crossopterum* has three branches at the tip of each ray in the second dorsal fin, the third branch elongated. The second (soft) dorsal fin is black with a white fringe. Otherwise, it is similar to other members of this spottail darter group. It grows to over 3 inches (Page et al. 1992).<br><br>The fringed darter is wide-ranging from Bear Creek and Obion River tributaries of the Mississippi River to portions of the Cumberland, Duck, Buffalo, and Shoal Rivers of Tennessee, Alabama and Kentucky.<br><br>*E. (C.) crossopterum* is found in slab-rock pools in waters ranging from creeks to medium-sized rivers. |
| *Etheostoma (Catonotus) forbesi*, Barrens darter | *E. (C.) forbesi* has three yellow branches at the tip of each ray in the black second dorsal fin, the first branch short and separate from the longer and adnate (attached) second and third branches. The nuptial male is colored similarly to other members of the group, black with yellow bands in the tail fin (Page et al. 1992). It grows to 2¾ inches.<br><br>The Barrens darter occurs in slab-rock pools of creeks in tributaries of Barren Fork, in the Collins River of the Caney Fork drainage in Cannon County, Tennessee.<br><br>*E. (C.) forbesi* has been recommended for federal protection. Inquire of state game and fish personnel before conducting collections of any darters in Barren Fork. If available, handle like *E. (C.) squamiceps*. The Barrens darter is a good candidate for captive breeding. |
| *Etheostoma (Catonotus) neopterum*, lollypop darter | *E. (C.) neopterum* has a yellow knob at the tip of each doubled ray in the second dorsal fin. The tail fin is black with ten concentric yellow bands. It attains 2¼ inches.<br><br>The lollypop darter occurs in the Shoal Creek system at the Alabama-Tennessee border, in slab-rock pools of small, clear, unpolluted creeks. |
| *Etheostoma (Catonotus) nigripinne*, blackfin darter | *E. (C.) nigripinne* has three branches at the tip of each ray in the second dorsal fin, the first branch short and separate from the longer, adnate (attached) second and third branches. There are eight dorsal spines. The second dorsal fin is black to the |

Lollypop darter, *Etheostoma neopterum*, Shoal Cr., Ala. WFR

edge with no knobs at the tips. Three basicaudal spots are fused into a bar. The tail fin is black with yellow concentric rings.

The blackfin darter is widely distributed in Tennessee River tributaries from Cub and Cypress Creeks in Tennessee to the Flint and Paint Rock Rivers in Tennessee and Alabama. It is also in the Duck River system. It is absent from Cypress Creek and most of Shoal Creek in Tennessee (Page et al. 1992).

*E. (C.) nigripinne* is always in slab-rock pools of medium to large rivers.

| | |
|---|---|
| *Etheostoma (Catonotus) olivaceum,* sooty or dirty darter | *E. (C.) olivaceum* is olive to dark green, greenish black in the nuptial male. It is the only member of this group with four white branches (forming a continuous fringe) at the tip of each of the 12 or 13 rays in the black second dorsal fin; a few rows of golden crescent-shaped marks occur between the rays deep in the fin. It has a dark tail fin with five to nine concentric rows of gold crescents forming wavy lines. It grows up to 2½ inches (Braasch and Page 1979). |

*E. (C.) olivaceum* occurs in small tributaries of the Cumberland River and lower Caney Fork system in central Tennessee (Braasch and Page 1979).

The sooty darter inhabits shallow (sometimes < 2 in.) pools of small slab-rock and bedrock creeks. It feeds mostly on midge (bloodworm) and mayfly larvae, other insect larvae, and small invertebrates. It breeds at age one during April and May on the roof of a cave under flat rocks, tiles, and tin cans and other smooth-surface trash. Five hundred 2 mm eggs from multiple females may form a single compact layer over a large surface (Page 1980).

| | |
|---|---|
| *Etheostoma (Catonotus) oophylax,* guardian darter | *E. (C.) oophylax* has eight spines in the first dorsal fin and a large, yellow knob at the far tip of each elongated ray in the second dorsal fin. Otherwise, it is similar to *E. (C.) pseudovulatum*. It grows to 2¾ inches (Page et al. 1992). |

The guardian darter occurs in lower Tennessee River tributaries (except Duck Creek) from Perry and Decatur Counties in Tennessee to the Ohio River.

*E. (C.) oophylax* inhabits slab-rock pools in waters ranging from creeks to medium-sized rivers.

| | |
|---|---|
| *Etheostoma (Catonotus) pseudovulatum,* egg-mimic darter | *E. (C.) pseudovulatum* has a large, yellow knob (an egg mimic) at the tip of each ray in the second dorsal fin. The fins of the nuptial male are black and the tail fin has concentric yellow rings. It grows to 2½ inches (Page et al. 1992). |

The egg-mimic darter is limited to Piney River, Beaverdam Creek, Little Piney Creek, and Happy Hollow Creek, all tributaries of the Duck River in Tennessee.

E. (C.) pseudovulatum is found in slab-rock pools of creeks and small rivers.

## Subgenus *Etheostoma (Etheostoma)*

Members of *E. (Etheostoma)* have a completely pored lateral line and large pectoral fins; the upper lip is unattached above or has a thin frenum; they have a broad and blunt head and four to seven conspicuous dorsal saddles, the first well back from the nape. There are five groups in this subgenus. The *sellare* group contains just *E. (E.) sellare,* the Maryland darter, based on a scale pattern and head shape unlike other saddled darters. Stephens et al. (1994) suggested the subgenus *Mooreichthys* for this species, but did not publish a diagnosis for that name.

## *Etheostoma (Etheostoma) sellare,* Maryland darter

E. (E.) sellare is robust and moderately sized, with four bold saddles extending below the lateral line. It is mostly tan and brown, with yellow in the fins and an orange mark at the base of the pelvic fin.

The Maryland darter was previously known from a few locales at the north end of Chesapeake Bay in small, sand and gravel streams at riffles (Knapp et al. 1963). It is the only saddled darter in its geographic area. Urbanization of Chesapeake Bay and changes in hydrology of the Susquehanna watershed has eliminated whatever earlier habitat existed.

Kuehne and Barbour (1983) stated, "Artificial propagation and stocking of the Maryland darter are justifiable, since otherwise it is only a matter of time before some chance pollution event wipes out the species." The U.S. Fish & Wildlife Service may have delayed action too long.

E. (E.) sellare is a rare and endangered (if not extinct) species. It cannot be collected and is unlikely to be seen.

The *variatum* group *(variatum, euzonum, tetrazonum, kanawhae,* and *osburni)* all have a slightly produced snout, four major dorsal saddles, nuptial tubercles in both sexes, and a spiny dorsal fin with a red edge and black or white submargins. They are all gravel spawners. They are most abundant in big rivers that are difficult to seine due to depth or current. Their agility often outperforms the agility of collectors trying to hold their nets and balance on slippery, diatom-covered rocks in a raging current. They are also difficult to keep in good health and to spawn in captivity, but it has been done. Their extraordinary beauty makes the effort worthwhile.

## *Etheostoma (Etheostoma) variatum,* variegate darter

E. (E.) variatum (**plate 66**) has four saddles that extend downward and forward to the lateral line on a dark blue-green to green body. Six orange lines occur on the flank in the rear half of the body, behind the orange breast. It is darker than *E. (E.) kanawhae,* and not nearly as colorful as *E. (E.) osburni,* related species found near its upstream limits of distribution. It is most similar to *E. (E.) tetrazonum* of Missouri.

The variegate darter ranges from the Kentucky, Whitewater, and Blue Rivers (Ohio River drainage) to the New River and other headwaters of the Monongahela and Allegheny Rivers, going from extreme western New York and western Pennsylvania through Ohio, Kentucky, and West Virginia to southern Indiana (Kuehne and Barbour 1983).

E. (E.) variatum occurs in larger rivers, avoiding headwaters and creeks. It migrates downstream to deeper pools in midwinter when temperatures on the riffles approach freezing, and returns to riffles during spring. It occupies clean sand behind boulders, and spawns when temperatures exceed 50°F during April and May.

A 29-gallon aquarium with strong flow from powerheads, large rocks, and 1 inch of sand will maintain six fish. Feed heavily on frozen bloodworms and moderately on blackworms, and change one-third of the water or more twice a week.

The female darts up into the water column to get the attention of males, then descends to a selected sandy bottom where she buries her head and is mounted slightly crosswise by a male. Eggs are buried in sand and hatch in two weeks; larvae are planktonic for four to six weeks, but are able to consume *Artemia* nauplii during this time and are raised easily (Kuehne and Barbour 1983). Unless newly captured adult fish are fed immediately with live blackworms and frozen *Artemia* and bloodworms, preferably in the company of darters already accustomed to feeding in aquaria, they may refuse to feed in captivity.

---

*Etheostoma (Etheostoma) kanawhae,*
Kanawha darter

*E. (E.) kanawhae* **(plate 67)** is a pretty fish with an orange breast and belly, a yellow mark on the cheek, ten thin red-orange bands on the flank, and blue-green and orange pigmentation over much of the body and fins. Page and Burr (1991) illustrated the Kanawha darter with orange in the middle of the anal fin, a character not found in *E. (E.) osburni;* whether this is a real difference or an unintentional distinction by the artist is unknown. For those with dissecting microscopes, *E. (E.) kanawhae* has larger and fewer scales than *E. (E.) osburni.* It is typically 2½–3 inches.

The Kanawha darter is identified mostly by its precise geographic range in the upper New River (above Kanawha Falls) in western North Carolina and Carroll County, Virginia. In Carroll County, it occurs in Big Reed Island Creek where it empties into the New River; on the opposite side of the river is Reed Creek, which contains the closely related and similar *E. (E.) osburni.* Other records in Virginia include Little Reed Island Creek (Carroll County), Crooked Creek, Snake Creek, Chestnut Creek, and the West Fork of the Little River in Floyd and Grayson Counties (Raney 1941).

---

*Etheostoma (Etheostoma) osburni,*
candy or finescale saddled darter

*E. (E.) osburni* **(plate 68)** has five dark saddles above, alternating red and green lines on the flank, and a bright orange belly with pigment extending onto the gill cover to join the forward bands on the flank. The fins are brightly colored; the spiny dorsal fin has a red edge; the soft dorsal, pectoral, and tail fins have rows of red spots; and the anal fin has a red submargin. It is beautiful and ". . . may be [the] most vivid freshwater fish in North America" (Page and Burr 1991). The average adult length is 3 inches.

The candy darter occurs in the lower (northern) half of the New River drainage in West Virginia and Virginia, downstream of Reed Creek. Upstream (southward) of the Greenbrier and New River confluence, it is replaced by *E. (E.) kanawhae,* which extends into North Carolina. Kanawha Falls on the New River has prevented *E. (E.) variatum,* widespread in the Ohio River drainage, from invading the upper part of the New (= Kanawha) system occupied by both *E. (E.) osburni* and *E. (E.) kanawhae* (McKeown et al. 1984); all three species are closely related.

*E. (E.) osburni* inhabits clear, medium to large, fast-flowing rivers in shallow but violent, rubble riffles and boulder-strewn pools to 3 feet deep (Kuehne and

Barbour 1983), a difficult habitat in which to seine. It has spawned in gravel while in captivity at 58°F (Katula 1991a).

The candy darter may be protected. Inquire of West Virginia and Virginia agencies before attempting collection.

---

*Etheostoma (Etheostoma) tetrazonum,*
Missouri saddled darter

*E. (E.) tetrazonum* (**plate 69**) has four dark saddles on the back that extend down and forward toward the lateral line. The male has an iridescent blue-green flank, an orange belly, a blue-green breast, and orange and green vertical lines alternating on the side. The fins are equally colorful. The female is similarly marked but far less colorful. It commonly grows to 3 inches.

The Missouri saddled darter occurs in the northern Ozarks of Missouri from the Pomme de Terre and Niangua (Osage River) and Moreau Rivers in the west to the Meramec River in the east (Pflieger 1975). The only similar darter in the Ozarks is the Arkansas saddled darter, *E. (E.) euzonum,* which is much larger, not as brightly colored, has a larger head, and occurs in the southern Ozarks.

*E. (E.) tetrazonum* inhabits the deep riffles and rocky runs of larger, clear, fast-flowing rivers.

The Missouri saddled darter breeds from late March when the water temperature is in the mid-50s (°F) through July; the activity sometimes is interrupted by spring flooding. The spawning site is thought to be gravel behind large rocks in riffles. The male matures at age two or three and females at age one. Maximum life expectancy is just over four years (Taber and Taber 1983).

Care as for *E. (Oligocephalus) caeruleum* and *E. (N.) juliae.* Feed frozen bloodworms, supplemented with live blackworms, whiteworms, and frozen adult brine shrimp. *E. (E.) tetrazonum* is not spawned easily in aquaria, but adults can be stripped for eggs and milt during the spring. The 2 mm eggs are clear and sticky and hatch in six days at 73°F (Taber and Taber 1983).

---

*Etheostoma (Etheostoma) euzonum,*
Arkansas saddled darter

*E. (E.) euzonum* (**plate 70**) has a large head and eyes. The snout is depressed and the dull tan body is elongate. The most striking character, other than its large size, is the group of four bold saddles that extend down and forward from the back to the midflank; there are no lateral bars or blotches, with saddles occupying that space. The nuptial male has widely spaced, thin orange vertical lines and spots along the lower and central flank; the belly and chest are orange. The spiny dorsal fin is orange-edged; the soft dorsal and tail fins are orange-spotted. The breeding male is the least colorful member of this group. The Arkansas saddled darter is also the largest member of its group, commonly attaining 4 inches.

Two subspecies are recognized based on river system, shape of the snout (elongate or blunt), and scales on the cheek and breast. This darter is restricted to southward flowing White River tributaries of the Missouri River on the Ozark Plateau of Missouri and Arkansas. *E. e. euzonum* is western, in the extreme upper White, lower White, Buffalo, North Fork, and Little Red Rivers; it has the blunter snout. *E. e. erizonum* occurs in the Current River system to the east. Intergrades occur in the Black River below the Current River (Strawberry, Spring, and Fourche Rivers). The subspecies were separated when the Black River, which originally flowed into the Mississippi, was diverted and began flowing directly into the White (Page and Cordes 1983). The Black and White Rivers meet on the Coastal Plain-like lowlands of the upper Mississippi embayment, a barrier to this upland species.

The Arkansas saddled darter inhabits rocky riffles and rock and boulder-strewn runs of fast-flowing, medium-sized rivers, usually at depths of 1 foot or more. Although locally abundant, I have never taken more than three individuals in a seine haul, and usually not even one. It prefers a neutral to slightly alkaline pH and a temperature of 60 to 75°F. *E. (E.) euzonum* has spawned in captivity at 60 to 68°F, but is difficult to breed.

A 29-gallon aquarium will support four males and ten females. Cover the bottom with gravel; plants are optional, but omit large rocks (they take up too much surface). Supply current from one end by the effluent of an outside power filter or a submersed powerhead. Feed only live foods such as *Daphnia* and whiteworms. The fish has a small mouth and cannot take earthworms or euphausiid shrimp, and often ignores dead foods which then foul the water.

*E. (E.) euzonum* is a gravel spawner. Each male establishes a territory over a section of bottom. Males threaten each other but rarely battle. As the females pass in and out of the territories, they are courted by the males. When a female remains in a territory, the male begins to undulate, stirring the gravel and litter on the bottom. The excited female joins alongside the male who mounts her and a few short, jerky, undulations occur.

The eggs are deposited on the gravel surface, some of them picked up and carried by the current. Group spawning lasts until all females lose interest, and the males then abandon their spawning territories. Adults should be transferred to another aquarium after spawning, and the power filter or powerhead turned off to prevent injury to the fry. Eggs hatch in 14 days at 70°F. The fry require small foods, such as ciliates, rotifers, infusoria, microworms, vinegar eels, or ostracods; *Artemia* nauplii are not attractive to either the fry or juveniles and will die uneaten (and could foul the tank).

The *thalassinum* group *(thalassinum, blennius, swannanoa,* and *inscriptum)* have a short snout, nuptial tubercles in the male only, six or seven saddles (but four in *blennius),* and a spiny dorsal fin with a rusty margin and no submargin. Their spawning modes are not completely known.

---

*Etheostoma (Etheostoma) inscriptum,* turquoise darter

E. (E.) inscriptum **(plate 71)** has six dorsal blotches that extend back to the base of the tail fin. The scales on the flank have tiny dark red centers that form horizontal rows of dots. The body is colored various shades of green with six dark blotches on the flank; the face, cheek, and breast are turquoise; the belly is white but not immaculate; there is a dark teardrop; and a black band (prepectoral spot) occurs at the base of the pectoral fins. The unpaired fins are turquoise at the base and red toward the outside (Richards 1966; Rohde et al. 1994).

The turquoise darter occurs in the Ocmulgee and Oconee Rivers (Altamaha River system) and Savannah River in the Piedmont and occasionally the upper Coastal Plain of Georgia, and in the Edisto and Ogeechee Rivers of South Carolina.

*E. (E.) inscriptum* inhabits large creeks and small rivers in the Piedmont, in gravel and rubble or bedrock riffles near large stones in water 2 to 12 inches deep. It is presumed to feed on midges and other aquatic insects and to spawn during April and May, but the spawning mode is unknown (Kuehne and Barbour 1983).

Swannanoa darter, *Etheostoma swannanoa*, Swannanoa R., Tenn. WFR

Seagreen darter, *Etheostoma thalassinum*, Santee R., N.C. WFR

*Etheostoma (Etheostoma) swannanoa,*
Swannanoa darter

*E. (E.) swannanoa* has six square dorsal blotches that do not expand downward in the manner of saddles. The body is green above, on the flank, and below. Ten blotches on the flank are reduced to narrow vertical bars toward the front. Scale centers on the flank are red, forming prominent rows of red spots. The spiny dorsal fin is orange at the base and submarginally. The pectoral fins are overall green but orange at the base in nuptial fish of both sexes. The head is green with a dark bar through the eye. It grows to 2¾ inches (Richards 1966).

The Swannanoa darter occurs in the Tennessee and North Carolina mountains and extends into western Virginia. It is found in the Tennessee River system, sporadically in the headwater Clinch, Holston, Watauga, Nolichucky, and Swannanoa Rivers, and more commonly in the French Broad (Richards 1966).

*E. (E.) swannanoa* inhabits medium to large, fast-flowing clear mountain rivers, occurring among boulders and large rocks on gravel-rubble riffles. These habitats are fast disappearing beneath new reservoirs or have suffered nutrient loading from industrial wastewater and agricultural discharges. Food habits are unknown. Breeding habits also are unknown, but the Swannanoa darter probably spawns during April and May in riffles 1 foot deep (Kuehne and Barbour 1983). It is a fairly large darter, up to 3 inches, requiring strong current, depth, and clean, cool water.

A 29-gallon aquarium is recommended for three to six fish, with a coarse gravel bottom, pebbles, and large rocks.

*Etheostoma (Etheostoma)*
*thalassinum,* seagreen darter

*E. (E.) thalassinum* is tan to green; the dorsum has seven dark blotches (not saddles), the last on the base of the tail fin. Nine dark bars on the flank, green in the nuptial male, extend all the way to the base of the anal fin or even onto the belly. Scattered dull red spots on the flank do not form lines. Dark marks surround the eye, with another at the front base of the pectoral fin (prepectoral spot). The spiny dorsal fin has a thin white margin and a broad orange band below; the soft dorsal and tail fins are spotted; the tail fin is dark at its base, orange outside and adjacent, and green above and below; the anal fin is green (Richards 1966).

The seagreen darter occurs in the Congaree and Wateree-Catawba drainages, two widely separated arms of the Santee River (above and below the gradually sloping fall line of South Carolina and above the steep fall line in North Carolina).

*E. (E.) thalassinum* inhabits rocky creeks and rivers, often among submersed branches or around rocks. I collected seagreen darters by backpack electroshocker

Blenny darter, *Etheostoma blennius,* Buffalo R., Tenn. WFR

in Peters Creek near Spartanburg, South Carolina during a preconstruction environmental survey in 1967, and followed up with benthic macroinvertebrate studies during and post-construction. This stream was 15 to 25 feet wide and 1½ to 3 feet deep, with a rock, coarse sand, and gravel bottom, with riffles, pools, and silt behind the large rocks. Vegetation was primarily thick algal growth on large rocks. The dominant predator was *Lepomis auritus.* Caddisflies (30%) and midges (53%) made up most of the benthic macroinvertebrates before a wastewater discharge system was installed, while caddisflies, midges, craneflies, and oligochaetes (tubificids) made up 54 percent after the discharge began operating. The increase in tubificids and proportional decrease in aquatic insects was associated with silt brought in by construction. Subsequent study showed stream recovery, and no deleterious effects from the discharge of treated wastewater.

Care as for related riffle-inhabiting darters such as *E. (E.) blennius,* but the spawning mode ( e.g., in gravel, on algae) is unknown.

---

*Etheostoma (Etheostoma) blennius,* blenny darter

*E. (E.) blennius* is robust in front with a snub-nosed snout and a body that tapers behind; four blue-black saddles may fuse with seven to nine dark blotches on the flank, or the blotches may fade in the breeding male; the scales on the flank have red centers, giving a red-spotted appearance; the dorsal fins are red to purple; the spiny dorsal fin has a submarginal red-orange band and the soft dorsal fin has a white margin; the mouth and lips are blue-green; the breast is blue-black to purple. The female is not as brightly colored (overall greener). It grows to 2½ inches.

The eastern subspecies, *E. b. sequatchiense,* has dark lines on the upper sides, is slightly smaller than the western subspecies, *E. b. blennius,* and has slightly fewer scales along the lateral line (Burr 1979b).

The blenny darter occurs in tributaries of the Tennessee River system in Tennessee and northern Alabama. The western *E. b. blennius* occurs in White Oak Creek, the upper and lower (but not middle) Duck River, and Buffalo River (all in Tennessee), and in Cypress-Shoal Creek in Alabama and Tennessee. The eastern *E. b. sequatchiense* occurs in the Sequatchie River of Tennessee. Intergrades occur in Second Creek and the Elk River on the Alabama-Tennessee border (Burr 1979b).

*E. (E.) blennius* inhabits rocky, fast-flowing creeks and small, clear rivers. It feeds on aquatic insect larvae, mostly midges and mayflies, and some blackflies. It spawns during March and April on fast gravel and rubble riffles following a period of cold temperatures. It lives two to three years (Burr 1979b; Kuehne and Barbour 1983).

Place captive fish in outdoor pools during the winter and bring them inside early in spring. A 55-gallon aquarium with a gravel bottom, a few rocks at the outside margins, and a temperature of 68°F will support three males and eight females. The aquarium should be mostly free of structure; the large gravel area is required for spawning. Provide moderate current with a submersed powerhead or the effluent from an outside power filter. Condition with abundant daphnia, bloodworms, earthworms, blackworms, and mosquito larvae.

The blenny darter spawns over shallow pits excavated by the male. A female is lured into the pit by an elaborate display or dance. The male aligns alongside the female, eggs released and fertilized with each clasp. Spawning continues from several hours to a few days. When it begins, the power filters should be turned off to prevent eggs from being captured by the filter. Adults should be removed after spawning.

Eggs hatch in ten days at 70°F. The fry require rotifers, infusoria, or ciliates; brine shrimp nauplii are too large, die uneaten, and foul the water, killing the fry.

The *blennioides* group *(blennioides, lynceum, rupestre, histrio,* and *zonale)* have a snubnosed snout, usually no tubercles in either sex, six or seven saddles, typically four basicaudal spots, and a green band in the margin and a red band at the base of the spiny dorsal fin. They are plant spawners.

| | |
|---|---|
| *Etheostoma (Etheostoma) blennioides,* greenside darter | E. (E.) blennioides **(plate 72)** is a complex of species. The snout, with its covered premaxilla, distinguishes it from all other darters. On the head, the skin completely covers the upper lip or premaxilla; the head seems to end at the teeth with no intervening ring of tissue. The lower jaw is normal, with a clearly distinguishable lip. The greenside is elongate, robust in the forward part of the body. Overall, the body is white, speckled with black on the upper flank, and the dorsal fin is distinctly green-edged on the outside and red-edged at its base. A black zigzag or U-pattern of dark marks appears on the side, and bright green vertical bars occur in the nuptial male. The saddles are not prominent. The blunt head with an inferior mouth resembles the snubnosed darters (subgenus *Ulocentra),* but they are much smaller (usually 2 inches or half the length of *E. (E.) blennioides).* The greenside darter is among the largest *E. (Etheostoma),* frequently more than 4 inches. |

There are four subspecies, based on the presence or absence of a weak frenum, the extent of scales over the gill cover and belly, and the scale and fin ray counts. The subspecies have distinct distributions (although intergrades occur where they meet) (Schwartz 1965; Miller 1968; Denoncourt, Potter, and Stauffer 1977), and some will be elevated to species rank.

*E. b. newmani* occurs from southern Virginia and western North Carolina through Tennessee and northern Alabama, ranging across the Mississippi River to the Ozark Plateau of southern Missouri, Arkansas, and Oklahoma. It occurs in most of the Tennessee River and Cumberland River drainages east of the Mississippi River, and west of the Mississippi in the St. Francis, Arkansas, upper White, Current-Black, Saline, and Ouachita Rivers. This subspecies will be elevated to species rank.

*E. b. gutselli* occurs only in the southeastern corner of the range occupied by *E. b. newmani,* at the headwaters of the Little Tennessee River and a few tributaries of the Pigeon River in western North Carolina, mostly in Oconaluftee and Tuckasegee Creeks on the Little Tennessee, and Johnathan's and Richland Creeks of the Pigeon River. In the Hiwassee River of North Carolina, it hybridizes with *E. b. newmani.* This subspecies also will be elevated to species rank.

*E. b. blennioides* ranges through the Ohio River valley from western New York south to western Virginia, and continues westward through West Virginia, Pennsylvania, Ohio, and Kentucky. It is generally north and east of *E. b. newmani.* Its river range is from the upper Genesee River of New York and the Potomac River of Maryland westward and southward through the Ohio basin, including the Salt, Allegheny, Monongahela, Kentucky, Miami, Big Sandy, Kanawha, and Scioto Rivers.

*E. b. pholidotum* is the most northerly of the group, and is disjunct on both sides of the Mississippi River. One race occurs north of *E. b. blennioides* in the southern drainages of the Great Lakes and extends into the Mohawk and Wabash Rivers of western New York, Michigan, Indiana, and northern Ohio. The other occurs in the Osage and other tributaries of the Missouri River in Missouri and eastern Kansas. In central Missouri, it hybridizes with the Ozarkian *E. b. newmani* (Miller 1968).

The greenside darter inhabits fast-flowing, clear waters in medium-sized creeks to large rivers, typically on shallow rock or cobble riffles with attached vegetation (usually not in pools, in emergent vegetation, or in backwaters). It is most common among algae-covered rocks in the shallowest and swiftest riffles. A catholic feeder, it takes mostly chironomids of the subfamily Orthocladiinae (95% of its diet), with notable amounts of mayflies and caddisflies (10%) and lesser amounts of beetles, worms, and small crustaceans (Turner 1921; Hlohowsky and White 1983). In nature, it spawns in vegetation, typically *Cladophora, Myriophyllum,* and *Fontinalis* (Winn 1958), and has been suggested to spawn in sand where vegetation is absent (Schwartz 1965).

Provide at least a 10-gallon aquarium for one or two males and two or three females. Feed frozen bloodworms and brine shrimp, supplemented with blackworms, daphnia, chopped earthworms, whiteworms, or amphipods. Spawning occurs at 65 to 72°F or less, but this probably varies with the collection locale and whether the fish were in full spawning condition immediately before capture during late winter or early spring.

I provided an artificial algal riffle by lowering the water level in the aquarium and tying a spawning mop to an outside power filter so that the filaments were in the return flow from the filter as water cascaded back to the aquarium. The dominant (largest and most colorful) male spawned with the females in the mop fibers. The large, 2 mm eggs were removed from the mop and incubated in a jar of well-aerated and clean water. The large, newly hatched fry took *Artemia* nauplii at once, growing rapidly but at different rates. Sallie Boggs spawned them in a bare, aerated tank filled with *Vesicularia* (java moss), so artificial riffles are not essential (S. Boggs, pers. comm.).

| | |
|---|---|
| *Etheostoma (Etheostoma) rupestre,* rock darter | *E. (E.) rupestre* is almost identical to *E. (E.) blennioides,* but has a clear upper lip, six small dorsal blotches, four spots rather than two blotches at the base of the tail fin, and only seven green bands on the side. It attains less than 3 inches. |

Banded darter, *Etheostoma zonale,* White R., Missouri. WFR

The rock darter occurs in the Mobile River drainage. Two races (Tsai 1968b) were formerly considered subspecies (Tsai 1967). The northern race occurs in the Tallapoosa, Cahaba, and upper Coosa Rivers of the Alabama River system in the mountains of northern Georgia, ranging southward into the Coastal Plain of central and eastern Alabama; it is occasionally above (as in the Etowah) but usually below the fall line. The southern race occurs just below the fall line in the Black Warrior, Sipsey, and other upper tributaries of the Tombigbee River drainage in western and southern Alabama, and just enters northeastern Mississippi. Intergrades occur in the North River (Black Warrior system); subspecies status for the two races is not appropriate (Tsai 1968b).

E. (E.) rupestre inhabits rocky riffles of medium to large rivers. Breeding occurs during March and April (Tsai 1968b), presumably on algal strands on rocks in riffles, as in *E. (E.) blennioides.*

*Etheostoma (Etheostoma) zonale,* banded darter

E. (E.) zonale (**plate 73**) is smaller than *E. blennioides* and has dark, iridescent green bars all the way to the belly that are contiguous with those of the other side; the green bars are wider than the light interbar spaces. Dark blotches occur along the lateral line within the interbar spaces (Page and Burr 1991). It is similar to *E. (E.) lynceum,* but the female has fine speckling and no saddles or bands. It grows to 2½ inches.

There are three separate populations, with two consisting of numerous races. The population in the highlands east of the Mississippi River consists of an Ohio River race ranging from Pennsylvania through Ohio to Indiana, and continuing southward to West Virginia and eastern Kentucky. Several Tennessee River races occur southward through the southern Appalachians to Tennessee, including the mountains of the Carolinas, Georgia, and Alabama. These races may represent new species (Tsai and Raney 1974). West of the Mississippi, the northern population is a single race occurring west and south of Lake Michigan in Wisconsin, Minnesota, Iowa, northern Indiana, and Illinois. Four southwestern races comprise the third population in the Ozark Plateau of Missouri, Arkansas, Oklahoma, and Kansas (Tsai and Raney 1974).

The banded darter is an upland species of moderate to large rivers, typically occurring in swift riffles over gravel with chert rock or boulders on gravel (or bedrock and gravel); it is usually associated with filamentous algae-covered rocks or in-stream vegetation in swift, clear water, and typically associated with *E. (E.) blennioides,* which shares a similar range, habitat, and foods. The banded darter feeds at all hours of the day, 60–96 percent on midges (Cordes and Page 1980). The leech, *Piscicolaria reducta,* which occurs on northwestern banded darters and on other darter species (Erickson 1976, 1978), can be removed with forceps (tweezers).

Katula (1993a) spawned banded darters in an aquarium with dark colored gravel and abundant *Hydrocotyle* and *Ambulia* for spawning sites. Vigorous aeration substituted for strong current, and the fish were fed frozen chironomids, live adult brine shrimp, whiteworms, and occasionally, live mayfly larvae. After one week together, the emerald green color of the male had intensified and the abdomen of the female had swollen considerably with roe. The female selected the spawning site and then remained stationary, after which the male approached from behind and began to vibrate rapidly. The acrobatic parents laid eggs both right side up and upside down on vegetation, with one to three eggs per episode.

Most spawning occurred during mid-May at 58°F. In addition to plants, the parents also used the walls of the aquarium and the gravel as spawning sites. At 56 to 62°F, the eggs hatched in 14 days. Within 24 hours the mostly pelagic fry had absorbed their yolk sacs and began feeding on newly hatched *Artemia* nauplii in the water column. Growing quickly, the banded pattern appeared by two months of age, and green pigmentation developed between three and six months. At one year of age, Katula had tank-raised 45 adults (average 1½ in.), but stated that he could easily have quadupled production had he known the fish were that easy to spawn and raise.

| *Etheostoma (Etheostoma) lynceum,* brighteye darter | *E. (E.) lynceum* has eight dark green bands on the flank that are continuous with those of the other side above and below. The fins are red on the basal half and green on the outer half of the spiny dorsal and central third of the soft dorsal. The caudal fin is flushed green and the lower fins are green. The male is similar to *E. (E.) zonale. E. (E.) lynceum* was previously considered a subspecies of *E. (E.) zonale* (Tsai and Raney 1974), but is now considered a distinct species (Etnier and Starnes 1986). In *E. (E.) zonale,* dark blotches occur on the lateral line in the light interspaces between the dark green vertical bars, but those midlateral blotches are indistinct or absent in *E. (E.) lynceum,* which also has dark mottling below the lateral line (these darker markings are most apparent in preserved specimens). There are 40 pored scales in the lateral line of *E. (E.) lynceum,* and 50 in *E. (E.) zonale* (Etnier and Starnes 1986). In living *E. (E.) lynceum,* the green vertical bars are equal in width to the light interbar spaces, but wider than the light spaces in *E. (E.) zonale* (Page and Burr 1991). The female of *E. (E.) lynceum* is unlike that of *E. (E.) zonale,* with dark bands that are more like blotches (separate from saddles) and having extensive black mottling on the lower half. The average adult length is 2 inches. |

The brighteye darter occurs in the lower Mississippi River basin, including but not limited to the Tangipahoa, Tallahatchie, Pearl, Homochitto (Bayou Pierre, Big Black River), Pascagoula (Leaf, Red, Black, Chickasawhay), and Yazoo (Obio, Hatchie, Wolf) Rivers, from extreme western Kentucky southward through Mississippi and Louisiana to the Gulf Coast (between Mobile and New Orleans, an area known as the Mississippi embayment).

*E. (E.) lynceum* inhabits second- and third-order (small to medium) Coastal Plain or Mississippi embayment streams with low gradient over sand, fine gravel, mud, and silt (Tsai and Raney 1974; Etnier and Starnes 1986), where the water is sluggish and frequently turbid. Here, it occurs in sluggish pools, swift gravel runs created by fallen timber (the runs often with aquatic plants), but sometimes where exposed bedrock riffles occur as in Bayou Pierre in Mississippi. In sandy habitats, it occurs with *Etheostoma (Oligocephalus) swaini* and *Percina (Hadropterus) nigrofasciata,* whereas on bedrock riffles it has been found with *E. (E.) histrio, E. (N.) rubrum, P. (I.) vigil,* and *P. (Hadropterus) sciera* (Kuehne and Barbour 1983).

## *Etheostoma (Etheostoma) histrio,* harlequin darter

*E. (E.) histrio* has dark green flank bars that expand into confluent blotches, virtually obliterating the lighter interbar space. Overall, it is dark green to green-brown and has a dark head, a dark teardrop, and two dark basicaudal blotches. The fins are either heavily speckled (pectorals, caudals, second dorsal) or dark overall (others).

The harlequin darter occurs in the lower Mississippi valley from the Missouri bootheel, Illinois, and western Kentucky southward to the Gulf Coast from western Florida to eastern Texas. It ranges from the Embarras River (Wabash drainage of the Ohio system) of Illinois to many eastern and western tributaries of the Mississippi River, continuing eastward to Tennessee and the Green River of Kentucky. It occurs as far west as Oklahoma, Arkansas, Texas, and Louisiana. It occupies Gulf Coast rivers from the Escambia of Florida to the Sabine and Neches of Texas (Tsai 1968a).

*E. (E.) histrio* inhabits swift rock or gravel riffles of medium-sized rivers above the fall line, where it is found in brush, leaves, and debris over sand and gravel bottoms in raceways and riffles. It occupies chutes below snags in slow-moving, sometimes turbid, Coastal Plain streams (Kuehne and Barbour 1983; Page 1983). The harlequin darter prefers blackwater habitats with a pH of 6.0 or lower, where it browses among leaf litter and detritus for aquatic insect larvae and crustaceans. The fish is not well known because its preferred habitat is difficult to seine, but it can be locally common.

Place a small group in a 20- to 29-gallon aquarium with a gravel or sand bottom, an air-driven undergravel filter, and dead hardwood tree leaves to acidify the water and provide hiding and browsing areas. Feed live daphnia and blackworms, supplemented with frozen bloodworms in moderation. Acidic water is usually soft and unstable. Be careful not to overfeed, which can elevate ammonia concentrations to lethal levels.

It spawns in early spring. Spawning occasionally takes place over dead leaves, but gravel or loose sand is preferred. In aquaria, it spawns on gravel. After spawning, remove the adults to another aquarium and watch for the appearance of fry in two weeks.

Because the harlequin darter is protected in states at the periphery of its range, state wildlife officials should be consulted before collection is attempted.

## Subgenus *Etheostoma (Hololepis)*

Members of *E. (Hololepis)* are the swamp darters. The lateral line is arched upward and incompletely pored; the pore system of the head and body scale arrangement are specific to the group (Collette 1962; Page 1983); the premaxillary frenum is broad; nuptial tubercles occur on the anal fin rays and underside of the pelvic fin rays of males; and the male is usually smaller than the female. They inhabit slow-moving waters such as swamps, stream backwaters, and lakes, where they spawn mostly on twigs.

Page (1983) added *Etheostoma exile* to the group of species previously placed in *E. (Hololepis)* by others, and resurrected the subgenus *E. (Boleichthys)* for the group. This was not accepted by Bailey and Etnier (1988), whom I follow in using the traditional definition for *E. (Hololepis)* as offered by Collette (1962) based on Hubbs and Cannon (1935); the species within the subgenus *E. (Hololepis)* and the spelling of some of the species names have been brought up to date herein. *E. exile* is retained in *E. (Oligocephalus).*

### *Etheostoma (Hololepis) gracile,* slough darter

*E. (H.) gracile* (**plate 74**) is robust in front with a blunt snout, the elongate body tapering to the rear. The nuptial male has a brilliant orange submarginal band in the spiny dorsal fin and ten iridescent green narrow bands on the flank. There are no similar darters in its range.

The slough darter occurs in Gulf Coast drainages from the Nueces River in Texas eastward to the Mississippi River. It ranges northward to Illinois, Indiana, and Kentucky in lowlands and foothills (Collette 1962).

*E. (H.) gracile* occurs in sluggish or moderately flowing, clear to turbid water on mud- or silt-bottom beaver and farm ponds, ditches, bayous, swamps, and lowland backwaters, usually near submersed vegetation such as *Myriophyllum, Ceratophyllum, Typha, Potamogeton, Azolla, Cabomba, Ludwigia, Nuphar,* and algae. It feeds mostly on chironomids, supplemented by mayfly larvae, copepods, amphipods, and cladocerans. Its broad geographic range assures it will be found with a great many associated species. It spawns from March through May on twigs, the stems of dead hardwood leaves, and other vegetation (Collette 1962; Braasch and Smith 1967).

A 10-gallon aquarium is sufficient for one male (the males fight) and two or three females. Provide gentle sponge or outside filtration, and sand and peat moss on the bottom, overlaid with dead hardwood leaves. Vegetation covering the surface is desirable. Feed frozen bloodworms and adult brine shrimp, and live blackworms, whiteworms, and *Artemia* nauplii. The slough darter spawns on twigs, leaf stems, and even the lift tube of a filter. Eggs hatch in one week to ten days at room temperature.

### *Etheostoma (Hololepis) zonifer,* backwater darter

*E. (H.) zonifer* resembles the slough darter, *E. (H.) gracile,* but is less colorful. The spiny dorsal fin has an orange-red submarginal band, and the flanks are crossed by a series of gray-blue or blue-green vertical bars (Collette 1962). In other literature it is called *E. zoniferum* (Page 1983; Kuehne and Barbour 1983).

The backwater darter is restricted to the Alabama and Tombigbee Rivers (Mobile Bay drainage) below the fall line in central Alabama and just into eastern Mississippi (Collette 1962).

*E. (H.) zonifer* inhabits pools in a creek with mud or gravel bottom (4 feet deep, with the alga *Chara*) in both clear and murky water (Hubbs and Cannon 1935). It probably breeds during spring.

### *Etheostoma (Hololepis) fusiforme,* swamp darter

*E. (H.) fusiforme* has two anal spines. It is heavily mottled and spotted on the head and flank, sometimes with spots on the belly. The male has black membranes in front and sometimes the rear of the spiny dorsal fin.

There are two subspecies. *E. f. fusiforme* is the northern form, ranging from southern Maine to the Cape Fear River of North Carolina, and often has three basicaudal spots. *E. f. barratti* extends from the Pee Dee drainage of southern North Carolina through all of Florida, continuing westward through southern Georgia, Alabama, Mississippi, and most of Louisiana (except near the coast) to extreme eastern Texas, then northward in the Mississippi River valley as far as western Ten-

Swamp darter, *Etheostoma fusiforme*, Wolf Swamp Cr., Jasper Co., S.C.
FCR

Sawcheek darter, *Etheostoma serrifer*, male, White Oak R., N.C. FCR

Sawcheek darter, *Etheostoma serrifer*, female with protruding ovipositor, Northeast Cape Fear R., N.C. FCR

nessee, the bootheel of Missouri, and adjacent areas in Kentucky; it typically has
four basicaudal spots (Collette 1962).

South of New England, the swamp darter occurs below the fall line; in New
England, its distribution is more complex. Throughout its range it inhabits densely
vegetated or detritus-, stick-, and leaf-littered ponds, small lakes, sluggish stream
edges, backwaters, drainage ditches, and pools. Swamp darters in streams probably
come from pond populations (Schmidt and Whitworth 1979). It tolerates a wide
range of pH and feeds mostly on chironomids and cladocerans (*Daphnia* and its relatives). It spawns on leaves from March through May.

A 10- to 20-gallon aquarium is sufficient for six individuals. Include a sand bottom, frequent partial water changes, vegetation, and aeration, but not strong currents. The swamp darter adapts well to captivity but may not spawn for a year. It
spawns in and at the base of vegetation when the temperature drops into the upper
60s (°F). Provide synthetic yarn mops for higher egg yields and ease of harvest. The
small, amber eggs should be incubated in shallow water and in darkness (but without dyes or medicaments), and hatch in less than two weeks. The fry take *Artemia*
nauplii, microworms, or vinegar eels as a first food.

---

*Etheostoma (Hololepis) serrifer,*
sawcheek darter

*E. (H.) serrifer* is sometimes called *E. serriferum*. It is a swamp darter with a black
midlateral band from the snout to the tail that often is interspersed with red flushes

and dots; it has four basicaudal spots at the base of the tail fin, sometimes surrounded by red pigment, and the fins have black and red-brown spots and lines. The female is spotted but lacks a midlateral band (Hubbs and Cannon 1935).

The sawcheek darter occurs on the Coastal Plain from the Roanoke River and Dismal Swamp of southern Virginia through the Altamaha River system of central Georgia.

*E. (H.) serrifer* inhabits sluggish streams, backwaters, ponds, lakes, and impoundments, often in clumps of weed on sand or silt bottoms, in slow to moderate currents, or no current at all. It breeds during March and April (Collette 1962). Feed tubificid worms, whiteworms, and chopped earthworms.

---

**Etheostoma (Hololepis) collis, Carolina darter**

*E. (H.) collis* has one anal spine and no bright colors. Small dark blotches appear along the flank and a dark teardrop is present. It is heavily speckled on the head and upper body, but the belly is unspotted. The male is darker than the female, and sometimes has a dark band in his dorsal fin.

There are two subspecies. *E. c. lepidinion* is more northerly, occurring in the Neuse and Tar Rivers of North Carolina and the Roanoke River in northern North Carolina, extending just into Virginia. *E. c. collis* occurs in the Pee Dee and Catawba Rivers (Santee drainage) of southern North Carolina and extreme northern South Carolina. The form from the Saluda and Broad Rivers of South Carolina will be resurrected as the valid species, *E. (H.) saludae*.

The Carolina darter is found only in the Piedmont. I found no differences among streams in which it occurred and those in which it did not. In general, it is present in small, cooler upland streams, often around woody debris or beneath undercut banks, wherever the current is reduced, and more often on sand than on silt or mud. It probably feeds mostly on chironomids. It appears to breed during March or April, and is likely to be a plant or twig spawner.

*E. (H.) collis* is state protected in North Carolina, and uncommon to rare everywhere in its narrow range. If available, see *E. (H.) fusiforme* or *E. (H.) gracile* for recommendations on care.

---

**Subgenus Etheostoma (Microperca)**

The characteristics uniting this plant-spawning group of darters are an average of less than nine dorsal spines, ten or fewer pectoral rays, a distinctive ovipositor, indented eggs, and a modified pelvic fin in nuptial males.

Members of *E. (Microperca)* are bred easily in small aquaria with twigs and vegetation, but one species, *E. (M.) fonticola*, is protected and not available. Although indented eggs are characteristic, they also occur in some unrelated *E. (Catonotus)* species (Burr and Ellinger 1980). This book follows Buth et al. (1980) and Bailey and Etnier (1988) in retaining this subgenus for *E. (M.) fonticola*, *E. (M.) proeliare*, and *E. (M.) microperca*, which are related by their isozyme patterns and the characters identified above. This is not the system offered by Page (1983), who placed these three species in *E. (Boleichthys)* together with a group of species in the subgenus *E. (Hololepis)* and the aberrant species *E. exile* [placed in *E. (Oligocephalus)* in this book].

---

**Etheostoma (Microperca) microperca, least darter**

*E. (M.) microperca* is small, brown, and has black scale edges that give it a spotted appearance. A distinct black line runs through the nose and eye, and a dark teardrop is present; a series of dark blotches occurs along the flank. The enlarged, rich orange pelvic and anal fins of the nuptial male are distinctive, particularly the flap on the leading edge of the pelvic fins. During this period, the male becomes dark green and the flank blotches turn intensely black with iridescent green scales; the second dorsal fin and the caudal fin become milky white with charcoal gray bands, and black blotches appear on the belly, breast and chin. The female does not develop pelvic flaps or color, but her ovipositor becomes enlarged (Burr and Page 1979).

The least darter is densely distributed around the Great Lakes, but erratically distributed in Mississippi River streams from Minnesota and Wisconsin to the Ozarks of Missouri and Oklahoma (Burr and Page 1979). The Ozark population differs from the northern form in isozyme pattern, indicating genetic differences (Buth et al. 1980).

E. (M.) microperca inhabits heavily vegetated, slow-moving small to large streams, and shallow vegetated edges of lakes, and in springs, over gravel, sand, or (most often) muck bottoms. It is associated with filamentous algae, *Elodea, Myriophyllum, Ceratophyllum* or other plants, often in open sunlight with little to no canopy (but below overhanging grassy banks). It feeds during the day mostly on copepods (it is a small fish) supplemented with chironomid larvae. Spawning occurs from April through June at 60 to 70°F; the characteristically indented eggs are adhered one at a time to strands of algae, leaves, or twigs (Burr and Page 1979; Cordes and Page 1980).

In aquaria, the least darter spawns on leaves, twigs, algae, and the vertical glass sides off the bottom. The egg-laden substrata can be moved to an aerated 1-gallon jar for hatching and the fry fed baby brine shrimp to supplement the protozoa that will bloom in the absence of adult fish. *Artemia* nauplii and *Ceriodaphnia* should provide the main portion of the adult diet, supplemented with grindal worms and mosquito larvae newly hatched from egg rafts.

---

*Etheostoma (Microperca) proeliare,*
cypress darter

E. (M.) proeliare (**plate 75**) is small and brown, with elongate dark dashes along the flank, a distinct teardrop, and a dark stripe across the snout. The nuptial male has an enlarged flap on the leading edge of the pelvic fins. A bright red spot adorns the leading edge of the spiny dorsal fin, and a dull red spot on the rear edge. There are light red bands in the soft dorsal and caudal fins. The female is plain, lacking red coloration and enlarged flaps on the pelvic fins; her ovipositor is distinctive.

The cypress darter is widespread throughout the Mississippi embayment northward to southern Illinois, and ranges westward to eastern Oklahoma and the San Jacinto River of Texas, and eastward to the Choctawhatchee River in Florida (Kuehne and Barbour 1983).

E. (M.) proeliare occurs in sloughs, river backwaters, lake edges, ponds, and other quiet waters. It is found on gravel riffles and in muck pools, wherever the bottom is richly vegetated or filled with sticks, leaf litter, or debris, or the banks are densely vegetated with fine tree roots that extend into the undercuts. The diet is dominated by chironomids, copepods, cladocerans, isopods, and amphipods.

The cypress darter spawns from March through June at 50 to 60°F on twigs, leaves, and vegetation well above the bottom. At 60 to 74°F, the deeply indented eggs hatch in 5½ to 12½ days (Burr and Page 1978).

---

*Etheostoma (Microperca) fonticola,*
fountain darter

E. (M.) fonticola is a dull brown fish with black scale edges that give it an appearance of crosshatching. A black line through the nose and eye continues as a series

Fountain darter, *Etheostoma fonticola,* San Marcos R., Tex. WFR

of dashes along the lateral line, ending in a single basicaudal spot; a teardrop is present. The spiny dorsal fin is black at the outer edge and along the lower half, with a broad red band in between; otherwise, the fins are speckled. It is small at 1½–1¾ inches, the same as *E. (N.) tippecanoe,* but is much slimmer and weighs only half as much (Page and Burr 1979).

The fountain darter is endemic to the spring-fed Comal and San Marcos Rivers, arising from the Edwards Aquifer of south-central Texas. Extirpated from the Comal River, it was later successfully reintroduced (Schenck and Whiteside 1976). It is being propagated at the Dexter National Fish Hatchery in New Mexico. In the San Marcos, it occurs in Spring Lake and the upper (first) 2 miles of the river.

*E. (M.) fonticola* is found in clear, hard water springs and their rivers in dense bottom vegetation; it prefers the filamentous alga *Rhyzoclonium,* but is also found with *Hydrilla* (Florida *Elodea*), *Ludwigia, Vallisneria, Potamogeton,* or *Zizania* (wild rice).

The fountain darter spawns year-round, with peaks in August and again during February and March. Because its habitat has a constant temperature, spawning peaks are probably related to a slight decrease in flow (Schenck and Whiteside 1976, 1977a). It feeds during the day, the smallest darters on copepods and the largest on mayfly larvae; all sizes take small amphipods and bloodworms (Schenck and Whiteside 1977b). In aquaria, it has spawned on filamentous algae.

The fountain darter is a federally and state endangered species.

**Subgenus *Etheostoma (Nothonotus)***

Members of *E. (Nothonotus)* are robust [except *E. (N.) denoncourti* and *E. (N.) tippecanoe*], slab-sided, deep-bodied darters with deep caudal peduncles and snouts that are pointed or angled, never blunt. The vomer and palatine bones of the mouth have teeth, and all except the smallest *[E. (N.) tippecanoe, E. (N.) denoncourti]* have a completely pored lateral line. A wide frenum attaches the upper lip (premaxilla) to the snout, and nuptial tubercles do not occur in either sex. All the species are colorful, and [except *E. (N.) juliae*] are sexually dichromatic. Dark and light scale edges on the body form horizontal lines. The front base of the spiny dorsal fin is dark to black in the male and sometimes the female. The breast is blue-green in the nuptial male of most species (Bailey 1959).

All are found in rivers feeding into Gulf Coast drainages, usually midstream in steep, moderate to large, clear, highly oxygenated rivers. They spawn in gravel out in the open or place their eggs in clumps in the gravel beneath rocks. The distribution is marked by a high degree of endemism. Today, two species occur in the Ozark Plateau or central highlands, one in a Coastal Plain tributary to the lower Mississippi River, four in the Mobile River basin, and twelve across the rivers of the eastern highlands of Ohio, Kentucky, West Virginia and surrounding areas.

Wood (1996) placed *E. (N.) juliae* as the basal type, and accounted for the *E. (N.) tippecanoe/denoncourti* species pair, the *E. (N.) camurum/chlorobranchium* species pair, and other related species pairs as the result of divergence when historic connections between the Tennessee River basin and the Mobile River basin were severed.

| | |
|---|---|
| *Etheostoma (Nothonotus) juliae,* yoke darter | *E. (N.) juliae* **(plate 76)** is moderately stout and is not obviously sexually dimorphic or dichromatic, although the male develops an orange-edged black spiny dorsal fin during the May through July spawning season. Otherwise, the male and female are similar. The body is yellow with alternating horizontal rows of dark and light scales on the flank. It has three or four bold, black saddles, the first on the nape being most prominent and giving rise to the common name. The teardrop is present. The fins are orange-edged to orange throughout, and black at the base in the front part of the spiny dorsal fin. An iridescent green humeral spot adorns the angle of the gill cover above the pectoral fin. Often attaining 2½ inches, it is a large darter. |

The yoke darter is endemic to the White River system of Missouri and Arkansas on the Ozark Plateau. The only other member of *E. (Nothonotus)* west of the Mississippi River is *E. (N.) moorei*.

*E. (N.) juliae* inhabits fast riffles and chutes of clear, medium-sized, high gradient rivers with fast flow. It appears from near shore to 2 feet deep, on diatom-glazed bedrock, among large boulders, and on rocky riffles with small patches of gravel. The yoke darter occurs in lower velocity water near shore, and alone wherever current velocity is high and excludes other darters. Seining varies from difficult to dangerous to impossible; here, the yoke darter may become common.

Spawning was observed from mid-May through mid-July at water temperatures of 68 to 72°F. Spawning occurred on deep riffles, on gravel behind large rocks in 1 to 2 feet of water. Eggs were buried in the gravel (James and Taber 1986). Egg diameters, numbers, and depth reported from field observations by James and Taber are not given here, because they may represent *E. (E.) euzonum,* which may have been spawning simultaneously at that location.

Hill (1968) used statistical techniques to validate seven age classes in the yoke darter and other observations to indicate a February to July spawning season; his conclusions have been discredited because the yoke darter spawns in late spring or early summer and lives only three years. The yoke darter might be stripped during its May to July spawning season.

A deep aquarium should be provided (29 gal.) for a group, and strong currents maintained by submersed powerheads. A large rock or two should rest on at least 1 inch of gravel. Feeding should be heavy with chopped earthworms, bloodworms, and live blackworms; *Noturus* (madtoms) or crayfish included as scavengers will eliminate excess food.

If spawning is suspected, a net filled with gravel should be removed downcurrent from a rock and poured into a glass dish for inspection. Inspect under a bright light with a magnifier and look for adhesive yellow eggs 1 to 2 mm in diameter. It is possible that this fish spawns beneath submersed boulders or flat rocks; these too should be provided and periodically removed for inspection.

| *Etheostoma (Nothonotus) tippecanoe*, Tippecanoe darter | *E. (N.) tippecanoe* (**plate 77**), the Tippecanoe darter, is the smallest *E. (Nothonotus)* at 1 to 1½ inches maximum size. It is sexually dichromatic. The female is yellow-brown with black vertical bands and black speckling on the fins. The male is lemon yellow to red-brown to black in front, and bright yellow-orange with blue-black vertical bands on the flank; these bands disappear during spawning. |

The Tippecanoe darter is widespread from French Creek and the Allegheny River in Pennsylvania southward and westward to the Muskingum and Scioto Rivers in Ohio and the Wabash and White Rivers in Indiana. It is found in the Licking, Kentucky, and Green drainages of Kentucky, and in the East Fork of Stones River and Harpeth River in the Cumberland system of Tennessee (Zorach 1969). The fish in the Clinch River (upper Tennessee system) in Tennessee is probably *E. (N.) denoncourti*.

*E. (N.) tippecanoe* inhabits medium-sized rivers on large, slowly to moderately flowing waters of riffles, on gravel and sand with scattered rocks. Due to its great geographic range, it occurs with a large number of darter species and other fishes.

A 10-gallon aquarium is sufficient for five males and five females. Provide 2 to 4 inches of gravel and half buried or partially exposed flat rocks. Aeration from air-release stones is sufficient, but a small powerhead offers better circulation. Feed chironomids and *Artemia* supplemented with blackworms and whiteworms.

Spawning in aquaria has been reported (Warren et al. 1986). The females were buried completely in the coarse gravel for ten minutes or more. Males mounted above the females, but did not appear to make contact at the time of flaring and gaping, interpreted as the time of ejaculation. Eggs were later found attached in groups to flat rocks buried in the gravel, sperm apparently driven down into the substratum by the thrashing movements of the males. Spawning occurred at 80°F (July spawning season) and the eggs hatched in nine days at 75°F.

| *Etheostoma (Nothonotus) denoncourti*, golden darter | *E. (N.) denoncourti* was recently separated from *E. (N.) tippecanoe* by geographic location, the scales on the operculum, and by typical (not absolute) dorsal fin counts of XIII/11 vs. XII/12 in *E. (N.) tippecanoe*. The nuptial male is yellow to golden orange with seven to nine black bars (most intense in the front and the rear, orange spots between the paired fins, and a gray or black but usually blue chest. The head is brown above, orange below, and yellow to green on the side, with three indistinct black marks around the eye. The dorsal fin has an orange margin, and the other fins are faint orange (Stauffer and van Snik 1997). The *E. (N.) tippecanoe* description in Jenkins and Burkhead (1994) refers to *E. (N.) denoncourti*. |

The golden darter occurs in the Clinch and Sequatchie Rivers of the upper Tennessee River drainage in northeastern Tennessee and southwestern Virginia; historically, it was reported from the Duck and Buffalo Rivers, in which its status is unknown. It feeds on mayfly, caddisfly, and midge larvae. An egg-burier, it breeds during late July and early August on riffles and runs of sand and gravel.

*E. (N.) denoncourti* needs only a small aquarium (≤ 10 gal.) and moderate cur-

Bluebreast darter, *Etheostoma camurum,* Cumberland R., Tenn. RB

rent. One male will mount several females over time as they bury themselves almost completely in the gravel.

| | |
|---|---|
| *Etheostoma (Nothonotus) chlorobranchium,* greenfin darter | *E. (N.) chlorobranchium* (**plate 78**) is sexually dichromatic, with a yellow female and a light green or dark green male, depending on origin. Alternating horizontal rows of dark and light scales along the flank are overlaid by scattered red-brown spots and 10–12 dark vertical uniform bands (male) or broken and erratic bands (female); the teardrop is obscure in the dark-headed male. The breast is light green to pink in front and orange to green behind. The fins are yellow (female) or dark green (male); the soft dorsal, anal, and tail fins have dark margins and a light submargin; the spiny dorsal has a dark blotch in front, a dark margin, and no submargin. The female may have patch of green in the unpaired fins (Zorach 1972). *E. (N.) chlorobranchium* is large (to 3½ in.). |

The greenfin darter occurs in the Watauga, French Broad, Nolichucky, Hiwassee, and Little Tennessee Rivers of the upper Tennessee River system in the mountains of North Carolina, Tennessee, and Georgia (Zorach 1972).

It inhabits moderate to large, clear streams in fast riffles with large stones, on gravel at depths of 3½ to 12 inches. It presumably spawns in gravel against or beneath rocks at 70 to 75°F during June.

| | |
|---|---|
| *Etheostoma (Nothonotus) camurum,* bluebreast darter | *E. (N.) camurum* was previously suspected of being identical to *E. (N.) chlorobranchium.* Work by Eisenhour (1995) supports their separation. The basal area of the pelvic fins is black or orange, but never green as in the closely related *E. (N.) chlorobranchium.* The basal area of the medial fins (dorsal, anal, caudal) is brick red but green in *E. (N.) chlorobranchium.* The throat and breast are bright blue, but black, green or turquoise (never bright blue) in *E. (N.) chlorobranchium.* The body is robust, the snout moderately pointed, and the teardrop present. Alternating rows of light and dark scales along the side give a horizontal, lined appearance; red (male) or brown (female) scales are scattered irregularly along the flank. The breast of the nuptial male in front of the pelvic fins is bright blue to blue-black, the chest orange. A black mark appears at the base where the spiny dorsal fin originates in both sexes. The fins are orange-red in the male and yellow in the female; there is a black margin and yellow submargin on the soft (second) dorsal, anal, and caudal fins of both sexes. There are no basicaudal markings, and no central light or dark portion |

in the uniformly colored tail fin, other than in the margin and submargin. *E. (N.) camurum* grows to 3 inches.

The bluebreast darter occurs in lower elevations of the Ohio and Tennessee River systems, while the related *E. (N.) chlorobranchium* occupies upper elevation streams; only minor areas of contact and hybridization are evident in the Nolichucky River (Eisenhour 1995). *E. (N.) camurum* ranges from French Creek and the Allegheny River in western Pennsylvania westward to the Walhonding and Scioto Rivers in Ohio. It continues on to the Tippecanoe River in Indiana and the Vermilion River in Illinois. It extends southward in the Cheat and Little Kanawha Rivers below the falls in West Virginia and the Kentucky River and the Cumberland River system below Cumberland Falls in Kentucky, ranging southwestward to the East Fork Stones River in Tennessee. In the Tennessee River system, it occurs in the Clinch, South and North Forks of the Holston, Pigeon, Little Pigeon, Little, and Elk River drainages (Zorach 1972). The bluebreast darter has been declining throughout much of its range, and is most abundant in the Allegheny system of Pennsylvania, below the Cumberland Falls in Kentucky and in the upper Tennessee basin (Kuehne and Barbour 1983).

*E. (N.) camurum* is found at a depth of 4 to 12 inches in fast riffles of large, clear streams during the May–June spawning season, when water temperatures are 70–75°F. It buries its eggs in fine gravel around the bases of 12- to 20-inch-diameter boulders near the crests of riffles. Eggs hatch in seven to ten days (Mount 1959; Zorach 1972; Kuehne and Barbour 1983).

Katula (1990a) had reported spawning bluebreast darters before they were clearly separated from *E. (N.) chlorobranchium*. His description of medial fins as red with black edges confirms that he was describing *E. (N.) camurum*. Adults were fed live tubificids, *Artemia*, *Daphnia*, and *Drosophila*, and frozen chaoborids (glass worms). Males placed in a 26-gallon high aquarium began to establish territories around large rocks in the flow of strong current. Spawning occurred at the beginning of March at 64°F and pH 8.0, with eggs being laid in pebbled areas around the bases of large stones. Females buried their ventral halves only before being mounted. About 40 eggs were laid in adhesive clumps at the bases of rocks where they received the strongest flow. Eggs began hatching on day 12 postspawning.

After the first spawning activity, subsequent clumps were removed to a 10-gallon hatching and rearing tank. The pelagic fry began feeding on *Artemia* nauplii on day 3 posthatching, but all fry in this aquarium died within two weeks. The others allowed to remain in the 26-gallon aquarium transformed to a benthic habit after five weeks, and took chopped adult *Artemia* at six to seven weeks. Males began developing a turquoise breast and red spots at eight months.

There are many more species of *E. (Nothonotus)* and most can be divided into two groups. The historic connection between the Duck River and the Green and Cumberland Rivers apparently occurred when the species pairs of the *maculatum* group diverged. Although *aquali, maculatum, microlepidum, moorei, rubrum, sanguifluum, vulneratum,* and *wapiti* have been thought to make up the distinctive *maculatum* group (Etnier and Williams 1989), and *jordani, acuticeps, chuckwachatte, douglasi,* and *etowahae* to make up the *jordani* group (Wood and Mayden 1993), the more recent analysis by Wood (1996) suggests that zoogeography and physiological attributes can provide an alternative interpretation, supported by the known ages of early connections and severances of historic rivers. Nonetheless, they will be presented below based on those two species groups.

The following eight species are generally considered to make up the *E. (N.) maculatum* group.

| | |
|---|---|
| *Etheostoma (Nothonotus) rubrum,* bayou darter | *E. (N.) rubrum* is dichromatic, with a dark teardrop, bold saddle on the nape, and a distinctive double basicaudal spot in both sexes. The female is brown with horizontal rows of dark-edged scales that alternate with light rows and scattered red to russet and white spots; there are irregular dark and light areas on the flank that are neither blotching nor bars; all fins are densely spotted with some red and russet, but mostly black spots; and the fins may be black-edged. The male has a dark body that obscures horizontal rows of dark scale edges and scattered white spots; the black spot at the base of the spiny dorsal fin contrasts with a dark, double basicaudal spot. All his fins are unspotted and red-orange; the unpaired fins are margined in black; the spiny and soft dorsal fins have a dusky central band below the red-orange zone; and the breast and anal spines are blue-green (Raney and Suttkus 1966; Johnson 1987). This is the third smallest *E. (Nothonotus),* growing only to 2 inches. |

The bayou darter occurs in White Oak, Turkey, and Foster Creeks of the Bayou Pierre River in southwestern Mississippi, east of the Mississippi River. It is absent from the Little Bayou Pierre River (a southern tributary), Tallahalla Creek, and the far upstream reaches of Turkey Creek (Ross et al. 1992).

*E. (N.) rubrum* is found midriver in larger streams and the main stem of the Bayou Pierre River, in the swiftest shallow, coarse gravel, and pebble riffles containing large rocks and boulders or large logs; it avoids tributaries containing limestone silt. It seeks out fast water behind boulders during the winter, and may migrate some distance annually within its limited geographic range. It spawns from April through June with a peak in May. The male takes up station on coarse gravel (16–32 mm) in fast water (30 in./sec.). The habitat of the bayou darter is vulnerable to sedimentation from development, which could destroy the species.

Investigators set up a large, compartmentalized tray with current provided by an electric trolling motor. The female attracted the male to a coarse (1–2 mm) sand eddy behind sticks, where she then buried partially and turned sideways, her head exposed above the sand. The male came alongside above the sand and they spawned. The female remained buried for 15 to 50 seconds before coming out of the sand, while the male stayed in the area displaying. Multiple spawnings occurred, sometimes with multiple females. Each time a half dozen to more than a dozen 1.7 mm eggs were buried in an adhesive clump. At 72°F, the eggs hatched in one week, but the larvae were not raised (Ross and Wilkins 1993).

*E. (N.) rubrum* is a threatened species under the Federal Endangered Species Act. It is also state-protected in Mississippi and unavailable to collectors.

| | |
|---|---|
| *Etheostoma (Nothonotus) maculatum,* spotted darter | *E. (N.) maculatum* (**plate 79**) is strongly sexually dichromatic. In both sexes, the teardrop is weak to absent, and an indistinct basicaudal mark with two or four black spots tends to be obscured by the overall dark coloration (which led to one of the earlier synonyms, *"E. niger,"* for this species). The male *E. (N.) maculatum* has a sharp snout, a rounded tail fin, a laterally compressed and dark body, a few scattered red spots on the flank, and a blue-green breast. The spiny dorsal fin has a dark mark at the origin. The pectoral fin is short and not fanlike. The pelvic and anal fins may |

have a rich blue-green flush. All unpaired fins have a thin white edge, and there is no red in any fins. The female's body and tail fin are heavily spotted, but she never has any red spots (Zorach and Raney 1967).

E. (N.) maculatum previously consisted of three subspecies, E. m. maculatum, E. m. vulneratum, and E. m. sanguifluum; however, these three forms, all from different river systems, are now regarded as full species, and a fourth has been discovered, E. (N.) wapiti.

The spotted darter occurs in the Ohio River system (including the Wabash and Green River drainages), from western Pennsylvania just south of Lake Erie southwestward into Ohio, Indiana, and Kentucky. It is not common anywhere and probably has been extirpated from most of its historic range. Its demise may be attributable to silt in runoff from development.

E. (N.) maculatum requires fast, clear, unsilted rivers with abundant high profile rocks close together that provide crevices between adjacent rocks and below, where rocks rest on other rocks. The compressed body of the spotted darter is adapted to occupying crevices among rocks in midstream during periods of strong flow. Silt clogs and eliminates these refuges, and the fish cannot adapt to other habitats (Kessler and Thorpe 1993). It feeds on insect larvae associated with rocky substrata. When the water temperature is in the 60s (°F) during June, it spawns clumps of eggs several layers deep on the underside of rocks above the gravel; however, these are old observations and verification is needed.

The spotted darter is a threatened species in Kentucky and protected there and perhaps elsewhere; check with state agencies before attempting collection.

---

*Etheostoma (Nothonotus) sanguifluum,* bloodfin darter

E. (N.) sanguifluum is strongly sexually dichromatic, but both sexes have a black, pronounced teardrop. The bloodfin darter is distinguished from E. (N.) maculatum by a blunter snout, red spots on the flank of the female, fanlike pectoral fins, dark spots at the upper and lower corners of the tail fin (slightly in advance of the two basicaudal spots), the absence of a blue-green breast in the male, white edges on unpaired fins [as in E. (N.) maculatum but not E. (N.) vulneratum], red unpaired fins [as in E. (N.) vulneratum but not E. (N.) maculatum], and red spots at the origin of the spiny dorsal fin [black in E. (N.) maculatum]. E. (N.) wapiti has been recognized recently as a separate species.

The bloodfin darter occurs in the upper Cumberland River system below the Cumberland Falls of Kentucky and Tennessee.

E. (N.) sanguifluum inhabits rocky riffles of medium, clear, fast-flowing rivers, among large rocks and boulders.

---

*Etheostoma (Nothonotus) wapiti,* boulder darter

E. (N.) wapiti recently has been described and found distinct from E. (N.) sanguifluum. It differs from other members of its group by lacking red on all fins except the caudal fin, and resembles only E. (N.) vulneratum in having black edging on the anal, soft dorsal, and tail fins. The juvenile male may have dirty red spots on the flank, a thin red margin on the spiny dorsal fin, and red-orange on the tail fin, but the adult male tends to lose the red color. Otherwise, the boulder darter is a gray fish with a gray breast, and black teardrops in both sexes. The female has spotted fins and otherwise is less colorful than the male (Etnier and Williams 1989).

The boulder darter is rare in the Elk River system of Tennessee and Shoal Creek in Alabama.

*E. (N.) wapiti* inhabits limestone boulder-strewn, deep gravel riffles of medium-sized rivers.

Efforts to breed the boulder darter have not been successful; only one spawning has occurred in captivity and the young were eventually lost. Based on the assumption that it deposits clumps of eggs beneath boulders, Etnier and Williams (1989) suggested adding limestone boulders in suitable streams to provide more spawning habitat.

This federally endangered species cannot not be collected.

| | |
|---|---|
| *Etheostoma (Nothonotus) vulneratum,* wounded darter | *E. (N.) vulneratum* (**plate 80**) is strongly sexually dichromatic. Characteristics include a blunt snout, fanlike pectoral fins, a pronounced teardrop, red spots on the body of the female, a red mark at the origin of the spiny dorsal fin of the male [all as in *E. (N.) sanguifluum* but not *E. (N.) maculatum*], and narrow black edging to the unpaired fins (found in neither of the other two species) (Zorach and Raney 1967). |

The wounded darter occurs in the upper Tennessee River system of North Carolina, Virginia, and Tennessee, including the French Broad, South and North Forks Holston, Obed, Clinch, Little Tennessee, Little Pigeon, Abrams Creek, Oconoluftee, and Little Rivers.

*E. (N.) vulneratum* is found in medium-sized streams with strong currents, over rocky and boulder-strewn riffles midriver. It presumably feeds on a variety of aquatic insect larvae, and may spawn on the undersurface of rocks above the gravel.

| | |
|---|---|
| *Etheostoma (Nothonotus) moorei,* yellowcheek darter | *E. (N.) moorei* (**plate 81**) is strongly sexually dichromatic. Both sexes have a black, pronounced teardrop. The female is yellow-brown with dense black horizontal lines on the flank; her gill covers are dark, but are yellow on the lower area of the cheek extending to the breast; her fins are yellow, densely spotted dark brown to black, and black-edged. The male is a dark blue-brown with dense black horizontal lines on the flank; his fins are edged in black with broad submarginal orange-red zones and a dark base; his anal spines are green, and a green band runs between the black base and orange-red submarginal zone in his spiny dorsal fin. This darter often attains 2½ inches. |

The yellowcheek darter occurs in the Little Red River, a tributary of the White River system in Cleburne and adjacent Van Buren Counties of north-central Arkansas, but has been extirpated from most of its range by construction of the Greers Ferry Dam (Raney and Suttkus 1964). It is one of two *E. (Nothonotus)* members (the other is *E. (N.) juliae*) found west of the Mississippi River.

*E. (N.) moorei* inhabits faster sections of riffles over gravel, rubble, and boulder-strewn bottoms at depths of 12 inches and more, often near *Podostemon* (Raney and Suttkus 1964). The yellowcheek darter has suffered from habitat fragmentation, and is a good candidate for captive breeding and introduction into nearby habitats currently unoccupied by any other *E. (Nothonotus)* species.

| | |
|---|---|
| *Etheostoma (Nothonotus) microlepidum,* smallscale darter | *E. (N.) microlepidum* is strongly sexually dichromatic. A black teardrop mark appears in both sexes. The female has densely spotted unpaired fins, blotched or mottled dark markings on a yellow body, and a distinctive, double basicaudal spot. The male is dark, with horizontal rows of dark-edged scales and scattered red spots with black edges on the flanks; his fins lack spots; his unpaired fins are two-thirds green and |

surrounded by a broad orange-red band and a thin black margin that is lacking in the spiny dorsal fin. This darter often attains 2 inches.

The smallscale darter occurs in the lower Cumberland River system below the falls (Stones, Harpeth, Red, and Little Rivers) in Kentucky and Tennessee (Kuehne and Barbour 1983; Page 1983), but not the Duck River as reported by Raney and Zorach (1967).

E. (N.) microlepidum inhabits rivers 30 to 50 feet wide, on gravel and small rubble (not boulder-strewn) riffles in midriver, 2 to 3 feet deep (Raney and Zorach 1967).

---

**Etheostoma (Nothonotus) aquali, coppercheek darter**

E. (N.) aquali has a stocky body and a moderately long snout and there is no sub-ocular bar (teardrop). It is yellow-brown with alternating light and dark scale edges in horizontal rows, and ten dark smudges along the midline that are compact in the male and expansive and irregular in the female. The body and fins are densely dark-spotted in the female. The body has irregularly scattered red scales in the male and unspotted fins. Double dark spots occur at the base of the tail fin in both sexes, larger in the male. The male pelvic, anal, and tail fins are bright red, his soft dorsal is red on the outer portion, and his spiny dorsal has a bright red spot at its origin and another at its termination. Two red streaks appear on the cheek of the male coppercheek darter, but not the female. A green humeral (armpit) spot occurs in the male. The coppercheek darter grows to over 2 inches.

E. (N.) aquali occurs in the Buffalo and Duck Rivers of central Tennessee, midstream in large, fast-flowing moderately sized rivers over gravel and rubble.

Provide a large aquarium (40-gallon long) for a group, or not less than a 20-gallon long aquarium for one male and one or two females. The water should be less than 8 inches deep and a strong current supplied by a powerhead or water pump. Add 2 inches of coarse gravel, scattered large rocks, and a trickle or canister filter to maintain good water quality. Feed frozen bloodworms, frozen brine shrimp, chopped earthworms, chopped frozen euphausiid shrimp (not freeze-dried), and live blackworms, daphnia, and whiteworms.

The next five species comprise the E. (N.) jordani group of E. (Nothonotus). They typically have 3–11 faint vertical bars on the flank and no dark horizontal bands. The care and handling described for E. (N.) aquali also applies to all five species of the E. (N.) jordani group.

---

**Etheostoma (Nothonotus) jordani, greenbreast darter**

E. (N.) jordani (plate 82) has a broad submarginal red band on the tail fin, red spots on the flank and scales on the operculum, but lacks red in the anal fin or on the lips. It is strongly sexually dichromatic. The female is yellow-brown with dusky or spotted and black-margined fins, diffuse horizontal lines on her flank, and a checkerboard pattern of square black blotches on the middle and upper flank. The male is light- to white-bodied, with red-brown lines and scattered checkerboard black spots above, blue-green on the gill plate, throat, and the anal and pelvic fins. His caudal fin is mostly red, margined in black and submarginal in yellow-white. His spiny dorsal fin has a black blotch at the origin of the base and a marginal red band. He also has a submarginal black band in his soft dorsal, with the entire dorsal dusky toward the base.

The greenbreast darter occurs above the fall line in the Conasauga, Coosawattee, Cahaba, and Tallapoosa Rivers of the Coosa River system (Zorach 1969; Wood and Mayden 1993) in small to large rivers over fast, shallow riffles of mostly rock and rubble on small amounts of gravel. It feeds on mayfly, fly (chironomid and blackfly), and stonefly larvae. Its peak spawning period is April and May. The female selects the spawning site. The eggs are buried in sand.

| | |
|---|---|
| *Etheostoma (Nothonotus) douglasi*, Tuscaloosa darter | *E. (N.) douglasi* differs from *E. (N.) jordani* in lacking red spots on the flank (Wood and Mayden 1993).<br><br>The Tuscaloosa darter occurs in the upper Black Warrior River system of Alabama on gravel or cobble riffles in moderate to strong current. It probably buries clumps of eggs under rocks from April through June. |
| *Etheostoma (Nothonotus) etowahae*, Etowah darter | *E. (N.) etowahae* differs from *E. (N.) jordani* in lacking red spots on the flank, and from *E. (N.) douglasi* by having scales on the opercle, and 11 to 14 rows of scales from top to bottom rather than 14 to 16 rows (Wood and Mayden 1993).<br><br>The Etowah darter occurs in the Etowah River system of Georgia (upstream of Lake Altoona) on gravel and cobble riffles in moderate to strong current. |
| *Etheostoma (Nothonotus) chuckwachatte*, lipstick darter | *E. (N.) chuckwachatte* differs from *E. (N.) jordani* in having bright red lips (jaws), and a broad red band in the anal fin (Wood and Mayden 1993).<br><br>The lipstick darter inhabits the Tallapoosa River system above the fall line in Alabama and Georgia. It occurs on gravel or cobble riffles with moderate to strong current. It feeds on aquatic fly (mostly chironomids and blackflies), mayfly, and stonefly larvae. It spawns from April through June at 68 to 78°F and is probably an egg burier like other *E. (Nothonotus)* that bury clumps of eggs in gravel beneath rocks. |
| *Etheostoma (Nothonotus) acuticeps*, sharphead darter | *E. (N.) acuticeps* (plate 83) has a sharp snout and a scaleless head and nape. It grows to 2½ inches (Bailey 1959). It has no red pigment or scales on the gill cover. The body is brown (male) to yellow (female), with 12 to 14 dark vertical bands on the flank and many alternating horizontal lines of dark- and light-edged scales; the subocular band (teardrop) is faint; the fins lack dark edging. The female has a dark spot at the upper and another at the lower base of the caudal fin, a dark spot at the base of the spiny dorsal fin, and a white breast and belly. The nuptial male is a bright blue-green with a blue breast, a dark blotch at the base of the spiny dorsal fin, and blue-green fins.<br><br>The sharphead darter occurs in the Toe and Nolichucky Rivers of the Tennessee drainage in northeastern Tennessee and extreme western North Carolina. It probably has been extirpated from the Holston River in Virginia. Only two populations survive; its historic sites have been destroyed by reservoir construction and siltation.<br><br>*E. (N.) acuticeps* is found midstream in medium to large, high velocity rivers in riffles and chutes with a substratum of boulders, rocks, rubble, and coarse gravel. It feeds on blackflies, mayflies, and midges, spawns after age one during July and August, and lives less than three years (Page 1981; Kuehne and Barbour 1983).<br><br>The sharphead darter is rare and protected in North Carolina and Tennessee. |

Orangefin darter, *Etheostoma bellum,* Green R., Ky. WFR

Although it is not available to aquarists, it is an excellent candidate for captive breeding and restocking.

*Etheostoma (Nothonotus) bellum,*
orangefin darter

*E. (N.) bellum* is robust, with a slightly pointed snout, distinct subocular bar (teardrop), intensely dark scale edges that form horizontal rows of spots, and black-edged unpaired fins. Eight dark smudges on the flank are weak and compact in the male and dark and irregular in the female. There are two light spots at the upper and lower base of the tail fin, continuous with the light submargin that surrounds the dark central part of the fin. In the nuptial male, the dark central part of the caudal fin is surrounded by bright orange. The fins of the female are dull yellow, and bright orange in the male. The male has a blue-green breast and scattered red scales on the flank.

The orangefin darter occurs in the Green River drainage of Kentucky above its confluence with the Barren River, and in the Barren River of Kentucky and Tennessee (Zorach 1968).

*E. (N.) bellum* inhabits 3- to 6-inch-deep riffles over small gravel (also among rocks) in small to moderate, clear, fast-flowing tributaries (Zorach 1968). It is tolerant of many substratum types because its robust body and strong pectoral fins enable it to withstand strong currents, freeing it from reliance on rock crevices for refuge (Kessler and Thorpe 1993).

Katula (1990a) spawned a pair of orangefin darters in a 10-gallon aquarium between May and August. He interpreted a frayed second dorsal fin on the female as evidence of mounting activity, which was later confirmed. The male displayed by erecting his fins from a position on a high rock. When the female approached, the male would move to her side and continue to display while circling. The female would bury with only her caudal fin above the gravel, and the male would mount and quiver while stroking the exposed caudal region of the female. Oviposition was estimated at 15 seconds, although the female remained buried up to 30 minutes.

No affinity for large rocks was seen; rather, eggs were laid in open areas of gravel, and sometimes near the undergravel filter lift tube. Three adhesive clumps contained 16, 20, and 33 eggs each. Eggs hatched in 11 to 14 days at 72 to 74°F. At 3 days, the pelagic fry had difficulty swallowing *Artemia* nauplii but readily accepted microworms, and fed on both foods after the first week. Pelagic for five to eight weeks, they required a strong current to keep station in the water column. Zoller (1998) had better luck by starting the fry on half-hatched brine shrimp nauplii, and doing partial water changes. He noted that massive water changes often killed the fry. Zoller (1998) also induced spawning with an artificial spring, accomplished by increasing the photo-period slowly to 16 hours a day and gradually increasing temperature.

| | |
|---|---|
| *Etheostoma (Nothonotus) rufilineatum,* redline darter | *E. (N.) rufilineatum* **(plate 84)** is sexually dichromatic and has no teardrop. Many dark horizontal dashes appear on the gill cover (more apparent in the female), the cream-colored basicaudal band is narrowest at the center (hourglass-shaped), and the body is yellow with black blotches and horizontal rows of dark-edged scales. The fins of the female are densely spotted (sometimes dark-edged), and her body has few or no red spots. The male has many scattered red spots, but they do not form rows or lines despite the common name. The central zone of the black-edged tail fin is wide and dark, and surrounded by red-orange except in front, where it abuts a cream colored, hourglass-shaped mark. The anal and second dorsal fins are black-edged with a thin light submargin, a wide orange-red central band, and a dusky zone near the body. The paired fins are red-orange, unspotted, and unmargined. |

The redline darter is widespread and common in the Cumberland and Tennessee River systems of Tennessee and adjacent states east of the Mississippi River. Its range extends from most of Tennessee into western North Carolina, southwestern Virginia, southern Kentucky, and northern Georgia and Alabama.

*E. (N.) rufilineatum* inhabits rivers and creeks of all sizes, occurring among rocks, rubble, bedrock, and boulders, typically where stones break up the flow in gravel riffles. It occurs with many other *E. (Nothonotus)* and other darters, including *E. (N.) acuticeps, E. (N.) aquali, E. (N.) chlorobranchium, E. (N.) vulneratum, E. (N.) sanguifluum, E. (N.) microlepidum, E. (N.) tippecanoe,* and *E. (N.) denoncourti.* It feeds mostly on chironomids, secondarily on mayflies and caddisflies, and consumes other small benthic aquatic animals. Spawning is similar to *E. (N.) camurum;* eggs are buried in gravel and the female spends considerable time beneath the gravel during each ovipositing episode (Kuehne and Barbour 1983; Page 1983).

Gravid fish collected in late April spawned in captivity during late May. A 30-gallon aquarium with black gravel and stones above an undergravel filter (provided with supplementary aeration-driven currents) was used. The pH was high (8.4) and the temperature held to the low 70s (°F). After several weeks, an adhesive clump of eggs was found at the base of a large rock; however, other eggs that were not located and removed subsequently hatched in the aquarium. The fry appeared at the rate of a few per day, indicating daily spawning by the parents (Katula 1990a).

Redline darter fry are small and pelagic, remaining in the water column current provided by aeration. They remain pelagic for six weeks, at which time they are ¼-inch long and settle to a benthic habit. Several other darters [not *E. (Nothonotus)*] reach this size and habit in just a few days.

The fry consumed *Artemia* nauplii upon yolk resorption and grew slowly, taking chopped frozen adult *Artemia* at ten weeks. The first hint of red colors in the male occurred at eight months of age, but nuptial coloration and spawning of the captively bred generation occurred at one year of age, at which time egg clumps were once more found at the bases of large stones in a steady current (Katula 1990a).

*E. (Oligocephalus)* is monophyletic (of a single evolutionary line) according to Bailey and Etnier (1988), based on anatomy and physiology, and Turner (1997), relying on analyses of DNA sequences. The subgenus currently includes *E. (O.) asprigene, australe, bison, burri, caeruleum, collettei, ditrema, exile, fragi, grahami, hopkinsi, kantuckeense, lepidum, luteovinctum, nuchale, okaloosae, pottsi, radiosum, spectabile, tecumsehi,* and *uniporum.*

Members of *E. (Oligocephalus)* share the following characteristics: the first dorsal fin has a blue or green marginal band and usually an orange or red submarginal or lower band; the lateral line is straight and usually not completely pored; a premaxillary frenum is present that connects the snout to the upper lip (Page 1983).

*E. (Oligocephalus)* typically are found in gravel or rubble riffles. There are two spawning modes: spawning in gravel by some species and spawning among vegetation by other species. Were it not for the DNA evidence, it would be tempting to divide this subgenus further. The plant spawners will be examined first.

## *Etheostoma (Oligocephalus) exile,* Iowa darter

*E. (Oligocephalus) exile* is elongate and unlikely to be confused with any other species in its range. The nuptial male has bright orange or yellow on the belly and chest that extends up the flank to the lateral line; a dozen bright blue bars traverse the flank; the spiny dorsal fin has a bright orange submarginal band surrounded by blue bands above and below; the teardrop is prominent. The female lacks bright colors and is densely spotted.

The Iowa darter occurs in the Allegheny River drainage of New York and in the Great Lakes through Ohio, Nebraska, Iowa, Montana, and Colorado. In Canada, it ranges from Quebec to Edson in northern Alberta. *E. (Oligocephalus) exile* is the most northerly and westerly of all the darters (Scott and Crossman 1973).

The Iowa darter inhabits densely vegetated and clear, cold lakes, ponds, and river backwaters, usually over litter, peat, plants, or sand mixed with organic material.

*E. (Oligocephalus) exile* spawns from April through June on submersed aquatic plants and tree roots in shallow water. The 1.1 mm eggs hatch in 9 to 21 days (according to temperature), and the 3.7 mm long larvae are pelagic and attracted to light at night. The larvae eat cladocerans and copepods. Adults feed on chironomids and other dipteran (fly) larvae, mayfly and caddisfly larvae, amphipods, fish eggs, and small snails (Scott and Crossman 1973; Simon and Faber 1987; Katula 1996).

Iowa darters have club cells in the epidermis containing an alarm substance that acts like (but is not necessarily identical in structure to) the alarm substance found in the more primitive Ostariophysian fishes (e.g., minnows, tetras, catfishes). When the club cells are breached (as when a fish is wounded), the chemical stimulates a "fright and escape" response in other Iowa darters (R.J.F. Smith 1979).

Katula (1996) placed Iowa darters in a 20-gallon aquarium half filled with melted snow to replicate natural soft water. The bottom was sand, and the corners were provided with leaves and twigs or a green synthetic yarn spawning mop. Water changes were provided with melted snow. The fish were fed live tubificids, fairy shrimp, and daphnia. Over 30 days, the temperature was slowly raised from 45 to 65°F. At about 54°F, eggs began to appear on the spawning mop and on the twigs and leaves, hatching within 18 days. The small fry required infusoria (ciliates and other protozoans) for several weeks before weaning onto *Artemia* nauplii. By one year of age, the fish had attained 2–2½ inches in length and were mature. Captive fish survive up to five years, two more than expected in the wild.

| | |
|---|---|
| *Etheostoma (Oligocephalus) ditrema,* coldwater darter | *E. (Oligocephalus) ditrema* (**plate 85**) has an orange belly, a densely mottled body, and an absence of vertical bars on the flank; the latter character distinguishes it from *E. (Oligocephalus) swaini* of the Gulf Coast. The fins are spotted; the spiny dorsal has a thin marginal blue band, a prominent red submarginal band with a wide dusky blue band below it, and an obscure red basal band; the soft dorsal is mostly dusky blue; the anal fin is dusky blue with a medial orange band. There are three bold basi-caudal spots. The female lacks orange on the belly; red in her dorsal fin is subdued (Ramsey and Suttkus 1965). It is a minute darter, growing to 1½ inches.

The coldwater darter occurs in the Chattooga, Etowah, and Choccolocco River drainages above the fall line of the Coosa River system in Georgia and Alabama.

*E. (Oligocephalus) ditrema* inhabits large (30 ft. wide, 6 ft. deep), strongly flowing (30–100 cu. ft./sec.) limestone springs with a silt bottom; it is always associated with lush growths of *Fontinalis, Myriophyllum, Sparganium,* or *Fissidens* at a temperature between 60 and 64°F (Ramsey and Suttkus 1965). It apparently spawns on vegetation during June.

A chiller may be necessary to maintain year-round temperatures in the low 60s (°F). A 29-gallon aquarium will suffice for a group of four to six fish, and should have a dolomite substratum, abundant *Vesicularia* or *Nitella,* diatomaceous-earth canister filtration, and supplementary current provided by powerheads. Feed frozen bloodworms, live blackworms, and daphnia. Move vegetation to a separate, heavily aerated aquarium to allow the eggs to hatch in safety, and begin the fry on *Artemia* nauplii and microworms or vinegar eels. |
| *Etheostoma (Oligocephalus) grahami,* Rio Grande darter | *E. (Oligocephalus) grahami* has a few well-developed saddles on the back. It is yellow with green vertical bands, fine black speckling, and scattered red dots on the flank. The fins are lightly speckled, becoming weakly reddish in the nuptial male, without any bright blue or green margin. It is short and stubby, usually about 1½ inches or slightly more.

The Rio Grande darter occurs at the Texas–Mexico border in the Rio Grande drainage between Del Rio and Laredo. It is found in the lower Pecos and Devils Rivers, San Felipe, Sycamore, and Dolan Creeks, and Howard Springs in Texas. In Mexico, it occupies the Rio Salado and Rio San Juan in the state of Coahuila (Kuehne and Barbour 1983; Page and Burr 1991).

*E. (Oligocephalus) grahami* inhabits gravel and rubble riffles and vegetated pools of springs and their outlets, often hidden among leaves and twigs. A plant-spawner on twigs and leaves, it prefers hard water and a temperature of 70°F for optimal production. Fry are easily raised on *Artemia* nauplii, reaching maturity in six months. As with other Texas darters from stenothermal (constant, narrow temperature range) environments (Hubbs 1985), good water, and abundant food should assure year-round breeding activity. |
| *Etheostoma (Oligocephalus) lepidum,* greenthroat darter | *E. (Oligocephalus) lepidum* (**plate 86**) resembles the Christmas darter, *E. (Oligocephalus) hopkinsi,* of the eastern seaboard, but the red banding on the green body of the male is reduced to red spots, and the female has alternating brown and yellow bands. Within its range, it resembles a small orangethroat darter, *E. (Oligo-* |

*cephalus) spectabile,* but the cheeks and breast are blue-green and the belly is orange. It is usually less than 2 inches.

The greenthroat darter has a disjunct distribution. It occurs in the Pecos River of southwestern New Mexico and on the Edwards Plateau (Nueces, Guadalupe, and Colorado Rivers) in south-central Texas, with females in the two populations producing different sized eggs (1.3 mm in New Mexico vs. 1.5 mm in Texas) (Hubbs et al. 1968).

*E. (Oligocephalus) lepidum* inhabits vegetated riffles, springs, and spring pools. It often occurs with *E. (Oligocephalus) spectabile,* with which it may hybridize in aquaria, even though the latter is normally an egg burier in gravel. Eggs of the greenthroat darter are laid on the surface of vegetation or beneath rocks, apparently on any structure (Page 1983). They hatch in 25 days at 54°F and in 3 days at 80°F; agitation at colder temperatures speeds up development (Hubbs et al. 1969). The spawning season appears to be virtually year-round in stenothermal (constant, narrow temperature range) spring environments at 68°F, with eggs laid at five-day intervals between spawnings, during daylight (Hubbs 1985). It requires clear, moderately hard, spring-quality, cool water.

---

*Etheostoma (Oligocephalus) luteovinctum,* redband darter

*E. (Oligocephalus) luteovinctum* (**plates 87 and 88**) is spectacular. The flank of the nuptial male is traversed by intense, dark greenish blue-black (bronze) bands that alternate with red bands margined in yellow. The head, the midline of the entire flank, and the pelvics are black. The margin of the spiny dorsal fin and the entire anal fin is blue-green; the lower half of the spiny dorsal and most of the soft dorsal is light red. The teardrop is intense in both sexes, but is obscured by the dark head of the male. The female has a black midline on the flank that traverses a row of dark bars, and black speckles in her fins.

The redband darter occurs in the Duck, Caney Fork, and Stones Rivers of central Tennessee (Tennessee and Cumberland drainages).

*E. (Oligocephalus) luteovinctum* inhabits springs and large creeks, sometimes in riffles and often in pools, and frequently is associated with vegetation (Kuenhe and Barbour 1983). It may spawn in riffles during March, but its association with vegetation across all habitats suggests that it may be a plant spawner rather than an egg burier in gravel or, like the greenthroat darter, may use both substrata.

---

*Etheostoma (Oligocephalus) nuchale,* watercress darter

*E. (Oligocephalus) nuchale* (**plate 89**) is small, averaging 1½ to 1¾ inches.

The watercress darter occurs in the Black Warrior River system in northern Alabama.

*E. (Oligocephalus) nuchale* inhabits densely vegetated springs and their outlets where the year-round water temperature is 61–64°F. It rests and feeds among the stems and leaves of watercress, consuming aquatic insect larvae, snails, cladocerans, and amphipods. It is thought to breed from March to July, but its stenothermal habitat is consistent with year-round spawning.

The watercress darter is an endangered species because of its small, isolated populations and the vulnerability of its habitats. If allowed to be propagated in public aquaria, it should be maintained in hard water at 61 to 64°F and provided live vegetation as the spawning substratum. Egg-laden plants should be moved to a hatching and rearing aquarium and aerated; the fry should be offered *Artemia* nauplii and cultured ciliates as first foods.

Okaloosa darter, *Etheostoma okaloosae,* Choctawatchee Bay, Fla. WFR

---

*Etheostoma (Oligocephalus) asprigene,* mud darter

*E. (Oligocephalus) asprigene* is dark, with dark blotchlike bands most pronounced toward the rear of the body. The belly of the nuptial male is bright red or orange; his spiny dorsal fin has a blue margin, an orange submarginal band, and a dark blue area in the rear third. The soft dorsal fin has a medial orange band in both sexes. The average length is 2 inches.

The mud darter occurs in the Mississippi River drainage from Louisiana to Wisconsin and Minnesota, and just enters the Ohio River. On the Gulf Coast, it ranges from the Mississippi River westward to the Sabine and Neches Rivers of eastern Texas.

*E. (Oligocephalus) asprigene* inhabits quiet waters of lakes, river backwaters, ponds, and stream pools, over dense vegetation or leaf and branch debris. It spawns on vegetation.

Two of these plant spawning members of *E. (Oligocephalus)* are or should be protected.

---

*Etheostoma (Oligocephalus) okaloosae,* Okaloosa darter

*E. (Oligocephalus) okaloosae* is devoid of bright colors. It is generally yellow-brown, with a series of square or dash-shaped marks along the lateral line and rows of many small, dark spots over the entire flank. The lack of pretty reds, blues, and greens on the dorsal fin and throat, or occurring as iridescent bars on the flank, is unusual in this subgenus. It attains a small size (2 in.).

The Okaloosa darter is found only in streams draining into Choctawhatchee Bay near Fort Walton Beach and Eglin Air Force Base on the Gulf Coast (Okaloosa and Walton Counties in western Florida) (Kuehne and Barbour 1983; Page 1983; Page and Burr 1991).

*E. (Oligocephalus) okaloosae* inhabits clear, sand-bottom, forest streams with a slow to moderate current, where it occurs around and spawns on *Nitella* and other vegetation. These forested streams are rich in snail and crayfish populations, and the fishes are usually infested with black-spot *(Neascus)* trematode larvae in the skin.

Mette (1977) suggested that *E. (O.) okaloosae* is being displaced from a much wider original range by *E. (O.) edwini.* If true, additional populations may exist in small streams elsewhere in the extensive national forests of western Florida. Because pollution from Eglin Air Force Base could be eliminating the Okaloosa darter throughout the perimeter of the base, officials plan to collect the related *E. (O.) ed-*

*wini* and test it for susceptibility to base runoff. Carter Gilbert, however, suggests that *E. (O.) edwini* is more tolerant of reduced current and increased siltation resulting from human alteration of the environment; thus, it is not outcompeting *E. (Oligocephalus) okaloosae,* but is expanding because it is better adapted to the same degrading environment that is reducing the range of the Okaloosa darter (C. Gilbert, pers. comm.).

E. (Oligocephalus) okaloosae is a protected species not available to aquarists; if it becomes available, it can probably be spawned easily on vegetation in small aquaria.

| | |
|---|---|
| *Etheostoma (Oligocephalus) pottsi,* Chihuahua darter | E. (Oligocephalus) pottsi is included here as probable trading material from Mexican aquarists. It is distinguished from its relatives by a lack of scales on the gill cover, nape, and breast, interrupted sensory canals on the head, and no distinct, broad bars on the body. The nuptial male has a blue marginal and red submarginal band on the dusky red to orange spiny dorsal fin, a green body with dark green blotches and mottles on the top and sides (orange below from the pelvics to the anal fin), and mostly orange fins. |

The Chihuahua darter occupies headwater streams of the Sierra Madre Occidental Mountains in western Mexico. It occurs in the Rio Conchos (tributary to the Rio Grande), Rio Nazas (entirely distinct drainage), Rio Aquanaval (upper part of the entirely distinct Rio Trujillo drainage), and at least historically in the Rio Mezquital (the latter a Pacific drainage stream) in the states of Chihuahua, Durango, and Zacatecas, Mexico (Page 1981, 1983; Kuehne and Barbour 1983; Smith et al. 1984). The population in the Rio Mezquital are the only darters on the western side of the Continental Divide; it is probable that this river was once part of the Rio Grande but has shifted its outlet through stream capture of headwaters from the Rio Nazas.

E. (Oligocephalus) pottsi inhabits slow to moderately flowing, shallow, sand or rubble, mountain headwater streams; it does not occur in fast riffles, but in pools and channels with dense beds of *Potamogeton, Nasturtium,* or algae attached to rubble (Smith et al. 1984).

The status of this fish is in doubt, and American ichthyologists have recommended that it be protected.

The remaining members of the subgenus are probably all gravel spawners.

| | |
|---|---|
| *Etheostoma (Oligocephalus) caeruleum,* rainbow darter | E. (Oligocephalus) caeruleum (plates 90, 91, and 92) is the best-known darter throughout the hobby in the United States and abroad. The rainbow darter was described by Storer 50 years before it was remarked upon by Jordan and Evermann in 1896 as probably the gaudiest American freshwater fish. Typically the males have brilliant spiny dorsal fins, blue at the wide margin and red through the remainder of the fin; the body is tan above to bright orange below and toward the rear and traversed by 6 to 12 brilliant blue bands. In some populations, the body is light with red speckles on the flank, and, in others, the anal fin is all blue. Generally, the rainbow darter has a bicolored anal fin, blue outside, and red-orange near the body. If in doubt, use a hand lens or microscope to examine the pectoral fins; the rainbow darter has 13 rays. The female is plain tan and brown-mottled; in some populations, it is readily separated from the orangethroat by lacking the black dashes on the flank. There is also a subtle difference in body proportions between the two species: the |

rainbow is thickest in the middle under the spiny dorsal fin (pot-bellied) and the orangethroat is thickest just in front of the spiny dorsal fin (barrel-chested). The male rainbow darter attains 3 inches and the female, 2 inches.

The rainbow darter is widespread and variable in different river systems, but no subspecies are recognized. The major contiguous range is from Tennessee and adjacent regions of northern Georgia and western North Carolina northward through the Great Lakes drainages into Quebec and then westward to Minnesota and southward to southern Illinois. A separate western population occurs on the Ozark Plateau of Missouri, Arkansas, and eastern Oklahoma and Kansas. Finally, a disjunct population occurs in a small area of southwestern Mississippi and eastern Louisiana. Rainbow darters in different drainages occupy the upper portions of rivers.

*E. (Oligocephalus) caeruleum* inhabits clean, clear, fast-flowing waters of large creeks to medium-sized rivers at depths of a few inches to 2 feet, over gravel riffles, rubble on gravel, and sometimes on bedrock or among boulders. It prefers swift, clean, and second-order or larger waters and avoids leaf litter, silted backwaters, the smallest spring branches, and first-order streams. It is a riffle and run fish that feeds only during the day and exclusively on and beneath rocks on chironomids, black-flies, mayflies, caddisflies, and other benthic insect larvae; it does not feed on drift insects (e.g., hatched mayflies) that normally occur at night. Throughout the year, it consumes mostly chironomids, but divides the remaining insect larval types with its neighbor darter species (Wynes and Wissing 1982; Hlohowsky and White 1983) through a selection behavior called resource partitioning.

During winter, when temperatures are their lowest, the males are at their most brilliant. As early spring advances, males concentrate on the shallowest coarse gravel clearings in riffles, each of the largest attempting to defend a territory of 1 to 2 square feet. This can prove difficult when there may be two dozen males to a square yard.

Females are not residents of these gravel spawning areas, but enter one or two at a time to investigate the males. As a female enters a territory, it is immediately courted by a male with head-shaking, fin and gill flaring, and other clear examples of strutting. This is followed by gentle nipping of the female or the male beating the side of the female with his tail. When sufficiently excited, the female pushes her nose into the gravel and plows forward, burying the lower half of her body and pectoral fins before raising her snout.

The male (and often a group of adjacent males) attempts to spawn by mounting the female. The male places his pectorals against the flank of the female or presses his tail against her tail. He proceeds to shake his snout and shudder his entire body, at which time a small number of adhesive eggs is emitted and fertilized. The eggs adhere to grains of gravel, and are thus protected from being swept away by the strong currents or from settling into low-oxygen backwaters or pools.

Spawning seasons, clutch size, and egg diameters were reviewed by Heins et al. (1996), who noted that early reports sometimes mixed observations of rainbow and orangethroat darters before the two species were recognized as distinct. One of the earliest reports of "rainbow darter" breeding was that of Reeves (1907), who probably observed orangethroat darters, at the time not known to be a separate species.

A 20-gallon long aquarium is sufficient for six males and six females. The bottom should be a mixture of pea-sized gravel and dolomite. Hard, slightly alkaline water is preferred. A strong current and good filtration should be supplied by vigorous aeration and an outside power or canister filter. Feed heavily on frozen bloodworms, adult brine shrimp, and live blackworms. Because of the heavy feeding, frequent partial water changes are essential to maintain high quality water; no amount of activated carbon will get the water as clean as it is in the rivers of its natural habitat.

Spawning should begin within one week of collection during late winter or early spring. One method is to allow the fish to spawn for one week, and then move the adults to another aquarium; the fry will hatch, rise from the gravel, and can be raised in the original spawning aquarium. An alternative method is to stir the gravel vigorously twice a week to loosen eggs and swirl them into the water column, where they can be collected with an aquarium net for incubation in shallow dishes with cool water containing acriflavine. The fry hatch in less than two weeks at room temperature and are easily raised on *Artemia* nauplii as the first food.

| *Etheostoma (Oligocephalus) spectabile,* orangethroat darter | *E. (Oligocephalus) spectabile* **(plates 93, 94, 95, and 96)** is similar to the rainbow darter, but usually has an all-blue anal fin. Otherwise, it has bright red and blue banded flanks, an orange cheek and throat, and a spiny dorsal fin banded in blue and orange. Several populations have recently been elevated to species rank and more will join them (Ceas and Page 1997). |

The orangethroat darter occurs east of the Mississippi River in stream systems of Illinois, Indiana, Michigan, and Ohio. It also occupies most of the stream systems in Kentucky, but not the Cumberland, Dix, Green, Salt, and Tennessee drainages. West of the Mississippi River, it occurs in the Osage River drainage of Missouri and Kansas, the Gasconade and Meramec River drainages in Missouri and Arkansas, and some minor streams in Iowa and Missouri that flow directly into the lower Missouri River or the Mississippi River. Aquarists should not mix "orangethroat" darters from different locations; they may be different species.

*E. (Oligocephalus) spectabile* inhabits gravel, sand, and rubble headwater riffles of small to large rivers, from first- to fourth-order streams in shallow waters. The orangethroat darter occurs mostly in the smallest streams; it is the most abundant darter (when present) in small streams. It prefers gently to moderately flowing water on a bottom of small rocks (cobble) over gravel, usually away from vegetation; it also occurs in leaf litter of silted river backwaters and occasionally in vegetated springs. It is a group riffle spawner that buries its eggs in gravel. The spawning season may begin as early as October in Texas, extending to May or June (2–7 mo.); it begins earlier in the South but ends the same time everywhere (Hubbs 1985).

A 10-gallon aquarium is suitable for three males and six females. Feed frozen bloodworms and adult brine shrimp, and live whiteworms, blackworms, and mosquito larvae. Put a thin layer of gravel on the bottom, and a margarine container filled with gravel on a rock below the discharge of an outside power filter. The elevated cup of gravel in the effluent stream simulates a riffle. A dominant male will take over the cup and females will enter for spawning, burying eggs in the cup's gravel.

Twice a week, remove the cup, pour the gravel into a clean plastic pail, and swirl the gravel with cold tap water. Pour the washings through a nylon aquarium net to retain debris and the 1 mm amber eggs. Remove and wash the gravel frequently; it must be clean or the buried eggs will die. Discard the debris before replacing the gravel in the cup. Incubate the eggs in shallow dishes with acriflavine until hatching ten days later. The fry are raised easily on *Artemia* nauplii as a first food. Growth is rapid, with the young reaching maturity in the first year.

The orangethroat darter previously consisted of five subspecies: *E. (O.) squamosum, E. (O.) pulchellum, E. (O.) spectabile, E. (O.) uniporum,* and *E. (O.) fragi,* distinguishable by counts, head pores, and pattern (Distler 1968), by isozyme differentiation (Wiseman et al. 1978), and by range (Page and Burr 1991). Both *E. (O.) uniporum* and *E. (O.) fragi* recently have been elevated to species rank. Four additional species have been recognized from this complex (Ceas 1994; Ceas and Page 1997): *E. (O.) tecumsehi* in the Pond River of Kentucky, *E. (O.) bison* in the Buffalo River of Tennessee, *E. (O.) kantuckeense* in the upper Barren River system, and *E. (O.) burri* in the upper Black River of Missouri.

---

*Etheostoma (Oligocephalus) uniporum,* Current darter

*E. (Oligocephalus) uniporum* has a wide turquoise band above the base of the first dorsal fin, no horizontal dashes below the lateral line with faint dashes (if any) above it, and eight to ten transverse bands on the side meeting at the belly; the spaces between the bands are blue-gray.

The Current darter occurs in the Black River system from Cane Creek (Butler County) in Missouri southward to Flat Creek (Lawrence County) in Arkansas, including Cane and Fourche Creeks, and the Little Black, Current, Eleven Point, and Spring Rivers (Ceas and Page 1997).

*E. (Oligocephalus) uniporum* usually occupies shallow, first- or second-order clear streams of moderate gradient over a rock and gravel bottom.

---

*Etheostoma (Oligocephalus) fragi,* strawberry darter

*E. (O.) fragi* is typical of the complex, except the female has a distinctive medial orange band in the first dorsal fin and transverse bars are often prominent. The medial orange band in first dorsal fin of the nuptial male is much wider than the blue bands above and below, and have a series of orange V-markings (chevrons) that cross the belly. The horizontal dashes on the flank are faint, but extend a few rows below the lateral line.

The strawberry darter occurs in the upland headwaters of the Strawberry River (Black River drainage) in Missouri and Arkansas.

*E. (O.) fragi* usually inhabits shallow, first-order clear streams of moderate to high gradient over a rock and gravel bottom, where it is abundant.

---

*Etheostoma (Oligocephalus) tecumsehi,* Shawnee darter

*E. (O.) tecumsehi* is a striking member of this complex in which orange is the predominant color. The body and belly are bright orange, including the spaces between all the transverse blue bars, not just those in front (Ceas and Page 1997).

The Shawnee darter is endemic to the upper tributaries of the Pond River (Green River system) in Christian, Todd, and Hopkins Counties in Kentucky.

*E. (O.) tecumsehi* usually occupies shallow, first- or second-order clear streams of moderate gradient over a rock and gravel bottom. It is common now, but its small range is precariously vulnerable to damage by development. The Shawnee darter has been recommended for protection.

---

*Etheostoma (Oligocephalus) bison,* buffalo darter

*E. (O.) bison* is a stocky, deep-bodied member of the complex in which the nuptial male develops a nuchal hump. His flanks are covered with long, dark dashes above the lateral line, with the outer (marginal) blue band being the widest band in the first dorsal fin. The six to nine transverse bands are reduced to squarish blotches. The buffalo darter usually has eight anal rays, whereas other members of the group usually have six or seven (Ceas and Page 1997).

The buffalo darter occurs in tributaries of the lower Duck and lower Tennessee Rivers, from southern to northern Tennessee and just into Kentucky.

*E. (O.) bison* usually inhabits shallow, first- or second-order clear streams of moderate gradient over a rock and gravel bottom.

---

| *Etheostoma (Oligocephalus) burri,* brook darter | The nuptial male of *E. (O.) burri* has a brick red throat, chin, and belly. The first dorsal fin is broadly edged in dark blue; six to nine transverse bars may be reduced to lateral blotches; and moderately distinct horizontal dashes appear above and below the lateral line (Ceas and Page 1997). |
|---|---|

The brook darter occurs in small upland streams of the long, narrow, upper Black River system from Reynolds and Iron Counties to where the river joins the lowland Mississippi River valley in Butler County of Missouri.

*E. (O.) burri* usually inhabits shallow, first- or second-order clear streams of moderate gradient over a rock and gravel bottom. Because many of these small streams are dry much of the year, the fish is widespread but not abundant.

---

| *Etheostoma (Oligocephalus) kantuckeense,* Highland Rim darter | *E. (O.) kantuckeense* (**plate 97**) is a robust, densely pigmented member of the complex with a powder blue belly. The first dorsal fin is almost completely pigmented by the broad, blue-black band that contrasts with an equally broad orange band dominating the second dorsal fin. The body is richly spotted with orange. Blue-black pigment appears on top of the head and on the pectoral fins, and there are about eight dark, blue-black transverse bands that do not extend to the top or to the belly. The horizontal dashes are reduced to spots (Ceas and Page 1997). |
|---|---|

The Highland Rim darter is endemic to Drakes Creek and other streams of the upper Barren River system in Kentucky and Tennessee. Two other species now known to be endemic to this river system are *E. (U.) barrenense,* and the sucker, *Thoburnia atripinnis.*

*E. (O.) kantuckeense* usually inhabits shallow, first- or second-order clear streams of moderate gradient over a rock and gravel bottom.

The "orangethroat" darters of the middle Cumberland–upper Green, Salt, lower Cumberland, Caney Fork, and Dix River systems of Tennessee and Kentucky, and of the White, Bayou des Arc, and St. Francis River systems of Arkansas and Missouri also appear to be taxonomically distinct but have not yet been described under new names. The remaining members of *E. (Oligocephalus)* are few and quite pretty.

---

| *Etheostoma (Oligocephalus) collettei,* creole darter | *E. (O.) collettei* (**plate 98**) was previously considered a subspecies of *E. (O.) asprigene,* which it resembles. The nuptial male has eight or nine saddles above (four prominent); the flank has five to eight blue vertical bars (most pronounced toward the rear); two orange spots mark the base of an otherwise colorless tail fin; a bright orange bar adorns the insertion of the pectorals; the belly and lower flank are bright orange; the spiny dorsal fin has a narrow outer blue margin, followed by a wide orange band below, a narrow blue band below that, and a narrow orange band at the |
|---|---|

base; the soft dorsal fin is dark at the outer margin, followed by a wide orange area with a thin, dusky blue line or two at the base; and the anal and pelvic fins are greenish or dusky blue. The female is similar, except mottled rather than barred on the flank, and color intensity is reduced (Birdsong and Knapp 1969).

The creole darter occurs in the Ouachita and Red River drainages of Arkansas, the Ouachita, Little, Red, and Sabine River drainages of Louisiana, and the Little River (Red River drainage) in Sevier County of Oklahoma (Matthews and Robison 1982).

*E. (O.) collettei* inhabits moderate to fast riffles and chutes over gravel, rock, or hard soil covered with logs and stumps. Typical streams are small, shallow, and shaded by a wooded canopy. It prefers both barren riffles and heavy growths of *Podostemum ceratophyllum* (Birdsong and Knapp 1969).

A pair spawned in the early spring in an outdoor 10 gallon aquarium supplied with vigorous aeration, a gravel bottom, and artificial plants (Katula 1991a). The long, slender genital papilla of the female appeared prior to spawning. Spawning was not observed, but occurred at 53 to 60°F, after which 78 eggs were retrieved from deep within the gravel. Additional spawning apparently occurred after these eggs were retrieved, based on indentations on the surface of the gravel. The newly hatched larvae immediately assumed a benthic habit, as has been seen in other *E. (Oligocephalus).*

---

*Etheostoma (Oligocephalus) swaini,* Gulf darter

*E. (O.) swaini* (**plate 99**) resembles *E. (O.) collettei,* but lacks the prominent blue bands on the flank. The nuptial male has a bright orange belly; the sides are darkly mottled, blotched, or banded in brown; the lower fins are dusky to bright blue; the spiny and soft dorsals are bright blue at the narrow outer margin, followed by a wide orange area, a narrow blue area, and a narrow orange area at the base; the caudal fin is spotted in the center, with blue above and below; and two orange spots adorn the base of the tail. The female is heavily spotted brown and has a white belly and dark basicaudal spots. The teardrop is prominent in both sexes.

The Gulf darter is widespread on the central Gulf Coast below the fall line. It ranges from the Ochlockonee River near Tallahassee, Florida northward to Macon, Georgia. It continues westward to Fort Campbell, Kentucky, and southward to Lake Pontchartrain near Baton Rouge, Louisiana.

*E. (O.) swaini* prefers clear, blackwater streams and small rivers with a sand or sand-silt bottom, leaf litter, organic debris, or dense vegetation *(Sparganium americanum, Orontium aquaticum, Mayaca fluviatilis,* and *Eleocharis),* where it feeds mostly on chironomids, cladocerans, caddisfly and mayfly larvae, copepods, and isopods. It spawns during March (Ruple et al. 1984). Eggs are deposited on large leaves in the bottom litter, on the filter tube, or any hard surface off the bottom.

---

*Etheostoma (Oligocephalus) hopkinsi,* Christmas darter

*E. (O.) hopkinsi* (**plate 100**) has an entirely green body with a dozen bars on the flank that are red in the nuptial male and yellow in the female. The spiny dorsal fin is green with a broad, dark red submarginal band; the anal fin is blue-green.

There are two subspecies. *E. h. binotatum* has two distinctive, rectangular dark blotches (giving rise to the specific epithet *binotatum*) on the nape in front of the dorsal fin. It occurs in the Savannah River drainage of Georgia and South Carolina and in Twentythree Mile Creek in South Carolina. *E. h. hopkinsi* has two faded, irregular dark blotches (if any) on the nape and occurs to the southwest in the Altamaha and Ogeechee Rivers of Georgia (Bailey and Richards 1963).

The Christmas darter occurs above and below the fall line on rock and gravel riffles of creeks to medium-sized rivers. It is found in medium to fast current (occasionally slower currents in vegetation). It usually is located behind and below stones, where it feeds on aquatic insect larvae. It breeds at age one and lives three years. It probably spawns during April and May (Rohde et al. 1994) in gravel.

---

*Etheostoma (Oligocephalus) whipplei,*
redfin darter

*E. (O.) whipplei* (**plate 101**) is a beauty. The nuptial male has a bright orange belly, bright orange spots on the entire flank, and eight saddles on the back. The pectorals are clear, the pelvics are blue, and the unpaired fins have a broad blue margin. The orange below the blue margin varies from a thin row of spots (spiny dorsal) to a broad band (soft dorsal and tail fin) to most of the remainder of the fin (anal). The female has clear to yellow plaques (spaces) on a dusky flank and her fins are mostly colorless. The redfin darter grows to 3 inches.

The original literature (Hubbs and Black 1941) described four subspecies: *E. (O.) w. radiosum, E. (O.) w. whipplei, E. (O.) w. montanum,* and *E. (O.) w. artesiae.* Later authors recognized *E. (O.) radiosum* as a distinct species. Retzer et al. (1986) clarified the relationships of the remaining three taxa, recognizing just two subspecies: *E. (O.) w. whipplei* above the fall line in the White and Arkansas systems of Kansas, Missouri, Arkansas, and Oklahoma (including *montanus* as not distinct); and *E. (O.) w. artesiae* mostly below the fall line (except for an area in central Georgia) from the Neches River of eastern Texas through the Mobile basin in Georgia. The ranges of the two subspecies, recognizable by their scale counts, overlap slightly in the Ouachita River system and possibly in the Red River system.

The redfin darter inhabits shallow, gravel and rubble riffles of headwaters, creeks, and slow-moving small rivers, only occasionally occurring on sand and mud or in current-swept vegetation. It spawns mostly during March and April (Heins and Machado 1993).

---

*Etheostoma (Oligocephalus) radiosum,*
orangebelly darter

*E. (O.) radiosum* (**plate 102**) is gorgeous, the illustrations in Kuehne and Barbour (1983), Page (1983), and Page and Burr (1991) not doing it justice. The nuptial male has four offset rows of blotches from the lateral line to the back (the saddles and lateral line are most distinct); the unpaired fins have blue margins, orange submargins, or are mostly orange (anal); the pelvics are blue; the pectorals are clear; and the throat and belly are bright orange. The female is blotched like the male, but her fins are not brightly colored.

Historically, *E. (O.) radiosum* has been considered a subspecies of *E. (O.) whipplei* (based on preserved specimens), but the living fishes are clearly different. It hybridizes in nature with *E. (O.) spectabile,* but the hybrids are too few to affect the genetic integrity of the populations of either species.

The orangebelly darter is restricted to a narrow band in Arkansas and Oklahoma. Three subspecies have evolved due to genetic drift, the process by which a small founding population provides all the genetic material for a later expanded population. *E. (O.) r. cyanorum* occurs in the Blue River (a tributary of the Red River) of Oklahoma; *E. (O.) r. paludosus* occurs in the Muddy Boggy and Kiamichi Rivers (tributaries of the Red River) of Oklahoma; and *E. (O.) r. radiosum* occurs in the Little and Ouachita Rivers of Oklahoma and Arkansas. The three subspecies differ in isozyme patterns, a good indicator of genetic differentiation. It is thought that the muddy Red River itself may be the barrier to mixing of the populations (Echelle et al. 1975), although the inherent lack of movement by the fish could also play a role. Movement appears to be a response to temperature extremes (Hill and Matthews 1980).

The best known subspecies, *E. (O.) r. cyanorum,* is common in clear, rocky bottom, Blue River raceways, in the shallow areas between riffles (with two or three fish/sq. yd.). The fish seem to move only within the one raceway, crossing neither riffles nor pools (Scalet 1973b). The Blue River is 100 miles long with a gradient of 7½ feet per mile, moderately swift, clear, and with a small floodplain.

The parasites of orangebelly darters include a leech *(Illinobdella moorei),* an adult trematode in the stomach *(Crepidostomum cooperi),* and a larval trematode *(Uvulifer ambloplitis)* that causes black-spot deposits in the skin (Scalet 1971). Centrarchids are not important predators of *E. (O.) radiosum,* based on lack of darters in predator stomachs (Scalet 1974).

*E. (O.) radiosum* spawns in raceways from mid-March through mid-April when a year old. Fish collected in the fall and given abundant food developed nuptial coloration and spawned before the end of the year at 63 to 79°F. Two or three fish were placed in half-filled, 2-gallon aquaria with 3 inches of water, rocks at one end, sand and gravel, and fed whiteworms, mosquito larvae, daphnia, and copepods (Linder 1958). In the wild, the youngest juveniles feed on copepods and cladocerans (daphnia), and the larger fish eat aquatic insect larvae, mostly chironomids, mayflies, caddisflies, and blackflies (Scalet 1972).

The female dives under the gravel and is mounted by the male on a territory only millimeters in diameter (Scalet 1973a). The male follows the female, pokes the female with his snout, dashes away, returns, nips, and rests alongside. The male then stops in front of the female, erects his dorsal fin, and vibrates his pectorals. Eventually, the female dives head-first into the sand bottom. Holding her body at a 45 degree angle, she rapidly and violently moves her tail fin, splashing water and sand on the inner aquarium walls to form a small depression in the sand and gravel, then sinks into the depression. When she begins vibrating, the male mounts, clasping with his pelvic fins and bending his tail downward against the female. The female bends her tail and head upward. All this takes seconds, and then both fish stop moving except for rapid vibrating of the gill covers. The female then moves away and prepares a new sand pit; the act is repeated, although sometimes eggs are laid on the bare aquarium bottom. The adhesive eggs were normally stuck to gravel. One female *E. (O.) radiosum* produced 76 eggs in a single day, and another produced 272 over 82 days. These numbers underestimate production, because not all eggs were seen, and many eggs were eaten by the breeders (Linder 1958).

---

*Etheostoma (Oligocephalus) australe,*
Conchos darter

*E. (O.) australe* is included as highly desirable trading material from Mexico (Page 1981a). It has one large, thick anal spine, a broad frenum, small size, and brightly colored bars. The nuptial male is dark red-brown with ten wide green bars on the flank; the interbar spaces are either red or brown, or they may be yellow and contain red blotches. There are dark green saddles on the back, and the breast and belly are green. His spiny dorsal fin is dark-edged, red below, and dark at the base; the anal and pelvics are green at the base and yellow to red beyond; the soft dorsal and

Goldstripe darter, *Etheostoma parvipinne*, Black Warrior R., Ala. FCR

caudal fins are dull red; and a teardrop is present. The female is similar but much subdued in coloration, generally green above and yellow below; her fins are mostly yellow with a dark band on the spiny dorsal; and her flank bars are not bright. *E. (O.) australe* grows to 2 inches.

The Conchos darter occurs in Rio Conchos (state of Chihuahua) and possibly extends southward into the state of Durango, Mexico. The Rio Conchos is a southern tributary of the Rio Grande.

*E. (O.) australe* inhabits riffles of shallow, clear, fast-flowing streams. It breeds during May and June at least.

### Subgenus *Etheostoma (Fuscatelum)*

*E. (Fuscatelum)* was erected by Page (1981b) for a single colorless species with many characters of the subgenus *E. (Oligocephalus)*, plus breeding tubercles on the anal fin of the male as in *E. (Ozarka)*, a premaxillary (upper lip) frenum, and an incompletely pored and straight lateral line.

### *Etheostoma (Fuscatelum) parvipinne*, goldstripe darter

*E. (F.) parvipinne* is the only species in *E. (Fuscatelum)*. It lacks bright colors, but has breeding tubercles on the anal fin of the nuptial male, and one or two anal spines. It is slim and grows to 2 inches. Bailey and Etnier (1988) make much of the tubercles on the anal fin, even suggesting that *E. (F.) parvipinne* be regarded as a somber-colored *E. (Ozarka)* pending elucidation of its breeding mode. However, *Ozarka* has more than one mode, as we shall see. The body is reddish brown above with a dark brown band along the upper flank. A gold stripe marks the row of lateral line scales, and indistinct blotches are below, above a generally white belly. A horizontal, black eyebar and vertical teardrop mark the face, but otherwise, the female and nonnuptial male are tan to brown above, white below, and stippled with fine dots.

The goldstripe darter is widespread in Gulf Coast drainages below the fall line from the Red River in Oklahoma to the Brazos River in eastern Texas. It ranges to the Altamaha and Apalachicola Rivers in southwestern Georgia and the Florida panhandle near Tallahassee, continuing northward in the Mississippi basin to the bootheel of Missouri and adjacent western Kentucky (Robison 1977).

Its apparent rarity in locations other than Mississippi and western Tennessee is probably due to its preference for small, shallow waters frequently overlooked by ichthyologists; in fact, the first specimens from the Apalachicola drainage in Florida were collected by Bruce Means while searching on hands and knees for salamanders in water 1 inch deep (C. Gilbert, pers. comm.).

E. (F.) parvipinne inhabits seeps and pools of springs and small (6 in. to 8 ft. wide) spring-fed creeks, often with sand, gravel, and rubble bottoms. It usually is found near filamentous algae, but sometimes occurs beneath overhanging bank vegetation and among leaf litter and woody debris in slight to moderate current close to the source spring. The water is frequently stained by tannins, but clear. Eggs are attached to vegetation and woody debris.

Fish collected from vegetated spring pool margins during April spawned in 20-gallon aquaria. Males darkened to brown with an intense black teardrop through the eye, black bars, and brilliant red eyes. The females remained mottled brown. No territories or courtship were observed, and males pursued females throughout the aquarium. Eggs were deposited practically everywhere, on rocks, glass, the top of the gravel, plants, but were not buried. The 0.85 to 1.1 mm diameter eggs hatched in eight days at 68°F (Johnston 1994).

---

**Subgenus *Etheostoma (Ozarka)***

Members of E. (Ozarka) are generally colorful and robust, medium-sized darters characterized by scale distribution and pore pattern, neither of which is easy for an aquarist to discern. The nuptial male has a black-edged, orange-banded spiny dorsal fin [except in E. (Ozarka) trisella], an orange flank and belly, and breeding tubercles on the anal fin. The female is speckled.

Members of E. (Ozarka) occur in small, shallow springs, seeps, or creeks, usually first- or second-order streams. E. (O.) boschungi and E. (O.) trisella lay eggs on vegetation in seeps, but E. (O.) punctulatum buries its eggs in gravel. Other species in this subgenus are E. (O.) cragini, E. (O.) pallididorsum, and the sunburst darter, an unnamed species that is herein referred to as E. (O.) cf. punctulatum.

---

**Etheostoma (Ozarka) boschungi, slackwater darter**

E. (O.) boschungi is a plant spawner. The nuptial male is tan with black blotches on the back and along the upper flank, a black mask and a large, well-developed teardrop marking, orange lips and the entire area below the lateral line, spotted unpaired fins, and a spiny dorsal that is dark-edged with a broad orange band and green at the base. The female is tan with blotches and speckles on the body and fins.

The slackwater darter occurs in second- and third-order streams in Shoal Creek, Cypress Creek, and the Flint River of the Tennessee River system in northern Alabama, and is known from one locality in the Buffalo River of southern Tennessee (Wall and Williams 1974).

E. (O.) boschungi inhabits 2- to 5-foot-deep pools in small, 20-foot-wide streams with gravel or coarse sand bottoms covered with leaf litter and branch debris or dense roots (Wall and Williams 1974). From January through March, as the water rises above 55°F, the fish move out of the streams into streamside seeps in open pastures, where eggs are attached to vegetation (Kuehne and Barbour 1983).

The slackwater darter is not available to aquarists. It is federally endangered and may not be collected.

---

**Etheostoma (Ozarka) trisella, trispot darter**

E. (O.) trisella (**plate 103**) has one anal spine, three dark saddles on the back, a black mask on the face, and contiguous black blotches all along the flank with a separate one on the base of the tail. The blotching is distinct in the male, but reduced to stippling in the female. The nuptial male is golden overall, but mostly from the lips to the chest and belly and to the base of the tail. He has green blotches on the flank and a row of red spots in the spiny dorsal fin; otherwise, all fins are dusky throughout.

The trispot darter occurs in the upper Coosa River basin of Alabama, Georgia, and Tennessee, but is rare outside the Conasauga River of Tennessee.

*E. (O.) trisella* inhabits small, sluggish creeks with sand and gravel bottoms in open (nonforested) areas, and in larger streams and small rivers. It spawns on vegetation in spring seeps feeding first-order streams. Search headwater streams of the Conasauga system, especially pools with leaf litter and vegetation.

The original locality, Cowans Creek, no longer exists, having been flooded by construction of the Weiss Lake dam and reservoir of the Alabama Power Company. At the time, Cowans Creek was a small, sluggish stream heavily overgrown with *Dianthera;* the bottom was silt and sand mixed with fine gravel (Bailey and Richards 1963). Other historic locales have been silted by highway construction, and the species remains rare and deserving of protection in its remaining streams (Howell and Caldwell 1967).

Set up as for *E. (Ozarka) punctulatum,* but include spawning mops and hardwood tree leaves. Feed blackworms and bloodworms.

Determine protected status before attempting collection.

---

**Etheostoma (Ozarka) pallididorsum, paleback darter**

*E. (O.) pallididorsum* (**plate 104**) has a light line along the length of the back, giving rise to the common and scientific names.

The paleback darter occurs in the upper Caddo River and Hallmans Creek, headwaters of the Ouachita River in central Arkansas. This river system is the large, adjacent drainage south of the Arkansas River, to which *E. (O.) cragini* is restricted (Kuehne and Barbour 1983; Page 1983).

*E. (O.) pallididorsum* inhabits small, vegetated streams connected to springs and seeps, in pools containing rocks over mud (sometimes among leaf litter). Its most common associate is *E. (Oligocephalus) radiosum.* It feeds on midges, mayflies, other aquatic insect larvae, and cladocerans. It probably breeds during March after entering streamside seeps, similar to *E. (Ozarka) boschungi.*

The paleback darter is not likely to be legally available.

---

**Etheostoma (Ozarka) punctulatum, stippled darter**

*E. (O.) punctulatum* is a gravel spawner. It has been confused in the literature with another, as yet unnamed, species referred to herein as *E. (Ozarka)* cf. *punctulatum.* A photograph of a nuptial male of the true *E. (O.) punctulatum* appears on the cover of Page's (1983) *Handbook of Darters.* The female is tan with black blotches and barely discernible black stippling, while the male is unstippled and brilliant orange below, from the lower jaw to the base of the tail. There is a bold, black teardrop, a black saddle becoming a band from the nape to just behind the gill cover, and a broad, elongate, iridescent dark greenish patch in the rear one-fourth of the body. The spiny dorsal fin is banded in orange and green-black. The stippled darter grows to over 3 inches.

It occurs in the northward-flowing Osage River drainage of the Ozark Plateau in Missouri. Robust, it is typically the only large common darter in its habitat. The fish present in the southward-flowing White River system is another (unnamed) species (Mayden 1987), distinguished by genetic and morphological characters and

Stippled darter, *Etheostoma punctulatum,* male, Osage R., Mo. RJG

Stippled darter, *Etheostoma punctulatum,* female, Osage R., Mo. RJG

social structure. The White River stippled darter reported from southeastern Kansas, northeastern Oklahoma, and northern Arkansas represents the unnamed species.

I have collected the true stippled darter from tributaries of the Osage River in Missouri almost yearly from 1978 through 1993, but never from the White River system. They were always in small, probably second-order, shallow (< 1½ ft. deep), moderately wide (20 ft.), slow-moving, clear streams with mixed bottoms of cobble, large flat rocks, gravel, and accumulations of leaf litter and woody debris along sandy backwaters and shores. *E. (Oligocephalus) spectabile* was usually the only other darter present and often abundant, whereas *E. (Ozarka) punctulatum* occurred in only small numbers (seldom two fish in a seine haul, and rarely more than six fish in a collection from one stream). Males and females were most often in different parts of the stream in December, the females among leaf litter and near shallow shores and the males under boulders in deeper pools created by concrete road crossings.

A 15- to 20-gallon aquarium is suitable for one or two males and two or three females. The aquarium should be half filled to provide shallow habitat, and the bottom prepared with sand, gravel, a few rocks, dead hardwood tree leaves, woody debris (twigs), and rooted or potted plants as hiding places for females. A plastic shoe box or margarine container should be filled with pebbles or coarse gravel and placed on top of the substratum so that its gravel is in shallower water than the surrounding gravel. An outside magnetic drive filter, without filter floss to interfere with flow, should be installed on the tank rim with its outflow directed onto the shoe box or margarine container to create an artificial riffle. Feed live blackworms, frozen bloodworms, and frozen adult brine shrimp.

The male makes no forays from its territory. A female will occasionally enter the territory and bury all but her head and tail in the gravel, at which time the male moves above her and spawning occurs. Fish that I collected in late December spawned in aquaria within two months at 65 to 70°F. A dominant male took up position on the artificial riffle, and displayed to and bit an intruding male, with the two occasionally locking jaws.

Eggs were removed from the pebbles by swirling, but better results ensued from removing the container, dumping its contents into a larger container, and adding cold tap water while swirling. I then poured the washings through an aquar-

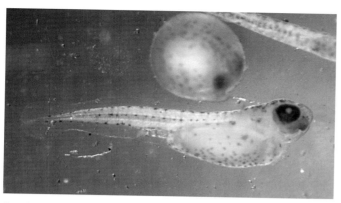

Stippled darter, *Etheostoma punctulatum,* eggs and fry. RJG

ium net to retain the darter eggs. The large (2 mm) eggs were placed in shallow dishes without fungicide. They hatched in two weeks, and the 5 mm fry could take *Artemia* nauplii a few days later as a first food. They grew at various rates and required separation by size. Maturity was attained in the first year.

*Etheostoma (Ozarka)* cf. *punctulatum,* sunburst darter

E. (O.) cf. *punctulatum* (**plate 105**) is far more robust (less streamlined) than *E. (O.) punctulatum.* The female is tan with dense black stippling, while the male is also heavily stippled and has dark saddles and yellow on the chest and belly. There is a bold, black teardrop, a dusky black saddle becoming a band from the nape to just behind the gill cover, and no green patch on the rear of the body. The spiny dorsal fin is banded in light orange and dusky black. This darter grows to over 3 inches.

The sunburst darter occurs in the White River system of Missouri and northern Arkansas (Mayden 1987), and ranges to southeastern Kansas and northeastern Oklahoma.

E. (O.) cf. *punctulatum* inhabits small, steep-sided, vegetated seepage creeks with *E. (O.) cragini, E. (Oligocephalus) spectabile, E. (M.) microperca,* and other darters. Adults are often abundant; six or more in a seine haul is not unusual. It is not difficult to take dozens from a single small stream, along with other species of darters. Males and females occur together, usually beneath undercut banks. Hotalling and Taber (1987), inadvertently discussing this species, reported that maturity occurs by the end of the first year and the fish live four years; spawning was not observed but was estimated as occurring from February through May, based on the maturity of eggs in fish collected over a period of months. Food consisted of 67 percent (by volume) isopods (the most abundant macroinvertebrate food source found in the stream leaf litter), plus lesser amounts of mayfly and caddisfly larvae. Other foods included earthworms, crayfish, and amphipods, but bloodworms (midges) surprisingly were not reported in the diet. Hotalling and Taber (1987) hand-stripped gametes, and reported that water hardened eggs were 1.6 mm in diameter and adhesive.

Katula (1988) spawned *E. (Ozarka)* cf. *punctulatum* collected from Shoal Creek in the White River system. Wild adults fed on live adult brine shrimp, live tubificid worms, and frozen chironomids, but live daphnia were ignored. Adults preferred caves in aquaria. During December and January, the adults were moved to a 30-gallon, cool aquarium with a black gravel substratum on an undergravel filter,

Sunburst darter, *Etheostoma* cf. *punctulatum*, habitat. RJG

artificial plants in the rear, and rocks forming caves at both ends. A single air-diffuser stone provided moderate turbulence.

Two males divided the aquarium territory and occupied the end caves. If a female approached (females were not pursued), the male would court by bumping his head against that of the female. The male then jerked his body and often circled the female or the pair circled one another. The female buried in the gravel, with her head and tail protruding, and the male mounted with his head and fins erect. Spawning was indicated by the male vibrating, followed by dismounting. Two or three episodes of mounting were observed, and the female remained buried to spawn for as long as 30 minutes. The male then retreated to his cave.

The large eggs hatched in 12 to 14 days at 63°F, and the 75–85 semipelagic fry consumed live *Artemia* nauplii at once. After a week or two, they assumed a strictly benthic habit. At six weeks, they were weaned onto chopped frozen adult brine shrimp and sifted daphnia; at eight weeks, however, unexplained severe losses were incurred, despite vigorous feeding and regular partial water changes. A second round of spawning during April or May produced more eggs and fry with better survival. At ten months of age, the young females became swollen with roe, promising a captively bred generation.

## *Etheostoma (Ozarka) cragini,* Arkansas darter

*E. (O.) cragini* (**plate 106**) is a gravel spawner with two anal spines and a dark teardrop. The female is dull tan to cream colored, with reduced blotches along the body and dense spotting on the body and fins. The male is also richly spotted and dark above, but develops a bright yellow-orange belly from the nose to the tail. It is a small member of this subgenus, growing only to about 2½ inches.

The Arkansas darter occurs in the Arkansas River drainage from southwestern Missouri and extreme northwestern Arkansas westward into northeastern Oklahoma, and continuing across southern Kansas into eastern Colorado. It is abundant in the Spring River drainage of the Ozark Plateau, but is less common westward.

Tuscumbia darter, *Etheostoma tuscumbia,* Moss Springs, Ala. FCR

*E. (O.) cragini* inhabits small (10 ft. wide), spring-fed streams and creeks with slow to moderate current and alternating pools and riffles. It prefers steep, over-hanging vegetated banks over a bottom of coarse gravel and sand that lies beneath cobble and rock with attached filamentous algae and accumulations of leaf litter or woody debris. Rick Edwards and I have collected them most often from un-dercut banks. It feeds primarily on isopods (60% by stomach volume) apparently taken from litter and debris, supplemented by mayfly larvae and only a small amount of midges. It spawns in gravel from late February through early July at 50 to 60°F.

Males do not fight and may jointly spawn with a single female burying in the gravel. The eggs are deposited 1 cm deep. Maturity is reached in the first year and most fish live less than two years (Page 1983; Taber et al. 1986). Provide a diet rich in amphipods, adult brine shrimp, or chopped euphausiid plankton to provide the nutrients associated with a predominantly crustacean diet.

## Subgenus *Etheostoma (Psychromaster)*

Members of *E. (Psychromaster)* have a single anal spine, an incomplete but straight lateral line, and scales on top of the head and on the branchiostegal membranes.

The relationships of this monotypic subgenus are not clear (Bailey and Etnier 1988).

## *Etheostoma (Psychromaster) tuscumbia,* Tuscumbia darter

*E. (P.) tuscumbia* is the only species in this subgenus, and is identified by one anal spine, scales on top of the short head, and a large underslung mouth. The remark by Kuehne and Barbour (1983) that the mouth is small is an error. The Tuscumbia darter is speckled or mottled with a red iris and a hint of red in the spiny dorsal fin. It occasionally attains 2 inches.

The Tuscumbia darter occurs in northwestern Alabama along the southern bend of the Tennessee River, and just enters southern Tennessee; however, it prob-ably has been extirpated from the latter locale (Kuehne and Barbour 1983).

*E. (P.) tuscumbia* inhabits densely vegetated limestone springs and their brooks, under mats of *Nasturtium* and *Myriophyllum* where it feeds mostly on amphipods, snails, and chironomids (Armstrong and Williams 1971). There is no information on breeding, but the long breeding tube of the male suggests a mode unique among darters, perhaps crevice spawning or the utilization of freshwater mussels.

The Tuscumbia darter is a protected species.

This book follows Bailey and Etnier (1988), who divided the species in the subgenus *Nanostoma* of Page (1983) into the subgenera *Ulocentra* and *Etheostoma*.

---

**Subgenus *Etheostoma* (*Ulocentra*)**

Members of *E. (Ulocentra)* are small- to medium-sized, snubnosed darters. They have a completely pored lateral line, large pectoral fins, a red spot in the front of the spiny dorsal fin in males (sometimes females), two spines in the anal fin, no nuptial tubercles, and an upper lip that is either free or attached by a thin frenum (a bridge of tissue between the snout and upper lip).

*E. (Ulocentra)* are found in both shallow water and deep pools of small to medium, clear, foothill streams east of the Mississippi River, south of the Ohio River, and west of the Appalachian Mountains. The snubnosed darters spawn in deep pools, laying one or a few eggs at a time on the vertical sides of flat rocks or boulders.

There are about 20 species in 2 species groups: the northeastern *E. (U.) duryi* group with no frenum and having vomerine teeth, and the southwestern *E. (U.) simoterum* group with no frenum or a thin one (and other technical characters). The *E. (U.) duryi* species group includes *E. (U.) duryi, brevirostrum, bellator, chermocki, colorosum, etnieri, flavum, lachneri, pyrrhogaster, ramseyi, raneyi,* and *tallapoosae,* but they probably are not all valid species. The *E. (U.) simoterum* group contains the remaining members of the subgenus.

---

*Etheostoma (Ulocentra) simoterum,*
Tennessee snubnose darter

*E. (U.) simoterum* (**plate 107**) has eight dark green saddles separated from corresponding black lateral blotches by a two- or three-scale wide white zone containing one or two rows of orange scales; the belly is orange; the lips, chin, and lower fins are blue-green. The first dorsal fin is red at the margin and the rear and black below; the center of the second dorsal is a diffuse red; the caudal fin has a red center. The breeding male is deep green to blue-green with a red-orange patch or spots on the body; both dorsal fins are bright red. It grows to 2½ inches (Page and Mayden 1981; Kuehne and Barbour 1983; Page and Burr 1991).

There are two subspecies. *E. (U.) s. atripinne* (**plate 108**) occurs in the middle (but not upper or lower) Cumberland River drainage of Tennessee, just enters southern Virginia, and is absent from much of Caney Fork in the Cumberland system; *E. (U.) s. simoterum* has a broader distribution, ranging in the upper Tennessee basin from western Kentucky through eastern and central Tennessee southward to the tip of northwestern Georgia and most of northern Alabama (Kuehne and Barbour 1983).

*E. (U.) simoterum* inhabits deeper pools of small to medium creeks on gravel and cobble, occupying crevices on bedrock. It feeds mostly on chironomids, somewhat less on mayflies and caddisflies, and on just a few cladocerans. It breeds at age one and probably does not live beyond age two.

Spawning occurs during April at 66°F on vertical surfaces of large rocks (Page and Mayden 1981). Wild fish collected during the spawning season (Page and Mayden 1981) at 66°F spawned immediately in aquaria at 78°F. Eggs were laid one or two at a time on the sides of large stones, sometimes on top of the stone, and occasionally on the gravel adjacent to the stone; gravel-spawned eggs were likely to be eaten by the female.

Provide a deep aquarium with a gravel bottom, and feed bloodworms and blackworms, supplemented with frozen adult brine shrimp. A group of three males and eight females is optimal for a 29- to 55-gallon aquarium. Include rocks, some stacked to provide crevices for egg deposition, and moderate current from an outside power filter.

Spawning in captivity occurs erratically. Courting behavior is triggered by a temperature of 65°F and adequate food. The male establishes an aquarium territory at the base of a rock. Females roam, stopping for a suitable male. Eggs are attached to the lower vertical surfaces of the rocks, seldom beneath. The male guards his territory for eight to ten days, then loses interest and returns to browse for food. Occasionally, a male or rogue female eats the eggs.

Remove egg-laden rocks to a smaller container with water from the parental aquarium. Eggs hatch in 14 days. Only the smallest live foods, such as rotifers, infusoria, or ciliates, are taken; *Artemia* nauplii are ignored. Do not overfeed; the fry will die from a drop in pH and elevated ammonia. As soon as the fry can swim, add snails to clean up uneaten food. The fry grow slowly.

| | |
|---|---|
| *Etheostoma (Ulocentra) duryi,* blackside snubnose darter | *E. (U.) duryi* (**plate 109**) is a spectacular member of the southwestern *E. (U.)* group. It has eight deep black dorsal saddles; 10–12 black blotches on the flank fuse into a broad, scalloped, intensely black band; the chest, throat, and belly to the caudal peduncle is bright orange; the unpaired fins and the upper side are orange-spotted; the nape, upper cheek, teardrop, and lower fins are black. It grows to about 2 inches.

The blackside snubnose darter is widely distributed from the Clinch to Duck Rivers, including the Sequatchie and Elk Rivers and Shoal Creek of the Tennessee River basin in Tennessee and northern Georgia (Kuehne and Barbour 1983).

*E. (U.) duryi* inhabits pools of small to medium clear streams with moderate flow and large rocks on a gravel bottom. It probably spawns during April. Eggs are deposited on vertical surfaces of rocks on the downstream side of the current.

Care and spawning is the same as for *E. (U.) simoterum.* |
| *Etheostoma (Ulocentra) brevirostrum,* holiday darter | *E. (U.) brevirostrum,* recently described by Suttkus and Etnier (1991), may be a complex of species. It has been illustrated and discussed in Page and Burr (1991) as the Ellijay darter, and in Kuehne and Barbour (1983) as the upland snubnose darter. The female is unremarkable. The nuptial male has a medial red band in the green anal fin and a narrow red band in the middle of the soft dorsal fin; vertically divided (hourglass) red bands appear on the green sides, with each band surrounded by a white to yellow halo, unlike any other darter, but reminiscent of the pattern in the needle-nosed *E. (L.) nianguae.* It grows to 2 inches.

The holiday darter occurs in the Conasauga River of Georgia and Tennessee, the Coosawattee and Etowah Rivers of Georgia, all extreme headwaters of the Coosa River system in northern Georgia and southern Tennessee, and in the Valley and Ridge and the Blue Ridge physiographic provinces (illustrated on geologic maps of the southern Appalachians available from the U.S. Geological Survey); it is disjunct far to the west in Choccolocco Creek of Cleburne County in Alabama (still in the Coosa system) (Suttkus and Etnier 1991).

Because the holiday darter may in fact consist of two or three separate but closely related species, specimens from the different drainages should not be housed together. The type locality in Alabama is a clear, fast-flowing creek, 30 to 60 feet wide, with a bottom of boulders, gravel, rubble, sand, and beds of *Justicia* in the summer. |

Saffron darter, *Etheostoma flavum,* Duck R., Tenn. WFR

The microhabitat appears to be boulders on sand in 2 to 3 feet of water, 6 feet or more from the heavily wooded bank. It probably spawns during April and May (Suttkus and Etnier 1991) on the sides of large rocks.

**Etheostoma (Ulocentra) flavum, saffron darter**

*E. (U.) flavum* generally has nine black saddles and an equal number of dark blotches that tend to fuse on the flank over the lateral line. The flank above the lateral line is dark gray and saffron yellow below the lateral line. The pelvics and outer anal fin are black; the upper and lower edges of the tail fin base are blue-green; the dorsal fins are dark reddish brown; the spiny dorsal has a dark red outer margin and row of dark spots at the base. The saffron darter is diagnosed by a single and undivided dark basicaudal spot; it has almost no red coloration and no more than 25 combined dorsal saddles and lateral blotches; it has yellow-orange lips; no red blotch appears in front of the spiny dorsal fin; and the lower flank is yellow (Etnier and Bailey 1989).

The saffron darter occurs in the lower Cumberland and Tennessee River drainages of Kentucky and Tennessee, including the Duck, Buffalo, Indian Creek, Stones, Harpeth, Caney Fork, and Elk Rivers.

*E. (U.) flavum* inhabits pools containing large rocks in fast-flowing, clear streams. It spawns on the vertical surface of large, flat rocks, depositing one to four eggs per spawning clasp in nooks and crannies on the rock surface (Keevin et al. 1989).

**Etheostoma (Ulocentra) coosae, Coosa darter**

*E. (U.) coosae* (**plate 110**) is a member of the southwestern group. It has a row (sometimes two) of dark red spots on the spiny dorsal fin, a diffuse red soft dorsal fin, nine dark saddles on the back, nine dark bars on the flank, mottling between saddles and bars, a teardrop, and dark spots above and below a basicaudal spot. The throat and cheeks are blue-green. The top and bottom margins of the dorsal fins are blue-green and the tail fin and paired fins have a blue-green tint. It often attains 2 inches.

The Coosa darter occurs in the Coosa River drainage (part of the Alabama River system) of northern Alabama, northern Georgia, and southern Tennessee. Within this area, *E. (U.) coosae* is confined to the lower Etowah River, and the sibling *E. (U.) scotti* to the upper Etowah.

The Coosa darter inhabits small to medium, shallow tributaries of the Coosa River with permanent moderate flow, and a bottom mainly of rocks and boulders on gravel and small stones (little sand). Spawning is presumed to occur in deep pools during early spring (Kuehne and Barbour 1983).

A 29- to 55-gallon aquarium is suitable for up to eight fish. Spread a thin layer of gravel on the bottom and provide outside filtration and supplementary strong current with a powerhead. *E. (Ulocentra)* spawns on the sides of large rocks in pools where water depth is at least 16 inches; it lays one egg at a time from the base of the rock to a distance well off the bottom when the temperature reaches 68–70°F (Winn 1958; Bailey and Etnier 1988). Rest a large piece of shale or slate against one side of the aquarium, extending to the top. Feed frozen bloodworms and brine shrimp supplemented with live daphnia and small amounts of live blackworms.

The dominant male will spawn with several females over a period of days, the male mounting the female on a vertical surface but only when there is sufficient water depth. The rock containing the eggs should be removed after a sufficient number of eggs are produced because the nonspawning darters will eat them. Invert the rock in a separate container of cool water with aeration played directly over the eggs. Alternatively, the eggs can be rolled off the rock with fingers, and the rock returned to the aquarium. The fry should be given *Artemia* nauplii.

---

*Etheostoma (Ulocentra) scotti,*
Cherokee darter

*E. (U.) scotti* differs from *E. (U.) coosae,* from which it has recently been separated, by a prominent, broad red band in the spiny dorsal fin of the male, in having more rows of scales, and by locality. It differs from *E. (U.) brevirostrum, E. (U.) ramseyi,* and *E. (U.) tallapoosae* in lacking oblique median orange-red bands in the soft (second) dorsal and anal fins, and in lacking orange or red on the body (Bauer et al. 1995).

The Cherokee darter occurs in the upper Etowah River of the Coosa River drainage (Alabama River system). Its range includes streams in Cherokee, Bartow, Pickens, Dawson, Lumpkin, and Paulding Counties, all in Georgia.

*E. (U.) scotti* inhabits small to medium, shallow tributaries with a permanent moderate flow and a bottom mainly of rocks and boulders on large gravel and small stones; it rarely occurs on fine gravel, sand, or bedrock. As with other members of the subgenus, pairs spawn on vertical surfaces of rocks (seldom horizontally); one egg is produced per clasp, which the female then rubs off onto the rock.

---

*Etheostoma (Ulocentra) tallapoosae,*
Tallapoosa darter

*E. (U.) tallapoosae* **(plate 111)** was recently described by Suttkus and Etnier (1991). It was discussed in Kuehne and Barbour (1983) as the Tallapoosa snubnose darter and in Page and Burr (1991) as the Tallapoosa darter. The female is unremarkable. The nuptial male has eight or nine vertically elongate blotches along the flank; it is brown in front and becomes orange toward the rear, merging with the orange belly bands from below; the bands sometimes are separated by green pigment. The tail has two bright orange spots. The soft dorsal fin has a broad red band through the middle; the spiny dorsal has a bright red band medially toward the rear, fading to dull red in front; there is no red spot in front of the dorsal.

The Tallapoosa darter is widespread throughout the Tallapoosa River system above the fall line in Alabama and Georgia and in the Blue Ridge and Piedmont physiographic provinces.

*E. (U.) tallapoosae* inhabits small, clear streams with a bottom of rubble, boulders, gravel, and sand. It probably spawns during March and April (Suttkus and Etnier 1991).

## Etheostoma (Ulocentra) rafinesquei, Kentucky snubnose darter

*E. (U.) rafinesquei* (plate 112) is a member of the northeastern group with eight or nine minor saddles on the back that are separated from ten black, vertically ovoid blotches on the flank by rows of dark-edged scales on the upper sides. The entire lower flank appears red-spotted due to red-edged scales; the lower midline is white; and the lower fins and cheeks are blue-green. A red spot in the spiny dorsal fin is prominent, but the entire fin of the nuptial male is red.

The Kentucky snubnose darter occurs in the upper tributaries of the Green River above Nolin River and in the Gasper River of the Barren River drainage (Kuehne and Barbour 1983; Page and Burr 1991). Its distribution in Kentucky is not discernible according to Clay (1975). In the Nolin River (Green River system), the Kentucky snubnose darter occupies the same type of habitat as *E. (U.) barrenense,* and hybridizes with it in aquaria (Winn 1958).

*E. (U.) rafinesquei* spawns on high-relief rock surfaces (sometimes on gravel) from late March through mid-May, initiated by increasing day length and temperature beginning in the 50s (°F). Spawning increases in frequency when temperatures are in the 60s (°F) and abruptly terminates at 70°F. Spawning occurs in bouts of consecutive days interrupted by resting intervals. During the six-week season, one female might produce 1,000 eggs (Weddle and Burr 1991).

The preference for vertical surfaces was documented by Weddle (1990) who noted that captive females spawned on vertical, inclined, and horizontal surfaces at a ratio (in order) of roughly 15:6:1. At all ages, chironomids are the predominant food items, with microcrustaceans a secondary food for juveniles (Weddle 1992). The diet should be primarily insectivorous and at least 80 percent bloodworms. Insect larvae are fattier and richer in calories than crustaceans such as brine shrimp. Spawning will cease if insufficient food is provided (Weddle and Burr 1991).

## Etheostoma (Ulocentra) baileyi, emerald darter

*E. (U.) baileyi* (plate 113) is a member of the northeastern group. It has an overall greenish cast, with diffuse saddles on the back and nine emerald green bars on the side that resemble *E. (E.) zonale* in pattern and iridescence. The first dorsal fin of the male has a broad red margin (red-brown in the female). The teardrop is indistinct. The average adult length is less than 2 inches.

The emerald darter occurs in the Laurel, Rock Castle, Dix, Big South Fork, and Red Rivers, with a distribution similar to *E. (L.) sagitta,* in the upper Kentucky (Ohio River basin) and the upper Cumberland Rivers of the Cumberland Plateau. It ranges both above and well below Cumberland Falls. It continues from Kentucky southward into northern Tennessee. Clay (1975), referring to it as an unnamed *Etheostoma* species, incorrectly believed it restricted to Kentucky.

*E. (U.) baileyi* is common in pools of small to medium streams with rubble and gravel bottoms. It probably spawns during May (Kuehne and Barbour 1983).

## Etheostoma (Ulocentra) barrenense, splendid darter

*E. (U.) barrenense* (plate 114) is a spectacular member of the northeastern group, with eight or nine black flank blotches that fuse into a broad horizontal band surrounded by red scales above and below to the breast. A red spot on the first dorsal fin is prominent in both sexes; the teardrop and dorsal saddles are present; red occurs in the spiny and soft dorsal fins; the spiny dorsal is dark at the base; and the head and lower fins are blue-green.

The splendid darter is endemic to the Barren River (Green River system) of

Kentucky and Tennessee (Kuehne and Barbour 1983), but not the Gasper River (Page and Burr 1991).

E. (U.) barrenense inhabits small to medium clear streams with rocky pools, bedrock, and gravel and rock riffles. It spawns during April, in the third and last year of life for the dominant males and in the second year for females. Spawning occurs on vertical or near vertical rock walls, in pools and limestone bedrock runs 2 to 3 feet deep; the currents must be swift enough to keep the habitat silt-free.

Winn (1958) noted that females kept swimming up the sides of an 8-inch-deep aquarium, but did not spawn. When he moved the fish to 16-inch-deep aquaria, they began to spawn on the slate walls, a large granite rock, and a piece of slate resting at an angle against the wall of the aquarium. The male mounted the female, balancing on his pectoral fins, as the female proceeded up the rock wall laying one egg at a time on the hard angular surface.

| *Etheostoma (Ulocentra) etnieri,* cherry darter | E. (U.) etnieri **(plate 115)** is a member of the southwestern group. The female is generally straw colored with minor black pigment and white below. The nuptial male is brilliantly colored, with a green head, cheek, breast, and upper and lower parts of the tail fin. He has eight large, dark, and wide dorsal saddles, eight irregular, sometimes contiguous lateral blotches, and between the saddles and lateral blotches, a series of thin, dark, horizontal lines that are unlike the pattern in any other E. (Ulocentra). The middle section of the second dorsal, caudal, and anal fins have a broad red area. The lower body is blood red, the color continuous to above the lateral blotches or separated from the lateral blotches by a white area. It grows to 2½ inches (Kuehne and Barbour 1983; Page and Burr 1991). |

The cherry darter occurs in the upper Caney Fork of the middle Cumberland River system in Tennessee, in streams flowing over the Mississippian limestones of the eastern Highland Rim (Bouchard 1977).

E. (U.) etnieri inhabits river edges, bedrock pools, but most often is found in small to medium streams, 15 to 30 feet wide, occupying riffles and runs of low turbulence over gravel with scattered rocks. It probably breeds during April. Not abundant, it is locally common (Bouchard 1977; Kuehne and Barbour 1983; Page 1983).

| *Etheostoma (Ulocentra) pyrrhogaster,* firebelly darter | E. (U.) pyrrhogaster **(plate 116)** is a member of the southwestern group. The head, chest, and pelvic fins are blue-green. The body is tan above and brilliant red below and on the sides, especially toward the rear. A broad, scalloped black band in the front half of the fish obscures an underlying horizontal row of black blotches on the midline that reappears toward the rear. The unpaired fins are mostly red; the anal has a blue-green border, the second dorsal has a clear border, and both dorsals have a blue-green base (Page and Burr 1991). |

The firebelly darter is limited to a small disturbed area of southwestern Kentucky and western Tennessee in the Obion and Forked Deer River drainages.

In Terrapin Creek (Obion River drainage), the habitat is a small stream (5 to 15 ft. wide and 4 to 5 ft. deep) of low to moderate gradient with a sand and gravel bottom. E. (U.) pyrrhogaster is uncommon throughout its small range. It occupies deeper parts of the creek, typically in sandy pools or undercut banks among tree roots, where it feeds mostly on chironomids, with a minor amount of mayfly and caddisfly larvae (Carney and Burr 1989).

*E. (U.) pyrrhogaster* is a "species of special concern" and cannot be collected. Ichthyologists with permits to investigate this species could provide specimens to aquarists cooperating in research projects. If this can be accomplished, set up a deep (≥ 16 in.) aquarium with a gravel bottom and a tall rock extending to the surface. Feed frozen bloodworms, optionally supplemented with daphnia, fruit flies, or *Artemia*. Low temperatures in the 50s and 60s (°F) are important to induce spawning activity. The firebelly darter has spawned in aquaria after injection with 50 IU of human chorionic gonadotropin (HCG), selecting the vertical aquarium corners and high rocks (Carney and Burr 1989).

---

*Etheostoma (Ulocentra) zonistium,* bandfin darter

*E. (U.) zonistium* (**plate 117**) is a member of the southwestern group. The male is light yellow, with a prominent red spot in the spiny dorsal fin. He has 7 small saddles well separated from a lateral row of 10 to 12 small black marks. These small black marks are obscured in the front half of the body by a superimposed brown-black band (darker in front) on the midline. The band is broken by a white line through the lateral line but once again appears toward the rear. The entire head is green, from the nape to the nose and from the chin to the cheeks. The spiny dorsal fin has a green margin. Both dorsal fins have rows of black spots. All other fins are green. The belly and upper rear flank are orange. The nuptial male is dark red on the upper flank and orange-red on the lower flank and belly.

According to Carney and Burr (1989), the bandfin darter is common but restricted to the lower western tributaries of the Tennessee River drainage in western Kentucky and western Tennessee, and just enters Mississippi and Alabama. It is also found in the Hatchie River of Tennessee and the Black Warrior system of Alabama.

*E. (U.) zonistium* inhabits the margins of small riffle and pool streams with a moderate gradient and a sand or gravel bottom, often among the rush, *Juncus effusus,* tree roots and brush piles, at depths to 16 inches. The diet is mostly chironomid larvae (bloodworms). It spawns from March through late May when water temperatures are in the 50s and 60s (°F) (Carney and Burr 1989).

Provide a deep (16 in.) aquarium with a sand or gravel bottom, and a high profile rock or plants as the spawning substratum. Feed frozen bloodworms, supplemented with live daphnia or frozen *Artemia*.

The male approaches the female, crossing her back in a zigzag motion and rubbing her nape. The pair moves to a vertical spawning site, which may be the corner wall of the aquarium, a crevice in a rock, or a bushy plant such as hornwort *(Ceratophyllum demersum)*. Occasionally, the fish will spawn on the surface of the gravel (eggs are not buried) if this is the only source of crevices. The male assumes the S-shape, typical of males adhering their bodies against females to bring the vents close together. The pair tense, vibrate, and one egg is laid at a clasp. The eggs are abandoned and may be eaten by other darters. The 1.7 mm eggs hatch in one week and the 4 mm larvae are large enough to take *Artemia* nauplii (Carney and Burr 1989).

---

Subgenus *Etheostoma (Villora)*

Hubbs and Cannon (1935) originally defined *E. (Villora)* by an ovipositor with brushlike fringes (villi), but this was an artifact of too much probing of a delicate connecting membrane (Collette and Yerger 1962). In fact, the ovipositor is a low tube with rugae (ridges or elongate folds) terminating in short free ends at the opening, and not markedly different from the wrinkled pads on most darter ovipositors. Other characters of the subgenus include a lack of nuptial tubercles in the male, the male much larger than the female, two anal spines (the first thicker than the second), a distinctive pore pattern on the head, and, most importantly, the shape of the lateral line. *E. (Villora)* is monotypic (Page 1983; Bailey and Etnier 1988).

*Etheostoma (Villora) edwini,*
brown darter

*E. (V.) edwini* (**plate 118**) is the only member of its subgenus. It has a broad frenum connecting the upper lip to the snout and three often indistinct basicaudal spots. The male has large orange to red spots over the entire body and on the fins, his spiny dorsal fin has a red submarginal band and a dark blotch at the rear, and there is a series of dark blotches below the light colored, arched lateral line. A teardrop occurs below the eye and horizontal dark lines occur throughout the eye. The name "brown darter" is misleading, and "redspot darter" has been suggested (Collette and Yerger 1962). The female is plain, dark spotted, and sometimes has additional red spots; her fins are clear to dark-spotted.

The brown darter occurs in the lower (northern) St. Johns and Suwannee Rivers of northern Florida, and ranges from the Ochlockonee and Apalachicola Rivers of Florida to the Perdido River on the Alabama state line. It continues northward into Georgia (where the Apalachicola becomes the Chattahoochee) below the fall line (Collette and Yerger 1962). This region of the Gulf Coast resembles the Sandhills of the Carolinas but with barely discernible low hills and many widely scattered, deep sinkholes in the limestone base. The land is sandy, and the dominant trees are pine, scrub oak, and mixed hardwoods.

*E. (V.) edwini* lives in clear rivers and streams with dense stands of *Vallisneria americana* and alder, wax myrtle, black gum, pine, and oak along the banks. These waters have moderate to swift current over clean white sand and pockets of gravel and detritus in the faster and slower regions, respectively. Depths range up to 4 feet, and widths from 5 to 40 feet.

The specific habitats for *E. (V.) edwini* were the clear to slightly turbid streams, 6 inches to 3 feet deep, with a bottom of sand and occasional overlay of fine silt, patches of gravel, and rocky outcrops. The pH ranged from 6.4 in leaf concentrations to 7.8 near limestone springs. Vegetation included *Ludwigia, Scirpus, Orontium, Nitella,* and *Batrachospermum,* a red alga forming thick clumps. In aquaria, *E. (V.) edwini* attached adhesive eggs to aquatic plants, one egg at a time, when mounted by the wall (Williams 1976).

## Family Cichlidae, the Cichlids

The cichlids are perchlike fishes similar in appearance to the Centrarchidae. Our sole native species is *Cichlasoma cyanoguttatum,* a member of the *Herichthys* group. Its closest relatives in Mexico are differentiated by their teeth. The family occurs in Africa, Asia, and in South, Central, and North America, with more than 1,000 species worldwide. Several exotic cichlids have been introduced accidentally in Florida and elsewhere in the United States, but they are not covered in this book.

**Genus *Cichlasoma***
*Cichlasoma cyanoguttatum,*
Texas or Rio Grande cichlid

*C. cyanoguttatum* is a high-backed, slab-sided fish with a large mouth, a large eye, compressed and enlarged outer teeth, well-developed dorsal and anal fins, and a nuchal hump in large males. Coloration is brown to pale with a dark spot at the base of the tail, another spot midflank, and iridescent blue-green scales over the entire body and the bases of the fins. Juveniles have smaller blue spots and more pronounced black body marks.

Rio Grande cichlid, *Cichlasoma cyanoguttatum,* San Marcos R., Tex. WFR

The Texas or Rio Grande cichlid is native to the Usumacinta Province (Atlantic slope) of Mexico. It ranges northward to the Rio Grande and has been introduced into adjacent drainages in Texas and into some waters of Florida. It is almost identical to other members of the *Herichthys* group (e.g., *boucourti, geddesi,* and *pearsei*) in Mexico, but these others do not range into the United States.

*C. cyanoguttatum* occurs on sand bottom of deep, clear rivers with submersed and emersed vegetation near the banks. It frequently occurs in deeper waters of rivers where sunfishes (Centrarchidae) occupy the shallows. It spawns in sand pits or on hard bottoms at one year of age and 4 inches long. Both parents guard the young.

Athough it is a peaceful fish, it requires at least a 29-gallon aquarium to breed. Feed flake and pellet foods, supplemented with chopped earthworms, crushed snails, adult brine shrimp, meal worms, and/or tubificids. Pair bonding follows a ritual that includes lateral wagging displays and often jaw locking.

The adhesive eggs are spawned on a flat rock, inside a flowerpot, or on a bare-bottom of the aquarium. Both parents fan the eggs until hatching, and then move the fry to a pit in the sand, where they adhere to the sand and each other by cement glands on the head until they are free-swimming. Upon swim-up, the shoaling fry take *Artemia* nauplii as a first food. They grow rapidly. The Texas cichlid hybridizes in aquaria with *C. nigrofasciatum.*

See Goldstein (1973) for the biology and breeding of cichlids.

## Coastal Fishes

Ordinary aquarium hydrometers (medical urinometers) read the concentration of salt in specific gravity (sp. gr.), whereas scientists utilize expensive electronic meters reporting salinity in parts per thousand (ppt). Hydrometers, unfortunately, are inaccurate, requiring that closely spaced lines be interpreted at the optically indistinct meniscus. Thus, a hydrometer reading of sp. gr. 1.01 might mean anything from 0 to 20 ppt.

A better alternative is to make up full-strength sea water from commercial salt mixes according to the package directions, which indicate that a pound of salt makes just over 8 gallons of synthetic sea water. This will provide water of sp. gr. 1.025 (36 ppt), equal in salinity to natural sea water. If you require 50 percent sea water, then use ½ full-strength sea water and ½ tap water. This will provide 18 ppt brackish water without the need for an instrument. It is simpler to keep a 30-gallon plastic barrel of full-strength stock sea water on hand, diluting as much as required when needed, than to calculate and weigh out the required amount of salt to be mixed with a particular volume of water each time a different salinity is required. For these reasons, the information presented is often given in percent of full-strength sea water.

## Family Blenniidae, the Combtooth Blennies

Within the perciform fishes, the combtooth blennies are most similar to the marine clinids, pricklebacks, and gunnels, but their habits and habitats are most similar to that of the gobies. They are small, almost entirely marine bottom fishes with high-backed or snakelike bodies, long dorsal and anal fins, and a single row of comblike curved teeth. They sometimes have knobby or branching growths above the eyes or elsewhere on the head.

During the breeding season, the male develops swellings on the front of the anal and sometimes the dorsal fin. There are usually separate color patterns for the nonbreeding, spawning, and brooding phases. The male is typically larger with a bigger head, and has anal fin swellings that enlarge and perhaps emit a pheromone to supplement his displays of head-bobbing and lateral weaving.

Blennies spawn in a crevice or cavity, the female laying a few hundred eggs attached by adhesive threads after the male first pastes his sperm on the surface. Thresher (1984) recommended using twice as many females as males in breeding aquaria and PVC pipes partially buried in the gravel as spawning burrows. The eggs are often 1 mm long, oval, flattened, and pigmented, and hatch in nine days at dusk. The phototropic, planktonic larvae are 3.5 to 5.0 mm long. Larvae of a Japanese blenny took *Brachionus* (rotifers) and *Balanus amphitrite* (barnacle) larvae at first, and accepted *Artemia* nauplii thereafter, requiring 40 days to metamorphose and assume a benthic mode of life (Shiogaki and Dotsu 1973).

Many blennies have pouches and sacs on the male reproductive system which add viscous substances to the seminal fluid (Rasotto 1995), perhaps to help glue the sperm to the substratum in advance of female oviposition. Alternatively, the viscous material may be a colloid that prevents sperm activation until contact with eggs is made, as has been hypothesized for mouthbrooding *Tilapia*.

Blennies occur in all warm and some temperate seas. In North America, they occur from both Canadian coasts to the coasts of Mexico and southward. They usually live among shallow water rocks, oyster bars, mussel beds, or other hard structures. The European *Blennius fluviatilis* enters fresh water, and other marine blennies may enter low salinity or even fresh water around the Black Sea.

Blennies are easy to collect. Tipping a clump of oysters (oyster rock) or mussels onto a fine-mesh dip net often yields blennies; scraping a long-handled dip net along pilings, stanchions, or breakwaters also works; baited hooks are sometimes effective; dragging a modified oyster dredge behind a small boat yields blennies and other marine organisms. (An oyster dredge is a box-shaped, heavy gauge wire basket on a steel frame, 2 feet square with an opening 4–6 inches in height, and is sometimes available from a coastal fish house.) Modify the dredge by attaching ¼-inch mesh hardware cloth (wire) inside the rear of the unit; finer mesh will clog.

Collecting blennies among oyster rocks can cause cuts to hands and feet. Especially in Gulf of Mexico waters in the summer, cuts may become infected with life-threatening *Vibrio* bacteria in immunosuppressed individuals. If you are elderly, have a depressed immune system, or are taking steroids, and fever, rash, and/or nausea develops after collecting, consult a physician immediately.

Striped blenny, *Chasmodes bosquianus,* N.C. RJG

In U.S. and Canadian waters, the Blenniidae contains 8 genera and 18 species, of which 12 are of interest to aquarists.

**Genus *Chasmodes***
*Chasmodes bosquianus,*
striped blenny

*C. bosquianus* has a smooth contour in the margin of the dorsal fin (no notch is distinguishable midway). Decorative growths are limited to slight expansions of the lips. The sexually active male has a swollen urogenital papilla, and enlarged, rough-surfaced swellings at the tips of the first two anal spines. Maximum length is about 3–4 inches (Smith-Vaniz 1980).

The striped blenny is almost a disjunct species (Springer 1959), ranging from Chesapeake Bay to northern Florida and from western Florida to Texas, but absent from most of the Florida peninsula. Around Mobile Bay, Alabama, it overlaps with *C. saburrae;* in this area, the two are easily distinguished. The phenomenon of distinguishing features becoming accentuated where closely related species overlap is called character displacement.

*C. bosquianus* occurs in inshore oyster beds at a depth of less than 1 foot during summer, but occurs offshore during the winter. It feeds on zooplankton, small crustaceans, worms, and other motile small animals. During April or May, the male defends a spawning territory such as an empty oyster shell within a clump, never an isolated shell. The selection is based on the gape (opening), which restricts the size of potential egg predators (Crabtree and Middaugh 1982); males may nest close together (Phillips 1973).

A 10-gallon aquarium is adequate for a pair. Use brackish to full-strength synthetic sea water (sp. gr. 0.015–1.035). Provide an undergravel filter with the discharge driven by a powerhead, and a substratum of gravel, sand, rocks, and shells. Include attached growth of *Caulerpa* and illuminate for 12 to 14 hours. The striped blenny thrives on live and frozen *Artemia* supplemented with flake food, and grazes on algae. Remove the planktonic fry with a cup and provide moderate aeration. Feed rotifers as the first food, followed by *Artemia* nauplii. If rotifers are not available, feed sifted wild plankton.

*Chasmodes saburrae,* Florida blenny

*C. saburrae* is high-backed with a smooth contour in the dorsal fin (no notch is distinguishable midway). It resembles the striped blenny, but its head is steeper and its body more spotted and less streaked. Decorative growths on the head are limited to slight expansions of the lips. The anal fin swellings of the male are smaller than in *C. bosquianus* and the teeth differ as well.

The Florida blenny is found on the Florida and the Gulf Coasts westward to Mississippi, occurring between and separating the two populations of *C. bosquianus* (Springer 1959).

*C. saburrae* occurs in inshore oyster beds, among rocks, on sea walls, in debris, and on mangrove roots, in water only inches deep.

Feeding requirements and breeding conditions are those described for *C. bosquianus*.

## Genus *Hypleurochilus*

Members of this genus have filaments above the eyes (cirri) and usually have canine teeth in the rear of the upper and lower jaws. The genus was recently revised and contains an additional five species (Bath 1994), two in west Africa *(H. aequipinnis* and *H. pseudoaequipinnis)* and three in North America, that are not covered in this book.

## *Hypleurochilus caudovittatus*, zebratail blenny

*H. caudovittatus* has distinct bands in the tail fin.

The zebratail blenny occurs in the eastern Gulf of Mexico from St. Andrews Bay, Florida southward along the coast of peninsular Florida.

*H. caudovittatus* prefers brackish shallows among oyster shells, but also occurs in marine shallows at rocks, mangroves, grass beds, pier pilings and floating docks.

Because the genus was revised recently, historical summaries should be reevaluated as they may have been compiled from a complex of species from different areas. These different populations may have different behaviors and preferences in salinity, food, and habitats.

## *Hypleurochilus geminatus*, crested blenny

*H. geminatus* was previously placed in *Hypsoblennius*. It has protruding eyes, a dip in the contour of the dorsal fin, and a dark spot at the front of the fin. The body and fins are dark brown with spots and marbling. The female has square dark blotches and a lighter body. The breeding male develops a brightly colored chin and throat and decorative growths (cirri) above the eyes. The average length is 3–4 inches.

The crested blenny ranges from North Carolina to eastern peninsular Florida.

*H. geminatus* selects an oyster shell of narrow gape, always within a clump of shells. Shells with large gapes are avoided as they are too vulnerable to predators of the eggs.

## *Hypleurochilus gentilis*, bay blenny

*H. gentilis* has a bluntly rounded head with a serrated (sawtoothed) rear edge on the cirrus (filament) above the eye. It is brown and green with reddish spotting and a reddish throat (Miller and Lea 1976). A black-and-red spot appears on the front of the dorsal fin.

The bay blenny ranges from Monterey Bay to the Gulf of California (Eschmeyer and Herald 1983) where it inhabits intertidal zone bays and estuaries, on hard bottoms, and feeds on small animals and some algae.

A 20-gallon aquarium with full-strength synthetic sea water (sp. gr. 1.025) is adequate for a pair or small group. Feed them chopped clam and shrimp. Remove the planktonic fry with a cup and place them in a separate aquarium with aeration. Feed rotifers or sifted wild plankton as the first food.

Feather blenny, *Hypsoblennius hentz*, Ocracoke Island, N.C. RJG     Freckled blenny, *Hypsoblennius ionthas*, Cape Fear R., N.C. FCR

| | |
|---|---|
| *Hypleurochilus gilberti,* rockpool or notchbrow blenny | In *H. gilberti* the cirrus is divided into branched filaments, and the head is deeply notched behind the eye. The body is olive with dark saddles along the back (Eschmeyer and Herald 1983). It grows to 4 inches or more.<br><br>The rockpool or notchbrow blenny ranges from Point Conception in California to Magdalena Bay in Baja California.<br><br>*H. gilberti* inhabits intertidal to deeper water, often among tubeworm colonies on rocks, and feeds mostly on limpets, crustaceans, and algae. It breeds from June to August, the male defending 600–1,800 adhesive eggs. The fry hatch in 5 to 18 days (Fitch and Lavenberg 1975). |
| *Hypleurochilus multifilis,* plumed blenny | *H. multifilis* resembles the crested blenny, but the large cirrus above each eye of the male has four more branching cirri at the base, whereas the cirri are not prominent in the female. In the male, the front of the dorsal fin and contiguous shoulder above the pectoral fin is black, and four square clusters of black blotches adorn the orange spotted flank.<br><br>This is the "crested blenny" population of the Gulf Coast. The renamed plumed blenny ranges from Choctawhatchee Bay in Florida westward to Texas.<br><br>*H. multifilis* is most common in estuaries with oyster rocks and reefs, on other hard debris and substrata, and around jetties, but is not abundant. |
| **Genus *Hypsoblennius***<br>*Hypsoblennius hentz,* feather blenny | *H. hentz* has spots, five obscure and oblique bands, and a prominent branched cirrus above the eye. It averages 3–4 inches long.<br><br>The feather blenny ranges from New Jersey to Texas, including southern Florida and occurs in typical blenny habitat. |
| *Hypsoblennius ionthas,* freckled blenny | *H. ionthas* resembles the feather blenny, but has either an unbranched cirrus or at most one branch at the base and another at the tip. It has a dark bar on the cheek with a black edge (Robins and Ray 1986).<br><br>The freckled blenny ranges from South Carolina through southern Florida to Texas, and is more common than the feather blenny along the Gulf Coast. |
| *Hypsoblennius jenkinsi,* mussel blenny | *H. jenkinsi* resembles the bay and rockpool blennies, but has a smooth head contour (no dip behind the eye) and the cirrus is divided into multiple filaments at the |

Molly Miller, *Scartella cristata*, Fla. FCR

tip. The body is brown with a tinge of red, and there is a curved dark stripe on the cheek. It grows to an average length of 3–4 inches.

The mussel blenny ranges from southern California to Baja California of Mexico where it occupies subtidal holes, burrows, crevices, and often mussel beds. It feeds on amphipods, copepods, worms, crustaceans, and other small benthic animals.

Collect a clump of mussels and shake it over a bucket of water; it is more difficult to remove them from burrows. Care as for *H. gilberti*.

**Genus *Parablennius***
*Parablennius marmoreus*,
seaweed blenny

*P. marmoreus* and has a branched growth above each eye. It is tan to orange above and lighter below, with orange honeycomb marks on the cheek and clusters of orange to brown spots on the body (Randall 1968). A dark band from the eye passes over the yellow pectoral fin and fades before reaching midflank. A dark spot marks the origin of the dorsal fin. It attains 3 inches.

The seaweed blenny ranges from New York to Florida, and in the northeastern Gulf of Mexico on shallow hard bottoms, not always with vegetation.

**Genus *Scartella***
*Scartella cristata*, Molly Miller

*S. cristata* was previously placed in *Blennius*. Cirri above the eyes surround a fringe of cirri on the midline from the head to the dorsal fin. It is olive with dark blotches on the upper side that extend into the dorsal fin, and scattered white spots. Adults often attain 4 inches.

The Molly Miller occurs in Florida and the Gulf of Mexico, ranging into Mexico.

*S. cristata* inhabits rocky areas close to shore. It is herbivorous (Randall 1968; Smith 1974).

A 5- to 10-gallon aquarium is adequate for a pair. See also *H. gentilis*. Include a rich growth of *Caulerpa* for food, and illuminate for 12 to 14 hours or more with incandescent light.

# Family Gobiidae, the Gobies

The family Gobiidae contains more than 2,000 species worldwide of mostly small, nearshore marine fishes, with a few exclusively in fresh water. The most popular freshwater gobies in the aquarium hobby are the bumblebee fish of Asia *(Brachygobius xanthozona, B. doriae, B. aggregatus, and B. nunus)*, the mudskippers of Africa

(*Periophthalmus barbarus*) and Asia (*P. chrysospilos*), and the Australian desert goby (*Chlamydogobius eremius*) and peacock gudgeon (*Tateurndina ocellicauda*). A recent reorganization of the gobies places the family within the Superfamily Gobioidea, which now contains the families Eleotridae, Kraemeriidae, Microdesmidae, Xenisthmidae, and Gobiidae; the Gobiidae contains the subfamilies Amblyopinae, Gobiinae, Gobionellinae, Oxudercinae, and Sicydiinae (Pezold 1993).

The pelvic fins of gobies are usually fused into an adhesive disk with which they can adhere to a substratum even in strong currents. The pelvic fins of the closely related sleepers (Eleotridae) are always separated.

Gobies occur in rocky tide pools, at rock jetties, on sandy beach slopes, on pilings, in aquatic beds in silt or mud, in burrows, crevices, depressions, among vegetation, or in the open. In some species, the male is distinguished by greater fin development or more intense pigmentation, and the female by a smaller size or swollen appearance when gravid. Where differences are difficult to detect, the fish should be inverted in a damp net and examined with a magnifying lens. The male typically has a pointed urogenital papilla whereas the papilla of the female has a blunt tip.

The pair spawns with the female depositing adhesive eggs in a secretive nest inside a burrow, rock crevice, depression, sponge, or bivalve shell defended by the male. Upon hatching, the larvae are initially pelagic, planktonic in the ocean, and require the finest living foods until they metamorphose and assume a benthic mode of life.

Some North American gobies occur as adults in fresh water and move to marine water for spawning, but most gobies worldwide are always brackish or marine. The brackish forms may require an increased or decreased salinity or an increased temperature to trigger aquarium spawning.

Of some 70 gobies on our Atlantic and Pacific Coasts, 19 species in 14 genera are sufficiently common and inshore to be considered potential aquarium fishes. Uncommon species have been excluded from this book, although the general conditions for holding and spawning related fishes should apply. The introduced yellowfin goby (*Acanthogobius flavimanus*) has become common in San Francisco Bay, but exotics are not covered in this book, and neither are the popular marine gobies available in pet stores.

All the common gobies can be collected with a baited minnow trap, bucket trap, dip net, or seine.

---

**Genus *Bathygobius***
*Bathygobius soporator,* frillfin goby

*B. soporator* is blunt-headed and the upper rays of the pectoral fin are free of connecting fin membranes. The body is sand colored (tan) with black dots and squares aligned mostly horizontally. The male frillfin goby often has a light edge on the unpaired fins. Two related species in the Caribbean are virtually identical. This is a moderately large and robust goby at 3 or 4 inches.

The frillfin goby occurs in Florida and Texas.

*B. soporator* ranges southward on open sandy beaches with vegetation, in drainage canals (typically with vegetation or submersed timber debris), and around rock jetties.

A 10-gallon marine aquarium (100% sea water is recommended, although the fish will accept ≤ 50%) is sufficient for one male and two females. The substratum should be a 1-inch layer of shell hash or aragonite gravel over an undergravel fil-

Arrow goby, *Clevelandia ios,* male, Los Angeles Co., Calif. RJG

Arrow goby, *Clevelandia ios,* female, Los Angeles Co., Calif. RJG

ter, and the tank provided with supplemental filtration (outside power or inside sponge). Include a 4-inch-long by 1½-inch-diameter PVC tube as a spawning site, and hiding places (rocks, other tubes) for the nonspawning females. The frillfin goby gorges on flake foods, but should also have fish, shrimp, clam, crushed snails, and other meats in its diet.

The eggs, numbering a thousand, are laid throughout the interior of the PVC tube and are guarded by the male until hatching. The fry are exceedingly small and pelagic, and cannot take *Artemia* nauplii as a first food. My attempts to rear them indoors in 30-gallon aquaria on *Brachionus* rotifers failed, although Delmonte et al. (1968) managed to raise three fry out of thousands of a related goby (*B. andrei*) by placing the spawn in a 200-gallon outdoor tank. Either the fry need food smaller than *Brachionus,* or else they remain in a nonfeeding prolarval stage for so long that their own metabolites pollute the water before they are old enough to feed.

**Genus *Clevelandia***

*Clevelandia ios,* arrow goby

*C. ios* is so dimorphic that the two sexes look like different species. Both sexes have a wide mouth with the angle of the jaw extending to the rear of the eye. The female is tubular-elongate, even arrow-shaped, and pink to flesh colored with low, clear fins. The larger male is large-headed and robust like a typical goby, has a heavily pigmented gray-black body, spotted and striped dorsal fins, and a black band on the anal fin. The male grows to about 2 inches, the female slightly less.

The arrow goby is a Pacific species ranging from British Columbia to Baja California.

*C. ios* burrows in mud or silt everywhere in coastal waters in marine water and fresh water, in tidal lagoons, inlets, and bays.

The arrow goby can be collected at low tide by digging out its burrows in mud (Eschmeyer and Herald 1983), or by seining on sand-mud bottoms in shallow quiet water. Unlike other gobies, it was said to scatter its eggs and provide no parental care (Eschmeyer and Herald 1983); however, I had them spawn twice in narrow (¾ inch) PVC tubes in aquaria at low salinities, producing a single layer of large, adhesive eggs. The eggs did not hatch, possibly damaged by light from the photographic strobe. There is no information on raising the larvae, but the eggs were large enough that I suspect the fry would take *Artemia* nauplii as a first food.

**Genus *Coryphopterus***

*Coryphopterus nicholsi,*
blackeye goby

*C. nicholsi* is light tan with green speckles. Its eye is black above with a blue spot below. The top of the dorsal fin is black, the scales are large, and a thickened ridge on the head runs from the eyes to the dorsal fin. The nuptial male has black pelvic fins (the adhesive disc). They attain 3–4 inches normally.

The blackeye goby is a Pacific species that ranges from the Queen Charlotte Islands of British Columbia to Rompiente Point in Baja California.

*C. nicholsi* occurs among rock rubble interspersed with sand and shell fragments, often at the base of rock jetties and walls where the dominant food items are snails, tiny crabs, shrimp, amphipods, and isopods.

From March through late July, nuptial males (recognized by their black pelvic discs) display for the drab females. The largest and most aggressive males are dominant and attract females for spawning, while the other males are reproductively inactive. Spawning occurs on the roof of a rock cave. Eggs number 1,000–2,000, are light pink at first, and darken with development while guarded by the male (Fitch and Lavenberg 1975). After hatching, the larvae are pelagic.

This fish is large enough to capture by hook-and-line. If a large, dominant male cannot be found, take whatever is available. *C. nicholsi* is a protogynous hermaphrodite, a fish that is female early in life and later becomes male (Cole 1982).

Fill a 10-gallon or larger aquarium with 100 percent sea water, rocks, gravel, and shell hash and an undergravel filter. Supply PVC tubes of different diameters as spawning sites. A dominant male will prevent other males from nesting. Two days after hatching, offer the fry rotifers and their motile algae food source. The pelagic larvae, upon metamorphosis, drop from the plankton and become benthic. At this time they are difficult to see and will require *Artemia* nauplii.

**Genus *Ctenogobius***

*Ctenogobius boleosoma,* darter goby

*C. boleosoma* was previously considered a member of *Gobionellus,* but species with coarse (large) scales were recently moved to this new genus (Birdsong et al. 1988). A large black blotch always occurs on the shoulder, another only sometimes at the base of the tail fin. The tail fin is pointed. The body of both sexes is tan with scattered dark dashes, V-shaped marks, and blotches (more vivid in the male). Orange, red, or yellow stripes or edges appear on the pectoral, second dorsal, and tail fins of the male; his fins are otherwise often dusky. The usual length is about 2 inches.

The darter goby is rarely found as far north as Buzzard's Bay, Massachusetts (Hoff 1976), but is common from Beaufort, North Carolina, to Texas; it ranges southward to Brazil.

*C. boleosoma* is ubiquitous in shallow, low-salinity bays and estuarine marshes on a silt or mud bottom (Hoese and Moore 1977; Pezold and Cashner 1983), where it is often the most common scaled goby (Ginsburg 1932).

The standard ¼-inch mesh minnow seine may allow darter gobies to pass through; ⅛-inch mesh is better, or seine with a plastic window screen.

*Ctenogobius shufeldti,*
freshwater goby

*C. shufeldti* has five square, diffuse dark blotches on the flank that are not connected to dorsal markings; there is no shoulder spot and no V-markings; a horizontal dark band appears on the cheek. It has an elongate tail fin and lacks filaments on the dorsal fin. It grows to 2 or 3 inches (Ginsburg 1932).

The freshwater goby ranges from North Carolina through all of Florida westward through Galveston Island, Texas. A population in Brazil previously thought to be this species is now considered distinct (F. Pezold, pers. comm.).

*C. shufeldti* inhabits shallow coastal fresh waters and low-salinity upper estuaries (Pezold and Cashner 1983). Although collected in fresh water, it does not breed in fresh water.

## Genus *Evorthodus*
*Evorthodus lyricus,* lyre goby

*E. lyricus* is an elongate gray goby with a bluntly rounded head, an inferior (underslung) mouth, a pointed tail, and two dark spots separated by a light spot (all three spots in vertical alignment) on the base of the tail. It resembles members of *Ctenogobius*. The first dorsal fin has elongate filaments in the male and a dark blotch in the female (Ginsburg 1932, 1935; Hoese and Moore 1977).

The lyre goby ranges from Chesapeake Bay to Rio de Janeiro. It is most common in the United States along the Georgia and Louisiana coasts.

*E. lyricus* inhabits low salinity, silt or mud bottom tidal ponds and ditches connected to estuaries, generally among smooth cordgrass or other dense, emersed low salinity coastal vegetation.

The lyre goby feeds by biting the bottom and presumably sifting the ingested sediments through a pharyngeal sieve that consists of the interdigitation of fleshy tabs on the side of each gill arch to the elongate rakers on the preceding arch (Wyanski and Targett 1985). The chewing action is completed when the sifted debris is expelled through the gill openings. During a slow forward progression over the bottom marked by biting, sifting, biting, the lyre goby captures and swallows small benthic animals (meiofauna) living in and on sand, mud, or silt sediments, bits of vegetation, and detritus. This behavior begins at early juvenile stages and extends through adulthood. The lyre goby has been collected by trawl from deeper parts of estuaries, suggesting it moves to high salinity water for spawning.

A 10-gallon aquarium with 5 to 20 percent sea water (salinity up to 7 or 8 ppt) is sufficient. Provide an undergravel filter below 1 or 2 inches of fine sand, an overhead light, and vegetation *(Vallisneria, Sagittaria, Myriophyllum, Nitella, Vesicularia)* only at lower salinities. The lyre goby should be provided frozen adult *Artemia,* live *Artemia* nauplii, frozen bloodworms, live daphnia, and live blackworms. The absence of a sand or silt bottom could cause starvation, because the fish needs to scoop its food and filter it from the soft bottom. A gravel or dolomite bottom could wound its delicate skin, resulting in fungal infection.

A higher salinity is necessary to spawn; see *Gobioides broussoneti* for instructions on inducing spawning behavior.

## Genus *Gillichthys*
*Gillichthys mirabilis,*
longjaw mudsucker

*G. mirabilis* has a huge mouth, the angle of the jaw extending back to the lower edge of the operculum. It is olive brown above and yellow below, with mottling. It is a large goby (5–7 in.).

The longjaw mudsucker ranges from the Salton Sea and Tomales Bay of northern California to Magdalena Bay of Baja California.

*G. mirabilis* inhabits the shallow mud flats of bays, lagoons, and estuaries, including industrial salt ponds, where it seeks preferred temperatures (De Vlaming 1971). It feeds on diverse worms and mollusks living in and on mud flats. The longjaw mudsucker nests in mud depressions, with the female producing thousands of eggs that hatch in 10 to 12 days. The pelagic larvae soon settle out of the plankton (Fitch and Lavenberg 1975).

The longjaw mudsucker sometimes can be purchased from bait dealers. Provide a 20-gallon aquarium (minimum) with marine or brackish water over a fine sand bottom. Feed blackworms, crushed snails, and bits of clam. It can survive for days out of water if kept damp, and can be shipped, like *Rivulus* species, in a plastic bag wrapped in a wet spawning mop. It should not be shipped during summer as it is intolerant of high temperature.

**Genus *Gobioides***
*Gobioides broussoneti,* violet goby

*G. broussoneti* is elongate and wormlike, with tiny eyes on top of the head. It has a basketlike, upturned mouth, and continuous finnage along the midline of the body. It is silvery, with a dark band below the dorsal fin and violet iridescence. The sexes are similar, but distinguishable by the urogenital papillae. Usually 6–12 inches, it attains 18 inches.

The violet goby occurs in the mouth of the St. Johns River, and in all Gulf of Mexico river estuaries southward to Brazil.

Most of the time, the violet goby is a resident of low salinity mud bottoms in salt marshes, estuaries, and river mouths, but periodically is trawled offshore. It probably spawns in higher salinity waters in the deeper parts of the estuary or slightly offshore in the spring. It is most common in the middle of the Gulf Coast, and is sometimes collected by seining or pulling a trawl behind a boat in mud-bottom areas. Shrimp trawlers might be persuaded to save them. It is sold in some pet stores as the dragon fish or dragon goby.

According to Rod Harper, a 15- to 20-gallon aquarium is suitable for 3 or 4 fish, but only one male as males are territorial. Water quality parameters should be pH 7.6–8.2, salinity 20–30 ppt (sp. gr. 1.01–1.02 or 50–80% sea water), and temperature 65–75°F. The aquarium bottom should be fine sand or bare, complemented with two or more halved flower pots or PVC tubes; the male will choose one for its nest, and the other will provide refuge for the females. Despite its fearsome appearance and large mouth, the violet goby is not a predator on smaller fishes. Offer small live foods (*Gammarus, Daphnia, Artemia,* blackworms), supplemented with frozen foods.

The violet goby feeds by ingesting small foods from the water column or scooping them from the substratum. It chews clumsily and then disgorges leftovers or waste detritus and mud from the gill openings, apparently filtering and grinding the food with pharyngeal teeth. Do not use coarse or sharp gravel in the aquarium, which will irritate the soft bottom of this silt-inhabiting fish and result in fungal infections and death.

All violet gobies in the hobby are wild fish that must be acclimated to aquarium foods. Spawning can be induced at any time in captivity by manipulating the salinity and availability of food. The group should be starved for four or five days while the salinity is reduced 5 ppt by removing one or two gallons a day for five days; replace with dechlorinated tap water. Live food should again be added to the tank following the fasting and dilution period, and the salinity gradually raised 5–10 ppt (to 80% or more sea water) during the next 5 days by removing 10 percent by volume (one or two gallons of water) daily and replacing it with 100 percent sea water.

The male should begin to display at the entrance to his PVC pipe or flower pot cave, and finally spawn with females over a 12-hour period. After spawning, the females should be removed as the male becomes aggressive.

The eggs hatch in 36 hours, the larvae appearing as a mass of wriggling slivers of gold. The male can be removed now or allowed to guard the fry until they are free-swimming. After the fry absorb the yolk sac, they descend and hop around the bottom of the aquarium. They cannot yet take *Artemia* nauplii, and should be fed marine rotifers *(Brachionus plicatilis),* supplemented with motile algae such as *Isocrysis* and *Tetraselmis* (ordinarily on hand because they are cultured to feed the rotifers). After 4 weeks, *Artemia* nauplii are accepted. After 8 weeks, larval mysid shrimp, small amphipods, and some prepared flakes can be added to the diet.

---

**Genus *Gobionellus***
*Gobionellus oceanicus,* sharptail goby

*G. oceanicus* is elongate but not wormlike, with a pointed tail, elongate filaments on the first dorsal fin, a bold ocellus (brown oval ringed with white) behind the pectoral fin, sometimes divided, and often another dark spot on the base of the tail. It was previously known as *G. hastatus* and *G. gracillimus,* both names now junior synonyms (Pezold and Grady 1990). Adults are 4 to 7 inches.

The sharptail goby occurs from North Carolina throughout Florida, ranging westward to Texas and Campeche, Mexico.

*G. oceanicus* is found on mud bottoms of estuaries and inshore in the Gulf of Mexico, but is difficult to collect.

---

**Genus *Gobiosoma***
*Gobiosoma bosc,* naked goby

*G. bosc* is a short, rounded goby with a rounded tail, ten broad, dark vertical bands on the flank, and an overall dark color. It is usually 1 inch, but attains 2 inches.

The naked goby and its close relatives (to be discussed below) have been extensively studied (Ginsburg 1933; Dawson 1966; Hoese 1966; Dahlberg and Conyers 1973; Crabtree and Middaugh 1982).

The naked goby ranges from New York to Texas, and is most common from the Chesapeake Bay southward, but is absent from Florida south of Jacksonville.

*G. bosc* is found on oyster rocks and bars, on shallow, inshore sand or muck bottoms, and only occasionally in *Zostera* marine grass beds if oyster reefs and isolated shells are not available (Hoese 1966); it also occurs in fouling communities of hydroids, barnacles, and sea squirts on wooden structures (Dahlberg and Conyers 1973), and typically in lower salinity (5–20 ppt) portions of estuaries (Dawson 1966).

I collected this common goby in a great variety of shallow estuarine habitats, including a low-salinity embayment in southern Virginia rich in *Myriophyllum brasiliensis;* Carter Gilbert reports it well up into fresh water in Florida (C. Gilbert, pers. comm.).

The naked goby spawns in empty oyster shells with a narrow gape, which helps protect the eggs of this small fish from larger predators (Crabtree and Middaugh 1982). It is cold tolerant, but moves offshore to slightly deeper water during winter. Otherwise, its spawning season is correlated with water temperature from north to south; it occupies inshore habitats ranging from shallow fresh to shallow marine water, but is most common in estuaries. It spawns in higher salinity waters, but the pelagic larvae migrate to low salinity waters upstream, moving to higher salinities after metamorphosis. The naked goby makes clicking sounds to threaten intruders and predators, mostly after dark; these sounds are not uttered during spawning (Mok 1981).

I found that elevating the salinity of Atlantic Coast stock induced spawning. I used a 10-gallon aquarium for a group of six fish. One male in the group spawned with females when the temperature and salinity were elevated to the middle 70s (°F) and full-strength sea water.

Prior to spawning in a PVC tube, the male would wag back and forth and move in a backward direction, fins erect, while the female would twitch her head. There was never any biting of the substratum, a normal cleaning procedure in other kinds of fishes. As spawning began, the female became light colored and stopped head twitching. The female bumped and twitched vertically while making contact with the substratum, giving the illusion of coughing from the ovipositor. Both fish continued to move back and forth, fins erect. The now dark male clasped the female in the rear, and broke away sharply after each group of one or two eggs was laid.

The first eggs were laid on a vertical surface, and the remainder on various surfaces. Eggs were attached by long filaments, and fanned by the male wagging his rear body and tail. If approached, the male rushed the intruder. The fry hatched in ten days at 74°F and were pelagic and phototropic, darting with jerky movements through the water. Initially, the fry were 3.1 mm long, and at four days, 4.6 mm long. They metamorphosed in 10 to 12 days, when they dropped to the bottom and hid in crevices. At this point I lost mine, but Rod Harper raised some of the young that were produced in his tanks. He fed rotifers *(Brachionus plicatilis)* for the first two or three weeks, after which the fry accepted *Artemia* nauplii. We both noted that a guarding male will eat the eggs of other guarding males, and any of the adults will feed on the pelagic fry. Remove the spawning tube when the eggs are ready to hatch, aerate the eggs, and let the fry hatch in their own rearing tank with sponge filtration.

Do not confuse disappearance of the pelagic fry with death from starvation (as I did), but continue to protect the larval rearing tank and begin feeding rotifers followed later by small numbers of *Artemia* nauplii. Lowering salinity while doing water changes may increase survival by reproducing the transport of pelagic fry to the upper estuaries.

| | |
|---|---|
| *Gobiosoma ginsburgi,* seaboard goby | *G. ginsburgi* can be distinguished from *G. bosc* by wavy rather than vertical dark bands on the flank. It resembles *G. longipala* of the Gulf Coast, but has broader pale spaces between the bands on the flanks and 11 anal fin rays. |

*G. ginsburgi* can be distinguished from *G. bosc* by wavy rather than vertical dark bands on the flank. It resembles *G. longipala* of the Gulf Coast, but has broader pale spaces between the bands on the flanks and 11 anal fin rays.

The seaboard goby ranges from Massachusetts to Georgia. It occurs in oyster reef habitats but avoids fouling communities and low salinities.

*G. ginsburgi* is found on hard bottoms, occasionally near shore but is more common in deeper water to 180 feet. It feeds on harpacticoid copepods and other benthic invertebrates (Dahlberg and Conyers 1973; Munroe and Lotspeich 1979).

*Gobiosoma longipala,* twoscale goby

*G. longipala* resembles the naked goby, but has two fringed (ctenoid) scales on the caudal peduncle that extend rearward. It is similar to *G. ginsburgi* of the Atlantic Coast, but has ten anal fin rays. The body is yellow-brown and crossed by seven or eight dark brown vertical bars; it is black at the dorsal midline and at the midline of the flank (resembling a series of dashes). The average length is 1 inch.

The twoscale goby occurs along the entire Gulf Coast from western Florida to Texas. It was regarded as possibly identical to *G. ginsburgi* of the Atlantic Coast (Hoese and Moore 1977), but C. R. Robins, an expert on gobies, considered it distinct (Robins and Ray 1986).

*G. longipala* inhabits hard bottoms (oyster reefs, rocks), and is uncommon near shore but fairly common in deep water.

A 10-gallon aquarium with a fine sand bottom is recommended. It is sensitive to high nitrites, and trickle filtration is recommended. Water parameters should be pH 7.4–8.2, salinity 20–30 ppt (sp. gr. 1.01–1.02 or 50–80% sea water), and temperature 65–80°F. Spawning can be induced as described for *Gobioides broussoneti*. The males are aggressive during spawning. Remove females after spawning and isolate them in a recovery tank.

---

*Gobiosoma robustum,* code goby

*G. robustum* resembles *G. bosc,* but has a horizontal row of dark dashes along the midline.

The code goby ranges from Cape Canaveral to the Florida Keys and the entire coast of the Gulf of Mexico.

*G. robustum* inhabits high-salinity (22–32 ppt or 60–90% sea water), muddy or sandy estuaries in seagrass beds of *Ruppia maritima, Diplantheria wrighti, Thalassia testudinum, Cymdocia,* and the alga *Padina* (Hoese 1966). It also occurs in mangrove forests and on oyster bars, typically in association with *Syngnathus scovelli* (Gulf pipefish) and *S. floridae* (dusky pipefish). It feeds on benthic macroinvertebrates, principally amphipods, mysids, copepods, chironomid larvae, decapod and mysid shrimp, ostracods, small mollusks, gammarids, and some detritus and algal filaments (possibly picked up during carnivory).

The code goby spawns throughout the year with peaks during the spring and fall, but does not spawn in summer when temperatures are high (Springer and McErlean 1961). In hypersaline Texas estuaries, it spawns when the salinity falls below 45 0/oo; in Florida, it spawns at intermediate salinities of 19–23 0/oo.

The 1.3 to 1.7 mm eggs are attached by filaments to the undersides of sponge shells or on seagrasses, and guarded by the male. The young, at 7 to 15 mm, feed on copepods, juvenile mysids, cumaceans, and diatoms. Maturity is reached in several months, and the fish lives only one year if not preyed upon by (mostly) inshore lizardfish *(Synodus foetens),* various seatrout *(Cynoscion* spp.), gray snapper *(Lutjanus griseus),* and other piscivores (Patillo et al. 1997).

Care as for *G. bosc*. High temperatures and salinities inhibit spawning behavior.

---

**Genus *Lepidogobius***
*Lepidogobius lepidus,* bay goby

*L. lepidus* has glisteningly smooth, small scales, and is tan to rusty brown with dark blotches (sometimes absent) and a black edge on the tip of the first dorsal. The average length is 3 inches.

The bay goby ranges along the Pacific Coast from British Columbia to Baja California, where it is found on intertidal mud bottoms. Care as for *Gillichthys mirabilis*.

---

**Genus *Lophogobius***
*Lophogobius cyprinoides,*
crested goby

*L. cyprinoides* is dark brown with an elevated ridge (crest) on the head. The nuptial male is blackish violet, with a black dorsal fin containing orange blotches (Robins and Ray 1986). It averages 3 to 4 inches long.

The crested goby ranges from southern Florida to Venezuela. This abundant goby occurs in tidal creeks, drainage and navigation canals, mangrove swamps, and coastal fresh waters, usually around shells, rocks, and algae. It is omnivorous and opportunistic on algae, amphipods, isopods, copepods, ostracods, worms, mollusks, barnacles, and insects (Darcy 1981).

A 20-gallon aquarium with brackish water and undergravel and sponge filtration should be provided with a variety of wide PVC tubes and rocks. Either daylight or 25-watt incandescent lighting is recommended; the fish abhors bright lights. The diet should be based on a vegetable flake food, supplemented with *Artemia,* bloodworms (chironomids), and bits of shrimp or clam. A combination of a commercially prepared fry food and green water (*Dunnaliella* sp.) in an outdoor pool proved successful in raising 15 percent of the fry (Delmonte et al. 1968).

**Genus *Microgobius***
*Microgobius gulosus,* clown goby

*M. gulosus* is elongate with a pointed tail and filamentous extensions of the dorsal fin spines in the male. There is an iridescent blue-green horizontal band under the eye and another angled band behind the pectoral fin. There are eight or nine dark blotches along the back and upper side (darker in the female). The unpaired fins of the male have horizontal bands, and those of the female have spots or blotches. The second dorsal fin of the male has a blue band and a median row of orange-red spots below, his tail fin has a red tinge, and his upper jaw is much larger than the female's (Ginsburg 1934; Birdsong 1981). The clown goby is less than 3 inches long.

It ranges from northern Florida on the Atlantic coast southward and continues along the Gulf Coast to Texas. In Alabama and northwestern Florida, *M. gulosus* was collected over clean white sand where it constructed shallow burrows (Birdsong 1981).

*M. gulosus* is among the most common gobies on the Gulf Coast (Ginsburg 1934) in low-salinity bayous and inland estuarine ponds, small coves of sounds and bays, on mud and sometimes grassy bottom, and in burrows 2 to 5 inches long (with openings at both ends) and located 1 to 2 inches below the surface mud or marl (Birdsong 1981). It feeds on copepods, mysid shrimp, amphipods, polychaete worms, bivalves, and chironomid larvae (bloodworms).

The clown goby is particular about water quality and, if the sand is not deep enough, it will not build a burrow or attempt to spawn. Should some of the sand become anaerobic, indicated by a dark patch, it should be vigorously stirred to aerate the noxious zone, and the aquarium water partially changed to remove gases and soluble organic wastes released from the sand.

Set up the aquarium with an undergravel filter, cover the filter plate with filter fiber to hold back the sand, and then add at least 2 inches of clean, fine sand. Provide PVC half tubes. The male constructs a shallow burrow beneath the PVC tube, then guards the entrance to the cave. Water quality parameters should be pH 7.8–8.2, salinity 27–32 ppt (sp. gr. 1.02 or 75–90% sea water), and temperature 65–80°F.

To breed, nitrite levels must be low, accomplished most easily with trickle filtration. Condition by starving for a few days, followed by live foods only, as described for *Gobioides broussoneti.*

The males are not particularly territorial, and a small breeding group of three males and ten females can be housed in a 30-gallon aquarium. Lowering the temperature overnight often triggers spawning behavior. They spawn over a 12-hour period, after which all adults should be removed; the males may eat the eggs. The eggs hatch in three days, and the larvae require rotifers as the first food, as in *Gobioides broussoneti.*

*Microgobius thalassinus,* green goby

*M. thalassinus* is uncommon but attractive. The male is a lustrous blue or green with two narrow blue-green lines that run obliquely across the cheek below the eye; there are three oblique bars on the shoulder; the dorsal fin is white or clear with rows of large red-brown spots or a reddish overall hue and bold dark spots at the rear margin; the upper part of the tail fin is edged in red-brown. Both sexes may have golden oblique bars across the body, a pointed tail, and a dark spot at the base of the tail. The female has a red spot on the dorsal fin. They are usually less than 2 inches.

The green goby ranges from Chesapeake Bay to Texas, but its distribution is scattered and erratic; it is absent from eastern Florida below Cape Canaveral. Inconsistencies in color descriptions by various authors suggest location, population, or taxonomic differences (perhaps more than one species) and stocks from different locales should be kept separately.

*M. thalassinus* is found at salinities of 1 to 33 ppt, with a preference for the middle range. It occurs in tide pools and ponds, over mud and sand bottoms, often with *Microgobius gulosus,* and in association with the sponge *Microciona.* It ranges into deeper water, but also is present in shallow grassy areas (Ginsburg 1934; Birdsong 1981).

## Genus *Quietula*
*Quietula y-cauda,* shadow goby

*Quietula y-cauda* is distinctive with a series of dashes on the flank and an arrowhead mark on the base of the tail pointing forward (also called a sideways Y-mark, the base of the Y pointing to the tail). The male has a dark stripe on the anal fin. This goby averages 2½ inches (Eschmeyer and Herald 1983).

The shadow goby occurs in central and southern California and in the Gulf of California.

*Quietula y-cauda* inhabits worm and shrimp holes and crevices in hard structures on mud flats of estuaries and coastal rivers.

Care as for *Gillichthys mirabilis,* but a 10-gallon aquarium is adequate for this species. It is not tolerant of polluted water.

## Genus *Tridentiger*
*Tridentiger trigonocephalus,* chameleon goby

The pectoral fin of *T. trigonocephalus* is black at the base and then white beyond; a black spot appears above the middle of the caudal peduncle; and there is usually one (sometimes two) dark horizontal band. The anal fin is dark-edged. The chameleon goby is able to change its color pattern rapidly (Eschmeyer and Herald 1983). It grows to 3 or 4 inches.

This Asian goby was introduced to California during the 1960s in the ballast of a ship, currently ranges from San Francisco to Los Angeles, and is spreading. *T. trigonocephalus* inhabits oyster shells, crevices, rocks, and other hard irregular bottoms in marine, brackish, and fresh water.

Provide a 10- to 20-gallon aquarium with 50 percent or more sea water, a thick shell hash substratum over an undergravel filter, and a diet of mixed meats (*Artemia,* clam, fish, blackworms) supplemented with flake foods. Include rocks and PVC tubes for spawning substrata.

This exotic has adapted well to the Pacific Coast, but the ecological effects it may have on native species is not known, including the potential elimination of competitors. It would be foolish to risk the inadvertent introduction of so adaptable a species to the Atlantic or Gulf Coasts.

## Genus *Typhlogobius*
*Typhlogobius californiensis,* blind goby

*T. californiensis* is pink, has no scales, and the tiny eyes of juveniles disappear in the adult. It grows to 2 or 3 inches.

The blind goby ranges from San Simeon Point of California to Magdalena Bay of Baja California.

*T. californiensis* is found on cobble or rocky bottoms in shallow coastal waters, under and in holes of rocks. In captivity, they are omnivorous on bits of shrimp, clam, fish, vegetables, *Artemia,* and rotted plants. They spawn within the burrows or cavities of the ghost shrimp, *Callianassa affinis.* Shovel out shrimp burrows for goby pairs and turn over rocks and cobble for individuals in intertidal shallows. Attempt to collect the ghost shrimp simultaneously. A rock or shell within the shrimp burrow is the spawning substratum for 1,500 to 2,500 eggs. Eggs hatch in 10 to 12 days, and the larvae are briefly pelagic (Fitch and Lavenberg 1975).

A 5- or 10-gallon aquarium filled with 100 percent sea water is recommended, with ghost shrimp if available. Provide undergravel filtration beneath shell hash and rocks, supplementary sponge filtration, and an outside power filter or a powerhead to provide current to duplicate the surge of the surf zone. If spawning occurs, turn off the filters and powerhead. Either siphon the fry to feed in a bare container, or remove the adults.

## Family Eleotridae, the Sleepers

Members of the family Eleotridae differ from most gobies in having widely spaced pelvic fins that are never joined or modified into a sucking disk.

In Central America, many eleotrid species coexist in estuaries in which salinity ranges from 0 to 2 ppt and the water is virtually fresh. They can be moved to brackish (5–25 ppt) or full-strength (35 ppt) marine water with no indications of stress (Nordlie 1979; Nordlie and Haney 1993). This ability of sleepers to live in fresh, brackish, or marine water is linked to an enzyme in gill epithelium called "sodium-potassium-activated ATPase," the activity of which is triggered by immersion in salt-containing water. The enzyme promotes the discharge of sodium ions from the gills, allowing the fish to maintain osmotic balance in sea water (Evans and Mallery 1975). The enzyme activity turns off (i.e., the fish stops extruding sodium ions) when the fish returns to fresh water.

Sleepers occur worldwide in coastal zones. They typically spawn large numbers of eggs on hard substrata on the bottom in cryptic or shaded localities. The fry of at least some species are light sensitive (Mashiko 1976).

Five species of estuarine sleepers are commonly found in the United States. A sixth, the emerald sleeper, *Erotelis smaragdus,* is unusual in inhabiting a strictly marine environment; it is known from the northern Gulf of Mexico, southeastern Florida, the Caribbean, and the tropical western Atlantic to Brazil. Although its young occur in Texas estuaries, it is unlikely to be collected and thus is excluded from coverage.

Sleepers are best taken by baited minnow trap, but have also been taken on occasion by seine or cast net. Because most sleepers are cryptic, a good trap is a 10-inch length of 2-inch-diameter PVC pipe with plastic window screening attached over one opening with a heavy rubber band. Pipe traps should be laid among rocks or in emersed grasses in shoreline shallows and canal banks of low-salinity upper estuaries.

### Genus *Dormitator*
*Dormitator maculatus,* fat sleeper

*D. maculatus* is a large, stocky, bottom dweller with a dark blue smudge above the pectoral fin at the upper margin of the gill cover; dark lines radiate from behind the eye onto the cheek; it often has horizontal rows of spots that sometimes develop into a dark line on the body. The anal fin has blue bars and a white margin. The body is dark brown to olive, mottled with brown, blue, or green. Maturity is reached at four years. It attains 12 inches (Dahlberg 1975; Hoese and Moore 1977; Sterba 1983; Robins and Ray 1986).

The fat sleeper ranges from Wilmington, North Carolina, to Brazil. *D. maculatus* inhabits freshwater ponds, fresh or brackish marshes, low salinity tidal pools, and coastal mangrove swamps. It feeds on copepods, ostracods, and insects among water hyacinth roots, ingesting plant material while feeding; this led to the impression that it is omnivorous (Nordlie 1979, 1981), when in fact it is simply an overqualified predator in a habitat of small prey.

A 20- to 29-gallon aquarium is recommended for a pair. Fresh water in a heavily vegetated aquarium is adequate, but 25 percent sea water (salinity 9–10 ppt) is better, resulting in more vigorous fry. Use both sponge and outside filtration. Provide a sand bottom, hiding places (rocks, large half PVC pipes), refuge from direct light, and a diet of daphnia, bloodworms, earthworms, adult *Artemia*, and crushed snails. The fat sleeper thrives on flake foods. Sleepers engorge on all foods, but do not require all they can consume.

Two hundred tiny, golden, oblong eggs are laid on a hard surface. The eggs hatch in 48 to 96 hours, and the fry absorb the yolk sac in 24 hours. The male can be trusted to guard the eggs and young for two weeks. Larger hatches will result if the male is removed and the eggs provided aeration until they hatch. The fry take *Artemia* naupili at once. Growth is slow, and sexual maturity is reached by 18 months. Sleepers are prolific breeders, but the offspring are generally not wanted by other aquarists or pet stores in the numbers produced. Excess young, especially newly hatched fry, are useful as live food for other fishes.

---

### *Dormitator latifrons,* Pacific fat sleeper

*D. latifrons* is similar to the fat sleeper and both were probably derived from a common ancestor before a land bridge appeared in Central America. Dark lines radiate onto the cheek from behind the eye, and a dark blue smudge occurs at the upper angle of the gill cover above the pectoral fin. It is brown to reddish brown with red-brown spots and green iridescence on the flank.

The Pacific fat sleeper ranges from southern California, where it is rare, to Ecuador (Eschmeyer and Herald 1983).

Adults live in shallow fresh waters and in brackish and marine water at the coast. Juveniles often ascend fresh waters well up into the mountains on the Pacific coast of Mexico, far from the sea. Although it spawns at 4 inches, the Pacific fat sleeper may attain a length of 2 feet.

---

### Genus *Eleotris*
### *Eleotris "pisonis,"* spinycheek sleeper

*E. "pisonis"* is light tan above and on the head, which contrasts sharply with the dark brown flank. The body is elongate and the head is flattened. A dark spot appears above the pectoral fin, and dark lines radiate from behind the eye onto the cheek. It averages 6–8 inches.

The spinycheek sleeper ranges from South Carolina and Bermuda to Mexico to Brazil. Pezold (pers. comm.) is revising the New World species of *Eleotris,* and will restrict the name *pisonis* to a Brazilian form (F. Pezold, pers. comm.). The U.S. Atlantic Coast species should be known as *E. abacurus* and *E. perniger.* A more southerly species, *E. amblyopsis,* occasionally enters the United States in southern Florida.

*E. "pisonis"* inhabits freshwater ponds, streams, and coastal marshes, more often in fresh water than not. In Costa Rica, it is found among water hyacinth root mats, and appears to prefer the upper levels of the water column. Opportunistic, it feeds on invertebrates and fish among root mats, ingesting vegetation during predation. It apparently moves coastward to higher salinities for spawning.

Spinycheek sleeper, *Eleotris "pisonis,"* New Hanover Co., N.C. Photo by S. W. Ross.

Provide large quarters (20–29 gallons for a pair), 50 percent sea water (18 ppt) to induce spawning, good filtration, and a diet of small live fishes supplemented with crushed snails and bits of shrimp. Do not feed flake foods. The spinycheek sleeper spawns like the fat sleeper, but not as readily, and the fry take *Artemia* nauplii at once. This is a predatory fish.

| | |
|---|---|
| *Eleotris picta,* spotted sleeper | *E. picta* is elongate but otherwise identical to the spinycheek sleeper. It attains more than 18 inches in length. |

*E. picta* is elongate but otherwise identical to the spinycheek sleeper. It attains more than 18 inches in length.

The spotted sleeper is the Pacific cousin of the spinycheek sleeper and possibly hybridizes with it inside the locks of the Panama Canal (Lee et al. 1980). It occurs along the tropical and subtropical Pacific Coast from extreme southern California to Peru, and is known from a single locality within North America, the Colorado River near Winterhaven, California.

*E. picta* inhabits fresh and brackish water coastal ponds, ditches, and streams, and is probably a predaceous piscivore.

**Genus *Gobiomorus***
*Gobiomorus dormitor,*
bigmouth sleeper

*G. dormitor* is the fish discussed under the name *Eleotris abacurus* in Carr and Goin (1959). It has an elongate body and is olive with dark mottling on the flank and a dark smudge on the first dorsal fin, the mouth is wide, dark lines radiate from behind the eye, and there are horizontal rows of spots on the flank. It is usually less than 1 foot but sometimes 2 feet in length.

The bigmouth sleeper ranges from southern Florida and southern Texas to Central America, but is absent from most of the Gulf Coast.

*G. dormitor* inhabits freshwater ponds, lakes, rivers, stormwater ditches, and pools, often well inland, but also in estuarine waters. A bottom dweller, it feeds largely on fish, shrimp, and larval insects (Nordlie 1979, 1981), including Ephemeroptera, Odonata, and chironomids (mayflies, dragonflies, and midges or bloodworms).

Care as for *D. maculatus,* but provide a more diverse diet, including fish and shrimp. Because of its potentially great size, the best field decision would be to return it to the wild if unable to provide it with the space, food, and water quality required to assure health and promote propagation.

# Literature Cited

Able, K. W. 1976. Cleaning behavior in the cyprinodontid fishes: *Fundulus majalis, Cyprinodon variegatus,* and *Lucania parva. Chesapeake Sci.* 17:35–39.

Anonymous. 1998. Haff disease associated with eating buffalo fish— United States, 1997. *Morbidity and Mortality Weekly Reports* 47:1091–93.

Armstrong, J. G., and J. D. Williams. 1971. Cave and spring fishes of the southern bend of the Tennessee River. *J. Tenn. Acad. Sci.* 46:107–15.

Atmar, G. L., and K. W. Stewart. 1972. Food, feeding selectivity and ecological efficiencies of *Fundulus notatus. Am. Midl. Nat.* 88:76–89.

Ayvazian, S. G. 1993. Observations of asymmetric reproduction along a morphocline of the blackspotted stickleback, *Gasterosteus wheatlandi. Can. J. Zool.* 71:1477–79.

Ayvazian, S. G., and W. H. Krueger. 1992. Lateral plate ontogeny in the North American ninespine stickleback, *Pungitius occidentalis. Copeia* 1992:209–14.

Bagarinao, T., and R. D. Vetter. 1993. Sulphide tolerance and adaptation in the California killifish, *Fundulus parvipinnis,* a salt marsh resident. *J. Fish Biol.* 42:729–48.

Bailey, R. M. 1941a. Geographic variation in *Mesogonistius chaetodon* (Baird), with description of a new subspecies from Georgia and Florida. Occas. Pap. Mus. Zool. no. 454 (cited in Jenkins et al. 1975). Ann Arbor: University of Michigan.

———. 1941b. *Hadropterus nasutus,* a new darter from Arkansas. Occas. Pap. Mus. Zool. no. 440. Ann Arbor: University of Michigan. 8 pp.

———. 1948. Status, relationships, and characters of the percid fish, *Poecilichthys sagitta* Jordan and Swain. *Copeia* 1948:77–85.

———. 1959. *Etheostoma acuticeps,* a new darter from the Tennessee River system, with remarks on the subgenus *Nothonotus.* Occas. Pap. Mus. Zool. no. 603. Ann Arbor: University of Michigan. 10 pp.

Bailey, R. M., and M. O. Allum. 1962. Fishes of South Dakota, Misc. Pub. Mus. Zool. no. 119. Ann Arbor: University of Michigan. 131 pp.

Bailey, R. M., and D. A. Etnier. 1988. Comments on the subgenera of darters (Percidae) with descriptions of two new species of *Etheostoma (Ulocentra)* from southeastern United States. Misc. Pub. Mus. Zool. no. 175. Ann Arbor: University of Michigan. 48 pp.

Bailey, R. M., and W. J. Richards. 1963. Status of *Poecilichthys hopkinsi* Fowler and *Etheostoma trisella,* new species, percid fishes from Alabama, Georgia, and South Carolina. Occas. Pap. Mus. Zool. no. 630. Ann Arbor: University of Michigan. 21 pp.

Bailey, R. M., and R. D. Suttkus. 1952. *Notropis signipinnis,* a new cyprinid fish from southeastern United States. Occas. Pap. Mus. Zool. no. 542. Ann Arbor: University of Michigan. 15 pp.

Bart, H. L., Jr. 1992. Spawning behavior of *Etheostoma davisoni* Hay. *Copeia* 1992:537–39.

Bart, H. L., Jr., and L. M. Page. 1991. Morphology and adaptive significance of fin knobs in egg-clustering darters. *Copeia* 1991:80–86.

Bath, H. 1994. Untersuchung der Arten *Hypleurochilus geminatus* (Wood 1825), *H. fissicornis* (Quoy & Gaimard 1824) und *H. aequipinnis* (Guenther 1861), mit Revalidation von *Hypleurochilus multifilis* (Girard 1858) und Beschreigung von zwei neuen Arten. *Senckenbergiana Biologica* 74:59–85.

Bauer, B. H., D. A. Etnier, and N. M. Burkhead. 1995. *Etheostoma (Ulocentra) scotti,* a new darter from Etowah River system in Georgia. *Bull. Ala. Mus. Nat. Hist.* 17:1–16.

Baxter, G. T., and M. D. Stone. 1995. *Fishes of Wyoming.* Cheyenne: Game and Fish Department. 290 pp.

Beach, M. L. 1974. Food habits and reproduction of the taillight shiner, *Notropis maculatus,* in central Florida. *Fla. Sci.* 37:5–16.

Beamesderfer, R. C. 1992. Reproduction and early life history of northern squawfish, *Ptychocheilus oregonensis,* in Idaho's St. Joe River. *Environ. Biol. Fishes* 35:231–41.

Bell, M. A. 1976. Evolution of phenotypic diversity in *Gasterosteus aculeatus* superspecies on the Pacific coast of North America. *Syst. Zool.* 25:211–27.

Bell, M. A., and S. A. Foster, eds. 1994. *The evolutionary biology of the threespine stickleback.* New York: Oxford University Press. 571 pp.

Bengtson, D. A. 1980. A partial bibliography of *Cyprinodon variegatus. Gulf Res. Rept.* 6:349–57.

Bennett, D. H., and R. W. McFarlane. 1983. The fishes of the Savannah River Plant: National Environmental Research Park. Aiken, S.C.: Savannah River Ecology Laboratory, University of Georgia. 152 pp.

Bestgen, K. R., and D. L. Propst. 1996. Redescription, geographic variation, and taxonomic status of Rio Grande silvery minnow, *Hybognathus amarus. Copeia* 1996:41–55.

Birdsong, R. S. 1981. A review of the gobiid fish genus *Microgobius* Poey. *Bull. Mar. Sci.* 31:267–306.

Birdsong, R. S., and L. W. Knapp. 1969. *Etheostoma collettei,* a new darter of the subgenus *Oligocephalus* from Louisiana and Arkansas. *Tulane Stud. Zool. Bot.* 15:106–12.

Birdsong, R. S., E. O. Murdy, and F. L. Pezold. 1988. A study of the vertebral column and median fin osteology in gobioid fishes with comments on gobioid relationships. *Bull. Mar. Sci.* 42:174–214.

Birstein, V. J. 1993a. Is *Acipenser medirostris* one or two species? *Sturgeon Quart.* 1(2):8.

———. 1993b. Sturgeons and paddlefishes: Threatened fishes in need of conservation. *Conserv. Biol.* 7:773–87.

Birstein, V. J., A. I. Poletaev, and B. F. Goncharov. 1993. DNA content in Eurasian sturgeon species determined by flow cytometry. *Cytometry* 14:377–83.

Blinn, D. W., J. White, T. Pradetto, and J. O'Brien. 1998. Reproductive ecology and growth of a captive population of Little Colorado spinedace (*Lepomeda vittata*: Cyprinidae). *Copeia* 1998:1010–15.

Bockstael, J. 1983. Spawning the logperch, a native Canadian darter. *Am. Currents* (July–August):5–7.

———. 1984. Spawning the pumpkinseed sunfish (*Lepomis gibbosus*). *Am. Currents* (June):6–8.

Boltz, J. M., and J. R. Stauffer Jr. 1986. Branchial brooding in the pirate perch, *Aphredoderus sayanus*. *Copeia* 1986:1030–31.

Bond, C. E. 1994. *Keys to Oregon freshwater fishes*. Corvallis: Department of Wildlife and Fisheries, Oregon State University. 53 pp.

Boschung, H. T. 1992. Catalogue of freshwater and marine fishes of Alabama. *Bull. Ala. Mus. Nat. Hist.* 14:1–266.

Bouchard, R. W. 1977. *Etheostoma etnieri*, a new percid fish from the Caney Fork (Cumberland) River system, Tennessee, with a redescription of the subgenus *Ulocentra*. *Tulane Stud. Zool. Bot.* 19:105–30.

Bouguenec, V. 1992. Oligochaetes (Tubificidae and Enchytraeidae) as food in fish rearing: a review and preliminary tests. *Aquaculture* 102:201–17.

Boyer, R. L., G. W. Luker, and R. J. Tafanelli. 1977. Observations on the ecology of *Micropterus treculi* in the Guadalupe River. *Tex. J. Sci.* 28:361–62.

Braasch, M. E., and L. M. Page. 1979. Systematic studies of darters of the subgenus *Catonotus*, with the description of a new species from Caney Fork, Tennessee. Occas. Pap. Mus. Nat. Hist. no. 78. Lawrence: University of Kansas. 10 pp.

Braasch, M. E., and P. W. Smith. 1967. The life history of the slough darter, *Etheostoma gracile*. Ill. Nat. Hist. Surv. Biol. Notes no. 58. Champaign: University of Illinois. 12 pp.

Branchaud, A., and A. D. Gendron. 1993. Artificial spawning and rearing of the copper redhorse, *Moxostoma hubbsi*. *Can. Field-Nat.* 107:279–82.

Browman, H. I., and W. J. O'Brien. 1992. Foraging and prey search behavior of golden shiner (*Notemigonus crysoleucas*) larvae. *Can. J. Fish. Aq. Sci.* 49:813–19.

Brown, C. J. D. 1971. *Fishes of Montana*. Bozeman: Montana State University Press. 207 pp.

Brown, J. H., and C. R. Feldmeth. 1971. Evolution in constant and fluctuating environments: Thermal tolerances of desert pupfish (*Cyprinodon*). *Evolution* 25:390–98.

Brummett, A. R. 1966. Observations on the eggs and breeding season of *Fundulus heteroclitus* at Beaufort, North Carolina. *Copeia* 1966:616–20.

Bruner, J. C. 1976. Variation in the caudal skeleton of *Etheostoma nigrum*. *Trans. Ill. State Acad. Sci.* 69:87–90.

———. 1991. Bibliography of the family Catostomidae. Nat. Hist. Occas. Pap. 14. Edmonton: Provincial Museum of Alberta.

Buchanan, T. 1973. *Key to the fishes of Arkansas*. Little Rock: Arkansas Game and Fish Commission. 68 pp. (198 maps)

Buckley, J., and B. Kynard. 1985a. Yearly movements of shortnose sturgeons in the Connecticut River. *Trans. Am. Fish. Soc.* 114:813–20.

———. 1985b. Habitat use and behavior of pre-spawning and spawning shortnose sturgeon, *Acipenser brevirostrum*, in the Connecticut River. In *North American sturgeons*, edited by F. P. Binkowski and S. I. Doroshov, pp. 111–17. Dordrecht, the Netherlands: Dr W. Junk Publishers.

———. 1985c. Spawning and rearing of shortnose sturgeon from the Connecticut River. *Prog. Fish-Culturist* 43:74–76.

Burgess, W. E. 1989. *An Atlas of Freshwater and Marine Catfishes*. Neptune City, N.J.: T.F.H. Publications. 784 pp.

Burggren, W. W., and W. E. Bemis. 1992. Metabolism and ram gill ventilation in juvenile paddlefish, *Polyodon spathula*. *Physiol. Zool.* 65:515–39.

Burr, B. M. 1977. The bantam sunfish, *Lepomis symmetricus*: Systematics and distribution, and life history in Wolf Lake, Illinois. *Ill. Nat. Hist. Surv. Bull.* 31:437–66.

———. 1979a. Observations on spawning and breeding coloration of *Moxostoma lachneri* in Chattahoochee River, Georgia. *Ga. J. Sci.* 37:205–207.

———. 1979b. Systematics and life history aspects of the percid fish *Etheostoma blennius* with description of a new subspecies from Sequatchie River, Tennessee. *Copeia* 1979:191–203.

Burr, B. M., and D. A. Carney. 1984. The blacktail redhorse, *Moxostoma poecilurum*, in Kentucky, with other additions to the state ichthyofauna. *Trans. Ky. Acad. Sci.* 45:73–74.

Burr, B. M., and R. C. Cashner. 1983. *Campostoma pauciradii*, a new cyprinid fish from southeastern United States, with a review of related forms. *Copeia* 1983:101–16.

Burr, B. M., and W. W. Dimmick. 1981. Nests, eggs, and larvae of the elegant madtom *Noturus elegans* from Barren River drainage, Kentucky. *Trans. Ky. Acad. Sci.* 42:116–18.

Burr, B. M., and M. S. Ellinger. 1980. Distinctive egg morphology and its relationship to development in the percid fish *Etheostoma proeliare*. *Copeia* 1980:556–59.

Burr, B. M., and R. L. Mayden. 1981. Systematics, distribution and life history notes on *Notropis chihuahua*. *Copeia* 1981:255–65.

———. 1982a. Status of the cypress minnow, *Hybognathus hayi* Jordan, in Illinois. Chicago Academy of Science no. 215, Nat. Hist. Misc. 10 pp.

———. 1982b. Life history of the freckled madtom, *Noturus nocturnus*, in Mill Creek, Illinois. *Occas. Pap. Mus. Nat. Hist., Univ. Kans.* 98:1–15.

———. 1982c. Life history of the brindled madtom *Noturus miurus* in Mill Creek, Illinois. *Am. Midl. Nat.* 107:25–41.

———. 1984. Reproductive biology of the checkered madtom (*Noturus flavater*) with observations on nesting in the Ozark (*N. albater*) and slender (*N. exilis*) madtoms. *Am. Midl. Nat.* 112:408–14.

Burr, B. M., and M. A. Morris. 1977. Spawning behavior of the shorthead redhorse, *Moxostoma macrolepidotum*, in Big Rock Creek, Illinois. *Trans. Am. Fish. Soc.* 106:80–82.

Burr, B. M., and L. M. Page. 1978. The life history of the cypress darter, *Etheostoma proeliare*, in Max Creek, Illinois. Ill. Nat. Hist. Surv. Biol. Notes no. 106. Champaign: University of Illinois. 15 pp.

———. 1979. The life history of the least darter, *Etheostoma microperca*, in the Iroquois River, Illinois. Ill.Nat. Hist. Surv. Biol. Notes no. 112. Champaign: University of Illinois. 15 pp.

———. 1993. A new species of *Percina (Odontopholis)* from Kentucky and Tennessee with comparisons to *Percina cymatotaenia*. Bull. Ala. Mus. Nat. Hist. 16:15–28.

Burr, B. M., and M. L. Warren Jr. 1986. A distributional atlas of Kentucky fishes. Sci. Tech. Ser. no. 4. Frankfort: Kentucky Nature Preserves Commission. 398 pp.

———. 1988. Nests, eggs, and larvae of the Ozark sculpin, *Cottus hypselurus*. Copeia 1988:1089–92.

Burr, B. M., R. C. Cashner, and W. L. Pflieger. 1979. *Campostoma oligolepis* and *Notropis ozarcanus*, two additions to the known fish fauna of the Illinois River, Arkansas and Oklahoma. *Southwest. Nat.* 24:371–96.

Burr, B. M., B. R. Kuhadja, W. W. Dimmick, and J. M. Grady. 1989. Distribution, biology, and conservation status of the Carolina madtom, *Noturus furiosus*, an endemic North Carolina catfish. *Brimleyana* 15:57–86.

Burtson, V. 1987. An unexpected spawning of speckled dace. *Am. Currents* (June–August):10.

Buth, D. G., B. M. Burr, and J. R. Schenck. 1980. Electrophoretic evidence for relationships and differentiation among members of the percid subgenus *Microperca*. *Biochem. Syst. Ecol.* 8:297–304.

Buth, D. G., T. R. Haglund, and W. L. Minckley. 1992. Duplicate gene expression and allozyme divergence diagnostic for *Catostomus tahoensis* and the endangered *Chasmistes cujus* in Pyramid Lake, Nevada. *Copeia* 1992:935–41.

Buynak, G. L., and H. W. Mohr Jr. 1979. Larval development of the shorthead redhorse (*Moxostoma macrolepidotum*) from the Susquehanna River. *Trans. Am. Fish. Soc.* 108:161–65.

———. 1980a. Larval development of stoneroller, cutlips minnow, and river chub with diagnostic keys, including four additional cyprinids. *Prog. Fish-Culturist* 42:127–35.

———. 1980b. Larval development of golden shiner and comely shiner from northeastern Pennsylvania. *Prog. Fish-Culturist* 42:206–11.

Byrne, D. M. 1978. Life history of the spotfin killifish, *Fundulus luciae*, in Fox Creek Marsh, Virginia. *Estuaries* 1:211–27.

Carlander, K. D. 1969. *Handbook of freshwater fishery biology*. Vol. 1. Ames: Iowa State University Press. 752 pp.

———. 1977. *Handbook of freshwater fishery biology*. Vol. 2. Ames: Iowa State University Press. 431 pp.

Carney, D. A., and B. M. Burr. 1989. Life histories of the bandfin darter, *Etheostoma zonistium*, and the firebelly darter, *Etheostoma pyrrhogaster*, in western Kentucky. Ill. Nat. Hist. Surv. Biol. Notes no. 134. Champaign: University of Illinois. 16 pp.

Carney, D. A., and L. M. Page. 1990. Meristic characteristics and zoogeography of the genus *Ptychocheilus*. *Copeia* 1990:171–81.

Carr, A., and C. J. Goin. 1959. *Guide to the reptiles, amphibians, and freshwater fishes of Florida*. Gainesville: University of Florida Press. 341 pp.

Carter, H. C. 1963. The behavior of the pumpkinseed sunfish, *Lepomis gibbosus*, with notes on the behavior of other species of *Lepomis* and the pygmy sunfish, *Elassoma evergladei*. *Behaviour* 22:7–151.

Cashner, R. C. 1974. A systematic study of the genus *Ambloplites*, with comparisons to other members of the tribe Ambloplitini. Ph.D. dissertation, Tulane University, New Orleans.

Cashner, R. C., and R. E. Jenkins. 1982. Systematics of the Roanoke bass, *Ambloplites cavifrons*. *Copeia* 1982:581–94.

Cashner, R. C., and R. D. Suttkus. 1977. *Ambloplites constellatus*, a new species of rock bass from the Ozark upland of Arkansas and Missouri with a review of western rock bass populations. *Am. Midl. Nat.* 98:147–61.

Cashner, R. C., B. M. Burr, and J. S. Rogers. 1989. Geographic variation of the mud sunfish, *Acantharchus pomotis*. *Copeia* 1989:129–41.

Casterlin, M. E., and W. W. Reynolds. 1979. Thermoregulatory behavior of the bluespotted sunfish, *Enneacanthus gloriosus*. *Hydrobiologia* 64:3–4.

Ceas, P. A. 1994. Descriptions of six species within the *Etheostoma spectabile* complex. Los Angeles: American Society of Ichthyologists and Herpetologists, 74th annual meeting, abstract no. 46.

Ceas, P. A., and L. M. Page. 1997. Systematic studies of the *Etheostoma spectabile* complex, with descriptions of four new species. *Copeia* 1997:496–522.

Chart, T. E., and E. P. Bergersen. 1992. Impact of mainstream impoundment on the distribution and movements of the resident flannelmouth sucker population in the White River, Colorado. *Southwest. Nat.* 37:9–15.

Chilton, E. W., II. 1998. *Freshwater fishes of Texas*. Austin: Texas Parks and Wildlife Dept. 104 pp.

Clancey, P., B. Gardner, and A. Tews. 1993. Population status and habitat use of pallid sturgeon in the upper Misouri River system of Montana and North Dakota. *Sturgeon Quart.* 1(2):7.

Clay, W. M. 1975. *The fishes of Kentucky*. Frankfort: Kentucky Department of Fish and Wildlife Resources. 416 pp.

Cleveland, A. 1994. Nest site habitat preference and competition in *Gasterosteus aculeatus* and *G. wheatlandi*. *Copeia* 1994:698–704.

Cofer, L. M. 1995. Invalidation of the Wichita spotted bass, *Micropterus punctulatus wichitae*, subspecies theory. *Copeia* 1995:487–90.

Cole, C. F. 1965. Additional evidence for separation of *Etheostoma olmstedi* Storer from *Etheostoma nigrum* Rafinesque. *Copeia* 1965:8–13.

———. 1967. A study of the eastern johnny darter, *Etheostoma olmstedi* Storer. *Chesapeake Sci.* 8:28–51.

———. 1971. Status of the darters, *Etheostoma nigrum*, *E. longimanum* and *E. podostomone* in Atlantic drainages. In *The distributional history of the southern Appalachians*, edited by P. C. Holt, pp. 119–38. Blacksburg: Virginia Polytechnic University.

Cole, K. S. 1982. Male reproductive behavior and spawning success in a temperate zone goby, *Coryphopterus nicholsi*. *Can. J. Zool.* 60:2309–16.

Cole, K. S., and R. J. F. Smith. 1992. Attraction of female fathead minnows, *Pimephales promelas*, to chemical stimuli from breeding males. *J. Chem. Ecol.* 18:1269–84.

Collette, B. B. 1962. The swamp darters of the subgenus *Hololepis*. *Tulane Stud. Zool.* 9:115–211.

Collette, B. B., and P. Banarescu. 1977. Systematics and zoogeography of the fishes of the family Percidae. *J. Fish. Res. Board Can.* 34:1450–63.

Collette, B. B., and R. W. Yerger. 1962. The American percid fishes of the subgenus *Villora*. *Tulane Stud. Zool.* 9:213–30.

Constantz, G. D. 1979. Social dynamics and parental care in the tessellated darter. *Proc. Acad. Nat. Sci. Phila.* 131:131–38.

Contreras-Balderas, S., and M. de Lourdes Lozano. 1994. *Cyprinella alvarezdelvillari*, a new cyprinid fish from Rio Nazas of Mexico, with a key to the *lepida* clade. *Copeia* 1994:897–906.

Cook, F. A. 1959. *Freshwater fishes of Mississippi*. Jackson: Mississippi Game and Fish Commission. 239 pp.

Cook, J. A., K. R. Bestgen, D. L. Propst, and T. L. Yates. 1992. Allozymic divergence and systematics of the Rio Grande silvery minnow, *Hybognathus amarus*. *Copeia* 1992:36–44.

Cooper, E. L. 1983. *Fishes of Pennsylvania and the northeastern United States*. University Park: Pennsylvania State University Press. 252 pp.

Cooper, J. E. 1979. Description of eggs and larvae of fantail *(Etheostoma flabellare)* and rainbow *(E. caeruleum)* darters from Lake Erie tributaries. *Trans. Am. Fish. Soc.* 108:46–56.

Cooper, J. E., and R. A. Kuehne. 1974. *Speoplatyrhinus poulsoni*, a new genus and species of subterranean fish from Alabama. *Copeia* 1974:486–93.

Copeland, D. E. 1969. Fine structural study of gas secretion in the physoclistous swim bladder of *Fundulus heteroclitus* and *Gadus callarias* and in the euphysoclistous swim bladder of *Opsanus tau*. *Zeitschrift für Zellforschung* 93:305–31.

Cordes, L. E., and L. M. Page. 1980. Feeding chronology and diet composition of two darters in the Iroquois River system, Illinois. *Am. Midl. Nat.* 104:202–206.

Cowell, B. C., and C. H. Resico Jr. 1975. Life history patterns in the coastal shiner, *Notropis petersoni* Fowler. *Fla. Sci.* 38:113–21.

Crabtree, R. E., and D. P. Middaugh. 1982. Oyster shell size and the selection of spawning sites by *Chasmodes bosquianus, Hypleurochilus geminatus, Hypsoblennius ionthas* (Pisces, Blenniidae) and *Gobiosoma bosci* (Pisces, Gobiidae) in two South Carolina estuaries. *Estuaries* 5:150–55.

Crawford, R. W. 1956. A study of the distribution and taxonomy of the percid fish *Percina nigrofasciata*. *Tulane Stud. Zool.* 4:1–55.

Crear, D., and I. Haydock. 1971. Laboratory rearing of the desert pupfish, *Cyprinodon macularius*. *Fish. Bull.* 69:151–56.

Dahlberg, M. D. 1975. *Guide to the coastal fishes of Georgia and nearby states*. Athens: University of Georgia Press. 186 pp.

Dahlberg, M. D., and J. C. Conyers. 1973. An ecological study of *Gobiosoma bosci* and *G. ginsburgi* on the Georgia coast. *Fish. Bull.* 71:279–87.

Dahlberg, M. D., and D. C. Scott. 1971. The freshwater fishes of Georgia. *Bull. Ga. Acad. Sci.* 29:1–64.

Daniels, R. A. 1993. Habitat of the eastern sand darter, *Ammocrypta pellucida*. *J. Freshw. Ecol.* 8:287–95.

Darcy, G. H. 1981. Food habits of the crested goby, *Lophogobius cyprinoides*, in two Dade County, Florida, waterways. *Bull. Mar. Sci.* 31:928–32.

Davis, R. M. 1974. *Key to the freshwater fishes of Maryland*. Lavale: Department of Natural Resources, University of Maryland. 48 pp.

Davis, W. P., D. S. Taylor, and B. J. Turner. 1990. Field observations of the ecology and habits of mangrove rivulus *(Rivulus marmoratus)* in Belize and Florida. *Ichthyol.Explor. Freshw.* 1:123–34.

Dawson, C. E. 1966. Studies on the gobies of Mississippi Sound and adjacent waters. 1. *Gobiosoma. Am. Midl. Nat.* 76:379–409.

Delmonte, P. J., I. Rubinoff, and R. W. Rubinoff. 1968. Laboratory rearing through metamorphosis of some Panamanian gobies. *Copeia* 1968:411–12.

DeMarais, B. D. 1991. *Gila eremica*, a new cyprinid fish from northwestern Sonora, Mexico. *Copeia* 1991:178–89.

DeMarais, B. D., and W. L. Minckley. 1992. Hybridization in native cyprinid fishes, *Gila ditaenia* and *Gila* sp., in northwestern Mexico. *Copeia* 1992:697–703.

Denoncourt, R. F. 1976. Sexual dimorphism and geographic variation in the bronze darter, *Percina palmaris*. *Copeia* 1976:54–59.

Denoncourt, R. F., C. H. Hocutt, and J. R. Stauffer Jr. 1977. Notes on the habitat, description and distribution of the sharpnose darter, *Percina oxyrhyncha*. *Copeia* 1977:168–71.

Denoncourt, R. F., W. A. Potter, and J. R. Stauffer Jr. 1977. Records of the greenside darter, *Etheostoma blennioides*, from the Susquehanna River drainage in Pennsylvania. *Oh. J. Sci.* 77:38–42.

Denoncourt, R. F., T. W. Robbins, and J. R. Stauffer Jr. 1976. A description of xanthic tessellated darters, *Etheostoma olmstedi. Copeia* 1976:813–15.

De Vlaming, V. L. 1971. Thermal selection behavior in the estuarine goby *Gillichthys mirabilis*. *J. Fish Biol.* 3:277–86.

———. 1975. Effects of photoperiod and temperature on gonadal activity in the cyprinid teleost, *Notemigonus crysoleucas*. *Biol. Bull.* 148:402–15.

DiMichele, L., and M. H. Taylor. 1981. The mechanism of hatching in *Fundulus heteroclitus*: development and physiology. *J. Exp. Zool.* 217:73–79.

Dimmick, W. W., and L. M. Page. 1992. Systematic significance of lactate dehydrogenase variation at the generic level in percids. *Copeia* 1992:535–37.

Dimmick, W. W., K. L. Fiorino, and B. M. Burr. 1996. Reevaluation of the *Lythrurus ardens* complex with recognition of three evolutionary species. *Copeia* 1996:813–23.

Dion, R. 1994. Spawning patterns and interspecific matings of sympatric white *(Catostomus commersoni)* and longnose *(C. catostomus)* suckers from the Gouin reservoir system, Quebec. *Can. J. Zool.* 72:195–200.

Distler, D. A. 1968. Distribution and variation of *Etheostoma spectabile*. *Univ. Kans. Sci. Bull.* 48:143–208.

Douglas, M. E. 1993. Analysis of sexual dimorphism in an endangered cyprinid fish (*Gila cypha* Miller) using video image technology. *Copeia* 1993:334–43.

Douglas, M. E., and P. C. Marsh. 1994. Population estimates/population movements of *Gila cypha*, an endangered cyprinid fish in the Grand Canyon region of Arizona. Programs and Abstracts. Los Angeles: American Society of Ichthyologists and Herpetologists, 74th annual meeting, abstract no. 67.

Douglas, M. E., and P. C. Marsh. 1998. Population and survival estimates of *Catostomus latipinnis* in northern Grand Canyon, with distribution and abundance of hybrids with *Xyrauchen texanus*. *Copeia* 1998:915–25.

Douglas, M. E., P. C. Marsh, and W. L. Minckley. 1994. Indigenous fishes of western North America and the hypothesis of competitive displacement: *Meda fulgida* (Cyprinidae) as a case study. *Copeia* 1994:9–19.

Douglas, N. H. 1974. *Freshwater fishes of Louisiana*. Baton Rouge: Claitor's Publishing Division. 443 pp.

Dowling, T. E., and G. J. P. Naylor. 1997. Evolutionary relationships of minnows in the genus *Luxilus* as determined from cytochrome *b* sequences. *Copeia* 1997:758–65.

Downhower, J. F., and L. Brown. 1979. Seasonal changes in the social structure of a mottled sculpin *(Cottus bairdi)* population. *Anim. Behav.* 27:451–58.

Dryer, M. P., and A. J. Sandvol. 1993. Recovery plan for the pallid sturgeon, *Scaphirhynchus albus*. Bismarck, North Dakota: U.S. Fish and Wildlife Service. 55 pp.

Duggans, C. F., Jr., A. A. Karlin, T. A. Mousseau, and K. G. Relyea. 1995. Analysis of a hybrid zone in *Fundulus majalis* in a northeastern Florida ecotone. *Heredity* 74:117–28.

DuRant, D. F., J. V. Shireman, and R. D. Gasaway. 1979. Reproduction, growth and food habits of Seminole killifish, *Fundulus seminolis,* from two central Florida lakes. *Am. Midl. Nat.* 102:127–33.

Eccleston, J. 1982. Spawning the eastern mudminnow *(Umbra pygmaea)*. *Am. Currents* (July–August):14–16.

Echelle, A. A. 1975. A multivariate analysis of variation in an endangered fish, *Cyprinodon elegans,* with an assessment of populational status. *Tex. J. Sci.* 26:529–38.

Echelle, A. A., and A. F. Echelle. 1978. The Pecos River pupfish, *Cyprinodon pecosensis* n.sp. (Cyprinodontidae), with comments on its evolutionary origin. *Copeia* 1978:569–82.

Echelle, A. A., and A. F. Echelle. 1998. Evolutionary relationships of pupfishes in the *Cyprinodon eximius* complex. *Copeia* 1998:852–65.

Echelle, A. A., A. F. Echelle, and L. G. Hill. 1972. Interspecific interactions and limiting factors of abundance and distribution in the Red River pupfish, *Cyprinodon rubrofluviatilis*. *Am. Midl. Nat.* 88:109–30.

Echelle, A. A., A. F. Echelle, M. H. Smith, and L. G. Hill. 1975. Analysis of genic continuity in a headwater fish, *Etheostoma radiosum*. *Copeia* 1975:197–204.

Echelle, A. A., C. Hubbs, and A. F. Echelle. 1972. Developmental rates and tolerances of the Red River pupfish, *Cyprinodon rubrofluviatilis*. *Southwest. Nat.* 17:55–60.

Echelle, A. F., and A. A. Echelle. 1994. Assessment of genetic introgression between two pupfish species, *Cyprinodon elegans* and *C. variegatus,* after more than 20 years of secondary contact. *Copeia* 1994:590–97.

Eddy, S. 1969. *How to know the freshwater fishes*. Dubuque, Iowa: William C. Brown, Publishers. 286 pp.

Eddy, S., and J. C. Underhill. 1974. *Northern fishes*. Minneapolis: University of Minnesota Press. 414 pp.

Eisenhour, D. J. 1995. Systematics of *Etheostoma camurum* and *E. chlorobranchium* in the Tennessee and Cumberland River drainages with analysis of hybridization in the Nolichucky River system. *Copeia* 1995:368–79.

Elser, A. A., M. W. Gorges, and L. M. Morris. 1980. *Distribution of fishes in southeastern Montana*. Helena: Montana Department of Fish, Wildlife and Parks and U.S. Department of Interior, Bureau of Land Management. 136 pp.

Emlen, J. M., T. A. Strekal, and C. C. Buchanan. 1993. Probabilistic projections for recovery of the endangered cui-ui. *N. Am. J. Fish. Manage.* 13:467–74.

Erickson, J. E. 1976. New host and distribution records for *Piscicolaria reducta* Meyer 1940. *J. Parasitol.* 62:409.

———. 1978. Parasites of the banded darter, *Etheostoma zonale*. *J. Parasitol.* 64:899.

Eschmeyer, W. N. 1990. *Catalog of the genera of recent fishes*. San Francisco: California Academy of Sciences. 697 pp.

Eschmeyer, W. N., and E. S. Herald. 1983. *A field guide to Pacific Coast fishes*. Boston: Houghton Mifflin Company. 336 pp.

Etnier, D. A., and R. M. Bailey. 1989. *Etheostoma (Ulocentra) flavum,* a new darter from the Tennessee and Cumberland River drainages. Occas. Pap. Mus. Zool. no. 717. Ann Arbor: University of Michigan. 24 pp.

Etnier, D. A., and R. E. Jenkins. 1980. *Noturus stanauli,* a new madtom catfish from the Clinch and Duck Rivers, Tennessee. *Bull. Ala. Mus. Nat. Hist.* 5:17–22.

Etnier, D. A., and W. C. Starnes. 1986. *Etheostoma lynceum* removed from the synonymy of *E. zonale*. *Copeia* 1986:832–36.

———. 1993. *The fishes of Tennessee*. Knoxville: University of Tennessee Press. 681 pp.

Etnier, D. A., and J. D. Williams. 1989. *Etheostoma (Nothonotus) wapiti,* a new darter from the Southern Bend of the Tennessee River system in Alabama and Tennessee. *Proc. Biol. Soc. Wash.* 102:987–1000.

Evans, D. H., and C. H. Mallery. 1975. Time course of sea water acclimation by the euryhaline teleost, *Dormitator maculatus:* Correlation between potassium stimulation of sodium efflux and Na/K activated ATPase activity. *J. Comp. Physiol.* 96:117–22.

Everhart, W. H. 1966. *Fishes of Maine*. Augusta: Department of Inland Fisheries and Wildlife. 96 pp.

Fanara, D. M. 1964. Notes on the biology of a salt marsh minnow, *Cyprinodon variegatus*. *Proc. 51st Annu. Meet. N.J. Mosquito Exterm. Assoc.*:152–59.

Feldmeth, C. R., E. A. Stone, and J. H. Brown. 1974. An increased scope for thermal tolerance upon acclimating pupfish *(Cyprinodon)* to cycling temperatures. *J. Comp. Physiol.* 89:39–44.

Fisher, J. W. 1981. Ecology of *Fundulus catenatus* in three interconnected stream orders. *Am. Midl. Nat.* 106:372–78.

Fitch, J. E., and R. J. Lavenberg. 1975. *Tidepool and nearshore fishes of California*. Calif. Nat. Hist. Guides: 38. Berkeley: University of California Press. 156 pp.

Fletcher, D. E. 1993. Nest association of dusky shiner *(Notropis cummingsae)* and redbreast sunfish *(Lepomis auritus),* a potentially parasitic relationship. *Copeia* 1993:159–67.

Fletcher, D. E., and B. M. Burr. 1992. Reproductive biology, larval description, and diet of the North American bluehead shiner, *Pteronotropis hubbsi,* with comments on conservation status. *Ichthyol. Explor. Freshw.* 3:193–218.

Fletcher, D. E., S. D. Wilkins, and R. J. Paul. 1994. Experimental evidence of host-specific costs from nest association with dusky shiners, *Notropis cummingsae*. Los Angeles: American Society of Ichthyologists and Herpetologists, 74th annual meeting, abstract no. 88.

Flynn, R. B., and R. D. Hoyt. 1979. The life history of the teardrop darter, *Etheostoma barbouri* Kuehne and Small. *Am. Midl. Nat.* 101:127–41.

Foster, N. R. 1966. Origin and development of reproductive behavior in the flagfish, *Jordanella floridae*. *Am. Zool.* 6:34.

———. 1967. Trends in the evolution of reproductive behavior in killifishes. *Stud. Trop. Oceanogr.* 5:549–66.

———. 1969. The flagfish, *Jordanella floridae*, as a laboratory animal for behavioral bioassay studies. *Proc. Acad. Nat. Sci. Phila.* 121:129–52.

Fowler, J. F., and C. A. Taber. 1985. Food habits and feeding periodicity in two sympatric stonerollers. *Am. Midl. Nat.* 113:217–24.

Gach, M. H. 1996. Geographic variation in mitochondrial DNA and biogeography of *Culea inconstans*. *Copeia* 1996:563–75.

Gagen, C. J., W. E. Sharpe, and R. F. Carline. 1993. Mortality of brook trout, mottled sculpins, and slimy sculpins during acidic episodes. *Trans. Am. Fish. Soc.* 122:616–28.

Gagen, C. J., R. W. Standage, and J. N. Stoeckel. 1998. Ouachita madtom *(Noturus lachneri)* metapopulation dynamics in intermittent Ouachita Mountain streams. *Copeia* 1998:874–82.

Galat, D. L., and B. Robertson. 1992. Response of endangered *Poeciliopsis occidentalis sonoriensis* in the Rio Yaqui drainage, Arizona, to introduced *Gambusia affinis*. *Environ. Biol. Fishes* 33:249–64.

Garrett, G. P., R. J. Edwards, and A. H. Price. 1992. Distribution and status of the Devils River minnow, *Dionda diaboli*. *Southwest. Nat.* 37:259–67.

Gee, J. H. 1980. Respiratory patterns and antipredator responses in the central mudminnow, *Umbra limi*, a continuous, facultative, air-breathing fish. *Can. J. Zool.* 58:819–27.

George, S. G. 1994. Life history of the crystal darter, *Crystallaria asprella* (Jordan) of south central Arkansas. Los Angeles: American Society of Ichthyologists and Herpetologists, 74th annual meeting, abstract no. 94.

George, S. G., W. T. Slack, and N. H. Douglas. 1996. Demography, habitat, reproduction, and sexual dimorphism of the crystal darter, *Crystallaria asprella*, from south-central Arkansas. *Copeia* 1996:68–78.

Getter, C. D. 1982. Temperature limitations to the distribution of mangrove mosquitofish in Florida. *Fla. Sci.* 45:196–200.

Ghedotti, M. J., and M. J. Grose. 1997. Phylogenetic relationships of the *Fundulus notti* species group as inferred from Cytochrome *b* gene. *Copeia* 1997:858–62.

Gilbert, C. R. 1979. Part 4. Fishes. In *Rare and endangered biota of Florida*, edited by P. C. H. Pritchard, pp. 1–58. Gainesville: State of Florida Game and Freshwater Fish Commission, Gainesville and University Presses of Florida.

———. 1997. *Type catalogue of recent and fossil North American freshwater fishes: Families Cyprinidae, Catostomidae, Ictaluridae, Centrarchidae and Elassomatidae*. Spec. Pub. Gainesville: Florida Museum of Natural History. 360 pp.

Gilbert, C. R., R. C. Cashner, and E. O. Wiley. 1992. Taxonomic and nomenclatural status of the banded topminnow, *Fundulus cingulatus* (Cyprinodontiformes: Cyprinodontidae). *Copeia* 1992:747–59.

Ginsburg, I. 1932. A revision of the genus *Gobionellus*. *Bull. Bingham Oceanogr. Coll.* 4:1–51.

———. 1933. A revision of the genus *Gobiosoma*. *Bull. Bingham Oceanogr. Coll.* 4:1–59.

———. 1934. The distinguishing characters of two common species of *Microgobius* from the east coast of the United States. *Copeia* 1934:35–39.

———. 1935. Juvenile and sex characters of *Evorthodus lyricus*. *Bull. Bur. Fish.* 47:117–24.

Glascock, J. 1994. Live foods. *Fish Flash* (Greater Portland Aquarium Society) 9 (November):9.

Glazier, J. R., and C. A. Taber. 1980. Reproductive biology and age and growth of the Ozark minnow, *Dionda nubila*. *Copeia* 1980:547–50.

Gleason, C. A., and T. M. Berra. 1993. Demonstration of reproductive isolation and observation of mismatings in *Luxilus cornutus* and *L. chrysocephalus* in sympatry. *Copeia* 1993:614–28.

Goddard, K. A., and R. J. Schultz. 1993. Aclonal reproduction by polyploid members of the clonal hybrid species *Phoxinus eos-neogaeus*. *Copeia* 1993:650–60.

Goin, C. 1942. A method for collecting the vertebrates associated with water hyacinths. *Copeia* 1942:183–84.

Gold, J. R., and Y. Li. 1994. Chromosomal NOR karyotypes and genome size variation among squawfishes of the genus *Ptychocheilus*. *Copeia* 1994:60–65.

Goldstein, R. J. 1973. *Cichlids of the world*. Neptune City, N.J.: T.F.H. Publications. 382 pp.

———. 1997a. Spawning *Cyprinella* spp. on a standard substratum. *Prog. Fish-Culturist* 59:256–57.

———. 1997b. *Marine reef aquarium handbook*. Hauppage, N.Y.: Barron's Educational Series. 198 pp.

Gould, W. R., and C. Kaya. 1991. Pharyngeal teeth in the endangered Kendall Warm Springs dace *(Rhinichthys osculus thermalis)*. *Copeia* 1991:227–29.

Grady, J. M. 1988. Evolutionary relationships among the madtom catfishes, genus *Noturus*, based on allozymic data. Lawrence, Kans.: American Society of Ichthyologists and Herpetologists, 68th annual meeting. P. 99.

Grady, J. M., and W. H. LeGrande. 1992. Phylogenetic relationships, modes of speciation, and historical biogeography of the madtom catfishes, genus *Noturus*. In *Systematics, historical ecology, and North American freshwater fishes*, edited by R. L. Mayden, pp. 747–77. Stanford, Calif.: Stanford University Press.

Grant, E. C., and B. R. Riddle. 1995. Are the endangered springfish *(Crenichthys* Hubbs) and poolfish *(Empetrichthys* Gilbert) fundulines or goodeids?: A mitochondrial DNA assessment. *Copeia* 1995:209–12.

Griffin, R. W. 1974a. Environment and salinity tolerance in the genus *Fundulus*. *Copeia* 1974:319–31.

———. 1974b. Pituitary control of adaptation to fresh water in the teleost genus *Fundulus*. *Biol. Bull.* 146:357–76.

Grizzle, J. M., and M. R. Curd. 1978. Posthatching histological development of the digestive system and swim bladder of logperch, *Percina caprodes*. *Copeia* 1978:448–55.

Gross, M. R., and A. M. MacMillan. 1981. Predation and the evolution of colonial nesting in bluegill sunfish *(Lepomis macrochirus)*. *Behav. Ecol. Sociobiol.* 8:163–74.

Guillory, V. 1980. *Gambusia gaigei* Hubbs, Big Bend gambusia. In *Atlas of North American freshwater fishes,* edited by D. S. Lee et al., p. 540. Raleigh: North Carolina State Museum of Natural History. 854 pp.

Hagen, D. W., G. E. E. Moodie, and P. F. Moodie. 1972. Territoriality and courtship in the Olympic mudminnow (*Novumbra hubbsi*). *Can. J. Zool.* 50:1111–15.

Haglund, T. R., D. G. Buth, and R. Lawson. 1992. Allozyme variation and phylogenetic relationships of Asian, North American, and European ninespine sticklebacks, *Pungitius pungitius.* In *Systematics, historical ecology, and North American freshwater fishes,* edited by R. L. Mayden, pp. 437–52. Stanford, Calif.: Stanford University Press.

Hale, J. G. 1970. White sucker spawning and culture of the young in the laboratory. *Prog. Fish-Culturist* 32:169.

Hamman, R. L. 1985. Induced spawning of hatchery-reared razorback sucker. *Prog. Fish-Culturist* 47:187–89.

Harlan, J. R., and E. B. Speaker. 1951. *Iowa fish and fishing.* Des Moines: Department of Natural Resources. 237 pp.

Harrington, R. W., Jr. 1959. Delayed hatching in stranded eggs of marsh killifish, *Fundulus confluentus. Ecology* 40:430–37.

———. 1967. Environmentally controlled induction of primary male gonochorists from eggs of the self-fertilizing hermaphroditic fish, *Rivulus marmoratus* Poey. *Biol. Bull.* 132:174–99.

———. 1968. Delimitation of the thermolabile phenocritical period of sex determination and differentiation in the ontogeny of the normally hermaphroditic fish *Rivulus marmoratus* Poey. *Physiol. Zool.* 41:447–60.

Harrington, R. W., Jr., and K. D. Kallman. 1968. The homozygosity of clones of the self-fertilizing hermaphroditic fish *Rivulus marmoratus* Poey. *Am. Nat.* 102:337–43.

Hart, J. L. 1973. Pacific fishes of Canada. Bull. 180. Ottawa: Fishery Research Board of Canada. 740 pp.

Hastings, R. W. 1969. *Rivulus marmoratus* Poey from the west coast of Florida. *Quart. J. Fla. Acad. Sci.* 32:37–38.

Heins, D. C., and M. D. Machado. 1993. Spawning season, clutch characteristics, sexual dimorphism and sex ratio in the redfin darter *Etheostoma whipplei. Am. Midl. Nat.* 129:161–71.

Heins, D. C., J. A. Baker, and D. J. Tylicki. 1996. Reproductive season, clutch size, and egg size of the rainbow darter, *Etheostoma caeruleum,* from the Homochitto River, Mississippi, with an evaluation of data from the literature. *Copeia* 1996:1005–10.

Hellwig, M. 1994. *Cyprinella* (formerly *Notropis*) *lutrensis,* the red shiner, a native jewel. *Darter* (Mo. Aq. Soc.) (January–February):16–18.

Henry, C. J., and R. Ruelle. 1992. A study of pallid sturgeon and shovelnose sturgeon reproduction. Pierre, S.D.: U.S. Fish and Wildlife Service, Fish and Wildlife Enhancement. 19 pp.

Hill, L. G. 1968. Inter- and intrapopulational variation of vertebral numbers of the yoke darter, *Etheostoma juliae. Southwest. Nat.* 13:175–91.

Hill, L. G., and W. J. Matthews. 1980. Temperature selection by the darters *Etheostoma spectabile* and *Etheostoma radiosum. Am. Midl. Nat.* 104:412–15.

Hlohowsky, I., and A. M. White. 1983. Food resource partitioning and selectivity by the greenside, rainbow, and fantail darters. *Oh. J. Sci.* 83:201–208.

Hocutt, C. H., and E. O. Wiley, eds. 1986. *The zoogeography of North American freshwater fishes.* New York: John Wiley & Sons, Inc.

Hoese, H. D. 1966. Habitat segregation in aquaria between two sympatric species of *Gobiosoma. Pub. Inst. Mar. Sci. Tex.* 11:7–11.

Hoese, H. D., and R. H. Moore. 1977. *Fishes of the Gulf of Mexico: Texas, Louisiana, and adjacent waters.* College Station: Texas A&M University Press. 327 pp.

Hoff, J. G. 1976. A first record of *Gobionellus boleosoma* for New England. *Chesapeake Sci.* 17:65.

Holt, P. C., ed. 1971. *The distributional history of the southern Appalachians. Part III. Vertebrates.* Res. Div. Monogr. 4. Blacksburg: Virginia Polytechnic Institute and State University. 306 pp.

Hotalling, D. R., and C. A. Taber. 1987. Aspects of the life history of the stippled darter *Etheostoma punctulatum. Am. Midl. Nat.* 117:428–34.

Howard, J. H., and R. P. Morgan II. 1993. Allozyme variation in the mottled sculpin (*Cottus bairdi*): A test of stream capture hypotheses. *Copeia* 1993:870–75.

Howell, W. M., and R. D. Caldwell. 1967. Discovery of a second specimen of the darter, *Etheostoma trisella. Copeia* 1967:235–36.

Hubbs, C. 1985. Darter reproductive seasons. *Copeia* 1985:56–68.

———. 1995. Springs and spring runs as unique aquatic habitats. *Copeia* 1995:989–91.

Hubbs, C., R. J. Edwards, and G. P. Garrett. 1991. An annotated checklist of the freshwater fishes of Texas, with keys to identification of species. *Tex. J. Sci.* (suppl.) 43:1–56.

Hubbs, C., A. E. Peden, and M. M. Stevenson. 1969. The developmental rate of the greenthroat darter, *Etheostoma lepidum. Am. Midl. Nat.* 81:182–88.

Hubbs, C., M. M. Stevenson, and A. E. Peden. 1968. Fecundity and egg size in two central Texas darter populations. *Southwest. Nat.* 13:301–24.

Hubbs, C. L. 1954. A new Texas subspecies, *apristis,* of the darter *Hadropterus scierus,* with a discussion of variation within the species. *Am. Midl. Nat.* 52:211–20.

———. 1971. Survival of intergroup Percid hybrids. *Jpn. J. Ichthyol.* 18:65–75.

Hubbs, C. L., and J. D. Black. 1941. The subspecies of the American percid fish, *Poecilichthys whipplii.* Occas. Pap. Mus. Zool. no. 429. Ann Arbor: University of Michigan. 27 pp.

———. 1954. Status and synonymy of the American percid fish *Hadropterus scierus. Am. Midl. Nat.* 52:201–10.

Hubbs, C. L., and M. D. Cannon. 1935. The darters of the genera *Hololepis* and *Villora.* Mus. Zool. Misc. Pub. no. 30. Ann Arbor: University of Michigan. 93 pp.

Hubbs, C. L., and K. F. Lagler. 1958. *Fishes of the Great Lakes region.* Ann Arbor: University of Michigan Press. 213 pp.

Hubbs, C. L., and E. C. Raney. 1939. *Hadropterus oxyrhynchus,* a new percid fish from Virginia and West Virginia. Occas. Pap. Mus. Zool. no. 396. Ann Arbor: University of Michigan. 9 pp.

Humphries, J. M., and R. C. Cashner. 1994. *Notropis suttkusi,* a new cyprinid from the Ouachita uplands of Oklahoma and Arkansas, with comments on the status of Ozarkian populations of *N. rubellus. Copeia* 1994:82–90.

Ingersoll, C. G., and D. L. Claussen. 1984. Temperature selection and critical thermal maxima of the fantail darter, *Etheostoma flabellare,* and johnny darter, *E. nigrum,* related to habitat and season. *Environ. Biol. Fishes* 11:131–38.

Ingersoll, C. G., I. Hlohowskyj, and J. D. Mundahl. 1984. Movements and densities of the darters *Etheostoma flabellare, E. spectabile,* and *E. nigrum* during spring spawning. *J. Freshw. Ecol.* 2:345–51.

Inglis, E. 1994. Redbelly dace—*Phoxinus eos. Calquarium* (Alberta, Canada) (December):2.

Innes, W. T. 1951. *Exotic aquarium fishes.* 12th edition. Philadelphia: Innes Publishing Company. 521 pp.

Isgro, T. 1982. The flagfish, quick and easy. *Am. Currents* (July–August):16–17.

Itzkowitz, M. 1974. The effects of other fish on the reproductive behavior of the male *Cyprinodon variegatus. Behaviour* 48:1–22.

James, P. W., and C. A. Taber. 1986. Reproductive biology and age and growth of the yoke darter, *Etheostoma juliae. Copeia* 1986:536–40.

Janovy, J., Jr., M. A. McDowll, and M. T. Ferdig. 1991. The niche of *Salsuginus thalkeni,* a gill parasite of *Fundulus zebrinus. J. Parasitol.* 77:697–702.

Jean, R., and E. T. Garside. 1974. Selective elevation of the upper lethal temperature of the mummichog *Fundulus heteroclitus,* with a statement of its application to fish culture. *Can. J. Zool.* 52:433–35.

Jenkins, R. E., and N. M. Burkhead. 1994. *Freshwater fishes of Virginia.* Bethesda, Md.: American Fisheries Society. 1079 pp.

Jenkins, R. E., and T. Zorach. 1970. Zoogeography and characters of the American cyprinid fish *Notropis bifrenatus. Chesapeake Sci.* 11:174–82.

Jenkins, R. E., L. A. Revelle, and T. Zorach. 1975. Records of the blackbanded sunfish, *Enneacanthus chaetodon,* and comments on the southeastern Virginia freshwater ichthyofauna. *Va. J. Sci.* 26:128–34.

Johnson, G. D., and V. G. Springer. 1997. *Elassoma:* Another look. Abstr. Seattle: 77th annual ASIH meetings. p. 176.

Johnson, J. E. 1987. *Protected fishes of the United States and Canada.* Bethesda, Md.: American Fisheries Society. 42 pp.

Johnson, J. E., M. G. Pardew, and M. M. Lyttle. 1993. Predator recognition and avoidance by larval razorback sucker and northern hog sucker. *Trans. Am. Fish. Soc.* 122:1139–45.

Johnston, C. E. 1989. Spawning in the eastern sand darter, *Ammocrypta pellucida,* with comments on the phylogeny of *Ammocrypta* and related taxa. *Trans. Ill. Acad. Sci.* 82(3–4):163–68.

———. 1991. Spawning activities of *Notropis chlorocephalus, Notropis chiliticus,* and *Hybopsis hypsinotus,* nest associates of *Nocomis leptocephalus* in the southeastern United States, with comments on nest association. *Brimleyana* 17:77–88.

———. 1994. Spawning behavior of the goldstripe darter (*Etheostoma parvipinne* Gilbert and Swain). *Copeia* 1994:823–25.

Johnston, C. E., and W. S. Birkhead. 1988. Spawning of the bandfin shiner, *Notropis zonistius. J. Ala. Acad. Sci.* 59(2):30–33.

Johnston, C. E., and K. J. Kleiner. 1994. Reproductive behavior of the rainbow shiner (*Notropis chrosomus*) and the rough shiner (*Notropis baileyi*), nest associates of the bluehead chub (*Nocomis leptocephalus*) in the Alabama River drainage. *J. Ala. Acad. Sci.* 65:230–38.

Johnston, C. E., and L. M. Page. 1992. The evolution of complex reproductive strategies in North American minnows (Cyprinidae). In *Systematics, historical ecology, and North American freshwater fishes,* edited by R. L. Mayden. Stanford, Calif.: Stanford University Press. 969 pp.

Jones, S. R., and C. A. Taber. 1985. A range revision for western populations of the southern cavefish, *Typhlichthys subterraneus. Am. Midl. Nat.* 113:413–15.

Jordan, C. M., and E. T. Garside. 1972. Upper lethal temperatures of threespine stickleback, *Gasterosteus aculeatus,* in relation to thermal and osmotic acclimation, ambient salinity, and size. *Can. J. Zool.* 50:1405–11.

Jordan, D. S., and B. W. Evermann. 1896. The fishes of North and Middle America: a descriptive catalogue of the species of fish-like vertebrates found in the waters of North America, north of the Isthmus of Panama. *U.S. National Museum Bulletin* 47, no. 1, 1240 pp.

Jordan, F., D. C. Haney, and F. G. Nodlie. 1993. Plasma osmotic regulation and routine metabolism in the Eustis pupfish, *Cyprinodon variegatus hubbsi. Copeia* 1993:784–89.

Kaighn, M. E. 1964. A biochemical study of the hatching process in *Fundulus heteroclitus. Dev. Biol.* 9:56–80.

Kaiser, M. J., and R. N. Hughes. 1993. Factors affecting the behavioral mechanisms of diet selection in fishes. *Mar. Behav. Physiol.* 23:105–18.

Kaiser, M. J., A. P. Westhead, R. N. Hughes, and R. N. Gibson. 1992. Are digestive characteristics important contributors to the profitability of prey? *Oecologia* 90:61–69.

Katula, R. 1987a. Northern redbelly dace in Wisconsin. *Am. Currents* (February):4–5.

———. 1987b. Crossbreeding of river darter and blackside darter (*Percina shumardi* and *P. maculata*). *Am. Currents* (October/November/December):20–22.

———. 1988. Spawning of an Ozark endemic, the stippled darter. *Freshw. Mar. Aq.* 11 (September):104–107.

———. 1990a. Spawning of three *Nothonotus* darter species. *Freshw. Mar. Aq.* 13 (August):16–22.

———. 1990b. Notes on spawning of the johnny darter. *Am. Currents* (September–November):21–22.

———. 1991a. Observations of spawning methods of the creole darter and the finescale saddled darter (*Etheostoma collettei* and *Etheostoma osburni*). *Am. Currents* (summer):15–16.

———. 1991b. Spawning of the reticulate sculpin. *Am. Currents* (December–February):13–15.

———. 1992a. The spawning mode of the pirate perch. *Trop. Fish Hobbyist* (August):156–59.

———. 1992b. The northwestern *Percopsis,* the sand roller. *Am. Currents* (spring):32–34.

———. 1993a. Spawning the green banded darter, *Etheostoma zonale. Freshw. Mar. Aq.* 16 (month undetermined):27–29.

———. 1993b. Spawning a "winged minnow"—the broadstripe shiner. *Am. Currents* (spring):20–21, 30.

———. 1996. Keeping the great northerner, the Iowa darter, *Etheostoma exile. Trop. Fish Hobbyist* (July):168–74.

Keenlyne, K. D., and L. G. Jenkins. 1993. Age at sexual maturity of the pallid sturgeon. *Trans. Am. Fish. Soc.* 122:393–96.

Keevin, T. M., L. M. Page, and C. E. Johnston. 1989. The spawning behavior of the saffron darter (*Etheostoma flavum*). *Trans. Ky. Acad. Sci.* 50:55–58.

Keivany, Y., J. S. Nelson, and P. S. Economidis. 1997. Validity of *Pungitius hellenicus* Stephanidis, 1971, a stickleback fish from Greece. *Copeia* 1997:558–64.

Kendall, A. W., Jr., and A. J. Mearns. 1996. Egg and larval development in relation to systematics of *Novumbra hubbsi*, the Olympic mudminnow. *Copeia* 1996:684–95.

Kessler, R. K., and J. H. Thorpe. 1993. Microhabitat segregation of the threatened spotted darter *(Etheostoma maculatum)* and closely related orangefin darter *(E. bellum)*. *Can. J. Fish. Aq. Sci.* 50:1084–91.

Kieffer, M. C., and B. Kynard. 1993. Annual movements of shortnose and Atlantic sturgeons in the Merrimack River, Massachusetts. *Trans. Am. Fish. Soc.* 122:1088–1103.

———. 1996. Spawning of shortnose sturgeons in the Merrimack River, Massachusetts. *Trans. Am. Fish. Soc.* 12:179–86.

Knapp, F. T. 1953. *Fishes found in the fresh waters of Texas.* Brunswick, Ga.: Ragland Studio and Lithograph Printing Company. 166 pp.

Knapp, L. W., W. J. Richards, R. V. Miller, and N. R. Foster. 1963. Rediscovery of the percid *fish Etheostoma sellare*. *Copeia* 1963:455.

Kneib, R. T., and A. E. Stiven. 1978. Growth, reproduction, and feeding of *Fundulus heteroclitus* on a North Carolina salt marsh. *J. Exp. Mar. Biol. Ecol.* 31:121–40.

Kodric-Brown, A., and P. Mazzolini. 1992. The breeding system of pupfish, *Cyprinodon pecosensis*: Effects of density and interspecific interactions with the killifish, *Fundulus zebrinus*. *Environ. Biol. Fishes* 35:169–76.

Koenig, C. C., and R. J. Livingston. 1976. The embryological development of the diamond killifish *(Adinia xenica)*. *Copeia* 1976:435–45.

Kristmundsdottir, A. Y., and J. R. Gold. 1996. Systematics of the blacktail shiner *(Cyprinella venusta)* inferred from analysis of mitochondrial DNA. *Copeia* 1996:773–83.

Kroll, K. J., J. P. Van Eenennaam, and S. I. Doroshov. 1992. Effect of water temperature and formulated diets on growth and survival of larval paddlefish. *Trans. Am. Fish. Soc.* 121:538–43.

Kubista, I. 1980. Minnesota bait farmer contributes to multi-million dollar state crop. *Aquacult. Mag.* (September–October):28–30.

Kuchnow, K. P., and R. S. Foster IV. 1976. Thermal tolerance of stored *Fundulus heteroclitus* gametes: Fertilizability and survival of embryos. *J. Fish. Res. Board Can.* 33:676–80.

Kuehne, R. A., and R. M. Bailey. 1961. Stream capture and the distribution of the percid fish *Etheostoma sagitta*, with geologic and taxonomic considerations. *Copeia* 1961:1–8.

Kuehne, R. A., and R. W. Barbour. 1983. *The American darters.* Frankfort: University Press of Kentucky. 177 pp.

Kuehne, R. A., and J. W. Small Jr. 1971. *Etheostoma barbouri*, a new darter from the Green River with notes on the subgenus *Catonotus. Copeia* 1971:18–26.

LaBounty, J. F., and J. E. Deacon. 1972. *Cyprinodon milleri*, a new species of pupfish from Death Valley, California. *Copeia* 1972:769–80.

LaHaye, M., A. Branchaud, M. Gendron, R. Verdon, and R. Fortin. 1992. Reproduction, early life history, and characteristics of the spawning grounds of the lake sturgeon *(Acipenser fulvescens)* in Des Praries and L'Assomption Rivers, near Montreal, Quebec. *Can. J. Zool.* 70:1681–89.

Lambinon, J. 1994. Keeping and breeding the red shiner. *Aquarist and Pondkeeper* (July):69–71.

LaRivers, I. 1962. *Fish and fisheries of Nevada.* Carson City: Game and Fish Commission. 782 pp.

Layman, S. R. 1984. The duskytail darter, *Etheostoma (Catonotus)* sp., confirmed as an egg-clusterer. *Copeia* 1984:992–94.

———. 1993. Life history of the Savannah darter, *Etheostoma fricksium*, in the Savannah River drainage, South Carolina. *Copeia* 1993:959–68.

Layzer, J. B., and R. J. Reed. 1978. Food, age and growth of the tessellated darter, *Etheostoma olmstedi*, in Massachusetts. *Am. Midl. Nat.* 100:459–62.

Lee, D. S., and B. M. Burr. 1985. Observation on life history of the dollar sunfish, *Lepomis marginatus. ASB Bull.* 32:58(abstract).

Lee, D. S., C. G. Gilbert, C. H. Hocutt, R. E. Jenkins, D. E. McAllister, and J. R. Stauffer Jr. 1980. *Atlas of North American freshwater fishes.* Raleigh: North Carolina State Museum of Natural History. 854 pp.

Leidy, R. A. 1992. Microhabitat selection by the johnny darter, *Etheostoma nigrum* Rafinesque, in a Wyoming stream. *Great Basin Nat.* 52:68–74.

Leim, A. H., and W. B. Scott. 1966. *Fishes of the Atlantic coast of Canada.* Bull. 155. Ottawa: Fisheries Research Board of Canada. 485 pp.

Levin, C. B., and N. R. Foster. 1972. Cytotaxonomic studies in Cyprinodontidae: multiple sex chromosomes in *Garmanella pulchra. Notulae Naturae of the Academy of Natural Sciences of Philadelphia,* no. 446. 5 pp.

Linder, A. D. 1955. The fishes of Blue River in Oklahoma with descriptions of two new percid hybrid combinations. *Am. Midl. Nat.* 54:173–91.

———. 1958. Behavior and hybridization of two species of *Etheostoma. Trans. Kans. Acad. Sci.* 61:195–212.

———. 1959. The American percid fishes *Ammocrypta clara* Jordan and *Ammocrypta pellucida* (Baird). *Southwest. Nat.* 4:176–84.

Lindquist, D. G., J. R. Shute, and P. W. Shute. 1981. Spawning and nesting behavior of the Waccamaw darter, *Etheostoma perlongum. Environ. Biol. Fishes* 6:177–91.

Lindquist, D. G., J. R. Shute, P. W. Shute, and L. M. Jones. 1984. Selection of sites for egg deposition and spawning dynamics in the Waccamaw darter. *Environ. Biol. Fishes* 11:107–12.

Loos, J. J., and W. S. Woolcott. 1969. Hybridization and behavior in two species of *Percina. Copeia* 1969:374–85.

Lowe, C. H., and W. G. Heath. 1969. Behavioral and physiological responses to temperature in the desert pupfish, *Cyprinodon macularius. Physiol. Zool.* 42:53–59.

Lowe, C. H., D. S. Hinds, and E. A. Halpern. 1967. Experimental catastrophic selection and tolerances to low oxygen concentration in native Arizona freshwater fishes. *Ecology* 48:1013–17.

Ludwig, G. M. 1997. Induced spawning in captive white sucker, *Catostomus commersoni*, and spotted sucker, *Minytrema melanops. J. Appl. Aquacult.* 7(3):7–17.

Lydeard, C., M. C. Wooten, and M. H. Smith. 1991. Occurrence of *Gambusia affinis* in the Savannah and Chattahoochee drainages: Previously undescribed geographic contacts between *G. affinis* and *G. holbrooki. Copeia* 1991:1111–16.

Lynch, J. M., D. M. McElroy, and M. E. Douglas. 1994. Every picture tells a story: Geometric morphometrics and variation in upper Colorado River chub. Los Angeles: American Society of Ichthyologists and Herpetologists, 74th annual meeting, abstract no. 167.

Makara, A., and I. Stranai. 1980. Rast a plodnost blatniaka (*Umbra krameri* Walbaum, 1792). *Biologia* (Bratislava) 35:131–35.

Markle, D. F., T. N. Pearsons, and D. T. Bills. 1991. Natural history of *Oregonichthys* (Pisces: Cyprinidae), with a description of a new species from the Umpqua River of Oregon. *Copeia* 1991:277–93.

Marsh, P. C., M. E. Douglas, W. L. Minckley, and R. J. Timmons. 1991. Rediscovery of Colorado squawfish, *Ptychocheilus lucius,* in Wyoming. *Copeia* 1991:1091–92.

Marshall, D. B., ed. 1992. Fishes. In *Sensitive vertebrates of Oregon*. Portland: Oregon Department of Fish and Wildlife. unpaginated.

Martin, F. D. 1968. Intraspecific variation in osmotic abilities of *Cyprinodon variegatus. Ecology* 49:1186–88.

———. 1972. Factors influencing local distribution of *Cyprinodon variegatus. Trans. Am. Fish. Soc.* 101:89–93.

Martin, R. A., and J. H. Finucane. 1968. Reproduction and ecology of the longnose killifish. *Quart. J. Fla. Acad. Sci.* 31:101–11.

Mashiko, K. 1976. Ecological study on breeding of an eleotrid goby, *Odontobutis obscurus,* under rearing conditions. *Jpn. J. Ecol.* 26:91–100.

Mathur, D. 1973a. Some aspects of life history of the blackbanded darter, *Percina nigrofasciata,* in Halawakee Creek, Alabama. *Am. Midl. Nat.* 89:381–93.

———. 1973b. Food habits and feeding chronology of the blackbanded darter, *Percina nigrofasciata,* in Halawakee Creek, Alabama. *Trans. Am. Fish. Soc.* 102:48–55.

———. 1977. Food habits and competitive relationships of the bandfin shiner in Halawakee Creek, Alabama. *Am. Midl. Nat.* 97:89–100.

Mathur, D., and J. S. Ramsey. 1974. Food habits of the rough shiner, *Notropis baileyi* Suttkus and Raney, in Halawakee Creek, Alabama. *Am. Midl. Nat.* 92:84–93.

Matthews, W. J., and H. W. Robison. 1982. Addition of *Etheostoma collettei* to the fish fauna of Oklahoma and of the Red River drainage in Arkansas. *Southwest. Nat.* 27:215–46.

Matthews, W. J., J. R. Bek, and E. Surat. 1982. Comparative ecology of the darters *Etheostoma podostemone, E. flabellare* and *Percina roanoka* in the upper Roanoke River drainage, Virginia. *Copeia* 1982:805–14.

Matthews, W. J., R. E. Jenkins, and J. T. Styron Jr. 1982. Systematics of two forms of blacknose dace, *Rhinichthys atratulus* in a zone of syntopy, with a review of the species group. *Copeia* 1982:902–20.

Maurakis, E. G., and W. S. Woolcott. 1992a. Spawning in *Semotilus corporalis* (fallfish). *Va. J. Sci.* 43:377–80.

———. 1992b. An intergeneric cyprinid hybrid, *Phoxinus oreas* × *Semotilus atromaculatus,* from the James River drainage, Virginia. *Copeia* 1992:548–53.

———. 1993. Spawning behaviors in *Luxilus albeolus* and *Luxilus cerasinus. Va. J. Sci.* 44:275–78.

———. 1996. Nocturnal breeding activities in *Nocomis leptocephalus* and *Nocomis micropogon. J. Elisha Mitchell Sci. Soc.* 112:119–20.

Maurakis, E. G., M. H. Sabaj, and W. S. Woolcott. 1993. Pebble nest construction and spawning behaviors in *Semotilus thoreauianus. ASB Bull.* 40:27–30.

Maurakis, E. G., W. S. Woolcott, and J. T. Magee. 1990. Pebble-nests of four *Semotilus* species. *Southeast. Fish. Council Proc.* 22:7–13.

Maurakis, E. G., W. S. Woolcott, and W. R. McGuire. 1995. Nocturnal reproductive behavior in *Semotilus atromaculatus. Southeast. Fish. Council Proc.* 31:1–3.

Maurakis, E. G., W. S. Woolcott, and M. H. Sabaj. 1991a. Reproductive-behavioral phylogenetics of *Nocomis* species-groups. *Am. Midl. Nat.* 126:103–10.

———. 1991b. Reproductive behavior of *Exoglossum* species. *Bull. Ala. Mus. Nat. Hist.* 10:11–16.

———. 1992. Water currents in spawning areas of pebble nests of *Nocomis leptocephalus. Southeast. Fish. Council Proc.* 25:1–3.

Maurakis, E. G., W. S. Woolcott, G. P. Radice, and W. R. McGuire. 1992. Myomere counts in larvae of three species of *Nocomis. ASB Bull.* 39:1–8.

Mayden, R. L. 1985. Nuptial structures in the subgenus *Catonotus,* genus *Etheostoma. Copeia* 1985:580–83.

———. 1987. Systematics of fishes in the *Etheostoma punctulatum* and *Notropis zonatus* species groups. Programs and Abstracts. Albany, N.Y.: American Society of Ichthyologists and Herpetologists, 67th annual meeting.

———. 1988. Systematics of the *Notropis zonatus* species group, with description of a new species from the interior highlands of North America. *Copeia* 1988:153–73.

———. 1989. Phylogenetic studies of North American minnows, with emphasis on the genus *Cyprinella.* Misc. Pub. no. 80. Lawrence: University of Kansas Museum of Natural History.

———, ed. 1992. *Systematics, historical ecology, and North American freshwater fishes.* Stanford, Calif.: Stanford University Press. 969 pp.

———. 1993. *Elassoma alabamae,* a new species of pygmy sunfish endemic to the Tennessee River drainage of Alabama. *Bull. Ala. Mus. Nat. Hist.* 16:1–14.

Mayden, R. L., and B. M. Burr. 1981. Life history of the slender madtom, *Noturus exilis,* in southern Illinois. *Occas. Pap. Mus. Nat. Hist., Univ. Kans.* 93:1–64.

Mayden, R. L., and D. M. Hillis. 1990. Natural history and systematics of the largemouth shiner, *Cyprinella bocagrande,* with comments on conservation status. *Copeia* 1990:1004–11.

Mayden, R. L., and B. R. Kuhajda. 1994. Reevaluation of the taxonomic, systematic, and conservation status of the Alabama sturgeon, *Scaphirhynchus suttkusi* Williams and Clemmer. Los Angeles: American Society of Ichthyologists and Herpetologists, 47th annual meeting, abstract no. 183.

Mayden, R. L., and R. H. Matson. 1992. Systematics and biogeography of the Tennessee shiner, *Notropis leuciodus. Copeia* 1992:954–68.

Mayden, R. L., and L. M. Page. 1979. Systematics of *Percina roanoka* and *P. crassa,* with comparisons to *P. peltata* and *P. notogramma. Copeia* 1979:413–26.

Mayden, R. L., and S. J. Walsh. 1984. Life history of the least madtom, *Noturus hildebrandi* with comparisons to related species. *Am. Midl. Nat.* 112:349–68.

Mayden, R. L., B. M. Burr, and S. L. Dewey. 1980. Aspects of the life history of the Ozark madtom, *Noturus albater,* in southeastern Missouri. *Am. Midl. Nat.* 104:335–40.

McAllister, D. E., B. J. Parker, and P. M. McKee. 1985. Rare, endangered, and extinct fishes in Canada. Syllogeus Series no. 54. Ottawa: National Museum of Natural Sciences, National Museums of Canada. 192 pp.

McCabe, G. T., Jr., R. L. Emmett, and S. A. Hinton. 1993. Feeding ecology of juvenile white sturgeon (*Acipenser transmontanus*) in the lower Columbia River. *Northwest Sci.* 67:170–80.

McCaskill, M. L., J. E. Thomerson, and P. R. Mills. 1972. Food of the northern studfish, *Fundulus catenatus*, in the Missouri Ozarks. *Trans. Am. Fish. Soc.* 101:375–77.

McDonnell, R. 1993. I love *lucie*. *J. Am. Killifish Assoc.* 26:79–82.

McElman, J. F., and E. K. Balon. 1979. Early ontogeny of walleye, *Stizostedion vitreum*, with steps of saltatory development. *Environ. Biol. Fishes* 4:309–48.

McGuire, W. R., W. S. Woolcott, and E. G. Maurakis. 1996. Histomorphology of external and internal mandubular and cheek epidermis in four species of North American pebble nest-building minnows. *ASB Bull.* 43:37–43.

McInerney, J. E. 1969. Reproductive behavior of the blackspotted stickleback, *Gasterosteus wheatlandi*. *J. Fish. Res. Board Can.* 26:2061–75.

McKenzie, J. 1969. A descriptive analysis of the aggressive behavior of the male brook stickleback, *Culaea inconstans*. *Can. J. Zool.* 47:1275–79.

McKeown, P. E., C. H. Hocutt, R. P. Morgan II, and J. H. Howard. 1984. An electrophoretic analysis of the *Etheostoma variatum* complex, with associated zoogeographic considerations. *Environ. Biol. Fishes* 11:85–95.

McLane, W. Mc. 1955. The fishes of the St. Johns River system. Unpublished Ph.D. dissertation, University of Florida, Gainesville. 360 pp.

McLennan, D. A. 1993. Phylogenetic relationships in the Gasterosteidae: An updated tree based on behavioral characters with a discussion of homoplasy. *Copeia* 1993:318–26.

McMaster, M. E., C. B. Portt, K. R. Minkittrick, and D. G. Dixon. 1992. Milt characteristics, reproductive performance, and larval survival and development of white sucker exposed to bleached kraft mill effluent. *Ecotoxicol. Environ. Safety* 23:103–17.

McNabb, R. A., and G. E. Pickford. 1970. Thyroid function in male killifish, *Fundulus heteroclitus*, adapted to high and low temperatures and to fresh water and sea water. *Comp. Biochem. Physiol.* 33:783–92.

Meagher, S., and T. E. Dowling. 1991. Hybridization between the cyprinid fishes *Luxilus albeolus*, *L. cornutus*, and *L. cerasinus* with comments on the proposed hybrid origin of *L. albeolus*. *Copeia* 1991:979–91.

Meffe, G. K., and F. F. Snelson Jr. 1989. An ecological overview of poeciliid fishes. In *Ecology and Evolution of Livebearing Fishes (Poeciliidae)*, edited by G. K. Meffe and F. F. Snelson Jr., pp. 13–31. Engelwood Cliffs, N.J.: Prentice Hall.

Menhinick, E. F. 1975. *The freshwater fishes of North Carolina*. Keys and distribution maps for all freshwater species, manuscript. Charlotte: Press of the University of North Carolina.

———. 1991. *The freshwater fishes of North Carolina*. Raleigh: North Carolina Wildlife Resources Commission. 227 pp.

Menhinick, E. F., T. M. Burton, and J. R. Bailey. 1974. An annotated checklist of the freshwater fishes of North Carolina. *J. Elisha Mitchell Sci. Soc.* 90(1):24–50.

Mettee, M. F. 1977. A study on the distribution of *Etheostoma okaloosae*, the Okaloosa darter, and *Etheostoma edwini*, the brown darter, in northwest Florida. *Journal of the Alabama Academy of Sciences* 48:65.

Mettee, M. F., P. E. O'Neil, and J. M. Pierson. 1996. *Fishes of Alabama and the Mobile basin*. Birmingham, Ala.: Oxmoor House. 820 pp.

Miller, D. J., and R. N. Lea. 1976. *Guide to the coastal marine fishes of California*. Sacramento: Department of Fish and Game Fish Bull. 157. 249 pp.

Miller, J. E., J. F. Savino, and R. K. Neely. 1992. Competition for food between crayfish (*Orconectes virilis*) and the slimy sculpin (*Cottus cognatus*). *J. Freshw. Ecol.* 7:127–36.

Miller, R. J. 1967. Nestbuilding and breeding activities of some Oklahoma fishes. *Southwest. Nat.* 12:463–68.

Miller, R. J., and H. W. Robison. 1973. *The Fishes of Oklahoma*. Stillwater: Oklahoma State University Press. 246 p.

Miller, R. R. 1991. Taxonomic status of two nominal species of Mexican freshwater fishes (Cyprinidae). *Copeia* 1991:225–27.

Miller, R. R., and G. R. Smith. 1981. Distribution and evolution of *Chasmistes* in western North America. *Occas. Pap. Mus. Zool., Univ. Mich.* 696:1–46.

Miller, R. R., and M. L. Smith. 1986. In *The zoogeography of North American freshwater fishes*, edited by C. H. Hocutt and E. O. Wiley, p. 495. New York: John Wiley & Sons, Inc.

Miller, R. R., and V. Walters. 1972. A new genus of Cyprinodontid fish from Nuevo Leon, Mexico. *Contributions in Science, Natural History Museum of Los Angeles County*, no. 233. 13 pp.

Miller, R. V. 1968. A systematic study of the greenside darter, *Etheostoma blennioides*. *Copeia* 1968:1–40.

Minckley, W. L. 1973. *Fishes of Arizona*. Phoenix: Arizona Game and Fish Department. 293 pp.

Minckley, W. L., and J. E. Deacon. 1968. Southwestern fishes and the enigma of "endangered species." *Science* 159:1424–32.

Mitten, J. B., and R. K. Koehn. 1976. Morphological adaptation to thermal stress in a marine fish, *Fundulus heteroclitus*. *Biol. Bull.* 151:548–59.

Mok, H. K. 1981. Chapter 22. Sound production in the naked goby, *Gobiosoma bosci*—A preliminary study. In *Hearing and sound communication in fishes*, edited by W. N. Tavolga and R. R. Fay, pp. 447–56. Proceedings in Life Sciences. New York: Springer-Verlag.

Morris, M. M., and L. M. Page. 1981. Variation in western logperches, with description of a new subspecies from the Ozarks. *Copeia* 1981:95–108.

Morrow, J. E. 1980. *The freshwater fishes of Alaska*. Anchorage: Alaska Northwest Publishing Company. 248 pp.

Mount, D. I. 1959. Spawning behavior of the bluebreast darter, *Etheostoma camurum*. *Copeia* 1959:240–43.

Moyle, P. B. 1976. *Inland fishes of California*. Berkeley: University of California Press. 405 pp.

Mueller, G., M. Horn, J. Kahl, T. Burke, and P. Marsh. 1993. Use of larval light traps to capture razorback sucker (*Xyrauchen texanus*) in Lake Mohave, Arizona-Nevada. *Southwest. Nat.* 38(4):399–402.

Mugford, P. S. 1969. *Illustrated manual of Massachusetts freshwater fish*. Boston: Massachusetts Division of Fish and Game. 127 pp.

Munroe, T. A., and R. A. Lotspeich. 1979. Some life history aspects of the seaboard goby (*Gobiosoma ginsburgi*) in Rhode Island. *Estuaries* 2:22–27.

Murphy, W. J., and G. E. Collier. 1997. A molecular phylogeny for Aplocheiloid fishes: The role of vicariance and the origins of annualism. *Mol. Biol. Evol.* 14:790–99.

Naiman, R. J. 1976. Productivity of a herbivorous pupfish population (*Cyprinodon nevadensis*) in a warm desert stream. *J. Fish. Biol.* 9:125–37.

Nelson, J. S., and M. J. Paetz. 1992. *The fishes of Alberta.* Alberta, Canada: University of Alberta Press. 437 pp.

Nelson, S. M., and L. C. Keenan. 1992. Use of an indigenous fish species, *Fundulus zebrinus*, in a mosquito abatement program: A field comparison with the mosquitofish, *Gambusia affinis*. *J. Am. Mosquito Control Assoc.* 8:301–304.

New, J. G. 1966. Reproductive behavior of the shield darter, *Percina peltata peltata*, in New York. *Copeia* 1966:20–28.

Nordlie, F. G. 1979. Niche specificities of eleotrid fishes in a tropical estuary. *Rev. Biol. Trop.* 27:35–50.

———. 1981. Feeding and reproductive biology of eleotrid fishes in a tropical estuary. *J. Fish Biol.* 18:97–110.

Nordlie, F. G., and D. C. Haney. 1993. Euryhaline adaptations in the fat sleeper, *Dormitator maculatus*. *J. Fish Biol.* 43:433–39.

North, J. A., R. C. Beamesderfer, and T. A. Rien. 1993. Distribution and movements of white sturgeon in three lower Columbia River reservoirs. *Northwest Sci.* 67:105–11.

Norton, S. F. 1991a. Capture success and diet of cottid fishes: the role of predator morphology and attack kinematics. *Ecology* 72:1807–19.

———. 1991b. Habitat use and community structure in an assemblage of cottid fishes. *Ecology* 72:2181–92.

Oakey, D. D., and M. E. Douglas. 1994. Phylogenetic analysis of *Rhinichthys osculus* in western North America. Los Angeles: American Society of Ichthyologists and Herpetologists, 74th annual meeting, abstract no. 225.

Ohguchi, O. 1981. Prey density and selection against oddity by three-spined sticklebacks. *Adv. Ethol.* 12:1–79.

Olin, P. 1993. Importing Live Organisms to Hawaii: Procedures and Permitting. UNIHI-SEAGRANT-FS –94-01. 6 pp.

Oliver, J. D. 1991. Consumption rates, evacuation rates, and diets of pygmy killifish, *Leptolucania ommata*, and mosquitofish, *Gambusia affinis*, in the Okefenokee Swamp. *Brimleyana* 17:89–103.

Ongarato, R. J., and E. J. Snucins. 1993. Aggression of guarding male smallmouth bass (*Micropterus dolomieui*) towards potential brood predators near the nest. *Can. J. Zool.* 71:437–40.

Ottinger, C. A., H. L. Holloway Jr., and T. M. Derrig. 1992. Maintenance of juvenile paddlefish as experimental animals. *Prog. Fish-Culturist* 54:121–24.

Otto, R. G., and S. D. Gerking. 1973. Heat tolerance of a Death Valley pupfish (*Cyprinodon*). *Physiol. Zool.* 46:43–49.

Page, L. M. 1973. An analysis of diversity in the darter genus *Percina*. Ph.D. dissertation, abstract 33, no. 10, University of Illinois, Champaign.

———. 1974a. The subgenera of *Percina*. *Copeia* 1974:66–86.

———. 1974b. The life history of the spottail darter, *Etheostoma squamiceps*, in Big Creek, Illinois, and Ferguson Creek, Kentucky. Ill. Nat. Hist. Surv. Biol. Notes no. 89. Champaign: University of Illinois. 20 pp.

———. 1975a. Relations among the darters of the subgenus *Catonotus* of *Etheostoma*. *Copeia* 1975:782–84.

———. 1975b. The life history of the stripetail darter, *Etheostoma kennicotti*, in Big Creek, Illinois. Ill. Nat. Hist. Surv. Biol. Notes no. 93. Champaign: University of Illinois. 15 pp.

———. 1976. The modified midventral scales of *Percina*. *J. Morph.* 148:255–64.

———. 1980. The life histories of *Etheostoma olivaceum* and *Etheostoma striatulum*, two species of darters in central Tennessee. Ill. Nat. Hist. Surv. Biol. Notes no. 113. Champaign: University of Illinois. 14 pp.

———. 1981a. Redescription of *Etheostoma australe* and a key for the identification of Mexican *Etheostoma*. Occas. Pap. Mus. Nat. Hist. no. 89. Lawrence: University of Kansas. 10 pp.

———. 1981b. The genera and subgenera of darters. *Occasional Papers of the Museum of Natural History, University of Kansas.* Number 90. 69 pp.

———. 1983. *Handbook of darters.* Neptune City, N.J.: T.F.H. Publications. 271 pp.

Page, L. M., and H. L. Bart Jr. 1989. Egg mimics in darters. *Copeia* 1989:514–18.

Page, L. M., and E. C. Beckham. 1987. *Notropis rupestris*, a new cyprinid from the middle Cumberland River system, Tennessee, with comments on variation in *Notropis heterolepis*. *Copeia* 1987:659–68.

Page, L. M., and M. E. Braasch. 1976. Systematic studies of darters of the subgenus *Catonotus*, with the description of a new species from the lower Cumblerland and Tennessee River systems. Pp. 1–18 in Occas. Pap. Mus. Nat. Hist., no. 60. Lawrence: University of Kansas.

———. 1977. Systematic studies of darters of the subgenus *Catonotus*, with the description of a new species from the Duck River system. Pp. 1–18 in Occas. Pap. Mus. Nat. Hist., no. 63. Lawrence: University of Kansas.

Page, L. M., and B. M. Burr. 1976. The life history of the slabrock darter, *Etheostoma smithi*, in Ferguson Creek, Kentucky. Ill. Nat. Hist. Surv. Biol. Notes no. 99. Champaign: University of Illinois. 12 pp.

———. 1979. The smallest species of darter. *Am. Midl. Nat.* 101:452–53.

———. 1991. *A field guide to freshwater fishes, North America north of Mexico.* Peterson Field Guide Series. Boston: Houghton Mifflin Company. 432 pp.

Page, L. M., and P. A. Ceas. 1989. Egg attachment in *Pimephales*. *Copeia* 1989:1074–77.

Page, L. M., and L. E. Cordes. 1983. Variation and systematics of *Etheostoma euzonum*, the Arkansas saddled darter. *Copeia* 1983:1042–50.

Page, L. M., and C. E. Johnston. 1990a. The breeding behavior of *Opsopoeodus emiliae* and its phylogenetic implications. *Copeia* 1990:1176–80.

———. 1990b. Spawning in the creek chubsucker, *Erimyzon oblongus*, with a review of spawning behavior in suckers (Catostomidae). *Environ. Biol. Fishes* 27:265–72.

Page, L. M., and R. L. Mayden. 1981. The life history of the Tennessee snubnose darter, *Etheostoma simoterum*, in Brush Creek, Tennessee. Ill. Nat. Hist. Surv. Biol. Notes no. 117. Champaign: University of Illinois. 11 pp.

Page, L. M., and D. W. Schemske. 1978. The effect of interspecific competition on the distribution and size of darters of the subgenus *Catonotus. Copeia* 1978:406–12.

Page, L. M., and P. W. Smith. 1970. The life history of the dusky darter, *Percina sciera,* in the Embarras River, Illinois. Ill. Nat. Hist. Surv. Biol. Notes no. 69. Champaign: University of Illinois. 15 pp.

———. 1971. The life history of the slenderhead darter, *Percina phox-ocephala,* in the Embarras River, Illinois. Ill. Nat. Hist. Surv. Biol. Notes no. 74. Champaign: University of Illinois. 14 pp.

———. 1976. Variation and systematics of the stripetail darter, *Etheostoma kennicotti. Copeia* 1976:532–41.

Page, L. M., and D. L. Swofford. 1984. Morphological correlates of ecological specialization in darters. *Environ. Biol. Fishes* 11:139–59.

Page, L. M., and G. S. Whitt. 1973. Lactate dehydrogenase isozymes of darters and the inclusiveness of the genus *Percina.* Ill. Nat. Hist. Surv. Biol. Notes no. 82. Champaign: University of Illinois. 7 pp.

Page, L. M., B. M. Burr, and P. W. Smith. 1976. The spottail darter, *Etheostoma squamiceps,* in Indiana. *Am. Midl. Nat.* 95:478–79.

Page, L. M., P. A. Ceas, D. L. Swofford, and D. G. Buth. 1992. Evolutionary relationships within the *Etheostoma squamiceps* complex with descriptions of five new species. *Copeia* 1992:615–46.

Pardue, G. B. 1993. Life history and ecology of the mud sunfish *(Acantharchus pomotis). Copeia* 1993(2):533–40.

Parenti, L. R. 1981. A phylogenetic analysis of Cyprinodontiform fishes. Bull. *Am. Mus. Nat. Hist.* 168:335–557.

Parker, A., and I. Kornfield. 1995. Molecular perspective on evolution and zoogeography of cyprinodontid killifishes. *Copeia* 1995:8–21.

Paszkowski, C. A., and W. M. Tonn. 1992. An experimental study of factors affecting the distribution of yellow perch and central mud-minnows along a species richness gradient. *Environ. Biol. Fishes* 33:399–404.

Patillo, M. E., T. E. Czapia, D. M. Nelson, and M. E. Monaco. 1997. *Distribution and abundance of fishes and invertebrates in Gulf of Mexico estuaries. Vol. II: Species life history summaries.* Estuarine Living Marine Resources Report Number 11. Silver Spring, Md.: NOAA/NOS Stategic Environmental Assessments Division. 377 pp.

Patrick, R. 1994–96. *Rivers of the United States* (six volumes). New York: John Wiley & Sons, Inc.

Peeke, H. V. S. 1969. Habituation of conspecific aggression in the three-spined stickleback *(Gasterosteus aculeatus). Behaviour* 35:137–56.

Pezold, F. 1993. Evidence for a monophyletic Gobiinae. *Copeia* 1993:634–43.

Pezold, F., and R. C. Cashner. 1983. A character analysis of *Gobionellus boleosoma* and *G. shufeldti* from the north-central Gulf of Mexico. *Northeast Gulf Sci.* 6:71–77.

Pezold, F., and J. M. Grady. 1990. A morphological and allozymic analysis of species in the *Gobionellus oceanicus* complex. *Bull. Mar. Sci.* 45:648–63.

Pflieger, W. L. 1975. *The fishes of Missouri.* Jefferson City: Missouri Department of Conservation. 343 pp.

Pflieger, W. L., and L. C. Belusz. 1982. *An introduction to Missouri fishes.* Jefferson City: Missouri Department of Conservation. 16 pp.

Phillips, R. R. 1973. The relationship between social behavior and the use of space in the benthic fish *Chasmodes bosquianus* Lacepede. III. The interaction between attraction/repulsion and prior social experience. *Behaviour* 49:206–26.

Pickford, G. E., P. K. T. Pang, J. G. Stanley, and W. K. Fleming. 1966. Calcium and fresh-water survival in the euryhaline cyprinodonts, *Fundulus kansae* and *Fundulus heteroclitus. Comp. Biochem. Physiol.* 18:503–509.

Pittman, E. 1987. Spawning *Gila orcutti. Am. Currents* (October–December):29–31.

Platania, S. P., and C. S. Altenbach. 1998. Reproductive strategies and egg types of seven Rio Grande basin cyprinids. *Copeia* 1998:559–69.

Poly, W. J., and M. H. Sabaj. 1998. Lack of evidence for the validity of *Rhinichthys bowersi. Copeia* 1998:1081–85.

Potter, R. L., and G. W. Fleischer. 1992. Reappearance of spoonhead sculpins *(Cottus ricei)* in Lake Michigan. *J. Great Lakes Res.* 18:755–58.

Poulson, T. L. 1963. Cave adaptation in Amblyopsid fishes. *Am. Midl. Nat.* 70:257–90.

Pratt, D. M., W. H. Blust, and J. H. Selgeby. 1992. Ruffe, *Gymnocephalus cernuus:* Newly introduced in North America. *Can. J. Fish. Aq. Sci.* 49:1616–18.

Pressley, P. H. 1981. Parental effort and the evolution of nest-guarding tactics in the threespine stickleback, *Gasterosteus aculeatus. Evolution* 35:282–95.

Prinslow, T. E., and I. Valiela. 1974. The effect of detritus and ration size on the growth of *Fundulus heteroclitus. J. Exp. Mar. Biol. Ecol.* 16:1–10.

Propst, D. L., and K. R. Bestgen. 1991. Habitat and biology of the loach minnow, *Tiaroga cobitis,* in New Mexico. *Copeia* 1991:29–38.

Ramsey, J. S., and R. D. Suttkus. 1965. *Etheostoma ditrema,* a new darter of the subgenus *Oligocephalus* from springs of the Alabama River basin in Alabama and Georgia. *Tulane Stud. Zool.* 12:65–77.

Randall, J. E. 1968. *Caribbean reef fishes.* Neptune City, N.J.: T.F.H. Publications. 318 pp.

Raney, E. C. 1941. *Poecilichthys kanawhae,* a new darter from the upper New River system in North Carolina and Virginia. Occas. Pap. Mus. Zool., no. 434. Ann Arbor: University of Michigan. 16 pp.

Raney, E. C., and C. L. Hubbs. 1948. *Hadropterus notogrammus,* a new percid fish from Maryland, Virginia, and West Virginia. Occas. Pap. Mus. Zool., no. 512. Ann Arbor: University of Michigan. 26 pp., pl. 1–2.

Raney, E. C., and R. D. Suttkus. 1964. *Etheostoma moorei,* a new darter of the subgenus *Nothonotus* from the White River system, Arkansas. *Copeia* 1964:130–39.

———. 1966. *Etheostoma rubrum,* a new percid fish of the subgenus *Nothonotus* from Bayou Pierre, Mississippi. *Tulane Stud. Zool.* 13:95–102.

Raney, E. C., and T. Zorach. 1967. *Etheostoma microlepidum,* a new percid fish of the subgenus *Nothonotus* from the Cumberland and Tennessee River systems. *Am. Midl. Nat.* 77:93–103.

Raney, E. C., R. H. Backus, R. W. Crawford, and C. R. Robins. 1953. Reproductive behavior in *Cyprinodon variegatus* in Florida. *Zoologica* 38:97–104.

Rasotto, M. B. 1995. Male reproductive apparatus of some Blennioidei. *Copeia* 1995:907–14.

Reed, B. C., W. E. Kelso, and D. A. Rutherford. 1992. Growth, fecundity, and mortality of paddlefish in Louisiana. *Trans. Am. Fish. Soc.* 121:378–84.

Reeves, C. 1907. The breeding habits of the rainbow darter (*Etheostoma caeruleum* Storer), a study in sexual selection. *Biol. Bull.* 14:35–59.

Reimchen, T. E. 1991. Trout foraging failures and the evolution of body size in stickleback. *Copeia* 1991:1098–1104.

———. 1992. Extended longevity in a large-bodied stickleback, *Gasterosteus,* population. *Can. Field-Nat.* 106:122–25.

Reisman, H. M., and T. J. Cade. 1967. Physiological and behavioral aspects of reproduction in the brook stickleback, *Culaea inconstans. Am. Midl. Nat.* 77:257–95.

Relyea, K. J. 1965. Taxonomic studies of the cyprinodont fishes, *Fundulus confluentus* (Goode and Bean) and *Fundulus pulvereus* (Evermann). Unpublished Master's thesis, Florida State University, Tallahassee.

Renfro, J. L., and L. G. Hill. 1971. Osmotic acclimation in the Red River pupfish, *Cyprinodon rubrofluviatilis. Comp. Biochem. Physiol.* 40A:711–14.

Retzer, M. E., L. M. Page, and D. L. Swofford. 1986. Variation and systematics of *Etheostoma whipplei,* the redfin darter. *Copeia* 1986:631–41.

Rhodes, K., and C. Hubbs. 1992. Recovery of Pecos River fishes from a red tide fish kill. *Southwest. Nat.* 37:178–87.

Richards, C. E., and R. L. Bailey. 1967. Occurrence of *Fundulus luciae,* spotfin killifish, on the seaside of Virginia's eastern shore. *Chesapeake Sci.* 8:200–205.

Richards, S. W., and A. M. McBean. 1966. Comparison of postlarvae and juveniles of *Fundulus heteroclitus* and *Fundulus majalis. Trans. Am. Fish. Soc.* 95:218–26.

Richards, W. J. 1966. Systematics of the percid fishes of the *Etheostoma thalassinum* species group with comments on the subgenus *Etheostoma. Copeia* 1966:823–38.

Richards, W. J., and L. W. Knapp. 1964. *Percina lenticula,* a new percid fish, with a redescription of the subgenus *Hadropterus. Copeia* 1964:690–701.

Richardson, L. R., and J. R. Gold. 1995. Evolution of the *Cyprinella lutrensis* species-complex. II. Systematics and biogeography of the Edwards Plateau shiner, *Cyprinella lepida. Copeia* 1995:28–37.

Richmond, A. M., and B. Kynard. 1995. Ontogenetic behavior of shortnose sturgeon, *Acipenser brevirostrum. Copeia* 1995:172–82.

Rinne, J. N., and W. L. Minckley. 1991. Native fishes of arid lands: A dwindling resource of the desert southwest. USDA For. Serv. Gen. Tech. Rept. RM –206. Fort Collins, Colo.: USDA Rocky Mountain Forest and Range Experiment Station. 45 pp.

Robins, C. R., and G. C. Ray. 1986. *A field guide to Atlantic coast fishes of North America.* Peterson Field Guide Series. Boston: Houghton Mifflin Company. 354 pp.

Robins, C. R., and H. W. Robison. 1985. *Cottus hypselurus,* a new cottid fish from the Ozark uplands, Arkansas and Missouri. *Am. Midl. Nat.* 114:360–73.

Robins, C. R., R. M. Bailey, C. E. Bond, J. R. Brooker, E. A. Lachner, R. N. Lea, and W. B. Scott. 1991. Common and scientific names of fishes from the United States and Canada. Spec. Pub. no. 20. Bethesda, Md.: American Fisheries Society. 183 pp.

Robison, H. W. 1977. Distribution, habitat, variation, and status of the goldstripe darter, *Etheostoma parvipinne* Gilbert and Swain, in Arkansas. *Southwest. Nat.* 22:435–42.

———. 1978. Status of the leopard darter. Endangered Spp. Rept. no. 3. Albuquerque, N.M.: U.S. Fish and Wildlife Service. 28 pp.

Robison, H. W., and T. M. Buchanan. 1988. *Fishes of Arkansas.* Fayetteville: University of Arkansas Press. 536 pp.

Rohde, F. C., and R. G. Arndt. 1987. Two new species of pygmy sunfishes (Elassomatidae, *Elassoma*) from the Carolinas. *Proc. Acad. Nat. Sci. Phila.* 139:65–85.

———. 1991. Distribution and status of the sandhills chub, *Semotilus lumbee,* and the pinewoods darter, *Etheostoma mariae. J. Elisha Mitchell Sci. Soc.* 107:61–70.

Rohde, F. C., and S. W. Ross. 1987. Life history of the pinewoods darter, *Etheostoma mariae,* a fish endemic to the Carolina Sandhills. *Brimleyana* 13:1–20.

Rohde, F. C., R. G. Arndt, D. G. Lindquist, and J. F. Parnell. 1994. *Freshwater fishes of the Carolinas, Virginia, Maryland, and Delaware.* Chapel Hill: University of North Carolina Press. 222 pp.

Rollo, P. R. 1994a. Successfully spawning and raising the green sunfish, *Lepomis cyanellus. Fin-Fax* (Del. Co. Aq. Soc.): unpaginated.

Rollo, P. R. 1994b. Successfully spawning and raising the banded sunfish (*Enneacanthus obesus*). *Am. Currents* (fall):30–36.

Ross, M. R., and R. J. Reed. 1978. The reproductive behavior of the fallfish *Semotilus corporalis. Copeia* 1978:215–21.

Ross, S. T., and S. D. Wilkins. 1993. Reproductive behavior and larval characteristics of the threatened bayou darter (*Etheostoma rubrum*) in Mississippi. *Copeia* 1993:1127–32.

Ross, S. T., J. G. Knight, and S. D. Wilkins. 1992. Distribution and microhabitat dynamics of the threatened bayou darter, *Etheostoma rubrum. Copeia* 1992:658–71.

Rubenstein, D. I. 1981a. Population density, resource patterning, and territoriality in the Everglades pygmy sunfish. *Anim. Behav.* 29:155–72.

———. 1981b. Combat and communication in the Everglades pygmy sunfish. *Anim. Behav.* 29:249–58.

Ruelle, R., and K. D. Keenlyne. 1993. Contaminants in Missouri River pallid sturgeon. *Bull. Environ. Contam. Toxicol.* 50:898–906.

Ruple, D. L., R. H. McMichael Jr., and J. A. Baker. 1984. Life history of the Gulf darter, *Etheostoma swaini. Environ. Biol. Fishes* 11:121–30.

Sabat, A. M. 1994a. Mating success in brood-guarding male rock bass, *Ambloplites rupestris:* The effect of body size. *Environ. Biol. Fishes* 39:411–15.

———. 1994b. Costs and benefits of parental effort in a brood-guarding fish (*Ambloplites rupestris,* Centrarchidae). *Behav. Ecol.* 5:195–201.

Scalet, C. G. 1971. Parasites of the orangebelly darter, *Etheostoma radiosum. J. Parasitol.* 57:900.

———. 1972. Food habits of the orangebelly darter, *Etheostoma radiosum cyanorum. Am. Midl. Nat.* 87:515–22.

———. 1973a. Reproduction of the orangebelly darter, *Etheostoma radiosum cyanorum. Am. Midl. Nat.* 89:156–65.

———. 1973b. Stream movements and population density of the orangebelly darter, *Etheostoma radiosum cyanorum. Southwest. Nat.* 17:381–87.

———. 1974. Lack of piscine predation on the orangebelly darter, *Etheostoma radiosum cyanorum. Am. Midl. Nat.* 92:510–12.

Scarola, J. F. 1973. *Freshwater fishes of New Hampshire.* Concord: Fish and Game Department. 131 pp.

Schenck, J. R., and B. G. Whiteside. 1976. Distribution, habitat preference and population size estimate of *Etheostoma fonticola. Copeia* 1976:697–703.

———. 1977a. Reproduction, fecundity, sexual dimorphism and sex ratio of *Etheostoma fonticola. Am. Midl. Nat.* 98:365–75.

———. 1977b. Food habits and feeding behavior of the fountain darter, *Etheostoma fonticola. Southwest. Nat.* 21:487–92.

Schmidt, K. 1984. Glassworms: a native food for native fish. *Am. Currents* (December):12.

Schmidt, R. E., and W. R. Whitworth. 1979. Distribution and habitat of the swamp darter *(Etheostoma fusiforme)* in southern New England. *Am. Midl. Nat.* 102:408–13.

Schmidt, T. R. 1994. Phylogenetic relationships of the genus *Hybognathus. Copeia* 1994:622–30.

Schmidt, T. R., J. P. Bielawski, and J. R. Gold. 1998. Molecular phylogenetics and evolution of the cytochrome *b* gene in the cyprinid genus *Lythrurus. Copeia* 1998:14–22.

Schmidt, T. R., and J. C. Gold. 1993. Complete sequence of the mitochrondrial cytochrome *b* gene in the cherryfin shiner, *Lythrurus roseipinnis. Copeia* 1993:880–83.

———. 1994. Molecular evolution of notropine minnows inferred from sequences of the cytochrome *b* gene. Los Angeles: American Society of Ichthyologists and Herpetologists 74th annual meeting, abstract no. 260.

———. 1995. Systematic affinities of *Notropis topeka* (Topeka shiner) inferred from sequences of the cytochrome *b* gene. *Copeia* 1995:199–204.

Schultz, T. W., S. Davis, and J. N. Dumont. 1978. Toxicity of coal-conversion gasifier condensate to the fathead minnow. *Bull. Environ. Contam. Toxicol.* 19:237–43.

Schwartz, F. J. 1958. The breeding behavior of the southern blacknose dace, *Rhinichthys atratulus obtusus. Copeia* 1958:141–43.

———. 1961. Food, age, growth, and morphology of the blackbanded sunfish, *Enneacanthus c. chaetodon,* in Smithville Pond, Maryland. *Chesapeake Sci.* 2:82–88.

———. 1962. Artificial pike hybrids, *Esox americanus vermiculatus* × *E. lucius. Trans. Am. Fish. Soc.* 91:229–30.

———. 1965. The distribution and probable postglacial dispersal of the percid fish, *Etheostoma b. blennioides,* in the Potomac River. *Copeia* 1965:285–90.

Scott, W. B., and E. J. Crossman. 1973. Freshwater fishes of Canada. Bull. 184. Ottawa: Fisheries Research Board of Canada. 966 pp.

Semmens, K. J. 1985. Induced spawning of the blue sucker *(Cycleptus elongatus). Prog. Fish-Culturist* 47:119–20.

Settles, W. H., and R. D. Hoyt. 1976. Age structure, growth patterns, and food habits of the southern redbelly dace *Chrosomus erythrogaster* in Kentucky. *Trans. Am. Fish. Soc.* 37:1–10.

———. 1978. The reproductive biology of the southern redbelly dace, *Chrosomus erythrogaster* Rafinesque, in a spring-fed Kentucky stream. *Am. Midl. Nat.* 99:290–98.

Shepard, T. E., and B. M. Burr. 1984. Systematics, status, and life his-

tory aspects of the ashy darter, *Etheostoma cinereum. Proc. Biol. Soc. Wash.* 97:693–715.

Shiogaki, M., and Y. Dotsu. 1973. The egg development and larva rearing of the tripterygiid blenny, *Tripterygion etheostoma. Jpn. J. Ichthyol.* 20:42–46.

Shrode, J. n.d. Developmental temperature tolerance of a Death Valley pupfish. (Journal unknown):378–89. Photocopy in author's possession.

Shute, J. R., P. W. Shute, and P. L. Rakes. 1993. Captive propagation and population monitoring of rare southeastern fishes by Conservation Fisheries, Inc. Nashville: Final Report to Tennessee Wildlife Resources Agency, November 29, 1993. 27 pp. (2 figs.)

Sigler, W. S., and J. Sigler. 1987. *Fishes of the Great Basin: A Natural History.* Reno: University of Nevada Press. 448 pp.

Simon, T. P. 1987. Description of eggs, larvae and early juveniles of the stripetail darter, *Etheostoma kennicotti* and spottail darter, *E. squamiceps* from tributaries of the Ohio River. *Copeia* 1987:433–42.

———. 1997. Ontogeny of the darter subgenus *Doration* with comments on intrasubgeneric relationships. *Copeia* 1997:60–69.

Simon, T. P., and D. J. Faber. 1987. Descriptions of eggs, larvae, and early juveniles of the Iowa darter, *Etheostoma exile,* from Lac Heney, Quebec. *Can. J. Zool.* 65:1264–69.

Simons, A. M. 1991. Phylogenetic relationships of the crystal darter, *Crystallaria asprella. Copeia* 1991:927–36.

Simonson, T. D., and R. J. Neves. 1992. Habitat suitability and reproductive traits of the orangefin madtom *Noturus gilberti. Am. Midl. Nat.* 127:115–24.

Simpson, J. C., and R. L. Wallace. 1978. *Fishes of Idaho.* Moscow: University of Idaho Press. 237 pp.

Smeltzer, J. F., and S. A. Flickinger. 1991. Culture, handling, and feeding techniques for black crappie fingerlings. *N. Am. J. Fish. Manage.* 11:485–91.

Smith, C. L. 1986. *The inland fishes of New York State.* Albany: New York Department of Environmental Conservation. 523 pp.

Smith, G. R. 1966. Distribution and evolution of the North American catostomid fishes of the subgenus *Pantosteus,* genus *Catostomus. Misc. Pub. Mus. Zool., Univ. Mich.* 129:5–132, pl. 1.

———. 1992. Chapter 28. Phylogeny and biogeography of the Catostomidae, freshwater fishes of North America and Asia. In *Systematics, historical ecology, and North American freshwater fishes,* edited by R. L. Mayden, pp. 778–826. Stanford, Calif.: Stanford University Press.

Smith, H. M. 1907. *The fishes of North Carolina.* Vol. 2. Raleigh: North Carolina Geological and Economic Survey. 453 pp.

Smith, M. L., J. Song, and R. R. Miller. 1984. Redescription, variation, and zoogeography of the Mexican darter *Etheostoma pottsi. Southwest. Nat.* 29:395–402.

Smith, P. W. 1979. *The fishes of Illinois.* Champaign: University of Illinois Press. 314 pp.

Smith, R. J. F. 1979. Alarm reaction of Iowa and johnny darters *(Etheostoma)* to chemicals from injured conspecifics. *Can. J. Zool.* 57:1278–82.

Smith, R. L. 1974. On the biology of *Blennius cristatus* with special reference to anal fin morphology. *Bull. Mar. Sci.* 24:595–605.

Smith, W. E. 1973. A cyprinodontid fish, *Jordanella floridae,* as laboratory animal for rapid chronic bioassays. *J. Fish. Res. Board Can.* 30:329–30.

Smith-Vaniz, W. F. 1980. Revision of the western Atlantic species of the blenniid fish genus *Hypsoblennius. Proc. Acad. Nat. Sci. Phila.* 132:285–305.

Snelson, F. F., Jr. 1990. Redescription, geographic variation, and subspecies of the minnow *Notropis ardens. Copeia* 1990:966–84.

Snyder, D. E., M. B. M. Snyder, and S. C. Douglas. 1977. Identification of golden shiner, *Notemigonus crysoleucas,* spotfin shiner, *Notropis spilopterus,* and fathead minnow, *Pimephales promelas,* larvae. *J. Fish. Res. Board Can.* 34:1397–1409.

Snyder, J. A., G. C. Garman, and R. W. Chapman. 1996. Mitochondrial DNA variation in native and introduced populations of smallmouth bass, *Micropterus dolomieu. Copeia* 1996:995–98.

Springer, V. G. 1959. Blenniid fishes of the genus *Chasmodes. Tex. J. Sci.* 11:321–34.

Springer, V. G., and A. J. McErlean. 1961. Spawning seasons and growth of the code goby, *Gobiosoma robustum,* in the Tampa Bay area. *Tulane Stud. Zool.* 9:87–98.

Stabile, J., J. R. Waldman, F. Parauka, and I. Wirgin. 1996. Stock structure and homing fidelity in Gulf of Mexico sturgeon *(Acipenser oxyrinchus desotoi)* based on restriction fragment length polymorphism and sequence analyses of mitochondrial DNA. *Genetics* 144:767–75.

Starnes, W. C., D. A. Etnier, L. B. Starnes, and N. H. Douglas. 1977. Zoogeographic implications of the rediscovery of the percid genus *Ammocrypta* in the Tennessee River drainage. *Copeia* 1977:783–86.

Stauffer, J. R., Jr., and E. S. van Snik. 1997. New species of *Etheostoma* from the upper Tennessee River. *Copeia* 1997:116–22.

Stauffer, J. R., Jr., J. M. Boltz, and L. R. White. 1995. *The fishes of West Virginia.* Philadelphia: Academy of Natural Sciences of Philadelphia. 400 pp.

Stauffer, J. R., Jr., C. H. Hocutt, and R. L. Mayden. 1997. *Pararhinichthys,* a new monotypic genus of minnows of hybrid origin from eastern North America. *Ichthyol. Explor. Freshw.* 7:327–36.

Stephens, R. R., L. M. Page, and M. E. Retzer. 1994. A reevaluation of phylogenetic relationships of species of *Etheostoma* recently referred to the subgenera *Etheostoma, Nanostoma,* and *Ulocentra.* Los Angeles: American Society of Ichthyologists and Herpetologists 74th annual meeting, abstract no. 281.

Sterba, G. 1983. *The aquarium encyclopedia.* Cambridge, Mass.: MIT Press. 605 pp.

Sternburg, J. 1986. Aquarium spawning and rearing of the southern redbelly dace. *Am. Currents* (October):7–9.

———. 1991. Breeding the blackbanded sunfish and its relatives. Pp. 25–26 in *Champaign* (Ill.) *Area Fish Exchange,* March (reprinted in *Tropic Tank Talk,* September 1991).

Stone, N., and G. M. Ludwig. 1993. Estimating numbers of golden shiner eggs on spawning mats. *Prog. Fish-Culturist* 55:53–54.

Strange, R. M. 1993. Season feeding ecology of the fantail darter, *Etheostoma flabellare,* from Stinking Fork, Indiana. *J. Freshw. Ecol.* 8:13–18.

Strauss, R. E. 1993. Relationships among the cottid genera *Artedius, Clinocottus,* and *Oligocottus. Copeia* 1993:518–22.

Sublette, J. D., M. D. Hatch, and M. Sublette. 1990. *The fishes of New Mexico.* Albuquerque: University of New Mexico Press. 393 pp.

Suttkus, R. D. 1991. *Notropis rafinesquei,* a new cyprinid fish from the Yazoo River system in Mississippi. *Bull. Ala. Mus. Nat. Hist.* 10:1–9, figs. 1–2.

Suttkus, R. D., and D. A. Etnier. 1991. *Etheostoma tallapoosae* and *E. brevirostrum,* two new darters, subgenus *Ulocentra,* from the Alabama River drainage. *Tulane Stud. Zool. Bot.* 28:1–24.

Suttkus, R. D., and J. S. Ramsey. 1967. *Percina aurolineata,* a new percid fish from the Alabama River system and a discussion of ecology, distribution, and hybridization of darters of the subgenus *Hadropterus. Tulane Stud. Zool.* 13:129–45.

Suttkus, R. D., B. A. Thompson, and H. L. Bart Jr. 1994. Two new darters, *Percina (Cottogaster),* from the southeastern United States, with a review of the subgenus. *Occas. Pap., Tulane Univ. Mus. Nat. Hist.* 4:1–46.

Sweet, J. G., and O. Kinne. 1964. The effects of various temperature-salinity combinations on the body form of newly hatched *Cyprinodon macularius.* Helgolandt Wissenschaften Meesesuntersuchung 11:49–69.

Symons, P. E. K., J. L. Metcalfe, and G. D. Harding. 1976. Upper lethal and preferred temperatures of the slimy sculpin, *Cottus cognatus. J. Fish. Res. Board Can.* 33:180–83.

Taber, C. A., and B. A. Taber. 1983. Reproductive biology and age and growth of the Missouri saddled darter *Etheostoma tetrazonum. Am. Midl. Nat.* 109:222–29.

Taber, C. A., B. A. Taber, and M. S. Topping. 1986. Population structure, growth and reproduction of the Arkansas darter, *Etheostoma cragini. Southwest. Nat.* 31:207–14.

Tagatz, M. E. 1967. Fishes of the St. Johns River, Florida. *Quart. J. Fla. Acad. Sci.* 30:25–50.

Taylor, B. E., and W. Gabriel. 1993. Optimal adult growth of *Daphnia* in a seasonal environment. *Functional Ecology* 7:513–21.

Taylor, M. C., G. J. Leach, L. DiMichele, W. M. Levitan, and W. F. Jacob. 1979. Lunar spawning cycle in the mummichog, *Fundulus heteroclitus. Copeia* 1979:291–97.

Taylor, W. R. 1969. A revision of the catfish genus *Noturus* Rafinesque with an analysis of higher groups in the Ictaluridae. Bull. 282. Washington, D.C.: U.S. National Museum. 315 pp.

Thomas, D. L. 1970. An ecological study of four darters of the genus *Percina* in the Kaskaskia River, Illinois. Ill. Nat. Hist. Surv. Biol. Notes no. 70. Champaign: University of Illinois. 18 pp.

Thomerson, J. E. 1966a. A collection of madtom catfish, *Noturus funebris,* from western Florida. *Trans. Ill. State Acad. Sci.* 59:397–98.

———. 1966b. *Rivulus marmoratus,* a rare and unusual killifish from Florida. *J. Am. Killifish Assoc.* 3:48–51.

———. 1966c. A comparative biosystematic study of *Fundulus notatus* and *Fundulus olivaceus. Tulane Stud. Zool.* 1:29–47.

———. 1967. Hybrids between the cyprinodontid fishes, *Fundulus notatus* and *Fundulus olivaceus* in southern Illinois. *Trans. Ill. State Acad. Sci.* 60:375–79.

Thresher, R. E. 1984. *Reproduction in reef fishes.* Neptune City, N.J.: T.F.H. Publications. 399 pp.

Tippie, D., J. E. Deacon, and C.-H. Ho. 1991. Effects of convict cichlids on growth and recruitment of White River springfish. *Great Basin Nat.* 51:256–60.

Tomelleri, J. R., and M. E. Eberle. 1990. *Fishes of the central United States.* Lawrence: University Press of Kansas. 226 pp.

Trautman, M. B. 1981. *The fishes of Ohio.* 2nd edition. Columbus: Ohio State University Press. 782 pp.

Tsai, C. 1968a. Distribution of the harlequin darter, *Etheostoma histrio. Copeia* 1968:178–81.

———. 1968b. Variation and distribution of the rock darter, *Etheostoma rupestre. Copeia* 1968:346–53.

———. 1972. Life history of the eastern johnny darter, *Etheostoma olmstedi,* in cold tailwater and sewage-polluted water. *Trans. Am. Fish. Soc.* 101:80–88.

Tsai, C., and E. C. Raney. 1974. Systematics of the banded darter, *Etheostoma zonale. Copeia* 1974:1–24.

Turner, B. J., W. P. Davis, and D. S. Taylor. 1992. Abundant males in populations of a selfing hermaphrodite fish, *Rivulus marmoratus,* from some Belize cays. *J. Fish Biol.* 40:307–10.

Turner, C. L. 1921. Food of the common Ohio darters. *Oh. J. Sci.* 22:41–62.

Turner, T. T. 1997. Mitochondrial control region sequences and phylogenetic systematics of darters. *Copeia* 1997:319–38.

Tyus, H. M. 1998. Early records of the endangered fish *Gila cypha,* Miller from the Yampa River of Colorado with notes on its decline. *Copeia* 1998:190–93.

Tyler, J. A. 1993. Effects of water velocity, group size, and prey availability on the stream-drift capture efficiency of blacknose dace, *Rhinichthys atratulus. Can. J. Fish. Aq. Sci.* 50:1055–61.

Umminger, B. L. 1970. Osmoregulation by the killifish, *Fundulus heteroclitus,* in fresh water at temperatures near freezing. *Nature* 225:294–95.

———. 1971. Chemical studies of cold death in the Gulf killifish, *Fundulus grandis. Comp. Biochem. Physiol.* 39A:625–32.

Vrijenhoek, R. C. 1985. Homozygosity and interstrain variation in the self-fertilizing hermaphroditic fish, *Rivulus marmoratus. J. Hered.* 76:82–84.

Wall, B. R., Jr., and J. D. Williams. 1974. *Etheostoma boschungi,* a new percid fish from the Tennessee River drainage in northern Alabama and western Tennessee. *Tulane Stud. Zool. Bot.* 18:172–82.

Wallin, J. E. 1992. The symbiotic nest association of yellowfin shiners, *Notropis lutipinnis,* and bluehead chubs, *Nocomis leptocephalus. Environ. Biol. Fishes* 33:287–92.

Walsh, S. J., and B. M. Burr. 1984a. Life history of the banded pygmy sunfish, *Elassoma zonatum* Jordan in western Kentucky. *Bull. Ala. Mus. Nat. Hist.* 8:31–52.

———. 1984b. Biology of the stonecat, *Noturus flavus,* in central Illinois and Missouri streams, and comparisons with Great Lakes populations and congeners. *Oh. J. Sci.* 85:85–96.

Walsh, S. J., and C. G. Gilbert. 1995. New species of troglobitic catfish of the genus *Prietella* from northeastern Mexico. *Copeia* 1995:850–61.

Warren, M. L., Jr. 1992. Variation of the spotted sunfish, *Lepomis punctatus* complex: Meristics, morphometrics, pigmentation and species limits. *Bull. Ala. Mus. Nat. Hist.* 12:1–47.

Warren, M. L., Jr., and B. M. Burr. 1989. Distribution, abundance, and status of the cypress minnow, *Hybognathus hayi,* an endangered Illinois species. *Nat. Areas J.* 9:163–68.

Warren, M. L., Jr., B. M. Burr, and J. M. Grady. 1994. *Notropis albizonatus,* a new cyprinid fish endemic to the Tennessee and Cumberland River drainages, with a phylogeny of the *Notropis procne* species group. *Copeia* 1994:868–86.

Warren, M. L., Jr., B. M. Burr, and B. R. Kuhajda. 1986. Aspects of the reproductive biology of *Etheostoma tippecanoe* with comments on egg-burying behavior. *Am. Midl. Nat.* 116:215–18.

Weber, A., and H. Wilkens. 1998. *Rhamdia macuspanensis:* a new species of troglobitic pimelodid catfish from a cave in Tabasco, Mexico. *Copeia* 1998:998–1004.

Weddle, G. K. 1990. Spawning orientation preferences of the Kentucky snubnose darter: An in-stream study of *Etheostoma rafinesquei. Trans. Ky. Acad. Sci.* 51:159–65.

———. 1992. Seasonal, sexual, and size class variation in the diet of the Kentucky darter, *Etheostoma rafinesquei,* in Middle Pitman Creek, Kentucky. *Trans. Ky. Acad. Sci.* 53:121–26.

Weddle, G. K., and B. M. Burr. 1991. Fecundity and the dynamics of multiple spawning in darters: An in-stream study of *Etheostoma rafinesque. Copeia* 1991:419–33.

Whitworth, W. R., P. L. Berrien, and W. T. Keller. 1968. *Freshwater fishes of Connecticut.* Bull. 101. Hartford, Conn.: State Geological and Natural History Survey. 134 pp.

Wilde, G. R., and A. A. Echelle. 1992. Genetic status of Pecos pupfish populations after establishment of a hybrid swarm involving an introduced cogener. *Trans. Am. Fish. Soc.* 121:277–86.

Wiley, E. O. 1977. The phylogeny and systematics of the *Fundulus nottii* species group. *Occas. Pap. Mus. Nat. Hist., Univ. Kans.* 66:1–31.

Williams, J. D. 1968. A new species of sculpin, *Cottus pygmaeus,* from a spring in the Alabama River basin. *Copeia* 1968:334–42.

———. 1975. Systematics of the percid fishes of the subgenus *Ammocrypta,* genus *Ammocrypta,* with descriptions of two new species. *Bull. Ala. Mus. Nat. Hist.* 1:1–56.

Williams, J. D., and G. H. Clemmer. 1991. *Scaphirhynchus suttkusi,* a new sturgeon from the Mobile Basin of Alabama and Mississippi. *Bull. Ala. Mus. Nat. Hist.* 10:17–31.

Williams, J. D., and D. A. Etnier. 1977. *Percina (Imostoma) antesella,* a new percid fish from the Coosa River system in Tennessee and Georgia. *Proc. Biol. Soc. Wash.* 90:6–18.

———. 1982. Description of a new species, *Fundulus julisia,* with a redescription of *Fundulus albolineatus* and a diagnosis of the subgenus *Xenisma. Occas. Pap. Mus. Nat. Hist., Univ. Kans.* 102:1–20.

Williams, J. D., and C. R. Robins. 1970. Variation in populations of the fish *Cottus carolinae* in the Alabama River system with description of a new subspecies from below the Fall Line. *Am. Midl. Nat.* 83:368–81.

Williams, J. S. 1976. Spawning behavior of *Etheostoma edwini. ASB Bulletin* 23:107.

Wilson, S., and C. Hubbs. 1972. Developmental rates and tolerances of the plains killifish, *Fundulus kansae,* and comparison with related fishes. *Tex. J. Sci.* 23:371–79.

Winn, H. E. 1958. Comparative reproductive behavior and ecology of fourteen species of darters. *Ecol. Monogr.* 28:155–91.

Wiseman, E. D., A. A. Echelle, and A. F. Echelle. 1978. Electrophoretic evidence for subspecific dierentiation and intergradation in *Etheostoma spectabile. Copeia* 1978:320–27.

Wolf, G. W., and B. A. Branson. 1979. Lactate dehydrogenase isozymes in six species of darters in the subgenus *Catonotus* Agassiz. *Am. Midl. Nat.* 102:392–94.

Wolf, G. W., B. A. Branson, and S. L. Jones. 1979. An electrophoretic investigation of six species of darters in the subgenus *Catonotus*. *Biochem. Syst. Ecol.* 7:81–85.

Wood, R. M. 1996. Phylogenetic systematics of the darter subgenus *Nothonotus. Copeia* 1996:300–18.

Wood, R. M., and R. L. Mayden. 1992. Systematics, evolution, and biogeography of *Notropis chlorocephalus* and *N. lutipinnis. Copeia* 1992:68–81.

———. 1993. Systematics of the *Etheostoma jordani* species group, with descriptions of three new species. *Bull. Ala. Mus. Nat. Hist.* 16:31–46.

———. 1997. Phylogenetic relationship among selected darter subgenera as inferred from analysis of allozymes. *Copeia* 1997:265–74.

Woodling, John. 1985. Colorado's Little Fish: A guide to the minnows and other lesser known fishes in the State of Colorado. Denver: Colorado Division of Wildlife. 77 pp.

Woolcott, W. S., and E. G. Maurakis. 1988. Pit-ridge nest construction and spawning behaviors of *Semotilus lumbee* and *Semotilus thoreauianus. Proc. Southeast. Fishes Council* 18:1–3.

Wootton, R. J. 1976. *The biology of the sticklebacks.* New York: Academic Press. 387 pp.

———. 1984. *A functional biology of sticklebacks.* Berkeley: University of California Press. 265 pp.

Wyanski, D. M., and T. E. Targett. 1985. Juvenile development of the lyre goby, *Evorthodus lyricus,* with a discussion of early life history. *Bull. Mar. Sci.* 36:115–23.

Wydoski, R. S., and R. R. Whitney. 1979. *Inland fishes of Washington.* Seattle: University of Washington Press. 220 pp.

Wynes, D. L., and T. E. Wissing. 1982. Resource sharing among darters in an Ohio stream. *Am. Midl. Nat.* 107:294–304.

Yeatman, H. C. 1966. *Argulus* parasitic on killifish. *J. Am. Killifish Assoc.* (spring): unpaginated.

Zoller, C. 1998. Collecting, spawning, and raising the orangefin darter, *Etheostoma bellum. Am. Currents* 24:1–3.

Zorach, T. 1968. *Etheostoma bellum,* a new darter of the subgenus *Nothonotus* from the Green River system, Kentucky and Tennessee. *Copeia* 1968:474–82.

———. 1969. *Etheostoma jordani* and *E. tippecanoe,* species of the subgenus *Nothonotus. Am. Midl. Nat.* 81:412–34.

———. 1971. Taxonomic status of the subspecies of the tessellated darter, *Etheostoma olmstedi* Storer, in southeastern Virginia. *Chesapeake Sci.* 11:254–63.

———. 1972. Systematics of the percid fishes, *Etheostoma camurum* and *E. chlorobranchium* new species, with a discussion of the subgenus *Nothonothus. Copeia* 1972:427–47.

Zorach, T., and E. C. Raney. 1967. Systematics of the percid fish, *Etheostoma maculatum* Kirtland, and related species of the subgenus *Nothonotus. Am. Midl. Nat.* 77:296–322.

# Index